THE ONE YEAR BOOK OF CHRISTIAN HISTORY

TYNDALE HOUSE PUBLISHERS, INC., Wheaton, Illinois

The ONE YEAR® BOOK OF CHRISTIAN HISTORY

E. MICHAEL AND SHARON RUSTEN

Library of Congress Cataloging-in-Publication Data

Rusten, E. Michael date.
  The one year book of Christian history / E. Michael Rusten and Sharon O. Rusten.
    p. cm.
  Includes bibliographical references and index.
  ISBN 0-8423-5507-3 (sc)
  1. Church history. 2. Christian biography. 3. Devotional calendars. I. Rusten, Sharon O. II. Title.
BR153.R79 2003
270—dc21   2002014504

Printed in the United States of America

09 08 07 06 05 04 03
8   7   6   5   4   3   2   1

*This book is dedicated
to our parents,
Carl and Mae Odmark,
Helen Rusten,
and to the memory of
Elmer M. Rusten, M.D.*

CONTENTS

ACKNOWLEDGMENTS

WE want to give our heartfelt thanks to the many who assisted us in this project: to our agent and lifelong friend, Al Youngren; to our patient and long-suffering editor, Susan Taylor; to those who served as research assistants, Martha Rusten, Carrie Zeman, Joyce Renick, Joe and Linnea Kickasola, Mark Ammerman, Dana Johnson, Greta Erickson, Katrina Costello, Michael Binder, Jack Riddle, Weyland Leach, and Kate Brand; and to Bob Taepke and Marta Rusten for helping to tabulate our dates. Thank you all for your help.

INTRODUCTION

All things happen just as [God] decided long ago. EPHESIANS 1:11

GOD is the author of history and as such is intimately involved with every detail of life. Just as we can learn from the lives of those whose stories are recorded in the Bible, there is much to learn from the lives of God's people down through the ages.

In this book we highlight an event associated with each day of the year. These events teach us something about God and his dealings with humankind. Our desire is to make the stories come alive by giving readers a glimpse of the real people behind the historical events. Each day ends with a Reflection designed to help readers interact with the historical account and learn the lessons God has for us.

In choosing the dates of events in the New Testament period, we have adopted those of Harold W. Hoehner.[1]

"Therefore, since we are surrounded by such a huge crowd of witnesses to the life of faith, let us strip off every weight that slows us down, especially the sin that so easily hinders our progress. And let us run with endurance the race that God has set before us. We do this by keeping our eyes on Jesus, on whom our faith depends from start to finish" (Hebrews 12:1-2).

Mike and Sharon Rusten

The ONE YEAR® BOOK OF

CHRISTIAN HISTORY

January 1

He fought for the faith.

BORN IN 1881, J. Gresham Machen grew up in an educated, well-to-do Presbyterian family in Baltimore. He majored in classics at Johns Hopkins University and graduated first in his class in 1901. He then entered the graduate program but after one year enrolled in Princeton Seminary. Following his graduation in 1905, he studied in Germany for a year and then returned to Princeton Seminary as a professor of New Testament in 1906.

Gresham Machen was known for his serious research and scholarly writing on various New Testament topics. He also became known for his defense of conservative theology, especially the authority of Scripture. After publishing *Christianity and Liberalism* in 1923, he became a nationally recognized figure. He maintained that liberalism was not a variety of Christianity but was instead an entirely different religion.

"Liberalism appeals to man's will, while Christianity announces, first, a gracious act of God." He argued that historical Christianity had always been rooted in the saving acts of Christ's death and resurrection, whereas liberal Protestantism reduced Christianity to a set of general religious principles regarding the moral teachings of Jesus.

These beliefs caused Machen to become a controversial figure both at Princeton Seminary and within his denomination, the Presbyterian Church U.S.A., as these institutions were beginning to shift toward a more liberal theological stance. Princeton's drift into liberalism was heartbreaking for Machen, who fought hard to keep the seminary committed to the creeds of the Presbyterian Church. He pleaded with the seminary faculty to stand for "the full truthfulness of the Bible as the Word of God and for the vigorous defense and propagation of the Reformed or Calvinistic system of doctrine, which is the system of doctrine that the Bible teaches."

It was a losing battle. Princeton officially reorganized in 1929 to ensure a more inclusive theological curriculum. This left Machen and other Reformed professors worried about the lack of evangelical training for future Presbyterian ministers. In response, Machen and other Reformed faculty members left Princeton and founded Philadelphia's Westminster Theological Seminary, an institution that would stand for theological orthodoxy and academic excellence. Gresham Machen was a professor of New Testament there until his death.

At Westminster, Machen continued to fight liberalism within the Presby-

STANDING FOR "THE FULL TRUTHFULNESS" OF THE BIBLE

terian Church. In 1933 he helped form the conservative Independent Board for Presbyterian Foreign Missions in order to counteract the liberalism that was infiltrating Presbyterian foreign missions. The Presbyterian General Assembly rejected this new mission board, and in 1935 Machen was tried and suspended from the ministry of the Presbyterian Church for refusing to break his ties to the Independent Board.

Machen then played a central role in founding a new denomination, the Presbyterian Church of America (later the Orthodox Presbyterian Church), which over time continued to uphold theological orthodoxy.

While speaking in Bismarck, North Dakota, in December 1936, Machen came down with pneumonia, yet he continued preaching even though it was extremely cold and he was very sick. Finally he was hospitalized. When a friend visited him New Year's Eve, Machen told him about a vision of heaven he had had in the hospital: "Sam, it was glorious, it was glorious." He died the next day on **January 1, 1937.**

Reflection

Respond to Gresham Machen's statement that "liberalism appeals to man's will, while Christianity announces . . . a gracious act of God." Where does your church or denomination stand on the conservative/liberal theological continuum? Where do you stand?

Yes, by God's grace, Jesus tasted death for everyone in all the world. And it was only right that God—who made everything and for whom everything was made—should bring his many children into glory. Through the suffering of Jesus, God made him a perfect leader, one fit to bring them into their salvation. HEBREWS 2:9-10

January 2

He wept with those who wept.

EDWARD D. GRIFFIN resigned his pastorate at the Newark Presbyterian Church, one of the largest churches in the nation, to become professor of pulpit eloquence at the newly established Andover Theological Seminary in Massachusetts.[1] When Griffin moved from New Jersey to Boston to assume his new position, he was accompanied by five students who would attend the new seminary. One of them, Lewis LeCount Conger, soon fell seriously ill, and Griffin, who had grown to love the young man deeply, sought to inform and comfort the family of the ailing seminary student. Griffin's poignant correspondence with those who loved Lewis Conger began:

> **January 2, 1810**
> *My Dear Sir,*
>   *How often have you and your dear family said, "The Lord reigneth, let the earth rejoice." What a blessing it is that he has the appointment of all our changes and trials. . . . You have given a son to Christ, and if he has work for him on the earth, he will preserve him and make him a blessing to the church; but if he has other designs, he will, I doubt not, take him to himself. . . . Lewis has the typhus fever. His mind is weak; but he loves to hear of the name of Christ, and will listen with deep interest and tender affection to every thing that is said about that blessed Savior. . . . I beseech you, my dear friends . . . Prepare for every thing which God has in store for you. . . . May God Almighty support you, my dear friends, under this trial, is my prayer.*

> *January 3, 1810*
> *We do little else but pray for him; and the whole college is crying with tears, "Spare him, spare him!" . . . I cannot but humbly and earnestly pray that God will spare him for your sakes, and for ours, and for the sake of Christ.*

> *January 6, 1810*
> *The Almighty God support you, my dear friends, under the trials you must feel. I wish with all my heart that I had something agreeable to communicate. And I have—Jesus of Nazareth reigns. The infinite God is happy. And our dear Lewis is happy. Ah, my heart, why this aching and trembling? The will of God is done. Lewis himself wished that the will of God might be done. And*

AN APPOINTMENT IN HEAVEN

I am confident that he does not wish to oppose it now. . . . Lewis left these abodes of pain this morning at 10 o'clock. . . .

No young man was ever more beloved. . . . He has not lived in vain. . . . He has been the means of good to some souls; and by his influence on the college, has probably been indirectly the means of some good to thousands. . . .

January 7, 1810
My friends, it is all the appointment of heaven. Eternal wisdom fixed it that he should die at this time and place. . . .

Think not my dear friends, that you have lost your pains in giving him an education. No, you have been fitting him for more than a pulpit—for a higher throne in heaven. . . . There he is! Think not of him on a bed of sickness, in a land of strangers. . . . Think of him on Mount Zion. There is all that is Lewis. The rest is mere dust. We have not lost him. He is only gone a little before us. . . . There we shall soon find him and enjoy him again, and forever—far more than we ever did in this world. . . .

Your afflicted and affectionate friend,
E. D. Griffin

Reflection

Have you lost a friend or loved one in the prime of life and wondered why God took that person? Can you think of any reasons why he took Lewis Conger? Is it really necessary for us to know why?

The righteous pass away; the godly often die before their time. And no one seems to care or wonder why. No one seems to understand that God is protecting them from the evil to come. For the godly who die will rest in peace. ISAIAH 57:1-2

January 3

Some choices have high stakes.

DELIVER US, Lord Jupiter!" shouted Trajanus Decius, emperor of Rome, as stones and arrows showered around him. "Deliver us, Lord Jupiter, for I have delivered all of Rome into your hands and the hands of our ancient gods!" cried the beleaguered monarch, as his horse stumbled forward through the dark waters of the tangled marshes of Dobruja. His men followed grimly, fighting as they fled.

Pressed violently on their left, assaulted mercilessly on their right, and pursued from behind, Decius's Roman troops bowed wearily and gradually succumbed to the fatal blows of the barbarian Goths of King Kniva. Decius fell at last, one dark form among so many, trampled underfoot by panic-stricken horses and pulled down by the sucking waters of the steaming swamp. His body was never found.

Decius had been emperor for fewer than three years. Coming to power in a time when political turmoil, military crisis, and economic instability threatened the Roman Empire, Decius sought to unite his subjects through forced submission to the ancient Roman gods. "Perhaps," he reasoned, "the gods will favor us once more, give us final victory over the pestilent Goths, and restore the glory of the empire."

On **January 3, 250,** he published an imperial edict commanding all citizens of the empire to sacrifice to the Roman gods. Those who did so were given certificates as evidence of their compliance while those who refused were imprisoned or executed.

Decius's edict initiated the first universal Roman persecution of the Christian church. Untold numbers of believers suffered the loss of family, freedom, and life itself. Among those martyred over the next two years were the bishops of Rome, Antioch, and Jerusalem.

When Decius died in battle against the Goths in June of 251, the pogrom ended, but the lull revealed a spiritual war within the ranks of the Christian community itself.

Many believers had sacrificed to the gods to save their lives, and others had illegally obtained certificates without sacrificing. And now thousands of lapsed Christians begged to be received back into the fellowship of the church.

A great controversy ensued. Some of those who had been imprisoned for their faith wrote letters of pardon to large numbers of those who had denied Christ. Some dishonest individuals produced amnesty papers in the name of dead martyrs.

Bishops were divided over how to treat the lapsed Christians. Some called for rigid excommunication. Some demanded a general amnesty. Eventually, they agreed that those who actually sacrificed to the gods should be readmitted to communion only when dying. Those who obtained a false Roman certificate but had not actually sacrificed to the gods could be readmitted upon repentance and penance. Without sorrow for their unfaithfulness, they would receive no grace. However, bitter dissensions over the matter continued with resulting schisms.

When another great persecution arose under Emperor Valerian in 257, a wider amnesty was offered to those who had defected during the days of Decius. This was not the sign of a weakened standard but rather a gracious opportunity for the shunned to stand where once they had fallen. Many returned to the fold. Many, in turn, sacrificed their lives for Christ.

Reflection

How do you feel the church should have dealt with Christians who sacrificed to the Roman gods or who obtained counterfeit certificates of compliance? How should churches today deal with members engaged in egregious sin?

∽❧∼

Dear brothers and sisters, if another Christian is overcome by some sin, you who are godly should gently and humbly help that person back onto the right path. And be careful not to fall into the same temptation yourself.   GALATIANS 6:1

January 4

He was an unlikely inquirer.

ALBERT CAMUS, the prominent existentialist thinker, struggled with religious issues like the meaning of life, the foundation for morality, the problem of suffering and evil, and the desire for eternal life. His major novels—*The Stranger* (1942), *The Plague* (1947), and *The Fall* (1956)—exhibited his conviction that God does not exist and that the world is without meaning.

Camus's main frustrations came from the issues of suffering and evil. Seeing pain and suffering all around him, he could not believe that a God who was good and all-powerful would watch such events and do nothing to alleviate them. Such a God, he felt, was not worth believing.

Camus could not merely sit by and watch the suffering of what he felt was a meaningless world. He tried to create meaning by showing compassion to the suffering and encouraging others to do so as well.

Howard Mumma, a Methodist pastor, was a guest minister at the American Church in Paris for several summers in the late 1950s. During these summers he was approached by Camus. Mumma was sworn to secrecy at the time, and his conversations with Camus were "irregular and occasional," but they had an impact. Mumma saw a man who had questions and doubts about his convictions. Camus told him, "I am searching for something I do not have, something I'm not sure I can define." Rather than try to point out the flaws in Camus's philosophy, Mumma commiserated with him and expressed his own inability to understand the world, man's existence, and purpose.

As their conversations continued, Camus began to read the Bible that Mumma gave him. As he read, something began to click in Camus's thought process.

At a later meeting Camus unexpectedly asked, "Howard, do you perform baptisms?" He also inquired what it meant to be born again. Mumma explained that "baptism is a symbolic commitment to God" and that being born again means "to enter anew or afresh into the process of spiritual growth . . . to receive forgiveness because you have asked God to forgive you of all your sins." Camus replied, "Howard, I am ready. I want this."

Camus wanted a private baptism, but Mumma would not agree to that. Instead he suggested that Camus continue to study his Bible and postpone his baptism until the two could agree on how to go about it. They parted for the season with Camus saying, "My friend, *mon cher*, thank you . . . I am going to keep striving for the Faith!"

A few months later, on **January 4, 1960,** Camus was killed in a car accident.

Reflection

Do you expect to meet Albert Camus in heaven? If you had been Howard Mumma, would you have done anything differently in talking with him?

⬿❧⬾

The Scriptures say, "I will destroy human wisdom and discard their most brilliant ideas." So where does this leave the philosophers, the scholars, and the world's brilliant debaters? God has made them all look foolish and has shown their wisdom to be useless nonsense. Since God in his wisdom saw to it that the world would never find him through human wisdom, he has used our foolish preaching to save all who believe. 1 CORINTHIANS 1:19-21

January 5

Some fathers deal with their sons eyeball-to-eyeball; others, nose-to-nose. My father dealt with me knee-to-knee.

JOHN ASHCROFT had just moved from the governor's mansion in Jefferson City, Missouri, to Washington, D.C., to become a United States senator.

"The night before I was sworn in to the Senate in 1995, my father arranged for some close friends and family—maybe fifteen to twenty people—to gather for dinner. My father eyed a piano in the corner of the room and said, 'John, why don't you play the piano, and we'll sing?' "

"Okay, Dad, you name it, I'll play it."

"Let's sing, 'We Are Standing on Holy Ground.' "

It was one of his father's favorites, but he was not engaging in some sentimental ploy by suggesting it. He had a profound purpose in his request.

The family gathered the next morning at a house not far from the Capitol that was maintained by a group of friends for the express purpose of bringing members of Congress together for spiritual enrichment. At the time Ashcroft did not realize how weak his father was. He later learned that his father had told an acquaintance of his, "I'm hanging on by a thread, and it's a thin thread at that, but I'm going to see John sworn in to the Senate."

As the family visited together, the earnestness of the senior Ashcroft's voice suddenly commanded everyone's attention. "John," he said, "please listen carefully." Everyone focused on John's dad.

"The spirit of Washington is arrogance," he said, "and the spirit of Christ is humility. Put on the spirit of Christ. Nothing of lasting value has ever been accomplished in arrogance. Someday I hope that someone will come up to you as you're fulfilling your duties as a senator, tug on your sleeve, and say, 'Senator, your spirit is showing.' "

John then knelt in front of the sofa where his father was seated, and everyone gathered closer. When John realized his father was struggling unsuccessfully to lift himself off the couch, John said, "Dad, you don't have to struggle to stand and pray over me with these friends."

"John," his father answered, "I'm not struggling to stand. I'm struggling to kneel." John felt overwhelmed, humbled, and inspired all at the same time.

John was sworn in to the Senate that afternoon. Early the next morning, on **January 5, 1995,** a friend awakened the Ashcrofts with the news that

John's father had died. "John," the friend said, "there's something you ought to know. This was not a surprise to your dad. Yesterday your father pulled me aside and said, 'Dick, I want you to assure me that when John gets to his assigned offices, you will have prayer with him, inviting the presence of God into those rooms.' "

"I looked at your father and said, 'We'll do just that. And, as a matter of fact, we'll call you up in Springfield, put you on the speakerphone, and you can join us for the consecration.'

"John, the next thing I knew, your father grabbed me by the arm and said, 'You don't understand. I'll be with you. But I won't be in Springfield.' He knew what was coming, John. He knew."

In 2001 Senator John Ashcroft left the Senate to become the attorney general of the United States.

Reflection

John Ashcroft is the product of a godly heritage. He would be the first to tell you that much of what he is today is due to his godly father. What heritage are you passing on to your children or to those whom God has placed in your life?

∾∾

The godly walk with integrity; blessed are their children after them.

PROVERBS 20:7

January 6

He came in to get out of the snow.

CHARLES SPURGEON was born in Kelvedon, Essex, England, in 1834 of Dutch ancestry. His father and grandfather were both independent pastors outside of the Church of England, and he was raised with a strict adherence to the Scriptures. In his father's and grandfather's studies, Charles pored over their books. *Foxe's Book of Martyrs* and Bunyan's *Pilgrim's Progress* were his early reading.

Despite knowing intellectually that "Christ died for our sins," Charles was so aware of his shortcomings that he could not believe that it applied to him. Turning to books such as Alleine's *Admonition to Unconverted Sinners* and Baxter's *Call to the Unconverted* only seemed to confirm his need for salvation.

He asked many different preachers the same question: "How can I get my sins forgiven?" No one provided an answer he understood, but on **January 6, 1850,** everything changed.

Fifteen-year-old Charles was headed to church during a snowstorm that Sunday morning when he ducked into a Primitive Methodist chapel to escape the snow. The congregation was sparse, and a lay preacher was filling in for the pastor. His text was "Look unto me, and be ye saved, all the ends of the earth." Charles loved to tell the story:

> He did not even pronounce the words rightly, but that did not matter. There was, I thought, a glimmer of hope for me in that text.
>
> The preacher began thus: "This is a very simple text indeed. It says 'Look.' Now lookin' don't take a deal of pain. It ain't liftin' your foot or your finger; it is just 'Look.' Well, a man needn't go to college to learn to look. You may be the biggest fool, and yet you can look. . . .
>
> When he had . . . managed to spin out about ten minutes or so, he was at the end of his tether. Then he looked at me under the gallery, and I daresay, with so few present, he knew me to be a stranger. Just fixing his eyes on me, as if he knew all my heart, he said, "Young man, you look very miserable." Well, I did, but I had not been accustomed to have remarks made from the pulpit on my personal appearance before. However, it was a good blow, struck right home. He continued, "And you will always be miserable—miserable in life and miserable in death—if you don't obey my text; but if you obey now, this moment,

you will be saved. . . . Young man, look to Jesus Christ. Look! Look! Look! You have nothing to do but look and live."

I saw at once the way of salvation. . . . I had been waiting to do fifty things, but when I heard that word "Look!" what a charming word it seemed to me. Oh! I looked until I could almost have looked my eyes away. There and then the cloud was gone, the darkness rolled away, and in that moment I saw the sun; and I could have risen that instant and sung with the most enthusiastic of them, of the precious blood of Christ, and the simple faith that looks to Him. Oh, that somebody had told me this before, "Trust Christ and you shall be saved." Yet it was no doubt, all wisely ordered, and now I can say—

> E'er since by faith I saw the stream
> Thy flowing wounds supply,
> Redeeming love has been my theme,
> And shall be till I die.

Charles Spurgeon did indeed keep looking to Jesus and went on to become the most famous preacher of his generation, ministering in London's Metropolitan Tabernacle.[2]

Reflection

Raised in a Christian family, Charles Spurgeon knew all the facts, but it wasn't until he was fifteen that God saved him. Regardless of your knowledge and background, there has to be a moment in time when the Holy Spirit opens your eyes and you look to Jesus for salvation. Have you looked?

Let all the world look to me for salvation! For I am God; there is no other.   ISAIAH 45:22

January 7

His life was changed by an ugly car, a pretty girl, and Mr. Pridgen.

By the age of thirteen, Johnny Hunt was already heavily abusing alcohol. His mother worked two jobs to provide for her family, and Johnny capitalized on the lack of adult supervision by getting into all kinds of trouble. When he was fourteen, he found a fake ID and gained entrance to the local poolroom, where he began playing pool five to eight hours a day. Johnny dropped out of school at sixteen and was hired as the manager of the poolroom.

His first car was an old beat-up junker that was so ugly he was embarrassed to be seen in it. So instead of driving it, he had his friend drive him home from work each day. One day when his friend was in a hurry, he dropped him off a few blocks away from his neighborhood, where Johnny saw a beautiful girl twirling a baton outside her house. After that, Johnny asked his friend to drop him off there every day, hoping to catch a glimpse of her as he walked by her house. His strategy paid off—they met and were married within the year!

His wife, Jan, soon began to talk about their need for church. Johnny was trying to be a good husband, but going to church was not part of his plan. Then a man named Mr. Pridgen began coming into the hardware store where Johnny had taken a part-time job. As Mr. Pridgen paid for his purchases each week, he would tell Johnny how Jesus had changed yet another life and invite him to church. Week after week Johnny was hounded by both Jan and Mr. Pridgen. He finally gave in.

They began attending Mr. Pridgen's church, and after a few weeks Johnny was surprised to feel the Lord working in his heart. "Things began to change. I went to church, and everything seemed fine so long as there was preaching or singing. But when the pastor would say, 'We're going to stand together and sing an invitation hymn,' I would begin to weep. While others bowed their heads in prayer, I'd ease out a handkerchief and wipe my tears."

During the morning service on **January 7, 1973,** Jan noticed his tears. She questioned him, but he didn't have words to describe what was happening to him.

That afternoon Johnny asked Jan whether she was interested in attending the evening service and added, "Jan, you know that I have tried to clean up my act, but I have failed. Well, if Jesus Christ can change my life, He's welcome to it." She could hardly believe her ears! That night, when the invitation was given, Johnny went forward and put his trust in Jesus.

FROM THE POOLROOM
TO THE PULPIT

From that moment on, Johnny Hunt was a changed young man. He went to all his old hangouts, sharing with his old friends what Jesus had done for him. When a skeptic asked him, "What are you going to do now that you're saved and going to heaven?" His answer came easily, "Take as many people with me as I can."

To achieve this goal, Johnny decided to become a pastor. He finished high school, attended college and then seminary, and became a Southern Baptist pastor. After years in the ministry he still has the same message: "Jesus took me from the poolroom to the pulpit, and he changed my life. He can change your life, too!"

He often prays, "Thank you, Lord, for rescuing this wayward son. Thank you for that ugly car, for that pretty girl, and for Mr. Pridgen."

Reflection

Have there been circumstances in your life that God has used to draw you closer to him? You may not have realized at the time that it was God working in your life. Thank him for where he has brought you and where he will take you!

∾⨀∾

Surely your goodness and unfailing love will pursue me all the days of my life.   PSALM 23:6

January 8

No one wanted to hear from God.

TWICE, King Nebuchadnezzar had deported Jews to Babylon. Ezekiel, a priest, had been part of the second deportation in 597 B.C.[3] In Babylon he had prophesied that God would send Nebuchadnezzar one more time to destroy Jerusalem completely because of the sins and apostasy of the Jewish people.[4] God even informed them of the day the siege began (Ezekiel 24:1-14).[5]

Then on **January 8, 585 B.C.**, a man who had escaped from Jerusalem came to Ezekiel in Babylon and told him, "The city is fallen." This news meant that more exiles were on the way.

Ezekiel then received a message from the Lord. The first part dealt with the Jews who had not been taken captive to Babylon and were living in the ruined cities of Judah. These people reasoned among themselves that if Abraham, a single person, had gained possession of the entire land of Israel, then they who were many people certainly deserved the whole land as their possession. God's message to them was this:

> You eat meat with blood in it, you worship idols, and you murder the innocent. Do you really think the land should be yours? Murderers! Idolaters! Adulterers! Should the land belong to you? . . .
> As surely as I live, those living in the ruins will die by the sword. Those living in the open fields will be eaten by wild animals. Those hiding in the forts and caves will die of disease. I will destroy the land and demolish her pride. Her arrogant power will come to an end. The mountains of Israel will be so ruined that no one will even travel through them. When I have ruined the land because of their disgusting sins, then they will know that I am the Lord. (Ezekiel 33:25-29)

The second part of the message dealt with the people in captivity in Babylon with Ezekiel. Regarding them, God said to Ezekiel:

> Son of man, your people are whispering behind your back. They talk about you in their houses and whisper about you at the doors, saying, "Come on, let's have some fun! Let's go hear the prophet tell us what the Lord is saying!" So they come pretending to be sincere and sit before you listening. But they have no intention of doing what I tell

16

them. They express love with their mouths, but their hearts seek only after money. You are very entertaining to them, like someone who sings love songs with a beautiful voice or plays fine music on an instrument. They hear what you say, but they don't do it! But when all these terrible things happen to them—as they certainly will—then they will know a prophet has been among them. (Ezekiel 33:30-33)

When God had originally called Ezekiel, he had warned him that the Jewish people of his day were rebellious, hard-hearted, and stubborn, but that Ezekiel should give God's message to them whether they listened or not (Ezekiel 2:3-5). Ezekiel was now experiencing the reality of what God had warned him about, for no one was listening!

Reflection

Why do you think the Jews of Ezekiel's day were so blatant in their disobedience to God's commandments? Why do you think the exiles in Babylon did not take seriously God's messages through the prophet Ezekiel? Can you think of situations in our world today that parallel those of Ezekiel's day? What lessons can we learn for ourselves?

∽∾

The Kingdom of God will be taken away from you and given to a nation that will produce the proper fruit.   MATTHEW 21:43

January 9

Their lives were like bright, short-lived flames.

NEW YEAR'S DAY 1956 was the day for the five missionaries to prepare for their upcoming attempt to contact the fierce Auca Indians of Ecuador.[6] Nate Saint, the pilot, was going to fly them to Palm Beach, where they had previously exchanged gifts with the Aucas from the air. As Jim Elliot, Pete Fleming, Ed McCully, and Roger Youdarian collected what they would need for their mission, Betty Elliot, Jim's wife, wondered, *Will this be the last time I'll help him pack?*

After breakfast and prayer on the day of their departure, January 3, the five men sang one of their favorite hymns:

> *We rest on thee, our Shield and our Defender,*
> *Thine is the battle, thine will be the praise.*
> *When passing through the gates of pearly splendor*
> *Victors, we rest with thee through endless days.*

Once on the beach, they built a tree house and prepared to contact the Aucas. On Friday, January 6, a visit from an Auca man and two women encouraged the missionaries. They spent several hours together and even gave the man a ride in the plane.

Saturday no Aucas appeared, but Sunday morning when Nate flew over the site, he spotted some Auca men walking toward their beach. At 12:30 P.M. Nate made his prearranged radio call to his wife, Marj, back at the mission station: "Looks like they'll be here for the early afternoon service. Pray for us. This is the day! Will contact you at 4:30."

When 4:30 came, the missionary wives switched on their radios. Silence. Five minutes went by and then ten. Sundown came, and still no word. The wives slept little that night.

Monday morning, **January 9, 1956,** Johnny Keenan, another missionary pilot, flew to the beach. As Betty Elliot awaited his report, Isaiah 43:2 ran through her mind: "When thou passest through the waters, I will be with thee; and through the rivers, they shall not overflow thee." She prayed, "Lord, let not the waters overflow."

At 9:30 A.M. the pilot's report came in. Marj Saint shared it with the other wives: "Johnny has found the plane on the beach. All the fabric is stripped off. There is no sign of the fellows."

Another pilot immediately contacted Lieutenant General William K. Harrison, commander in chief of the Caribbean Command, himself a Christian. Radio station HCJB in Ecuador flashed the news to the rest of the world: "Five men missing in Auca territory." By noon a ground party was organized to go to the site.

On Wednesday Johnny Keenan made his fourth flight over the beach. Marj Saint, who had hardly left her radio since Sunday, called the other wives, and as soon as she was able to speak, she said, "They found one body." Johnny had seen one body floating face down in the river.

In the afternoon Johnny radioed in again, "Another body sighted about two hundred feet below Palm Beach." The five wives had no idea whose bodies they were.

The search party located four of the five bodies, but Ed McCully's had been swept away by the river. The other four were buried on Palm Beach.

What happened to the Aucas? By the end of 1958 Betty Elliot and Rachel Saint, Nate's sister, were living among them, and one by one the Aucas put their faith in Jesus Christ.[7]

The five men who murdered the missionaries became not only Christians but also spiritual leaders among their people. After they believed, they shared how on that fateful day they heard singing from above the trees. Looking up they saw what appeared to be a canopy of bright lights. God was welcoming his children home.

Nine years later, in June 1965, two of Nate Saint's children, Kathy and Stephen, were baptized at Palm Beach by two of the men who had killed their father.

Reflection

In 1948 Jim Elliot wrote in his journal, "Saturate me with the oil of the Spirit that I may be a flame. But flame is often short-lived. Can thou bear this, my soul?" How would you answer that question?

∽❧∾

Those who turn many to righteousness will shine like stars forever.
DANIEL 12:3

January 10

It was a prayer meeting that ended in heaven.

DANIEL JAMES DRAPER, an English Methodist, went as a missionary to south Australia in 1836. There he witnessed the building of thirty new churches and under his leadership saw membership increase tenfold.

Draper and his wife made their first visit back to England twenty-nine years later. On January 5, 1866, they left Plymouth, England, to return to Australia aboard the *London*. As they sailed out at midnight, the sky and sea were calm. Two days later the wind increased but not enough to prevent Draper from holding a worship service in the ship's saloon. But within twenty-four hours the wind greatly increased, and much of the ship's rigging was blown away. The winds became so violent that the wreckage from the masts could not be cleared, making the ship rock even more, furthering the damage to the ship. The winds continued until they became a full-blown hurricane. By 3:00 P.M. Wednesday, **January 10, 1866,** the ship turned back toward Plymouth, sailing as quickly as it could in its damaged state in an attempt to reach safer, calmer waters.

At ten-thirty that night a "mountain of water" fell on the main deck, taking out the engine-room skylight, completely filling the engine room and extinguishing the engine fires. As the men worked furiously to repair the damage, nature showed no mercy. Finally, Captain Martin told his men to say their prayers, for the ship was doomed.

The darkness that night was an eerie forerunner of the deeper darkness that would soon engulf them. At midnight Draper began a prayer meeting in the saloon. All the passengers and crew not on duty gathered. In between the prayers Draper exhorted the people to come to Christ for salvation. Many brought their Bibles and read them with earnestness. Survivors later reported that mothers were weeping as they held their bewildered children and friends bid each other good-bye, but there was no hysteria.

At dawn Captain Martin calmly told the passengers and crew that all hope was lost. Draper broke the somber silence that followed this announcement by standing up to address the crowd once more. With tears flowing down his face, he said in a clear, strong voice, "The captain tells us there is no hope; that we must all perish. But I tell you there is hope, hope for all. Although we must die and shall never again see land, we may all make the port of heaven."

The survivors reported that from the beginning of the prayer meeting at midnight until the boat sank at two the next afternoon, Draper was ceaseless in his prayers, admonitions, and invitations. Among his last heard words were, "In a few moments we must all appear before our Great Judge. Let us prepare to meet him."

A survivor said that as he left the ship, he heard people singing:

> Rock of Ages, cleft for me,
> Let me hide myself in thee;
> Let the water and the blood,
> From thy wounded side which flowed,
> Be of sin the double cure,
> Save from wrath and make me pure.
>
> While I draw this fleeting breath,
> When my eyes shall close in death,
> When I rise to worlds unknown,
> And behold thee on thy throne,
> Rock of Ages, cleft for me,
> Let me hide myself in thee.[8]

Reflection

Daniel Draper's sole concern as the ship went down was making sure that everyone knew the way of salvation. What do you think you would do if you were on a sinking ship?

∞

God has given us the task of reconciling people to him. For God was in Christ, reconciling the world to himself, no longer counting people's sins against them. This is the wonderful message he has given us to tell others. 2 CORINTHIANS 5:18-19

21

January 11

"Where is Timothy?" his mother and father wondered once again.

THE LAD was often late for dinner and predictably hard to find. When at last his parents found him, seated under an apple tree, he was teaching the catechism to a rapt congregation of New England Indians, whom he had met in the street and invited to discuss the Christian religion. Completely absorbed in his endeavor, Timothy Dwight had forgotten the hour. The particular event, though not out of character for the little boy, was highly unusual for someone his age—he was four years old.

Born in 1752, Timothy Dwight, the grandson of Jonathan Edwards,[9] was a child prodigy. Between the ages of four and eleven, he was schooled in classical literature, taught himself Latin and studied geography, grammar, biblical history and the histories of England, Rome, and ancient Greece. At eleven he was tutored in Latin and Greek, and at thirteen he entered Yale. He graduated at seventeen, continued graduate study, and became a hired tutor at the college.

It was an amazing record—but with sorrowful side effects. The four-year-old who chose teaching the catechism to eating supper became an adult enslaved to intellectual achievement. He gave up physical exercise and cut back on eating and sleeping for increased study time. After ignoring his body for the sake of his mind, he was sick for months and nearly died. He was left nearly blind, never again to read without terrible pain and headaches or write without help to record his dictation.

But Dwight served a God who works good out of all things. Since he could no longer read, he went outdoors, where he could talk to people. Instead of learning from old dusty theology books, he learned from the man on the street. The long-term fruit of Dwight's personal suffering was an increased understanding of the life and labor of the common man.

When the American Revolution began, Dwight joined the Continental Army as a chaplain. He counseled, prayed, and exhorted men to faith and courage in the midst of fear and death. In the crucible of war, a pastoral heart was born.

In 1783 he accepted the pastorate of the church in Greenfield, Connecticut, where he shepherded his flock and taught at an academy. Still an intellectual, he began to speak and write against French deism. In 1794 he published *A Discourse on the Genuineness and Authenticity of the New Testament,* a defense

22

against the antibiblical French philosophies taking root at the university level throughout the newly formed United States.

In 1795 God called Timothy Dwight to a new chapter in his life. He became the president of his alma mater, Yale College, a growing hotbed of deism. Dwight found himself at war once more, but it was a war for which he was made. Prayerfully and confidently, he unsheathed the sword of the Spirit and stepped into the fray.

By 1802, after seven years of Dwight's solid biblical preaching, hearts were softened, deism's back was badly bent, and revival broke out on campus. One-third of Yale's 225 students were converted to Christ under his preaching, and many became instrumental in a larger revival that spread throughout New England, upstate New York, and onto the Western frontier. It was the beginning of the nation's Second Great Awakening.

When Timothy Dwight passed at last from this life into the next on **January 11, 1817,** he left behind a legacy of biblical scholarship and evangelical revival.

Reflection

How did God work his purposes through Timothy Dwight's loss of most of his eyesight? How might his life have been different if he had not had the problem with his eyes? Was it a positive or a negative for his life and ministry?

The Lord disciplines those he loves. HEBREWS 12:6

January 12

He started early.

HENRY ALFORD was born in 1810 in London, where his father was an Anglican vicar and his mother died in childbirth. From a young age, he showed an aptitude for artistic and scholarly pursuits and a commitment to his Lord. One of his hobbies as a boy was writing little books. When he was only five, he wrote a five-page book entitled *The Travels of St. Paul from his Conversion to his Death.* He was writing Latin odes before he was ten. At age ten he wrote *Looking unto Jesus, or, The Believers Support under Trials and Afflictions.* The first chapter began: "Looking unto Jesus is not, as some would suppose, looking to him with our bodily eyes, for we cannot see Jesus as the apostles did, and other holy men; but it is here taken in a spiritual sense, and means first, a looking unto him by faith, second, praying to him."

At twenty-two he graduated from Trinity College and was ordained the next year as his father's assistant. Two years later he married and became a fellow of Trinity College. While at Trinity he began his most ambitious work, *The Greek Testament.* This four-volume classic commentary on the New Testament, on which he worked for sixteen years, is still in use today. In 1835 he became vicar of Wymesworld and remained there for the next eighteen years.

In 1853 he became the minister of Quebec Chapel in London, and four years later he was appointed dean of Canterbury. He remained in that position for eighteen years until his death.

Few people in the history of the church have displayed the lifelong productivity and range of abilities of Henry Alford. In addition to his preaching, teaching, and research, Alford wrote and translated poetry and prose, and was a watercolor painter and wood-carver. He played and composed music for piano and organ and wrote the hymns "Come, Ye Thankful People Come" and "Ten Thousand Times Ten Thousand."

When Henry Alford died, on **January 12, 1871,** the much-loved dean was deeply mourned. The funeral procession wended its way from Canterbury Cathedral to St. Martin's Churchyard. There the graveside service ended with the singing of Alford's hymn:

> Ten thousand times ten thousand
> In sparkling raiment bright,
> The armies of the ransomed saints

A TRAVELER ON HIS WAY
TO JERUSALEM

Throng up the steeps of light;
'Tis finished, all is finished,
Their fight with death and sin;
Fling open wide the golden gates,
And let the victors in!

Bring near thy great salvation,
Thou Lamb for sinners slain;
Fill up the roll of thine elect,
Then take thy power and reign;
Appear, Desire of nations,
Thine exiles long for home;
Show in the heaven thy promised sign,
Thou Prince and Saviour, come!

Henry Alford had many accomplishments but little need for accolades. After his death the following memorandum from him was found: "When I am gone and a tomb is to be put up, let there be, besides any indication of who is lying below, these words and these only: *The Inn of a Traveler on His Way to Jerusalem.*"—Henry Alford

Reflection

How do you react when you hear of someone who wrote Latin odes before the age of ten and then grew up to be a famous author? God has given few people gifts like Henry Alford's, but he has equipped every one of his children to accomplish whatever he has purposed for them.

May the God of peace, who brought again from the dead our Lord Jesus, equip you with all you need for doing his will. May he produce in you, through the power of Jesus Christ, all that is pleasing to him.
HEBREWS 13:20-21

January 13

Enough is enough!

KING FRANCIS I had been very tolerant of those "Lutherans," as the Protestants in France were called in the early 1520s. Known as the "Father of Letters," Francis wished to be seen as a supporter of the Renaissance, encouraging Italian artists and new writers and building beautiful palaces.

He had been patient and sometimes even agreed with his sister, Marguerite of Angoulême, who was sympathetic to the Protestant cause and often pleaded its case. Francis resisted the increasing pressure from the center of scholarship, the Sorbonne, to censure the Protestant scholars and preachers. At first when the Parliament of Paris, the highest civil tribunal, joined the Sorbonne in the search for heresy, the king repeatedly rescued those who were targeted. However, when it became obvious that public peace was threatened, he changed his mind.

Francis became increasingly less tolerant of those Lutherans who were militant and pushy. He felt they were a threat to the lifestyle and politics of his kingdom. At the end of the 1520s and in the early 1530s, Protestants were walking a tightrope. Catholics and Protestants alike were becoming more rigid and insistent on the rightness of their respective causes.

Putting up large posters in public places had long been a part of Parisian life. However, an incident referred to as the "Affair of the Placards" angered Francis I so much that it became a watershed for Protestants. A poster entitled "True Articles Respecting the Horrible, Great and Insupportable Abuses of the Papal Mass" was written by Antoine Marcourt, a French refugee who had fled to Neuchâtel, Switzerland. The plastering of this scandalous document all over the streets of Paris on October 8, 1534, was bad enough, but the impertinence of placing one on the king's bedroom door in his castle at Amboise so infuriated Francis that from then on the king was fiercely intolerant of the Lutherans.

Protestant literature was everywhere in France and was winning many converts. Finally Francis I felt it was time to stop the nonsense once and for all, and on **January 13, 1535,** he sent an edict to the Parliament of Paris forbidding the printing of books of any kind. This was a move that the theologians of the Sorbonne had advised the king to make a year and a half earlier because of their alarm over the number of "heretical" books being printed.

After six weeks the king, perhaps remembering he was the "Father of Letters," had second thoughts about outlawing printing and opted for censorship instead. He set up a board of twelve censors that had to approve all books printed. In addition, books could be printed only in Paris.

Things went downhill from there for followers of the Reformation in France. In January 1535 six Protestants were burned to death, beginning the persecution of the Lutherans, later known as Huguenots. In June 1540 the Edict of Fontainebleau gave parliament control of determining what heresy was. In 1542 the Faculty of Theology of Paris issued an Index of Prohibited Books.

In spite of the king's opposition to the propagation of "heretical books," the publication of Christian literature and Bibles marched on, moving outside of Paris to Lyon, to Monbéliard, and also to Switzerland. Bibles were distributed throughout the countryside of France, providing the people with eye-opening access to Scripture until at one point France had become half Protestant.

Reflection

What is your reaction to the decision of King Francis I to outlaw the printing of books in an attempt to stem the tide of the Reformation? Why do people restrict the religious activities of those who believe differently than they do? Throughout history, religious freedom has been the most important of all civil rights.

∽❧∼

The Lord, the God of the Hebrews, has sent me to say, "Let my people go, so they can worship me in the wilderness." EXODUS 7:16

January 14

For years he labored without results.

GOD GAVE Dr. Walter L. Wilson, a Kansas City physician, a deep love for the Scriptures. After his conversion in 1896, Wilson diligently studied the Bible and applied himself to doing everything he found in God's Word. Yet it bothered him that his life did not seem to bear spiritual fruit. But others reassured him "not to look for results, but only to be busy at seed sowing."

So Wilson pressed on in his work as a physician and lay preacher. Then in 1913 a missionary from France visiting in his home challenged him with the question "What is the Holy Spirit to you?"

No stranger to theology, Wilson answered, "He is one of the persons of the Godhead, a Teacher, a Guide; the third person of the Trinity."

"He is just as great," the missionary said, "just as precious, just as needful as the other two Persons of the Trinity. But still you have not answered my question, What is He to you?"

"He is nothing to me," Wilson said, surprised at his own candor. "I have no contact with Him, no personal relationship, and could get along quite well without Him."

His visitor replied, "It is because of this that your life is so fruitless even though your efforts are so great. If you will seek personally to know the Holy Spirit, he will transform your life."

The missionary's words haunted Wilson into the next year. He wanted to bear the fruit of the Spirit but feared becoming a fanatic, giving an inferior place to Jesus Christ by overly exalting the Holy Spirit. A trusted Christian friend reassured him from the Bible that only by the Holy Spirit could Christ be made known to him and others.

Then on the evening of **January 14, 1914,** everything changed. Wilson heard Dr. James Gray, later the president of Moody Bible Institute, preach a sermon on Romans 12:1. Gray asked, "Have you noticed that this verse does not tell us to whom we should give our bodies? It is not the Lord Jesus. . . . He has his own body. It is not God the Father. . . . He remains upon His throne. Another has come to earth without a body. . . . God gives you the privilege and the indescribable honor of presenting your bodies to the Holy Spirit, to be His dwelling place on earth."

Wilson reported later that he said to the Holy Spirit, "My Lord, I have mistreated You all my Christian life. I have treated You like a servant. . . . I shall do so no more. Just now I give You this body of mine; from my head to my feet. I give You my hands, my limbs, my eyes and lips, my brain; all that I am within and without, I hand over to You for You to live in it the life that You please. You may send this body to Africa, or lay it on a bed with cancer. . . . It is Your body from this moment on. Help yourself to it. Thank You, my Lord, I believe You have accepted it, for in Romans twelve You said, 'acceptable unto God.' "

The next morning two women came to his office, as they had done before, selling advertising. Although he had never spoken to them about Christ before, that day he did, and both put their trust in him that morning. This was only the beginning of how mightily God used Dr. Walter Wilson. He went on to pastor Central Bible Church in Kansas City and cofounded and served as first president of Kansas City Bible College, now Calvary Bible College.

Walter Wilson, the "beloved physician," often testified, "With regard to my own experience with the Holy Spirit, I may say the transformation in my own life on **January 14, 1914,** was greater, much greater than the change that took place when I was saved December 21, 1896."

Reflection

What is your reaction to the story of Dr. Walter Wilson? Do you agree with Dr. Gray's sermon? Have you ever specifically given your body to God as a living sacrifice? God may use you in surprising ways just as he did Dr. Wilson.

Dear brothers and sisters, I plead with you to give your bodies to God. Let them be a living and holy sacrifice—the kind he will accept. When you think of what he has done for you, is this too much to ask?

ROMANS 12:1

January 15

He had a desire transplant.

THE SON of a respected Scottish minister, William Chalmers Burns was not interested in following in his father's footsteps. In 1831, after achieving success at the University of Aberdeen, Burns decided to study law. This was a great disappointment to his father, who as a minister of the Church of Scotland, desired that his son follow him into the ministry.

But his father's faith had affected him. Shortly after Burns decided to become a lawyer because they were "rich and with fine houses," he began to reevaluate the direction of his life.

Late one night when William heard his father praying, he whispered, "There can be no doubt where *his* heart is and where he is going." Not long after that, God changed him.

Burns later recalled, "When reading Pike's *Early Piety* on a Sabbath afternoon, I think about the middle of December 1831, an arrow from the quiver of the King of Zion was shot by his Almighty sovereign hand through my heart." It was about January 7, 1832, that "first the Spirit of God shone with full light upon the glory of Jesus as a Saviour for such as I was."

With Burns's faith came a loss of interest in studying law and, instead, a strong, deep desire to preach to those who had not heard the gospel. After studying for the ministry in Glasgow, he was accepted by the Church of Scotland as a missionary to India. But God had another plan, and Burns became involved in the Scottish revival, which began in 1839. He spent the next eight years preaching to crowds in Scotland, England, Ireland, and Canada.

In 1847, at the age of thirty-two, Burns went to China as the first missionary of the Presbyterian Church of England. He ministered in many port cities, but his heart was set on reaching the people of inland China. Leaving the coastal mission stations, Burns's practice was to build up native congregations, leave them in the care of other missionaries, and press on ever deeper into the heart of China. He was so dedicated to his mission work that his sole furlough lasted only one month before he returned to his work in China.

William Burns became terminally ill in December 1867 and wrote this farewell letter to his mother on **January 15, 1868.**

> *At the end of last year I got a severe chill which has not yet left the system, producing chilliness and fever every night, and for the last two nights this has*

been followed by perspiration, which rapidly diminished the strength. Unless it should please God to rebuke the disease, it is evident what the end must soon be, and I write these lines beforehand to say that I am happy, and ready through the abounding grace of God either to live or to die. May the God of all consolation comfort you when the tidings of my decease shall reach you, and through the redeeming blood of Jesus may we meet with joy before the throne above.

Reflection

When William Burns became a Christian, he lost his desire to make money and instead became burdened to make men and women rich in faith. In your life has God ever replaced a desire for wealth with a spiritual one? If so, how would you compare the satisfaction you received from trying to meet the respective desires?

Don't store up treasures here on earth, where they can be eaten by moths and get rusty, and where thieves break in and steal. Store your treasures in heaven, where they will never become moth-eaten or rusty and where they will be safe from thieves. MATTHEW 6:19-20

January 16

Motherhood brings joys and sorrows.

ELIZABETH PRENTISS, author of the hymn "More Love to Thee," was the wife of a pastor.[10] While they were serving a church in New York City, she gave birth to her first son, Eddy, on October 22, 1848. Frail from the beginning of his life, he was nonetheless a joy to Elizabeth. Her journal tells of three-year-old Eddy's Christmas:

> He enjoyed Christmas as much as I had reason to expect he would, in his state of health, and was busy among his new playthings all day. He had taken a fancy within a few weeks to kneel at family prayers with me at my chair, and would throw one little arm round my neck, while with the other hand he so prettily and seriously covered his eyes. As their heads [Eddy and his sister Annie] touched my face as they knelt, I observed that Eddy's felt hot when compared with A's; just enough so to increase my uneasiness. On entering in the nursery on New Year's morning, I was struck with his appearance as he lay in bed; his face being spotted all over. On asking Margaret [his nurse] about it, she said he had been crying, and that this occasioned the spots. This did not seem probable to me, for I had never seen anything of this kind on his face before. How little I knew that these were the last tears my darling would ever shed.

A few days later Elizabeth called for a doctor, as Eddy's symptoms only worsened with each passing day. All the doctor could suggest was a warm bath. Elizabeth tenderly cared for him as best she could.

> I knelt by the side of the cradle, rocking it very gently, and he asked me to tell him a story. I asked what about, and he said, "A little boy," on which I said something like this: Mamma knows a dear little boy who is very sick. His head ached and he felt sick all over. God said, "I must let that little lamb come into my fold; then his little head will never ache again, and he will be a very happy little lamb." I used the words little lamb because he was so fond of them. Often he would run to his nurse with his face full of animation and say, "Margaret! Mamma says I am her little lamb!" While I was telling the story his eyes were fixed

intelligently on my face. I then said, "Would you like to know the name of the boy?" With eagerness he said, "Yes, yes, mamma!" Taking his dear little hand in mine, and kissing it, I said, "It was Eddy."

On Friday, **January 16, 1852,** little Eddy died, his loving spirit ascending to that place where the Lord Jesus, thousands of other children, and a myriad of angels joyfully welcomed him. That day Elizabeth wrote the following poem:

To My Dying Eddy, January 16th:

Blest child! dear child! For thee is Jesus calling:
And of our household thee—and only thee!
Oh, hasten hence! to His embraces hasten!
Sweet shall thy rest and safe thy shelter be.

Reflection

As believers, how do we know that children who die in infancy are in heaven? The Bible indicates that they are in the story of the death of David and Bathsheba's little son. David fasted and prayed for the sick child until he died. Then he got up and went to the temple to worship, confident that one day he would be reunited with the child in heaven.

❧

David replied, "I fasted and wept while the child was alive, for I said, 'Perhaps the Lord will be gracious to me and let the child live.' But why should I fast when he is dead? Can I bring him back again? I will go to him one day, but he cannot return to me." 2 SAMUEL 12:22-23

January 17

He was a powerful emperor who showed he could be humble before God.

THE GREAT bronze statue of the Greek goddess Serapis had been worshiped for generations. Faithful worshipers now watched in fear as the soldiers of Theodosius raised heavy hammers against the giant metal effigy standing in the pagan temple in Alexandria.

At the first blow, the spectators fell upon their faces in fear of the divine wrath of Serapis. But no lightning fell upon the troops of the Christian emperor Theodosius I; no sound of rage and thunder filled the temple. Instead, as the hammers tore great holes in the battered bronze, a swarm of frightened rats poured out upon the ancient temple floor. It is said that on that day many pagans became Christians.

Son of a famous Roman general, Theodosius was born in Spain in 347. Early in life he distinguished himself in the military and then retired from public service. In 379 Emperor Gratian called Theodosius out of private life and made him fellow-emperor for the East. There he fought the Gothic War so effectively that in 380 he was able to sign a victorious peace treaty with the Goths. Earlier that year, stricken so ill that he feared death, he sought out the bishop of Thessalonica and was baptized.

Although Theodosius was raised a Christian, his baptism in 380 may have been a conversion experience. From 381 until his death, he was as militantly zealous for the apostolic doctrines of the church as he was for the governance of the empire.

In 381 and 385 he prohibited sacrifices for divination, effectually stopping all pagan sacrifice throughout the empire, authorized the destruction of some pagan temples or their conversion to Christian churches, and ordered the demolition of all temples in Alexandria following unrest between the Christians and the pagans.

In 391 he closed temples empirewide. The next year he effectively ended Roman paganism by prohibiting private pagan worship, threatening harsh punishment to frighten pagans into considering Christianity.

From the year of his baptism, Theodosius ordered his subjects to follow "that religion which Peter the Apostle transmitted to the Romans." Spiritually allied with Ambrose, the popular bishop of Milan, he fought vigorously against the long-standing heresy of Arianism, which denied the eternal existence of God the Son. All known Arians were expelled from Constantinople, and Arian chapels were closed throughout the East.

THEODOSIUS THE GREAT

Theodosius made one very serious mistake. In the summer of 390 a subversive riot broke out in Thessalonica, and the military commander of the city was murdered. Theodosius's desire for revenge led him to order a massacre of the city's inhabitants, the innocent along with the guilty. He soon repented of his anger and canceled the order—but too late! Seven thousand Thessalonicans, lured into the city's stadium by the false promise of a chariot race, were slaughtered by Roman troops.

Ambrose was horrified. As bishop and friend, he sent a personal but spiritually uncompromising letter to Theodosius. "If the priest does not speak to someone who errs," he wrote, "he who errs will die in his sin." Ambrose denied the emperor Communion until he truly repented and completed an eight-month period of penance.

Theodosius shut himself up in his palace and wept. Finally he went to Ambrose privately in humble brokenness. Pardoned at last and free to enter the sanctuary for worship, he showed his repentance publicly by throwing himself upon the floor, tearing his hair, and crying out loudly to both God and man for the forgiveness of his sin.

On **January 17, 395,** Theodosius I died. He was the last sovereign of the undivided Roman Empire. He officially arranged that after his death the East and the West would split into permanent empires for his two sons. As a result of his aggressive policies, he left behind a kingdom swept free of heresy and paganism. Posterity remembers him as Theodosius the Great.

Reflection

How do you evaluate the life of Theodosius? Was he right or wrong to destroy pagan temples and banish heretics? What were his strengths and weaknesses? Mistakes are part of the human condition, but, praise God, there is forgiveness for those showing genuine repentance!

❧

Zeal without knowledge is not good; a person who moves too quickly may go the wrong way. PROVERBS 19:2

January 18

You never know how God will answer.

Amy Carmichael was born in 1867 in Millisle, County Down, Northern Ireland. At the age of twelve, she was sent to a Wesleyan Methodist boarding school in Yorkshire, England. There at age fifteen during a children's service she heard the song "Jesus loves me this I know, for the Bible tells me so." In the quiet moments following the song, Amy realized that, in spite of her mother's teaching that Jesus loved her, she had never invited him into her life. "In His great mercy the Good Shepherd answered the prayers of my mother and my father and many other loving ones, and drew me, even me, into His fold."

After the death of her father, she went to England to live in the home of Robert Wilson, who was a cofounder and chairman of the Keswick Convention, a summer gathering of English evangelicals. Under Wilson's influence, Amy became interested in missions, and in 1893 she sailed for Japan as the first Keswick missionary with the Church Missionary Society. After spending less than two years in Japan and Ceylon, she was forced to return to England because of poor health.

In November 1895 Amy again left England to work with the Church of England Zenana Missionary Society in South India. Traveling on evangelistic trips throughout India, she became aware that many young Indian girls were offered by parents or guardians as temple prostitutes, a practice that was later outlawed. Touched by their plight, Amy began rescuing young girls from this fate.

By 1901 she, along with the Indian colleagues and converts from her many trips, settled in Dohnavur. In 1926 she founded the Dohnavur Fellowship, a home and school for rescued children. Here the Indian children were educated and trained to serve God as Christian nurses, teachers, and evangelists.

Amy was known at Dohnavur Fellowship as Amma or Mother. As the leader of the fellowship, she set high standards for herself and her colleagues. She established the Sisters of the Common Life, which approached being a Protestant order. Vows were not binding for life, but if a sister married, she was required to leave the association. So committed was Amy Carmichael to India that from the time she arrived in November 1895, she never returned to England.

On October 24, 1931, Amy visited a Dohnavur dispensary and was concerned about the Fellowship's financial support. Seeking God's guidance regarding money, she fell silent for a long time and then prayed, "Do anything, Lord, that will fit me to serve thee and to help my beloveds."

A LIFE-CHANGING PRAYER

Later that day she was driven to a house she had rented for another dispensary. There in the darkness she fell into a newly dug pit, breaking her leg, dislocating an ankle, and twisting her spine. As a result of her fall, she was bedridden her last twenty years. Yet from her bed she remained in charge of Dohnavur and also wrote the prose and poetry through which the work of Dohnavur became known around the world.

In 1938 Carmichael believed that God gave her a promise that she would die in her sleep. This she did on **January 18, 1951.**

Announcing her death, the bells of the House of Prayer at Dohnavur played the music she had requested, to which her words had been set:

One thing have I desired, my God, of Thee;
That will I seek: Thine house home to me.

I would not breathe an alien, other air;
I would be with Thee, O Thou fairest fair.

For I would see the beauty of my Lord
And hear Him speak, who is my heart's adored.

O Love of loves, and can such wonder dwell
In Thy great name of names, Immanuel?

Thou with Thy child; Thy child at home with Thee;
O Love of loves, I love, I worship Thee.

Reflection

Do you believe that Amy Carmichael's fall in 1931 was God's answer to her prayer earlier that day, "Do *anything*, Lord, that will fit me to serve thee and to help my beloveds"? Do you dare to pray such a prayer?

Mary responded, "I am the Lord's servant, and I am willing to accept whatever he wants."
LUKE 1:38

January 19

He had walked in their shoes—until the night he sold them.

THE SON of a saloon keeper, Mel Trotter had learned bartending from his father when his dad was too drunk to pour a drink at the bar. As a young man, Trotter had resolved to escape the saloon, leaving home to take up barbering. Unfortunately, he was so successful as a barber that the income gave him the opportunity to gamble and drink at will.

Trying to escape big city temptations, Mel Trotter moved to Iowa about 1890 and managed to stay sober long enough to marry. But his wife soon discovered that she was married to an alcoholic. He repeatedly vowed to straighten out his life, once staying sober for eleven months. But even the birth of a beloved son could not keep him from drinking. After one ten-day binge, Trotter returned home to find his wife weeping over the dead body of their two-year-old son.

Trotter left his son's funeral for a saloon. Then he hopped a train for Chicago, running from his failure, from alcohol, and from the certainty he couldn't conquer his addiction. He knew his life was running out, but he resolved to end it in anonymity.

The night of **January 19, 1897,** homeless, hatless, and coatless, Mel Trotter sold his shoes for one last drink before planning to commit suicide. The alcohol barely warmed him as he trudged barefoot through a Chicago blizzard, trying to find Lake Michigan so he could drown his sorrows forever. Passing the darkened businesses on Van Buren Street, Trotter stumbled. A young man stepped out of the doorway of the only lit building, helped Trotter up, and invited him inside. Trotter followed, too numb to read the sign over the door: Pacific Garden Mission.[11]

The man sat Trotter down in a warm room full of derelict men. The mission's superintendent, Harry Monroe, was in the middle of his evening message but broke off his comments when he saw Trotter. Monroe felt compelled to pray aloud, "Oh, God, save that poor, poor boy."

Monroe then shared the story of his own troubled life before he had met Christ. "Jesus loves you," he concluded, "and so do I. He wants to save you tonight. Put up your hand for prayer. Let God know you want to make room in your heart for Him." Barely understanding what he was doing, Trotter raised his hand. Something inside him rose up and accepted the invitation in simple faith. And in that moment the shackles of alcoholism and despair fell away.

Trotter spent the next forty-three years ministering to the men and women he met on the streets, as lost and hopeless as he had been. His message was simple: "God loves you in the midst of the deepest failure and despair, and his love has the power to change even the most ruined life." He was ordained in 1905 and for forty years served as the supervisor of a rescue mission in Grand Rapids, Michigan. Alumni of his mission founded sixty-eight other rescue missions across the United States, and Trotter became an international evangelist.

That dark night in Chicago Mel Trotter's life didn't end—it began!

Reflection

Have you ever struggled with an addiction, whether alcohol, drugs, sex, or something else? God is in the business of delivering men and women from addictions. He did it for Mel Trotter, and he can do it for you.

❧

He lifted me out of the pit of despair, out of the mud and the mire.
He set my feet on solid ground and steadied me as I walked along.

PSALM 40:2

January 20

God used him to bring the English Bible to England.

MILES COVERDALE was but four years old when Columbus discovered the New World in 1492. Born in York, England, he graduated from Cambridge, was ordained into the priesthood in 1514, and soon became an Augustinian friar. He belonged to a group of Cambridge scholars including William Tyndale,[12] Thomas Cranmer, Hugh Latimer,[13] and his prior, Robert Barnes, who met at the White Horse Tavern to discuss religious reform. A friend described what Coverdale was like in those days:

> Under the mastership of Robert Barnes he drank in good learning with a burning thirst. He was a young man of friendly and upright nature and very gentle spirit, and when the Church of England revived, he was one of the first to make a pure profession of Christ. Other men gave themselves in part, he gave himself wholly to propagating the truth of Jesus Christ's gospel and manifesting his glory.

In 1528 after preaching against the mass, confession, and images, Coverdale was forced to leave the Augustinians.

During his time abroad from 1528 to 1535 he worked with Tyndale in Hamburg and Antwerp on translations of the Old Testament. In October 1535 he published the first edition of his own Bible in Marburg, Germany. To prepare this first complete printed English Bible, Coverdale relied on the work of five translations, among them Tyndale's. The long dedication he wrote to Henry VIII[14] and Queen Anne[15] implies his expectation that the king would receive it favorably. With customary humility, Coverdale wrote,

> Considering now, most gracious prince, the inestimable treasure, fruit and prosperity everlasting that God giveth with his word, and trusting in his infinite goodness that he would bring my simple and rude labour herein to good effect, therefore, as the Holy Ghost moved men to do the cost hereof, so was I boldened in God to labour in the same. . . .
> I do with all humbleness submit mine understanding and my poor translation unto the spirit of truth in your grace, so make I this protestation, having God to record in my conscience, that I have neither wrested nor altered so much as one word for the maintenance

of any manner of sect, but have with a clear conscience purely and faithfully translated this out of five sundry interpreters, having only the manifest truth of the scripture before mine eyes.

Today's Bibles still retain some of his phrases, as well as the idea of chapter headings and of not including the Apocrypha with the other Old Testament books. The Coverdale Bible was so well received that the king's chancellor, Thomas Cromwell, asked Coverdale to go to Paris to supervise the publication of an official Bible to be placed in every parish church in England. Begun in Paris, this second Bible known as the Great Bible had to be finished in London when the inquisitor general of France forbade any further printing of the English Bible.[16] The Great Bible was presented to Henry VIII by Cromwell in 1539. It proved to be Coverdale's greatest achievement and had a significant influence on the translation of the King James Version in 1611.

Miles Coverdale died on **January 20, 1569,** having provided the English with Bibles in their own language.

Reflection

Because God has revealed himself in the Bible in words, it is of utmost importance to be able to read those words in one's own language in an accurate translation. But the work of scholars such as Miles Coverdale accomplishes little unless we actually read and study the Bible to know what God is saying to us.

I assure you, until heaven and earth disappear, even the smallest detail of God's law will remain until its purpose is achieved.

MATTHEW 5:18

January 21

What one does during life matters more than how long one lives.

BORN IN Scotland on **January 21, 1613,** George Gillespie attended the University of St. Andrews. He first came to prominence in 1637 when he anonymously published *A Dispute Against the English Popish Ceremonies, Obtruded Upon the Church of Scotland,* in which he criticized the Episcopalian innovations imposed by King Charles I on the Church of Scotland, which was Presbyterian.[17] In 1643, only one year after becoming the pastor of Greyfairs Church in Edinburgh, Gillespie was the youngest of the four Scottish ministers chosen to attend the Westminster Assembly, considered by many the greatest assembly of theologians of all time, called by the Puritan English Parliament to advise and guide it in promoting the Reformation.

In his day he was often referred to as the "Great Mr. Gillespie." He was the most able defender of Presbyterian Church government at the assembly, and he provided the material for many legends—some true and some exaggerated. Nevertheless, the legends illustrate the godly character of the meetings and Gillespie's role in them. One such story begins with the assembly wrestling with the question "What is God?" George Gillespie was asked to pray for guidance for the assembly. His prayer, "O God, thou who art a spirit, infinite, eternal, and unchangeable in thy being, wisdom, power, holiness, justice, goodness, and truth . . ." provided the Westminster Catechism's answer.

Another story tells of Gillespie's skill as an orator and thinker. During a debate on whether the church or the state had the authority to excommunicate, Samuel Rutherford,[18] Gillespie's older colleague, called upon Gillespie to respond, saying: "Rise, George, rise up, man, and defend the right of the Lord Jesus Christ to govern by His own laws." Gillespie began by summarizing the speech of his opponent, and then piece by piece he broke down his opponent's arguments. So convincing was his reasoning and oration that Gillespie's opponent exclaimed, "That young man, by this single speech has swept away the learning and labor of ten years of my life."

Perhaps the most reliable tale is the story of Gillespie's notebook. While listening to an opponent and preparing to respond, Gillespie appeared to be taking very detailed notes. After Gillespie presented his persuasive response, men sitting beside him found nothing about the speech in the notebook. Instead, they found in Latin such notes as: "Lord, send light," "Lord, give assistance," and "Lord, defend thine own cause."

THE GREAT GILLESPIE

Upon his return home from London, Gillespie was elected to serve in the High Church of Edinburgh in 1647 and was selected as moderator of the General Assembly of the Church of Scotland in Edinburgh in the summer of 1648.

Shortly thereafter Gillespie became gravely ill with tuberculosis at the age of thirty-six. During his last days he received a letter from his old friend and colleague Samuel Rutherford, who wrote to him from St. Andrews: "Be not heavy: the life of faith is now called for; doing was never reckoned in your account; though Christ in and by you hath done more than by twenty, yea, an hundred gray-haired and godly pastors. Believing now is your last. Look to that word, Galatians 2:20."

In 1661, twelve years after Gillespie's death, King Charles II forced the Episcopal government of the Church of England upon the Presbyterian Church of Scotland. To dramatize this event, Parliament removed Gillespie's tombstone from his grave and had it publicly broken to pieces.

His tombstone is no more, but the documents of the Westminster Assembly live on as a memorial to George Gillespie and the others who drafted them.

Reflection

When a gifted person dies at a young age, the world often laments, "If only he could have lived longer." None of us knows the number of days God will give us, yet we know that those days will be enough to do what he has planned for us. How are you using the time that God has granted to you?

So be careful how you live, not as fools but as those who are wise. Make the most of every opportunity for doing good in these evil days. Don't act thoughtlessly, but try to understand what the Lord wants you to do.
EPHESIANS 5:15-17

January 22

Being a pastor has its risks.

WHEN King Edward VI died at fifteen in 1553, England was thrown into religious turmoil. Crowned at the age of nine only six years earlier, King Edward had been a sincere Christian.[19] At that time the Reformation in England was only thirty years old and in its infancy.

At the death of Edward VI, his cousin Lady Jane Grey, an evangelical girl also fifteen, ascended the throne for nine days before she was deposed[20] and replaced by Mary Tudor, Edward's Roman Catholic half sister.[21] Determined to reestablish the order of the Catholic Church, Mary removed the legislation that protected Protestants from persecution. She imprisoned Jane Grey and seven weeks later executed her for treason.

John Bradford, like hundreds of other Protestant pastors in England, was forced in 1553 to yield his pulpit to the Catholic Church. Bradford's congregation was so opposed to its new bishop, Gilbert Bourne, that when Bourne came to preach in Bradford's church, Bradford had to stand behind him in the pulpit to stop the congregation's heckling. During the sermon that would change Bradford's life, someone hurled a dagger at Bishop Bourne, causing Bradford to step forward to admonish the unruly crowd. After the service Bourne fled out the back door with Bradford shielding him from sight of the angry crowd and shepherding him to safety.

Bourne survived the uproar, but Bradford did not. Three days later he was arrested on charges of sedition. Bradford remained imprisoned for sixteen months. Then on **January 22, 1555**, the Roman Catholic bishops questioned Bradford. They pronounced him guilty of fostering the attempt on Bourne's life and sentenced him to death by burning.

Bradford spent the next months preaching to his fellow prisoners twice a day. Then one afternoon the wife of the prison keeper came to him very troubled and said, "Oh, Mr. Bradford, I bring you heavy news. . . . Tomorrow you must be burned. Your chain is now a-buying, and soon you must go to Newgate."

Bradford took off his cap, and lifting up his eyes to heaven said, "I thank God for it; I have looked for the same a long time, and therefore it cometh not suddenly; the Lord make me worthy thereof."

Early that evening Bradford said good-bye to the friends he had made in prison and spent the evening alone in prayer. His captors moved him to

Newgate Prison late that night. The next morning about nine, Bradford was led out of Newgate to the field where heretics were burned.

When Bradford arrived at the stake, he lay face down on the ground and prayed silently. Then rising to his feet and removing his coat, he walked to the stake. Turning to the young man who was to be burned with him, he said, "Be of good comfort, brother; we shall have a merry supper with the Lord this night."

As he was tied to the stake, Bradford warned those around him, "Strait is the way and narrow is the gate that leadeth to eternal salvation, and few there be that find it."

Reflection

John Bradford was sentenced to die because of an incident in which he did the honorable thing. Have you ever been criticized for doing the right thing? How did you handle the criticism? Remember that Jesus lived a perfect life, yet he was crucified.

If you suffer for doing right and are patient beneath the blows, God is pleased with you. 1 PETER 2:20

January 23

His life spanned two continents.

Lott Carey didn't know the year of his birth because they didn't keep birth records for slaves. But it was around 1780 on a Virginia plantation near Richmond. An only child, Carey was brought up in an undivided slave family. While his parents worked, his grandmother, a devout Baptist, cared for him. She taught him the history of his people: the suffering of slaves brought to America and the need for those remaining in Africa to hear about Jesus.

As a young man working as a slave laborer in Richmond, Carey lived a godless life and showed no signs of espousing his family's faith. Then in 1807 Carey was in the gallery of the First Baptist Church in Richmond and heard a sermon about Jesus telling Nicodemus, a ruler of the Jews, that he must be born again.[22] Carey was profoundly moved by the sermon, and he put his trust in Jesus Christ for his salvation. After he was baptized, he determined to read the Bible himself. He taught himself to read and write and then continued his education in a night school started by William Crane, a white Baptist.

Carey earned repeated promotions at the Shockoe tobacco warehouse where he worked. Around age thirty-three he purchased freedom for himself and his two children for $850—much more than his annual salary. His first wife had died, and he later remarried.

Carey began preaching to gatherings of African Americans, eventually forming and becoming the pastor of a black church. Meanwhile, in his night classes with William Crane, he became interested in missions to Africa. In 1815 he worked with Crane to organize the Richmond African Missionary Society.

His church grew to over eight hundred members while he remained respected and secure in his position at the tobacco warehouse. Yet his burden for missions to Africa increased, and finally he determined to go to Africa himself.

In a final sermon to his congregation in Richmond, Carey said, "I am about to leave you and expect to see your faces no more. I long to preach to the poor Africans the way of life and salvation. I don't know what may befall me, whether I may find a grave in the ocean, or among the savage men, or more savage wild beasts on the coast of Africa; nor am I anxious what may become of me. I feel it my duty to go."

On **January 23, 1821,** Carey sailed with his family and several coworkers to Liberia. He was the first black missionary to Africa. The missionaries had the support of their home churches and the American Colonization Society, a group that worked to return freed slaves to Africa.

Carey's distinguished service in Liberia was varied. He founded and served as pastor of Providence Baptist Church. He helped to establish schools for both settlers and native children, and served as the first president of the Monrovia Baptist Missionary Society. When the white governor of the colony was forced to return home because of illness, he appointed Carey as provisional governor. In this role Carey defended the colony against attacks by hostile natives.

In 1829, as Carey was preparing a rescue mission to retrieve some of his men who had been imprisoned while negotiating with a native tribe, he and seven coworkers died in an explosion of gunpowder apparently set off by an overturned candle. It had been eight years since Carey had set sail for Africa, and about forty-nine years since he had been born a slave in America.

Reflection

God had vastly different plans for Lott Carey than did his slave master. Have you ever had lower expectations for a person because of his or her appearance or position? It is important that we see those around us from God's perspective.

Suppose someone comes into your meeting dressed in fancy clothes and expensive jewelry, and another comes in who is poor and dressed in shabby clothes. If you give special attention and a good seat to the rich person, but you say to the poor one, "You can stand over there, or else sit on the floor"—well, doesn't this discrimination show that you are guided by wrong motives?
                                                                    JAMES 2:2-4

January 24

He knew what was coming.

IN RWANDA Reverend Yona Kanamuzeyi was a Tutsi pastor who had established a network of twenty-four village churches that ministered to some six thousand people. In 1963 the Hutu, determined to rid their country of the hated Tutsi minority, drove Kanamuzeyi and thousands of other Tutsi still in Rwanda into refugee camps.

For a thousand years the central African territory known as Ruanda-Urundi was a feudal monarchy ruled by the Tutsi, a tall, proud people who had reduced the shorter Hutu to serfdom. Germany claimed the country in 1890; then the League of Nations awarded it to Belgium after World War I. Although the governments changed, the political system did not. The Tutsi, though just 15 percent of the population, continued to rule the Hutu majority as they had for centuries.

Missionaries began arriving in the late 1920s. By 1968 Rwanda in the north had 85,000 Anglicans, and in Burundi in the south, Swedish Pentecostals had won 160,000 to Christ.

Belgium was willing to grant independence, but in 1959 centuries of repression boiled over in Rwanda. The Hutu majority rebelled, massacring thousands of Tutsi and taking over the government. Belgium and the United Nations granted the Hutu rule of Rwanda in 1962 with the Tutsi retaining control of Burundi on Rwanda's southern border.

In the face of political and ethnic turmoil, many missionaries fled or were recalled to the safety of their homelands. But faithful native pastors, both Hutu and Tutsi, remained, ministering the gospel of peace.

On the morning of **January 24, 1964,** a jeep pulled up in front of Reverend Kanamuzeyi's home in the refugee camp. Armed Hutu soldiers ordered the pastor and his friend, Andrew Kayumba, into the jeep. Kanamuzeyi told his friend, "Let us surrender our lives into God's hands." The men were driven to a military camp, where Kanamuzeyi asked permission to write in his pocket diary. Then he handed the diary to the soldier in charge and asked him to deliver the little book to his wife. The soldier answered, "You had better pray to your God."

So Kanamuzeyi prayed aloud in front of the soldiers, "Lord God, you know we have not sinned against the government, and now I pray you, in your mercy, accept our lives. And we pray you to avenge our innocent blood and to help these soldiers who do not know what they are doing."

Both men were tied up, and as Kanamuzeyi was led away, he turned to ask Andrew one last question. "Do you believe, Brother?"

"Yes," Andrew replied.

Kanamuzeyi was taken to a bridge over a river and as he walked, Andrew heard him sing:

> There's a land that is fairer than day,
> And by faith we can see it afar:
> For the Father waits over the way,
> To prepare us a dwelling place there.

The crack of a gunshot ended the hymn. The soldiers picked up Kanamuzeyi's body and threw it into the river.

The soldiers put Andrew back into the jeep, their double message of murder and intimidation seemingly accomplished. "We're taking you home," they said. "But remember, if you tell anyone about the killing of the pastor, you, too, will be killed."

Pastor Kanamuzeyi's diary did reach his wife. In it he had inscribed, "We are going to Heaven."

Reflection

If you had been Yona Kanamuzeyi, do you think you would have been singing a hymn as you were led away to be killed? God provides peace to his children as they need it.

~∞~

Don't worry about anything; instead, pray about everything. Tell God what you need, and thank him for all he has done. If you do this, you will experience God's peace, which is far more wonderful than the human mind can understand. His peace will guard your hearts and minds as you live in Christ Jesus. PHILIPPIANS 4:6-7

January 25

God used a Roman emperor to change the life of an Egyptian Jew.

IT ALL began on **January 25, A.D. 42,** when Claudius became the fourth Roman emperor the day after the assassination of his nephew Emperor Gauis, better known by his nickname, Caligula. Claudius's accession to the throne was rather unconventional. Agrippa I, the grandson of King Herod the Great and king over northeastern Palestine, happened to be in Rome when Caligula was murdered and was influential in the choice of Claudius as the successor.[23]

Caligula had considered himself deity and had outraged the Jews by ordering a statue of himself to be placed in the Jerusalem temple. Claudius took a different approach toward the Jews, trying not to offend them, no doubt as a reward for King Agrippa's role in securing the throne for him. At the beginning of his reign, Claudius issued edicts favorable to the Jews, granting them freedom to observe their laws throughout the empire. The only exception to the policy was in Rome, where Jews, because they had become so numerous and were thus considered a threat, were not permitted to assemble.

Later in his reign, however, he expelled all the Jews from Rome. The Roman historian Suetonius reported that Claudius expelled them "for constant rioting at the instigation of Chrestus" (a common misspelling of Christ). If this is a reference to Christ, the riots were about him, not instigated by him.

Two of those expelled from Rome were a Jewish couple named Aquila and Priscilla who had likely become Christians while they were in Rome. They fled to Corinth, where they set up shop in their trade as tentmakers (Acts 18:1-3).

A short time after they arrived in Corinth, the apostle Paul arrived.[24] Paul soon met them, and since they shared the same trade, he lived and worked with them (Acts 18:3). Paul spent almost two years with Aquila and Priscilla, making them among the most well taught of any of Paul's disciples.

When Paul left Corinth, Aquila and Priscilla accompanied him as far as Ephesus (Acts 18:18-19). There they resumed their tentmaking business and at the same time became leaders in the Ephesian church (1 Corinthians 16:19).

While they were in Ephesus, a Jew named Apollos, an eloquent speaker who knew the Scriptures well, arrived from Alexandria, Egypt. He had learned about Jesus and talked to others with great enthusiasm about him; however, he knew only about the baptism of John the Baptist. He had not yet heard about the outpouring of the Holy Spirit and Christian baptism. When

A DIVINE STRING OF EVENTS

Priscilla and Aquila heard him preach boldly in the synagogue, they took him aside and explained the way of God to him more fully (Acts 18:24-26).

As a result of their instruction, Apollos became a mighty preacher of the gospel. He went from Ephesus to Corinth, and there he proved to be of great benefit to the believers. He debated publicly, refuting the Jews with powerful arguments. Using Old Testament Scripture, he convincingly explained to them, "The Messiah you are looking for is Jesus" (Acts 18:28).

And it all began with Claudius expelling the Jews from Rome.

Reflection

Claudius's persecution of the Jews and Christians in Rome started a divine string of events that prepared Apollos, a Jew from Alexandria, to become one of the great preachers in the New Testament church. In your experience have you seen God bring positive results out of persecution? Even when we aren't privileged to see immediate results, God is the One who causes everything to work for the good of those who love him (Romans 8:28).

⤮

The believers who had fled . . . went everywhere preaching the Good News about Jesus.

ACTS 8:4

January 26

They had never met but were so alike.

ISABEL ALISON grew up in Perth, Scotland, where she listened eagerly to the preaching of Donald Cargill, the leader of the persecuted Presbyterians called Covenanters.[25] She loved Jesus and defended his gospel in a day when King Charles II of England was trying to snuff out Scotland's Presbyterian Church. In 1680, after speaking out against the severe punishment inflicted on those who would not conform to the Anglican Church, Isabel was arrested in Perth and sent to Edinburgh for trial.

About the same time, near Borrowstounness, Scottish soldiers laid a trap to catch Donald Cargill. They caught instead a twenty-year-old maidservant, Marion Harvie, who had been converted under the preaching of Richard Cameron.[26] Marion, too, was sent to Edinburgh for trial and indicted as a Covenanter.

After two months of examination under threat of torture, Isabel and Marion were brought from their cells to the bishop of Edinburgh's chambers for their final hearing. He told Marion that although she had insisted that she would never listen to an Anglican clergyman pray, he was now going to force her to. But she outsmarted him and said to her fellow prisoner, "Come, Isabel, let us sing the Twenty-third Psalm," and their singing drowned out the priest's prayer.

With their song still ringing in the chamber, the bishop read a single indictment condemning both Isabel and Marion to death by hanging. Marion returned to her cell and wrote:

> I desire to bless the Lord for my lot. . . . It was but little I knew of Him
> before I came to prison; but now He has said to me, because He lives,
> I shall live also. . . . Kind has He been to me since He brought me out
> to witness for Him. I have never sought anything from Him but that
> was for His glory since I came to prison, but He granted me my desire.
> I have found Him in everything that hath come my way, ordering it to
> Himself for His own glory. And how I bless Him that thoughts of death
> are not terrible to me. He hath made me as willing to lay down my life
> for Him as ever I was willing to live in this world.

IN SEEKING, THEY FOUND

In her separate cell, Isabel wrote:

I lay down my life for owning and adhering to Jesus Christ. . . . But what shall I say to the commendation of Christ and His cross? I bless the Lord, praise to His holy name, that hath made my prison a palace to me. . . . Oh! How great is His love to me that He hath brought me forth to testify against the abominations of the times, and kept me from fainting hitherto, and hath made me rejoice in Him! Now I bless the Lord that ever He gave me a life to lay down for Him.

Isabel Alison and Marion Harvie laid down their lives together on the Grassmarket scaffold on **January 26, 1681.**

As Isabel went up the ladder she said, "Oh, ye His enemies, what will ye do, whither will ye fly in that day? For now there is a dreadful day coming on all the enemies of Jesus Christ."

Marion Harvie's words on the scaffold were, "I am come here today for avowing Christ to be head of his church and King in Zion. Oh! Seek Him, sirs; seek Him and ye shall find Him. I sought Him and found Him; I held Him and would not let Him go."

Reflection

Can you think of a time that you sought God? Did you find him? If you didn't, keep seeking him, and you will. Once you have found him, seek to know him even better.

∽≫∾

Keep on asking, and you will be given what you ask for. Keep on looking, and you will find. Keep on knocking, and the door will be opened. For everyone who asks, receives. Everyone who seeks, finds. And the door is opened to everyone who knocks. MATTHEW 7:7-8

January 27

People are drawn to doctrines that bolster their egos.

IT'S EASY to see the appeal of a doctrine propounded in the fifth century. It went like this: When Adam fell, he fell alone. His sin was his alone, and the consequences his alone. His children, born as innocent as the first dawn over Eden, came forth from the womb of Eve with pure souls and the God-given ability to live lives fully pleasing to their Creator. They could choose obedience, or they could follow the errant example of their father, Adam. There was nothing wicked in their nature to drag them toward the latter.

This heretical view taught by Pelagius, an influential Irish monk, was in direct opposition to the church's doctrine of original sin. Many people followed Pelagius. His views were like a plague upon the Christian church. Pelagianism spread from the British Isles to Rome and then to North Africa.

Augustine of Hippo, the greatest theologian of the early church,[27] fought it vigorously, debating and opposing its founder both privately and publicly. For twenty-five years a theological war was waged. Pelagius claimed that humanity was born without sin, free to obey or disobey the commandments of God. Augustine fired back that Adam's fall in the Garden resulted in original sin and the total depravity of humankind.

Pelagius conceded that sin appears to be universal but only because people give in to the evil example of others who have chosen to do wrong. He claimed that it is possible for a person to live a sinless life as Christ did when he set the example of complete obedience to God. Augustine countered that it is impossible to have victory over sin apart from the grace of God that operates in the Christian who is submitted to Jesus Christ.

Pelagius believed that anyone who chose to trust in Jesus and was baptized for the forgiveness of sins already committed could march obediently toward heaven in his or her own strength. Augustine preached that God alone called people to salvation, and that none could believe or obey apart from his wooing grace and the enabling power of his Holy Spirit.

Pelagius insisted that people had the freedom of choice and held their own fate in their hands. Augustine retorted that God's sovereignty and election are the first cause of each person's eternal destiny.

The rancorous debate continued until a local synod of sixty-four bishops in Carthage, North Africa, at the end of 416 asked Pope Innocent I to excommunicate Pelagius. Another North African church council in Mileve made the

HUMANITY: SINFUL OR INNOCENT AT BIRTH?

same request. Finally, on **January 27, 417,** the pope excommunicated Pelagius. Another council held in 418 seconded the censure of Pelagianism, and Zosimus, the succeeding pope, concurred.

Even after Pelagius's death, however, the battle continued against two of his principal disciples, Celestius and Julian of Eclanum. A definitive condemnation of Pelagianism was finally reached by the Council of Ephesus in 431, confirming it as a heresy.

Reflection

Who do you think was right, Pelagius or Augustine? Do you believe babies are born innocent or sinful? Is it possible for humans to live without sin? It is important to always confirm what you believe through Scripture, godly counsel, and prayer. Always seek God's perspectives on theological and cultural issues.

"No one is good—not even one. No one has real understanding; no one is seeking God. All have turned away from God; all have gone wrong. No one does good, not even one." . . . But now God has shown us a different way. . . . We are made right in God's sight when we trust in Jesus Christ to take away our sins. ROMANS 3:10-12, 21-22

January 28

It all began when he was sixteen.

OSWALD J. SMITH grew up in Embro, Ontario, a country stop on the Canadian Pacific Railway where his father was the telegraph operator. In the winter of 1906 when Oswald was sixteen, the daily Toronto newspapers that the train dropped off every day told of a great evangelistic crusade being conducted in Toronto by Dr. R. A. Torrey with Charles Alexander as the song leader and soloist. Dr. Torrey's messages were published word for word every day in the paper. The articles told how thirty-four hundred people were filling the hall nightly with many others being turned away.

After reading about the meetings for several days, Oswald and his younger brother Ernie asked their mother if they could go the ninety-four miles to Toronto to attend the meetings. She eagerly gave her permission, so the two brothers boarded a train in the cold prairie winter. They arrived in time to attend the final eight meetings, staying at their aunt's house. Smith tells what happened:

> The second to the last meeting came. We had made up our minds to accept Christ that afternoon. It was a special service for boys. There were 3,400 present. We did not know then that our mother had written to Dr. Torrey asking him to pray that her sons might be converted. We arrived early, and the Hall was crowded. What Dr. Torrey had to say I do not remember. But I will never forget the way he repeated his text, Isaiah 53:5—"But He was wounded for *my* transgressions; He was bruised for *my* iniquities, the chastisement of my peace was upon Him, and with His stripes *I* am healed."
>
> At the close of his message he asked those 25 and over who wanted to accept Christ to come forward. Some responded. Little by little he lowered the ages until I was included. But to my amazement I was turned into a chunk of lead. I did not know then about the power of Satan, but I have found out since. Presently my brother quietly nudged me, and that broke the spell. I sprang out of my seat and with a sober face I took the momentous step. For a moment I found myself alone at the front, then I grasped Dr. Torrey's hand and went down into the inquiry room in the basement where I sat on a chair. A man came and spoke to me and then left. But I saw no light and got nowhere, though he thought I was through.

THE MOMENTOUS STEP

Then suddenly, it happened. I cannot explain it even today. I just bowed my head, put my face between my hands and in a moment tears gushed through my fingers, and fell upon the chair, and there stole into my boyish heart a realization of the fact that the great change had taken place. Christ had entered and I was a new creature. I had been born again. There was no excitement, no unusual feeling, but I knew that something had happened, and that ever after all life would be different. That was **January 28th, 1906,** when I was 16 years of age, and it has lasted to this day. Yes, and it is going to last, praise God, throughout the countless ages of eternity.

Oswald went on to found and pastor Canada's largest church, the People's Church of Toronto. Throughout his ministry, he wrote twelve hundred hymns, published thirty-five books in 128 languages, raised twenty-three million dollars for missions, and helped send out hundreds of missionaries.

From that first step in Toronto, Oswald J. Smith walked with the Lord for three days short of eighty more years.

Reflection

"The longest journey begins with one step." For Smith, the journey was a lifetime of serving God in ministry. God used Oswald Smith mightily after his conversion at sixteen. Have you taken the first step toward God? Unfortunately many churches today teach a Christianity that doesn't include a conversion, but that was not the Christianity of Jesus or of Oswald Smith!

Then [Jesus] said, "I assure you, unless you turn from your sins and become as little children, you will never get into the Kingdom of Heaven."
MATTHEW 18:3

January 29

He honored his God and his country.

On **January 29, 1843,** America's future president William McKinley Jr. was born. Growing up in a devout Methodist family in Ohio, he trusted in Jesus at age ten when he went forward at a revival meeting. Six years later he became a full-fledged member of the Methodist Episcopal Church, the denomination in which he was active his entire life. His mother had hoped in vain that he would become a minister, but God had other designs for his life.

When McKinley was eighteen, the Civil War began. He joined the Twenty-third Ohio Volunteer Infantry Regiment, and by the end of the war had worked his way up to major. In contemplating the possibility that he could be killed in battle, he wrote in his diary: "Fall in a good cause and hope to fall in the arms of my blessed Redeemer. This record I want left behind, that I not only fell as a soldier for my Country, but also as a Soldier of Jesus. [McKinley's friends and relatives could be comforted with solace] that if we never meet again on earth, we will meet around God's throne in Heaven. Let my fate be what it may, I want to be ready and prepared."

After the war McKinley became a successful lawyer in Canton, where he married Ida Saxton, a temperance worker and Sunday school teacher. Unfortunately, the couple was stricken with great hardship. After the deaths of their two young children, Ida succumbed to a nervous disorder that left her a semi-invalid. McKinley cared for her the rest of his life, remaining a faithful and devoted husband.

Over the years McKinley held various offices within local and state government and in the House of Representatives, becoming a Republican Party leader. In 1896 he successfully ran for president and was inaugurated as the twenty-fifth president of the United States. During his inaugural address, he kissed his Bible that was opened to Solomon's prayer, "Give me now wisdom and knowledge, that I may go out and come in before this people: for who can judge this thy people, that is so great?" (2 Chronicles 1:10, KJV). He declared that he would be "relying upon the support of my countrymen and invoking the guidance of Almighty God. Our faith teaches that there is no safer reliance than upon the God of our fathers, who has so singularly favored the American people in every national trial, and who will not forsake us so long as we obey His commandments and walk humbly in His footsteps."

McKinley's faith was frequently reflected in his policies. When America seized control of the Philippine Islands from Spain in 1898 and it was unclear what to do next, McKinley prayed for divine guidance. He eventually felt guided to annex the islands to the United States, making sure to educate and evangelize the Filipinos who were "our fellowmen for whom Christ also died."

On September 6, 1901, McKinley was shot by an assassin, whom he then publicly forgave. McKinley held on to life with courage and dignity for a week, but his condition worsened steadily as infection spread. His doctors were keeping him alive with oxygen and heart stimulants, but finally he said, "It is useless, gentlemen. I think we ought to have prayer." He said good-bye to his wife and friends and then said weakly, "It is God's way. His will, not ours, be done." He then murmured his last words, lines from his favorite hymn, "Nearer My God to Thee."

Reflection

William McKinley took seriously the Christian's responsibility to serve God as citizen as well as family and church member. In what ways can you serve God as a citizen?

∽❧∾

Jesus called them together and said, "You know that in this world kings are tyrants, and officials lord it over the people beneath them. But among you it should be quite different. Whoever wants to be a leader among you must be your servant." MATTHEW 20:25-26

January 30

With God all things are possible.

Kurt Warner grew up in a poor, broken home in rural Iowa. His "salvation" was sports—a natural talent and intense desire to be the best brought him success, popularity, and happiness in high school. Committing his life to athletics, his life's goal was to play football in the National Football League (NFL).

In college at Northern Iowa, he didn't become starting quarterback on the football team until his senior year. Sitting on the bench during those years was incredibly difficult for a young man whose drive was to be the best. While at Northern Iowa he met Brenda, who was a Christian. As their relationship became more serious, she often pressed him regarding his beliefs about God. Although he admired Brenda's faith, he was not yet ready to give his own life to Christ.

Although Kurt held on to his dream of playing in the NFL, at times it seemed quite unrealistic. After college when he tried out for the Green Bay Packers, he was released at the end of training camp. After working in a grocery store to make ends meet, he finally found a job in the Arena Football League, playing for the Iowa Barnstormers. Although this was an unlikely pathway to the NFL, Kurt kept his dream.

Kurt's heart began to turn toward the Lord during his first season with the Barnstormers. His life was more settled, and he was more receptive to discussing spiritual matters with Brenda. He also became friends with Christian teammates and began regularly attending their Bible study. His interest in having a personal relationship with God grew.

"There was no single, magic moment where I shed my skin and emerged anew. Instead, it was a gradual feeling that probably evolved over the course of about ten months. I finally reached the point where I knew what I needed to do. I probably asked Jesus into my heart three or four times because I didn't really know when my official salvation would occur. It's like I wasn't sure which one was going to take. I'd pray and ask God to forgive me for all the times and ways I'd messed up in my life. I'd tell him I wanted him to come into my heart, and I'd promise to live for him."

It was during this time that Brenda's parents were tragically killed in an Arkansas tornado the night they were to have been baptized. Not until this tragedy did Kurt realize what had taken place in his own heart and life. During this difficult time Kurt found a new sense of peace and was able to support

Brenda spiritually. This role reversal was a new experience for the couple and brought them closer to God and to each other.

Over the next few years Kurt's dreams began to materialize. He married Brenda in 1997, and his success in the Arena Football League led to one season with NFL Europe and then finally back to the NFL in 1998 with the St. Louis Rams. He was determined not to let the outcome of the Packers training camp years before be repeated!

His hard work, patience, and determination paid off. He started training camp in 1998, fighting for the third-string quarterback position, and by the 1999 season he had become the Rams' starting quarterback. It was a fairy-tale season—an underdog team rising to the top with a quarterback no one had ever heard of.

On **January 30, 2000,** Kurt Warner's lifelong dream came true. His team, the St. Louis Rams, won the Super Bowl, defeating the Tennessee Titans 23-16. Not only that, but Kurt also passed for a record 414 yards and was named Most Valuable Player of the game!

Kurt Warner discovered that he didn't really become a winner until he figured out God's rules of the game.

Reflection

Kurt Warner discovered that once he had committed his life to Jesus Christ, all things were possible. That doesn't mean that every Christian is going to be the world champion in his or her specialty, but it does mean that once we have sincerely given our allegiance to Jesus, there are no limits on how he may choose to use us.

With God everything is possible.　　　　MATTHEW 19:26

January 31

A man of peace died in peace.

BORN IN 1496 in the small village of Witmarsum in the Dutch province of Friesland, Menno Simons grew up tending cattle on his father's dairy farm. At twenty-eight he was ordained to the Roman Catholic priesthood and appointed to a parish near his home.

He quickly settled into a routine that included saying Mass, baptizing newborns, playing cards, and drinking with his fellow priests. As he went about his days, Simons's active mind was entertaining doubts concerning certain tenets of the Catholic faith. He had been reading Luther[28] and was influenced by the region's strong anti-Catholic movement.

His first doubts centered on the Mass and whether bread and wine became the actual body and blood of Christ. This was a serious issue for a priest and not one easily ignored. His personal questions led him to an intense study of Scripture and the conclusion that the teachings of the church were wrong. Yet he remained a Catholic priest. It was a comfortable living. It paid the bills.

Then troubling news reached his ears. A man in a nearby town had been executed for adhering to an unusual new doctrine: rebaptism!

"It sounded strange to me," wrote Menno, "to hear of a second baptism."

The death of this "Anabaptist" (rebaptizer) drove Menno to a renewed search of the Scriptures. He could find no mention of infant baptism, and he became more and more convinced that "believer's baptism" was instead the true Christian model for baptism. Still he remained a Catholic. It was safe. It was secure.

But then Menno's peace was shattered. Members of his own congregation, his brother Pieter among them, staged a militant Anabaptist occupation of a local cloister and were captured and massacred by the authorities. Menno's soul was crushed. He realized that in his role as a spiritual leader he might have been able to discourage the group's violent enterprise. Had he been a good shepherd, he could have led them into peaceful pastures instead of stony graves.

"The blood of these people, although misled, fell so hot upon my heart that I could not stand it, nor find rest in my soul," he wrote.

He repented of his apathy and all his sins, begging God for grace and a clean heart. He prayed for the wisdom, spirit, and courage to "preach His exalted adorable name and holy Word in purity, and make known His truth to His glory." Menno Simons was reborn.

FROM APATHY TO COURAGE

As he began to preach the Bible from the pulpit and to those he met, Menno's life became increasingly at risk. In 1536 he quietly renounced his priesthood, was rebaptized, and began an itinerant career of radical biblical reform that lasted until his death.

During that time he rose to a place of revered pastoral and apostolic influence within the Anabaptist movement. His tireless traveling, his writing, and his spirit of moderation helped unite various Anabaptist groups into one distinctive Christian body. As neither Catholic nor identifiably Protestant, the Mennonites, as Simons's followers came to be called, maintained a view of the church as a pure bride for Christ, untainted by earthly political allegiance. Believing that Jesus called Christians to forsake the sword for the Word of God, they refused to accept secular offices or join an army. As such, authorities everywhere, both civil and religious, viewed them as traitorous and seditious. Many were martyred for their faithfulness to their understanding of the words and example of Jesus Christ.

But Menno Simons, a man of peace in a world of war, eluded capture to the end and died in his own bed on **January 31, 1561.**

Reflection

To what extent do you agree with Menno Simons's conclusions regarding baptism for believers only and pacifism? What do you feel are the best arguments for or against these convictions? If you had lived in the 1550s and 1560s, do you think you would have followed the teaching of Menno Simons? Why or why not?

God blesses those who work for peace, for they will be called the children of God.   MATTHEW 5:9

February 1

He was late for his own wedding.

JAMES TAYLOR awoke before dawn on his wedding day, a man without God. As he went about his morning work threshing wheat in his barn, deep in thought, his heart was being strangely pulled toward heaven. The words "As for me and my house, we will serve the Lord" kept running through his mind.

He knelt praying in the straw, unaware of the time as the sun rose higher toward noon. While James prayed, God gave him a glimpse into eternity, and he rose from the straw, a man reborn.

Suddenly he realized he was late for his wedding, and he ran out of the barn as fast as he could, down the long hill to the snowy valley of Croyden, where the pealing church bells sang a loud invitation to the marriage of James Taylor and Betty Johnson.

James Taylor, a young stonemason from Yorkshire in England's North Country, had heard Jesus' words all his life. Even before his wedding-day conversion he had served as a bell ringer and a member of the choir at Royston parish. But he had not known God personally until then.

How God began his awakening we don't know. It may have been the Gospel readings he heard weekly from the lips of the village vicar or the dramatic conversion of his neighbors, Joseph and Elizabeth Shaw, from whose cottage he could often hear hymns rising with the wind that crossed the ridge. The whole neighborhood knew of the strange and narrow-minded "Methodist" notions of the Shaws. They also knew that Elizabeth had once been crippled with rheumatism but was now hale and hearty and fully convinced that God had healed her instantly when she "trusted the Lord."

It may have been when young Taylor, at the Mapplewell Midsummer Fair, listened intently as the radical Methodist preacher John Wesley boldly warned his lukewarm hearers of "the wrath to come."

What we do know is that on the morning of **February 1, 1776,** while lost in contemplation of the eternal state of his soul and late for his own wedding, he said "I do" to the Lord Jesus Christ.

Betty Johnson had never intended to marry a Methodist, but the new bride soon followed her husband into the kingdom of God as part of the glorious revival that was sweeping Great Britain and Ireland. The Spirit of God was doing a mighty work among people at all levels of society.

After a serious accident some years later, James Taylor was forced to give up his career as a stonemason. The couple, now with a young family in tow, moved to a nearby mining town, where Taylor eventually became the Methodist preacher. His faithfulness in ministry in a spiritually resistant corner of the nation laid a strong foundation of Christian commitment for generations of Taylors to come.

On a day in May 1832, with the warm spring sun melting the late winter snows in the Yorkshire valleys, a baby boy was born. Great-grandson to the deceased stonemason and Methodist minister James Taylor, the child was named James Hudson Taylor. Hudson, as the boy was called, eventually became the first Protestant missionary to Inland China. But the story of Hudson Taylor, grand and glorious in the history of the church of Jesus Christ, is for another day.[1]

Reflection

Just as in the Old Testament God chose Abraham as the progenitor of a godly family and drew him to himself, so God chose James Taylor and drew him into a personal relationship with himself to found a godly family that would help change the world. If you are part of a family with a godly heritage, praise God for it. If not, start now, and ask God to begin this heritage with you.

The love of the Lord remains forever with those who fear him. His salvation extends to the children's children of those who are faithful to his covenant, of those who obey his commandments!

PSALM 103:17-18

February 2

Their meeting changed history.

POPE JOHN XII was one of the worst of a long line of reprobate Italian vicars. King Otto I was one of the best of a promising succession of strong German sovereigns. When their paths crossed, Pope John XII crowned Otto as Roman Emperor of the West on **February 2, 962,** and effectually signed his own political death warrant and the rebirth certificate of the Holy Roman Empire in one grand and ceremonious stroke.

The Holy Roman Empire was first born Christmas Day A.D. 800. On that day, while Charlemagne, the conquering king of western Europe, was quietly worshiping at St. Peter's Basilica in Rome, Pope Leo III stepped down from the altar and crowned him successor to the caesars of Rome.

But the heirs of Charlemagne could not maintain the empire he had built. Separate kingdoms once again arose with no central government to hold them together. Invading Norsemen splintered the kingdoms further. Robbers and looters roamed the land, and feudalism emerged as a system of local allegiance, alliance, and protection in an increasingly brutal age.

Near the end of the ninth century and through the first half of the tenth, the papacy fell into political subservience and moral decadence. Powerful secular leaders in Italy acquired control of Rome and the papacy, contaminating the highest offices of the church with greed, violence, and intrigue. Immoral popes were seated and deposed at whim, the lives of many of them ending with murder or imprisonment. During this infamous period John XII became pope in 955. His papal reign included drunken orgies in the Lateran Palace.

Meanwhile in Germany, young Otto I was growing in power and prestige. Wielding Christianity as a unifying sword, King Otto formed wise and careful alliances with other German tribes. Appointing bishops at the same time as he anointed civil authorities, he gave generous land grants to the German church, building it into a national institution independent of Rome.

At sword point he sought to bring the Wends, a western Slavic tribe, to the foot of the cross. Denmark, Poland, and Bohemia bowed to him as their feudal sovereign. And then, with his eye on the crown of the Holy Roman Empire, he led his army into Italy to rescue the widowed Adelaide, the former queen of Italy, whom King Berengar II (her late husband's successor) had imprisoned. Otto married Adelaide, reduced Berengar to a fief of the German crown, and returned to Germany.

THE HOLY ROMAN EMPIRE

Several years later Otto came up against Berengar again when Pope John XII sent an appeal for his help against the king. This time Otto rode into Italy at the head of a massive army, marched peaceably into Rome, and there, on **February 2, 962,** was crowned emperor of the Holy Roman Empire by John XII. In Rome Otto also witnessed firsthand the moral degradation of the papacy and was greatly alarmed at what he saw.

The next year Otto returned to Rome and summoned Pope John XII to stand trial before an ecclesiastical court. Cardinals charged the pope with adultery, incest, taking bribes for bishoprics, and turning the papal palace into a brothel. Refusing to appear before the court, John went hunting instead. The cardinals removed him from his papal office, replacing him with Otto's choice for the job, a capable but ecclesiastically unaccredited layman. The new pope, Leo VIII, and many successive popes would now answer to the Holy Roman Emperor.

Thus began a reformation of the papacy that lasted nearly three centuries. From Otto the Great, the "Charlemagne of Germany," the Holy Roman Empire would exist continuously until Napoleon Bonaparte replaced it with his Confederation of the Rhine in 1806.

Reflection

When you read of the corruption and misuse of power in the church in the Middle Ages, where do you see God fitting into the picture? Do you see any reason for the state ever to control the church? The prophet Daniel describes how the kingdom of heaven will replace the flawed kingdoms of this world.

∽❧∾

During the reigns of those kings, the God of heaven will set up a kingdom that will never be destroyed; no one will ever conquer it. It will shatter all these kingdoms into nothingness, but it will stand forever. DANIEL 2:44

February 3

He pursued peace with godly convictions.

DESCENDING from Presbyterian pastors on both sides of his family, Thomas Woodrow Wilson was born in Virginia in December 1856. His father, Dr. Joseph Ruggles Wilson, was a pastor and seminary professor. His parents were completely devoted to their son, homeschooling him, training him in daily Bible reading, and raising him to see the world from a Christian perspective. The Civil War dominated his childhood, undoubtedly influencing his lifelong quest for peace. During the winter of 1872–73, Wilson experienced a sobering conversion to Jesus Christ.

The integrating concept he learned from his parents was God's covenant with humanity. God made commandments that people are to live by, and he also made promises for those who trust in him. For Wilson, the covenantal framework meant that not only was there the call for strenuous obedience from individuals but also a bond between church and society. He admired John Calvin as "the greatest reforming Christian statesman."

After graduating from Princeton University, Wilson practiced law, motivated by his passion to see justice served. But as an attorney he found himself more interested in ideas than in acquiring clients. So he returned to graduate school at Johns Hopkins University, receiving a Ph.D. in history in 1886. Wilson's intellect shone in the academic sphere and led to an apointment as a history professor at Princeton in 1890.

He so distinguished himself over the next decade that in 1902 Princeton appointed him its president, the first layperson to hold the office. Great energy and zeal characterized all of his activities.

Central to Wilson's thinking was the belief that God ruled the world and that people were to become the servants of God's will in the world. This conviction motivated him throughout his life.

During his presidency at Princeton, Wilson had the first in a series of small strokes that began to harden his already forceful personality. As a leader he was unexcelled—except with people whose vision or ambition were at odds with his own.

In 1910 Wilson accepted the Democratic Party's nomination for govenor of New Jersey, winning easily. His success in reforming the state's social and political systems helped him get elected president of the United States just two years later. With a congressional majority of like-minded progressives, Wilson made rapid reform: creating the Federal Reserve System, reducing tariffs, and establishing the first nationwide child labor laws.

Wilson kept the United States out of the war that broke out in Europe in 1914 and was elected to a second term in 1916. However, he lost his majority in Congress and was increasingly frustrated by his inability to pass legislation. Then in April 1917, when Germany's aggression on the high seas threatened U.S. interests, Wilson, the man who revered peace above all, reluctantly led the nation into World War I.

A year and a half later the war's end gave Wilson the chance to leave his mark on world history. He proposed creating a League of Nations to promote higher standards of justice on an international scale. Many countries embraced the idea, but back home, Congress staunchly refused the United States' entry into the League. Undaunted, Wilson took his zeal on the road, determined to convince the American people of the rightness of his cause. But the tour ended abruptly when Wilson suffered a debilitating stroke in 1919.

Although his faith and convictions remained strong, he was disappointed with himself and died on **February 3, 1924,** disillusioned with politics. Yet friend and foe alike agreed that he was a man of great personal integrity.

Reflection

Whatever Wilson's flaws, his ideals were grounded in his Christian education and in the Christian faith that characterized his life. Were you surprised to read that Wilson was a Christian? Because many of our schools teach just the secular side of history, we sometimes hear only part of the story.

Fear of the Lord is the beginning of wisdom. Knowledge of the Holy One results in understanding. PROVERBS 9:10

February 4

She wrote a hymn that became her prayer.

FRANCES RIDLEY HAVERGAL was born in 1836 to a Christian family in England. She was a very bright child who read well at age three and was writing poetry at age seven. She memorized long passages of Scripture, learned several languages, and became an excellent pianist. Her father called her "Little Quicksilver."

Her mother became terminally ill when Frances was only eleven. On her deathbed she told her devastated, sensitive daughter, "Fanny dear, pray God to prepare *you* for all He is preparing *for* you." Fanny took her mother's words to heart and made this her lifelong prayer.

From her teen years she loved to write and sing, desiring to use her gifts to win others to her Savior. She once described her writing process: "Writing poetry is easy for me. Most of the time I just put down in verse a personal experience. Writing hymns is like praying, for I never seem to write even a verse by myself. I feel like a child writing. You know a child will look up at every sentence and ask, 'What shall I say next?' That is what I do. Every line and word and rhyme comes from God."

On **February 4, 1874,** Frances Ridley Havergal wrote the hymn "Take My Life and Let It Be." Frances was spending five days visiting in the home of some friends that included several unbelievers and lukewarm believers. She felt burdened for them and prayed, "Lord, give me all in this house." By the end of the visit her prayer was answered, and her friends were rejoicing together in the joy of knowing Christ personally. Fanny wrote to her sister of the event, "The last night of my visit I was too happy to sleep, and passed most of the night in praise and renewal of my consecration; and these little couplets formed themselves, and chimed in my heart one after another, till they finished with 'ever—only—ALL for thee!'

> *Take my life, and let it be*
> *Consecrated, Lord, to thee;*
> *Take my hands, and let them move*
> *At the impulse of thy love.*
>
> *Take my feet, and let them be*
> *Swift and beautiful for thee;*
> *Take my voice and let me sing*
> *Always, only, for my King.*

Take my lips, and let them be
Filled with messages for thee;
Take my silver and my gold,
Not a mite would I withhold.

Take my moments and my days,
Let them flow in ceaseless praise;
Take my intellect, and use
Every power as thou shalt choose.

Take my will, and make it thine;
It shall be no longer mine;
Take my heart—it is thine own!
It shall be thy royal throne.

Take my love, my Lord, I pour
At thy feet its treasure store;
Take myself, and I will be
Ever, only, all for thee!

Frances considered "Take My Life and Let It Be" to be an expression of her own commitment to Christ. She frequently reviewed the words prayerfully in order to consecrate herself to Jesus anew. She died four years after writing the hymn, at age forty-two, leaving a legacy of many hymns such as "Like a River Glorious," "Lord, Speak to Me That I May Speak," "I Am Trusting Thee, Lord Jesus," and "Who Is on the Lord's Side?"

Reflection

Is it your prayer that God would "take your life and let it be consecrated" to him? Use this hymn as a sincere prayer that God would work in your life today.

Give yourselves completely to God since you have been given new life.
And use your whole body as a tool to do what is right for the glory
of God.   ROMANS 6:13

February 5

He kept the faith.

Dr. Rowland Taylor was the Anglican rector of Hadleigh, England, in the 1500s, a priest who, unlike many in his day, actually lived among the people whom he pastored. He faithfully studied the Scriptures, desiring to fulfill Christ's command to Peter, "Feed my lambs, feed my sheep." Every Sunday he preached salvation through faith in Christ and frequently warned his people of papal corruptions. He cared for the poor, the sick, and the lonely. He was a loving husband and trained his nine children in the Scriptures.

When the young Protestant King Edward VI[2] died, Queen Mary,[3] a Roman Catholic, came to the throne, and shortly thereafter two of Taylor's enemies hired a Catholic priest to celebrate Mass in Taylor's church. Just before the Mass was to begin, Taylor rushed into his church and protested that the service was both illegal and idolatrous. Thereupon Taylor was forcibly removed from the church and the incident reported to the lord chancellor of England. Taylor was summoned to London by the chancellor and arrested. He was imprisoned and then sentenced to burn at the stake for refusing to submit to the pope.

On **February 5, 1555,** he gave his son a book in which he had written his legacy:

> I say to my wife and to my children, The Lord gave you unto me, and the Lord hath taken me from you and you from me: blessed be the name of the Lord! I believe that they are blessed which die in the Lord. God careth for sparrows, and for the hairs of our heads. I have ever found Him more faithful and favourable than is any father or husband. Trust ye, therefore, in Him by the means of our dear Savior Christ's merits. Believe, love, fear, and obey Him: pray to Him, for He hath promised to help. Count me not dead, for I shall certainly live and never die. I go before, and you shall follow after, to our long home. . . . I have bequeathed you to the only Omnipotent.
>
> I say to my dear friends . . . and to all others which have heard me preach, that I depart hence with a quiet conscience as touching my doctrine, for the which I pray you thank God with me. For I have, after my little talent, declared to others those lessons that I gathered out of God's Book, the blessed Bible. "Therefore, if I, or an angel from heaven, should preach to you any other Gospel than that ye have received," God's great curse be upon that preacher!

IF I, OR AN ANGEL FROM HEAVEN, SHOULD PREACH ANY OTHER GOSPEL . . .

Beware, for God's sake, that ye deny not God, neither decline from the word of faith, lest God decline from you, and so do ye everlastingly perish. For God's sake beware of Popery, for though it appear to have in it unity, yet the same is vanity and anti-Christianity, and not in Christ's faith and verity.

Beware of sin against the Holy Ghost, now after such a light opened so plainly and simply, truly, thoroughly, and generally to all England.

The Lord grant all men His good and Holy Spirit, increase of His wisdom, condemning the wicked world, hearty desire to be with God, and the heavenly company; through Jesus Christ, our only Mediator, Advocate, Righteousness, Life, Sanctification, and Hope. Amen. Amen. Pray. Pray.

Rowland Taylor, departing hence in sure hope, without all doubting of eternal salvation. I thank God, my heavenly Father, through Jesus Christ, my certain Saviour. Amen. **5th of February, anno 1555.**

Five days later, Dr. Rowland Taylor, father to nine, husband to one, and shepherd to many, was burned at the stake. Holding up both his hands, he called upon God, "Merciful Father of heaven, for Jesus Christ my Saviour's sake, receive my soul into Thy hands."

Reflection

If you had been Rowland Taylor, would you have intervened to prevent Mass from being celebrated in your church? Would you have chosen to be burned at the stake rather than to submit to the pope? Why or why not?

❧

Everyone who wants to live a godly life in Christ Jesus will suffer persecution.   2 TIMOTHY 3:12

February 6

God never stops doing good for his people.

GEORGE MÜLLER was a leader in the Plymouth Brethren movement, a faith mission advocate, and the founder and director of orphanages during the 1800s in Britain. He was known for his faith and prayer life. Never directly appealing for funds, Müller relied only on prayer for the support of his orphanages and his mission work. He never drew a salary, always trusting that God would meet his needs. His faith was rewarded—God always met the needs of his orphanages and mission organizations.[4]

Müller experienced a severe test of his faith when on **February 6, 1870,** his beloved wife, Mary, died of rheumatic fever. She had not been well for three years, and the rheumatic fever overcame her in her weakened state. After six days of terrible suffering, she died.

Müller wrote in his diary that day: "39 years and 4 months ago, the Lord gave me my most valuable, lovely and holy wife. Her value to me, and the blessing God made her to me, is beyond description. This blessing was continued to me till this day, when this afternoon, about four o'clock, the Lord took her to Himself."

February 11 he wrote: "To-day the earthly remains of my precious wife were laid in the grave. Many thousands of persons showed the deepest sympathy. About 1,400 of the orphans who were able to walk followed in the procession. . . . I myself, sustained by the Lord to the utmost, performed the service at the chapel, in the cemetery, etc."

He chose Psalm 119:68 as the text of the funeral sermon: "You are good, and do good." His message had three points: (1) The Lord was good, and did good, in giving her to me. (2) The Lord was good, and did good, in so long leaving her to me. (3) The Lord was good, and did good, in taking her from me.

In discussing his third point he told how he had prayed for her during her illness: "Yes, my Father, the times of my darling wife are in Thy hands. Thou wilt do the very best thing for her and for me, whether life or death. If it may be, raise up yet again my precious wife—Thou art able to do it, though she is so ill; but howsoever Thou dealest with me, only help me to continue to be perfectly satisfied with Thy holy will."

Müller felt that God had answered his prayer, both in how he dealt with Mary and how he dealt with his own heart:

THE LORD WAS GOOD
AND DID GOOD

Everyday I see more and more how great [is] her loss to the orphans. Yet, without an effort, my inmost soul habitually joys in the joy of that loved departed one. Her happiness gives joy to me. My dear daughter and I would not have her back, were it possible to produce it by the turn of the hand. God Himself has done it; we are satisfied with Him.

As a husband, I feel more and more every day that I am without this pleasant, useful, loving companion. As the Director of the Orphan Houses, I miss her in numberless ways and shall miss her yet more and more. But as a child of God, and as the servant of the Lord Jesus, I bow, I am satisfied with the will of my Heavenly Father, I seek by perfect submission to His holy will to glorify Him, I kiss continually the hand that has thus afflicted me; but I also say, I shall meet her again, to spend a happy eternity with her.

A close friend reported that after the funeral Müller sat at the vestry table, buried his face in his hands, and did not speak or move for two hours. But in his loneliness and grief he could still say to the Lord, "You are good and do good."

Reflection

If you look back at all the events of your life, can you say, "The Lord was good and did good"? Have any events caused you to doubt this promise? Why?

∽◈◞

I will make an everlasting covenant with them, promising not to stop doing good for them.   JEREMIAH 32:40

February 7

It was love at first sight.

RUTH BELL could never quite remember the first time she met Billy Graham,[5] but for Billy it was love at first sight.

One day in 1940 as Billy and a friend were driving through the streets of Wheaton, Illinois, talking about their girlfriends, Billy's friend told him he thought Ruth was beautiful. "She's the second nicest girl on campus, the nicest being my girl, of course."

The "second nicest girl" was the twenty-year-old daughter of Presbyterian missionaries to China. Ruth was studying to be a missionary as well. Billy, already an ordained Baptist minister at twenty-one, was also a student at Wheaton and felt called to be an evangelist.

Their first meeting in November was unremarkable for Ruth, but Billy remembered everything about it—the hallway, the friends she was chatting with, her slight smile. "I fell in love right that minute," he later told her, reconstructing the moment she could not remember.

A month later Billy mustered his courage and asked her out on their first date, a concert performance of Handel's *Messiah*. That night Billy made a more lasting impression. Ruth returned to her rooming house and wrote in her diary, "Bill is a real inspiration—because, I suppose, he is a man of one purpose & that one purpose controls his whole heart & life. He is dead in earnest yet richly endowed with the fruit of the Spirit. . . . Humble, thoughtful, unpretentious, courteous."

Then she closed her diary, knelt beside the bed, and prayed, "God, if you let me serve You with that man, I'd consider it the greatest privilege of my life."

Billy had already written home to his parents that Ruth was the girl he intended to marry. But his friends cautioned him to dampen his enthusiasm for Ruth lest he scare her away. So for the next six weeks Billy avoided her altogether. Ruth finally took matters into her own hands and invited him to a house party. Billy issued a counter-invitation: to come hear him preach in Chicago that same night, Friday, **February 7, 1941.**

That second date was unconventional. Ruth sat in a pew while Billy preached. "The authority with which he spoke," she later mused in her journal, "the humility, the fearlessness. . . . The star, seen and admired from afar became a human, personal thing, within reach."

Billy drove Ruth home, walked her to her door, said good night, and then hesitated. "There's something I'd like you to make a matter of definite prayer," he said. Ruth remembered even the cloud of breath that hung in the cold air between them. "I have been taking you out because I am more than interested in you and have been since the day we were introduced last fall. But I know you have been called to the mission field, and I'm not definite."

Truth be told, Billy felt a clear call to evangelism. But he later revealed that at that moment he was so in love with her that the most he could make himself admit was that he did not feel definitely called to foreign missions.

Ruth was smitten. That night she couldn't sleep and ended a dreamy journal entry with the thought, "Something big has happened."

In spite of their mutual love, Ruth wrestled with the thought of giving up missions to be the wife of an evangelist, foreseeing many more evenings like their second date, alone in the pew or at home while Billy preached. But as they prayed, God showed them that they were called to each other, and two and a half years later, Ruth Bell became Mrs. Billy Graham.

Reflection

Have you ever felt "something big" happening in your life? When you do, look to God for his direction and his answer. God is just as interested in your life choices as he is in the lives of Ruth and Billy Graham.

∽◉∾

Teach me to do your will, for you are my God. May your gracious Spirit lead me forward on a firm footing.   PSALM 143:10

February 8

His flattery got him nowhere in the end.

His NAME was Agrippa, and he was born in 10 B.C. His grandfather was King Herod the Great, the king of Judea at the birth of Jesus.

Herod the Great had five wives, including two named Mariamne. Agrippa's grandmother was the first Mariamne, a descendant of the Maccabees who freed the Jews from the Syrians.[6] Herod married Mariamne I in 37 B.C. Their wedded bliss lasted only eight years before Herod became suspicious of her loyalty and had her executed. Their union had produced two sons, Aristobulus and Alexander.

Aristobulus married his cousin Bernice, and they had two children, Agrippa and Herodias. In 7 B.C. Herod became suspicious of the loyalty of Aristobulus and Alexander and had both sons executed just as he had their mother.

After his father's death, Agrippa's mother brought him to Rome, where he was raised with members of the imperial family. When he reached adulthood, Agrippa became a spendthrift, and when his wealth was gone, he borrowed heavily. Finally falling out of favor with the imperial family, he left Rome, leaving behind many unhappy creditors.

By A.D. 36 Agrippa was back in Rome to seek his fortune. He made friends with Gaius Caligula, the adopted son of the emperor Tiberius. When Agrippa remarked that he wished Tiberius would give the throne to Caligula who would do a better job of ruling, Tiberius immediately had him arrested. However, fortunately for Agrippa, six months later Tiberius died and was succeeded by Caligula.

Caligula immediately released Agrippa from prison and gave him a gold chain, the same weight as the iron chain he had worn in prison. Caligula also made him king over the region of Philip the tetrarch, Agrippa's uncle, and also over the tetrarchy of Lysanias (Luke 3:1). Then in A.D. 39 when Caligula sent Herod Antipas, the tetrarch of Galilee and another of Agrippa's uncles, into exile, he gave his territory to Agrippa as well.

Agrippa happened to be in Rome in A.D. 41 when Caligula was assassinated, and ever the opportunist, he helped Claudius ascend to the throne.[7] Once he had become caesar, Claudius rewarded Agrippa by adding Judea and Samaria to his realm, making Agrippa's kingdom even greater than that of his grandfather, Herod the Great.

February 8, A.D. 41, Herod Agrippa, as he came to be known, sailed from

AN ILL-FATED EGOTIST

Rome to return to his enlarged kingdom. Once there, he began to persecute the church, trying to earn the favor of the Jews, and had the apostle James killed. When he saw how much this pleased the Jewish leaders, he arrested Peter during the Passover and imprisoned him with the intention of bringing him to trial after the feast. What Herod didn't know was that while Peter was in prison, the church was praying for his protection (Acts 12:1-5).

The night before Peter's trial he was awakened by an angel who said, "Put on your coat and follow me." Peter's chains fell off, and he left his cell, following the angel. The iron gate to the street opened all by itself, and Peter was free! He quickly went to thank those who had been praying for him. Meanwhile, Herod ordered a search for Peter, and when they couldn't find him, Herod sentenced the guards to death (Acts 12:6-19).

Later Herod Agrippa spoke to a delegation from Tyre and Sidon that was trying to win his favor. After the speech they gave him a loud ovation, shouting, "It is the voice of a god, not of a man!"

As Herod was basking in their flattery, an angel of the Lord suddenly afflicted him with a terrible malady because he accepted his audience's worship instead of giving the glory to God. He was consumed by worms and died five days later (Acts 12:20-23).

Reflection

Do you think that Herod Agrippa's persecution of the church and the murder of James were contributing factors in God's judgment on him? If nothing else, the story of Herod Agrippa's death underlines the importance of giving glory to God and not keeping it for ourselves.

I, the Lord your God, am a jealous God.   EXODUS 20:5

February 9

He almost didn't grow up.

On February 9, 1709, John Wesley,[8] then known as Jacky, was just five years old as he lay in his bed on the second floor of the rectory in Epworth, Lincolnshire, England.

Waking up, Jacky was puzzled to find the room filled with light, but the curtains on the four-poster bed were closed. He poked his head out and saw streaks of fire on the ceiling. Then he realized that his two sisters who shared the bed with him were gone. He looked over to the other bed, where the nurse slept with his sister Patty and baby Charles, and that, too, was empty. Jacky jumped out of bed and ran to the open door but found the floor in the hall on fire. He ran back into the room, climbed up on a chest of drawers, and opened the window latch so he could look out. Above him the thatched roof of the rectory was ablaze, fanned by a strong northeast wind. Below he could see a crowd of neighbors throwing buckets of water at the burning building with little effect. One of the men looked up and saw little Jacky edging his way out of the window along the windowsill and frantically called for someone to get a ladder.

"There will not be time!" another man yelled. Then a tall, burly neighbor leaned against the side of the burning house, and other neighbors helped a lighter man climb onto his shoulders. As the heat from the fire behind Jacky grew intense, the top man managed to stand upright, stretch out his arms, and pluck the little boy from the windowsill. Just then the house's roof caved in.

As the family was fleeing from the burning house, Mr. Wesley had realized that Jacky was missing, but when he tried to run back up the steps to get him, the stairs were on fire and wouldn't support his weight. In agony he had quickly knelt in the hallway and committed Jacky to God before fleeing with the rest of his family. When the rescuers carried Jacky to the neighboring house where the family had taken refuge, his father cried out with joy, "Come, neighbors! Let us give thanks to God! He has given me all eight children. Let the house go. I am rich enough!"

This event left an indelible mark on John Wesley's life. He took it as evidence that God had some particular purpose in sparing him. Later in his life as he led the Methodist revival in England, the incident became for him a picture of the world and his role in it. The burning house represented the perishing world. Each soul was symbolized by the perishing child who needed to be plucked from the fire.

A BRAND PLUCKED OUT
OF THE BURNING

On **February 9, 1750,** forty-one years after the fire, Wesley made this journal entry describing a Watch Night Service in London's West Street Chapel: "About eleven o'clock it came into my mind that this was the very day and hour on which . . . I was taken out of the flames. I stopped and gave a short account of that wonderful providence. The voice of praise and thanksgiving went upon high, and great was our rejoicing before the Lord."

Before he died, he wrote his own epitaph, which begins, "Here lieth the body of John Wesley, a brand plucked out of the burning."

Reflection

Can you relate to Wesley's analogy of a brand plucked out of the burning, representing souls being rescued out of a perishing world? How does your understanding of the world compare with Wesley's?

∽∾

Rescue others by snatching them from the flames of judgment.

JUDE 1:23

February 10

It was a marriage of different expectations.

JOHN WESLEY[9] thought he had found the perfect wife in the widow Molly Vazeille. He praised her for her "indefatigable industry . . . exact frugality . . . uncommon neatness and cleanness both in [her] person . . . clothes and all things around [her]." Molly was past the age of childbearing, so Wesley would not be bound by the responsibilities of fatherhood; she was financially independent, which would free Wesley from the need to support her and allow him to continue to give to the poor; and finally, she was not a member of high society, so he would not have to accommodate the prying eyes that had followed one of Wesley's earlier love interests.

In January 1751 John Wesley decided he would marry Molly. Before they were married, Wesley planned a preaching tour in north England. Early on **February 10, 1751,** Wesley set out, but he didn't get very far. On London Bridge he slipped on the ice and sprained his foot. So instead of preaching, he turned back, staying at Molly's home for a week so she could care for him.

During that fateful week he announced his intention to marry Mrs. Vazeille immediately. Previously John and his brother Charles had pledged that neither would marry without the other's approval. Now John merely wrote to his brother, announcing his decision. Although history is imprecise as to the exact date they married, brother Charles said the event "made us all hide our faces."

Two weeks after the wedding, Wesley set off to preach. Much to his disappointment, Molly did not write for at least "four whole days." He wrote, "My body is stronger and stronger—and so is my love to you. God grant it may never go beyond his will! O that we may continue to love one another as Christ has loved us."

Molly eventually tried traveling with John, working among the poor and attempting to help John's ministry, but the difficulties wore on her quickly. Wesley made no attempt to change his schedule, desiring that his wife show true compassion and godly obedience. Molly grew increasingly resentful of his absences and developed a violent temper.

As she became more unhappy, Molly sought to make Wesley's life unhappy as well. She destroyed some of his writings, publicly criticized him, and repeatedly accused him of adultery. In 1771 she abruptly left, only to return home three years later. Wesley was a small man, and shortly after Molly's return, a friend of Wesley's "entered a room unannounced to find Molly dragging her husband across the floor by his hair."

Things continued to deteriorate. Twice more the couple attempted to reconcile, but in the end Wesley was resolute in his rejection of his wife: "You have laid innumerable stumbling blocks in the way, . . . and increased the number of rebels, deists, atheists; and weakened the hands of those that love and fear God. If you were to live a thousand years twice told, you could not undo the mischief which you have done. And until you have done all you can towards it, I bid you Farewell!"

Never to speak or meet again, Wesley was not even informed when she died. In his diary he simply noted, "I came to London and was informed that my wife died on Monday. This evening she was buried, though I was not informed of it."

Reflection

Sometimes we think that a pastor's family should have it all together, but the stresses of ministry can wear a marriage thin. What do you believe caused the problems in the Wesleys' marriage? Do you think anything could have been done to save their marriage? What can we learn from their unfortunate example?

∽◌◞

Now, for those who are married I have a command that comes not from me, but from the Lord. A wife must not leave her husband. But if she does leave him, let her remain single or else go back to him. And the husband must not leave his wife.   1 CORINTHIANS 7:10-11

February 11

"Heaven is already rich with thine ingathered sheaves."

CHARLES HADDON SPURGEON was the greatest preacher of his day.[10] He served as pastor of Metropolitan Tabernacle in London from the age of nineteen until his death. For many years he was plagued by the painful condition of gout, which he described this way: "If you put your hand into a vice, and let a man press as hard as he can, that is rheumatism; if he can be got to press a little harder, that is gout."

In the fall of 1891, while recovering from influenza along with his usual suffering from the gout, he and Mrs. Spurgeon traveled to Mentone, their favorite spot in sunny southern France. During three restful months together at the Hôtel Beau Rivage, Spurgeon worked quietly on a New Testament commentary whenever he was able, and they enjoyed just being together in the soothing climate. At times it even seemed he was improving, but then on January 31, 1892, after a day of particularly severe pain, Spurgeon entered his eternal rest at the age of only fifty-seven.

On Monday evening, February 8, Spurgeon's casket arrived at Metropolitan Tabernacle and was placed below the preacher's platform, where he lay in state for three days. In lieu of flowers Mrs. Spurgeon had palm branches placed around the casket to signify victory. That Tuesday and Wednesday, one hundred thousand people filed by the coffin from 6:30 A.M. to 7:00 P.M. to pay their last respects. The mourners included members of Parliament, the poor from the slums, and everyone in between—all joining forces to bid farewell to the Prince of Preachers.

Four memorial services were held Wednesday, two of which were for the general public. Ira D. Sankey,[11] D. L. Moody's song leader, was the soloist. Following the funeral on Thursday, **February 11, 1892,** thousands of mourners lined the route of the funeral procession to pay tribute to the man whose words God had used in their lives.

Archibald Brown, pastor of East London Tabernacle, graduate of Spurgeon's College, and one of Charles Spurgeon's closest friends, spoke these words at the graveside service:

Beloved President, Faithful Pastor, Prince of Preachers, Brother
Beloved, Dear Spurgeon—we bid thee not "Farewell," but only for a
little while "Goodnight." Thou shalt rise soon at the first dawn of the

Resurrection Day of the redeemed. It is not the "Goodnight" ours to bid, but thine. It is we who linger in the darkness; thou art in God's own light. Our night, too, shall soon be past, and with it all our weeping. Then, with thine, our songs shall greet the morning of a day that knows no cloud nor close; for there is no night there. Hard worker in the field thy toil is ended. Straight has been the furrow thou hast ploughed. No looking back has marred thy course. Harvests have followed thy patient sowing, and heaven is already rich with thine ingathered sheaves, and shall be still enriched through years yet lying in eternity. Champion of God, thy battle long and nobly fought is over. The sword which clave to thy hand has dropped at last; the palm branch takes its place. No longer does the helmet press thy brow, or weary with its surging thoughts of battle; the victor's wreath from the Great Commander's hand has already proved thy full reward. Here for a little while shall rest thy precious dust. Then shall thy Well-beloved come, and at His voice thou shalt spring from thy couch on earth fashioned like unto His body in glory. Then spirit, soul and body shall magnify thy Lord's redemption. Until then, beloved, sleep. We praise God for thee, and by the blood of the everlasting covenant hope and expect to praise God with thee. Amen.

Reflection

What do you think will be said about you at your funeral? It is now while we are living that we determine our legacy. Only by trusting Jesus Christ as our Lord and Savior can we live fruitful lives that will produce eternal results.

☙

All of us must quickly carry out the tasks assigned us by the one who sent me, because there is little time left before the night falls and all work comes to an end.   JOHN 9:4

February 12

She was the queen of England at fifteen.

BORN IN 1537, Lady Jane Grey was the niece of King Henry VIII.[12] Her father was committed to the Reformation and made sure that Jane received the best Reformed education available. She learned Latin and Greek as a young child from the future bishop of London and even corresponded with Heinrich Bullinger,[13] the Swiss reformer—in Latin. She enjoyed academic studies so much that at the age of thirteen she announced that "whatsoever I do else but learning is full of grief, trouble, fear, and wholly misliking unto me."

Her father had hopes of her marrying her cousin, King Edward VI.[14] Lady Jane and Edward were exactly the same age and the closest of friends. Both were zealous Christians, desiring to use their influence and positions for God's glory. But Edward was terminally ill with tuberculosis, so her father had her marry Lord Guildford Dudley, the son of the most powerful man in the kingdom, John Dudley, duke of Northumberland.

Not long before King Edward died on July 6, 1553, at fifteen years of age, the duke of Northumberland, counselor to the king, convinced him to name his daughter-in-law Lady Jane Grey as his successor instead of the king's own sisters, Mary[15] and Elizabeth.[16] Apart from the duke's strong desire to see his son become king as the husband of Lady Jane, the stakes were great on another front. The Protestants feared that Mary would reinstate Catholicism.

On July 10 Lady Jane Grey was publicly proclaimed queen against her wishes, for becoming queen was one of those things "wholly misliking" to her. Jane felt that Mary was the rightful heir. In opposition to the duke of Northumberland's scheme, the nobility and much of the populace supported Mary, not Jane. After being queen for only nine days, Jane was deposed, and Mary, the oldest daughter of King Henry VIII, was proclaimed queen in her stead.

Less than two weeks after Mary was crowned queen, Parliament began with a Mass. Jane and her husband were arrested and imprisoned in the Tower of London. Mary was ambitious and ruthless, determined to reestablish Catholicism as the state religion of England. She repealed many religious freedoms previously accorded by Henry VIII and Edward VI. "Bloody Mary" reigned for five years, during which time hundreds of Protestants were burned at the stake and many clergymen went into exile.

Lady Jane and her husband were convicted of treason and sentenced to death. Two days before Lady Jane was to be beheaded, the queen sent the abbot of Westminster to persuade her to convert to Catholicism. But Jane was resolute. The abbot communicated how sorry he was for her, saying, "For I am sure that we two shall never meet."

Lady Jane answered, "True it is that we shall never meet, except God turn your heart, for you are in an evil case. And I pray God to send you his Holy Spirit; for he hath given you his great gift of utterance, if it pleased him also to open the eyes of your heart."

On **February 12, 1554,** Jane's husband was beheaded first. As she looked out her prison window, she saw his body being carted away from the execution site and cried out, "Oh Guildford! Guildford . . . that is nothing compared to the feast you and I shall this day partake of in Paradise."

When her turn came, she addressed the people surrounding the scaffold, "Good people, I pray you all to bear me witness that I die a true Christian woman, and that I look to be saved by no other mean[s] but the mercy of God in the blood of his only Son, Jesus Christ."

She knelt down, said a psalm, and died at the age of sixteen.

Reflection

Lady Jane Grey was truly a remarkable teenager. In the space of one year she was married, became queen, was imprisoned, and died for her faith. May God give us all the spiritual maturity that she had in her teens.

Let your roots grow down into him and draw up nourishment from him, so you will grow in faith, strong and vigorous in the truth you were taught. COLOSSIANS 2:7

February 13

Our times are in his hands.

ON SEPTEMBER 24, 1757, Aaron Burr Sr., the second president of Princeton College, died at the age of forty-one.[17] Four days later twenty-two students graduated at the college's first commencement in its new location in Princeton, New Jersey. The next day the board of trustees met and after a time of earnest prayer, elected Jonathan Edwards,[18] father-in-law of Aaron Burr Sr., as the college's next president.

Jonathan Edwards' career had begun brilliantly and early. At sixteen, he received a bachelor of arts degree from Yale College. With a master's degree at twenty-three as well, he accepted a call to minister in Northampton, Massachusetts, where he served for the next twenty-three years and was loved and respected. During these years he married, his family grew to ten children, and his writing and preaching received growing acclaim.

From Northampton, Edwards went to Stockbridge, Massachusetts, a frontier village, where for seven years he found contentment pastoring a small church made up of colonists and Indians.

John Brainerd, brother of David Brainerd[19] and one of Princeton's trustees, was one of two men sent to Stockbridge to inform Edwards of his election as president. Edwards was surprised, and though he was considered the greatest American theologian and philosopher of his generation, he questioned whether he was qualified. After a period of prayer and counsel from others, he reluctantly accepted the position.

With his wife and family remaining in Stockbridge until spring, Edwards left for Princeton in January. Two daughters, the recently widowed Esther Burr and Lucy, who was staying with her, were already in Princeton.

After his installation as president, Edwards began preaching every Sunday in the college chapel. He also taught theology to the senior class, and his classes quickly became very popular. Edwards became more convinced that God had called him to Princeton.

In February the smallpox epidemic sweeping the country reached Princeton. Since inoculation for the disease was proving successful, Edwards proposed that he be inoculated if his physician recommended it and the trustees approved. With the approval of both, Edwards was inoculaed on **February 13, 1758,** one month after he had assumed the presidency.

Unfortunately the inoculation did not produce the intended results, and soon Edwards developed smallpox in his throat, making it difficult to swallow. His condition deteriorated rapidly, and he knew he was dying. Realizing he would not see his wife again, he wrote to his daughter:

Dear Lucy, it seems to me to be the will of God that I must shortly leave you; therefore give my kindest love to my dear wife, and tell her, that the uncommon union which has so long subsisted between us, has been of such a nature as I trust is spiritual and therefore will continue forever; and I hope she will be supported under so great a trial, and submit cheerfully to the will of God. And as to my children, you are now to be left fatherless, which I hope will be an inducement to you all to seek a father who will never fail you.

Jonathan Edwards died on March 22, 1758. His physician had to write the difficult letter informing Sarah Edwards of her husband's death. Sarah found refuge in the same God her husband had preached. She wrote to her widowed and now fatherless daughter, Esther Burr: "What shall I say? A holy and good God has covered us with a dark cloud. O that we may kiss the rod, and lay our hands on our mouths! The Lord has done it. He has made me adore his goodness, that we had him so long. But my God lives, and he has my heart. O what a legacy my husband, and your father, has left us! We are all given to God, and there I am, and love to be."

Esther Burr, who had been inoculated at the same time as her father, died sixteen days later.

Reflection

What is your reaction to the letter of Sarah Edwards to her daughter, who, unknown to her, was about to die? What can you learn from it for your own life?

❦

The Lord has comforted his people and will have compassion on them in their sorrow.   ISAIAH 49:13

February 14

He had asked her to marry him on Valentine's Day.

ROBERTSON MCQUILKIN was president of Columbia Bible College and Seminary in Columbia, South Carolina. His wife, Muriel, was not only a devoted wife and mother, but also a painter, speaker, hostess for the college, fabulous cook, and host of her own radio program. Then Muriel was diagnosed with Alzheimer's. Initially the college board arranged for a companion to stay with her so that McQuilkin could go to the office each day. As her condition deteriorated, McQuilkin was faced with a choice between taking early retirement to care for his wife or putting her in an institution for the rest of her life. In McQuilkin's own words:

> When the time came, the decision was firm and it didn't take any heavy-duty calculation. . . . The decision was made, in a way, 42 years ago when I promised to care for Muriel "in sickness and in health . . . till death do us part." So, as I told the students and faculty, as a man of my word, integrity has something to do with it. But so does fairness. She has cared for me fully and sacrificially all these years; if I cared for her for the next 40 years I would not be out of her debt. . . . She is a delight to me. . . . I don't *have* to care for her. . . . I *get* to! It is a high honor to care for so wonderful a person. . . .
>
> It's more than keeping promises and being fair, however. As I watch her brave descent into oblivion, Muriel is the joy of my life. Daily I discern new manifestations of the kind of person she is, the wife I always loved. . . . I also see fresh manifestations of God's love—the God I long to love more fully.

In spite of her deterioration, McQuilkin stood by her and continued to love her deeply. Eventually she rarely did more than mumble "nonwords." He wondered if he would ever hear her sweet voice again.

Then came **February 14, 1995**. McQuilkin writes:

> Valentine's Day was always special at our house because that was the day in 1948 that Muriel accepted my marriage proposal. On the eve of Valentine's Day in 1995, . . . I bathed Muriel on her bed, kissed her good night . . . , and whispered a prayer over her, "Dear Jesus, you love

sweet Muriel more than I, so please keep my beloved through the night; may she hear the angel choirs. . . ."

The next morning I was peddling on my Exercycle at the foot of her bed and, while Muriel slowly emerged from sleep, I dipped into memories of some of the happy Lovers' Days long gone. Finally she popped awake and, as she often did, smiled at me. Then, for the first time in months, she spoke, calling out to me in a voice clear as a crystal chime, "Love . . . love . . . love . . ." I jumped from my cycle and ran to embrace her. "Honey, you really do love me, don't you?" Holding me with her eyes and patting my back, she responded with the only words she could find to express agreement. "I'm nice," she said.

Reflection

How do you evaluate Robertson McQuilkin's decision to resign from his position to take care of his wife? If you are married and your mate develops Alzheimer's, how do you think you will react? What do the marriage vows "in sickness and in health, till death do us part" mean to you?

You husbands must love your wives with the same love Christ showed the church. EPHESIANS 5:25

February 15

How do you motivate people to build a temple?

In 538 B.C. the Jewish people were in Babylon as a result of God's judgment on them. One of them was a young priest named Zechariah, who was born in Babylon during the seventy years of the Jewish captivity. Then King Cyrus of the Medo-Persian Empire overthrew Babylon and issued a proclamation for Jews to return to Jerusalem to rebuild their temple (Ezra 1:2-4).[20]

Zechariah was one of the approximately fifty thousand Jews who returned to Judah along with his grandfather Iddo (Zechariah 1:7; Nehemiah 12:4).

Within two years after the Jews returned, they rebuilt the foundation of the temple. But the Samaritans and other neighboring tribes, fearing that this signaled the beginning of a powerful Jewish state, successfully stopped the construction.

In 520 B.C. God spoke to the Jews in Jerusalem four times through the prophet Haggai, encouraging them to complete the temple,[21] and in September the work resumed.

In October and November 520 B.C., God also gave a message to Zechariah, making him now a prophet as well as a priest. The message was this: "I, the Lord, was very angry with your ancestors. Therefore, say to the people, 'This is what the Lord Almighty says: Return to me, and I will return to you,' says the Lord Almighty" (Zechariah 1:2-3).

After ten years of drought because they stopped their work on the temple (Ezra 4:24; Haggai 1:9-10), God desired to reassure the Jews after disciplining them. His reassurance was, "Return to me, and I will return to you" (Zechariah 1:3).

Then on **February 15, 520 B.C.**, the Lord sent another message to Zechariah (1:7). That night Zechariah had eight visions. It was a busy night, for these were not dreams—Zechariah was wide awake when he saw them.

The purpose of these visions was to motivate the Jews to rebuild the temple by revealing God's future plans for Israel. The visions spanned the ages from Zechariah's day to the Millennium following the second coming of Christ when, many Christians believe, God will restore the kingdom to Israel.

Zechariah's eight visions were symbolic, depicting God's anger and judgment on the nations that afflicted Israel, as well as God's future blessing on a restored Israel, cleansed from sin, reinstated as a priestly nation, and serving as a light to the nations under the Messiah, who will be a King-Priest (1:7–6:8).

At the end of the eight visions, Zechariah received a final message from God, who instructed him to place a crown of silver and gold on the current high priest, Joshua (in Greek "Jesus"). This was a symbol of the future Messiah, who will rebuild the millennial temple of God and rule over Israel as both Priest and King (6:9-15).

With this encouraging big picture of what God was going to do in the future, the Jews completed the rebuilding of their temple in just three and a half years.

Reflection

Studies in industrial psychology have shown that workers are more efficient and motivated when they understand how their work fits into the overall plan and mission of their employer. Similarly, when we understand how our role in life relates to accomplishing God's purposes, it not only motivates us but life also makes more sense.

God, the Lord, created the heavens and stretched them out. He created the earth and everything in it. He gives breath and life to everyone in all the world. And it is he who says, "I, the Lord, have called you to demonstrate my righteousness. . . . And you will be a light to guide all nations to me." ISAIAH 42:5-6

February 16

Teaching was his life.

BENJAMIN BRECKINRIDGE WARFIELD was the greatest theologian of his day.[22] He was professor of theology at Western Theological Seminary from 1879 to 1887. From 1887 until his death he was professor of theology at Princeton Seminary. No theologian of his day is as widely read today as he.

On Christmas Eve 1920 Dr. Warfield suffered a heart attack. He slowly recuperated over the following weeks, and when classes resumed after Christmas vacation, he was back teaching. On **February 16, 1921,** Warfield went to his regular afternoon class, but he did not stand to lead the opening prayer as was his usual custom, for he was still feeling weak. The passage for study that day was the third chapter of 1 John. When he began teaching, it was as if all of his weakness faded away.

When his exposition reached the sixteenth verse, "Hereby perceive we the love of God, because he laid down his life for us: and we ought to lay down our lives for the brethren," a student recalled, "All the eloquence of Dr. Warfield's Christian heart, all the wisdom of his ripened scholarship focused on the interpretation of that text." Dr. Warfield explained, "The laying down of His life in our stead was a great thing, but the wonder of the text is that He being all that He was, the Lord of glory, laid down His life for us, being what we are, mere creatures of His hand, guilty sinners deserving His wrath." He urged his students to realize their own sin and God's gift more fully which would deepen "our wonder at His grace and our wish to glorify His name."

After his lecture Warfield returned home. Later that evening he suffered another heart attack and died. He had taught his last class.

The day after Warfield's death, his Princeton colleague and good friend J. Gresham Machen[23] wrote a letter to his mother saying, "I am writing to tell you of the great loss which we have just sustained in the death of Dr. Warfield. Princeton will seem to be a very insipid place without him. He was really a great man. There is no one living in the Church capable of occupying one quarter of his place. To me, he was an incalculable help and support in a hundred different ways. This is a sorrowful day for us all."

Years earlier, when performing the funeral service of a friend, Dr. Warfield had described "the innumerable throng" that "have laid aside the trials and labors of earth, well-pleasing to their Lord, and entered into their rest with him." He continued, "while our farewell to them on this side of the separating gulf was sounding in their ears, the glad 'Hail!' of their Lord was welcoming them there. . . . May God grant each of us to follow them. May he give us his Holy Spirit to sanctify us wholly and enable us when we close our eyes in our long sleep to open them at once, not in terrified pain in torment, but in the soft, sweet light of Paradise, safe in the arms of Jesus!"

After teaching his last class, Warfield followed the "innumerable throng" into the safe arms of Jesus.

Reflection

The greatest attribute of B. B. Warfield was his great heart for God. To him, theology wasn't about lofty propositions; it was about a personal God who sent his Son to lay down his life in our stead that we may spend eternity in paradise with him. Do you think of Jesus as a theological concept, or do you know him personally as B. B. Warfield did?

We know what real love is because Christ gave up his life for us.

1 JOHN 3:16

February 17

Witnessing an execution was life changing.

BORN IN 1662 in Moniaive in Dumfriesshire, Scotland, James Renwick was the only surviving son of Christian parents. He graduated from Edinburgh University in 1681, and that same year he witnessed the execution of Donald Cargill,[24] a field preacher of the Covenanters, the persecuted Scottish Presbyterians who had covenanted together to maintain the Reformed faith in Scotland. Their struggle was against the imposition of the Church of England with its bishops on a land of Presbyterians.

The martyrdom of Cargill caused Renwick to align wholeheartedly with the Covenanters. With their assistance he studied theology in Holland at the University of Groningen and was ordained in 1683. He returned to Scotland, where he was called to be the minister of the United Societies, a Covenanter gathering in southwest Scotland.

The period from 1684 to 1688, known as the "Killing Time," was the height of Covenanter persecution. This coincided with Renwick's ministry. More than any other, he was responsible for guiding the resistance of the Covenanters.

James VII, a Roman Catholic, became king of Scotland in 1685. He issued indulgences guaranteeing freedom of worship if meetings were held in private homes, chapels, or places dedicated for this purpose. Conventicles—all other worship services, especially in secret and in open fields—were against the law and considered organized rebellion. Many ministers, tired of the struggle, accepted the conditions of the indulgences, but Renwick and a few others refused to be told where they could preach. Renwick continued to preach in the fields and villages, often to men, women, and children who were in hiding and wandering in the mountains to survive. In one year Renwick baptized six hundred children. Soon the government identified him as a traitor and issued an order for his arrest. But protected by so many friends, he was able to continue preaching without capture for three more years.

Finally one winter night he was seized at the Edinburgh home of a friend. The Privy Council condemned him to death for refusing to acknowledge the king's authority and for telling his followers to come armed to meetings. He agreed with the council that he was guilty of these charges. The council, attempting to entice him to change his allegiance, gave him a week's reprieve.

During his reprieve his mother asked him how he was doing. His reply, "I am well; but, since my last examination, I can hardly pray, being so much taken up with praising, and so ravished with the joy of the Lord."

The night before his execution he obtained pen, ink, and paper and wrote to his Christian friends: "He has strengthened me to brave man and face death, and I am now longing for the joyful hour of my dissolution, and there is nothing in the world that I am sorry to leave but you."

The morning of his death he said to his mother and young sisters, "Death is the king of terrors but not to me now, as it was some times in my hidings; but now let us be glad and rejoice. . . . Would ever I have thought that the fear of suffering and of death could be so taken from me?"

A huge crowd gathered in Grassmarket in Edinburgh on **February 17, 1688,** to witness the final minutes of James Renwick's life. From the gallows he sang Psalm 103, read Revelation 19, and prayed, "Lord, I die in the faith that Thou wilt not leave Scotland, but that Thou wilt make the blood of Thy witnesses the seed of Thy church, and return again and be glorious in our land. And now, Lord, I am ready."

James Renwick, just twenty-six years old, was the last Covenanter to be hanged in public. One year later the Catholic King James VII was in exile; the persecution was over.

Reflection

If you had lived in Scotland between 1684 and 1688, would you have been a Covenanter? If you had been in James Renwick's position, would you have done anything differently? What can you learn from his life?

❧

Cling tightly to your faith in Christ, and always keep your conscience clear. For some people have deliberately violated their consciences; as a result, their faith has been shipwrecked.   1 TIMOTHY 1:19

February 18

He wrote a classic of devotional literature.

FOR A century after it was first published, one book's popularity was exceeded only by that of the Bible. Yet its author was a tinker—a mender of pots and pans. Who was the country tinker whose story continues to inspire generation after generation?

When John Bunyan was sixteen, his mother and sister died within a three month span, and his father remarried. Unable to deal with the upheaval, he began acting out in what he would later term "wild and willful ways."

Bunyan owned no books before he was married, but his wife's dowry consisted of two Puritan books. Although she was a Christian, Bunyan was an unbeliever.

One Sunday afternoon with his friends on the village green, Bunyan heard a voice from heaven ask, "Wilt thou leave thy sins and go to Heaven, or keep thy sins and go to hell?" Bunyan "looked up to Heaven, and it was as if I had . . . seen the Lord Jesus looking down upon me."

Bunyan became severely depressed as a result of the vision. Feeling he might as well "be condemned for many sins as few," he spent the next month indulging in selfish pursuit. Then his feelings shifted, and he pursued righteousness with equal vigor. "Our neighbors," he wrote, "did take me to be a very godly man, a new and religious man . . . and indeed so it was, yet I knew not Christ, nor grace, not faith, nor hope."

Working as a tinker, Bunyan often overheard a group of women discussing the Bible. He later wrote, "I thought they spoke as if joy did make them speak. . . . They were to me as if they had found a new world." Irresistibly drawn by their conversations, one day he marveled "at a very great softness and tenderness of heart, which caused me to fall under the conviction of what by Scripture they asserted." Shortly thereafter he put his trust in the Lord Jesus as his Savior.

Bunyan's path after his conversion, however, was neither smooth nor straight. He struggled with assurance of salvation, his daughter's blindness, poverty, his wife's death, and his desire to preach the gospel when it was forbidden by law. In 1660, remarried and the father of six, John Bunyan was imprisoned for preaching in public without a license. He had been unable to get a license because he had little education and disagreed with the Church of England.

Intermittently in and out of prison for twelve years, he made shoelaces in his cell to support his family and spent many hours writing. His manuscript began, "As I was walking in the wilderness of this world . . . I dreamed, and behold I saw a man clothed with rags, a book in his hand, and a great burden upon his back. I looked, and saw him open the book and read therein, and as he read, he wept and trembled . . . and broke out with a lamentable cry saying, 'What shall I do to be saved?'" The manuscript, entitled *Pilgrim's Progress*, told the story of Pilgrim's quest to answer that question.

First licensed for print on **February 18, 1678**, *Pilgrim's Progress* is the best known of the fifty-eight books Bunyan wrote. It remains in print three hundred years later and has been translated into more than two hundred languages.

Bunyan died ten years later. In the words of *Pilgrim's Progress*, "Now at the end of this valley was another, called the Valley of the Shadow of Death, and Christian must needs go through it, because the way to the Celestial City lay in the midst of it."

Reflection

John Bunyan would probably be considered a most unlikely person to write a devotional classic. How do you think he was able to do it? Has God ever enabled you to do something beyond your abilities? God has the power to stretch any of us beyond what we think we can do.

I can do everything with the help of Christ who gives me the strength I need.   PHILIPPIANS 4:13

February 19

He walked through the shadows of tragedy and emerged stronger on the other side.

THOSE best qualified to teach us about suffering and hope are those who have walked through the shadows of tragedy and emerged stronger on the other side. Doug Herman is one such person. This is his story.

"In a two-month period my life and faith came to a crashing climax. Evon [my wife] was going to die. . . . My infant daughter Ashli . . . was an AIDS baby just six months of age. My grandfather—a wonderful Christian man—died of liver cancer. Then we found out that my youngest brother Dan had acute myeloblastic leukemia. . . . I had had enough. God was supposed to be my refuge and hiding place! I was a minister! I had given Him my life."

Doug and Evon Herman were high school sweethearts before their marriage in 1981. They had both loved the Lord since childhood and followed his calling into ministry together.

The Hermans were thrilled at the birth of their first child, Joshua, on **February 19, 1985.** In the hospital, as Doug wondered at the miracle of the new life in his arms, two units of blood dripped slowly into Evon's vein to replace blood lost during the delivery. Eighteen months later, they were shattered by the news that the blood had been contaminated with HIV. When the HIV tests came back, Doug's and Joshua's tests were negative, but Evon's was positive. They had a second baby, Ashli, who was also found to be positive.

Doug was tortured by the question, "Where was God during the blood transfusion that would eventually kill my wife?" Doug and Evon battled both physical and spiritual assaults. "All the while our faith was torn between the God of love we had known all our lives and the God who seemed so unconcerned. Instead of standing firm, our faith quaked."

Doug pleaded with God for answers, but God was silent. Fearing AIDS, Doug's church did not renew his pastoral call. A few months later two-year-old Ashli died in Doug's arms; Evon was too sick to be at her daughter's deathbed.

Nine months later, in September 1991, came the moment that Doug had dreaded. The doctor gently told him the choice for his wife was either two days of suffering hooked up to a machine and then death or two hours of suffering and death. As Doug sat before the doctor with tears streaming down his face, a voice flashed through his mind, "Evon has fought the good fight of faith. She has run her race in life. There is now laid up for her a crown of righteousness."

Doug turned to the doctor, "Let my wife go Home. I don't want her to suffer any longer." As Doug sat by Evon's side weeping, a single tear trickled down her cheek. Then she was gone, and Doug Herman became a bewildered, grieving, single parent.

One day Doug took six-year-old Joshua to the pediatrician's office for an inoculation. "I'm not sick, Daddy," Josh protested. "Please, Daddy, I don't want a shot!"

"It's going to be all right," Doug assured him, holding his son on the exam table.

"When they stuck him with the needle, Josh looked straight at me. Looking deep into my eyes as I firmly held his head he cried, 'Daddy!' It was only one word, but his look said a million words, 'Daddy, why the pain? Why are you letting them hurt me? It's not my fault. Why, Daddy? I thought you loved me?' "

"My eyes burned with tears as my mind suddenly raced to the familiar phrases I had uttered months before. 'Why, God? I thought you were my Father! Why, Daddy, why?' . . . Very clearly God spoke to my heart in that moment. He simply said, 'It's the same with you and me.' . . . God . . . has no desire to see His children suffer. But if this temporal suffering provides a greater blessing, whether we understand it or not, He will allow it. He sees what we cannot."

Reflection

Have you faced tragedy in your life? If you haven't yet, you will someday. What we often fail to realize is that the Christian life includes suffering. Rather than be surprised when we suffer, we should be surprised when we don't.

Though our bodies are dying, our spirits are being renewed every day. For our present troubles are quite small and won't last very long. . . . But the joys to come will last forever. 2 CORINTHIANS 4:16-18

February 20

Listening to the radio changed his life.

D. JAMES KENNEDY grew up in the 1930s in Chicago and attended the University of Tampa on a music scholarship. Big-band music was all the rage then, and many learned to dance at Arthur Murray studios. True to his pursuit of excellence in all areas, Jim mastered the steps, became an Arthur Murray dance instructor, and before long was a nationally competitive dancer.

When nineteen-year-old Anne Lewis entered the Tampa Arthur Murray Studio for a lesson one evening, Jim, then twenty-two, told a friend, "That's the girl I'm going to marry."

During their courtship, Anne, who was a Christian, challenged Jim about what he believed. Although he believed in God and assumed he was a Christian, Anne's questions threw him.

One Sunday afternoon in 1955, Jim woke up with a hangover. The radio was on and tuned to a message by Dr. Donald Grey Barnhouse from Tenth Presbyterian Church in Philadelphia.[25] Dr. Barnhouse asked, "Suppose that you were to die today and stand before God and He were to ask you, 'What right do you have to enter into My Heaven?'—what would you say?" Jim listened to Barnhouse's explanation of salvation and redemption. He recalls, "I was completely dumbfounded. I had never thought of such a thing as that. As I sat there on the edge of my bed with my mouth hanging open, I groped desperately for some answer." Realizing he had no right to enter heaven, he gave his life to Christ.

The transformation of his life was immediate and miraculous. He made an overnight, 180 degree turn away from his former lifestyle. "To this day I have friends . . . who do not know what happened to me. One moment there was a young man managing an Arthur Murray dance studio, his heart and affections fastened entirely upon the things of this world. Then suddenly, overnight, something happened: a new person was born and an old person died."

Shortly thereafter he drove to see Anne with an engagement ring in his pocket. He said, "I have quit my job at the studio, which means I'm almost flat broke. I am going into the ministry, and I know you always said you wouldn't want to be a preacher's wife. Will you marry me?" Anne was taken aback but said yes.

After graduating from seminary, he went to Fort Lauderdale in 1959 to start a church. The attendance at the first service of Coral Ridge Presbyterian

WHAT EVER HAPPENED TO THAT DANCING INSTRUCTOR?

Church was forty-five. After ten months, attendance was down to seventeen! Jim and Anne were discouraged but didn't give up. Jim went to Atlanta to conduct an evangelism conference with his seminary friend Kennedy Smartt. Observing his friend, Jim discovered what he felt were the tools for successful one-on-one evangelism. He went home to teach these tools to his little flock. In one month his church grew from 17 to 66, and then to 122 the next year. When they reached 200 members, they built a church, quickly becoming one of the fastest growing churches in America. By 1974 Coral Ridge had more than 3,000 members!

Pastors from all over wanted to know how he did it. In answer, Jim held his first Evangelism Explosion (EE) Clinic on **February 20, 1967,** to train pastors in his unique method of lay evangelism. Thirty-six pastors attended that first clinic. Since 1967 EE Clinics have trained thousands of pastors, and in 1996 EE International reached its goal of planting EE teams in all 211 of the world's nations.

James Kennedy continues to evangelize the world through Evangelism Explosion and through his radio and television ministries from Coral Ridge Presbyterian Church in Fort Lauderdale.

Reflection

The key questions of Evangelism Explosion are: Have you come to a place in your spiritual life where you can say you know for certain that if you were to die today you would go to heaven? Suppose that you were to die today and stand before God and he were to say to you, "Why should I let you into my heaven?" How would you answer these two questions?

≈∂≈

To all who believed him and accepted him, he gave the right to become children of God. They are reborn! This is not a physical birth resulting from human passion or plan—this rebirth comes from God.

JOHN 1:12-13

February 21

He ran the race set before him.

ON FRIDAY, July 11, 1924, twenty-one-year-old Eric Liddell won the four-hundred-meter dash at the Paris Olympics,[26] as chronicled in the Academy Award-winning movie *Chariots of Fire*. The next year he went to China to teach at the Anglo-Chinese College at Tientsin.

In 1937 Eric began working in Siaochang, traveling back and forth to Tientsin to be with his family. In 1941, sensing that the political climate was changing, Eric believed it was no longer safe for his family to remain in China. He sent his wife, Florence, who was expecting their third child, and their two daughters back to her parents' home in Canada. On March 12, 1943, Eric and hundreds of other "enemy nationals" were interned at a Japanese prisoner of war camp at Weihsien in Shantung Province.

About eighteen hundred people lived in the camp with buildings in shambles and streets littered with beds, radiators, desks, and more. The soup line stretched for seventy yards and typically entailed a forty-five minute wait. There were roll calls twice a day, but in between the prisoners were allowed to organize regular activities such as entertainment programs and church services.

Soon after Eric arrived at Weihsien, three hundred students from the Chefoo School of the China Inland Mission, all separated from their parents, arrived at the prison. These children became Eric's focus. He organized a school in the prison camp for the children and served as their mentor.

Among Eric's official tasks were teaching math and science at the school, administering camp athletics, and acting as chief translator. He was also a warden for 230 unattached men, women, boys, and girls, which meant he was responsible for their presence at roll call.

In January 1945 he began having debilitating headaches and went to the camp hospital. The doctors said the headaches were likely caused by influenza or severe sinusitis and sent him back to his living quarters. Annie Buchan, a nurse and longtime friend of Eric and his wife, had him readmitted to the hospital, where he began having severe neurological symptoms: halting speech and partial paralysis of his right leg. Even though they suspected that he might have a brain tumor, the doctors treated him for a stroke. He showed some signs of improvement.

Then on **February 21, 1945,** he had a spasm of choking and coughing. Later in the evening he had another attack and was attended by a doctor. Eric's friend Annie Buchan checked in on him. After observing him, she went to the next room where doctors were discussing Eric and said, "Do you realize Eric is dying?" They replied, "Nonsense." Annie returned to Eric's side and took him in her arms as he whispered, "Annie, it's complete surrender." As she watched with tears streaming down her face, he had a convulsion, then slipped into a coma and into the arms of Jesus. An autopsy the next day revealed that Eric had an inoperable tumor on the left side of his brain. He was only forty-three.

Ten days later the Weihsien prisoners held a memorial service for Eric. After his death a slip of paper was found. On his last afternoon he had written the first line of his favorite hymn, "Be Still, My Soul," on it. The mourners sang it together.

Be still, my soul! The Lord is on thy side;
Bear patiently the cross of grief or pain;
Leave to thy God to order and provide;
In every change He faithful will remain.
Be still, my soul! thy best, thy heavenly Friend
Through thorny ways leads to a joyful end.

Be still, my soul! the hour is hastening on
When we shall be forever with the Lord,
When disappointment, grief, and fear are gone,
Sorrow forgot, love's purest joys restored.
Be still, my soul! when change and tears are past,
All safe and blessed we shall meet at last.

Reflection

How do you react to the emergencies and tragedies of life? Are you able to rest in the fact that God is in control and that he does all things well?

❦

Be still in the presence of the Lord, and wait patiently for him to act.
PSALM 37:7

February 22

Through the same door, Martin Luther started the Reformation and passed into eternal rest.

In 1517 a Dominican friar named Johann Tetzel had been selling indulgences near Wittenberg to raise money for constructing St. Peter's in Rome. According to Tetzel, those who purchased an indulgence would receive remission of purgatory. Indulgences could also be purchased on behalf of dead relatives and friends. The punch line of Tetzel's sermon was, "As soon as the coin in the coffer rings, the soul from purgatory springs."

The sale of these indulgences infuriated Martin Luther,[27] the professor of biblical studies at the University of Wittenberg, and he decided to hold a disputation with other faculty members on the subject. A professor interested in holding a disputation would nail the theses to be discussed on the cathedral door. Luther posted his Ninety-five Theses on the great wooden door of Castle Church in Wittenberg, Germany, on October 31, 1517.

Some of Luther's points for discussion were: (1) "Our Lord and Master Jesus Christ in saying, 'Repent ye,' intended that the whole life of believers should be penitence." (32) "Those who believe that, through letters of pardon, they are made sure of their own salvation, will be eternally damned, together with their teachers." (37) "Every true Christian, whether living or dead, has a share in all the benefits of Christ and of the Church, given him by God, even without letters of pardon." (62) "The true treasure of the Church is the Holy Gospel of the glory and grace of God."

Luther knew from his own repentance and conversion that paying an indulgence could not achieve forgiveness of sins. Shortly before posting the Ninety-five Theses, Luther had begun studying the Greek New Testament, and his studies persuaded him that the Greek word for repentance, *metanoia,* meant a change of heart, not mere performance of outward works, as theologians of his day defined it.

Luther wrote the Ninety-five Theses in Latin, intending them to be discussed by scholars, not circulated among the populace. But as Luther himself acknowledged, "In a fortnight they flew all over Germany." Translated into German and sold as far away as Rome, the Ninety-five Theses became much more than a university exercise.

For the next two decades, Luther enjoyed seeing the Reformation grow. Many regions in Germany accepted the evangelical doctrines that Luther and

THE DOOR OF THE BEGINNING
AND THE END

other Reformers discovered in the Scriptures. Luther lived to see a second generation of evangelicals sing the hymns he had written, read his German translation of the Bible, and learn his catechism from their early childhood.

Throughout his life he preached and taught God's promise of redemption to the repentant sinner. On his deathbed he prayed, "O Lord Jesus Christ, I commend my poor soul to Thee. O Heavenly Father, I know that, although I shall be taken from this life, I shall live forever with Thee. God so loved the world that He gave His only begotten Son that whosoever believeth on Him should not perish, but have everlasting life. Father, into Thy hands I commend my spirit."

Luther died on February 18, 1546, at the age of sixty-two in Eisleben, the city where he was born. As word of his death spread to Wittenberg, bells tolled, and people crowded the streets, wanting to pay their last respects to their leader.

On Monday, **February 22, 1546,** accompanied by a caravan that included his wife, Katie, his four children, and a throng of his followers, Luther's casket was borne through the door of Castle Church in Wittenberg, on which, more than twenty-eight years before, the young monk had nailed his theses.

Reflection

Little did Martin Luther realize the forces that would be set in motion by the posting of his Ninety-five Theses. He merely felt it necessary to speak out against the error of his day. He was willing to stand up and be counted for truth, and God used him to change the world. Do you ever feel that you should speak out against error? There is no predicting how God will honor your faithfulness.

They should gently teach those who oppose the truth. Perhaps God will change those people's hearts, and they will believe the truth.

2 TIMOTHY 2:25

February 23

It was the worst persecution to date.

WHEN DIOCLETIAN became emperor of the Roman Empire in 284,[28] Christians were encouraged because of rumors that his wife, Prisca, and daughter Valeria were believers. And, in fact, during the first nineteen years of his reign, Christians lived in relative peace and prosperity, some even holding high positions in the emperor's court.

In civil affairs Diocletian had great organizational skills. To facilitate the rule of the Roman Empire, he established his tetrarchy with two senior emperors called *augusti* (himself and Maximian) and two junior emperors called *caesares* (Galerius, his son-in-law, and Constantius, the father of Constantine).

Gradually, life became more difficult for Christians. Deciding that religious unity would strengthen the empire, Diocletian published three edicts in an attempt to guarantee the supremacy of the Roman state religion.

On **February 23, 303,** the day of the Roman feast *Terminalia,* an edict was posted that ordered all copies of Scripture to be burned, all churches destroyed, their property confiscated, and Christian worship forbidden. Additional measures were decreed the next day: Christians who resisted no longer had legal recourse. Christians were deprived of any honors and public office, and Christians in the royal household would be enslaved if they did not recant. Thus the Great Persecution began, although it was not uniformly enforced by the four emperors. Many Christians first learned of the edicts as they watched their churches go up in smoke.

A third edict, ordering Christian clergy arrested, resulted in a state crisis when the prisons filled, crowding out real criminals. To deal with this problem, the next edict stated that Christian prisoners would be released if they sacrificed to Roman gods. The prison guards could compel them by any means possible to make these sacrifices. But the proclamations did not stop there. In early 304 another edict insisted that everyone in the Roman Empire—clergy and laity alike—sacrifice to the Roman gods. Every Christian was now in jeopardy.

In 305 Diocletian and Maximian abdicated in favor of Constantius and Galerius, effectively ending the persecution in the West since Constantius was not interested in enforcing the edict. The persecution continued in the East until 311, when shortly before his death Galerius relented and issued an edict of limited toleration, granting freedom of worship if Christians did not disturb the peace.

THE GREAT PERSECUTION

The years of the Great Persecution officially ended with a second edict of toleration, this time by Constantine[29] in 313. The Edict of Milan was a great historical event, for it granted religious liberty to Christians and pagans alike. Eusebius, the first church historian and a contemporary of these events, recorded the words of Constantine's edict:

> Perceiving long ago that religious liberty ought not to be denied, but that it ought to be granted to the judgment and desire of each individual to perform his religious duties according to his own choice, we had given orders that every man, Christians as well as others, should preserve the faith of his own sect and religion. . . . We resolved . . . to grant both to the Christians and to all men freedom to follow the religion which they choose, . . . And we decree still further in regard to the Christians, that their places, in which they were formerly accustomed to assemble . . . shall be restored to the said Christians, without demanding money or any other equivalent, with no delay or hesitation. . . . For by this means . . . the divine favor toward us which we have already experienced in many matters will continue sure through all time.

Reflection

What would you have done if you had been living in 304 and the Roman emperor decreed that everyone must sacrifice to the Roman gods? This issue may be more relevant than you think if you are alive when the Antichrist appears. He will demand to be worshiped and require the death penalty for those who refuse.

∼❧∼

Another beast . . . ordered the people of the world to make a great statue of the first beast, who was fatally wounded and then came back to life. He was permitted to give life to this statue so that it could speak. Then the statue commanded that anyone refusing to worship it must die.   REVELATION 13:11, 14-15

February 24

They took the road less traveled and more dangerous.

MICHAEL SATTLER was a Catholic priest in southern Germany in the 1520s, and Margaretha had a lay position in the Catholic Church. Boldly breaking their vows of celibacy to marry, they were of one mind regarding their faith in God and their love for each other.

As if this weren't scandal enough, their convictions led them to join the Anabaptists, a fledgling religious movement the ecclesiastical and magisterial powers deemed dangerous.[30]

The Anabaptists believed that obedience to God was primary and obedience to the state was secondary. This view attracted the Sattlers, and they also committed to the group's principle of seeking careful counsel of fellow believers before acting. Adult baptism and strict pacifism also attracted the Sattlers. These views were considered extreme at the time, but Michael and Margaretha consistently made choices against the norm.

When Michael became an Anabaptist leader, he saw a great need for structure within the movement, which was full of life and spirit but lacked direction and organization. It needed written guidelines in order to preserve freedom, set boundaries, and protect themselves against fanatics who might lead the group astray. On **February 24, 1527,** in Schleitheim, Germany, Michael Sattler brought together a small group of Anabaptist leaders who wrote and adopted seven articles of faith, which they called the "Brotherly Union." They now had an organized church.

Michael went to Rottenburg, where officials seized the "Brotherly Union" papers as well as other Anabaptist plans. Nineteen people, including Michael and Margaretha, were arrested and tried for violating Catholic doctrine and practice such as baptism, the Eucharist, unction, and veneration of the saints. Michael was also charged with leaving his monastery, marrying, and promoting a pacifist approach toward the Turks.

In court Michael refuted all the charges except the last, for he did believe in a pacifist approach to the Turks. He questioned the authorities regarding their persecution of other Christians. "The Turk knows nothing about the Christian faith; he is a Turk according to the flesh. But you want to be considered Christians, boast of being Christ's, and still persecute his pious witnesses. You are Turks according to the spirit."

He insisted that the Anabaptists had done nothing against the Bible and requested a debate with the Catholic leaders. Sattler asserted that if he and the other Anabaptists could be proved in error, they would gladly accept their punishment. "But if we are not shown to be in error, I hope to God that you will accept teaching and be converted." The court did not take kindly to the suggestion of his "teaching" them and returned with the sentence: "Michael Sattler shall be committed to the hangman, who shall take him to the square and there first cut out his tongue, then chain him to a wagon, tear his body twice with hot tongs there and five times more before the gate, then burn his body to powder as an arch-heretic."

As the executioner tied Michael to a ladder, Michael prayed with slurred speech, "Almighty, eternal God, Thou art the way and the truth; because I have not been shown to be in error, I will with Thy help on this day testify to the truth and seal it with my blood." After the fire burned the ropes off his hands, he raised his hands and struggled to form the words: "Father, I commend my spirit into Thy hands."

After Michael's death the authorities tried in vain to persuade Margaretha to recant her testimony, but she declared that she would forever remain true to her Lord and to her husband. Eight days after Michael's execution, Margaretha was drowned in the Neckar River that passes through Rottenburg.

Reflection

Do you tend to go along with the flow, taking the path of least resistance, or, like the Sattlers, do you take the more difficult, nonconformist road when your convictions call for it?

∽◦⌒

Hate what is wrong. Stand on the side of the good.   ROMANS 12:9

February 25

The question was whether Jesus had a beginning..

ARIANISM was a heresy dating to the early fourth century, when an Alexandrian named Arius denied the eternality of Jesus Christ, God the Son. Arius argued that, as a human who had a beginning and experienced development, Jesus could not have been eternal. In 325 the Council of Nicea condemned Arianism. This put an end to the controversy in the Roman Empire, but Arianism maintained a following among some Germanic peoples, such as the Vandals.

In 429 Gaiseric, then king of the Vandals, led his eighty thousand people out of Spain and conquered North Africa. The Roman Empire ceded part of the territory to the Vandals by treaty. Four years later Gaiseric took Carthage. At the height of the Vandals' power in 455, they sacked Rome.

Gaiseric was primarily interested in the wealth to be acquired through conquering North Africa; however, his son Huneric wished to promote Arianism. When Huneric first took power in 477 at his father's death, he showed some religious tolerance by allowing a Catholic bishop to be ordained in Carthage, the first time the position had been filled in twenty-four years. But near the end of his life he launched a brutal campaign to force Catholic Christians to convert to Arianism.

In 483 Huneric announced that beginning on February 1 of the following year, he would sponsor a debate that would decide the superior merit of either Arianism or Catholic Christianity. Hundreds of bishops from the two sides gathered in Carthage in spite of serious misgivings by the Catholics. It turned out the debate was a sham—in fact, it never took place, as the Arian bishops used technicalities to forestall discussion. On **February 25, 484,** Huneric published a decree accusing the Catholic bishops of "[taking] it upon themselves, with consummate foolhardiness, to throw everything into confusion with seditious shouting, with the intention of bringing it about that the debate did not take place." Huneric cancelled the debate and decreed that non-Arian worship be prohibited, all Catholic churches be turned over to the Arians, and all Catholic bishops convert to Arianism by June 1 of that year.

Hundreds of Catholic bishops were stripped of their possessions and exiled for their refusal to convert. Even in exile they were scourged, and some were killed. The Vandals divided families and subjected their victims, young and old, to beatings, mutilations, draggings, and hangings.

IS JESUS ETERNAL?

Huneric died in December 484, the same year of his decree, and his successors did not continue the violent persecution he had begun. The hold of Arianism and the strength of the Vandals waned. In 533, when the Vandals were defeated, North Africa once again became part of the Roman Empire, and orthodox Christianity was reestablished.

Reflection

Do you believe that God the Son always existed? If you do, how would you explain that to the next Jehovah's Witnesses (modern-day Arians) who come knocking on your door? Why not prepare your answer now so you are prepared when they come.

Christ is the visible image of the invisible God. He existed before God made anything at all and is supreme over all creation. Christ is the one through whom God created everything in heaven and earth. He made the things we can see and the things we can't see—kings, kingdoms, rulers, and authorities. Everything has been created through him and for him. He existed before everything else began, and he holds all creation together. COLOSSIANS 1:15-17

February 26

He went from healing the physical to healing the spiritual.

DAVID MARTYN LLOYD-JONES was born in Wales in 1899 and at twenty-two earned a medical degree under the most renowned physician in England. But Lloyd-Jones believed that there was a soul sickness that ran far deeper than any physical ailment. Shortly after becoming a physician, he became convinced that the real root of his patients' ailments went beyond the physical or psychological. He concluded that to live apart from God was death and what humanity needed most was life from God.

As he came to understand that through Christ's death on the cross people could have eternal life, Lloyd-Jones was born again. This experience changed his life—and its direction, from medicine to the pastorate. His theological education came from great theologians like John Owens and Jonathan Edwards. "I devoured these volumes and just read them and read them," Lloyd-Jones wrote. "It is certainly true that they helped me better than anything else." In 1927 he was ordained in George Whitefield's London Tabernacle as a Calvinistic Methodist.

After eleven years as an evangelist and preacher in south Wales, Lloyd-Jones was invited by the aging G. Campbell Morgan to become copastor at London's Westminster Chapel in 1938.

Spending the next thirty years preaching at the church, Lloyd-Jones saw it through the difficult war years, becoming the sole pastor when Morgan retired in 1943. Under his leadership, Westminster Chapel became recognized as the leading evangelical pulpit of England. Careful exposition of the Bible and uncompromising Reformed theology characterized his ministry there. At the same time, he was known for his genuine piety, thriving family life, sense of humor, skill as a counselor, and deep desire for renewal in the evangelical church. Thousands found Christ and grew in their faith under Lloyd-Jones's preaching.

In 1968 illness forced him to end his ministry at Westminster Chapel. But Lloyd-Jones was later convinced that God removed his preaching ministry so that he could write. He began editing his sermon transcripts for publication and wrote many books that still remain in print.

Lloyd-Jones was a student of church history, and among his most treasured thoughts was a statement by John Wesley, who said of the early Methododists, "Our people die well." Lloyd-Jones knew the power behind those words. Physical death did indeed lose its sting for those who were confident of their life in eternity.

His own turn to die came in the waning days of the winter of 1981. On Thursday evening, **February 26, 1981,** in a trembling hand, Lloyd-Jones wrote a note to his dear wife and children: "Do not pray for healing. Do not hold me back from glory." His request was honored. The next Sunday, Dr. David Martyn Lloyd-Jones entered glory to meet face-to-face the God he so cherished.

Reflection

God brought about a change of direction in the life of David Martyn Lloyd-Jones, from physician to pastor. Has God ever opened up a new door of opportunity in your life that you didn't expect? If he hasn't yet, be open to the possibility that he might!

∽✑✓

Lead me in the right path, O Lord, or my enemies will conquer me.
Tell me clearly what to do, and show me which way to turn.

PSALM 5:8

February 27

New York State had never seen anything like it.

ASAHEL NETTLETON was a leading figure in the American Second Great Awakening from the late 1790s to the early 1840s.[31] In April 1820 he wrote the following letter from Union College in Schenectady, New York, describing the revivals occurring in the area:

> *This region, and especially the county of Saratoga, has heretofore been as destitute of revivals of religion as any part of this State. . . . About forty have made a profession of religion. These include some of the most respectable characters in the village. Directly south is the town of Malta. For a number of years there has been no Presbyterian church in that place. But the year past, there has been a very interesting revival among that people. . . . A church has been recently organized, which now consists of one hundred and five members. You can hardly imagine the interest which this revival excited in the surrounding region. Although the inhabitants are scattered over a large extent, yet, I verily believe, I have seen more than fourteen hundred people assembled at once to hear the gospel. On the east of Malta is the town of Stillwater. . . . On the **27th of February** last (**1820**) one hundred and three publicly presented themselves a living sacrifice unto the Lord.*

Describing the revival at Union College and in Schenectady he wrote:

> *More than one hundred have been brought to rejoice in hope. Besides these, we had more than two hundred in our meeting of inquiry, anxious for their souls. . . . The room was so crowded, that we were obliged to request all who had recently found relief to retire below, and spend there time in prayer for those above. This evening will never be forgotten. The scene is beyond description. Did you ever witness two hundred sinners, with one accord, in one place, weeping for their sins? . . . I felt as though I was standing on the verge of the eternal world; while the floor under my feet was shaken by the trembling of anxious souls in view of a judgment to come. The solemnity was still heightened, when every knee was bent at the throne of grace; and the intervening silence of the voice of prayer was interrupted only by the sighs and sobs of anxious souls. . . . I only add that some of the most stout, hard-hearted, Heaven-daring rebels, have been in the most awful distress. Within*

a circle whose diameter would be twenty-four miles, not less than eight hundred souls have been hopefully born into the kingdom of Christ since last September.

A student from Union College corroborated Nettleton's account of these remarkable events.

It commenced then in Malta, about ten miles from this place, under the labours of a Mr. Nettleton, a missionary from Connecticut. . . . with such displays of the power of God's Spirit in crushing the opposition seldom seen. The Deist and Universalist, the Drunkard, the Gambler, and the Swearer, were alike made the subjects of this heart-breaking work. Four months ago, Christ had no church there. It was a place of great spiritual dearth; and like the top of Gilboa, had never been wet by rain or dew. But the Lord has now converted that wilderness into a fruitful field.

Reflection

It's inspiring to read of the revival of 1820. Why don't revivals like this occur more frequently? What can we learn from them?

I will send showers, showers of blessings, which will come just when they are needed.　　　　　　　　ÉZEKIEL 34:26

February 28

Only 25 percent of the Jews living in Holland survived the Holocaust.

GOD CHOSE to stop Hitler short of his "final solution" by using Gentile rescuers: human hands that hid, fed, and protected the Jews from the grisly Nazi onslaught. Two of those hands belonged to Corrie ten Boom. She later said she was simply "the skin on the hands of God."

February 28, 1944, started like many other days in the ten Boom family watch shop in Nazi-occupied Haarlem, Holland. Corrie, the first woman watchmaker in Europe, was helping her father, Casper, repair watches, and her sister, Betsie, was doing housework in their home attached to the back of the watch shop. The machine-gun-armed gestapo that patrolled the streets was unaware of the six Jews hidden in a crawl space behind a bookcase in the ten Boom house.

Corrie wasn't surprised when a stranger, under the pretense of showing her a broken watch, whispered that his family was also hiding Jews. His wife had just been arrested. Could she help? Believing that God called her to resist the evil embodied in the Third Reich, Corrie led a clandestine network of rescuers hiding Jews in Haarlem. By 1944 Jews still alive in Nazi-occupied countries had two choices: hide or die.

Corrie agreed to help the stranger, and then he left the shop.

During the night, sleep in the ten Boom house was shattered by a gestapo raid. That night Corrie, Betsie, Casper, and thirty-three other rescuers in their network were arrested, beaten, and charged with hiding Jews. But in spite of a two-day search, the gestapo never found the six people in the ten Boom's hiding place.

Casper ten Boom, Corrie's father, died in prison ten days after his arrest. Corrie and Betsie were transferred to the Ravensbruck death camp, where Betsie later died Christmas Day. The Jews behind Corrie's bookcase were freed, hidden again, and ultimately survived the Holocaust.

In June 1945, four months after her release from Ravensbruck, Corrie forced herself to write a letter that pained her greatly. It was to the Dutch stranger who had asked for help that day in the shop and whom Corrie now realized had betrayed her family to the Nazis.

I heard that most probably you are the one who betrayed me. I went through ten months of concentration camp. My father died . . . and my sister died in prison.

SKIN ON THE HANDS OF GOD

The harm you planned was turned into good for me by God. I came nearer to Him. I have prayed for you, that the Lord may accept you if you will repent. I have forgiven you everything. God will also forgive you everything if you ask Him.

Rescuing dozens of Jews in Holland turned out to be the beginning of her life's work. God led her first to forgive her betrayer, then sent her out at age fifty-four with a message to the postwar world.

She began in Haarlem, where Corrie established Christ-centered rehabilitation homes for people of all faiths scarred by the war.

Then she went to America, where her story of the Holocaust put a new face on the horror that many had managed to keep at arm's length. In Corrie they saw their grandmothers, their mothers, themselves. Many searched their hearts: Would they have hidden Jews? Could they have survived concentration camps? Corrie's message was: "My survival is not my personal miracle, but the reality of Jesus!"

Into Corrie's seventies and eighties, God gave her opportunities to speak to thousands of people who turned to him through her message. Her aged hands, scarred from the concentration camp, wrote five best-selling books. Several strokes took away her ability to speak, but her books continued to minister. She died in 1983 at the age of ninety-one.

Reflection

If you had been living in Holland at the time of the Nazi takeover, would you have hidden Jews in your home? Why or why not? Who around you right now might be in need of protection or help?

Love your neighbor as yourself. MATTHEW 22:39

February 29

He was Scotland's first Protestant martyr.

PATRICK HAMILTON, born about 1503, was from an important Scottish noble family and a distant relative of the Stuart king James V and therefore, technically, royalty. During his short life he passed a number of milestones in rapid succession. When a teenager, he was appointed the titular abbot of Ferne in Ross-shire, then entered the University of Paris, and graduated in 1520.

In Paris, Hamilton was exposed to the teachings of Martin Luther,[32] which were spreading across Europe. He returned to Scotland in 1523, unhappy with the Roman Catholic Church, but as the second son, he was expected to study theology. He entered St. Leonard's College at St. Andrews that same year, excited about Luther's teaching of justification by faith.

By 1525 books containing the heresies of Luther were forbidden by the Scottish Parliament. The next year Patrick Hamilton let it be known publicly that he believed those doctrines. In the space of a year Hamilton received three summonses from Archbishop Beaton. In response to the first accusation of heresy in 1527, he went abroad to avoid further problems with the church.

However, this trip served only to strengthen his resolve to follow Luther. He went to Wittenberg, Germany, and personally met both Luther and co-Reformer Philip Melanchthon. He also met William Tyndale, who was translating the Bible into English.[33] While in Germany he wrote a short book entitled *Common Places,* which explained the principles and doctrines of the Reformation, emphasizing, in particular, justification by faith in Christ alone.

Soon he was home again in Scotland, where he began preaching the doctrines of the Reformation. His preaching and family connections made him a considerable threat to the Roman Catholic Church, and in January 1528 Hamilton was called to meet with Archbishop Beaton and other Catholic theologians at St. Andrews. He was examined and then sent home—perhaps in the hope that he would further incriminate himself or that he would leave the country to save himself.

A month later he was again summoned to appear before the archbishop and his council on thirteen charges of heresy: the main charge being the position he took in *Common Places:* that "man is not justified by works, but by faith alone." Other charges concerned his positions on penance, confession, and purgatory. He was convicted and sentenced to be burned at the stake that very same day, **February 29, 1528**. The execution was carried out in such haste

THE REEK OF PATRICK HAMILTON

that there was not enough wood and powder on hand to produce a huge blaze. As a result, Hamilton suffered a slow and horrible death.

Hamilton's influence grew as word of his martyrdom spread, making him more popular in death than in life. Soon all of Scotland was discussing Reformed theology. One of his accusers, Alexander Alexius, was converted as a result of Hamilton's testimony and became a Reformation leader.

A witness of Hamilton's burning later remarked, "The reek [stench of the smoke] of Patrick Hamilton has infected as many as it did blow upon."

Reflection

If you had been raised a Roman Catholic at the beginning of the Reformation, how would you have reacted to Martin Luther's teaching that man is not justified by works but by faith alone? What about now? Do you know of justification by faith as merely a doctrine or as a personal experience?

∽⊗∼

If they are saved by God's kindness, then it is not by their good works. For in that case, God's wonderful kindness would not be what it really is—free and undeserved. ROMANS 11:6

March 1

Their loyalty was mutual.

ON **MARCH 1, 1973**, Billy Graham was at a White House state dinner to honor Prime Minister Golda Meir of Israel. A family friend tells the story:

> Just before the 8:00 P.M. dinner, the Grahams mingled with the other guests in the East Room. When Billy greeted the prime minister in the receiving line, she reached up and kissed him. At dinner, Meir sat between Nixon and Billy at table 12. Ruth sat at table 9 . . . where she watched the proceedings with a bit of bemusement. A Jewish woman sitting at Ruth's table stared suspiciously at Billy and Golda Meir, not realizing that the evangelist's wife was sitting inches away from her.
>
> "What is Billy Graham doing sitting next to Madame Golda?" the woman asked of no one in particular. . . . "Do you suppose that he is proselytizing her?"
>
> "I would put my money on Madame Golda Meir," Ruth replied dryly. "But never fear. When we get home tonight, I'll straighten him out."

Billy Graham and President Richard Nixon's friendship began after Nixon's mother told her son of the powerful young evangelist she had just heard preach. Nixon was in law school at the time, and the two did not meet until 1950 when Graham was in Washington, D.C., and was introduced to Nixon, a freshman congressman from California. They had become good friends by the time John F. Kennedy defeated Nixon in his first bid for the White House. Nixon often sought out Graham for counsel and prayer. Later when Nixon did become president, Graham preached at some White House worship services.

But in January 1973 at Nixon's second inauguration, Graham told his wife, Ruth, "The president does not look like himself. I've never seen him look or act that way." He later wrote, "Nixon was terribly preoccupied and hardly seemed to know we were present. I could tell by his eyes that he was under some severe strain. At the time I had no idea what was about to come nor did any of his other friends."

Shortly after the dinner with Prime Minister Meir, the Watergate scandal broke. Graham found the news "so discouraging that it almost made me physically sick." Graham was one of the few who distinguished between the sinner, his friend Nixon, and the sin of the Watergate cover-up. But the distinction was lost on many who condemned Graham for refusing to condemn Nixon. Graham remained loyal, but Nixon wouldn't return his phone calls.

When Nixon died in April 1994, his family asked Graham to preach at his funeral. Graham was honored and recalled another funeral that gave him hope that he would see his friend again in heaven:

"Before his mother's funeral service, he talked with me for a few minutes about her faith.

"'Dick, do you have that same kind of faith?' I asked.

"'I believe I do,' he said quietly . . . that was his Quaker way, to keep piety private. . . .

"'That's the only way you can be guided in life, and it's the only way you can get to heaven,' I said, and then I prayed for him. He later told me that was one of the great moments of his life, and I believe he meant it."

And the months of no communication in the wake of Watergate? It turned out that the silence was motivated by love for a friend. After months of long waiting, Graham learned Nixon had told his aides, "Don't let Billy Graham near me. I don't want him tarred with Watergate."[1]

Reflection

How do you think Graham felt when Nixon wouldn't talk to him after the scandal broke? Could you separate the sinner from the sin and remain faithful to a friend in a situation like that? It turned out that they were both faithful to each other in their own way.

Wounds from a friend are better than many kisses from an enemy.

PROVERBS 27:6

March 2

When a man dies, what he leaves behind bears testimony to who he was.

In 1791 John Wesley, the leader of the Methodist revival, was eighty-seven years old with failing health. He hadn't preached in the open air, as he loved to do, for some months.

On Wednesday, February 23, 1791, Wesley responded to the request of a wealthy London merchant named Belson, whom he hardly knew, to counsel him after his wife's death. The sixteen miles from Wesley's house in London to Belson's home in the village of Leatherhead was an arduous trip for an old man. After Wesley counseled him privately for an hour and a half, Belson then informed him that he had sent his servants into the village to invite everyone to come and hear Wesley preach. Crowding into the elegant house, the villagers listened intently as Wesley preached on Isaiah 55:6: "Seek ye the Lord while he may be found: call ye upon him while he is near" (KJV). This was to be John Wesley's last sermon.

On Thursday Wesley's assistant, James Rogers, read to him from a recently published tract by Gustavus Vassa, an African who was sold into slavery in Barbados but then was sent by his master to England, where he became a Christian. The story so moved Wesley that he dictated a letter to his friend William Wilberforce[2] who was actively fighting in Parliament to abolish the slave trade:

> O be not weary in well doing! Go on in the name of God and in the power of his might, till even American slavery (the vilest that ever saw the sun) shall vanish away from it. . . .
> That He who has guided you from youth up may continue to strengthen you in this and all things is the prayer of, dear sir,
> Your affectionate servant,
> John Wesley

Wesley had difficulty holding the pen to sign his name. This was to be his last letter.

By March 1, John Wesley, who had prepared so many for death, was himself happily awaiting his end. Although he had been speaking very little, that afternoon he decided to get up from bed. He surprised everyone by singing two stanzas of the metrical psalm of Isaac Watts[3] that begins, "I'll praise my Maker while I've breath." He was able to sit up a little while and then had to lie down once again. As his closest friends gathered around him he was able to say amen to their prayers. At one point Wesley surprised everyone by saying with a strong voice, "The best of all is, God is with us!"

On Wednesday, **March 2, 1791,** his family and friends knelt at his bedside; his last word was "Farewell." Their sadness was diminished by the knowledge he had entered into the joy of his Lord.

In his lifetime John Wesley had accomplished what few others have, and he died the most well-loved man in England. Beginning at thirty-six as an itinerant preacher, he traveled 250,000 miles on horseback and preached more than forty thousand sermons to crowds as large as twenty thousand. He regularly preached three times a day, often beginning at 5 A.M. At the time of his death, there were seventy-nine thousand Methodists in England and forty thousand in America. He was the "Father of the Religious Paperback," publishing about five thousand sermons, tracts, and pamphlets. During his lifetime he lived frugally, giving away nearly $150,000 out of his meager income to spread the gospel.

What he left behind was one well-worn coat, two silver teaspoons, and the Methodist Church.[4]

Reflection

Few men influenced their world for good like John Wesley. God used him to change the hearts of so many in England that many historians credit him with preventing the spread of the French Revolution to England. What lessons are there for us in John Wesley's life?

Honor the Lord and serve him wholeheartedly.   JOSHUA 24:14

March 3

Would God be fair?

As PART of God's judgment on his people, King Nebuchadnezzar had brought Jewish exiles to Babylon in two separate deportations in 605 and 597 B.C. In August 586 B.C.[5] Nebuchadnezzar destroyed Jerusalem. The exiles learned of this in January 585 B.C.[6] Realizing that God really did exist and that Jerusalem had been destroyed just as God had foretold, the exiles no doubt wondered whether God would also judge the heathen nations as he had promised. The Egyptians in particular were no doubt gloating over the destruction of Jerusalem and what they perceived to be their own self-sufficiency and power.

Then on **March 3, 585 B.C.**, the Lord sent a message for Pharaoh, the king of Egypt, to Ezekiel the prophet in Babylon[7] (Ezekiel 32:1). God's message, assuring the exiles that he would judge Egypt, came in the form of a funeral song that would be sung by all the nations at Egypt's death (v. 16).

God said to Pharaoh:

You think of yourself as a strong young lion among the nations, but you are really just a sea monster, heaving around in your own rivers, stirring up mud with your feet.

Therefore, this is what the Sovereign Lord says: I will send many people to catch you in my net and haul you out of the water. I will leave you stranded on the land to die. All the birds of the heavens will land on you, and the wild animals of the whole earth will gorge themselves on you. I will cover the hills with your flesh and fill the valleys with your bones. I will drench the earth with your gushing blood all the way to the mountains, filling the ravines to the brim. When I blot you out, I will veil the heavens and darken the stars. I will cover the sun with a cloud, and the moon will not give you its light. Yes, I will bring darkness everywhere across your land. Even the brightest stars will become dark above you. I, the Sovereign Lord, have spoken!

And when I bring your shattered remains to distant nations that you have never seen, I will disturb many hearts. Yes, I will bring terror to many lands, and their kings will be terrified because of all I do to you. They will shudder in fear for their lives as I brandish my sword before them on the day of your fall.

THE SWORD OF THE KING OF BABYLON IS AGAINST YOU

For this is what the Sovereign Lord says: The sword of the king of Babylon will come against you. I will destroy you with the swords of mighty warriors—the terror of the nations. They will shatter the pride of Egypt, and all its hordes will be destroyed. I will destroy all your flocks and herds that graze beside the streams. Never again will people or animals disturb those waters with their feet. Then I will let the waters of Egypt become calm again, and they will flow as smoothly as olive oil, says the Sovereign Lord. And when I destroy Egypt and wipe out everything you have and strike down all your people, then you will know that I am the Lord. (vv. 2-15)

God's judgment fell on Egypt when Nebuchadnezzar invaded in approximately 568 B.C. Just as the Babylonians defeated Judah, they conquered Egypt twenty years later (29:12). God was just in all his dealings with the nations.

Reflection

The Jews exiled in Babylon needed reassurance that God would deal justly with Egypt just as he had with Israel. Do you ever question whether God is dealing justly with some of the world's present nations? God may be patient with evil for a time, but there will be justice for all in the end.

～✍～

The Lord is coming to judge the earth. He will judge the world with justice, and the nations with fairness.　　　　　PSALM 98:9

March 4

Sometimes things get worse before they get better.

BORN IN 1516, Mary Tudor was the only surviving child of King Henry VIII[8] and his first wife, Catherine of Aragon. Since Mary's mother was Spanish, the daughter of King Ferdinand II of Aragon, and since her father, even after breaking with the Church of Rome, still maintained basically Roman Catholic beliefs, Mary was raised a Roman Catholic. When she was fifteen, her parents divorced, and she and her mother went into separate exiles, never to see each other again. At seventeen, after the birth of her half sister, Elizabeth,[9] and the declaration that her parents' marriage was void, Mary was declared a bastard, losing her title of princess and her right of succession to the throne. Since she believed her problems were primarily due to the Reformation in England, she clung tenaciously to Roman Catholicism, finding solace in her faith. After Parliament revoked her parents' annulment and restored her legitimacy, Mary returned to prominence and became vocal about her Catholicism.

In 1544 Henry VIII wrote his will, designating the order of succession to the throne after his death. It would be his only son, Edward, Mary, and then Elizabeth if either of the first two died without having produced an heir.

At the death of Henry VIII, his nine-year-old son, Edward, succeeded him, becoming King Edward VI.[10] A godly boy, Edward moved England decisively toward Protestantism. Mary liked him but not his evangelical faith. Suffering from congenital syphilis, he died from tuberculosis at fifteen. A few weeks before his death, without authorization from Parliament, he amended his father's will by naming his cousin Lady Jane Grey,[11] also an evangelical, as his successor instead of his sister Mary.

Jane Grey's reign lasted just nine days before she was replaced by Mary, who became Queen Mary I in 1553.

Upon becoming queen, Mary set about returning England to its Roman Catholic roots.[12] At first Mary dealt tolerantly with the Protestants, hoping to convert them to Catholicism. She declared that she would not "compel or constrain consciences" in the matter of religious beliefs. This was one of the first statements of religious tolerance by a modern government.

But within weeks her early popularity was gone as England came to view her as a Spaniard first and only second as an English Tudor. She was not overly attractive and, like Edward VI, had inherited congenital syphilis. This gave her severe headaches, poor eyesight, and chronic rhinitis that caused her perpetual foul breath. She endeared herself to no one.

Mary quickly realized that her lenient approach with the Protestants was not working. Although they were in the minority, they were financially powerful. Mary feared a Protestant revolt would place her Protestant half sister, Elizabeth, on the throne. Therefore, on **March 4, 1554,** Mary issued an edict that reinstated Catholic worship and outlawed Protestantism and other "heresies."

She earned the title "Bloody Mary" in enforcing the edict, following the advice of her advisers to kill anyone who threatened her. Lady Jane Grey, her husband, and her father were executed, as well as a hundred other rebels who were part of a Protestant plot to take back the throne. Mary also held her half sister, Elizabeth, in the Tower of London for months while investigating her role in the plot. Elizabeth survived, eventually succeeding Mary as queen.

In 1555 the reign of terror began with the execution of Protestant clergymen who refused to accept the reestablished Catholic creed. "Heretics" were given a chance to recant. If they did not, they were burned at the stake. Most prominent were Thomas Cranmer, archbishop of Canterbury, and deposed bishops Latimer and Ridley.[13] Many Protestant ministers and leaders were executed, but most martyrs were laypeople who had been converted to Christ as the Reformation spread through England.

In all, Bloody Mary's reign of terror claimed the lives of more than three hundred Protestants. It ended with her death in 1558.

Reflection

Bloody Mary ruled like a terrorist—she killed her opposition. What a contrast to Jesus Christ! He gave his life for those who were his enemies.

∽◎◇◎◦

You were his enemies, separated from him by your evil thoughts and actions, yet now he has brought you back as his friends. He has done this through his death.　Colossians 1:21-22

March 5

Twenty-five escaped; only he was recaptured.

IN THE 1600s English kings insisted on imposing the Anglican Church on the Presbyterians of Scotland. In protest approximately three hundred thousand Scots signed the National Covenant of 1638, vowing to defend Presbyterianism from governmental control. This marked the beginning of fifty years of bitter struggle between the Covenanters and the Church of England.

Forty-one years later in 1679, young John Dick, a recent graduate of the University of Edinburgh, escaped capture after fighting with the Covenanters at Bothwell Bridge[14] but was later betrayed in Edinburgh by a poor woman needing the reward. Put into prison during the fall of 1683, he was sentenced to death for high treason and imprisoned with twenty-four other Covenanters in two large upper prison cells. The prisoners planned a daring escape while friends prayed for its success.

They were in two cells, one above the other, and to prepare for the escape, the prisoners in the lower cell sawed through the iron window bars, while those above devised a way to drop down through the flooring. While they were sawing, a bar fell down into the street but miraculously the sentry below did not see it. The next morning a sympathetic visitor managed to return it to them so they could fit it back into the window frame and not be noticed until their escape. When the appointed day came, all twenty-five escaped.

John Dick was the only one recaptured, but during his six months of freedom he put his university education and theological studies to good use by writing a short book with a long title: *Testimony to the Doctrine, Worship, Discipline, and Government of the Church of Scotland and the Covenanted Work of Reformation in the Three Kingdoms*, published after his death.

At the beginning of March 1684 John Dick was arrested, brought to trial again, and ordered to be hanged at Grassmarket in Edinburgh on **March 5, 1684.** The night before his execution he wrote his father a letter:

> Dear Sir,
>   This hath been one of the pleasantest nights I have had in my lifetime; the competition is only betwixt it and that I got eleven years ago . . . [when] the Lord firmly laid the foundation stone of grace in my heart, by making me with my whole soul close with Him upon His own terms, . . . as also to give myself entirely without reserve, in soul, body, heart, affection, and the whole

faculties of my soul, and powers of my body, to be by Him disposed at His pleasure for the advancement of His glory. . . .

Your Affectionate son, and Christ's prisoner, John Dick.

P.S: I hope, ere I go Home, to get another sight of you. Let none see this till I be in my grave. The Lord gave me to you freely, so I entreat you, be frank in giving me to Him again. . . .

On the appointed day, as the crowds looked on and the drums rolled, John Dick proclaimed from the scaffold:

I am come here this day, and would not change my lot with the greatest in the world. I lay down my life willingly and cheerfully for Christ and His cause, and I heartily forgive all mine enemies. I forgive all them who gave me my sentence, and them who were the chief cause of my taking; and I forgive him who is behind me [the executioner]. I advise you who are the Lord's people, to be sincere in the way of godliness, and you who know little or nothing of the power thereof, to come to Him and trust God, He will not disappoint you. I say trust in the Lord, and He will support or strengthen you in whatever trouble or affliction you may meet with. I remember, when Abraham was about to sacrifice his son, Isaac said, "Here is the wood, and the fire, but where is the sacrifice?"

He looked up at the gallows, then out to the crowd, and continued, "Now blessed be the Lord, here is the sacrifice and free-will offering. Adieu, farewell all friends."

Reflection

How do you account for John Dick's attitude in facing death? How would you respond in a similar situation? How would you like to respond?

"God will provide a lamb, my son," Abraham answered. GENESIS 22:8

March 6

How would a twenty-three-year-old Oxford man spend two weeks on the rock of Gibraltar?

GEORGE WHITEFIELD was born in 1714 in humble circumstances—his parents ran the Bell Inn in Gloucester, England. He graduated from Oxford University in 1736, one year after his dramatic conversion to Christ.[15] He left for America aboard the *Whitaker* in February 1738, the day after his friend John Wesley arrived back in England after three discouraging years as a missionary in Georgia.[16] The ship stopped and anchored off Gibraltar for two weeks before continuing its journey across the Atlantic. Whitefield, ever eager to share the gospel, seized the opportunity and went ashore anticipating what God might have in store for him during his time there. Many English soldiers were stationed at the fort on Gibraltar, and Whitefield immediately began to preach and minister to them.[17] Whitefield wrote in his journal on **March 6, 1738,** about his last day there:

> Monday, Mar. 6. Had near, if not more than, a hundred at morning exposition; and it being the last day of my sojourning at Gibraltar, many came to me weeping, telling me what God had done for their souls, desiring my prayers, and promising me theirs in return. Others both gave and sent me tokens of their love, as cake, figs, wine, eggs, and other necessaries for my voyage, and seemed to want words to express their affection. The good Lord note their kindnesses in His book, and reward them a thousandfold!
>
> About twelve, went to the church, according to appointment, and made a farewell exhortation, as God gave me utterance, to a great number of weeping soldiers, women, etc. After which, we kneeled down, and having recommended each other to the care of God, I left them, and went and took my leave of the two Generals; visited the confined prisoner; dined at a gentlewoman's house of the town; left near fifty letters to be sent to England; and, about four, went on board, accompanied to the seaside with near two hundred soldiers, women, officers, etc., who sorrowed at my departure, and wished me good luck in the Name of the Lord. Surely I may now expect greater success abroad, having such an addition of intercessors in my behalf. O Lord put their tears into Thy bottle, and let their cry come unto Thee!

TWO WEEKS ON GIBRALTAR

Samson's riddle has been fulfilled at Gibraltar. "Out of the eater came forth meat; out of the strong came forth sweetness." Who more unlikely to be wrought upon than soldiers? And yet, amongst any set of people, I have not been where God has made His power more to be known. . . . This is the Lord's doing, and it is marvelous in our eyes. May He give a blessing to the books dispersed amongst them, and perfect the good work begun in their hearts, till the day of our Lord Jesus! May they be my joy and crown of rejoicing at the last day, and may God's mercies to me in every place make me more humble, more zealous, more thankful, and more steady to do or suffer whatever my dear Redeemer hath allotted for me.

Reflection

A two-week delay in his journey to America could have caused frustration, but instead young George Whitefield ministered to the soldiers stationed at Gibraltar. How do you react when your plans get interrupted? We can view interruptions as obstacles or opportunities—the choice is ours.

Live wisely among those who are not Christians, and make the most of every opportunity. Let your conversation be gracious and effective so that you will have the right answer for everyone.

COLOSSIANS 4:5-6

March 7

Society dictated that she obey her father, but she would not.

At the beginning of the third century, Vibia Perpetua, a twenty-two-year-old mother of an infant son, was the daughter of a noble family in Carthage (on the northern coast of present-day Tunisia). Perpetua, her brother, and her personal slave, Felicitas, were Christians, but the rest of her family were unbelievers. It is not known whether her husband believed.

In A.D. 202 the Roman emperor Septimius Severus issued an edict forbidding conversion to Christianity. Carthage was one of the cities where the edict was scrupulously enforced.

In Roman society, to defy the wishes of one's father was unthinkable. As a new Christian, Perpetua was preparing for baptism as a catechumen under a Christian man named Saturus. Because government officials equated baptism with conversion, Perpetua and four other catechumens were arrested. She wrote in her diary what happened next:

> While we were still under arrest, my father, out of love for me, was trying to persuade me and shake my resolution. "Father," I said, "do you see this vase here for example, or water pot or whatever?"
>
> "Yes, I do," said he.
>
> And I told him: "Could it be called by any other name than what it is?"
>
> And he said: "No."
>
> "Well, so too I cannot be called anything other than what I am, a Christian."

Apparently Perpetua and the others were held initially under house arrest. During this time Perpetua was baptized, a direct violation of the emperor's edict against conversion. Consequently these Christians were taken to prison and placed in a dungeon. After a time two deacons bribed the guards, who transferred her and the others to a better section of the prison. There she was able to nurse her baby and receive her mother's and brother's visits. Her brother advised, "Dear sister, you are greatly privileged; surely you might ask for a vision to discover whether you are to be condemned or freed." This she did.

Several days later the Christians were given a hearing to which her distraught father came. Again he tried to persuade Perpetua to think of her parents and her child and to give up her beliefs. Perpetua tried to comfort him, saying, "It will all happen in the prisoner's dock as God wills, for you may be sure that we are not left to ourselves but are all in his power."

Later Hilarianus, the governor, held a hearing during which her father appealed to her one last time to sacrifice to the Roman gods. However, Perpetua stood her ground and received her sentence. Perpetua records, "We were condemned to the beasts, and we returned to prison in high spirits."

On **March 7, 203,** the group was herded into the amphitheater to be killed. First a mad heifer mauled the women; then a leopard pounced upon Saturus, the catechist; and finally the gladiators completed the task with their swords. During her last moments Perpetua encouraged her brother and the catechumens: "You must all stand fast in the faith and love one another, and do not be weakened by what we have gone through."

The vision Perpetua requested and received of God while still in prison prepared her and the others for their deaths. She reported: "I saw a ladder of tremendous height . . . reaching all the way to the heavens, but it was so narrow that only one person could climb up it at a time. . . . Then I saw an immense garden, and in it a gray-haired man sat in shepherd's garb. . . . And standing around him were many thousands of people clad in white garments. He raised his head, looked at me, and said: "I am glad you have come, my child.""

Reflection

Most Christians go through their lives never receiving a vision or audible word from God. But every Christian does receive the Holy Spirit, who is able to strengthen and enable us to meet any problem or crisis.

∽✺∾

For God has not given us a spirit of fear and timidity, but of power, love, and self-discipline. So you must never be ashamed to tell others about our Lord. And don't be ashamed of me, either, even though I'm in prison for Christ. With the strength God gives you, be ready to suffer with me for the proclamation of the Good News.   2 TIMOTHY 1:7-8

March 8

It took only a few minutes to write, but its blessings will last forever.

Almost from the day she was born, **March 8, 1839,** in New York City, Phoebe Palmer showed a keen interest in music. Growing up in the church as the daughter of the Methodist evangelist Walter C. Palmer, she loved its music. At sixteen she married a prominent Sunday school worker named Joseph Fairchild Knapp, who achieved wealth and fame as the founder of the Metropolitan Life Insurance Company.

Mrs. Knapp made a name for herself in her day as a composer of both music and verse. One day when Mrs. Knapp had composed a new melody about which she was particularly excited, she wondered what her good friend Fanny Crosby, the prolific blind hymn writer,[18] would think of it. She immediately went to Fanny's house in Brooklyn, and after playing the tune once on the piano, Mrs. Knapp turned around to find Fanny kneeling in prayer. Thinking perhaps Fanny hadn't paid attention, she played it again. Fanny later wrote of that afternoon: "My friend, Mrs. Knapp, composed a melody, and played it over to me two or three times on the piano. She then asked me what it said, and I immediately replied 'Blessed Assurance, Jesus is mine! O what a foretaste of glory divine!' "

Within just a few minutes Fanny Crosby had written three verses and a chorus for Mrs. Knapp's new melody. Their joint effort, "Blessed Assurance," was first published in 1873. The music and verses that we sing today remain the same as the day they were created in Fanny Crosby's living room that afternoon:

> *Blessed assurance, Jesus is mine!*
> *O what a foretaste of glory divine!*
> *Heir of salvation, purchase of God,*
> *Born of His Spirit, washed in His blood.*
>
> *Perfect submission, perfect delight!*
> *Visions of rapture now burst on my sight;*
> *Angels descending bring from above*
> *Echoes of mercy, whispers of love.*
>
> *Perfect submission—all is at rest,*
> *I in my Savior am happy and blest;*

BLESSED ASSURANCE

Watching and waiting, looking above,
Filled with His goodness, lost in His love.

This is my story, this is my song,
Praising my Savior all the day long.

Mrs. Knapp published more than five hundred hymns during her lifetime, but of her many hymns only "Blessed Assurance" and "Open the Gates of the Temple" are commonly sung today. Both compositions are set to texts that Fanny Crosby wrote.

Of the nearly nine thousand hymns Fanny Crosby wrote in her lifetime, "Blessed Assurance" is one of her most beloved as well. The first verse of the hymn was chosen for the inscription on her headstone at her death in 1915.

Reflection

Phoebe Knapp and Fanny Crosby left a glorious legacy in the hymn "Blessed Assurance." Countless people across the world have been blessed and comforted by the inspiring words and beautiful melody combined that day by the two friends. Do you have the blessed assurance that Jesus is yours? If you do, praise your Savior "all the day long." If you don't, trust him today as your Savior, and you will be "born of His Spirit, washed in His blood."

We have this assurance: Those who belong to God will live; their bodies will rise again! Those who sleep in the earth will rise up and sing for joy!
                                                          Isaiah 26:19

March 9

They won against all odds.

ON DECEMBER 16, 167 B.C., the Syrian ruler Antiochus IV Epiphanes desecrated the Jewish temple in Jerusalem by offering the flesh of a pig as a sacrifice on an altar to Zeus constructed over the altar of burnt offering (1 Maccabees 1:41-64; 2 Maccabees 6:1-11; Daniel 11:31).[19]

The following year Antiochus decreed that everyone in Palestine sacrifice to the heathen gods under an imperial representative's supervision. Mattathias, an aged priest, had moved with his family from Jerusalem to the village of Modein, seventeen miles northwest of Jerusalem, to escape the idolatry of Antiochus. When Antiochus's officers finally came to Modein, they forced Mattathias, his five sons, and the other villagers to assemble before an altar the officers had built. The officers addressed Mattathias, "You are a leader, honored and great in this city, and supported by sons and brothers. Now be the first to come and do what the king commands" (1 Maccabees 2:1-18).

But in a loud voice Mattathias replied, "Even if all the nations that live under the rule of the king obey him, and have chosen to do his commandments, departing each one from the religion of his fathers, yet I and my sons and my brothers will live by the covenant of our fathers. Far be it from us to desert the law and the ordinances. We will not obey the king's words by turning aside from our religion to the right hand or to the left" (vv. 19-22).

When Mattathias finished speaking, a Jew came forward to offer his sacrifice and Mattathias ran up and killed him on the altar. He then killed the officer who had commanded them to sacrifice and tore down the altar (vv. 23-26).

Then Mattathias called out with a loud voice, "Let everyone who is zealous for the law and supports the covenant come out with me." With that battle cry, Mattathias and his sons fled into the hills, where many Jews followed them (vv. 27-30).

From the hills they conducted guerrilla warfare, with leadership passing to his son Judas, called Maccabeus, which means "hammer," because of the blows he inflicted on the Syrians. The name was applied to Judas's brothers and then to all who took part in the rebellion.

The first battles of the Maccabean Revolt during the 160s B.C. were against the Syrian army led by Nicanor. In 166 B.C. the Syrians were so sure that Nicanor would defeat Judas that they brought traders along to buy Jewish slaves. However, the Maccabees were victorious.

WHO WERE THE MACCABEES?

In 164 B.C., after three years of fighting, Judas won control of Jerusalem. He cleansed and rededicated the temple with "songs and harps and lutes, and cymbals" (4:54). The eight-day celebration was the beginning of Hanukkah, the Jewish Feast of Dedication, or Lights.

The fight was ongoing, though the leaders of Syria changed. Nicanor continued as commander in chief of the Syrian forces waging war against the Maccabees.

Finally in 161 B.C. the Syrian ruler, Demetrius I Soter, the nephew of Antiochus IV Epiphanes, sent Nicanor and his army one more time against Judas Maccabeus. On **March 9, 161** B.C., before the battle, Judas prayed, "O Sovereign of the heavens, send a good angel to carry terror and trembling before us. By the might of thy arm may these blasphemers who come against thy holy people be struck down" (2 Maccabees 15:23-24). God answered. Judas was victorious, and Nicanor was killed. The Jews celebrate this day, the thirteenth of Adar in the Jewish calendar, as Nicanor's Day.

Although as the years passed the Maccabean dynasty became less noble in their purposes, they set up an independent nation that lasted until 63 B.C. when Pompey established a Roman protectorate over Palestine.

Reflection

What was the reason for the success of the Maccabees? Before the final battle with Nicanor, Judas Maccabeus, "perceiving the hosts that were before him and the varied supply of arms and the savagery of the elephants, stretched out his hands toward heaven and called upon the Lord who works wonders; for he knew it is not by arms, but as the Lord decides, that he gains the victory for those who deserve it" (2 Maccabees 15:21).

By faith these people overthrew kingdoms, ruled with justice, and received what God had promised them. HEBREWS 11:33

March 10

They are in heaven together.

JOHN COWPER and his wife, Ann, had seven children, but only two survived infancy: William born in 1731 and John born in 1737. Ann was very frail and died six days after the birth of John. Their father was rector of Berkhamsted, Hertfordshire, England. The family was keenly evangelical. Not only were both parents Christians, but also many of the boys' aunts, uncles, and cousins. The one weakness that the Reverand Dr. Cowper passed on to his son William was chronic depression.

In 1764, during one of his hospitalizations, William was converted through the evangelistic efforts of his doctor, Dr. Nathaniel Cotton. Despite his lifelong battle with mental illness, he became one of England's greatest poets, authoring the lyrics to hymns such as "O for a Closer Walk with God" and "There Is a Fountain Filled with Blood." His brother, John, however, remained an unbeliever.

When John became ill in September 1769, his friends insisted that William come to Cambridge to visit him. After ten days John improved, and William returned to his home in Olney, mystified as to why his brother refused to trust in Jesus even when facing death.

The following February, William was again summoned because of John's failing health. John continued in great suffering until **March 10, 1770,** when William heard him quoting the words "Behold, I create new heavens and a new earth" to which he added, "Ay, and he is able to do it too."

The following day William wrote to a Christian friend of what had happened:

I am in haste to make you a partaker of my joy. . . . Yesterday, in the afternoon, my Brother suddenly burst into tears, and said with a loud cry, "Oh! forsake me not!" I went to his bed-side, and . . . found that he was in prayer. Then, turning to me, he said, . . . "I have felt that which I never felt before; and I am sure that God has visited me with this sickness, in order to teach me what I was too proud to learn in health. I never had satisfaction till now. The doctrines I had been used to referred me to myself for the foundation of my hope, and there I could find nothing to rest upon. The sheer anchor of the soul was wanting. I thought you wrong, yet wanted to believe as you did. I found myself unable to believe, yet always thought that I should one day be brought to do so. You suffered more than I have done, before you believed these truths, but our sufferings, though different in their kind and measure, were directed to the same end. . . . These things were foolishness to me once, I could not understand them, but now I have a solid foundation and am satisfied."

When I went to bid him good night, he resumed his discourse as follows—"I see the Rock of my salvation. I have peace, myself, and if I live, I hope it will be that I may be a messenger of the same peace to others. I have learnt that in a moment, which I could not have learnt by reading many books for many years. I have often studied these points, and studied them with great attention. . . . Now they appear so plain. . . . The evil I suffer, is the consequence of my descent from the corrupt original stock, and of my own transgressions. The good I enjoy, comes to me as the overflowing of his bounty. But the crown of all his mercies is this, that he has given me a Saviour, and not only the Saviour of mankind, but my Saviour."

John Cowper died ten days later.

Reflection

Do you know Jesus as *your* Savior? Many people call themselves Christians because they have learned facts about Jesus and the Christian faith. Yet the only way a person becomes a Christian is by trusting Christ personally. Make sure you trust him as your Savior so that you can experience the same joy as John Cowper.

I know that my Redeemer lives, and that . . . after my body has decayed, yet in my body I will see God! . . . I am overwhelmed at the thought!
JOB 18:25-27

March 11

He was cast down but not in despair.

WILLIAM CAREY, often called the "Father of Modern Missions," dedicated his life to spreading the gospel in India.[20] Serving as a missionary there from 1793 until his death in 1834, he never took a furlough.

Although he had little formal education, Carey was a gifted linguist who learned dozens of languages and dialects. His goal was to translate Scripture into as many Indian languages and dialects as possible. In order to meet this goal, Carey supervised the creation of India's first printing press. He established a large print shop in the city of Serampore, where he did his Bible translation. The building was two hundred by fifty feet, and twenty translators worked there in addition to typesetters, compositors, pressmen, binders, and other writers.

On **March 11, 1812**, Carey was teaching in Calcutta. While he was gone, a fire started in the printing room. His associate, William Ward, smelled smoke and called for help. Despite many hours of exhaustive efforts to fight the fire, the building burned to the ground. Just five pieces of equipment were saved.

Carey's entire library, his completed Sanskrit dictionary, part of his Bengal dictionary, two grammar books, and ten translations of the Bible were lost. Gone also were the type sets for printing fourteen different languages. Vast quantities of English paper, priceless dictionaries, deeds, and account books were all gone.

Another missionary interrupted Carey while he was teaching a class in Calcutta to inform him of the stunning and tragic events of the day before. When Carey returned to Serampore and surveyed the scene, he wept and said, "In one short evening the labours of years are consumed. How unsearchable are the ways of God. I had lately brought some things to the utmost perfection of which they seemed capable, and contemplated the missionary establishment with perhaps too much self-congratulation. The Lord has laid me low, that I may look more simply to him."

Although he was heartbroken, he did not take much time to mourn. With great resiliency Carey wrote, "The loss is heavy, but as traveling a road the second time is usually done with greater ease than the first time, so I trust the work will lose nothing of real value. We are not discouraged; indeed the work is already begun again in every language. We are cast down but not in despair."

IT BURNED, THEN RETURNED

Carey resolved to trust God that from the embers would come a better press and more scholarly translations. Within a few months Carey had set up shop in a warehouse.

Little did Carey know that the fire would bring him and his work to the attention of people all over Europe and America as well as India. In just fifty days in England and Scotland alone, about ten thousand pounds were raised for rebuilding Carey's publishing enterprise. So much money was coming in that Andrew Fuller, Carey's friend and a leader of his mission in England, told his committee when he returned from a fund-raising trip, "We must stop the contributions." Many volunteers came to India to help as well. By 1832 Carey's rebuilt and expanded printing operation had published complete Bibles or portions of the Bible in forty-four languages and dialects!

Reflection

Resiliency was William Carey's trademark throughout his life. In spite of difficulty and loss he never despaired. He once wrote, "There are grave difficulties on every hand, and more are looming ahead. Therefore we must go forward." Are there trials in your life that tempt you to despair? What can you learn from Carey's example of resiliency?

We are pressed on every side by troubles, but we are not crushed and broken. We are perplexed, but we don't give up and quit. We are hunted down, but God never abandons us. We get knocked down, but we get up again and keep going. 2 CORINTHIANS 4:8-9

March 12

They wondered why it didn't rain.

THE FIRST group of Jews returned from the Babylonian captivity in about 537 B.C., when Cyrus, the king of Persia, issued a decree authorizing them to return to Jerusalem to rebuild the temple the Babylonians had destroyed. After the construction began, the Samaritans and other neighboring tribes so intimidated the Jewish builders that they ceased work from 530–520 B.C.

When they stopped working on the temple, God sent a drought as his judgment on them (Haggai 1:5-6). At that time the prophets Haggai[21] and Zechariah[22] prophesied to the Jews of God's judgment on them for their failure to work on the temple. Zerubbabel, the governor of Judah, and Jeshua, the high priest, responded to the prophesies by motivating the people to resume working again (Ezra 5:1-2).

But Tattenai, governor of the province west of the Euphrates, and his colleagues, hearing construction had resumed, soon arrived in Jerusalem and asked, "Who gave you permission to rebuild this temple?" As if the drought weren't bad enough, now the Jews were being hassled by the government. The leaders of the Jews told Tattenai and his cohorts to write Darius, king of Persia, and let him verify that Cyrus had officially authorized the project. The Jewish leaders told the officials that they would continue to work until a reply was received from Darius (vv. 3-5).

Tattenai immediately wrote a letter to King Darius, asking him to search the royal archives in Babylon to discover whether King Cyrus ever issued a decree to rebuild the temple in Jerusalem (vv. 6-17).

Upon receipt of the letter, Darius issued orders to search the Babylonian archives. But it was at the fortress at Ecbatana in the province of Media that a scroll was found that said:

"Memorandum:
"In the first year of King Cyrus's reign, a decree was sent out concerning the Temple of God at Jerusalem. It must be rebuilt on the site where the Jews used to offer their sacrifices, retaining the original foundations. Its height will be ninety feet, and its width will be ninety feet. . . . All expenses will be paid by the royal treasury. And the gold and silver utensils, which were taken to Babylon by Nebuchadnezzar from the Temple of God in Jerusalem, will be taken back to Jerusalem and put into God's Temple as they were before."

FROM CURSE TO BLESSING

So King Darius sent this message:

"To Tattenai . . .

"Stay away from there! Do not disturb the construction of the Temple of God. Let it be rebuilt on its former site, and do not hinder the governor of Judah and the leaders of the Jews in their work. Moreover I hereby decree that you are to help these leaders of the Jews as they rebuild this Temple of God. You must pay the full construction costs without delay from my taxes collected in your province so that the work will not be discontinued. . . . And without fail, provide them with the wheat, salt, wine, and olive oil that they need each day. Then they will be able to offer acceptable sacrifices to the God of heaven and pray for me and my sons.

"Those who violate this decree in any way will have a beam pulled from their house. Then they will be tied to it and flogged, and their house will be reduced to a pile of rubble. May the God who has chosen the city of Jerusalem as the place to honor his name destroy any king or nation that violates this command and destroys this Temple. I, Darius, have issued this decree." (Ezra 6:3-12)

Tattenai did as he was told. The Jewish leaders continued their work and finished the temple on **March 12, 516 B.C.**, seventy years after its destruction in 586 B.C.[23] Then all who had returned to Jerusalem dedicated the Temple to God with great joy (vv. 13-16).

Reflection

The Jews went from experiencing a drought when they were disobedient to the blessing of the Persian government paying all their expenses when they were obedient. Have you experienced God's chastening when you were disobedient and his blessing when you were faithful?

As surely as the Lord your God has given you the good things he promised, he will also bring disaster on you if you disobey him.

JOSHUA 23:15

March 13

The media dubbed her "the grandmother next door."

VELMA BARFIELD was born in rural North Carolina in October 1932. As the oldest daughter, she became the target of her drunken father's abuse for trying to protect her younger siblings.

"A lot of those times I wanted to talk to somebody about all the bad feelings going on inside me, like all the anger and resentment," Velma recalled. "I didn't know who could do anything about it, anyhow. I just kept pushing it deeper inside." No one in the community knew what life was like in their home.

When she was seventeen, Velma escaped the horror at home by eloping with a young man from church. During the next four years she had a son and a daughter and experienced happiness for the first time in her life.

Then life began to fall apart. Hospitalized after an accident caused by a drunk driver, Velma suffered her first bout of depression. About the same time, her husband began to drink and became abusive. Velma supported their family by working two full-time jobs. Worn down by stress and lack of sleep, she suffered a nervous breakdown in 1968.

Velma found some relief from the pain and shame that had hounded her from childhood through the drugs the doctors prescribed for her depression. Soon she was addicted to prescription tranquilizers and painkillers and supported her habit by fraud, hiding the drugs and her pain from everyone. Only her children suspected she had a problem.

Then on **March 13, 1978,** Velma Barfield, "the grandmother next door," confessed to poisoning the man she hoped to marry. Later it was revealed that she had murdered three others as well, all with arsenic. Although aware that each had died, in her drug-induced fog, Velma could only remember wanting painful people to go away.

Coming off drugs nearly killed her during the five months of solitary confinement while she awaited trial, and Velma was at the bleakest point of her life. Her one thought was, *I want to die.*

Outside Velma's cell a guard regularly listened to a Christian radio station. One night an evangelist invited everyone who could hear his voice to accept the forgiveness of Jesus Christ.

Velma later said, "The horror of my life, ever since childhood, had been unbearable. . . . But the marvelous revelation was that God knew that. He

A PRISON DOOR TO ETERNAL LIFE

knew that I was helpless without Him. And that's why He sent His only Son. Jesus was blameless, paid the penalty for me because I couldn't. . . . I couldn't undo my grievous sins. I couldn't bring those people back to life. It was too late to go back. But I realized at that time that I could go *forward*."

Going forward was not easy, even with Christ. Velma was convicted of first-degree murder and sentenced to death. The next five years of appeals and stays of execution were a time appointed by God for the redemption of many. Velma joined a prison Bible study and led many young women to Christ. She corresponded with hundreds of people from death row and wrote her autobiography, testifying to the transforming power of God.

But God did not choose to stop her execution. Anne Graham Lotz, Billy Graham's daughter, had become a close friend of Velma's and later wrote, "I witnessed the execution of my dearly beloved sister in Christ on November 2, 1984, comforted by the knowledge that physical death is no interruption to a believer's relationship with Jesus Christ. It is merely a stepping over from a relationship based on faith, to one of sight. Velma Barfield, with peace and tranquility on her face, her lips moving in silent prayer, closed her eyes in death at 2:15 A.M., while opening them to the face of her beloved Savior and Lord for all eternity."

Reflection

The apostle Paul had participated in the murder of Stephen, yet he became the leader of the New Testament church. God specializes in saving those who need him the most.

For I am the least of all the apostles, and I am not worthy to be called an apostle after the way I persecuted the church of God. But whatever I am now, it is all because God poured out his special favor on me.

1 CORINTHIANS 15:9-10

March 14

It all began at a tea party.

In 1856 in Ulster, Ireland, James McQuilkin was invited to tea. There a visiting woman skirted the civilities of discussing the weather and spoke openly on a subject McQuilkin found uncomfortable: the condition of the soul. After another guest at the tea party described the nature of her Christian experience, the visitor said, "My dear, I don't believe you have ever known the Lord Jesus." McQuilkin later wrote, "I knew that she spoke what was true of *me*. I felt as if the ground were about to open beneath me and let me sink into hell. As soon as I could, I left the company. For two weeks I had no peace day or night. At the end of that time I found peace by trusting the Lord Jesus."

The following year McQuilkin felt burdened to pray for his neighbors. He asked three friends to join him. Once a week the four men gathered at the village schoolhouse to pray for each person in their community by name. The town was Ahogill, County Antrim, Ulster, Ireland. The date: September 1857.

Meanwhile, unbeknownst to them, God was laying the same burden on many hearts, and similar prayer groups started throughout northern Ireland. Pastors began preaching about revival.

In December 1857 McQuilkin's group rejoiced to see the first conversion in Ahogill. But widespread revival did not come. Still, God's people prayed—for nineteen more months. Then one morning in the city of Ballymena, just six miles from Ahogill, a young man fell prostrate in the crowded marketplace and called out, "Unclean! Unclean! God be merciful to me a sinner!"

The night of **March 14, 1859,** the McQuilkin group responded by inviting Christians to a prayer meeting at the Ahogill Presbyterian Church. The church was so crowded that they moved the meeting out into the street. There hundreds of people knelt in the mud and rain, confessing their sins and praising God. They were the first of one hundred thousand people God called to himself in 1859 in what became known as the Ulster Revival.

There was a great spiritual movement among young people. It was not uncommon for teenage boys to hold street meetings to reach their peers for Christ. At one such street meeting an Irish clergyman counted forty children and eighty adults listening to the preaching of twelve-year-old boys.

The results of the revival were remarkable. In 1860 in County Antrim the police had an empty jail and no crimes to investigate. Judges often had no cases to hear. With their owners converted, pubs closed and alcohol consumption fell so drastically that whiskey distilleries were sold. Gambling at horse races fell off by 95 percent.

A visitor to Ulster reported "thronged church services, abundant prayer meetings, increased family prayers, unmatched Scripture reading, increased giving, converts remaining steadfast." The Ulster movement touched off similar revivals in England, Scotland, and Wales.

God drew hundreds of thousands of people to himself, and it all began with a woman unafraid to speak spiritual truth over tea.

Reflection

We never know what will be the effect of our conversation with others. The woman at the tea had no idea that God was using her to launch a nationwide revival. Our responsibility is to faithfully share God's truths as we go about our daily lives and leave the results to him.

∽❧∾

I have not been afraid to speak out, as you, O Lord, well know. I have not kept this good news hidden in my heart; I have talked about your faithfulness and saving power.   PSALM 40:9-10

March 15

He died the way he hoped.

ONE EVENING at a gathering in his home, Julius Caesar was discussing the best way to die. He said that his preference was that his death be "a sudden one."

The next morning was the Ides of March, **March 15, 44 B.C.** As Caesar was about to leave for the Senate, his wife begged him not to go, telling him that she had seen him in a dream, covered with blood. His friend Brutus urged Caesar to ignore his wife and go. Caesar went, and the rest is history. Once at the Senate, Brutus and his coconspirators ambushed and assassinated Julius Caesar.

Julius Caesar had designated his grandnephew, Gaius Octavian, born in 63 B.C., as his heir to the throne. Caesar had noticed Octavian in 49 B.C. because of his leadership in a series of Italian civil wars in which Caesar was victorious. Julius Caesar was so impressed with his grandnephew that he adopted him as his son and in his will made him his heir.

Following the death of Julius Caesar, Octavian succeeded him but over a period of years had to prove himself continually against challengers who aspired to the throne. The naval battle at Actium in 31 B.C. finally eliminated his opposition when his fleet defeated the fleet of Mark Antony and Cleopatra. The next year Octavian made Egypt part of the Roman Empire, and Mark Antony and Cleopatra committed suicide. To celebrate his accomplishment the Senate awarded Octavian the title of "Caesar Augustus."

With all his brilliant accomplishments, Caesar Augustus never would have been able to predict how he would be remembered down through history. Perhaps the most familiar story of all time begins with the words "And it came to pass in those days, that there went out a decree from Caesar Augustus, that all the world should be taxed" (Luke 2:1, KJV). It is ironic that the name of one of the most powerful emperors of all time is linked with that of a baby born far away in humble circumstances.

When the passage speaks of "all the world," Luke is asserting Caesar's sovereignty over the known world. Yet when God sends his Son into the world he does not announce it to Caesar but to shepherds watching their flocks. This is the God who "has taken princes from their thrones and exalted the lowly," as Mary sang before Jesus' birth (1:52).

During his lifetime, Caesar Augustus did not support the veneration of himself as divine. Yet he asserted the deity of Julius Caesar, his adoptive father, and as his son permitted himself to be called the "Son of God," thus setting the stage for being deified after his death. Caesar Augustus also accepted the title of "Savior" and was honored for having brought peace to all the world. One inscription about him reads, "Divine Augustus Caesar, Son of God, Savior of all the world."

Yet that little baby in the manger whose birth is linked with Caesar Augustus was *the* Prince of Peace, *the* Son of God, and *the* Savior.

Reflection

To whom do you look as your savior? Is it a politician, technology, the latest wonder drug? Or is it the baby in the manger? If it is Jesus, do you see him as an example to follow or as your Lord and Savior to trust?

∽◈∾

For a child is born to us, a son is given to us. And the government will rest on his shoulders. These will be his royal titles: Wonderful Counselor, Mighty God, Everlasting Father, Prince of Peace. His ever expanding, peaceful government will never end. He will rule forever with fairness and justice from the throne of his ancestor David. The passionate commitment of the Lord Almighty will guarantee this!

ISAIAH 9:6-7

March 16

The kingdom of Judah ended badly.

THE SIGNIFICANT battle of the late 600s B.C. was fought at Carchemish, the modern city of Jerablus, Syria, on the Euphrates River near the border with Turkey. Carchemish had military importance because it guarded the primary ford of the Euphrates.

In 612 B.C. the Babylonians had destroyed Nineveh, the capital of the Assyrian Empire. Three years later Egypt marched northward against the Babylonians in an effort to shore up the weakened Assyrians. King Josiah of Judah, preferring a Babylonian presence to that of Egypt and Assyria, tried to stop the Egyptians at Megiddo but was slain. Then the people anointed his son Jehoahaz and made him king. After ruling only three months, he was imprisoned by Pharaoh Neco. The pharaoh then placed another of Josiah's sons, Jehoiakim, on the throne of Judah and made Judah a vassal state of Egypt (2 Kings 23:29-35). The Egyptian army continued northward to Carchemish, which it garrisoned with its army and the remnant of the Assyrian forces.

The year 605 B.C. was a decisive one in the history of the ancient Near East. Nebuchadnezzar II, crown prince of Babylon, became commander in chief of the armies of Babylon. In the spring of 605 he marched to Carchemish and defeated the Egyptians and Assyrians in hand-to-hand fighting. As a result, Babylon took control of Syria and Palestine.

From his victory at Carchemish, Nebuchadnezzar led his armies to Judah and besieged Jerusalem. Jehoiakim renounced Egypt and became a vassal of Babylon (24:1). Nebuchadnezzar took a number of Jewish leaders to Babylon, including Daniel (Daniel 1:3).

Jehoiakim, an evil king in God's eyes, remained loyal to Babylon for only three years, so Nebuchadnezzar, now king of Babylon, once again sent his armies to force Jehoiakim to submit to him. Jehoiakim then remained in subservience to Babylon until his death in 597 B.C. (2 Kings 24:1-6).

Jehoiakim was succeeded by his eighteen-year-old son, Jehoiachin, who also did not follow Jehovah and was as bad as his father, oppressing his own people (vv. 8-9). So despicable was he that God said through Jeremiah the prophet, who was living in Jerusalem:

"As surely as I live," says the Lord, "I will abandon you, Jehoiachin. . . .
I will hand you over to those who seek to kill you, of whom you are so

THE RESULTS OF NOT TAKING
GOD SERIOUSLY

desperately afraid—to King Nebuchadnezzar of Babylon and the mighty Babylonian army. I will expel you and your mother from this land, and you will die in a foreign country." (Jeremiah 22:24-26)

This prophesy was fulfilled only three months into Jehoiachin's reign on **March 16, 597 B.C.**, when Nebuchadnezzar, after besieging the city, accepted the surrender of King Jehoiachin, his mother, advisers, nobles, and officials.

Nebuchadnezzar took ten thousand people captive to Babylon, including the king. In addition, Nebuchadnezzar carried away all the treasures from the temple and the royal palace.

Eleven years later Nebuchadnezzar would return a final time, destroying the city and temple and taking all but the poorest of the remaining Jews captive to Babylon (2 Kings 25:1-21).[24]

Eight hundred years earlier God had declared: "If you refuse to listen to the Lord your God, and do not obey all the commands and laws I am giving to you today, all these curses will come and overwhelm you. . . . The Lord will bring a distant nation against you from the end of the earth. . . . Its armies will lay siege to your cities until all the fortified walls in your land—the walls you trusted to protect you—are knocked down. . . . The Lord will scatter you" (Deuteronomy 28:15-64).

Judah refused to listen to God, and God did just what he had promised.

Reflection

Just as God held the nation of Israel accountable for its disobedience, he holds us as individuals accountable for whether or not we give him our allegiance and obey him. What lessons from Judah's final days can you apply to your life?

Fear God and obey his commands, for this is the duty of every person. God will judge us for everything we do, including every secret thing, whether good or bad.   ECCLESIASTES 12:13-14

March 17

She wrote from her own experience.

BORN ON **March 17, 1789,** Charlotte Elliott grew up in a cultured, spiritual household in England. Her grandfather was the famous preacher Henry Venn, and her father and brother were also ministers.

When Charlotte was in her thirties, she experienced a serious illness that left her in poor health and in significant pain for the rest of her life. Feelings of weakness and helplessness that stemmed from her physical problems resulted in a lifelong struggle with depression.

One day in 1822 when Charlotte was especially depressed and irritable, Dr. Caesar Malan, a Swiss minister, musician, and old family friend, questioned her regarding her faith. He asked her whether she had ever experienced God's peace in the midst of her difficulties. She became upset and defensive, but his words nagged at her heart. Later, when she was feeling better, she sought out Dr. Malan and asked him for help, confessing her sense of alienation from God. She said, "I want to be saved; I want to come to Jesus, but I don't know how." He replied simply and sincerely, "Come to him just as you are." His words were from the Lord, and they spoke to Charlotte powerfully.

Charlotte did come to Jesus in faith that day, and peace filled her heart for the first time. She continued to struggle with depression as her physical problems plagued her, but now she had Jesus to help her through her difficulties.

On one particularly trying day she was unable to go to a church function she really wanted to attend because of her intense pain and weakness. She was deeply depressed, feeling she could do nothing to serve the Lord as a homebound invalid. In her misery she reached for a pen and paper and poured out her feelings. As she wrote, the words of Dr. Malan came back to her, and she felt as if her great burden was being lifted:

> Just as I am, without one plea,
> But that Thy blood was shed for me,
> And that Thou bidd'st me come to Thee,
> O Lamb of God, I come! I come!

Charlotte Elliott published the hymn anonymously in a small Christian newspaper. Unknown to Charlotte, over time the hymn gained popularity and was shared in churches and religious magazines. A wealthy woman was so moved by the hymn that she had it published on a leaflet and distributed throughout England. One day Charlotte's doctor handed her the leaflet, thinking that the poem might be of help to her. Imagine their collective surprise when she recognized the words as her own! Charlotte was amazed as she learned how many people were touched by her hymn. She realized then that writing was not only a source of comfort for her but that she also could bring comfort to others. She had found her ministry. She continued writing hymns through the years, and although she remained in significant pain, her hymns consistently demonstrated gentleness, patience, and spiritual strength.

Years later, when "Just As I Am" had become known throughout England, her brother, who was a pastor, commented that her single hymn may have borne more fruit than he had in his entire ministry.

A century later when young Billy Graham went forward to receive Christ at an evangelistic service, the first song of invitation was "Just As I Am."[25]

Reflection

Dr. Malan never could have guessed that his simple reply to Charlotte's question would be repeated again and again by countless Christians throughout the world. We never know how our words may impact others. Pray that God will use your words for his purposes.

My message and my preaching were very plain. I did not use wise and persuasive speeches, but the Holy Spirit was powerful among you. I did this so that you might trust the power of God rather than human wisdom.   1 CORINTHIANS 2:4-5

March 18

Why would intelligent, popular, and athletically gifted young men disdain lucrative careers and choose to be missionaries?

IN THE 1880s seven prominent Cambridge students made an impact not only on England but also on the world. Stanley Smith, Montague Beauchamp, Dixon Hoste, William Cassels, Cecil Polhill-Turner, Arthur Polhill-Turner, and C. T. Studd became known to the world as the "Cambridge Seven."

In 1873 Stanley Smith, son of a prominent London surgeon, had gone to a D. L. Moody crusade and put his faith in Christ but did not live for him. Once he arrived at Cambridge, rowing became the most important thing in his life. Montague Beauchamp, Smith's best friend from prep school and fellow member of the rowing team, was a nominal Christian, too. Under the influence of a mutual Christian friend, Smith rededicated his life to God in 1880. God had raised the first member of the Cambridge Seven. Beauchamp, however, remained uninterested in his friend's change of heart. After Smith and his friend Kynaston Studd committed to pray together fifteen minutes every day for their friend Beauchamp, their prayers were answered in 1881 when Beauchamp announced that he had finally "yielded all to Christ."

Dixon Hoste was the brother of Cambridge student William Hoste, a committed Christian who was on the rowing team with Smith and Beauchamp. William prayed for and shared his faith continually with Dixon, who eventually attended a D. L. Moody rally where he gave his life to Christ. Dixon, who at twenty-one was already a commissioned officer in the British army, returned to his post professing faith in Jesus.

William Cassels, also on the rowing team, was a quiet young man studying to become a minister. After Stanley Smith gave his life to Christ, he became good friends with Cassels. They frequently prayed together that they would be a Christian influence on the rowing team of which Smith was now the popular captain.

Arthur Polhill-Turner also found Jesus at a Moody crusade while at Cambridge.[26] Arthur then persuaded his brother Cecil, who was a commissioned officer in the British army, to go to a Moody crusade in London. Cecil was interested in Christianity but thought it would mean giving up his promising military career, which he was unwilling to do. Finally in 1884 he gave his life completely to Christ after a year-long spiritual struggle.

THE CAMBRIDGE SEVEN

Charles (C. T.) Studd was the younger brother of Kynaston Studd. Their father, a millionaire, was converted at a Moody rally in 1877. He had devoted the remaining two years of his life to spreading the gospel. All three of his sons were converted through his efforts. At Cambridge, C. T. Studd was the popular captain of the cricket team, receiving worldwide recognition as the greatest cricket player of all time. With his fame and success, C. T. drifted far from Christ for a few years. In 1883 his world was shaken when his brother George was sick. Faced with his own mortality and eternity, cricket began to look shallow to him. C. T. gave himself completely over to Christ and immediately began using his influence to reach others.

Independently each of these young men began seeking how God could use his life. Beauchamp was the first to learn of the China Inland Mission (CIM),[27] and through a series of events and common connections, all seven men decided to go together to China. Each of them was accepted as a CIM missionary. Before they sailed, the Cambridge Seven toured the campuses of England and Scotland, speaking nightly to packed auditoriums. Hundreds came to Christ through their meetings, bringing revival to England. At their farewell service in London thirty-five hundred gathered to say good-bye.

On **March 18, 1885,** the Cambridge Seven arrived in China, where they served for many years, some until their deaths.

Reflection

Why do you think these seven successful, prominent, well-to-do students went to China as missionaries? Have you ever considered whether God might want you to go to those who have never heard the good news of salvation? There are wonderful mission opportunities for all ages, from short-term ministries to career possibilities.

∽๑๏

My ambition has always been to preach the Good News where the name of Christ has never been heard, rather than where a church has already been started by someone else. ROMANS 15:20

March 19

Their parting was bittersweet.

LARS AND MAREN STAVIG lived on a farm near Stavik, Norway, with their three children, Andrew, Hans, and Magnus. Lars's father, a widower, had remarried and was raising a second family. Lars was especially close to his younger half brother, Knut, and half sister, Sirianna. But he knew there was no long-term future for him on the farm.

Lars and Maren made the difficult decision to go to America. In May 1876 their family and friends gathered to bid them farewell on the pier in Bergen, realizing that they would likely never see one another again.

In June 1876 the family arrived in Starbuck, Minnesota, and settled two miles north of town, where they farmed until 1884, when Lars learned that Day County in the Dakota Territory was opening up for homesteading. The family journeyed by ox-drawn covered wagon and settled in what is now northeastern South Dakota. Lars became a successful farmer on his 320 acres and was blessed with four more children, Peder, Edwin, Anna, and Louise, but he deeply missed his family back in Norway. They were linked by the letters they exchanged, their deep mutual faith in Jesus, and the hope of their reunion in heaven one day.

Eventually Lars sold his farm, retired, and went to live with one of his sons in Sisseton, South Dakota. There in his old age he continued to exchange letters with his brother and sister in Norway.

Sisseton, February 19, 1923
Old honorable brother, Knut Stavig,

> *I have received many greetings from you lately and I want to thank you for them.*

> *Last summer I was very sick. I guess I was near death. I had two doctors who attended me and they did not think I had any chance of surviving. I have not been my old self since then but I thank God for each day that has passed.*

> *I hope and trust that my Savior who paid so much for me has found a home for me in His Father's house. He will come and bring us to Him and He does it all out of grace. . . .*

> *I am sending you a small gift but it is too small to be of much help.*
> *Live well.*
> *Wishes from your brother,*
> *Lars A. Stavig*

LINKED BY THE PEN
AND THE SAVIOR

Apparently Lars also sent some money to his half sister, Sirianna:

Aas, **March 19, 1923**
Good Brother,

Grace to you and peace from God our Father and our Lord Jesus Christ, He who hanged himself for our sins in order that He could free us from the evil in this world according to our God and Father's Will. To Him be honor in all eternity! Amen. Oh, you wonderful God, you can bend hearts like a running brook, thanks and praise. So I will tell you that I received the letter March 7. I should go to Tornes but didn't have any money. The hired girl should loan me a crown. Just then the mail came with a letter for me. I went in and opened the letter, but think, think, I was so overcome I had to cry. . . .

It is best to hold to the cross tree, to Jesus and ask for grace and compassion because He has said, "Call on me on the day of grace so I will set you free and you shall praise me." I don't have the strength by myself. It was Jesus who gave me everything good.

So I will thank you for remembering that we are brother and sister. Yes, we are after a kind father. Yes, he was kind. Blessed be his memory. We must get to meet him in heaven, there where all are happy. . . .

Friendly greetings from your sister,
Sirianna Aas

Reflection

How did the Stavig family's faith help them deal with their separation? Do you look forward to meeting your loved ones in heaven?

∽∾

There are many rooms in my Father's home, and I am going to prepare a place for you. JOHN 14:2

March 20

He was one of Scotland's greatest theologians.

SAMUEL RUTHERFORD was born in 1600 in Nisbet, Scotland, educated at the University of Edinburgh, and then appointed professor of Latin.

After just a few years Rutherford left academia to become a minister in Anworth, Scotland, a community and parish he loved deeply. However, his quiet country life was disrupted when he published a book against Arminianism, the theology that was challenging the Calvinism of the Church of Scotland. The publication brought him recognition as a gifted theologian and scholar but also the scrutiny of the Arminian Anglican bishops King Charles I had forced on the Church of Scotland. As a result, in 1636 the Anglican High Commission judged him to be a Nonconformist, removed him from his parish, exiled him to Aberdeen, and barred him from preaching in Scotland. However, in 1638 the Presbyterian party took control of the Church of Scotland, and the National Covenant was signed in which Scots vowed to defend the Reformed faith and to keep the church free from governmental control. With this political change, Rutherford was made professor of divinity at St. Andrew's University. Later appointed as a member of the Westminster Assembly, which wrote the Westminster Confession,[28] Rutherford continued to study and write, becoming one of Scotland's greatest theological writers.

The restoration of the English monarchy in 1660 brought the reinstitution of the Anglican Church in Scotland. Rutherford lost his teaching position, and his books were publicly burned. In 1661 he received a summons to appear before Parliament to answer the charge of high treason. Realizing he was terminally ill, Rutherford responded to the court, "I have got summons already before a Superior Judge and Judicatory; . . . and ere your day come, I will be where few kings and great folks come."

While Rutherford was on his deathbed, a friend asked him, "What think ye now of Christ?" Rutherford replied, "Oh, that all my brethren in the land may know what a Master I have served, and what peace I have this day! I shall sleep in Christ, and when I awake, I shall be satisfied with his likeness. This night shall close the door, and put my anchor within the vail; and I shall go away in a sleep by five of the clock in the morning. Glory! Glory to my Creator and my Redeemer forever! . . . Glory! Glory dwelleth in Immanuel's land!"

Just as Rutherford predicted, he died in his sleep early on **March 20, 1661.** Rutherford's dying words were developed into a poetic tract called "The

GLORY DWELLETH IN
IMMANUEL'S LAND

Last Words of Samuel Rutherford" by Anne Ross Cousin, and a hymn was compiled from it: "The Sands of Time Are Sinking."[29]

> *The sands of time are sinking,*
> *The dawn of heaven breaks;*
> *The summer morn I've sighed for,*
> *The fair, sweet morn, awakes:*
> *Dark, dark hath been the midnight,*
> *But dayspring is at hand,*
> *And glory, glory dwelleth*
> *In Immanuel's land.*

> *O Christ! He is the fountain,*
> *The deep, sweet well of love!*
> *The streams on earth I've tasted,*
> *More deep I'll drink above:*
> *There, to an ocean fullness,*
> *His mercy doth expand,*
> *And glory, glory dwelleth*
> *In Immanuel's land.*

Reflection

Samuel Rutherford's faith was unwavering despite religious persecution and personal setbacks. Standing in the face of death, he looked expectantly and joyously into the glory awaiting him in heaven. What can Rutherford's life teach you about living your life and facing death?

He took me in spirit to a great, high mountain, and he showed me the holy city, Jerusalem, descending out of heaven from God. It was filled with the glory of God and sparkled like a precious gem, crystal clear like jasper.   REVELATION 21:10-11

March 21

"I once was lost but now am found."

JOHN NEWTON, the son of a sea captain, was born in London in 1725. When he was six, he lost his mother, but before she died, she prayed that he would become a minister. Choosing another path, Newton went to sea with his father at age eleven. After an unsuccessful stint in the Royal Navy, he went to work for a slave trader. As things went from bad to worse in his life, he hit bottom as the slave of a white slave trader's black mistress on one of the Plantain Islands off the Sierra Leone coast. For two long years he was hungry and destitute. Then in 1747 he began working once more on a slave ship.

In March 1748 Newton had an experience that changed him forever. He wrote in his journal: "Among the few books we had on board, one was Stanhope's Thomas à Kempis; I carefully took it up, as I had often done before, to pass away the time; but I had still read it with the same indifference as if it was entirely a romance. However, while I was reading this time, an involuntary suggestion arose in my mind—what if these things should be true?"

He went to bed that night but was awakened by a fierce storm. Within a few minutes the ship was a virtual wreck, filling with water. Working frantically, the crew finally plugged the leaks. In his exhaustion, Newton heard himself say to the captain, "If this will not do, the Lord have mercy upon us." Newton was instantly taken aback by his own words. This was the first time he had desired God's mercy in years. Then the thought went through his mind, *What mercy can there be for me?*

The next day, **March 21, 1748,** the storm continued. Newton was summoned to the helm, where he had time to reflect. He sadly concluded that there had never been a sinner as wicked as he and that his sins were too great and too many to be forgiven.

His journal records the deliverance from the storm and his spiritual deliverance as well: "[This] is a day much to be remembered by me, and I have never suffered it to pass wholly unnoticed since the year 1748. On that day the Lord sent from on high and delivered me out of the deep waters. . . ."

Later he wrote: "I stood in need of an Almighty Saviour, and such a one I found described in the New Testament. . . . I was no longer an infidel; I heartily renounced my former profaneness, and I had taken up some right notions; was seriously disposed, and sincerely touched with a sense of the undeserved mercy I had received, in being brought safe through so many dangers."

Although he continued sailing and working in the slave trade for a time, he studied the Bible, prayed, read Christian books, and finally left the sea behind. In 1764 at age thirty-nine John Newton began a new life as a minister in the Church of England, later writing his autobiographical hymn, "Amazing Grace."

Throughout his life, he stopped to thank God on the anniversary of his conversion. The last entry in his journal was written on **March 21, 1805,** the anniversary of his deliverance, "Not well able to write; but I endeavor to observe the return of this day with humiliation, prayer and praise."[30]

Reflection

Often God will use danger or tragedy to get our attention. Has that ever been your experience? If so, did the experience produce a permanent result similar to John Newton's?

∽

Suddenly, there was a great earthquake, and the prison was shaken to its foundations. All the doors flew open, and the chains of every prisoner fell off! The jailer woke up to see the prison doors wide open. He assumed the prisoners had escaped, so he drew his sword to kill himself. But Paul shouted to him, "Don't do it! We are all here!"

Trembling with fear, the jailer called for lights and ran to the dungeon and fell down before Paul and Silas. He brought them out and asked, "Sirs, what must I do to be saved?" Acts 16:26-30

March 22

In 1620, when many people were considering whether to go to the New World, one person had a unique reason—he was trying to go home.

AN AMERICAN Indian named Tisquantum (Squanto for short) had come to England via the slave trade. In 1605 Captain George Weymouth captured Squanto and took him to England, where he learned English. Spending nine years in England before returning to his people, the Patuxets on Cape Cod, he traveled home in 1614 on Captain John Smith's vessel. He was not home long before Captain Thomas Hunt, part of Smith's expedition, lured Squanto and twenty-six other unsuspecting Indians aboard his vessel under the pretext of trading with them. Once the Indians were onboard, Hunt's crew clamped them in irons and took them to Spain, where they were sold into slavery. Many never returned to their homeland. Squanto was delivered into the hands of local friars, who introduced him to the Christian faith.

Squanto did not remain long with the Spanish monks. Making his way to England, he managed to get passage on the American-bound ship of Captain Dermer in 1619. When Squanto arrived back on Cape Cod, he learned that every single person in his tribe had died. In 1617 smallpox had ravaged his people, and no one had survived.

In early November 1620, the Pilgrims reached the shores of Cape Cod. They had been members of that Separatist congregation of Scrooby, England, that refused to conform to the Church of England and as a result, had fled to Holland. Twelve years later, they set sail for America to build a new life, fearing their children would lose their English identity. They settled in a place they called Plymouth, named after the town in England where they started their voyage.[31]

The settlers soon discovered that Indians had cleared the land at Plymouth but had not farmed it for some time. One March day, after a devastating winter of hardship and sickness, an English-speaking Indian named Samoset walked into Plymouth. He had learned English from fishermen he had met along the Maine coast. From Samoset the Pilgrims learned that they had settled on the homeland of the Patuxets, the tribe that disease had wiped out four years earlier. Samoset informed the Pilgrims that the Patuxets had been a large, hostile tribe that viciously murdered any white man who encroached upon their shores. After the death of the Patuxets, no other Indians had inhabited the land for fear of the death curse that might fall on any who settled there. So it came about that God led the Pilgrims to perhaps the one plot of un-inhabited land on the East Coast, the very land where Squanto had grown up.

Samoset introduced the Pilgrims to Squanto on **March 22, 1621.** Squanto brought news that the great Massasoit, chief of the Wampanoag and leader of most of the surrounding tribes, was coming to visit the settlers that very day. When Massasoit arrived, Squanto helped the Pilgrims agree to a peace treaty with Massasoit that would last for decades.

When Squanto arrived in Plymouth, the Pilgrims were in desperate straits. Nearly half had died during the previous winter, lacking the skills for survival in their new land. Squanto showed the Pilgrims how to fertilize and protect the corn they planted, how to catch fish from the streams, and how to harvest the food the land provided. If God had not sent Squanto, the Pilgrims would never have survived. One of the Pilgrim leaders called him "a special in-strument sent of God for our good, beyond our expectation."

Reflection

Who has God used to profoundly influence you? God always provides the help his children need. Look around you, and you might be surprised at whom God wants to use in your life.

Abraham named the place "The Lord Will Provide."   GENESIS 22:14

March 23

What would a revival be like among the Delaware Indians in 1746?

DAVID BRAINERD, at twenty-eight, had been a missionary to the Indians for four years. Now he was ministering to the Delaware Indians of Crossweek-sung, New Jersey.

His diary records the events of **March 23, 1746**:

There being about fifteen strangers, adult persons, come among us in the week past—divers of whom had never been in any religious meeting till now—I thought it proper to discourse this day in a manner peculiarly suited to their circumstances and capacities; and accordingly attempted it from Hosea 13:9, "O Israel, thou hast destroyed thyself. . . ." In the forenoon, I opened in the plainest manner I could man's apostasy and ruined state, after having spoken some things respecting the being and perfections of God, and His creation of man in a state of uprightness and happiness. In the afternoon, endeavored to open the glorious provision God has made for the redemption of apostate creatures, by giving His own dear Son to suffer for them and satisfy divine justice on their behalf. There was not that affection and concern in the assembly that has been common among us, although there was a desirable attention appearing in general, and even in most of the strangers.

Near sunset I felt an uncommon concern upon my mind, especially for the poor strangers, that God had so much withheld His presence, and the powerful influence of His Spirit, from the assembly in the exercises of the day; and thereby denied them that degree of conviction which I hoped they might have had. In this frame I visited sundry houses and discoursed with some concern and affection to divers persons particularly, but without much appearance of success, till I came to a house where divers of the strangers were. There the solemn truths I discoursed of appeared to take effect, first upon some children, then upon divers adult persons that had been somewhat awakened before, and afterwards upon several of the pagan strangers.

I continued my discourse, with some fervency, till almost every one in the house was melted into tears; and divers wept aloud and appeared earnestly concerned to obtain an interest in Christ. Upon this, numbers soon gathered from all the houses round about and so thronged the place that we were obliged to remove to the house where we usually meet for public worship. The congregation gathered immediately, and many appeared remarkably affected. I discoursed some time from Luke 19:10. "For the Son of man is come to seek and to save that which was lost." . . .

There was much visible concern and affection in the assembly; and I doubt not but that a divine influence accompanied what was spoken to the hearts of many. There were five or six of the strangers, men and women, who appeared to be considerably awakened. And in particular one very rugged young man, who seemed as if nothing would move him, was now brought to . . . weep a long time.

David Brainerd died of tuberculosis just a year and a half later. He went on ahead to heaven where he would later welcome all the Indians he had led to Christ.[32]

Reflection

Revival broke out among the Indians because Brainerd felt God's leading to visit their homes in the evening after the worship service. Do you ever feel that God is leading you to do something? Do you follow that leading? You may not experience miraculous results like Brainerd did, but if you will follow God's leading, you will have the satisfaction of being faithful.

∽✑↷

All who are led by the Spirit of God are children of God.

ROMANS 8:14

March 24

Through its pages millions came to know God personally.

FOR FORTY-FIVE years Queen Elizabeth reigned over England. She had neither husband nor children and grew increasingly lonely in her last days. Queen Elizabeth's devotion to her country characterized her reign, and when her life finally ended on **March 24, 1603,** the coronation ring, a symbol of her marriage to England, had to be filed from her finger. It had seemingly become one with her, one of England's greatest devotees.

It was in the midst of the nation's mourning that the state's trumpets announced the reign of King James I. Already serving as King James VI of Scotland, he brought the two nations under one ruler. James took the throne in the midst of the growing pains of the Church of England. The church had labored to free itself of Roman Catholicism, and the Puritans sought to continue to liberate the church from additional remnants of Rome they felt still existed. In an effort to show his willingness to listen to the petitions of his new subjects, King James convened the Hampton Court Conference on January 14, 1604, to hear the concerns of the Puritans. Anxious to prove his own prowess in matters of the church, the king began the conference with a five-hour critique of the corruptions of the Church of England. The following day he heard the concerns of the Puritan leaders, who had been encouraged by the king's criticisms, but he disappointed them when he dismissed each of their requests and called instead for uniformity within the Church of England.

The king used the Hampton Court Conference to establish his control over the Church of England and to make clear his desire for unity. The one tangible result of the conference, however, was the decision to produce a new translation of the English Bible, one that would express the ancient text in the common vernacular, and unite his subjects through their access to the Scriptures. The king approved a list of fifty-four scholars divided into six translation teams that were to meet separately at Westminster, Oxford, and Cambridge. The translators were mostly middle-aged scholars, all but one members of the Church of England, chosen for their skill in the ancient languages of the Bible, knowledge of theology, and biblical scholarship.

This learned group of men spent two years and nine months creating the most accurate translation possible, drawing on every resource available to them. The result was a biblical translation that was not materially revised until nearly three centuries later when the Revised Version was published in 1885.

THE BEST-SELLING BOOK OF ALL TIME

The work of these men had a profound literary influence, setting a criterion of "Bible English," which helped standardize the English language. For three hundred years nearly every English-speaking Protestant family in the world had a King James Bible. Through its pages, millions came to know God personally. It is the single best-selling book of all time.

Reflection

Owning a Bible is one thing; reading it is another. The Bible is God's primary message to us. Reading and studying it has revolutionized millions of lives—it can revolutionize your life too.

❧

Jesus' disciples saw him do many other miraculous signs besides the ones recorded in this book. But these are written so that you may believe that Jesus is the Messiah, the Son of God, and that by believing in him you will have life. JOHN 20:30-31

March 25

Memorizing Scripture became a way of life for many because of his influence.

DAWSON TROTMAN was born prematurely in Arizona on **March 25, 1906.** He was not expected to live. His mother attributed her son's survival to God, while his father attributed it to luck. This wasn't their first difference of opinion. The family moved to California, and eventually Dawson's parents divorced.

In high school Daws was a natural leader. Both president and valedictorian of his class, he also led the Christian Endeavor Society at Lomita Presbyterian Church. But he was living a double life. After graduating from high school, he immersed himself in the Roaring Twenties, living a reckless life of alcohol and gambling.

Dawson Trotman was nearing rock bottom even before the day he and his girlfriend nearly drowned while swimming. When she was unable to swim back to shore, Daws tried to rescue her, but then they both began to sink. A couple in a nearby boat saved their lives.

A month later the police picked up Daws for drunkenness. His mother asked a Christian neighbor to pray for her wayward son. The next day the neighbor called her back, saying, "We spent the night praying, and the Lord showed me a vision of Dawson holding a Bible, speaking to a large group of people. And the burden has lifted. Don't worry about Dawson any more."

Two nights later Daws went back to visit his old Christian Endeavor group at church. Their Scripture memorization contest captivated his interest, and over the next two weeks, he memorized twenty verses. One of those verses blazed into his consciousness as he walked to work one day: "Verily, verily, I say unto you, He that heareth my word, and believeth on him that sent me, hath everlasting life" (John 5:24, KJV). The concept of eternal life intrigued Daws. He prayed, "O God, whatever this means, I want to have it." Immediately another memorized verse flashed into his mind: "As many as received him, to them gave he power to become the sons of God, even to them that believe on his name." He prayed a simple prayer: "O God, whatever it means to receive Jesus, I want to do it now."

After committing his life to Christ, Dawson joined a personal evangelism group. He discovered that the words of God he had memorized were a powerful witness, which compelled him to learn even more. Bible memorization became a discipline that would shape his future life and ministry.

After starting a discipling group Daws called the "Minute Men," he met a sailor, and their meeting crystallized Trotman's vision. Thousands of young men were spending months at sea aboard ships, and Daws saw the potential of training sailors to disciple their comrades. God began raising up men who wanted to disciple their shipmates, and in 1933 the Minute Men became the Navigators. Their motto: "To Know Christ and to Make Him Known." By 1945 there were Bible-memorizing Navigators on more than eight hundred navy ships, stations, and army bases. When World War II ended, thousands of former sailors went to college on the GI Bill, and the Navigators followed them onto campuses across the United States.

In 1950 Billy Graham asked Dawson to develop a follow-up program for crusade converts.[33] The Navigators' philosophy significantly impacted other ministries as well, including Wycliffe Bible Translators,[34] Operation Mobilization, Mission Aviation Fellowship, and Campus Crusade for Christ.[35]

In 1956 at the Navigators annual summer conference at Schroon Lake in the Adirondacks of New York, Dawson saw a girl fall out of a speedboat and dove into the lake to rescue her. He held her above water long enough for others to pull her out but then sank himself. Before anyone could reach him, Dawson Trotman drowned.

The caption under his obituary photo in *Time* magazine said simply, "Always holding someone up."

Reflection

Central to Dawson Trotman's vision and to the ministry of the Navigators is memorizing Scripture. Committing Bible verses to memory is an excellent way of making them part of your life. If you have never memorized God's Word, begin today.

❧

When I learn your righteous laws, I will thank you by living as I should!
PSALM 119:7

March 26

He was burned at the stake for reading the Bible.

WILLIAM HUNTER, a young follower of the Reformation, went to London in 1553 to apprentice as a silk weaver. That year the young Protestant king Edward VI died,[36] and his sister Mary ascended to the throne.[37] Mary was a staunch Catholic who was determined to purge England of evangelical heresy and to reestablish the Roman Catholic Church as the state religion. After losing his job for refusing to receive Communion in the Catholic Church, William returned to his home village, Burntwood. His brother later wrote about what happened after the local priest found William reading the Bible:

> "What meddlest thou with the Bible?" he asked William. "Canst thou expound the Scriptures?"
>
> "Father, I take not upon me to expound the Scriptures," William replied. "But I, finding the Bible here when I came, read in it to my comfort."
>
> "It was never merry world [sic] since the Bible came abroad in English," the priest said. "I perceive your mind well enough: you are one of them that misliketh the queen's laws. You must turn another leaf, or else you and a great sort more heretics will broil for this gear, I warrant you."
>
> "God give me grace that I may believe his word, and confess his name, whatsoever may come thereof."

The priest walked out of the chapel in a fury and had nineteen-year-old William arrested and sent to a London prison. The bishop told William that he had been arrested in order to restore him to the Catholic faith. William answered, "I am not fallen from the Catholic Faith of Christ, but confess it with all my heart." Over the next nine months he refused to recant on twelve occasions. Finally the bishop sentenced him to death by burning, and the queen, Bloody Mary, signed his death warrant.

The morning of **March 26, 1555,** was dark as William was led to the stake erected in the center of Burntwood. His brother recounted his last moments:

> His father . . . spake to his son, weeping and saying, "God be with thee, son William." And William said, "God be with you, good father, and be

of good comfort; for we shall meet again when we shall be merry."
Then William knelt and said the 51st Psalm.

Then said the Sheriff, "Here is a letter from the Queen. If thou wilt
recant, thou shalt live." "No," quoth William, "I will not recant." Then
William rose and went to the stake and stood upright to it. Then came
a bailiff and made fast the chain about William. . . . Then said William,
"Pray for me while you see me alive, good people, and I will pray for
you. . . . Son of God, shine on me"; and immediately the sun in the
element shone out of a dark cloud so full in his face that he was con-
strained to look another way; whereat the people mused, because it
had been so dark a little time before. . . .

Immediately fire was made. Then William cast his psalter into his
brother's hand, who said, "William, think on the passion of Christ and
be not afraid." William answered, "I am not afraid." Then he lift [sic]
up his hands and said, "Lord, Lord, Lord, receive my spirit"; and
casting down his head again into the smothering smoke, he yielded
up his life for the truth.

Reflection

Although we may take for granted the freedom to read the Bible, it has
not always been so. Even today in many Muslim nations Bibles are
outlawed as Christian propaganda. Would you die for the privilege of
reading your Bible? Do you value Bible reading enough to do it daily?

*For the word of God is full of living power. It is sharper than the
sharpest knife, cutting deep into our innermost thoughts and desires.
It exposes us for what we really are.*   HEBREWS 4:12

March 27

What would become of the next generation?

In 458 B.C. Ezra arrived in Jerusalem from Persia with a large group of exiles, joining those who had returned earlier from the Babylonian captivity.[38] Ezra, a Jewish priest, likely held an office in the Persian government equivalent to the commissioner for Jewish affairs. He was responsible for enforcing the observance of the law of Moses (Ezra 7:1–8:36).[39]

Four months after Ezra's arrival the Jewish leaders came to him complaining: "Many of the people of Israel, and even some of the priests and Levites, have not kept themselves separate from the other peoples living in the land. . . . For the men of Israel have married women from these people and have taken them as wives for their sons. . . . To make matters worse, the officials and leaders are some of the worst offenders" (9:1-2).

Intermarriage would be catastrophic for the Jews because foreign wives committed to the gods of their own nations would influence their children and threaten the survival of the Jewish faith. At best it might result in a religion mingled with idolatry that God would certainly judge.

When Ezra heard the report, he expressed his distress in the custom of the day, tearing his clothing and pulling hair from his head and beard. He sat in shock until the evening sacrifice in the temple and then fell to his knees, lifted up his hands to God, and prayed:

> O my God, . . . Our guilt has reached to the heavens. Our whole history has been one of great sin. That is why we and our kings and our priests have been at the mercy of the pagan kings of the land. . . .
> And now, O our God, . . . once again we have ignored your commands! Your servants the prophets warned us that the land we would possess was totally defiled by the detestable practices of the people living there. . . . Now we are again breaking your commands and intermarrying with people who do these detestable things. (9:6-14)

As Ezra prayed this prayer of confession, a large crowd of people gathered around him and wept. Then one of the leaders of Israel said to Ezra: "We confess that we have been unfaithful to our God, for we have married these pagan women of the land. But there is hope for Israel in spite of this. Let us now make a covenant with our God to divorce our pagan wives and to send them away. . . . We will obey the law of God" (10:2-3).

In response, Ezra stood up and demanded that they all do as their leader suggested, and they all agreed with a solemn oath. A proclamation was then circulated throughout the area ordering all returned exiles to come to Jerusalem. "Those who failed to come within three days would, if the leaders and elders so decided, forfeit all their property and be expelled from the assembly of the exiles" (10:5-8).

Within the three days everyone had gathered in Jerusalem's temple square, scared to death. Ezra stood before them and intoned: "You have sinned, for you have married pagan women. . . . Confess your sin to the Lord, the God of your ancestors, and do what he demands. Separate yourselves from the people of the land and from these pagan women" (10:10-11).

Then everyone cried out in response, "Yes, you are right; we must do as you say!" (10:12).

By **March 27, 457** B.C., their leaders verified that all the men who had married pagan wives had divorced them (10:17).

Reflection

What is your reaction to Ezra's requiring the Jewish men to divorce their pagan wives? Without this drastic step, the next generation of Jews would have been taught to worship foreign gods by their mothers.

∽◎◠

Do not make treaties of any kind with the people living in the land. . . . If you make peace with them, they will invite you to go with them to worship their gods, and you are likely to do it. And you will accept their daughters, who worship other gods, as wives for your sons. Then they will cause your sons to commit adultery against me by worshiping other gods. EXODUS 34:15-16

March 28

She gladly gave up her most valuable possession.

THE YEAR was A.D. 33, and the Feast of Passover was approaching when every Jewish male was required to come to Jerusalem.⁴⁰ Six days before the Passover, Jesus arrived in Bethany, the hometown of Lazarus, the friend he had raised from the dead only a short time before. On the far side of the Mount of Olives, Bethany was less than two miles from Jerusalem and an easy walk to the temple.

That night, **March 28, A.D. 33,** a dinner was prepared in Jesus' honor at the home of Simon the leper (Mark 14:3). Martha, the sister of Lazarus, served the food, and Lazarus, of course, was among the guests (John 12:2).⁴¹

The custom was for the Jewish men to eat together, reclining on thin mats around a low table and leaning on their left arms with their feet radiating out from the table.

As they reclined around the table that evening, Mary, the other sister of Lazarus, brought out a twelve-ounce jar of extremely expensive perfume made from essence of nard and imported from India. Breaking open the jar, she went over to Jesus and anointed him. The whole house was filled with the wonderful fragrance.

Judas Iscariot immediately objected, "That perfume was worth a small fortune. It should have been sold and the money given to the poor" (12:4). The perfume was, in fact, very costly—worth three hundred denarii, the equivalent of a year's wages for the average working man of Jesus' day.

The ugly truth was that Judas was not burdened for the poor but had an ulterior motive. Serving as treasurer for Jesus and his disciples, Judas was in charge of the disciples' funds and often took some for himself (12:16). He was no doubt thinking, *If we can get some big contributions like this coming in, I can make myself rich.*

How did Jesus react? "Leave her alone," he replied. "She did it in preparation for my burial. You will always have the poor among you, but I will not be here with you much longer" (12:7-8).

Mary did not know that Jesus was about to die, yet her act symbolized more than she knew. In the culture of Jesus' day it was not thought inappropriate to spend extravagant amounts on a funeral, especially for expensive perfumes that would mask the smell of decay. Mary lavishly anointed Jesus while he was still alive, just as Joseph of Arimathea and Nicodemus would six days later after his death (19:38-40).[42] Her act of amazing devotion was both appropriate and timely. Jesus knew that his death and burial were imminent and that, as God the Son, he was due the same honor as God the Father (5:23). He knew that in six days he would become the perfect Passover Lamb, removing the power of sin forever by his sacrificial death—something all previous Passover lambs had been unable to do.

Reflection

The perfume Mary used to anoint Jesus undoubtedly represented a significant portion of her net worth. Yet in her complete devotion to Jesus, she never questioned that this was the obvious thing to do. How great is your devotion to Jesus? How much are you willing to give to him?

Wherever your treasure is, there your heart and thoughts will also be.
MATTHEW 6:21

March 29

He didn't rush to help.

In the winter of A.D. 32–33 a man named Lazarus fell sick. He lived in Bethany on the far side of the Mount of Olives from Jerusalem with his two sisters, Mary and Martha. They were among Jesus' closest friends. When Lazarus became sick, his sisters sent a message to Jesus:[43] "Lord, the one you love is very sick" (John 11:1-3).

One would have thought that when Jesus received the message he would have rushed to the side of his sick friend, but instead he stayed where he was for two more days. Finally he said to his disciples, "Let's go to Judea again. . . . Our friend Lazarus has fallen asleep, but now I will go and wake him up."

"The disciples said, 'Lord, if he is sleeping, that means he is getting better!' They thought Jesus meant Lazarus was having a good night's rest, but Jesus meant Lazarus had died.

"Then he told them plainly, 'Lazarus is dead. And for your sake, I am glad I wasn't there, because this will give you another opportunity to believe in me. Come, let's go see him'" (John 11:5-15).

When Jesus arrived at Bethany, he was told that Lazarus had been in his grave for four days. When Martha got word that Jesus was coming, she ran out to meet him and said, "Lord, if you had been here, my brother would not have died" (11:17-21).

When Jesus told her that her brother would rise again, Martha responded, "Yes, when everyone else rises, on resurrection day."

"Jesus told her, 'I am the resurrection and the life. Those who believe in me, even though they die like everyone else, will live again. They are given eternal life for believing in me and will never perish. Do you believe this, Martha?'

"'Yes, Lord,' she told him. 'I have always believed you are the Messiah, the Son of God'" (11:27).

Jesus then went to the grave. It was a cave with a stone rolled across its entrance. "Roll the stone aside," Jesus said.

Martha objected and said, "The smell will be terrible."

"Jesus responded, 'Didn't I tell you that you will see God's glory if you believe?' So they rolled the stone aside. Then Jesus looked up to heaven and said, 'Father, thank you for hearing me. . . . Then Jesus shouted, 'Lazarus, come out!' To everyone's astonishment Lazarus came out, bound in his graveclothes, and Jesus commanded, "Unwrap him and let him go!" (11:38-44).

THE DOWNSIDE OF MIRACLES

Many people believed in Jesus when they witnessed this miracle. But some went to the Pharisees to report what Jesus had done. In response, the chief priests and Pharisees called a meeting of the Sanhedrin to discuss what they deemed a troubling situation. They feared everyone in their nation would become followers of Jesus, causing the Romans to send their army to kill them all. Then Caiaphas, the high priest said, "How can you be so stupid? Why should the whole nation be destroyed? Let this one man die for the people" (11:45-50).

Because the religious leaders were plotting to kill Jesus, he and his disciples left Jerusalem and went to a safer place. Shortly thereafter it was time for Passover, when every Jewish man was required to go to Jerusalem, so Jesus and his disciples went back to Bethany to stay at the home of Lazarus (11:53–12:1).

The second day he was there, **March 29, A.D. 33,** the people learned of Jesus' arrival and flocked to see him and Lazarus, the man Jesus had raised from the dead (12:9).

The chief priests then decided that their only solution to the popularity of Jesus was to kill not only Jesus but Lazarus as well (12:9-11).

Reflection

Why do you think the religious leaders wanted to kill both Jesus and Lazarus? A mighty miracle had taken place, and they wanted to do away with the evidence.

∽◎∽

This prophecy that Jesus should die for the entire nation came from Caiaphas in his position as high priest. He didn't think of it himself; he was inspired to say it. It was a prediction that Jesus' death would be not for Israel only, but for the gathering together of all the children of God scattered around the world. John 11:51-52

March 30

THE DAY was **March 30, A.D. 33**, four days before Passover. As Jesus[44] set out for Jerusalem from Bethany on the eastern slope of the Mount of Olives, he sent two disciples on ahead.

> "Go into the village over there," he said, "and you will see a donkey tied there, with its colt beside it. Untie them and bring them here. If anyone asks what you are doing, just say, 'The Lord needs them,' and he will immediately send them." This was done to fulfill the prophecy, "Tell the people of Israel, 'Look, your King is coming to you. He is humble, riding on a donkey—even on a donkey's colt.'"

The two disciples did as Jesus said. They brought the animals to him and threw their garments over the colt, and he sat on it. (Matthew 21:2-7)

[As Jesus rode the donkey toward Jerusalem,] the crowds spread out their coats on the road ahead [to honor him]. As they reached the place where the road started down from the Mount of Olives, all of his followers began to shout and sing as they walked along, praising God for all the wonderful miracles they had seen. "Bless the King who comes in the name of the Lord! Peace in heaven and glory in highest heaven!"

But some of the Pharisees among the crowd said, "Teacher, rebuke your followers for saying things like that!"

He replied, "If they kept quiet, the stones along the road would burst into cheers!" (Luke 19:36-40)

This was the official entry of the Messiah-King into Jerusalem. Just as David's son Solomon had ridden a donkey at his presentation as king to Jerusalem's cheering crowds a little over a millennium earlier (1 Kings 1:33-46), so Jesus entered Jerusalem riding a donkey to proclaim publicly that he was the greater Son of David who would sit on David's throne.

As Jesus drew nearer to Jerusalem and saw the city ahead, he began to cry. "Before long your enemies will build ramparts against your walls and encircle you and close in on you. They will crush you to the ground, and your children with you. Your enemies will not leave a single stone in place, because you have rejected the opportunity God offered you" (19:41-44).

This prophecy of Jesus was fulfilled in A.D. 70 when the Roman armies conquered the Jewish people, destroyed the city of Jerusalem, and left not one stone standing upon another (21:6, 20-24).[45]

More than five hundred years earlier God had revealed to the prophet Daniel that 483 years after the command to rebuild Jerusalem the Messiah would come (Daniel 9:25). King Artaxerxes of Persia gave the command to rebuild Jerusalem in the month of Nisan in the twentieth year of his reign (Nehemiah 2:1). The Jews did not use a solar calendar as we do today, and in biblical prophecies the years are composed of 360 days (Revelation 11:2, 3; 12:6; 13:5). The exact day of the month is not given, but if the command to rebuild Jerusalem was given on the first of Nisan, March 5, 444 B.C., it was 483 years of 360 days later to the day, **March 30, A.D. 33,** that Jesus formally entered the city as the Messiah. The prophecy likely was fulfilled to the day!

Something else also happened on that day. It was the day when the lambs to be slain at Passover were selected. In his triumphal entry Jesus was presenting himself as *the* Passover Lamb.

Reflection

The Jews of Jesus' day had to decide whether or not they would commit themselves to Jesus as their Messiah, King, and Passover Lamb. The issue for us today is the same.

John saw Jesus coming toward him and said, "Look! There is the Lamb of God who takes away the sin of the world!" JOHN 1:29

March 31

Jesus used visual parables.

THE MORNING after Jesus' triumphal entry into Jerusalem, on **March 31, A.D. 33,** as Jesus[46] and his disciples were leaving Bethany, where they had spent the night, Jesus was hungry. He noticed a fig tree covered with leaves a little way off the road. He went over to it to see if it had any figs, but since it was early in the season, it had only leaves. Jesus said to the tree, "May no one ever eat your fruit again!" (Mark 11:12-14).

Was Jesus having a temper tantrum because the tree had no fruit for his breakfast? Certainly he knew that it was too early in the season for figs, so he used the opportunity for a visual parable. Several passages in the Old Testament liken Israel to a fig tree. Just as the leaves concealed the lack of fruit on the tree, so the magnificence of the temple concealed the fact that Israel did not have the fruit of righteousness God required. Both the fig tree and the temple looked attractive from a distance, but on closer inspection both had no fruit. Jesus' cursing of the fig tree symbolized the curse that would soon fall on Judaism and its temple.

When Jesus and the disciples arrived in Jerusalem, Jesus entered the temple and found the court of the Gentiles filled with merchants. When Jews traveled to Jerusalem to sacrifice at the temple, they needed to purchase animals for their sacrifices. In addition, they had to pay the temple tax of one shekel. In those days the shekel of the city of Tyre was the closest equivalent to the old Hebrew shekel, so money changers were needed to change Roman currency into Tyrian shekels. For years these various transactions were made at four markets on the Mount of Olives. But around A.D. 30, Caiaphas, the high priest, decided to set up a market in the court of the Gentiles to compete with the markets on the Mount of Olives. The result was that the court of the Gentiles looked like an Oriental bazaar.

When Jesus saw all this commerce, he began to drive out the merchants and their customers, knocking over the tables of the money changers and the stalls of those selling doves, and stopping everyone from bringing in more merchandise. To explain himself, he announced, "The Scriptures declare, 'My Temple will be called a place of prayer for all nations,' but you have turned it into a den of thieves" (11:15-17).

To Jesus, turning any part of the temple into a market was an abomination. The court of the Gentiles was supposed to be the "place of prayer for all nations," but there was no room for Gentiles to pray when it was filled with merchants. This was his temple, and he was not about to allow buying and selling within it.

When the chief priests and teachers of Jewish law heard what Jesus had done, they intensified their plotting to kill him. Nevertheless they were afraid of him because the people were so enthusiastic about his teaching (11:18).

The next morning as Jesus and his disciples passed by the fig tree he had cursed, the disciples noticed that its leaves had dried up. Peter remembered what Jesus had said to the tree on the day before and exclaimed, "Look, Teacher! The fig tree you cursed has withered" (11:21).

Reflection

When Jesus saw the fig tree from a distance, it looked beautiful, but when he looked more closely, there was no fruit. The temple also looked magnificent from a distance, but upon closer examination, it had become a shopping mall. Jesus cursed the fig tree and in A.D. 70 sent the Roman armies to destroy his temple, forty years after Caiaphas had set up the market in it.

Jesus replied, "These magnificent buildings will be so completely demolished that not one stone will be left on top of another."

MARK 13:2

April 1

Jesus summarized the rest of world history.

ON **APRIL 1, A.D. 33,** as Jesus[1] was leaving the temple grounds in Jerusalem, his disciples began talking about the beautiful stonework of the temple. But Jesus said to them, "The time is coming when all these things will be so completely demolished that not one stone will be left on top of another" (Luke 21:5-6). In A.D. 70 the Roman legions completely destroyed the temple,[2] fulfilling Jesus' prediction.

Later that day when Jesus was sitting on the Mount of Olives, his disciples, still thinking about the destruction of the temple, asked,

"Teacher, when will all this take place? And will there be any sign ahead of time?"

He replied, "Don't let anyone mislead you. For many will come in my name, claiming to be the Messiah and saying, 'The time has come!' But don't believe them. And when you hear of wars and insurrections, don't panic. Yes, these things must come, but the end won't follow immediately." Then he added, "Nations and kingdoms will proclaim war against each other. There will be great earthquakes, and there will be famines and epidemics in many lands, and there will be terrifying things and great miraculous signs in the heavens.

"But before all this occurs, there will be a time of great persecution. You will be dragged into synagogues and prisons, and you will be accused before kings and governors of being my followers. This will be your opportunity to tell them about me. So don't worry about how to answer the charges against you, for I will give you the right words and such wisdom that none of your opponents will be able to reply! Even those closest to you—your parents, brothers, relatives, and friends— will betray you. And some of you will be killed. And everyone will hate you because of your allegiance to me. But not a hair of your head will perish! By standing firm, you will win your souls.

"And when you see Jerusalem surrounded by armies, then you will know that the time of its destruction has arrived. Then those in Judea must flee to the hills. Let those in Jerusalem escape, and those outside the city should not enter it for shelter." (Luke 21:7-21)

WHAT THE FUTURE HOLDS

Eusebius, the first Christian church historian, tells us that when the Roman armies were about to surround Jerusalem in A.D. 70, the Christians living in Jerusalem received a divine revelation telling them to flee, and all escaped to the city of Pella. The divine revelation they received instructing them to flee was no doubt from Luke's Gospel.

Jesus continued:

"Those will be days of God's vengeance, and the prophetic words of the Scriptures will be fulfilled. How terrible it will be for pregnant women and for mothers nursing their babies. For there will be great distress in the land and wrath upon this people. They will be brutally killed by the sword or sent away as captives to all the nations of the world. And Jerusalem will be conquered and trampled down by the Gentiles until the age of the Gentiles comes to an end. . . .

"Then everyone will see the Son of Man arrive on the clouds with power and great glory." (Luke 21:22-24, 27)

Jesus tells us that between the destruction of Jerusalem in A.D. 70 and his second coming is a period called the age of the Gentiles. That is the time in which we are now living, when the church is made up primarily of Gentiles, not Jews. This age will end with the return of Jesus "on the clouds with power and great glory."

Reflection

Do you believe that Jesus will come again? If you do, how does that affect your life?

∽≫

Watch out! Don't let me find you living in careless ease and drunkenness, and filled with the worries of this life. Don't let that day catch you unaware, as in a trap. For that day will come upon everyone living on earth. Keep a constant watch. LUKE 21:34-36

April 2

It was the night before Jesus' crucifixion.

On **April 2, a.d. 33,** Jesus[3] sent Peter and John to prepare the Passover meal for him to eat with his disciples (Luke 22:7-13).[4]

At the Last Supper Jesus instituted the New Covenant, replacing the Old Covenant of Mount Sinai. At the institution of the Old Covenant, Moses, Aaron, Aaron's sons, Nadab and Abihu, and seventy of the elders of Israel had gone up to the top of Mount Sinai, where they saw God and shared a meal in God's presence (Exodus 24:9-11). Which person of the Trinity did they see and eat with? It was God the Son whose role is to represent the Godhead visibly to humanity (John 1:18). Thus, the Old Covenant was instituted at a meal between God the Son and the elders of Israel. The New Covenant was instituted in the upper room at a meal between God the Son and the disciples, the elders of the church (cf. 1 Peter 5:1; 2 John 1:1; 3 John 1:1).

At the Last Supper when Jesus said, "This is my blood, which seals the covenant" (Matthew 26:28), the words (except for *my*) were identical to the Greek Septuagint translation of Moses' words at the institution of the Old Covenant (Exodus 24:8). Clearly Jesus was instituting a New Covenant to replace the Old Covenant.

Bible covenants were treaties between God and his people. Thus, it is significant that Jesus said, "This wine is the token of God's new covenant to save you—an agreement sealed with the blood I will pour out for you" (Luke 22:20). Since the time of Homer, nations poured out a cup of wine to seal treaties. This ritual was so central to treaty making, the Greek word for "libation" became the word for "treaty." Thus, Jesus used this contemporary treaty symbolism to make sure that everyone understood that he was instituting a New Covenant, or treaty, with his people.

Since the Old Covenant contained commandments, one would expect that the New Covenant would contain a new commandment. Thus, at the Last Supper Jesus says, "Now I am giving you a new commandment: Love each other. Just as I have loved you, you should love each other" (John 13:34).

After Jesus had identified Judas Iscariot as the one who would betray him and Simon Peter as the one who would deny him (John 13:18-38), he led the disciples across the Kidron Valley to the Garden of Gethsemane (John 18:1; Matthew 26:36).

In the garden Jesus prayed while the disciples slept (Matthew 26:36-45).

THE LAST SUPPER

Then Judas Iscariot led Roman soldiers to the garden to arrest Jesus. Jesus was taken first to Annas, the former high priest and father-in-law of Caiaphas, the current high priest (John 18:12-24). From there he was taken to Caiaphas and the Sanhedrin (Mark 14:53-65). After an all-night session, the Sanhedrin decided to accuse Jesus of treason before Pontius Pilate (Mark 15:1). Pilate decided that Jesus was innocent, yet when the crowds continued to shout, "Crucify him," he gave in and sentenced Jesus to die (Luke 23:1-24).[5]

Reflection

Within less than twenty-four hours Jesus went from eating the Passover meal to dying as the "Lamb of God." The New Covenant that Jesus instituted at the Last Supper is his kingdom's constitution, the legal framework that explains how his kingdom functions. Jesus poured out his blood when he died for us as the Passover "Lamb of God who takes away the sin of the world" (John 1:29). We can be part of his kingdom through faith by declaring our allegiance to him as our Lord and Savior.

All praise to him who loves us and has freed us from our sins by shedding his blood for us. He has made us his kingdom and his priests who serve before God his Father. Give to him everlasting glory! He rules forever and ever! Amen! REVELATION 1:5-6

April 3

They crucified their King.

THE PREVIOUS night the chief priests and Pharisees had sent a battalion of Roman soldiers with Judas to arrest Jesus[6] in the Garden of Gethsemane and take him to trial before the high priest and the Sanhedrin.[7]

After the trial ended in the early hours of the morning of **April 3, A.D. 33,** Jesus was taken to Pontius Pilate, the Roman governor.

"Are you the King of the Jews?" he asked him. . . .

Jesus answered, "I am not an earthly king. If I were, my followers would have fought when I was arrested by the Jewish leaders. But my Kingdom is not of this world."

Pilate replied, "You are a king then?"

"You say that I am a king, and you are right," Jesus said. . . .

Then [Pilate] went out again to the people and told them, "He is not guilty of any crime. But you have a custom of asking me to release someone from prison each year at Passover. So if you want me to, I'll release the King of the Jews."

But they shouted back, "No! Not this man but Barabbas!" (Barabbas was a criminal.)

"But if I release Barabbas," Pilate asked them, "what should I do with Jesus who is called the Messiah?"

And they all shouted, "Crucify him!"

Pilate saw that he wasn't getting anywhere . . . so he sent for a bowl of water and washed his hands before the crowd, saying, "I am innocent of the blood of this man. The responsibility is yours!"

And all the people yelled back, "We will take responsibility for his death—we and our children!"

So Pilate released Barabbas to them. He ordered Jesus flogged with a lead-tipped whip, and then turned him over to the Roman soldiers to crucify him. (John 18:33-40; Matthew 27:22-26)

The next event was truly remarkable. Though Jesus had been born to be king and had been anointed by the Holy Spirit following his baptism (Acts 10:38), he had never been officially crowned. After the soldiers beat Jesus, they coronated him—using all the major features of the coronation of a caesar.

THE CRUCIFIXION

In the Roman Empire, the soldiers frequently chose the next caesar. Here the soldiers set a crown of thorns on Jesus' head and put a royal purple robe on him (John 19:2). (At this time becoming caesar was known as "donning the purple.") They placed a stick in his right hand as a scepter and knelt before him in mockery, yelling, "Hail! King of the Jews" (Matthew 27:29).

"Then Pilate went outside again and said to the people, 'I am going to bring him out to you now, but understand that I find him not guilty.' Then Jesus came out wearing the crown of thorns and the purple robe. And Pilate said, 'Here is the man!'

"When they saw him, the leading priests and Temple guards began shouting, 'Crucify! Crucify!' So they took Jesus and led him away" (John 19:4-6, 16).

On Skull Hill (in Hebrew, "Golgotha") they crucified him between two thieves. Pilate had a sign placed over him that said, "Jesus of Nazareth, the King of the Jews." At three in the afternoon an earthquake shook Jerusalem as he died, just as the Passover lambs were being slain all over Jerusalem (John 19:19-30; Matthew 27:33-51). The apostle Paul later wrote, "When he was hung on the cross, he took upon himself the curse for our wrongdoing. For it is written in the Scriptures, 'Cursed is everyone who is hung on a tree' " (Galatians 3:13). Jesus paid the penalty for the sins of his people so that they might be forgiven on a just basis.

Reflection

April 3, A.D. 33, was the most important date in human history because on the cross the newly crowned King of kings suffered and died, paying the penalty for all the sins of his people. All who trust him as their Savior and King receive forgiveness of sin and eternal life. Have you trusted him?

The Roman officer and the other soldiers at the crucifixion were terrified by the earthquake and all that had happened. They said, "Truly, this was the Son of God!" MATTHEW 27:54

April 4

Two wrongs never make a right.

THE DAY after the Crucifixion, **April 4, A.D. 33,** was the Sabbath. Although Jesus[8] rested in death on the Sabbath, his enemies did not.

The chief priests and Pharisees went to see Pilate on that Sabbath day. They told him, "Sir, we remember what that deceiver once said while he was still alive: 'After three days I will be raised from the dead.' So we request that you seal the tomb until the third day. This will prevent his disciples from coming and stealing his body and then telling everyone he came back to life! If that happens, we'll be worse off than we were at first."

Pilate replied, "Take guards and secure it the best you can." Pilate answered cynically, remembering their fear of Jesus when he was alive and recognizing their fear even after his death.

So they sealed the tomb with official seals that if broken would attest that the tomb had been violated. Roman soldiers were then posted to guard it (Matthew 27:62-66).

Early the next morning there was an earthquake when an angel of the Lord came down from heaven and rolled aside the stone sealing the tomb.[9] As he sat on the stone, the face of the angel shone like lightning and his clothing was as white as snow. When the guards saw him, they were terrified and fell in a dead faint (28:1-4). How ironic that those assigned to guard a dead man themselves appeared dead and the One who was dead was made alive.

Once they were conscious again, some of the guards went immediately to the chief priests to report what had happened. The religious leaders met and decided to bribe the soldiers not to tell what had occurred. Once again the Jewish leaders were not concerned with the truth but with expediency and self-protection. They told the soldiers, "You must say, 'Jesus' disciples came during the night while we were sleeping, and they stole his body'" (28:12-13).

The story they made up shows how desperate they were. They proposed the very scenario against which they were trying to protect themselves. Yet their story was not plausible. If the guards were indeed asleep, they would not have seen the disciples. On the other hand, if one of them had awakened and seen the crime being committed, he would have awakened the other guards, and they would have arrested the body snatchers. The Jewish leaders must have offered the guards a very large bribe to say they were asleep because the penalty for falling asleep on watch was death. That is why they promised, "If the governor hears about it, we'll stand up for you and everything will be all right" (28:14).

The soldiers accepted the bribe and said what they were told to say. What a day it had been for those soldiers! They had seen an angel roll a stone away from the tomb. They had seen that the tomb was empty. And then instead of being sent to Pilate for punishment, they walked back to their barracks with their pockets full of money!

The deception was effective. More than one hundred years later Justin Martyr (c. 100–165) reported that the Jewish people were still saying that Jesus' disciples stole the body.

Reflection

Imagine the consternation of the Jewish religious leaders when the Roman soldiers reported that an angel had rolled the stone away and the tomb was empty. How do you think they rationalized the soldiers' report with the lie they bribed them to tell? Does this reveal anything about how humanity searches for truth?

∽୧❀

The Lord looks down from heaven on the entire human race; he looks to see if there is even one with real understanding, one who seeks for God. But no, all have turned away from God; all have become corrupt. No one does good, not even one!   PSALM 14:2-3

April 5

It's the story of an empty tomb.

EARLY ON Sunday morning, **April 5, A.D. 33,** Mary Magdalene and several other women went to Jesus' tomb.[10] To their great surprise they found that the stone covering the entrance had been rolled aside.[11] They entered the tomb, but there was no body, only the linen wrappings, with the cloth that had covered Jesus' head folded up and lying to the side. They could not fathom what had happened to Jesus' body.

Then suddenly two angels appeared to them, clothed in dazzling robes. The women were terrified and bowed down before them. The angels asked, "Why are you looking in a tomb for someone who is alive? He isn't here! He has risen from the dead! Don't you remember what he told you back in Galilee, that the Son of Man must be betrayed into the hands of sinful men and be crucified, and that he would rise again the third day?"

Then they remembered that he had said this. So they rushed back to tell his disciples what had happened, but their story sounded so preposterous the disciples didn't believe it. However, Peter and John ran to the tomb to see for themselves. They saw the empty linen graveclothes and went back, wondering what had happened (Matthew 28:1-10; Mark 16:1-8; Luke 24:1-12; John 20:1-18).

> That same day two of Jesus' followers were walking to the village of Emmaus, seven miles out of Jerusalem. . . . Suddenly, Jesus himself came along and joined them. But they didn't realize who he was because God kept them from recognizing him. [They told him how Jesus' body was missing from his tomb.]
>
> Then Jesus said to them, "You are such foolish people! You find it so hard to believe all that the prophets wrote in the Scriptures. Wasn't it clearly predicted by the prophets that the Messiah would have to suffer all these things before entering his time of glory?" Then Jesus quoted passages from Moses and all the prophets, explaining what all the Scriptures said about himself. Then suddenly . . . their eyes were opened, and they recognized Jesus. And at that moment he disappeared! . . .
>
> Within the hour they were on their way back to Jerusalem, where the eleven disciples and the other followers of Jesus were gathered.

When they arrived, they were greeted with the report, "The Lord has really risen! He appeared to Peter!" Then the two from Emmaus told their story. . . .

As they spoke, Jesus was suddenly standing there among them. He said, "Peace be with you." But the whole group was terribly frightened, thinking they were seeing a ghost! "Why are you frightened?" he asked. "Why do you doubt who I am? Look at my hands. Look at my feet. You can see that it's really me. Touch me and make sure that I am not a ghost, because ghosts don't have bodies, as you see that I do!" As he spoke, he held out his hands for them to see, and he showed them his feet. . . .

Then he said, "When I was with you before, I told you that everything written about me by Moses and the prophets and in the Psalms must all come true." Then he opened their minds to understand these many Scriptures. And he said, "Yes, it was written long ago that the Messiah must suffer and die and rise again from the dead on the third day. With my authority, take this message of repentance to all the nations, beginning in Jerusalem: 'There is forgiveness of sins for all who turn to me.' You are witnesses of all these things." (Luke 24:13-48)

Reflection

Do you believe that Jesus rose from the dead? If you don't, how do you explain the growth of Christianity stemming from the disciples' claim they had seen the risen Christ and their willingness to die for their convictions?

He was raised from the dead on the third day. . . . He was seen by Peter and then by the twelve apostles. After that, he was seen by more than five hundred of his followers at one time, most of whom are still alive.   1 CORINTHIANS 15:4-6

April 6

It's amazing what can result from unsubstantiated claims.

In 1820 a fourteen-year-old boy named Joseph Smith Jr. claimed to have received a vision in which God the Father and God the Son appeared to him and told him that they had chosen him to help restore true Christianity. Apparently not overly moved by this revelation, he went back to digging for Captain Kidd's treasure with his father and brother.

When he was seventeen, he claimed to have been visited by an angel named Moroni, who told him that he would receive the "golden plates" of *The Book of Mormon* to translate. In 1827 Smith alleged that he unearthed the plates in Cumorah, a hill near Palmyra, New York. Smith said he translated the "reformed Egyptian hieroglyphics" with the help of miraculous glasses he supposedly received from Moroni. Oliver Cowdery, a schoolteacher and a convert of Smith's, assisted in his translation, although no one but Smith ever saw the golden tablets. In 1829 during the translation, the "Prophet," as Smith liked to be called, alleged that John the Baptist was sent by Peter, James, and John to bestow the "Aaronic priesthood" on himself and Oliver. Early in 1830 they completed their translation, and *The Book of Mormon* was published and copyrighted.

On **April 6, 1830,** Joseph Smith Jr., his two brothers, Hyrum and Samuel, Oliver Cowdery, and David and Peter Whitmer Jr. met in Fayette, New York, to found a new religious society they called "The Church of Christ." Eventually known as the Church of Jesus Christ of Latter-day Saints, the Mormon Church was begun.

Soon after, the Mormons moved to Kirtland, Ohio, where they attracted many new followers. In six years they grew to more than sixteen thousand members. Because of Smith's reputation as a charlatan and accusations that his religion was a hoax, the new church had to move several times. Next they moved to Jackson County, Missouri, and then on to Nauvoo, Illinois, but their problems followed them to each new location. The trouble intensified in Nauvoo when their practice of polygamy became public. The exact number of Smith's wives is not known, but it has been estimated to be as high as fifty. When Smith called for the destruction of a newspaper that was outspokenly anti-Mormon, the state of Illinois stepped in to control the dispute and jailed Joseph Smith and his brother Hyrum. On June 27, 1844, an angry mob stormed the jail and murdered both men.

LATTER-DAY SAINTS?

After the death of Joseph Smith, Brigham Young became the leader of the Mormons.[12] Young led the group across the Great Plains and over the Rocky Mountains to the Salt Lake Valley in 1846. Finally, the Mormons were granted recognition as a legitimate religion. Brigham Young had twenty-seven wives and fifty-six children.

Today the Mormons claim more than 11 million members, more than half who live outside the United States.

What do they believe? Simply stated, Mormons teach that all gods were originally men and that all men have the potential to become gods. Being a king and priest to God is a step toward becoming a god. They believe that all persons were preexistent and, depending on their good works, go to one of three levels of heaven: telestial (for unbelievers), terrestial (for ignorant but good people), and celestial (for good Mormons). Jesus, who is the Jehovah of the Old Testament, will reign over a millennial kingdom from Independence, Missouri.

Reflection

How do you evaluate the beliefs of the Mormons? Do you believe that they are latter-day saints, as their name claims? How would you defend your answer to a Mormon?

∽⊘〜

Let God's curse fall on anyone, including myself, who preaches any other message than the one we told you about. Even if an angel comes from heaven and preaches any other message, let him be forever cursed.   GALATIANS 1:8

April 7

How can one enter God's Kingdom?

ON APRIL 7, A.D. 30, Jesus[13] was in Jerusalem for the Feast of the Passover, the first since he had begun his public ministry.[14] Since he had been performing miracles, many people believed he was indeed the Messiah. But Jesus didn't trust them because he knew that they were just following him because of the miracles (John 2:23-24).

Then one dark evening while Jesus was still in Jerusalem, a sincere seeker came to him. His name was Nicodemus, a leader of the Pharisees, the legalist followers of the law of Moses, and a member of the Sanhedrin, Judaism's ruling body.

"Teacher," he said, "we all know that God has sent you to teach us. Your miraculous signs are proof enough that God is with you."

Jesus replied, "I assure you, unless you are born again, you can never see the kingdom of God."

"What do you mean?" exclaimed Nicodemus. "How can an old man go back into his mother's womb and be born again?"

Jesus replied, "The truth is, no one can enter the Kingdom of God without being born of water and the Spirit. Humans can reproduce only human life, but the Holy Spirit gives new life from heaven. So don't be surprised at my statement that you must be born again. . . . "

"What do you mean?" Nicodemus asked.

Jesus replied, "You are a respected Jewish teacher, and yet you don't understand these things? . . . If you don't even believe me when I tell you about things that happen here on earth, how can you possibly believe if I tell you what is going on in heaven? For only I, the Son of Man, have come to earth and will return to heaven again. And as Moses lifted up the bronze snake on a pole in the wilderness, so I, the Son of Man, must be lifted up on a pole, so that everyone who believes in me will have eternal life.

"For God so loved the world, that he gave his only Son, so that everyone who believes in him will not perish but have eternal life. God did not send his Son into the world to condemn it, but to save it.

"There is no judgment awaiting those who trust him. But those who do not trust him have already been judged for not believing in the only Son of God. Their judgment is based on this fact: The light from heaven came into the world but they loved the darkness more than the light, for their actions were evil. They hate the light because they want to sin in the darkness. They stay away from the light for fear their sins will be exposed and they will be punished. But those who do what is right come to the light gladly, so everyone can see that they are doing what God wants." (John 3:1-21)

Nicodemus next appears in Scripture defending Jesus before the Pharisees. They asked, "Is there a single one of us rulers or Pharisees who believes in him?"

Nicodemus spoke up on his behalf. "Is it legal to convict a man before he is given a hearing?" he asked.

The Pharisees, suspecting something in his question, replied, "Are you from Galilee, too?" (John 7:47-52).

Nicodemus is last seen following the Crucifixion, bringing seventy-five pounds of embalming ointment to Jesus' tomb and then helping Joseph of Arimathea, another secret believer, prepare Jesus' body for burial (John 19:38-42).

Reflection

What does being born again mean to you? God gives eternal life to those who truly believe in Jesus, and the beginning of eternal life is what Jesus terms being born again. It is being born into God's family and becoming his child forever. Have you been born again? How do you know?

To all who believed him and accepted him, he gave the right to become children of God. They are reborn! This is not a physical birth resulting from human passion or plan—this rebirth comes from God.

JOHN 1:12-13

April 8

They had little in common with one another.

DWIGHT L. MOODY, the famous evangelist,[15] had two very different sons.

William Moody and his younger brother, Paul, were both dearly loved by their father, yet they had little in common with one another. William, ten years older than Paul, grew up to be serious and formal with conservative theological beliefs. Paul, a theological liberal, had a very easygoing nature and a reputation as a practical joker.

In addition to the large campaigns for which he is so well known, in his later years D. L. Moody shifted his focus to Christian education as a tool to bring the gospel to the masses. In 1879 Moody started Northfield Seminary for girls and in 1881 Mount Hermon School for boys in his birthplace of Northfield, Massachusetts, where he had resettled a few years earlier. His home was on the campus of the girls seminary. They became known as "The Northfield Schools," which remains their formal title today. He loved these schools dearly and threw himself into planning, building, developing, and managing them. Then in 1887 Moody launched the Bible-Work Institute of the Chicago Evangelization Society, renamed Moody Bible Institute shortly after his death.

Both William and Paul graduated from Yale. Moody intended that his sons would jointly manage the Northfield Schools after his death, with Will in charge of Mount Hermon School, and Paul, Northfield Seminary. However, soon after their father's death, the brothers became estranged, their differing theologies causing them continual conflict.

Believing that Paul would change the school's theology if he could, Will decided to force Paul out of leadership by consolidating the two schools. On **April 8, 1912,** a bill proposing the merger was presented to the Committee on Mercantile Affairs of the commonwealth of Massachusetts and was passed. Paul was in Chicago at the time and did not have a chance to voice his opinion.

Will ended up serving in a general leadership capacity over both the Northfield Schools and the Moody Bible Institute. He also published the first official biography of his father's life.

Paul achieved a distinguished career for himself outside of the Moody enterprises, becoming an influential voice in the liberal wing of American Protestantism. He graduated from Hartford Theological Seminary and became pastor of a church in Vermont. During World War I he served as senior chaplain of the American Expeditionary Forces. After the war he served as president of

Middlebury College for twenty-one years. Like his brother, Paul published a biography of his father's life.

Whereas the Northfield Schools evolved into typical New England private academies, Moody Bible Institute became America's premier Bible institute. By the late 1920s it had one thousand students in its day and evening programs. In 2000 it had fourteen hundred day students and eighteen thousand in its extension and correspondence programs. Moody Bible Institute has trained more foreign missionaries than any school in the world.

Reflection

Do you believe that Will Moody did the right thing by forcing his brother out of the leadership of their father's schools? What would you have done in that situation?

∾

They will act as if they are religious, but they will reject the power that could make them godly. You must stay away from people like that.   2 TIMOTHY 3:5

April 9

His accomplishments were great, but his time was short.

BORN IN 1887, William Whiting Borden grew up in a wealthy Chicago family that was heir to the Borden Dairy fortune. Bill was a precocious and mature boy for his age. When he was six, his mother had Bill and a number of his cousins write down what they wanted to be when they grew up and then sealed their responses in envelopes. Ten years later they were opened, and Bill's read, "I want to be an honest man when I grow up, a true and loving and kind and faithful man."

When Bill was about seven, his mother had a conversion experience that dramatically changed her life and deeply affected him. She became a joyful committed Christian. After the family transferred to Moody Memorial Church in Chicago, Bill flourished under the ministry of pastor Reuben A. Torrey. In a service when Bill was quite young, Dr. Torrey asked all who wished to dedicate their lives to Christian service to rise for prayer. Bill, in a little blue sailor suit, stood resolutely and never wavered from that point forward in his dedication to the service of Christ.

Bill became focused on world missions when he was seventeen and on a journey around the world following his high school graduation. Spending the year traveling through parts of the Orient, Europe, and the Middle East, he saw firsthand the spiritual needs of the people in these countries. His heart especially went out to the Chinese, and he returned home determined to bring the news of his Savior to the people of China.

After his trip he entered Yale University. While there he became involved in the Student Volunteer Movement. At one of its conventions, he sat under the teaching of Dr. Samuel Zwemer, who was fervent about reaching Muslims for Christ. Bill learned that there were fifteen million Muslims in northwest China, yet not a single missionary had been sent to reach them. He was astounded that there were more Muslims in China than in Egypt, Persia, or even Arabia, and yet no one was sharing the gospel with them. That night Borden dedicated his life to reaching Chinese Muslims. He never wavered from his passionate pursuit of this goal.

After graduating from Yale, he went to Princeton Seminary. He was extremely busy with his rigorous studies, volunteer ministries, and management of his family's financial interests. In addition, he had many responsibilities outside of Princeton. He had recently been made a trustee of Moody Bible Institute in Chicago, a member of the North American Council of the China Inland Mission (CIM), a delegate to the Edinburgh Missionary Conference for the CIM, a director of the National Bible Institute of New York City, and a member of the American Committee of the Nile Mission Press. He truly was a young man spiritually mature beyond his years!

Borden joined the China Inland Mission[16] and set sail for Cairo to study Arabic before going to China. He had his heart set on evangelizing the Kansu people of China. Upon his arrival in Cairo in 1913, he immediately threw himself into his studies and community service. He was quickly beloved by many.

Unfortunately, he soon contracted cerebral meningitis and became seriously ill. Suffering greatly for a few weeks, he died on **April 9, 1913,** at the age of just twenty-five. He never made it to China. He left his fortune of almost one million dollars to various home and foreign missions agencies. After his death, friends found a paper under his pillow scrawled with the words "No Reserve! No Retreat! No Regrets!"

Young Bill Borden's death was covered by many newspapers throughout the world as a testimony to Christ. Memorial services were held for him in many parts of the world: Princeton, Yale, New York, Chicago, Cairo, Japan, Korea, India, and South Africa. Although Bill Borden's financial legacy was substantial, it was his spiritual legacy of total dedication and self-sacrifice that had a lasting effect on people around the world.

Reflection

According to the world's standards, many see Borden's life and untimely death as a tragic "waste." How do you see it?

∽≫

He enjoyed a close relationship with God throughout his life. Then suddenly . . . God took him. GENESIS 5:24

April 10

His release never came.

SHU-TSU NEE was born in 1903 in southern China. Shu-tsu's mother, Peace Lin, was unhappy in her arranged marriage and took it out on her children. She was obsessed with ambition and social connections, often at the expense of her family, and Shu-tsu resented her for it.

When Shu-tsu was seventeen, his mother attended an evangelistic meeting led by Dora Yu, a prominent woman who had abandoned a lucrative career as a physician to become a preacher. Peace Lin was filled with admiration for Dora Yu and found her words cutting through to her angry soul. Asking forgiveness for her self-serving pursuits, Peace Lin gave her life to Christ. Shu-tsu could not believe the change he saw in his mother. Although Shu-tsu had a general disdain for religion, he was curious enough to go hear Dora Yu for himself, for he knew that what he saw in his mother was more than empty religion. After hearing Dora Yu preach, he confessed his sins and accepted Jesus as his Savior and Lord.

As is customary when Chinese reach a turning point in their lives, he chose a new name for himself, Nee To-sheng, or Watchman Nee in English. His life was indeed forever changed. He vowed to "give Christ all of my life, my loyalty, and my love." He became a preacher, even though he had previously called it "the most despised and base of all occupations."

Watchman found a mentor in Margaret Barber, an Anglican missionary. She was strong willed, fearless, and intensely passionate for God's Word. His lifelong motto came from her example: "I want nothing for myself; I want everything for the Lord."

During the 1930s under Chiang Kai-shek's leadership, China experienced a transportation boom. With this new opportunity, Watchman and his coworkers envisioned evangelizing all of China. He relentlessly encouraged Shanghai Christians to share their faith. His words were hard to ignore: "Because you are not witnessing, many have not heard the gospel. They will be eternally separated from God. What a consequence of our apathy! . . . This is my challenge to you. Witness to at least one person a day. Witness to whomever you meet. . . . It is time for us to put feet to our faith."

In 1934 Watchman married his childhood sweetheart, Charity, also a committed Christian, and they loved each other deeply.

During the 1930s and 1940s, China was embroiled in war. The civil war between Chiang Kai-shek's Nationalist Party and Mao Tse-tung's Communist Party was temporarily suspended by the war with Japan. During the wars Watchman and Charity continued undaunted in their efforts to evangelize China. After the war the Communist Party drove out the Nationalists, expelled the foreign missionaries, and outlawed Christianity. Evangelism became very dangerous. On Black Saturday, April 27, 1951, thousands of Shanghai intellectuals were arrested by the Communists and subjected to "thought reform." Some of those taken were Watchman's coworkers. Watchman fearlessly continued his work and began preparing materials for underground churches to use after his inevitable imprisonment by the Communists.

On **April 10, 1952,** Watchman was arrested and charged as a lawless capitalist. The communist media informed the world of the "crimes of Watchman Nee," citing many hundreds of alleged crimes and vices. He received a fifteen-year sentence but was not released at the end of his term. His days were divided into three 8-hour segments: hard labor, "reeducation," and solitary confinement. During his first twenty years in prison, he was allowed no communication, so he knew nothing of what had happened to his wife. During his twentieth year in prison he became sick, and his captors allowed him limited communication. He found out that Charity had also been arrested and had died years earlier. On June 1, 1972, Watchman also died in prison after spending twenty years in chains for the gospel.

Reflection

Watchman Nee did not let the prospect of imprisonment curb his zeal for Christ. He worked fearlessly for the Lord in spite of the arrest he knew was coming. What can you learn from his life?

I have worked harder, been put in jail more often, been whipped times without number, and faced death again and again.

2 CORINTHIANS 11:23

April 11

He fought for another kind of victory.

ALTHOUGH a convinced abolitionist, D. L. Moody did not enlist in the Union Army during the Civil War, claiming, "There has never been a time in my life when I felt that I could take a gun and shoot down a fellow-being. In this respect I am a Quaker."

In his adopted city of Chicago, he helped to establish the city's YMCA as its first full-time employee. Yearning to teach the Bible, he went to the streets looking for children and street people to fill his Sunday school class at the North Wells Street Mission. By 1861 he was working full time in both Sunday school and the YMCA, supported by Cyrus McCormick and others.

When the Civil War broke out, Camp Douglas was established in Chicago. Seeing the need to hold services there, Moody helped form a YMCA Army and Navy Committee and led daily services at the camp. At Camp Douglas thousands of Confederate soldiers were interned, Union soldiers were constantly coming and going, and new recruits were gathered and instructed. Moody ministered to as many soldiers as he could. Among the new recruits were a large number of "Moody boys."

On Sunday and Monday, April 6–7, 1862, the second great battle of the Civil War and one of the bloodiest—the battle of Shiloh or Pittsburg Landing—was fought in southern Tennessee. The Confederates lost 10,700 soldiers, while Grant's army lost 13,000. Over 100,000 were wounded.

An emergency call went out for extra doctors, nurses, medical students, and volunteers. The news reached Chicago on Tuesday, and Moody quickly volunteered to be on the trainload of help dispatched from the city. Arriving at Pittsburg Landing on **April 11, 1862,** Moody recounted,

> We were taking a large number of wounded men down the Tennessee River. . . . A number of young men of the Christian Commission were with me, and I told them that we must not let a man die on the boat that night without telling him of Christ and Heaven.
>
> You know the cry of a wounded man is "Water! Water!" As we passed along from one to another giving them water, we tried to tell them of the water of life, of which if they would drink they would never die. I came to a man who had about as fine a face as I ever saw. I spoke to him, but he did not answer. . . .

I sat down beside him and gave him brandy and water every now and then. . . . I said to myself that I could not let him die without getting a message for [his] mother. Presently he opened his eyes, and I said: . . . "Yes, you are on your way home, . . . but the doctor says you won't reach your earthly home. I thought I'd like to ask you if you had any message for your mother."

His face lighted up with an unearthly glow as he said: "Oh, yes, tell my mother that I died trusting in Jesus!"

It was one of the sweetest messages I ever heard in my life!

D. L. Moody did deliver the message to the soldier's mother, and he made eight more trips to the front lines during the war.[17]

Reflection

D. L. Moody was a pacifist, but that did not deter him from ministering during the Civil War. What is your attitude toward war? Do you believe that there are just wars?

The authorities are established by God for that very purpose,
to punish those who do wrong.   ROMANS 13:4

April 12

They paid a terrible price.

AFTER THIRTY-SEVEN years as a missionary to Burma, Adoniram Judson could look back not only on good times but also on extremely difficult times. He had struggled against intense persecution, imprisonment, disease, and discouragement. Yet at the end of Judson's labors, he could look with satisfaction on a complete Burmese translation of the Scriptures; a Burmese-English dictionary; sixty-three churches among the Burmese and Karens; and best of all, seven thousand Burmese Christians.[18]

In November 1849 Judson was caring for his convalescing wife, Emily, as she recovered from a debilitating disease. After a cold night of caring for a sick child as well, Judson found himself ill. At first it seemed a mere cold, but dysentery and congestive fever followed. Though pregnant with their second child, Emily steadfastly ministered to him day and night as he lay in bed, wracked with unbearable pain.

After a time it became clear that he would not recover in the stifling Burmese climate. Together they decided his only chance to survive was an extended sea voyage out into the clean, ocean air, away from the pestilence of the jungle. As they talked about the possibility of his death, he remarked, "I am not tired of my work, neither am I tired of the world; yet when Christ calls me home, I shall go with the gladness of a boy bounding away from his school." On the ship he'd have friends and doctors with him, while upon land he'd have praying friends and family. By the time he left on April 3, 1850, Judson had difficulty walking and speaking. Emily kissed his silent yet grateful lips, and he was carried to the ship.

Emily prayed hard and long, but she knew in her heart that her husband's death was near. On April 22, their son Charlie was born but did not survive the day. Emily poured out her grief through a poem she entitled "Angel Charlie."

> *He came—a beauteous vision—*
> *Then vanished from my sight,*
> *His wing one moment cleaving*
> *The blackness of my night;*
> *My glad ear caught its rustle,*
> *Then sweeping by, he stole*
> *The dew-drop that his coming*
> *Had cherished in my soul.*

A WELCOME TO HEAVEN

Oh, he had been my solace
When grief my spirit swayed,
And on his fragile being
Had tender hopes been stayed;
Where thought, where feeling lingered
His form was sure to glide,
And in the lone night-watches
'Twas ever by my side.

He came; but as the blossom
Its petals closes up,
And hides them from the tempest
Within its sheltering cup,
So he his spirit gathered
Back to his frightened breast,
And passed from earth's grim threshold,
To be the Saviour's guest.

Emily didn't find out until several months later that Adoniram had died at sea on **April 12, 1850**, ten days before Charlie was born. He was in heaven to welcome his little son.

Reflection

Many Christians like Adoniram Judson have paid a profound price for serving Jesus. Yet because of him and missionaries like him, there are more than 2.3 million Christian believers in Burma (modern Myanmar) today. If God calls you to do so, are you willing to suffer for him?

∽❧∾

[God said,] "Saul is my chosen instrument to take my message to the Gentiles and to kings, as well as to the people of Israel. And I will show him how much he must suffer for me." Acts 9:15-16

April 13

The Christians of Chad rejoiced to have a Christian president.

THE AFRICAN nation of Chad had been a fruitful field for missionaries. Victor Veary and his wife went to Chad in 1926 under the Sudan United Mission. Their forty-two years of ministry resulted in 258 churches and 168 chapels, forty-two thousand evangelical Christians, and a typical Sunday church attendance of sixty-two thousand. Baptist Mid-Missions came to Chad at about the same time and had similar results.

Christians rejoiced when Chad gained independence in 1960. The first president, N'Garta Tombalbaye, was even a professing Christian! He testified that he had been converted through a Baptist missionary. Before entering politics he had taught at a Baptist elementary school. Yet some encouraged caution regarding him, remembering that he had once been excommunicated from his home church for "unchristian behavior."

Tombalbaye was a member of the Sara tribe, which constituted one-fourth of the country's population. The Sara and other southern tribes had a background of spirit worship. The northern tribes were Muslim, and for centuries there had been friction between north and south. The southern tribes never forgot that in the past, northern tribesmen had enslaved some of their people.

No sooner had independence been declared than rebel activity began in the north. In response President Tombalbaye assumed dictatorial powers. To pacify nationalists he began an "authenticity" campaign. The first step was to replace all Christian names with African names. Muslims, however, were allowed to keep their Islamic names. The capital of Chad, Fort Lamy, was renamed N'djamena, meaning "Leave Us Alone." Simultaneous with the political turmoil, a six-year drought led to starvation for thousands.

Next all citizens were ordered to submit to "Yondo," an ancient pagan initiation that included sacrifices to ancestral spirits, circumcision, and a pagan "rebirth." Secret ceremonies called for whippings, facial scarring, mock burials, and the use of drugs. Tombalbaye insisted that bizarre tests of willpower—such as crawling naked through a bed of termites—would also create authentic national unity.

This presidential decree was particularly enforced in Baptist towns. Apparently the president was trying to get back at the church that had disciplined him in his younger days.

Christians who refused to comply had their homes ransacked and their lives threatened. Some Christian children were taken by force to initiation camps. A pastor who refused to let his sons participate was killed.

A dozen Baptist missionaries and their families were arrested and deported. All Baptist churches and schools among the Sara tribe were closed. Still Tombalbaye insisted that he was a Christian, explaining that while the blood of Christ atoned for sin, the initiations completed the cleansing.

Tombalbaye next set up a state church called the Evangelical Church of Chad, headed by two pastors whom the Baptists had disciplined. Regional committees, each of which included a pastor, were set up and made responsible for enforcing the initiations. The committees also sponsored self-accusation meetings, in which punishments were meted out.

The persecution intensified, and many were buried alive with one leg sticking out of the ground. Others were buried with just their heads above ground, leaving them exposed to insects and the insufferable heat. Friends were told that the same would happen to them if they dug them out.

Finally on **April 13, 1975,** a group of dissident soldiers stormed the presidential palace and assassinated President Tombalbaye.

The persecution ended, and the expelled missionaries returned. Today, although the political situation continues to be tense, over one million evangelical believers live in Chad.

Reflection

For Christians in Chad, what were the spiritual implications of participating in the pagan initiations? Can you think of anything in our culture that would be analogous to those initiations?

∽೭ల∾

All who are victorious will inherit all these blessings, and I will be their God, and they will be my children. But cowards who turn away from me, and unbelievers, and the corrupt, and murderers, and the immoral, and those who practice witchcraft, and idol worshipers, and all liars—their doom is in the lake that burns with fire and sulfur.

REVELATION 21:7-8

April 14

He served a good master.

ANDREW DUNCAN was ordained into the Presbyterian ministry in Scotland in 1597, a difficult time to be a Presbyterian. In 1603 James I of England began a campaign to place Anglican bishops over the Church of Scotland, which was Presbyterian.[19] In 1605 Duncan and five other prominent Presbyterian ministers were arrested for defying the king by attending a general assembly of the Church of Scotland in Aberdeen. They were imprisoned for fourteen months and then banished to France. After about six years Duncan was allowed to return to his church in Scotland but soon fell into disfavor again, suffering multiple imprisonments and finally exile.

Once while living in lonely exile, Duncan and his family ran out of food. With his wife and children in tears, Duncan prayed and then told them that God would provide. After his family went to bed that night, a stranger came to the house and gave Duncan a sack of food for the family. He left without giving his name. Duncan brought the sack to his wife saying, "See what a good Master I serve."

Andrew Duncan and his family suffered great hardships for their faith, but Duncan remained steadfast. Nearing the end of his life, he wrote his last will and testament:

I, Andrew Duncan, . . . set down the declaration of my latter will, concerning these things, which God hath lent me in this world; in manner following,—First, as touching myself, body and soul; my soul I leave to Christ Jesus, who gave it, and when it was lost, redeemed it, that He may send His holy angels to transport it to the bosom of Abraham, there to enjoy all happiness and contentment; and as for this frail body, I commend it to the grave, there to sleep and rest, as in a sweet bed, until the day of refreshment, when it shall be reunited to the soul, and shall be set down at the table with the holy patriarchs, prophets, and apostles; yea, shall be placed on the throne with Christ, and get the crown of glory on my head. As for the children whom God hath given me, for which I thank His Majesty, I leave them to His providence, to be governed and cared for by Him, beseeching Him to be the tutor, curator, and agent, in all their adoes, yea, and a father; and that He would lead them by His gracious Spirit, through this evil world; that they be profitable instruments . . . holding their course to heaven, and comforting themselves with the glorious and fair-to-look-on heritage, which Christ hath conquered for them, and for all that love Him. Under God, I leave John Duncan, my eldest son, to be tutor to my youngest daughter, Bessie Duncan, his youngest sister, to take a care of her, and to see that all turns go right, touching her person and gear. My executors I leave my three sons, John, William, and David Duncan, to do my turns after me, and to put in practice my directions; requesting them to be good and comfortable to their sisters, but chiefly to the two that are at home, as they would have God's blessing and mine. As concerning my temporal goods, the baggage and blathrie of the earth, as I have gotten them in the world off God's liberal hand, so I leave them behind me in the world; giving most humble and hearty thanks unto my heavenly Father for so long and comfortable loan of the same."—**14th April, 1626**

Reflection

How do you regard your possessions? Do you see them as something you own, or do you see yourself as a steward of what God has entrusted to you?

∽❧∾

Don't worry about having enough food or drink or clothing. Why be like the pagans who are so deeply concerned about these things? Your heavenly Father already knows all your needs, and he will give you all you need from day to day if you live for him and make the Kingdom of God your primary concern.   MATTHEW 6:31-33

April 15

He nearly drowned three times.

JOHN HARPER was born in Scotland in 1872 to a Christian family. When he was presented with the message of John 3:16 at the age of thirteen, he believed in Jesus and received everlasting life. When he was eighteen, he had a powerful vision of the cross of Christ. At that moment he committed his life to bringing the message of the Cross to others. The very next day he began to preach in his village, urging all his hearers to be reconciled to God. He made every street corner his pulpit.

His desire to win souls to Christ was unmatched, becoming his all-consuming purpose. An evangelist friend, W. D. Dunn, recalled often seeing Harper lying on his face before God, pleading with him to "give me souls, or I die," sobbing as if his heart would break.

At thirty-two he had a near-drowning experience when he was caught on a leaky ship in the Mediterranean. He said of the experience, "The fear of death did not for one minute disturb me. I believed that sudden death would be sudden glory."

In 1911 he spent three months preaching at Moody Memorial Church in Chicago during a revival and received an enthusiastic response. He was asked to return for three more months of meetings beginning in April 1912. Originally scheduled to sail on the *Lusitania*, he sailed on the *Titanic* after a schedule change.

When he informed his church of his intent to return to Chicago, a parishioner begged him not to go, saying that he had been praying and felt strongly that something ominous would happen if he went. He pleaded with Harper but to no avail. Harper felt that there was a divine purpose for his trip, and Harper went ahead with his plans. The night before the ship sank, Harper was seen leading a man to Christ on the deck. Afterward, he looked to the west, and seeing a glint of red in the sunset he said, "It will be beautiful in the morning."

Moments later the *Titanic* struck an iceberg, and the sea poured in. Mayhem ensued as most people struggled to save their own lives. As they loaded the lifeboats, John Harper shouted, "Let the women, children, and the unsaved into the lifeboats." He then removed his life preserver and gave it to another man.

At 2:20 A.M. on **April 15, 1912,** the *Titanic* disappeared beneath the water. Harper and many others were left floundering in the icy waters.

A HERO OF THE TITANIC

One man, who was clinging to a piece of wood, saw Harper struggling in the water. Harper shouted, "Are you saved?" When the man answered no, Harper quoted Acts 16:31, "Believe on the Lord Jesus Christ and thou shalt be saved." The man did not respond, and they lost sight of each other. A few minutes later the current brought them together again. Harper asked the same question again, urging the man to believe in Jesus, and received the same answer again. Harper then slipped beneath the water, never to resurface. The man did put his faith in Jesus Christ and was later rescued by a lifeboat. He testified that he was John Harper's last convert.

After the sinking of the ship, relatives and friends of the passengers gathered outside the White Star office in Liverpool, England. As news came in about the passengers, names were placed on one of two lists, "Known to Be Saved" or "Known to Be Lost." The voyage had begun with three classes of passengers, but now it was reduced to only two—saved or lost. John Harper's name was placed on the list for those "Known to Be Lost," but it was on the "Saved" list in heaven.

Reflection

John Harper faced death heroically and without fear because he never lost sight of his passionate purpose in life—to win souls for Christ. Imagine those last horrifying moments aboard the *Titanic*. If you had been there, what do you think you would have done?

Perfect love expels all fear.   1 JOHN 4:18

April 16

He learned from his father.

JOHN GIBSON PATON was born in a Christian home near Dumfries, Scotland, in 1824. From an early age he had a special awareness of a closet in the three-room cottage, where he lived with his parents and ten brothers and sisters. He described it thus:

> The closet was . . . the Sanctuary of that cottage home. Thither daily, and oftentimes a day . . . we saw our father retire, and "shut the door"; and we children got to understand by a sort of spiritual instinct . . . that prayers were being poured out there for us. . . . We knew whence came that happy light as of a new-born smile that always was dawning on my father's face: it was a reflection from the Divine Presence, in the consciousness of which he lived. . . . My soul would wander back to those early scenes, and, hearing still the echoes of those cries to God, would hurl back all doubt with the victorious appeal, "He walked with God, why may not I?"

Before the age of twelve, Paton had begun learning his father's trade of making stockings, but he had already given his "soul to God, and was resolved to aim at being a Missionary of the Cross, or a Minister of the Gospel."

Paton applied for a position as a tract distributor, which included one year of training at the Free Church Normal Seminary in Glasgow. When it was time to leave for Glasgow, his father walked with him for the first six miles of his journey. Paton recalled:

> His counsels and tears and heavenly conversation on that parting journey are in my heart as if it had been but yesterday. . . . For the last half-mile or so we walked on together in almost unbroken silence. . . . His lips kept moving in silent prayers for me . . . on reaching the appointed parting-place, he grasped my hand firmly for a minute in silence, and then solemnly and affectionately, said: "God bless you, my son! Your father's God prosper you, and keep you from all evil!"
>   Unable to say more, his lips kept moving in silent prayers; in tears we embraced, and parted. . . . I was soon out of sight. But my heart was too full, so I darted into the side of the road and wept for a time.

Then, rising up cautiously, I climbed the dyke to see if he yet stood where I had left him; and just at that moment I caught a glimpse of him climbing the dyke and looking out for me! He did not see me, and after he had gazed eagerly in my direction, he got down [and] set his gaze toward home. . . . I watched through blinding tears, till his form faded from my gaze; and then, hastening on my way, vowed deeply and oft, by the help of God, to live and act so as never to grieve or dishonour such a father and mother as he had given me.

After ten years of city mission work and theological studies, on **April 16, 1858,** Paton and his wife left Glasgow to do mission work in the New Hebrides (present-day Vanuatu), where he became the pioneer missionary to the island of Tanna. Within the year his wife died in childbirth, and his newborn son was quick to follow. Paton left the island in 1862 to raise funds and more recruits, returning in 1866 to the island of Aniwa. There during his next fifteen years of ministry most of the island's inhabitants put their faith in Jesus.

The heritage Paton received from his father lived on, as three generations of his family served in Vanuatu until 1970.

Reflection

In what ways did John Paton's father influence his life? If you are a parent, how are you influencing your children's lives? If you are not a parent, what can you do to influence the children and youth around you?

Don't make your children angry by the way you treat them. Rather, bring them up with the discipline and instruction approved by the Lord. EPHESIANS 6:4

April 17

It wasn't some kind of crazy fad diet.

DURING the early 1500s Europe was in a great state of flux. A revived interest in pre-Christian Greek and Roman culture launched the Renaissance, which celebrated humanism and somewhat undermined contemporary Christian culture. Another threat to contemporary Christian culture came from within the church in the form of the outspoken Martin Luther, a professor at the University of Wittenberg in Germany. He was becoming known for his bold criticism of the Roman Catholic Church and his forthright convictions regarding justification by faith, papal authority, and the sacraments. The Reformation had begun when Luther nailed his Ninety-five Theses to the door of the Wittenberg Cathedral in 1517. The Theses consisted of ninety-five distinct propositions arguing against the supreme power of the pope, the greed within the church, and the abuse of indulgences. As a result, the Roman Catholic Church excommunicated Luther in January 1521. This move served to fuel public support for Luther rather than to diminish it.

Because of Luther's great popularity, Charles V, emperor of the Holy Roman Empire, agreed to hear his arguments at a diet, a meeting of the empire parliament, which was scheduled for the spring of 1521 in Worms, Germany. Church representatives wanted Luther arrested and condemned to death as a heretic without a trial. However, Luther was promised that he would be protected and given a lawful trial at the diet.

At 4:00 P.M. on **April 17, 1521,** Luther arrived triumphantly in Worms. It was a dramatic contrast: Luther, a simple monk, standing before the powerful sovereign of the Holy Roman Empire. When he was immediately confronted with a pile of his books and asked whether he acknowledged their authorship, he quietly responded, "The books are all mine." They pressed him further, asking whether he would stand by them or recant anything in them. Luther was shocked because he had been promised a hearing of his beliefs, not a demand for recantation. Luther replied, "This touches God and his Word. This affects the salvation of souls. Of this Christ said, 'He who denies me before men, him will I deny before my Father.' To say too little or too much would be dangerous. I beg you, give me time to think it over." After some deliberation, even though they felt he didn't deserve it, Luther was granted a one-day delay.

Martin Luther spent the evening in prayer, carefully preparing his response. At 6:00 P.M. the following day he gave his famous answer: "Unless I am convinced by the testimony of Scripture or by clear reason (for I trust neither pope nor council alone, since it is well known that they have often erred and contradicted themselves), I am bound by the Scriptures I have cited, for my conscience is captive to the Word of God. I cannot and will not recant anything since to act against one's conscience is neither safe nor right. I cannot do otherwise. Here I stand, may God help me. Amen."

These famous words reverberated throughout the Reformation, inspiring many others to take their stand as well.[20]

Reflection

God called upon Martin Luther to take a stand before the emperor of the Holy Roman Empire. Where might God call upon you to stand up for your convictions? What can you do to prepare yourself for those eventualities?

I assure you of this: If anyone acknowledges me publicly here on earth, I, the Son of Man, will openly acknowledge that person in the presence of God's angels. But if anyone denies me here on earth, I will deny that person before God's angels. LUKE 12:8-9

April 18

And "the scales fell off. . . ."

GEORGE WHITEFIELD, the great preacher and evangelist of the 1700s, kept a daily journal throughout much of his life.[21] In it he chronicled how God was dealing with him personally, as well as writing about the fruits of his ministry.

On **April 18, 1739,** when he was twenty-four years old, he wrote about a recently converted Cambridge man:

> Several persons came to see me, amongst whom was Mr. Benjamin Seward, whom God has been pleased to call by His free grace very lately. His circumstances both before and in conversion, much resemble those of St. Paul. For he was bred up at the feet of Gamaliel, being at Cambridge for some years. As touching the law, so far as outward morality went, he was blameless; concerning zeal, opposing the Church. My proceedings he could by no means approve, and he had once a mind, he said, to write against Mr. Law's enthusiastic notions in his Christian Perfection.
>
> But lately, it has pleased God to reveal His dear Son in him, and to cast him down to the earth, as he did Saul, by eight days' sickness, in which time he scarce ever ate, or drank, or slept, and underwent great inward agonies and tortures. After this, the scales fell more and more from the eyes of his mind. God sent a poor traveling woman, that came to sell straw toys, to instruct him in the nature of the second birth, and now he is resolved to prepare for Holy Orders, and to preach Christ and those truths straightway in every synagogue, which once he endeavoured to destroy. He is a gentleman of a very large fortune, which he has now devoted to God.
>
> I write this to shew how far a man may go, and yet know nothing of Jesus Christ. Behold, here was one who constantly attended on the means of grace, was exact in his morals, humane and courteous in his conversation, who gave much in alms, was frequent in private duties; and yet, till about six weeks ago, as destitute of any saving experimental knowledge of Jesus Christ as those on whom His Name was never called, and who still sit in darkness and the shadow of death. Blessed be God, that although not many rich, not many mighty, not many noble are called, yet some are.

THE COMPLETE CAMBRIDGE MAN

Who would but be accounted a fool for Christ's sake? How often has my companion and honoured friend, Mr. William Seward, been deemed a madman even by this very brother, for going to Georgia; but now God has made him an instrument of converting his brother. This more and more convinces me, that we must be despised, before we can be vessels fit for God's use. As for my own part, I find by happy experience, the more I am condemned, the more God delights to honour me in bringing home souls to Christ. And I write this for the encouragement of my fellow labourers, who have all manner of evil spoken against them falsely for Christ's sake. Let them not be afraid, but rejoice and be exceeding glad, for the Spirit of God and of glory shall rest upon their souls.

Reflection

Benjamin Seward had all the world has to offer—wealth, education, and social status. Yet he discovered that the only way to discover real satisfaction was through faith in Jesus Christ. Take a moment to consider your own life. What brings you satisfaction? You can experience the same satisfaction Benjamin Seward found by trusting the same Savior he did.

∽≫

We believe that we are all saved the same way, by the special favor of the Lord Jesus. ACTS 15:11

April 19

In 1775 the American colonies were in uproar.

THE BRITISH were taxing the colonists without representation; King George III, a devout evangelical Christian, had recently declared himself and parliament sovereign over the colonies in "all cases whatsoever"; and British troops had just arrived in Boston to enforce royal supremacy. During this turbulent time the colonists, more than ever, turned to their ministers for guidance, thereby giving them a unique role in history. They not only were preaching the gospel but also helping to create a nation. Their roles were both prophets and statesmen.

In Concord, Massachusetts, William Emerson (grandfather of Ralph Waldo Emerson) was one such prophet and statesman. As a minister he tried to analyze the rapidly changing events in the light of Scripture. In the spring of 1775 he was quickly propelled from being an ordinary country preacher into taking part in what he called "the greatest events taking place in the present age."

By March, Emerson and other patriots in Concord were aware that British spies had infiltrated their town and had informed General Thomas Gage about a hidden armory, where the local "Sons of Liberty" were stockpiling weapons. Emerson began to fear for the safety of his town. On March 13 he preached a sermon to the Concord militia that would alter the course of history.

He had the power to either promote or discourage a call to arms. What should he say? Was it God's will for America to fight for independence? After much prayer and study, he came down on the side of armed resistance.

He reminded the militia of the inevitable "approaching storm of war and bloodshed." He asked them if they were ready for "real service." He explained that readiness depended not only on military skill and weapons but also on moral and spiritual resolve. He challenged them to believe wholeheartedly in what they were fighting for and to trust in God's power to uphold them, or else they would end up running in fear from the British.

He argued for colonial resistance on the grounds that they had been standing by their liberties and trusting only in God yet had been "cruelly charged with rebellion and sedition" by the Crown. "For my own part, the more I reflect upon the movements of the British nation . . . the more satisfied I am that our military preparation here for our own defense is . . . justified in the eyes of the impartial world. Nay, for should we neglect to defend ourselves by military preparation, we never could answer it to God and to our own consciences of the rising [generations]." The colonists should go forth into war, assured that "the Lord will cover your head in the day of battle and carry you on from victory to victory." Emerson was convinced that in the end the whole world would realize "that there is a God in America."

On **April 19, 1775,** British troops marched as predicted on Lexington and Concord. Before they reached Concord, patriot silversmith Paul Revere had made his famous ride into town, warning of the approaching redcoats. Because the colonists were warned, Emerson and other minutemen from nearby towns were assembled and ready. The first shot, the famed "shot heard 'round the world," was fired, and the war for independence began. Three Americans and twelve British soldiers were casualties in that first battle.

Throughout the war for independence, ministers such as Emerson were the single most influential voice of inspiration and encouragement for the fighting colonists. For many ministers, the religious aspect of the war was exactly the point of revolution—gaining freedom in order to create a new order in which God's principles would rule.[22]

Reflection

Do you believe there was a biblical basis for waging a war of independence against England? Was "taxation without representation" a sufficient reason for a just war? Should the disciples have started a war against Rome in the first century because they had "taxation without representation"?

You must obey the government for two reasons: to keep from being punished and to keep a clear conscience. Pay your taxes, too, for these same reasons.   ROMANS 13:5-6

April 20

God gave us a glimpse of the future.

RACHEL SCOTT was just eight when her father, Pastor Darrell Scott, walked out on her mother, Beth, leaving her with five children. A year later Rachel's grandparents helped her mom move to Littleton, Colorado, and buy a home.

When Rachel was twelve, she had a life-changing spiritual encounter. She later wrote in her journal, "Everyone was there at the altar, and I felt so drawn to it. You have to understand that I was so young . . . to be drawn that way, it was nothing short of God. . . . That night I accepted Jesus into my heart. I was saved." From that time on her family saw a spiritual depth beginning to develop in Rachel.

Two years later Rachel's mother remarried. During this difficult adjustment Rachel became increasingly withdrawn and private. When she was sixteen, her mother gave her a journal, the first of many. Rachel began to chronicle her spiritual journey and commitment to Christ—a commitment that cost her deeply. She broke up with the boy she loved in order to keep herself chaste and later was rejected by five of her closest friends for talking openly about her faith. On **April 20, 1998,** one year to the day before she died, she wrote these words: "I have no more personal friends at school. But you know what . . . it's all worth it to me. . . . If I have to sacrifice everything I will." Rachel had no idea of the sacrifice she would ultimately make.

On **April 20, 1999,** Rachel sat outside the cafeteria when two troubled students armed with guns came up the stairs at Columbine High School. They opened fire, hitting her three times. After leaving to find more victims, they returned to where Rachel lay crying in pain. One of them lifted her head by her ponytail and jeered, "Do you believe in God?" She answered, "Yes." He put the gun to her temple and killed her.

About a month after Rachel's funeral, her father received a phone call from a stranger who told him about a dream he had. As Darrell recalled it, "He dreamed about her eyes and a flow of tears that were watering something that he couldn't quite see in the dream. He was adamant about the eyes and tears and wanted to know if that meant anything to me. . . . He told me that the dream had haunted him for days, and he knew there was a reason for it."

Her father had no idea what the dream could mean. Several days later he picked up Rachel's backpack from the sheriff's office. Inside were two journals, one with a bullet hole through it. He turned to the last page of her most recent diary and was dumbfounded to see a drawing of her eyes with a stream of thirteen tears watering a rose. The tears appeared to turn into drops of blood as they touched the rose. The number of tears matched the number of victims at Columbine. It practically took his breath away to see in Rachel's final diary exactly what the stranger had described to him a week earlier.

Looking in previous diaries, her parents discovered that same rose drawn a year before Rachel's death. The earlier drawing simply showed the rose with the bloodlike drops, not her eyes or the clear tears, and it showed the rose growing up out of a columbine plant, the state flower from which Columbine High School got its name.

Rachel's diaries reveal the heart of a young woman who loved her Lord. When the time came to put her faith on the line, she was prepared to pay the ultimate sacrifice.

Reflection

Are you willing to put your faith on the line and speak boldly of your Savior? If we follow Rachel's example of committing ourselves completely to Christ, we too will be willing to sacrifice all if called upon to do so.

~~

If you try to keep your life for yourself, you will lose it. But if you give up your life for me, you will find true life. LUKE 9:24

April 21

It is a city with a past.

THE ROMAN annalist Titus Livius set the traditional date for the founding of Rome as **April 21, 753 B.C.** The oldest settlement was seventeen miles up from the mouth of the Tiber River on a cluster of seven hills.

Initially Rome was ruled by Latin kings, but in about 600 B.C. Etruscans from modern-day Tuscany along the northwestern coast of Italy took control.

About 509 B.C. the Romans revolted against the Etruscans and established the Roman republic. The republic's chief officers were two consuls, elected annually and assisted by other elected administrative officials. The defining moment for the republic came in 387 B.C. when the Gauls ransacked Rome. Determined to be vulnerable no longer to outside attack, the Romans took up the sword and, by so doing, united all of Italy south of the Po River into a confederation. Rome became so strong that the city stood inviolate for eight centuries.

The republic ended in 27 B.C. when Caesar Augustus became emperor and the Roman Empire began.[23] At this time the population of Rome was well over one million.

The first two hundred years of the Roman Empire are called the *Pax Romana*, the Roman Peace, reflecting the empire's internal and external peace. During this time of peace, Christians first appeared in Rome. Initially they were not differentiated from the Jews, as we know Christians Aquila and Priscilla had to leave Rome when Emperor Claudius forced the Jews out of the city.[24]

In A.D. 57 when the apostle Paul wrote his epistle to the Romans, there was a church there. Paul was imprisoned in Rome from 59 until 62 and then a second time in 67 or 68. He was finally martyred there as was the apostle Peter.

Six different caesars of the first two centuries persecuted Christians. Then from the third century until Constantine in 313, there were five periods of persecution.[25] During this period the *Pax Romana* disappeared. There were twenty-eight claimants to the imperial throne in the Roman Empire between Commodus (180–192) and Diocletian (284–305). Only one died a natural death, and only one reigned for more than ten years.

It was during these turbulent times that the Christians of Rome retreated to the catacombs, the subterranean cemeteries outside Rome's city walls. In these underground labyrinths Christians not only buried their dead but also worshiped during times of persecution.

In 313 Constantine issued the Edict of Milan, giving Christians freedom of worship.[26] At this time there were approximately forty churches in Rome. But Constantine also moved the capital of the empire to Constantinople (Istanbul), leaving Rome as the capital of only the Western empire. Rome weakened, and in 410 the Visigoths, a Germanic tribe, sacked the city. In 476 the Western Roman Empire fell to another Germanic tribe, the Ostrogoths. As the city of Rome weakened politically, the church grew in power and came to dominate Rome.

In 847 Pope Leo IV built a wall of defense around St. Peter's Basilica, and it became the center of a Christian Rome. At this same time the title "Pope" from the Latin *papa*, meaning "father," came to be reserved for the bishop of Rome. Previously it had applied to all bishops. Except for a period between 1305 and 1377 when the popes were captives of the French kings and ruled from Avignon, France, the Vatican in Rome has been the pope's residence and the Roman Catholic Church headquarters.

Reflection

The New Testament book of Revelation contains references to the city of Rome. A woman called "Babylon the Great, Mother of all Prostitutes and Obscenities in the World," symbolizing false religion, is pictured as sitting on "the seven hills of the city where this woman rules" (Revelation 17:5, 9). The woman herself "represents the great city that rules over the kings of the earth" (Revelation 17:18). In A.D. 95 when the book of Revelation was written, this description obviously applied to Rome. What do you think is the significance of these references to Rome?

I will show you the judgment that is going to come on the great prostitute.
REVELATION 17:1

April 22

He went where he didn't want to go.

In 1536 John Calvin no longer felt safe in his native France,[27] so he left for Strasbourg, a free city situated between France and Germany that had declared itself Protestant. On his way there he stopped for the night in Geneva, Switzerland. Just two months earlier Geneva had given its allegiance to Protestantism as a result of the labors of William Farel, who had been ministering there for three years. That evening Farel met Calvin and immediately asked him to join in leading the church in Geneva. Calvin declined, saying he wanted to go to Strasbourg to study and write. Farel thundered at him that unless Calvin joined him in Geneva, God would bring down curses upon him. Somewhat intimidated by Farel's pronouncement, twenty-eight-year-old Calvin agreed to stay, even though his preference was to go on to Strasbourg.

Calvin's initial stay in Geneva, however, was short. In January 1537 Geneva's Council of Two Hundred zealously enacted a series of ordinances prohibiting immoral behavior, gambling, foolish songs, and desecration of Sunday with no thought as to how they would be enforced. In July the council ordered all citizens to assent to a confession of faith. In November the council ordered banishment for anyone who refused to swear to the confession. This was more than the man on the street could stomach, and in the city council election three days later, a majority of anticlerical councilmen were elected.

The new city council and Calvin and Farel locked horns when the council ordered the two pastors to administer the Lord's Supper to everyone, regardless of their spiritual condition. On Easter while preaching in separate churches, both Calvin and Farel announced that they would not give the Lord's Supper to such a rebellious city. Many in the audiences drew their swords, and without the aid of friends, neither pastor would have made it safely home.

The Council of Two Hundred met the following day, **April 22, 1538,** to decide their fate. The meeting stretched into a second day, at which time the order was given to Calvin and Farel to leave Geneva within three days. Farel went to Neuchâtel, and Calvin returned to his original plan and went to Strasbourg.

In Strasbourg Calvin became pastor of the Church of the Strangers, a French refugee church. There he met and married Idelette deBure, the widow of an Anabaptist. Calvin was content in Strasbourg and probably would have spent the rest of his life there had it not been for the Roman Catholic cardinal's efforts to bring Geneva back into the fold of the Catholic Church. In 1539 the cardinal wrote to the Genevans, inviting them to return to the pope. No one in Geneva felt qualified to answer the letter, so it was sent to Calvin to respond, which he did very effectively.

Meanwhile Geneva was not doing well in his absence. A new election had placed the city government back into the hands of friends who feared that the only way to save the city from anarchy was to bring Calvin back. As a result, in October 1540 the Council of Two Hundred voted to invite him back to Geneva.

Once again Calvin's personal desire was not to go to Geneva. He wrote to a friend, "There is no place in the world which I fear more; not because I hate it; but because I feel unequal to the difficulties which await me there." And once again it was through the counsel and persuasion of Farel, who himself was not invited back, that Calvin was convinced to return.

He returned to Geneva in September 1541 and ministered there the rest of his life, making Geneva the center for the Reformed faith.[28]

Reflection

John Calvin spent most of his life in a place where he would rather not have been. Yet he was convinced that God wanted him in Geneva, so that is where he ministered. Do you put geographical limitations on where you will serve God? We will always be happiest when we are in the center of God's will, regardless of where that may be.

With my authority, take this message of repentance to all the nations, beginning in Jerusalem.   LUKE 24:47

April 23

God sometimes tells us ahead of time what is going to happen.

In 536 B.C. Daniel was a very old man living in Persia. He had been deported from Jerusalem sixty-nine years earlier with the first group of captives and taken to Babylon.[29] In Babylon Daniel rose to the top in government service, serving under Nebuchadnezzar, Darius the Mede, and perhaps also Cyrus the king of Persia.[30] Under Nebuchadnezzar Daniel became the governor of the province of Babylon. Belshazzar, son of Nebuchadnezzar, appointed him to be the third ruler in his kingdom, and Darius made him one of three presidents to whom his 120 satraps reported.

Three years earlier, after a time of prayer and mourning over the sins of his people, Daniel had received a vision from the angel Gabriel who gave him a message that included the timing of the future events in the history of God's people (Daniel 9:20-27).

Now once again Daniel was in prayer and mourning. In particular he prayed for greater understanding of the visions he had already received. For three weeks as he prayed, he ate no rich food or meat and drank no wine. Then suddenly on **April 23, 536 B.C.**, as the old man was standing beside the Tigris River, he looked up and saw a vision of "a man dressed in linen clothing, with a belt of pure gold around his waist. His body looked like a dazzling gem. From his face came flashes like lightning, and his eyes were like flaming torches. His arms and feet shone like polished bronze, and his voice was like the roaring of a vast multitude of people" (10:4-6).

Daniel was the only person who saw this vision. The men who were with him saw nothing but became so terrified that they ran away to hide. So Daniel was left all alone to watch the awesome vision. He began feeling very weak, and when the man began to speak, Daniel fainted, falling facedown on the ground. Then the man's hand touched Daniel and lifted him, still trembling, to his hands and knees. The man said, "O Daniel, greatly loved of God, listen carefully to what I have to say to you. Stand up, for I have been sent to you" (10:11). When he said this, Daniel stood up, still trembling with fear.

Then the man said, "Don't be afraid, Daniel. Since the first day you began to pray for understanding and to humble yourself before your God, your request has been heard in heaven. I have come in answer to your prayer. But for twenty-one days the spirit prince of the kingdom of Persia blocked my way. Then Michael, one of the archangels, came to help me, and I left him there with the spirit prince of the kingdom of Persia. Now I am here to explain what will happen to your people in the future, for this vision concerns a time yet to come" (10:12-14).

Daniel was then given a summary of the future kings of the Persian Empire (11:2) and told of the appearance of Alexander the Great[31] (11:3) and the division of Alexander's kingdom into four lesser kingdoms (11:4). Daniel is next told of the continuing struggle between Syria (the king of the north) and Egypt (the king of the south) from 323 B.C. to 167 B.C. when Antiochus IV Epiphanes, the Syrian ruler, erected an altar to Zeus on top of the brazen altar in the temple in Jerusalem and there offered a pig as a sacrifice[32] (11:5-32). This is followed by a description of the Maccabean revolt in which the Jews were able to win independence from Syria[33] (11:35).

The vision then fast forwards to the future Antichrist, a person similar to Antiochus Epiphanes in many ways, and describes the battles of the end times (11:36–12:13).

The message to Daniel and the book itself ended with the words "You will rest, and then at the end of the days, you will rise again to receive the inheritance set aside for you" (12:13).

Reflection

When God describes the future, what does that tell you about him? God is not only the author of the Bible but also the author of history—past, present, and future.

God rules the kingdoms of the world and appoints anyone he desires to rule over them.
DANIEL 5:21

April 24

He was the nineteenth century's greatest seminary professor.

CHARLES HODGE was born in Philadelphia on December 27, 1797, and raised by his mother because his father died six months after Charles's birth. A gifted student, Charles entered the College of New Jersey, later Princeton University, in 1812 at that age of fourteen. As a senior he publicly confessed his faith in Christ during a campus revival, where over half of the student body gave their allegiance to Jesus. After entering Princeton Seminary in 1816, he excelled in his studies and graduated at age twenty-two. A year later he became professor of biblical languages at the school and the seminary's third professor.

Hodge taught at Princeton Seminary for over fifty years and became America's leading Reformed theologian of the nineteenth century.[34] His three-volume *Systematic Theology* remains in print today.

On **April 24, 1872,** a unique celebration took place in Princeton to honor Charles Hodge for his fifty years of teaching. On that day all the shops in town closed, and people from near and far gathered in the First Presbyterian Church to honor the town's most distinguished citizen. Present were Charles's wife, Mary, their eight children, and a large number of grandchildren. Also in attendance were four hundred graduates of the seminary, almost 15 percent of the total alumni of the school. There were presidents and faculty representatives from many other colleges and seminaries as well as officials from virtually every denomination.

That day Henry Boardman spoke on behalf of the seminary trustees. He pointed out that celebrations for national heroes were not uncommon, but here was "the spontaneous homage paid to a simple teacher of God's Word and defender of its truth." Then addressing Dr. Hodge he said:

> What honor, beloved Brother, has God put upon you! For fifty years you have been training men to preach the glorious gospel of the grace of God to their fellow-sinners. The teacher of teachers, your pupils have become professors in numerous Colleges and Seminaries at home and abroad. Not to speak of one or two thousand pastors, who are exerting an ameliorating influence upon this nation more potent than that of an equal number of men belonging to any other calling, you are helping, through your students, to educate a great body of Christian

ministers, not a few of whom are to be employed in laying the foundations of Christianity on pagan lands.

At that time Charles Hodge had personally taught twenty-seven hundred students—no other seminary in the country had even enrolled that many. In his address Boardman pointed out that there were men scattered around the world who honored Hodge for the gifted mind God had given him and who "love him for his still greater heart."

During the program the seventy-five-year-old Hodge sat on a sofa off to the side of the platform, out of sight of the audience. Almost overcome by emotion after fifteen men had spoken their words of tribute, he came to the lectern to respond: "When I say thank you for all your respect, confidence and love, I am nothing, I am powerless. I can only bow down before you with tearful gratitude, and call on God to bless you, and to reward you a hundred-fold for all your goodness."

That night before retiring, the tired but grateful Hodge summed up the day by writing in his journal: "April 24th. The apex of my life . . . altogether affording an imposing and most affecting testimony of the unity of the faith, and of common love to the same gospel, and to our common God and Saviour Jesus Christ."

Reflection

Most of us are not gifted scholars or teachers like Charles Hodge, but God intends for us to impact the lives of those around us. God placed thousands of students in Hodge's life. He may place only one or two people in your life to disciple. It isn't the number that matters; it is the faithfulness with which you invest yourself.

❧

We are telling you about what we ourselves have actually seen and heard, so that you may have fellowship with us. And our fellowship is with the Father and with his Son, Jesus Christ.   1 JOHN 1:3

April 25

He was the great theologian of the Reformation.

WE KNOW him as John Calvin, but he was born Jean Cauvin on July 10, 1509, in Picardy, France. He studied law in Paris and was converted in 1533. He later wrote, "God drew me from obscure and lowly beginnings and conferred on me the most honorable office of herald and minister of the gospel. . . . What happened first was that by an unexpected conversion he tamed to teachableness a mind too stubborn for its years." Three years later at age twenty-six, he wrote the first edition of his *Institutes of the Christian Religion*, probably the most influential systematic theology of all time.

In 1536 he left Catholic France to avoid persecution and went to Geneva. Except for an interlude of three years, he remained in Geneva until his death.

John Calvin was the leader of the French Reformation, the father of the theology called Calvinism, and the founder of the Reformed churches of the world. He lived modestly, never owned his own home, had few possessions, and refused salary increases. Plagued with ill health, he nevertheless preached an average of five sermons a week and wrote commentaries on nearly every book of the Bible. When his associates were concerned for his health and encouraged him to rest, he shot back: "What! Would you have the Lord find me idle when he comes?"

During the last few months of his life, he slowed down but refused to give up. He was carried to the church to preach his last sermon on February 6, 1564. Two months later, on **April 25, 1564,** feeling it was time to make his will, he called Peter Chenalat, notary of Geneva, to his home and dictated to him:

> In the name of the Lord, Amen. I, John Calvin, minister of the Word of God in this Church of Geneva, being afflicted and oppressed with various diseases . . . give thanks to God, that taking mercy on me, whom He had created and placed in this world. . . . And I testify and declare, that it is my intention to spend what yet remains of my life in the same faith and religion which He has delivered to me by His gospel. . . . With my whole soul I embrace the mercy which He has exercised towards me through Jesus Christ, atoning for my sins . . . that under His shadow I may be able to stand at the judgment-seat. I likewise declare, that . . . I have endeavored, both in my sermons

and also in my writings and commentaries, to preach His Word purely and chastely, and faithfully to interpret His sacred Scriptures. . . . I also testify and declare, that . . . with the enemies of the gospel, I have acted candidly and sincerely in defending the truth. But, woe is me! . . . I confess I have failed innumerable times to execute my office properly, and had not He, of His boundless goodness, assisted me, all that zeal had been fleeting and vain. . . . As God is the Father of mercy, He will show Himself such a Father to me, who acknowledge myself to be a miserable sinner.

The second half of the will is devoted to distribution of the "slender patrimony which God has bestowed upon me" to various family members and friends. In the next month he quickly declined and died on May 27, 1564, shortly before his fifty-fifth birthday.

John Calvin worked tirelessly, almost up to his death, literally using up his life in the service of his Savior.[35]

Reflection

John Calvin's legacy was much more than the few possessions he left to family and friends. His real legacy was the Reformed faith and the Reformed churches of the world. When you depart this life, what will you leave behind? In addition to your material possessions, what will be the primary contributions you will have made? What will you leave to your family and friends?

I have fought a good fight, I have finished the race, and I have remained faithful.   2 TIMOTHY 4:7

April 26

Adoniram Judson, pioneer missionary to Burma, gave up everything for Christ.

ADONIRAM JUDSON had buried his only son in Burma and barely survived a horrifying seventeen-month imprisonment.[36] During the fall of 1826, he was separated from his family for a few months while assisting the English government in negotiations with the Burmese king. Back at their mission station his wife, Ann, became very sick. While preparing to return to her, Judson received the following letter from the mission: "My Dear Sir: To one who has suffered so much, and with such exemplary fortitude, there needs but little preface to tell a tale of distress. It were cruel indeed to torture you with doubt and suspense. To sum up the unhappy tidings in a few words, Mrs. Judson is no more."

After receiving this devastating news, Judson wrote to Ann's mother: "Dear Mother Hasseltine: this letter, though intended for the whole family, I address particularly to you; for it is a mother's heart that will be most deeply interested in its melancholy details. I propose to give you, at different times, some account of my great, irreparable loss, of which you will have heard before receiving this letter."

He went on to describe the great work Ann had been accomplishing in Amherst, Burma, building a school and taking care of their sick two-year-old, Maria. He described his immense pain at not being able to comfort her during her sudden illness and death. He ended with this outpouring of grief and hope:

> I will not trouble you, my dear mother, with an account of my own private feelings—the bitter, heart-rending anguish, which for some days would admit of no mitigation, and the comfort which the Gospel subsequently afforded. . . . Blessed assurance—and let us apply it afresh to our hearts,—that, while I am writing and you perusing these lines, her spirit is resting and rejoicing in the heavenly paradise,—
>
> > Where glories shine, and pleasures roll
> > That charm, delight, transport the soul;
> > And every panting wish shall be
> > Possessed of boundless bliss in Thee.
>
> And there, my dear mother, we also shall soon be, uniting and participating in the felicities of heaven with her for whom we now mourn. 'Amen. Even so, come, Lord Jesus.'

LEFT ALONE

Although Maria seemed to recover after her mother's death, she died just a few months later. At the age of thirty-nine, Judson found himself alone, his wife and two children buried in Burma. He again wrote to his mother-in-law:

*Amherst, **April 26, 1827***

My little Maria lies by the side of her fond mother. The complaint to which she was subject several months proved incurable. She had the best medical advice; and the kind care of Mrs. Wade could not have been, in any respect, exceeded by that of her own mother. But . . . the work of death went forward, and after the usual process, excruciating to a parent's heart, she ceased to breathe on the 24th instant, at 3 o'clock P.M., aged two years and three months. . . . The next morning we made her last bed in the small enclosure that surrounds her mother's lonely grave. Together they rest in hope . . . and together, I trust, their spirits are rejoicing after a short separation of precisely six months.

And I am left alone in the wide world. My own dear family I have buried; one in Rangoon, and two in Amherst. What remains for me but to hold myself in readiness to follow the dear departed to that blessed world,

Where my best friends, my kindred dwell,
Where God, my Saviour, reigns.

Reflection

If you were to have an experience like Adoniram Judson's, how do you think you would react? What hope do you have to hold on to?

∽๛๛∾

If we have hope in Christ only for this life, we are the most miserable people in the world. But the fact is that Christ has been raised from the dead. He has become the first of a great harvest of those who will be raised to life again. 1 CORINTHIANS 15:19-20

April 27

His dream was realized, but he wasn't there to see it.

MILO P. JEWETT was born in Vermont on **April 27, 1808.** He graduated from Dartmouth College, planning to become an attorney. However, after two years he abandoned law and entered Andover Theological Seminary. He had a great interest in education and during his vacations from Andover achieved prominence lecturing on the value of "common-school" systems. He was one of the first proponents of quality public school education for all.

Deciding that God intended him to be a teacher rather than a preacher, after seminary he took a teaching position at Marietta College in Ohio. While there, he was influential in developing Ohio's public school system.

In addition to public schooling, Jewett was interested in education for girls, which he felt was neglected. In 1839 he changed his view of baptism and became a Baptist, leading him to resign from Marietta College. He then moved to Alabama, where he founded Judson Female Institute, which became the South's most successful school for women.

In 1856 Jewett met the wealthy Matthew Vassar at the Baptist Church of Poughkeepsie, New York, and the two men became friends. As their friendship deepened, Jewett talked to his friend about a rich man's duty "to use his property for the glory of God." In response, Vassar excitedly told Jewett of his plan to will his significant estate for the formation of a hospital after his death. Much to Vassar's disappointment, Jewett did not share his excitement. Instead, Jewett shared his dream that Vassar would help him build and endow a Christian college for young women, that would be for them what Yale and Harvard were for young men.

Jewett campaigned hard, appealing to Vassar's interest in Sunday schools and missions. He appealed to his Christian duty to found a Christian school. He also appealed to his pride in Poughkeepsie, New York, and the opportunity to name the college after himself.

Jewett succeeded in convincing Vassar to change his plans and his will. Vassar decided to use his wealth to found a women's college in his name in Poughkeepsie during his lifetime. He abandoned his plans for the hospital and instead gave $400,000 to start Vassar Female College.

Jewett and Vassar worked together for the next few years planning the school, with Jewett as chief adviser in every area. There were some disagreements. Jewett wanted at least eight of the thirteen trustees to be Baptists. Although Vassar wanted an evangelical school, he did not want it to be sectarian. In the end he created a board of trustees from various denominations but made it self-perpetuating so that it would remain true to its evangelical purpose. In 1861 Vassar's charter was granted, and Jewett was named Vassar Female College's first president.

The school had six areas of emphasis that the founders felt were lacking in current women's education. One of them was moral and religious education. Vassar was to have ethics classes, two chapels daily, Sunday services, Bible classes, and social-religious organizations.

Unfortunately tension arose between the visionary and the benefactor. In 1864 Jewett resigned as president before the school even enrolled its first students. After years of work Jewett walked away from the school that had been his dream from the beginning.

After Vassar, Jewett moved to Milwaukee, eventually becoming the commissioner of public schools. His only other known contact with Vassar College was a gracious letter he wrote in 1873 to a Vassar trustee approving the course the college had taken. He expressed happiness in "the humble part I was permitted to bear in laying the foundations and building the rough scaffolding of the grand temple. I never could have overcome the obstacles you have vanquished in rearing the superstructure. Being advised of these from year to year, I have long been persuaded that it was best for myself, as well as for the college, that I left in 1864."

Reflection

Milo Jewett was not able to see his vision for Vassar College through to completion. Have you experienced not realizing some of your dreams? In hindsight have you been able to see the reasons why they weren't fulfilled? In some cases we'll only understand in the next life.

◦◦◦

We can make our plans, but the Lord determines our steps.

PROVERBS 16:9

April 28

What will Jerusalem be like in the future?

EZEKIEL was a priest and prophet who had been taken into captivity in Jerusalem and brought to Babylon in 597 B.C. by King Nebuchadnezzar.[37] In Babylon Ezekiel had seen a vision in which the glory of God departed from the temple in Jerusalem before it was destroyed (Ezekiel 10:1-22).[38] Then in 586 B.C. King Nebuchadnezzar destroyed the temple in Jerusalem and took most of the remaining residents captive to Babylon.[39]

Ezekiel encouraged his fellow exiles with six messages proclaiming the hope of their restoration to Israel (33:21–39:29). Some of these prophesies looked beyond their return from Babylon to their return from exile throughout the world before the final consummation of history. For example, God says through Ezekiel: "I will gather you up from all the nations and bring you home again to your land. Then I will sprinkle clean water on you, and you will be clean. Your filth will be washed away, and you will no longer worship idols. And I will give you a new heart with new and right desires, and I will put a new spirit in you. I will take out your stony heart of sin and give you a new, obedient heart. And I will put my Spirit in you so you will obey my laws and do whatever I command" (36:24-27).

The prophet Zechariah gives more details of this future time when God will put his Spirit in the Jewish people. The Lord says through him, "I will pour out a spirit of grace and prayer on the family of David and on all the people of Jerusalem. They will look on me whom they have pierced and mourn for him as for an only son" (Zechariah 12:10). The book of Revelation quotes this verse from Zechariah and applies it to Jesus' second coming: "Look! He comes with the clouds of heaven. And everyone will see him—even those who pierced him. And all the nations of the earth will weep because of him" (Revelation 1:7). In other words, when Jesus returns, the Jews living on the earth at that time will literally "look on [Jesus] whom they have pierced and mourn for him as for an only son." This is when God gives them his Holy Spirit and they are converted, receiving "a new obedient heart" (Ezekiel 36:26). The apostle Paul writes: "So all Israel will be saved. Do you remember what the prophets said about this? 'A Deliverer will come from Jerusalem, and he will turn Israel from all ungodliness. And then I will keep my covenant with them and take away their sins'" (Romans 11:26-27).

Since King Solomon's time when the Jewish people were under God's

THE GLORIOUS TEMPLE

blessing, they had a Temple in Jerusalem in which to worship. This will again be true in the millennial age following the second coming of Christ.

Then on **April 28, 573 B.C.**, God took Ezekiel from Babylon back to Jerusalem by means of a vision in which he showed him the final glorious temple that is to come. More important, just as Ezekiel had had a vision of God's glory leaving the temple of his day, now he sees the glory of the Lord returning to the future temple: "Suddenly, the glory of the God of Israel appeared from the east. . . . And the glory of the Lord came into the Temple through the east gateway. . . . And the glory of the Lord filled the Temple. . . . And the Lord said to me, 'Son of man, this is the place of my throne'" (Ezekiel 43:2-7).

Reflection

Does it surprise you that Israel will be converted to Christ in the future and will again have a temple in Jerusalem filled with the glory of the Lord? It is easy to accept Bible prophecies that have already been fulfilled and ignore those that are still in the future. But these future prophecies will be fulfilled just as surely as the earlier ones.

From that day the name of the city will be "The Lord Is There."
EZEKIEL 48:35

April 29

From boyhood, he continually astounded everyone with his wisdom.

EVERY YEAR Jesus' parents went to Jerusalem for the Passover festival. Every Jewish male was required to attend, but women who loved God came as well. It was a difficult eighty-mile trip from Nazareth, but Passover was the highlight of the year. Since highway robbers were a known danger, pilgrims on their way to Jerusalem usually traveled together in caravans for protection. Mary and Joseph traveled with a large group of friends and relatives.

When Jesus[40] was twelve years old, the Passover was on **April 29, A.D. 9,** and the whole family attended the festival as usual.[41] This was a highly significant period in Jesus' life because at age thirteen Jewish boys were considered to be responsible for themselves before God. The year prior to this was filled with intense instruction. (The custom of the bar mitzvah came after the time of Jesus.)

After the celebration was over, Mary and Joseph started home for Nazareth with their large group of fellow pilgrims. Without their knowledge, Jesus stayed behind in Jerusalem. His parents did not miss him at first because they assumed he was with friends elsewhere in their caravan. But when they stopped for the evening, they could not find him, and realized he was missing. So they returned to Jerusalem to search for him. Three days later they finally found him in the temple, sitting among the religious teachers, engaged in a question-and-answer session with them.

But Mary and Joseph were angry at what they perceived as his disobedience. They were relieved to find him but were understandably upset. Mary said, "Son! Why have you done this to us? Your father and I have been frantic, searching for you everywhere."

Jesus answered her, "But why did you need to search? You should have known that I would be in my Father's house."

In Jesus' Greco-Roman world, *house* or *household* was not only a designation of location but also of authority. Jesus was aligning himself with his heavenly Father's house even if it meant disrupting his relationship with his earthly parents. This was a foreshadowing of the pattern for the rest of his life. Mary and Joseph did not understand what he meant. They could not comprehend Jesus' understanding of who he was. But Mary stored all these things in her heart.

THE CHILD WHO KNEW MORE
THAN HIS PARENTS

Then, as an obedient twelve-year-old, Jesus returned to Nazareth with his parents and lived under their authority (Luke 2:41-52).

Reflection

Mary and Joseph were probably the very first persons to wrestle with the question of who Jesus was. Before his birth an angel had told Joseph that Mary's son would "save his people from their sins" (Matthew 1:21) and had told Mary her son "would be very great and [would] be called the Son of the Most High" (Luke 1:32). Yet Mary and Joseph did not completely understand the angels' messages. These were the things that Mary pondered in her heart. We, too, must answer the question, Who is Jesus? What is your answer?

So the baby born to you will be holy, and he will be called the Son of God.

LUKE 1:35

April 30

They were political casualties.

THAILAND was a difficult place to be a missionary in 1974. The Vietnam War had spilled over into Laos, Cambodia, and northern Thailand. In southern Thailand there was ongoing conflict between the military and Muslim liberation groups that wanted independence for Thailand's predominantly Muslim provinces. Malaysia, having a majority Muslim population, was supporting the Muslim rebels. The tense religious and political climate made missionary work difficult and dangerous.

Minka Hanskamp, a six-foot-tall Dutch woman who had grown up in Java as the daughter of missionaries, and Margaret Morgan, a nurse from a Welsh mining village, were missionary nurses with Overseas Missionary Fellowship (OMF). They had worked tirelessly in southern Thailand for sixteen and nine years respectively. They both had a special burden for those with leprosy. Their ministry involved cutting away rotten flesh, treating ulcerated sores that emitted a horrible stench, and washing many leprous feet.

Every two weeks the women held a leprosy clinic in the town of Pujud. On April 20, 1974, Minka's sixteenth anniversary at OMF, she and Margaret were lured away from Pujud by strangers who insisted they come with them to the mountains to treat some sick patients needing help.

On **April 30, 1974,** Ian Murray, the OMF representative for Thailand, received two devastating letters. One was a letter from Minka and Margaret stating that they had been kidnapped by "jungle people" but were well and "still praising." The second letter was from their captors. It demanded a half-million-dollar ransom. The kidnappers also demanded that an official letter be sent from OMF to the nation of Israel in support of Palestinian rights. OMF's policies did not allow them to comply with either demand. If they paid a ransom, every missionary would become more susceptible to abduction. It was also against OMF policy to become involved in political issues.

Instead Ian Murray met with Thai officials and representatives of the kidnappers, attempting to secure the release of Minka and Margaret. The meeting was unsuccessful. Violence in the area escalated over the next few days between Muslim separatists and the military. The Muslim gang that held the women issued a statement saying that they were not against OMF but against American and British support of Israel. The women would not be released unless the "Christian world stop any support to Israel against the Palestinian people."

This crisis received international attention and prayer, but the letters from the women soon stopped. Rumors of their executions spread but were not confirmed.

Finally in March 1975 a Malaysian man confessed that he had shot both missionaries in the head. The chief of the Muslim gang had decided that the women had to be killed in order to keep the respect of his underlings in the rebel movement. The man said that the nurses were calm when they were told they were going to die, saying only, "Give us a little time to read and pray." Although the Christian world hoped the story wasn't true, it was confirmed when two skeletons that physically matched the women were found in the jungle. They had been shot in the head five or six months earlier.

On May 15 hundreds attended their funeral, not only Christians but Buddhists and Muslims as well. Many were shocked and saddened by the violent murders of the women who had come to help them. One man testified at the funeral that he had been a former bandit killer but had become a Christian after Minka had tenderly placed his ulcerated foot on her lap as she treated it. Following the funeral, native pastors and missionaries received more inquiries about the Christian faith than ever before.

Reflection

Can you imagine yourself ministering to lepers as Minka and Margaret did? Are there areas of Christian ministry that you suspect you should participate in but that are outside your comfort zone?

Heal the sick, raise the dead, cure those with leprosy, and cast out demons. Give as freely as you have received! MATTHEW 10:8

May 1

The child on the moss she laid
And she stretched the cold limbs of the dead,
And drew the eyelid's shade,
And bound the corpse's shattered head,
And shrouded the martyr in his plaid;
And where the dead and living slept,
Sat in the wilderness and wept.

THIS POEM, written by Henry Inglis, tells the story of the death of John Brown, Covenanter martyr.

The Covenanters were Scottish Presbyterians who resisted the Episcopal system that Charles I, Charles II, and James VI imposed upon Scotland from 1637 to 1690. They opposed the divine right of kings, believing that limitless sovereignty belongs to God alone. When Presbyterianism was outlawed and replaced by episcopacy, the situation became very serious for the Covenanters, who were forced to choose between obedience to God or to the king. During the reign of Charles II they were hunted, jailed, and killed in large numbers.

John Brown was a poor farmer in Priesthill, Scotland, who aspired to be a Covenanter minister, but felt hampered by a problem with stammering. A brilliant man, Brown instead put his intellect and love of the Bible to work at home—teaching theology classes to local youth at his farm. Being a Covenanter meant being willing to give up his life for Christ at any moment, and Brown taught his students not to fear persecution but rather to consider it joy to suffer for Christ. Students came from miles around to be inspired by the gifted teacher.

In 1682 Covenanter pastor Alexander Peden performed the wedding ceremony for John Brown and Isabel Weir. After the ceremony Peden said to the bride, "Isabel, you have got a good man; but you will not enjoy him long. Prize his company and keep linen by you to be his winding sheet; for you will need it when you are not looking for it, and it will be a bloody one."

On **May 1, 1685,** the king's troops came to Priesthill looking for Peden. They surprised Brown in his field and brought him back to his house and ransacked it. Finding some Covenanter literature, they began to interrogate him. Speaking in a clear, stammer-free voice, Brown's confident answers made the chief officer ask whether he was a preacher. When told no, the officer replied, "Well, if he has never preached, much has he prayed in his time. Go to your prayers, for you shall immediately die."

THE DEATH OF JOHN BROWN

John Brown fell on his knees, asking God to spare a remnant of believers in Scotland. The officer cut him short, accusing him of preaching rather than praying. The officer later confessed that he could never forget John Brown's powerful prayer.

Brown then said to his wife, "Now, Isabel, the day is come that I told you would come when I spoke to you first of marrying me."

She said, "Indeed, John, I can willingly part with you."

He replied, "That is all I desire. I have no more to do but die. I have been ready to meet death for years past."

As he said his good-byes and kissed his wife and baby, the officer broke in and ordered the troops to shoot him. The soldiers were so moved by the scene that they would not comply. The officer angrily pulled out his pistol, walked over, and shot John Brown in the head.

"What do you think of your fine husband now?" he asked Isabel.

Through her tears she answered, "I ever thought much good of him, and more than ever now."

As the poem tells, Isabel laid her baby on the ground, bound up her beloved husband's head, straightened his body, covered him with a plaid blanket, and sat down and wept.

Peden was in a nearby Covenanter home and described seeing a meteor that morning, "a bright, clear, shining light [that] fell from heaven to the earth." He told his fellow believers, "And indeed there is a clear, shining light fallen this day, the greatest Christian that I ever conversed with."

Reflection

John and Isabel Brown's marriage was filled with love yet accompanied by the awful reality of the constant threat of death. Can you imagine what it would be like to live with martyrdom as a continual possibility? How would you live differently?

∽◌◠

You refused to deny me even when Antipas, my faithful witness, was martyred among you by Satan's followers. REVELATION 2:13

May 2

He had no idea what he was starting.

Peter Waldo was a wealthy twelfth-century merchant from Lyons, France, an important center of the silk industry. Waldo decided to take literally the words of Mark 10:21: "Go and sell all you have and give the money to the poor, and you will have treasure in heaven. Then come, follow me." He did precisely that.

Waldo never intended to found a movement; he merely wanted to follow Jesus as the disciples had done. He focused on Christ's poverty. His followers, known as the "Poor of Lyons," were sent out two by two to preach and teach the Bible. Waldo had sections of the Scriptures translated into the local dialect to use in their preaching. The Roman Catholic Church was threatened by this ministry of laymen and condemned them as heretics. The Poor of Lyons fled to Languedoc in southern France and across the Alps to Lombardy in northern Italy, suffering persecution along the way. A century later they were found in Germany, still experiencing intense persecution.

In 1689 the Waldensians, as they subsequently were called, began what has come to be known as their "glorious return" to the Alps of northern Italy, their adopted homeland. During this same period French Huguenots were also fleeing their country for the Italian Alps. High in the mountains a small group of Waldensian officers, together with their soldiers, made a solemn pact, called the Covenant of Sibaud:

> God by his grace, having brought us happily back to the heritages of our fathers, to re-establish there the pure service of our holy religion— in continuance and for the accomplishment of the great enterprise which this great God of armies hath hitherto carried on in our favor—
>
> We, pastors, captains, and other officers, swear and promise before the living God, and on the life of our souls, to keep union and order among ourselves; and not to separate and disunite ourselves from one another, whilst God shall preserve us in life, if we should be reduced even to three or four in number. . . .
>
> And we, soldiers, promise and swear this day before God to be obedient to the orders of our officers, and to continue faithful to them, even to the last drop of our blood. . . .
>
> And in order that union, which is the soul of all our affairs, may

remain always unbroken among us, the officers swear fidelity to the soldiers, and the soldiers to the officers;

All together promising to our Lord and Saviour Jesus Christ to rescue, as far as it is possible to us, the dispersed remnant of our brethren from the yoke which oppresses them, that along with them we may establish and maintain in these valleys the kingdom of the gospel, even unto death.

In witness whereof, we swear to observe this present engagement so long as we shall live.

Finally on **May 2, 1690,** their numbers reduced over the hard winter to three hundred men, the Waldensians were entrenched on the mountain crags. Lined up beneath them in the valley were four thousand French dragoons led by the Marquis de Feuquière. The marquis first attacked during a severe snowstorm, then commanded his artillery to roll its cannons up the slopes to attack the bedraggled remnant of men who climbed even higher, waiting for death. In his confidence, the marquis had already sent a victory message back to France. But then a miracle happened. A thick fog surrounded the Waldensians, allowing them to escape off the mountaintop during the night! They were saved by God's hand!

The Waldensian church later united with the Methodists and still exists today.

Reflection

Have you experienced God's intervention in your life? In the case of the Waldensians God did protect the final three hundred men but chose not to preserve those who died earlier in the winter. We should pray for God's protection, realizing that in some cases he protects his children by taking them to be with himself.

∽◦∾

This I declare of the Lord: He alone is my refuge, my place of safety; he is my God, and I am trusting him.   Psalm 91:2

May 3

Although Greenland was anything but green (actually 85 percent glacial icecap!), he didn't let that deter him. . . .

HANS EGEDE was born in northeastern Norway in 1686. While serving as a Lutheran minister in Vaagan, Norway, Egede began studying about the old Norse Christian settlements in Greenland. During the Middle Ages a bishop had sent Norwegian settlers there, and these settlers had not had any contact with Europe since 1410. Egede wondered what had become of their descendants.

Egede became fascinated with the idea of resuming contact with the settlers and evangelizing them if they were no longer followers of Jesus. He felt that it was the duty of Norway and Denmark to bring the gospel to the descendants of the settlers and whoever else might live on the island. He tried to interest both the Danish king and the bishops in a missionary effort to Greenland, but they were not interested. When Egede changed his proposition to include more commercial purposes, such as colonizing, setting up trading posts, and investigating the natural resources of Greenland, he found support. He eventually succeeded in founding a company that supported both commercial and missionary endeavors, and he set sail for Greenland with his wife and two sons on **May 3, 1721.**

Upon his arrival in Greenland, Egede was shocked to find no Norse communities. No Europeans had survived the centuries, and the island was inhabited solely by Eskimos. Although surprised, he maintained his missionary purpose and attempted to learn the language and culture of the Eskimo people and present the gospel to them. He initially had very limited success. However, his optimism was clear in his founding of the colonial town of Godthab, which means "Good Hope." Godthab today is known as the capital city of Nuuk.

The evangelistic tides turned in 1733 when a smallpox epidemic killed thousands of Eskimos on the island. The selfless way that Egede and his family cared for the sick and buried the dead had a profound impact on the Eskimos. All of a sudden his message was received eagerly and many were won to Christ. Due to the difficult time that Egede had experienced learning the Eskimo language, it was his son Paul who did most of the preaching and the winning of souls to Christ. Having grown up with the Eskimos, he spoke their language as his own. After his father left Greenland, Paul remained as a missionary. Hans, Egede's other son, Niels, his son-in-law, and two nephews also were missionaries to Greenland.

Hans Egede returned to Denmark in 1736 to found a school for the training of missionaries to Greenland. He wrote ethnographic books on the history, folklore, geography, and language of Greenland that are still respected today. With Paul's assistance he translated the New Testament into the Eskimo language and wrote an Eskimo grammar, a dictionary, and a catechism.

Moravian missionaries arrived in Greenland in 1733.[1] They carried on the work for Christ that Egede and his family had pioneered. Due to the missionary efforts of Hans Egede, his family, and the Moravian missionaries that followed, all of Greenland's Eskimos eventually became members of Christian churches!

Reflection

Hans Egede's ministry did not bear fruit quickly. Despite his initial lack of success, he trusted that God would reach the people of Greenland, and he did. It was Egede's selfless actions and not his words that earned him a hearing. What can you learn from Hans Egede to apply to your own life?

Be careful how you live among your unbelieving neighbors. Even if they accuse you of doing wrong, they will see your honorable behavior, and they will believe and give honor to God when he comes to judge the world.
1 PETER 2:12

May 4

She began a voyage to Australia—but ended up in paradise.

ON MAY 4, 1837, Jessie Hetherington began a letter to her mother that she never finished.

Several months earlier Jessie and Irving Hetherington had been married and immediately left Scotland for Sydney, Australia. Before their wedding, Irving had a fruitful ministry in the poor suburbs of Edinburgh. While involved in this work, he felt the call of God when he heard a request for preachers in New South Wales, Australia, even though he knew it might mean the end of his engagement to Jessie. Jessie, however, gladly agreed to accompany him: "Where *you* wish to take me, *there* I will go." Three months into the voyage to Sydney, Jessie caught scarlet fever and died just days later. The following is an excerpt from the letter Irving finished for his wife:

> I write now in Sydney, for, during our whole voyage, we met no opportunity in England; yet is my Jessie's every look and every tone as distinctly engraved on my memory—as fully remembered, as they were two months ago. O yes! I never can forget. And in particular will you be anxious to know what was her experience in the prospect of eternity. It was of the serenity of heaven. Let me die the death of the righteous, and let my last end be like hers. O, it was the most perfect peace! On the surgeon appraising me on Tuesday of her extreme danger, I thought it right to communicate this to her. She was quite collected at the time; and was looking at me in the affectionate manner that was so usual to her, and which will, I think, never cease to haunt my dreams. I said to her that Mr. Thompson did not give us reason to expect her recovery. "It is the Lord's will, and we must submit, Irving," she quietly answered. "And have you no fear, then, of death, Jessie?" "No, dear." "And how is it that you are not afraid to die?" "I have long taken Christ for my portion, and set my hopes on Him." I could but weep. Afterwards I asked her what word of God it was that then gave her the most comfort. "Come unto me, all ye that labor and are heavy laden, and I will give you rest," she replied, with much eagerness; and, after I had made some remarks on this, she bade me repeat some of those Scriptures in which salvation by grace is offered to sinners. This I continued to do, when I thought she was in a state of consciousness; and prayed with her day and night. Her spirit ascended as I was commending her to the God of grace. As assured do I feel of her blessedness, yea, as confident

that she is now with the God for whom she gave up so much, as I could be were an angel to bring to me tidings of her mingling with the choir above. To her, death was indeed unspeakable gain. But what a loss have I sustained!

Now alone, Irving Hetherington continued on to Australia and became the first evangelical minister in Singleton, New South Wales. It was a district fifty miles long by thirty miles wide. For several years he also was the superintendent of the area's school. Combined with these responsibilities he made weekly treks in all weather to settlers' houses to serve both them and their convict servants, doing much of his studying and sermon preparations on horseback. After nine years he was called as the minister of the Scott's Church in Melbourne, where he preached until just before his death in 1875.

Reflection

Have you ever lost a loved one? If it hasn't happened yet, it will in the future. When our loved ones have given their allegiance to Jesus, we can know that they are in God's presence. If you have loved ones who are not yet on the way to heaven, share with them that Jesus is the way.

Jesus told him, "I am the way, the truth, and the life. No one can come to the Father except through me." JOHN 14:6

May 5

It was a religious club that produced mostly poor results.

CHARLES WESLEY[2] and two friends began a small Christian group at Oxford University in 1728. John Wesley,[3] who had already graduated from Oxford, returned the following year as a tutor and assumed its leadership. Oxford students made fun of the group, referring to it as the "Holy Club" or "Methodists." By the time George Whitefield[4] joined the group in 1733, there were eight or nine dedicated members.

The focus of the Holy Club was on religious self-discipline. They woke up early for lengthy devotions, took Communion each Sunday, fasted every Wednesday and Friday, and observed Saturday as the Sabbath in preparation for the Lord's Day. Exhorting each other to live piously and do good works, they were motivated by the belief that they were working for the salvation of their souls. Yet their self-discipline brought them neither happiness nor salvation.

The lifestyle of the Holy Club had a catastrophic effect on the life of William Morgan, one of the founders. He lost his mind and eventually his life in his struggle to achieve self-disciplined perfection.

Whitefield was the first Holy Club member to question their practices. He read a book where, in his words,

> God showed me that I must be born again, or be damned! I learned that a man may go to church, say his prayers, receive the sacrament, and yet not be a Christian. Shall I burn this book? Shall I throw it down? Or shall I search it? I did search it; and, holding the book in my hand, thus addressed the God of heaven and earth: "Lord, if I am not a Christian, or if I am not a real one, for Jesus Christ's sake, show me what Christianity is that I may not be damned at last!" God soon showed me in reading a few lines further that "true religion is a union of the soul with God, and Christ formed within us," a ray of Divine light was instantaneously darted in upon my soul, and from that moment, but not till then, did I know that I must become a new creature.

His solution, however, was to try to become a new creature through further extremes of self-denial. During Lent in 1735 he only ate a little coarse bread with tea. By Holy Week he was so weak that he could not study or even walk up a flight of stairs. His grades began to suffer and his tutor wondered if he was going mad. His physician put him in bed, where he remained for seven weeks.

Having hit bottom in his efforts to earn his salvation, Whitefield described what happened next:

> God was pleased to remove the heavy load, to enable me to lay hold of his dear Son by a living faith, and by giving me the Spirit of adoption, to seal me, even to the day of everlasting redemption.
>
> O! With what joy—joy unspeakable—even joy that was full of and big with glory, was my soul filled when the weight of sin went off and an abiding sense of the love of God broke in upon my disconsolate soul! Surely it was a day to be had in everlasting remembrance. My joys were like a spring tide and overflowed the banks.

Later he declared, "I knew the place: it may be superstitious, perhaps, but whenever I go to Oxford I cannot help running to the place where Jesus Christ first revealed himself to me, and gave me the new birth."

On **May 5, 1735,** Whitefield wrote a letter to John Wesley, attempting to share what had happened to him. He wrote, "Into his all gracious arms, I blindly throw myself."

It would be three more years before the Wesleys found his gracious arms.

Reflection

Have you ever found yourself trying to earn your salvation? Salvation is a gift to be received from God, and there is nothing we can do to earn it. Good works do not lead us to Christ—it is out of our relationship with Christ that good works flow.

God saved you by his special favor when you believed. And you can't take credit for this; it is a gift from God. Salvation is not a reward for the good things we have done, so none of us can boast about it.

EPHESIANS 2:8-9

May 6

He proved that a good education isn't dependent upon lavish surroundings.

WILLIAM TENNENT was born in 1673, educated at the University of Edinburgh, where he received a master of arts degree, and eventually was ordained in the Anglican Church in Ireland. He had an independent streak and tended not to conform to the Anglican Church. Instead of leading his own parish as a typical clergyman, he served as a chaplain to an Irish nobleman.

In 1718 he and his family emigrated from Ireland to Philadelphia. Shortly after his arrival he petitioned the Presbyterian synod to allow him to become a Presbyterian minister. He renounced the Anglican Church because of disagreements over church government and the Arminian tendencies of its doctrines. His petition was accepted, and he was ordained as a Presbyterian minister without having to undergo further education.

He first took pastorates in New York and then in 1726 went to Neshaminy, Pennsylvania, to lead a church. He remained there for the rest of his life. Shortly after his arrival, he began informally tutoring his sons and some other young men who were preparing to enter the Presbyterian ministry. By 1735 he formalized his efforts by building a simple log building on his property to serve as his school. It came to be known as "Log College." His motivation for building the college was to increase the supply of Presbyterian ministers in America. Until this point candidates for the ministry had had to go to New England or abroad for training. Tennent was known for his excellent teaching skills, deep faith, and godly lifestyle.

Tennent's three younger sons, William, John, and Charles, were trained at Log College and went on to become Presbyterian ministers and leaders of the Great Awakening.

The college was not without its detractors. In fact, the name "Log College" was in itself a derogatory and derisive reference. Many within the Presbyterian Church were skeptical of the college's ability to provide adequate training because of its humble and remote surroundings. Additional tension came from the fact that those who were supporters of the college also tended to be more aggressively evangelistic. They embraced the great evangelist George Whitefield[5] and his methods, which were controversial at the time.

Although many demeaned the simplicity of the Log College, George Whitefield admired it. He wrote in his journal:

FROM LOG CABIN TO UNIVERSITY

The place wherein the young men study now, is in contempt called, the college. It is a log house, about twenty foot long, and near as many broad; and to me it seemed to resemble the school of the old prophets; for their habitations were mean; and that they sought not great things for themselves is plain. . . . All that we can say of most of our universities is, they are glorious without. From this despised place, seven or eight worthy ministers of Jesus have lately been sent forth; more are almost ready to be sent, and the foundation is now laying for the instruction of many others.

The Log College closed as old age and poor health claimed William Tennent. He died on **May 6, 1746.** That fall supporters of the Log College joined together with Presbyterians disillusioned with Yale's recent expulsion of David Brainerd[6] to form the College of New Jersey.[7] Four of the initial trustees were graduates of the Log College, including two of Tennent's sons. Another Log College graduate and initial trustee was Samuel Finley, who later became the fifth president of the college. Today we know the College of New Jersey, the successor of Log College, as Princeton University.

Princeton University was born in a log cabin!

Reflection

William Tennent's deep faith and his commitment to teaching others created a far-reaching legacy for the kingdom of Christ. Do you ever think about the legacy you will leave? Will it further God's kingdom?

Do not despise these small beginnings, for the Lord rejoices to see the work begin.   ZECHARIAH 4:10

May 7

He realized his boyhood dream.

As a boy, James Montgomery Boice attended Tenth Presbyterian Church in Philadelphia with his family. He idolized his pastor, Donald Grey Barnhouse,[8] and was an avid listener to Barnhouse's radio program, *The Bible Study Hour*. At the age of twelve Boice decided he wanted to become a minister. Little did he know how closely he would follow his beloved minister's footsteps.

Boice attended Harvard, where he received a degree in English literature. There he met his future wife, Linda Ann McNamara, at InterVarsity Christian Fellowship. She received a master of arts from Harvard, and they shared a dream of creating a Christian college preparatory school for needy inner-city youth.

After Harvard, Boice went to seminary to prepare himself for becoming a minister. He then married Linda, and they moved to Switzerland so Jim could study at the University of Basel. After he received his doctorate, they settled in Washington, D.C., where he worked for the magazine *Christianity Today*.

In 1968 Tenth Presbyterian Church in Philadelphia, the church of his youth, called him to be their senior pastor. In 1969 he also became the speaker for *The Bible Study Hour*. Boice continued Barnhouse's legacy of providing clear, intellectual, heartfelt expository preaching to the Tenth Presbyterian congregation. Under Boice's leadership the church grew in numbers, budget, and outreach programs. The church became ethnically diverse and intensely missions focused. Many of its ministries grew out of its inner-city location: ministries to internationals, HIV positive individuals, inner-city youth, women with crisis pregnancies, and the homeless. Jim and Linda achieved their dream of a Christian college preparatory school for needy inner-city youth with the creation of City Center Academy, which was started and run by Tenth Presbyterian. Despite the lack of parking in its downtown location, the church has well over a thousand members.

In the 1970s Boice started the Philadelphia Conference on Reformed Theology, which spawned many similar conferences in cities throughout the country. In 1977 he founded the International Council on Biblical Inerrancy, a topic on which he frequently wrote. In all he wrote or contributed to more than sixty books. Under Boice's leadership Tenth Presbyterian left the Presbyterian Church USA in 1981 and joined the Presbyterian Church in America, a denomination that conformed more closely to the church's Reformed theological beliefs.

On Good Friday 2000, two hours before he was to preach, Dr. Boice learned that he had an aggressive form of liver cancer. His prognosis was not good.

Jim Boice mounted the pulpit of Tenth Presbyterian for the last time on Sunday, **May 7, 2000.** He announced to his stunned congregation that he was rapidly dying of cancer. He said to them: "Should you pray for a miracle? Well, you're free to do that, of course. My general impression is that the God who is able to perform miracles—and he certainly can—is also able to keep you from getting the problem in the first place. . . . Above all, I would say pray for the glory of God. If you think of God glorifying himself in history and you say, 'Where in all of history has God most glorified himself?' the answer is that he did it at the cross of Jesus Christ, and it wasn't by delivering Jesus from the cross, though he could have. . . . And yet that's where God is most glorified."

On June 15, 2000, at the age of sixty-one, James Montgomery Boice died peacefully in his sleep, just eight weeks after his diagnosis.

Reflection

How do you think you would react if you were given news of your impending death? Dr. Boice's inclination was not to pray for a miracle but rather to pray that Christ be glorified in his death. What is your reaction to what Dr. Boice told his congregation?

∽℮∼

While we live, we live to please the Lord. And when we die, we go to be with the Lord. So in life and in death, we belong to the Lord.
ROMANS 14:8

May 8

She returned to her captors.

JUDY HYLAND grew up in a small town in northern Minnesota. She gave her life to Christ as a high school student and soon made a committment to world missions. On October 5, 1940, she set sail for China with nine other Lutheran missionaries.

Their ship did not reach China but was redirected to the Philippines because of Japan's war against China. They settled in the mountain city of Baguio and immersed themselves in the difficult task of learning Chinese, still hoping to go to China. They heard rumors that the war was spreading but were not concerned about themselves, as the U.S. high commissioner to the Philippines had assured them of their safety.

Thus it came as a total surprise when Japanese bombers attacked their city on the same day that the news of the Japanese attack on Pearl Harbor reached them.[9] Shortly thereafter, as the Japanese army marched toward the city of Baguio, the missionaries read Psalm 91 together: "He who dwells in the shelter of the Most High will rest in the shadow of the Almighty. I will say of the Lord, 'He is my refuge and my fortress, my God, in whom I trust.' Surely he will save you. . . . He will cover you with his feathers, and under his wings you will find refuge" (vv.1-4, NIV).

The Japanese captured Judy and approximately five hundred other Americans and held them captive from December 1941 to February 1945. They were held at a U.S. military rest camp in Baguio until May 1942, then in a Filipino camp in Baguio until December 1944, and finally in Old Bilibid Prison in Manila until February 1945. Crowded into austere barracks, they fought hunger and boredom constantly. They were cut off from all news of World War II, and for more than three years they did not know what was happening or whether they would ever be released. It was as if time stood still.

On February 4, 1945, American troops launched a surprise attack on the Japanese in Manila, and the American prisoners were freed! They were unable to return home immediately because the military had to focus on winning the war rather than transporting freed prisoners. The former prisoners used the time to learn about the last three years and to reorient themselves to American life. So much had changed that they were frightened about returning to their old life. They also struggled with feelings of hatred toward the Japanese. Could forgiveness come?

FROM ENEMIES TO FRIENDS

When the announcement finally came that they were going home, Judy was surprised by her lack of excitement. She knew she should be happy but was somewhat afraid to leave the life that had been reality for her for over three years. Resuming normal life seemed impossible. As they left, she later recalled, "There was no sentimental looking back, but there was also no joyful anticipation. We went through it all as if we were sleepwalking."

When the ship reached Los Angeles on **May 8, 1945,** and Judy disembarked, a Red Cross volunteer approached her and said, "My dear, you look tired. Would you like some coffee and a doughnut?" Judy's emotions burst forth like a flood. "Coffee and doughnuts! We had daydreamed about it, and it had been in our daily conversations. And now to actually hold coffee and doughnuts in my hands—and even more to receive the kindness and sympathy—was too much."

Returning to Minneapolis by train, she was met by her family, friends, and fiancé. With tears streaming down their faces they sang, "Now Thank We All Our God." She later wrote, "A foretaste of the great homecoming in glory! I went through it all, however, as if it were happening to someone else. But now after 40 years I cannot speak of that homecoming without tears."

Judy Hyland and her fiancé were married and became Lutheran missionaries in Japan, serving there for thirty years. Those who once were captors and enemies became dear friends.

Reflection

Judy found meaning in her suffering by ministering to the very people who had hurt her. God gave her a forgiving heart. Do you have trouble forgiving others? Judy Hyland's experience is an example of how through Christ we can forgive the most grievous wrongs.

❧

Forgive us our sins, just as we have forgiven those who have sinned against us.
MATTHEW 6:12

May 9

He was victorious in death.

BY THE 1600s, Scotland had fallen under English rule. For Scottish Presbyterians, their loss of religious freedom was even more galling than their loss of political freedom. The king of England was the head of the Church of England, yet to Scottish Presbyterians like John Paton, the true head of the church was King Jesus. This was no mere theological distinction. The Anglican Church in that day asserted its authority over individual conscience. In response, John Paton and many other Presbyterians in Scotland covenanted together to uphold and defend the principles of the Reformation and became known as the Scottish Covenanters.

Captain John Paton was born in the 1620s on a farm in rural Fenwick Parish in Ayer, Scotland. He became a professional soldier and fought under Gustavus Adolphus in Germany[10] and with the Covenanters at the battles of Marston Moor (1644),[11] Rullion Green (1667), and Bothwell Bridge (1679).[12]

Since he was a Covenanter, Paton spent most of his retirement in hiding. Finally in August 1683 he was arrested. He was tried and sentenced to death by hanging for treason against the Crown. But Paton remained fiercely loyal to a higher King. On **May 9, 1684,** from the scaffold, he read his last testimony:

Dear Friends and Spectators—
You are come here to look upon me a dying man. . . . I am a poor sinner, and could never merit anything but wrath, and have no righteousness of my own; all is Christ's and His alone; and I have laid claim to His righteousness and His sufferings by faith in Jesus Christ; through imputation they are mine; for I have accepted of His offer on His own terms, and sworn away myself to Him, to be at His disposal, both privately and publicly; and now I have put it upon Him to ratify in Heaven all that I have purposed to do on earth, and to do away with all my imperfections and failings, and to stay my heart on Him. . . .

I now leave my testimony, as a dying man, against the horrid usurpation of our Lord's prerogative and crown-right . . . for He is given by the Father to be the head of His Church. . . .

Oh! Be oft at the throne, and give God no rest. Make sure your soul's interest. Seek His pardon freely, and then He will come with peace. Seek all the graces of His spirit, the grace of love, the grace of holy fear and humility. . . .

THE CAPTAIN'S LAST WORDS

Now I desire to salute you, dear friends in the Lord Jesus Christ, both prisoned, banished, widow and fatherless, or wandering and cast out for Christ's sake and the Gospel's; even the blessings of Christ's sufferings be with you all, strengthen, establish, support, and settle you. . . .

Now as to my persecutors, I forgive all of them . . . but I wish they would seek forgiveness of Him who hath it to give. . . .

Now I leave my poor sympathizing wife and six small children upon the Almighty Father, Son, and Holy Ghost, who hath promised to be a father to the fatherless, and a husband to the widow, the widow and orphans' stay. Be Thou all in all to them, O Lord. . . .

And now farewell, wife and children. Farewell all friends and relations. Farewell all worldy enjoyments. Farewell sweet Scriptures, preaching, praying, reading, singing, and all duties. And welcome, Father, Son, and Holy Spirit. I desire to commit my soul to Thee in well-doing. Lord, receive my spirit.

Reflection

If you were about to be executed for your faith, what do you think would be your last words? God promises to give his children the words to say when the time comes.

You must stand trial before governors and kings because you are my followers. This will be your opportunity to tell them about me—yes, to witness to the world. When you are arrested, don't worry about what to say in your defense, because you will be given the right words at the right time. For it won't be you doing the talking—it will be the Spirit of your Father speaking through you. MATTHEW 10:18-20

May 10

The troops called him "Stonewall"; members of his church called him "Deacon."

THOMAS JONATHAN JACKSON was born in 1824 in Clarksburg, Virginia. He had a limited education and barely passed the entrance examination for West Point Military Academy. However, once in the academy he distinguished himself academically and went on to become one of the greatest tactical geniuses in military history.

His interest in the Christian faith began when he was a young boy and intensified while he was fighting in the Mexican War. On April 29, 1848, he publicly declared his faith and was baptized at an Episcopal church, though he made it clear that he was not joining the Episcopal Church because he was unsure which denomination he favored.

In 1851 he began ten years of teaching at the Virginia Military Institute. His students considered him to be too pious and inflexible and made him the object of many pranks. During this time he joined the Presbyterian church and became a deacon. He was extremely circumspect in his behavior and intense in his spiritual devotion.

In 1853 he married Elinor Judkin, but his joy was short-lived because she died in childbirth just a year later. This devastating loss was the first real test of his faith, causing him to rededicate himself to Christ. He believed strongly in God's will and found comfort in the fact that God's providence assured him there was a purpose in his loss.

Jackson did not support the secession of the southern states, yet he remained a loyal Virginian. When Virginia seceded from the Union in 1861, Jackson accepted a commission in the Army of Northern Virginia. He earned his famous nickname "Stonewall" in the first battle of Bull Run, when his brigade stood firm against attack—like a stone wall.

Jackson's great courage in battle didn't go unnoticed. Another officer asked how he managed to remain so calm. He replied, "Captain, my religious belief teaches me to feel as safe in battle as in bed. God has fixed the time for my death. I do not concern myself about that, but to always be ready, no matter when it may overtake me. Captain, that is the way all men should live, and then all would be equally brave."

Jackson always gave God the credit for his victories. "Without God's blessing I look for no success, and for every success my prayer is, that all glory may be given unto Him to whom it is properly due." He was also known as a man of prayer. He prayed passionately before making decisions, and on the eve of battle he would wake up several times during the night to ask for God's guidance.

From 1861 to 1863 Jackson demonstrated his tactical genius in multiple campaigns: the Peninsular campaign, the Shenandoah Valley, Seven Days' Battles, Cross Keys, Port Republic, the second battle of Bull Run, Antietam, Fredricksburg, and others. Some of the soldiers privately considered him to be a religious extremist, but they respected him as a general too much to ever make fun of him.

During the battle of Chancellorsville, Jackson was caught in the friendly fire of his own men and shot in the arm. It had to be amputated, and as he was recovering, he caught pneumonia. General Lee[13] wrote him saying, "Could I have directed events, I should have chosen for the good of the country to be disabled in your stead. I congratulate you on the victory." When the letter was read to him, Jackson replied, "General Lee is very kind, but he should give the praise to God."

Jackson's condition continued to worsen, and on **May 10, 1863,** he slipped in and out of consciousness and then clearly uttered his last words, "Let us cross over the river, and rest under the shade of the trees." Then the soul of the great general passed into the peace of God.

Reflection

Jackson's trust in God enabled him to be brave and hopeful in all circumstances, including the death of his wife, life-threatening battles, and in the face of his own death. How does your faith affect how you live your life?

❦

Every child of God defeats this evil world by trusting Christ to give the victory.   1 JOHN 5:4

May 11

They died to win.

MARGARET MACLACHLAN and Margaret Wilson, Covenanters in Wigtown, Scotland, were tried for their faith on April 13, 1865, for refusing to take the Oath of Abjuration, which stated that the Church of God is a department of the State. Found guilty of rebellion, attending field meetings, and worshiping in places other than a church, they were ordered to receive their sentences on their knees. When they refused to bow before anyone but God, they were forced down to their knees and then were sentenced to death by drowning.

Margaret MacLachlan was a seventy-year-old widow who was highly respected by fellow Christians for her unwavering faith and godly life. She had been on her knees worshiping God with her family when she was arrested. While in prison awaiting trial she suffered greatly without food, light, or bed.

By contrast, Margaret Wilson was an eighteen-year-old serving maid who along with her brother and sister had fled to the mountains to escape persecution because they were followers of Covenanter James Renwick.[14] Their parents suffered greatly for the godly convictions of their children. Margaret's thirteen-year-old sister, Agnes, was arrested at the same time as her sister, but their father was able to post a heavy bond for her in time. It was too late for him to rescue Margaret.

On **May 11, 1685,** the two faithful Margarets were tied to posts and staked in the sea as the tide was rising. The older Margaret was farther out; the younger was near the shore. They were given many chances to recant their beliefs, but they both stood firm and resolute.

Margaret MacLachlan remained silent with her eyes closed throughout the ordeal, communing with Christ until death. As the tide overtook her and her body went limp, the soldiers said to the younger Margaret, "What do you think of her now?"

She replied, "Think! I see Christ wrestling there. Think ye that we are sufferers? No; it is Christ in us."

As the tide rose eighteen-year-old Margaret Wilson began to sing a Covenanter rendition of Psalm 25:7:

> *My sins and faults of youth*
> *Do thou, O Lord, forget:*
> *After Thy mercy think on me,*

San Marco to be incorporated into a new grouping of convents that would be more subject to the authority of Rome. Savonarola defied the order.

Savonarola's spiritual influence over Florence was so strong that during the carnival season in 1497 children gathered indecent books and pictures and made a bonfire of them in the main square while singing hymns. This "bonfire of vanities" was an affront to many of the city's moderates.

With the passage of time, community support for Savonarola's strict views started to wane, and his power began to erode. Pope Alexander VI sensed the changing heart of the people toward Savonarola and decided to make the most of it.

On **May 13, 1497,** Alexander VI excommunicated Savonarola from the church on the grounds that he had disobeyed the pope's commands. The pope ordered Florence to silence Savonarola or send him to Rome for trial. The fickle public abandoned him as the city government changed hands. The new government arrested Savonarola in April 1498. He was tried for sedition and heresy and was brutally tortured. On May 23, 1498, he was publicly hanged and his body burned.

In the succeeding years the majority of citizens of Florence went back to their old ways, yet many permanently changed. One of those was a sculptor named Michelangelo.

Reflection

Savonarola insisted that all Christians, especially religious leaders, practice what they preach. Would your family and friends say you practice what you preach? In our own strength it is impossible to live a Christian life, but if we give our allegiance to Jesus Christ, he will enable us to live more like him.

∽❧

God knew his people in advance, and he chose them to become like his Son.   ROMANS 8:29

May 14

How did Jesus' three years of public ministry begin and end?

JESUS' MINISTRY is bracketed by two periods of forty days. In the forty-day period preceding his ministry, Jesus[15] was led out into the wilderness by the Holy Spirit to be tempted by the devil. He ate nothing during all that time and became very hungry.

> Then the Devil came and said to him, "If you are the Son of God, change these stones into loaves of bread."
> But Jesus told him, "No! The Scriptures say, 'People need more than bread for their life; they must feed on every word of God.' "
> Then the Devil took him to Jerusalem, to the highest point of the Temple, and said, "If you are the Son of God, jump off! For the Scriptures say, 'He orders his angels to protect you. And they will hold you with their hands to keep you from striking your foot on a stone.' "
> Jesus responded, "The Scriptures also say, 'Do not test the Lord your God.' "
> Next the Devil took him to the peak of a very high mountain and showed him the nations of the world and all their glory. "I will give it all to you," he said, "if you will only kneel down and worship me."
> "Get out of here, Satan," Jesus told him. "For the Scriptures say, 'You must worship the Lord your God; serve only him.' "
> Then the Devil went away, and angels came and cared for Jesus. (Matthew 4:3-11)

Jesus had won the first round of his confrontation with Satan. But the great victory came three years later at the end of his ministry. On the cross Christ died to pay the penalty for the sins of his people, all those who sincerely put their trust in him. Jesus was buried and then on Easter morning rose from the dead. "The Devil . . . had the power of death" (Hebrews 2:14), but by his resurrection Christ defeated Satan, demonstrating that death could not hold the victorious Son of God.

In order to make sure that all his followers knew that he had risen from the dead and defeated Satan, Jesus appeared to them time after time during the forty-day period following his resurrection (Acts 1:3).

At the end of this final forty days, on **May 14, A.D. 33,** Jesus led his disciples to the village of Bethany on the Mount of Olives. There, while lifting up his hands to heaven, he blessed them, and while they were watching, he was taken up into the sky and disappeared into a cloud. As his disciples strained to see him, two white-robed men suddenly stood there among them and said, "Men of Galilee, why are you standing here staring at the sky? Jesus has been taken away from you into heaven. And someday, just as you saw him go, he will return" (Acts 1:11).

Jesus was triumphant over Satan in the wilderness and defeated him by his resurrection. One day, after Jesus' return, the devil will be thrown into the lake of fire (Revelation 20:10), defeated to tempt no more.

Reflection

What wonderful news that Jesus Christ has defeated Satan! What relevance does this defeat have to you personally?

∽❧∼

Because God's children are human beings—made of flesh and blood—Jesus also became flesh and blood by being born in human form. For only as a human being could he die, and only by dying could he break the power of the Devil, who had the power of death. Only in this way could he deliver those who have lived all their lives as slaves to the fear of dying. HEBREWS 2:14-15

May 15

They came from all over the world.

IN 63 B.C. the Roman armies invaded the land of Israel and made it part of the Roman Empire. Then Jesus came, and in response to the Jews' rejection of him as their Messiah, he predicted just before his death in A.D. 33 that the Jewish temple would be completely destroyed (Luke 21:6).[16] In addition, he foretold that a foreign army would conquer Jerusalem and that the Jews would be dispersed throughout the world (Luke 21:20-24). This prediction was fulfilled in A.D. 70 when, in response to an earlier Jewish revolt, the Roman armies destroyed the city of Jerusalem and its temple, killing hundreds of thousands of Jews and taking most of the survivors away captive.[17] After a second revolt in A.D. 135, no Jews lived in Jerusalem, and they became scattered throughout the world.

Then in the late 1800s in response to anti-Semitism, particularly in eastern Europe, a Jewish movement called Zionism arose. Its goal was to create an independent Jewish state in Palestine. In 1917 in an attempt to win Jewish support for World War I, England issued the Balfour Declaration, declaring England's support for "the establishment in Palestine of a national home for the Jewish people."[18] Following World War I, the League of Nations placed Palestine under the control of England.

As the persecution of Jews by the Nazis increased during the 1930s, large numbers of refugees fled to Palestine. In response, the Palestinian Arabs revolted against the British from 1936 to 1939. In 1939 Britain decided to limit Jewish immigration, arousing militant Jewish resistance.

During World War II six million Jews were murdered by the Nazis in the Holocaust. Following the war the British continued to limit Jewish immigration to Palestine. In response, large-scale resistance organizations began operating in Palestine. In the summer of 1946, England decided to turn the problem of Palestine over to the United Nations after one such organization, under the direction of future Israeli prime minister Menachem Begin, blew up one wing of the King David Hotel in Jerusalem, killing ninety-one.

When the matter came to a vote in the UN on November 29, 1947, the General Assembly endorsed a plan to create separate Jewish and Arab states, with Jerusalem as an international zone, due largely to U.S. president Harry Truman's strong support.

The British Mandate was scheduled to end on **May 15, 1948,** at which time their troops would begin leaving. The day before, a historic meeting was held in the exhibition hall of the art museum in Tel Aviv. At exactly 4:00 P.M. the meeting was called to order by David Ben-Gurion. The audience rose and sang "Hatikvah," the Jewish national anthem, accompanied by the Palestine Symphony Orchestra. Then David Ben-Gurion read in Hebrew Israel's Declaration of Independence. It ended with the words "We . . . hereby proclaim the establishment of the Jewish State in Palestine, to be called Israel." Everyone in the audience stood to their feet and applauded, many with tears streaming down their faces.

For the first time in more than two thousand years there was an independent Jewish state of Israel.

Reflection

About 585 B.C. God gave the prophet Ezekiel a vision of a valley filled with dry bones. As Ezekiel watched, first the bones came together and were covered with muscles and skin and formed dead corpses. Then God gave breath to them, and they came alive. After Ezekiel had seen the vision, God explained to him that the forming of the bones into corpses was a prophecy of how God would in the future bring the Jews back from exile into their land. This prophecy was fulfilled when Israel declared its independence from the rule of England (Ezekiel 37:1-13). The very existence of present-day Israel is a reminder to us of God's faithfulness in keeping his promises.

O my people, I will open your graves of exile and cause you to rise again. Then I will bring you back to the land of Israel. EZEKIEL 37:12

May 16

He was a general who spent his spare time ministering to the poor.

CHARLES GORDON, a famous and beloved English general, was born in 1833.[19] His masterful tactical skills, heroic bravery, and tragic death are well known historically, but his unwavering faith in God and tireless work for the poor are less well remembered.

In 1868 Gordon wrote a document called "My experiences showing the order in which God revealed himself to me." He wrote:

1. Ever since I remember, I had a belief that Jesus was the Son of God, and used to have feelings of deep depression on account of my faults at that time.
2. I knew Jesus to be my Saviour, and had assurance but was not established till I had gone through 10 years of captivity commencing at the Crimean War till 1864.
3. At my father's death I was brought to think how vain the world was to give satisfaction, but after my brother-in-law's death, and consequent seclusion at Gosport for a month, God made me count the cost and conclude that His service should be *all* and that if *everything* was given up, He would abundantly repay me in this world.
4. After a long dreary struggle (looked back on with horror) for 8 or 9 months of very earnest work, God began to bring under my body in this way.
5. He gave me first to see that the fruits of the Spirit could be only had by abiding in Christ or being joined to Him, but how joined was still a mystery.
6. [There is no record of number 6.]
7. Next He showed me that He was glorified only so far as those fruits were produced.
8. Next that the Holy Ghost produced them.
9. Next the great truth that it was the Holy Ghost *in me* which produced them while myself was dead and incapable of producing anything good.
10. Next that God *in me* gave out faith as the fire gives out heat. . . .

Shortly thereafter he began ministering at a rescue mission in the slums. From then on, almost every waking moment not spent on military duties was devoted to evangelism and work among the poor.

Gordon rescued countless boys off the street, teaching them the Bible and how to read and write. He gave out several hundred suits a year, bought boots by the gross, and helped many find jobs, speaking fondly of his boys as "kings."

He also helped the elderly, prostitutes, criminals, and the terminally ill.

On **May 16, 1870,** he was called to the bedside of a dying girl. His tender heart is reflected in a letter he wrote:

> There is a very beautiful young girl dying to-night; in a few short hours she will glide into a bright balmy land, and see such sights as would pass our understanding. She suffers much poor thing and makes one feel Oh! If I could soften this pang what would I not do. But still it must be true that it is better for her, that she should; otherwise God who loves her so deeply would alter it.

Of another deathbed visit he wrote:

> I went to Polly's and saw her off to the Golden City. She left at ten minutes to 12, very happily and beautifully. "What are those bands playing for," she said just before her departure. It was the Harpers with their harps, harping the Song of Moses and the Lamb as she neared the riverbank. Tune, tune your harps Ye saints in glory. All is well.

Reflection

Christians die in different ways. For some, as with the first young girl, there is intense pain and suffering. A few like Polly are welcomed to heaven by the music of the hosts of heaven. Whatever our lot, God will be there.

∞

They were all holding harps that God had given them. And they were singing the song of Moses, the servant of God, and the song of the Lamb.   REVELATION 15:2-3

May 17

A father's fervent prayer was answered after his death.

WILLIAM GRIMSHAW was a well-known pastor and evangelist in Haworth, England, during the mid-eighteenth century.[20] He and his first wife, Sarah, had two children, John and Jane, before Sarah died at the age of twenty-nine.

In 1748, when John was twelve and Jane was eleven, William sent them to be educated at the Kingswood School in Bristol, a boarding school started by George Whitefield[21] for the children of miners. In 1740 John Wesley[22] had turned it into a school for the children of itinerant preachers. Jane became very sick and died there at the age of twelve. William Grimshaw was devastated not to have been with his daughter at her death but was comforted by the story of the last words she uttered before dying:

> *He hath loved me, I cried,*
> *He hath suffered and died*
> *To redeem such a rebel as me.*

John showed no interest in studying or in spiritual matters, and William thought he should at least learn a trade. After Jane's death he brought John home from school to become a weaver's apprentice. He also wanted the boy nearer to himself so that he could encourage him in spiritual matters.

After losing his mother when he was three, his stepmother when he was ten, and his sister when he was thirteen, John was a troubled teenager with no personal faith of his own. He had spent many of his years at his grandparents' home or at boarding school because of his father's travels. He and Jane had inherited all of his maternal grandparents' substantial estate. Knowing that he would be getting a substantial legacy when he turned twenty-one added to his difficulties. He had no motivation to master his trade or to study and became a heavy drinker, fathering a child out of wedlock.

William Grimshaw hoped and prayed fervently that his son might find Christ. In a spirit of hopefulness for his son's salvation he wrote: "What inconceivable, incomprehensible, eternally durable pleasure it will afford us to meet and dwell for ever with those in heaven (whether they have gone thither before us or shall follow after us). . . . O what exquisite pleasure to see their faces. . . . Parents departed hence in the Lord rejoice over the conversion of their children, whom they left behind in their sins."

A FATHER'S PRAYER

In March 1763 William contracted a fatal infection after visiting a sick parishioner. As he lay on his deathbed, many people came to visit him, risking their own health in order to pay their last respects to their beloved pastor and friend. One of the people who came to visit at his bedside was John, now twenty-seven years old and still a drunkard. We do not know what was said between them; we do know that John went away burdened by the realization of his sinfulness for the first time. William died shortly thereafter and was buried near the pulpit in his church as he had requested.

Memories of his father plagued John with guilt. He regretted his prodigal ways and the torment he had caused his father while he was alive. John inherited the horse that his father rode on his evangelistic travels, and when he rode the horse, he would often say, "Once you carried a saint, but now you carry a devil."

Over the next years the burden of his sinfulness became intolerable, and he began to search for the God his father knew and loved. When he was only thirty-one, he fell ill and soon was near death. Before he died, John finally found his Savior. His father's prayers had been answered.

Remembering his father's great burden and hope for his salvation, John exclaimed with joy just before he died on **May 17, 1766,** "What will my father say when he sees me in heaven?"

Reflection

William Grimshaw loved and prayed for his son for many years without seeing any visible results. Yet even after he died, William bore witness to his son. His faithfulness was finally rewarded, although not in his lifetime. We must be faithful in our prayers and our witness to our loved ones who are without Christ, for God brings people to himself in his own time.

I appointed you to go and produce fruit that will last, so that the Father will give you whatever you ask for, using my name.   JOHN 15:16

May 18

They trusted not in chariots or horsemen, but in the living God.

DURING THE Civil War a revival spread throughout the Confederate army and many soldiers came to know Christ.[23] This was largely because many of the generals were dedicated Christians. The soldiers had strong spiritual leaders as well as military leaders.

Lieutenant General Leonides Polk, an Episcopalian, was one of those influential generals. General Polk was spiritually mentored by two of his close friends, E. M. Bounds, a chaplain who was later known for his books on prayer, and Frank Lyon, a leading Christian layman. Polk became known as a man of God among his troops, influencing not only his soldiers but also other generals on spiritual matters.

General Polk and General Hood were riding side by side one day discussing battle plans. General Hood had lost his leg in the battle of Chickamauga and had to be tied to his horse. The conversation shifted to spiritual things, as it often did in the presence of Polk, and Hood asked if he would be willing to baptize him. That night he baptized Hood in front of the troops against the background of artillery fire. It was moving for the soldiers to see their one-legged general leaning on his crutches, affirming his faith in Jesus and committing his life to him.

The wife of General Joseph Johnston had heard about General Hood's baptism, and she wrote to General Polk:

> You are never too much occupied, I well know, to pause to perform a good deed, and will, I am sure, even while leading your troops on to victory lead my soldier nearer to God. General Johnston has never been baptized, and it is the dearest wish of my heart that he would be and that you should perform the ceremony. It would be a great gratification to me. I have written to him on the subject and am sure he only waits your leisure. I rejoice that you are near him in these trying times. May God crown all your efforts with success and stay your life for your country and your friends.

On **May 18, 1864,** Johnston confessed publicly his faith in Jesus and was baptized by General Polk. Polk wrote of it to his wife, "It was a deep, solemn scene, and what a passage for history! God seemed to be drawing our hearts to

THE GODLY GENERAL

Him. Our trust is not in chariots or horsemen, but in the living God. May He take and keep all our hearts until that day."

Just a few weeks later the troops of Generals Polk and Johnston were stretched too thinly across the mountains north of Marietta, Georgia, making them vulnerable. On June 14 General Sherman's Union forces fired several rounds of cannon fire up the mountain toward Polk's troops. One shot exploded near General Polk, and shrapnel tore through his chest, killing him. In his blood-stained pocket were found three copies of a tract entitled *Balm for the Weary and Wounded*. They were inscribed to Generals Johnston, Hood, and Harding, and each had been signed, "With the compliments of Lt. Gen. Leonides Polk, June 12, 1864." He had undoubtedly intended to give them to his friends that morning.

When presented with his tract, General Johnston tearfully said, "The autograph, and the noble blood that almost effaces it, makes it a souvenir truly precious, one which I shall cherish while the Almighty leaves me on earth."

Reflection

General Polk had a great ministry to those within his sphere of influence. Even in the height of battle his thoughts went to the spiritual needs of those around him. To whom within your sphere of influence do you believe God would have you minister? Who needs to hear the good news of salvation or to be encouraged in their Christian walk? Ask God, and he will open the doors and show you in whom you can invest your life.

Now wherever we go he uses us to tell others about the Lord and to spread the Good News like a sweet perfume.   2 CORINTHIANS 2:14

May 19

She was England's first evangelical queen.

THE DAUGHTER of an English earl, Anne Boleyn was born in 1507. She and her older sister, Mary, had the honor of going to France and serving as "children-in-waiting" to the sister of Henry VIII, Mary, who married King Louis XII of France. He died only eighty-two days after the wedding. Anne remained in France as an aide to Queen Claude, the fifteen-year-old wife of twenty-year-old Francis I, the king who succeeded Louis XII.

While ten-year-old Anne was in France, Martin Luther nailed his Ninety-five Theses to the door of the Wittenberg Church.[24] The Reformation quickly spread into France, reaching a number of the nobility. One of the persons with whom Anne became friends was Marguerite d'Angoulême, the sister of Frances I and future queen of Navarre, who became one of the leaders of the French Reformation. Whether it was through Marguerite or someone else, Anne became a devout Christian.

Recalled to England in 1521, Anne became part of King Henry VIII's court along with her sister, Mary, who became a mistress of the king. Within a year, when Anne was still fifteen, she caught the eye of King Henry VIII[25] who began plotting to marry her. The problem was that he was already married to Catherine of Aragon. Nearing the end of her childbearing years, Catherine had not yet produced the male heir that Henry desperately desired.

When Henry asked Anne to become his mistress, she fell on her knees before him, saying, "I think your majesty, most noble and worthy king, speaketh these words in mirth to prove me, without intent of defiling your princely self, who I find thinks nothing less than of such wickedness which would justly procure the hatred of God and of your good queen against us."

In 1527 Henry VIII determined to divorce Catherine. Informing Anne of his plan, she agreed to marry him after his divorce. However, in order to obtain a divorce Henry needed the permission of the pope, and negotiations were painfully slow.

Finally in 1532 the archbishop of Canterbury died, and the evangelical Boleyn family was able to get Thomas Cranmer, a convert of the Reformation, selected as the next archbishop.[26] Meanwhile, Cranmer was in Germany consulting the university theologians on Henry's divorce problems and himself marrying the niece of one of the Lutheran Reformers.

By November 1532, convinced that once Cranmer was archbishop of

Canterbury a divorce would be forthcoming, Anne began living with her future husband. By the end of December, she suspected that she was pregnant; and in January Anne and Henry were married secretly, since the king's divorce from his first wife had not yet been granted.

Thomas Cranmer was installed as archbishop of Canterbury on March 30, 1533. He immediately granted Henry's divorce, and Parliament severed the ties of the Church of England with Rome, making Henry VIII head of the church.

As queen, Anne was the first to demonstrate how royalty could aid the Reformation. She appointed evangelical bishops and aided the evangelical cause through her carefully chosen personal chaplains, Nicholas Ridley[27] and others. Her personal life demonstrated her faith. Whenever she dined with her husband, she would discuss the Bible with him. She also helped distribute Bibles. As long as she was alive every parish in England was required to have an English Bible in its church. More important, she was a student of the Bible, preferring to read the Bible in French, the language in which she first heard the gospel.

Henry's affection for Anne faded when during her three years as queen she failed to produce a male heir, giving birth to only a daughter, the future Queen Elizabeth I. Having fallen in love with Jane Seymour, the king conspired to have Anne falsely convicted of adultery, and on **May 19, 1536,** Anne Boleyn was beheaded. Her last words were: "To Christ I commend my soul, Jesu, receive my soul."

Reflection

Anne Boleyn was a great Christian, but like King David, she used poor judgment in the area of moral restraint and began living with Henry VIII before they were married. How do you react when a Christian young woman around you becomes pregnant out of wedlock?

∽◌∾

[Jesus] said, "All right, stone her. But let those who have never sinned throw the first stones!"
JOHN 8:7

May 20

They were missionaries while still themselves a mission field.

JOHN AND Charles Wesley were born in 1703 and 1707 respectively, the fifteenth and eighteenth children of Samuel and Susanna Wesley.[28]

At Oxford they met frequently with George Whitefield[29] and others for Bible study and reflection. John was the leader of their group, which was mockingly called the "Holy Club."[30]

In 1735 the Wesleys sailed to America to become missionaries in the colony of Georgia. During the long journey the ship was buffeted by a violent storm, and John was left cowering in fear of death. He was amazed at the peace of the Moravian Christians aboard the same ship[31] and was shaken, realizing that they had something he didn't have.

On January 24, 1738, he wrote in his journal, "I went to America to convert the Indians; but O! who shall convert me? Who, what is he that shall deliver me from this evil heart of unbelief? I can talk well; nay, and believe myself while no danger is near; but let death look me in the face, and my spirit is troubled. Nor can I say, 'to die is gain.'"

After a short unsuccessful time in America, the brothers returned to England, where they came under the influence of Peter Boehler, another Moravian. Boehler's teachings on justification by faith, not works, were convincing. The Wesleys began eagerly reading Martin Luther's writings on Galatians and Romans, coming to the realization that their theology had been resting on works, not faith. This doctrine was now clear in their minds, but they did not yet have it in their hearts.

On **May 20, 1738,** the brothers and some friends stayed up all night praying for Charles, who was quite ill. They also were praying that God would open their hearts so they could truly believe and have assurance of salvation. The next day Charles believed and gave his life to Christ for the first time. "I now found myself at peace with God, and rejoiced in hope of loving Christ."

For three days John wrestled with what happened to his brother. He wanted to believe but couldn't and became very depressed. Then on May 24, 1738, he wrote in his journal: "In the evening I went very unwillingly to a society in Aldersgate Street, where one was reading Luther's preface to the Epistle to the Romans. About a quarter before nine, while he was describing the change which God works in the heart through faith in Christ, I felt my heart strangely warmed. I felt I did trust in Christ, Christ alone for salvation; and an assurance was given to me that he had taken away my sins, even mine, and saved me from the law of sin and death."

When John went to Charles to tell him the good news, he found him up late writing a hymn to celebrate his own conversion. They sang the hymn together. That night John went to bed, hoping he would still believe in the morning. He said of the next morning, "The moment I awaked, 'Jesus, Master,' was in my heart and in my mouth, and I found all my strength lay in keeping my eye fixed upon him."

John and Charles Wesley went on to lead the great Methodist revival that changed English society. When Charles died in 1788, he had written almost eight thousand hymns. John preached nonstop until his death in 1791.

Reflection

John and Charles Wesley were very religious for a number of years before they became Christians. Justification by faith through grace was the amazing truth that at last brought the Wesleys' peace and assurance. With what in their experiences can you identify? Where are you in your spiritual pilgrimage? The lives of the Wesleys illustrate the fact that religious activity cannot get us into heaven. That comes only through personal faith in the Lord Jesus Christ.

On judgment day many will tell me, "Lord, Lord, we prophesied in your name and cast out demons in your name and performed many miracles in your name." But I will reply, "I never knew you. Go away."
MATTHEW 7:22-23

May 21

The loss of a brother gave the world a song.

In 1868 in Scotland, Elizabeth Clephane wrote a poem called "The Lost Sheep." Also called "The Ninety and Nine," it depicts the Good Shepherd leaving his flock of sheep to find the one that was lost.

Sixteen years before, Elizabeth's brother George had left the family and gone to Canada. There he collapsed on a country road in a drunken stupor and died the next day. Elizabeth had often thought about the story of the Good Shepherd, fantasizing that Christ the Shepherd had found her brother, the lost sheep, before his death. When asked to contribute a poem for a Christian magazine, she wrote this poem out of her grief and hope for her brother's salvation.

In 1874 D. L. Moody, the American evangelist,[32] and Ira Sankey, his song leader, went on an evangelistic tour of Scotland. On May 20 the two men were on their way to Edinburgh for two days of meetings. Sankey picked up a newspaper called the *Christian Age* to read on the train. In it, his eyes were drawn to Elizabeth Clephane's poem, "The Lost Sheep." Its words moved him deeply, and he thought it would make an excellent evangelistic hymn. He enthusiastically read it to Moody but then realized that Moody was busy reading a letter and had not listened to him. Nevertheless, Sankey ripped the poem out of the newspaper and began mulling over tunes in his head.

The next day, **May 21, 1874,** the theme for their meeting at the Free Church Assembly Hall was "The Good Shepherd." Moody and several other ministers spoke. The audience was deeply moved by the truths of Jesus as the Good Shepherd. After the messages Moody, as chairman of the meeting, turned to Sankey and said, "Have you a solo appropriate for this subject, to close the service with?"

Sankey was startled to be put on the spot and quickly tried to think of something. "At this moment I seemed to hear a voice saying: *Sing the hymn you found on the train!*" Sankey thought this was crazy because it was a poem without music, not a hymn! He had not yet had time to compose a tune. Moody and the audience waited, and again the thought came, *Sing that hymn!*

Sankey recalls, "Placing the little newspaper slip on the organ in front of me, I lifted my heart in prayer, asking God to help me so to sing that the people might hear and understand. Laying my hands upon the organ I struck the key of A flat and began to sing:

THE NINETY AND NINE

"There were ninety and nine that safely lay
In the shelter of the fold;
But one was out on the hills away,
Far off from the gates of gold—
Away on the mountains wild and bare,
Away from the tender Shepherd's care,
Away from the tender Shepherd's care."

After the first verse, Sankey was afraid the other verses would sound different from the first. But he prayed, and the Lord gave him the same tune for the other verses, note for note. His voice was triumphant as he sang the final verse:

"But all through the mountains, thunder riven,
And up from the rocky steep,
There arose a cry to the gate of heaven,
'Rejoice! I have found My sheep!'
And the angels echoed round the throne:
'Rejoice, for the Lord brings back His own!'
'Rejoice, for the Lord brings back His own!' "

The rapt audience was overcome with emotion, as was Moody. He said, "Sankey, where did you get that hymn? I never heard the like of it in my life!'

Sankey replied, "Mr. Moody, that's the hymn I read to you yesterday on the train, which you did not hear."

Reflection

The Lord seeks his lost sheep and rejoices when they are found. This story spoke powerfully to Elizabeth Clephane, Ira Sankey, D. L. Moody, and those present at the meeting on May 21, 1874. What does it mean to you? Are you a lost sheep or are you safe in the fold?

Heaven will be happier over one lost sinner who returns to God than over ninety-nine others who are righteous and haven't strayed away!

LUKE 15:7

May 22

It was to be his biggest crusade to date.

BILLY GRAHAM was born into a Christian family in 1918 near Charlotte, North Carolina.[33] He regularly attended church and held to the strong moral values his parents had instilled in him. When Billy was almost sixteen, a colorful evangelist named Mordecai Ham was conducting services in Charlotte. Billy grudgingly attended a meeting at the urging of his parents. The evangelist intrigued him with his keen sense of humor yet harsh condemnation of sin. Billy returned night after night.

Graham recalled: "I became deeply convicted about my sinfulness and rebellion. And confused. How could this evangelist be talking to me, of all people? I had been baptized as a baby, had learned the Shorter Catechism word perfect, and had been confirmed. . . . I was even the vice president of my youth group in our church. . . . What was slowly dawning on me during those weeks was the miserable realization that I did not know Jesus Christ for myself. I could not depend on my parents' faith."

One night when Dr. Ham gave the invitation to accept Jesus, Billy responded. He was guided through a simple prayer in which he committed himself to Christ. That night in his room he prayed for the first time without having been told to do so.

Graham felt called to be a preacher, and his evangelistic ministry expanded rapidly. He began holding citywide crusades by the late 1940s. He first attracted national attention at his 1949 Los Angeles Crusade in which several famous people were converted.

Five years later he was on his way to England for the Greater London Crusade. There had been many months of planning, and this was to be his largest and longest crusade yet. While on the boat, he was confronted by a radio news report that stated that a Labour member of Parliament would challenge in Commons the admission of Billy Graham to England on the grounds that he was interfering in British politics under the guise of religion.

Apparently material distributed in England about the upcoming crusade contained a statement condemning socialism. In Britain the term *socialism* was almost synonymous with the Labour Party. The English took this as a political insult. Graham issued apologies to Parliament and explained to the press that the publication condemned secularism in general, not a particular political view. Although the incident was stressful, it brought much more publicity to the crusade than ever could have been purchased!

March 1, 1954, the first day of the crusade, brought rain, sleet, and doubts. Graham wasn't sure if people would come. The arena held 12,000, but an hour before the crusade only 2,000 people had arrived. He and his staff continued to pray, and when he arrived at the arena, it was filled past capacity. At the invitation 200 came forward.

For three months Graham held nightly meetings. Each night brought larger crowds with the police turning thousands away. The press was amazed at Graham's ability to reach people from every facet of society.

May 22, 1954, the last day of the Greater London Crusade, Graham was exhausted. The final meeting was held in a stadium seating one hundred thousand. The weather was terrible, but every seat was filled, and an additional 22,000 were allowed to sit on the playing field. Graham preached on "Choose This Day Whom You Will Serve." He did not know where he was going to find the strength to preach, but as he looked out over the crowd of 122,000 wet, cold people, God gave him the strength. Over 2,000 people came forward that night.

In all, more than 38,000 people made professions of faith during the Greater London Crusade. As their bus slowly made its way through the shouting, waving crowds leaving the stadium, Graham and his team sang together, "Praise God from Whom All Blessings Flow."

Reflection

What do you believe has been the secret to Billy Graham's success? God called him to a role that is unique to him, but he has a role for each one of us. What can you learn from Billy Graham's life?

∽

Work at bringing others to Christ.   2 TIMOTHY 4:5

May 23

He was right under her nose.

MALLA MOE, a Norwegian immigrant to America, went to Swaziland, Africa, as a missionary with the Scandinavian Alliance Mission in 1892. She had no formal theological training but an incredible burden for lost souls. Her entire life was devoted to winning Africans to Christ. She served the Lord in Swaziland until her death in 1953, two months shy of her ninetieth birthday.

After a few years in Swaziland, Malla began to feel overwhelmed by the preaching and teaching demands of her ministry. While praying that God would send her a helper, she heard a voice say, "I will send someone to work with you," but so far God had sent no one. Little did she know that he was there all the time—in the kitchen!

Mapelepele Gamede, a teenager, was working in the kitchen of the mission. He liked working for the kind Norwegian-American missionary, and to please her he had been baptized and had changed his name to Johane. A few days after his baptism, Malla and a visiting missionary couple planned to travel back to Malla's former mission station with Johane serving as their guide. Before the group left, Johane had an argument with one of the missionaries about how much money he was owed. He became so angry that he refused to lead the group and instead set off on foot for his home, leaving the missionaries to make the difficult journey on their own.

A few days into the journey a humbled Johane caught up with the group. He had been attacked by two men who wanted money, and his leg had been injured. He said, "I know I did wrong in being angry. I kneeled down and asked God to forgive me, and He led me to you." Malla forgave him and patched up his leg. He led them the rest of the way, and on **May 23, 1895,** the group arrived safely at their destination, the Bulunga mission station.

In Bulunga Malla continued to pray that God would send her a helper. While praying, she heard the same voice as before saying, "There's your boy!" Immediately she knew that her helper would be Johane.

Johane, however, was not so easily convinced—he was a very timid young man who could not read and was petrified at the thought of preaching. He couldn't study the Bible because of his seeming lack of ability to learn to read. He was convinced he would never learn. "I have prayed, but it doesn't help. God does not want me to learn." He was so discouraged that Malla was afraid he would give up and leave her, but she continued to pray for him.

THE MIRACLE OF JOHANE

One night Johane had a vision in which a man in a white gown asked him how many days he had left. When Johane answered that he did not know, the man answered, "I know how many days you have, and you shall receive your reward from me." Johane was very frightened.

The next day Johane was nowhere to be found. Malla was worried that he had given up and had left the mission station. Much to Malla's relief, that night Johane walked into the mission with a triumphant smile on his face and his Bible in his hand. "God has taught me to read. I went up to the mountain and prayed to Him. He said He would teach me, and when I opened the book, I could read."

Much to Malla's amazement, he could read! It was truly a miracle. And just as miraculous was Johane's change of heart. He was a completely different person. Not only could he now read the Bible, but his faith was truly his own! Immediately he began preaching to his people with great boldness. In an instant he had become the helper she had been fervently praying for!

Reflection

Have you ever tried to act religious, only to find that it didn't work? Baptism and religious activity won't change our lives, as Johane discovered. Only Christ can do that, and it is he who is pursuing us.

And I, the Son of Man, have come to seek and save those . . . who are lost.   Luke 19:10

May 24

No one had ever seen anything like this before.

IT WAS Pentecost, **May 24, A.D. 33,** the fiftieth day after the Sabbath of Passover week. Pentecost marked the beginning of the Feast of Weeks, one of the three annual feasts when every male Jew was required to appear at the temple. It was a festival of joy with the presenting of the first fruits of the grain harvest to the Lord.

Just ten days earlier Jesus had ascended into heaven,[34] and in keeping with his instructions, the disciples had stayed on in Jerusalem. They were meeting together when suddenly they heard a loud roaring like a mighty wind, and it filled the house where they were meeting. Then they saw what looked like tongues of fire on each other's heads. They remembered how Jesus had spoken of a baptism of fire, and now here was a fire and they weren't being burned by it! (Acts 2:1-3).

And if the fire weren't miraculous enough, they began speaking in languages they didn't know! Jews from many nations were in Jerusalem at the time, and when they came running to see what all the ruckus was about—the roaring wind, the nonburning flames on the believers' heads, and preaching in many languages—they were bewildered to hear their own languages being spoken by the believers:

"How can this be?" they exclaimed. "These people are all from Galilee, and yet we hear them speaking the languages of the lands where we were born!" . . . But others in the crowd were mocking. "They're drunk, that's all!" they said.

Then Peter stepped forward with the eleven other apostles and shouted to the crowd, "Listen carefully, all of you, fellow Jews and residents of Jerusalem! Make no mistake about this. Some of you are saying these people are drunk. It isn't true! It's much too early for that. People don't get drunk by nine o'clock in the morning. No, what you see this morning was predicted centuries ago by the prophet Joel: 'In the last days, God said, I will pour out my Spirit upon all people. Your sons and daughters will prophesy. . . . And anyone who calls on the name of the Lord will be saved.'

"People of Israel, listen! God publicly endorsed Jesus of Nazareth by doing wonderful miracles, wonders, and signs through him, as you well know. But you followed God's prearranged plan. With the help of lawless Gentiles, you nailed him to the cross and murdered him. However, God released him from the horrors of death and raised him back to life again, for death could not keep him in its grip. . . ."

Peter's words convicted them deeply, and they said to him and to the other apostles, "Brothers, what should we do?"

Peter replied, "Each of you must turn from your sins and turn to God, and be baptized in the name of Jesus Christ for the forgiveness of your sins. Then you will receive the gift of the Holy Spirit. This promise is to you and to your children, and even to the Gentiles—all who have been called by the Lord our God. . . ."

Those who believed what Peter said were baptized and added to the church—about three thousand in all. They joined with the other believers and devoted themselves to the apostles' teaching and fellowship, sharing in the Lord's Supper and in prayer. (Acts 2:7-42)

It was a memorable day for the fledgling church, and Peter's instructions are just as true for the church today.

Reflection

Have you believed and been baptized like the converts on the day of Pentecost? Do you join with other believers in learning, fellowship, the Lord's Supper, and prayer? In which areas do you need to become more faithful?

All the believers met together constantly and shared everything they had. They sold their possessions and shared the proceeds with those in need. They . . . met in homes for the Lord's Supper, and shared their meals with great joy and generosity—all the while praising God and enjoying the goodwill of all the people. And each day the Lord added to their group those who were being saved. ACTS 2:44-47

May 25

What would you write in a last letter to an aging parent?

ARCHIBALD ALEXANDER was a Presbyterian pastor who became the first professor at Princeton Seminary in 1812.[35] His reputation for sound scholarship and his commitment to God and to his students followed him throughout his life.

When his aging mother was in failing health, he lovingly wrote the following letter to comfort her:

> *Princeton, May 25, 1823*
> *My Dear Mother:*
> *When I last saw you, it was very doubtful whether you would ever rise again from the bed to which you were confined. Indeed, considering your great age, it was not to be expected that you should entirely recover your usual health. I was much gratified to find that in the near prospect of eternity, your faith did not fail but that you could look death in the face without dismay, and felt willing, if it were the will of God, to depart from this world of sorrow and disappointment. But it has pleased your Heavenly Father to continue you a little longer in the world. I regret to learn that you have endured much pain from a disease of your eyes, and that you have been less comfortable than formerly. Bodily affliction you must expect to endure as long as you continue in the world. . . . While your Heavenly Father continues you in the troublesome world, he will, I trust, enable you to be resigned and contented and patient under the manifold afflictions which are incident to old age.*
> *The great secret of true comfort lies in a single word, TRUST. Cast your burdens on the Lord, and he will sustain them. If your evidences of being in the favour of God are obscured, if you are doubtful of your acceptance with him, still go directly to him by faith; that is, trust in his mercy and in Christ's merits. Rely simply on his word of promise. Be not afraid to exercise confidence. There can be no deception in depending entirely on the Word of God. It is not presumption to trust in him when he has commanded us to do so. We dishonour him by our fearfulness and want of confidence. We thus call in question his faithfulness and his goodness. Whether your mind is comfortable or distressed, flee for refuge to the outstretched wings of his protection and mercy. There is all fullness in him; there is all willingness to bestow what we*

need. He says, "My grace is sufficient for thee. My strength is made perfect in weakness. As the day is so shall thy strength be. I will never leave thee nor forsake thee. Though I walk through the valley of the shadow of death, I will fear no evil; for thou art with me; thy rod and thy staff they comfort me." Be not afraid of the pangs of death. Be not afraid that your Redeemer will then be afar off. Grace to die comfortable is not commonly given until the trial comes. Listen not to the tempter, when he endeavours to shake your faith, and destroy your comfort. Resist him, and he will flee from you. . . . My sincere prayer is, that your sun may set in serenity; that your latter end may be like that of the righteous; and that your remaining days, by the blessing of God's providence and grace, may be rendered tolerable and even comfortable.

It is not probable that we shall ever meet again in this world; and yet, as you have already seen one of your children go before you, you may possibly live to witness the departure of more of us. . . . May we all be ready! And may we all meet around the throne of God, where there is not separation for ever and ever! Amen!

I remain, your affectionate son,

A. A.

Reflection

Letter writing provides the writer with the opportunity to choose words carefully and the receiver the opportunity to read and reread the letter. If you were to write a final letter to a parent or loved one, what would you say in it? What truths or words of comfort would you particularly want to include?

Night and day I constantly remember you in my prayers.

2 TIMOTHY 1:3

May 26

Where is the joy?

ON WEDNESDAY, January 24, 1738, John Wesley grudgingly accompanied a friend to Aldersgate Street in London for a meeting of the Moravians, the followers of Count Nikolaus von Zinzendorf.[36] There the leader was reading Martin Luther's preface to his commentary on the book of Romans. In his journal Wesley recorded what happened that night: "I felt my heart strangely warmed. I felt I did trust in Christ, Christ alone, for salvation; and an assurance was given me that He had taken away my sins. . . .But it was not long before the enemy suggested, 'This cannot be faith; for where is thy joy?' "

That night John went to see his brother Charles, who himself had been converted just three days earlier.[37] Charles was overflowing with newfound joy, but John had no such feelings.

The next day after attending a service at St. Paul's Cathedral he recorded in his journal: "I could taste the good word of God in the anthem, which began, 'My song shall be always of the loving-kindness of the Lord: with my mouth will I ever be showing forth thy truth from one generation to another.' Yet the enemy injected a fear, 'If thou dost believe, why is there not a more sensible change?' I answered (yet not I), 'That I know not. But this I know, I have "now peace with God." ' "

Two days later on **May 26, 1738,** John, perplexed that he still did not have the joy he felt he should have, went to seek the counsel of John Toeltschig, an older Moravian friend who had befriended him during his missionary days in Georgia. Toeltschig was passing through London on his way back to Herrnhut, the Moravian headquarters in Saxony, Germany. Wesley explained to Toeltschig that he knew that he had experienced the new birth and that his salvation rested not on good works but on the death of Christ for him, but he had no joy and was still buffeted by temptations. "What should I do?" he asked his friend.

Toeltschig's answer was, "You must not fight them as you did before. You must flee from them the moment they appear and take shelter in the wounds of Jesus."

After his visit with Toeltschig, John Wesley went on to evensong at St. Paul's Cathedral, where he found further encouragement as the choir sang, "My soul truly waiteth still upon God, for of him cometh my salvation; he verily is my strength and my salvation, he is my defense, so that I shall not greatly fall."

THE ROLE OF EMOTION

Day after day he spent much time in prayer and found himself growing more in spiritual strength "so that though I was now assaulted by many temptations, I was more than conqueror, gaining more power thereby to trust and to rejoice in God my Saviour." Yet joy continued to elude him.

A few days later he wrote in his journal: "I determined, if God should permit, to retire for a short time into Germany. I had fully proposed, before I left Georgia, so to do, if it should please God to bring me back to Europe. And I now clearly saw the time was come. My weak mind could not bear to be thus sawn asunder. And I hoped the conversing with those holy men who were themselves living witnesses of the full power of faith, and yet able to bear with those that are weak, would be a means, under God, of so establishing my soul, that I might go on from faith to faith, and from strength to strength."

Three weeks after his conversion at the Aldersgate meeting, Wesley left with Toeltschig and several others to go to Herrnhut, the Moravian center in Saxony. There in Germany he grew in his newfound faith. When he returned to England three months later, the joy of the Lord had become his strength.[38]

Reflection

John Wesley learned a valuable lesson in the days immediately following his conversion. He learned that faith does not depend upon feeling. Some Christians experience great joy at conversion; others do not. Salvation is not a matter of emotions; it is wholeheartedly putting our trust in Jesus Christ as our Lord and Savior.

You will grow and experience the joy of your faith.   PHILIPPIANS 1:25

May 27

He crowned the king, and the king gave him an even better crown.

ONE OF the privy councillors of Scotland beginning in 1628 was Archibald Campbell, the eighth earl of Argyll. In February 1638 when Scottish people of all ranks signed the Scottish National Covenant, an oath that bound them to keep the church free of governmental control, Argyll did not sign it but tried to persuade the king to compromise with the signers, now called Covenanters. However, by November he had joined the Covenanters and immediately became one of their leaders. When King Charles I visited Scotland in 1641, he recognized Argyll's prominence by making him a marquis. Argyll helped write the Solemn League and Covenant of 1643 in which the signatories swore to maintain the Reformed faith in Scotland.

After the execution of King Charles I in England, Argyll, a supporter of the monarchy, personally crowned Charles II as king of Scotland at Scone on New Year's Day 1651, the last coronation of a king in Scotland. Cromwell's Commonwealth temporarily replaced the monarchy, but in 1660, Charles II was restored to the throne, and Argyll went to London to congratulate him. Friends warned him that there was danger ahead, and the king never gave him an audience. Instead, he ordered that the marquis of Argyll be imprisoned for treason in the Tower of London, where he was kept in chains throughout the summer and autumn. In December he was sent back to Scotland to stand trial before the Parliament in Edinburgh.

The verdict of the trial was a foregone conclusion, for the king wished him to be executed. The young lawyers who finally agreed to defend him were harassed and not given enough time to prepare a proper defense for the charges against him: that he was a Covenanter, that he had cooperated with Cromwell, and that he questioned the Divine Right of kings. He was found guilty of high treason and sentenced to be executed at Edinburgh on Monday, **May 27, 1661.** When denied a last petition to the king, he responded, "I had the honour to set the crown on the king's head, and now he hastens me to a better crown than his own."

He was allowed to spend his last weekend with his wife, and during those two days he felt a calm and courage he attributed to "the special mercy of God." He told her, "For my part, I am as content to be here as in the castle, and I was as content in the castle as in the Tower of London, and there I was as content as when at liberty; and I hope to be as content upon the scaffold as in any of them all."

On the fateful Monday he rose early to write letters and see friends. He warned his minister friends that they must "either suffer much or sin much." To his daughter-in-law he wrote, "What shall I say in this great day of the Lord, wherein in the midst of a cloud, I have found a fair sunshine. I can wish no more for you, but that the Lord may comfort you, and shine upon you as He does upon me, and give you that same sense of His love in staying in the world, as I have in going out of it." He wrote King Charles I, adding the prayer that "your Majesty and your successors may always sway the scepter of these nations, and that they may be a blessed people under your government."

When the two o'clock execution neared, he walked to the scaffold, a model of decorum. The ministers prayed, and he spoke his parting words: "I bless the Lord, I pardon all men, as I desire to be pardoned myself."

Reflection

Being involved in politics was dangerous business in the 1600s. To be on the losing side often meant a trip to the scaffold. Yet Archibald Campbell and many others like him were willing to give their lives to stand up for God's people and God's principles. How seriously do you take your role as citizen? Might God be asking you to do more than merely vote?

Whatever you do or say, let it be as a representative of the Lord Jesus.
COLOSSIANS 3:17

May 28

He tried to dispel the rumors about him.

PAUL'S THIRD missionary journey had been very rewarding. The Roman province of Asia, along the seacoast of modern Turkey, was now evangelized, and the churches of Greece were doing well.

His next objective was to go to Jerusalem with a collection for the poor (1 Corinthians 16:1-4). Paul[39] and his traveling companions arrived in Jerusalem, where they stayed at the home of Mnason, one of the early disciples. As the news of Paul's arrival spread, many Christians came to welcome him to Jerusalem.

On **May 28, A.D. 57**, the day after his arrival, Paul went with his traveling companions to meet with James, the brother of Jesus (Matthew 13:55) and leader of the church in Jerusalem. All the elders of the church in Jerusalem were also present.

Paul first gave a detailed account of the things God had accomplished among the Gentiles through his ministry (Acts 21:19). Then he presented to James the offering he had collected in the Gentile churches for the poor of the church in Jerusalem.

Paul's report and the generous gift caused the elders to praise God. But at the same time there was an issue they felt they needed to get off their chests. Many thousands of Jews in the Jerusalem church were trusting Jesus as their Messiah but also were very zealous for keeping the laws of the Old Testament. Among the Hebrew Christians of Jerusalem it was widely rumored that not only was Paul teaching his Gentile converts that they did not need to keep the Old Testament law, but he was also encouraging Jewish converts to stop following the law of Moses.

Eight years earlier the Jerusalem Council had officially determined that it was not necessary for Gentile Christians to keep the Old Testament Law, but that ruling was irrelevant to many of the Hebrew Christians of Jerusalem. There was so much opposition to Paul in the Jerusalem church over this issue that the leaders felt that Paul needed to do something to counter the rumors about himself. And the church leadership had a specific suggestion.

Four Hebrew Christians in the church of Jerusalem had taken a temporary Nazirite vow, a special Old Testament oath of consecration to God. Temporary Nazirite vows typically lasted thirty days. However, if the person became ceremonially unclean, by going near a dead body, for example, he had to undergo purification rites at the temple, shave his head on the seventh day, and start his vow all over again. Apparently these four had become unclean and needed purification. James and the elders therefore suggested to Paul, "Go with them to the Temple and join them in the purification ceremony, and pay for them to have their heads shaved. Then everyone will know that the rumors are all false and that you yourself observe the Jewish laws" (Acts 21:24). Then, fearing that Paul might think they were going back on the decision of the Jerusalem Council, they added, "As for the Gentile Christians, all we ask of them is what we already told them in a letter: They should not eat food offered to idols, nor consume blood, nor eat meat from strangled animals, and they should stay away from all sexual immorality" (Acts 21:25).

Paul agreed with their request in order to halt the rumors and went through the purification ritual with the four men.

Reflection

Do you think that Paul did the right thing in agreeing to go through this Jewish ritual? Paul's strategy was to observe the cultural norms of whatever group he was with so as not to alienate them from Christ.

I have become a servant of everyone so that I can bring them to Christ. When I am with the Jews, I become one of them so that I can bring them to Christ. When I am with those who follow the Jewish laws, I do the same, even though I am not subject to the law, so that I can bring them to Christ. When I am with the Gentiles who do not have the Jewish laws, I fit in with them as much as I can. In this way, I gain their confidence and bring them to Christ. 1 CORINTHIANS 9:19-20

May 29

They followed the star.

ANCIENT Persia had a priestly caste called Magi, who are mentioned by the prophet Daniel (Daniel 2:2, 4-5, 10). Astrology was very popular in the ancient Near East, and the magi were both astrologers and astronomers.

Early Jews also were interested in astrology. One of their messianic prophecies said, "A star will rise from Jacob" (Numbers 24:17). To them Jupiter was "the king's planet" and Saturn was Israel's "defender." An old Jewish proverb said, "God created Saturn to shield Israel."

Early astrologers observed that planets move in a belt in the heavens they termed the zodiac. They divided the zodiac into twelve equal blocks, or signs. According to Chaldean astrology, each sign represented a different nation. Pisces, the sign of the fish, represented Amurru, which included Syria and Palestine. To Jewish astrologers Pisces represented Judea. They predicted that the Messiah would appear when Saturn, their "defender," met Jupiter, "the king's planet" in Pisces. Since many of the Jews did not return from the Babylonian captivity and continued to live in Persia, the magi would have been familiar with Jewish astrological beliefs.

In 7 B.C. Jupiter and Saturn came together in Pisces for the first time in 853 years. Shortly before sunrise on April 12, 7 B.C., Jupiter and Saturn emerged together out of the dawn in Pisces. They began moving together until on **May 29, 7 B.C.**, they were in conjunction, passing within less than one degree of each other. Then they began moving apart. The magi no doubt watched this with great interest, knowing of the Jewish expectation.

In early August the two planets stopped moving apart, and in late September and early October began moving toward each other even more quickly this time for a second conjunction in Pisces.

October passed, and the planets continued to separate. After just a month they began approaching one another a third time. Finally on December 4, 7 B.C., the third conjunction of Jupiter and Saturn in Pisces occurred.

The magi would have tried to understand the significance of what they had seen. Something important was going to happen in Judea. Could it be the birth of the Jewish Messiah?

Then in February 6 B.C. something unexpected happened. Mars, which had been far away in the sky a few months earlier, now joined Jupiter and Saturn in Pisces. Again the attention of the astrologers was drawn to Judea. Mars was thought to represent war. Could this be indicating that the Messiah, the defender of Israel, was about to arise and defeat his enemy? This would be in line with the final prophecy of Balaam:

> *I see him, but not in the present time.*
> *I perceive him, but far in the distant future.*
> *A star will rise from Jacob; a scepter will emerge from Israel.*
> (Numbers 24:17)

One year later in February or early March 5 B.C., blazing across the sky from the east came a nova, a star that suddenly explodes, becoming ten thousand to one hundred thousand times brighter than it was before. The nova was heading toward Judea, and the magi decided to follow it. The nova was visible for more than ten weeks. If the magi left Persia shortly after it first appeared, they would have been able to reach Bethlehem while it was still visible.

When the magi reached Jerusalem, they apparently had lost sight of the star because they asked where the king of the Jews was to be born. This was no doubt caused by the fact that once a month the moon would hide the light of the nova.

When the nova reappeared, it would have been fifty degrees high due south of Jerusalem at dawn—directly over Bethlehem! When they saw the star, they were filled with joy and followed it to the house where Jesus and Mary were. There they fell down before Jesus and worshiped him (Matthew 2:1-11).

Reflection

How do you react to learning that astronomers have been able to figure out the signs in the heavens that apparently led the magi to worship Jesus? Does it surprise you? Will you join them in worshiping him?

∽❧

Then they opened their treasure chests and gave him gifts of gold, frankincense, and myrrh.　　　　MATTHEW 2:11

May 30

He was the loose cannon of church reform in Czechoslovakia.

JEROME of Prague was a tall, black-bearded, hotheaded, adventurous Reformer of the Catholic Church in the 1390s. His friend Jan Hus,[40] also a Reformer, had encouraged him to travel to England to study the teachings of John Wycliffe, the English Reformer. Jerome went to Oxford and immersed himself in the works of Wycliffe. Returning to Prague, he brought Wycliffe's books back to Hus and the other Czech Reformers.

Jerome had a restless and adventurous spirit. He loved to travel abroad, spreading his message of reform, but frequently returned home to his beloved Prague to reconnect with Hus. He traveled to Jerusalem, Paris, Poland, Lithuania, Heidelberg, Cologne, Vienna, Russia, and Hungary. His ability as an orator and his respect as one of the most able scholars of his day provided him opportunities to address university crowds. He created a commotion wherever he went with his fiery condemnation of the corruption within the Catholic Church. He barely escaped each city, always leaving behind enraged university masters and church authorities.

When Hus was arrested and brought to Constance in 1414, Jerome promised him he would come to his aid. Hus wrote to Jerome and warned him not to come. However, true to his daring spirit, Jerome secretly entered the city on April 4, 1415. He boldly posted inflammatory signs around the city demanding the right to speak before the council in his and Hus's defense and requested a pledge of protection. When he was given no assurance of security, he attempted to flee the city. He almost escaped but was captured and thrown into prison.

While Jerome was imprisoned in stocks and chains, Hus was burned at the stake as a heretic, remaining faithful to the end. After Hus's death, Jerome recanted all that he had previously proclaimed, expecting thereby to be set free. He confessed loyalty to the Catholic Church and pronounced Wycliffe and Hus to be heretics. To his dismay, Jerome was not set free after his recantation but kept in prison for many months. The council, believing that not even a recantation should save a heretic from execution, pressed for a new trial at which he could be condemned. Meanwhile Jerome was feeling great remorse over his disloyalty to his Lord. At the ensuing trial Jerome denounced his recantation, saying that he said those things "for fear of death," and he publicly resolved to defend God's truth until death. He demanded a hearing to plead his case, but the council refused to hear his defense. He angrily replied, "What iniquity is this! While I have languished for three hundred and fifty days in the most cruel prisons, in stench, squalor, excrements, and chains, lacking all things, you have ever heard my adversaries and slanderers; but me you now refuse to hear even for an hour! . . . For you have already in your minds condemned me as an unworthy man, before you could learn what I really am. But you are men, not gods, not immortals, but mortals!"

Jerome's impassioned speech impressed a few bystanders, but the council quickly condemned him to death.

For his execution he was made to wear a tall paper hat painted with red devils. Jerome said, "Our Lord Jesus Christ, when he suffered death for me, a most miserable sinner, did wear a crown of thorns upon his head; and I for his sake will wear this adorning of derision and blasphemy."

As he was led to the same place where Hus had been burned to death, Jerome sang hymns in Latin and Czech, continuing to sing as the wood was piled around him. On **May 30, 1416,** Jerome of Prague, wearing his paper crown, was burned at the stake.

Reflection

Jerome denied his Lord as the apostle Peter had done, yet he recanted and was forgiven. Have you ever denied your Lord? What factors caused you to do this? If we confess our denials to God as Peter and Jerome of Prague did, God can enable us not to do it again.

∽◦◦∾

If anyone acknowledges me publicly here on earth, I will openly acknowledge that person before my Father in heaven. But if anyone denies me here on earth, I will deny that person before my Father in heaven. MATTHEW 10:32-33

May 31

Contemporary ministers called him "the hare-brained enthusiast," but we know him as the father of modern missions.

WILLIAM CAREY was born in 1761 to a poor Anglican family in rural England.[41] He wanted to become a professional gardener, but a skin disease prevented him from working out in the sun. He therefore began training as a shoemaker's apprentice at the age of fourteen. This was a providential career shift because a fellow apprentice, John Warr, was a Christian.

Being from a staunch Anglican family that despised Dissenters, Carey was uneasy with the evangelical arguments Warr presented to him. However, over time Carey began to feel a "growing uneasiness and stings of conscience gradually increasing" with regard to Warr's beliefs. After a traumatic incident when Carey was caught trying to pass off a counterfeit coin as real money to his employer, he was so ashamed that for the first time he began to see himself as morally bankrupt and in need of salvation. Over the next two years he came to "depend on a crucified Saviour for pardon and salvation."

Although he did not attend high school or college, Carey possessed a keen intellect. He taught himself five languages, and by the end of his life knew dozens of languages and dialects.

Carey became a Calvinistic Baptist preacher and followed a rigid system of study. He studied the classics on Mondays, science and history on Tuesdays, and the Hebrew and Greek Scriptures the rest of the week. During this time he became increasingly burdened for overseas missions. He published a pamphlet called *An Enquiry into the Obligations of Christians to use Means for the Conversion of the Heathens.*

For years Carey tried to convince fellow Baptist ministers of the need to form a missionary society in order to spread the gospel across the world. Although the leaders of the denomination kept putting him off, he persisted.

On the evening of May 30, 1792, Carey preached at the annual Baptist association meeting. His text was Isaiah 54:2-3, and his theme was "Expect great things from God; attempt great things for God." He urged his fellow pastors to commit to venturing forth among the nations with the gospel, having confidence that God would bless the message and extend his kingdom. Carey's address made a profound impression on the ministers in attendance.

However, despite Carey's stirring sermon the day before, at the business meeting the next morning the ministers went about their annual agenda in the usual manner and were about to adjourn the meeting without acting on Carey's proposal for overseas missions. Carey was greatly distressed and gripped the arm of Andrew Fuller, imploring him, "Is nothing again going to be done?"

Whatever reservations Fuller and the others had, that day, **May 31, 1792,** they agreed to form the "Baptist Society for Propagating the Gospel among the Heathen." Fuller passed around his snuffbox to collect contributions for the new undertaking, later renamed the Baptist Missionary Society.

In 1793 Carey and two other men sailed for India as missionaries. Carey worked there until his death in 1834 without ever taking a furlough. His comprehensive approach to missions included evangelization, church planting, and Bible translation but also included working for social reform. He established schools, hospitals, and a savings bank; founded the Agricultural and Horticultural Society of India; started a Bengali newspaper; and supervised the start of India's first printing press, paper mill, and steam engine. He also taught languages at a local college, wrote a Bengali-English dictionary, and founded the first Christian college in Asia. In all, Carey translated the complete Bible into six languages and portions of it into twenty-nine others.

He expected great things from God, and attempted great things for God, and God brought them to pass.

Reflection

Do you expect great things from God? Do you attempt great things for God? If you do, God can bring them to pass just as he did for William Carey.

The truth is, anyone who believes in me will do the same works I have done, and even greater works, because I am going to be with the Father. You can ask for anything in my name, and I will do it, because the work of the Son brings glory to the Father. Yes, ask anything in my name, and I will do it!　　　　JOHN 14:12-14

June 1

He was a man who knew not only what he was living for but also what he was willing to die for.

JAMES GUTHRIE was born in a well-to-do Anglican family in Scotland in 1612. He attended St. Andrews University, where his soul was awakened as well as his mind. The two primary influences that God used to bring Guthrie to himself were weekly prayer meetings and his friendship with Samuel Rutherford,[1] one of Scotland's greatest theologians. Guthrie left St. Andrews in 1638 to enter the Presbyterian ministry.

In that same year Guthrie took a bold step in opposition to King Charles I by signing the National Covenant. The king was attempting to force Episcopalian government on the Scottish Church. The Scottish Presbyterians drew up a document called the National Covenant to oppose the king's plan. Those who signed the Covenant committed themselves to uphold the Reformed faith and Presbyterian government, and to keep the church free of all civil control. On his way to sign the Covenant, Guthrie chanced to meet the town hangman and took it as an ominous sign. Later that day he said, "I know that I shall die for what I have done this day, but I cannot die in a better cause."

Guthrie served as a pastor through the first and second English Civil Wars (1642–1648) and the resulting Puritan Commonwealth under Oliver Cromwell (1648–1660).[2] When Charles I was executed by the English Parliament in 1649, his son Charles II was proclaimed king in Scotland and took an oath to accept the National Covenant and to uphold Presbyterianism throughout his realm. However, in 1660 when Charles II was restored to the English throne following the end of the Puritan Commonwealth, he once again forced Episcopalian government on the Church of Scotland.

Guthrie led a group of twelve Scotsmen who petitioned the king to keep the oath he had previously sworn to uphold the Covenant and encouraged him to fill his government with godly men who were themselves committed to the Covenant. In response to their petition, Charles II threw Guthrie and the others into prison.

At his trial before the well-named Drunken Parliament, Guthrie declared, "It is not the extinguishing of me or of many others that will extinguish the Covenant or the work of the Reformation. My blood will contribute more for the propagation of these things than my life in liberty would do, though I should live many years."

A MAN OF PRINCIPLE

Guthrie was sentenced to be hanged, his head to be stuck on a pike and his estate to be confiscated. In prison he told his wife that he considered himself fortunate to be hanged on a tree as his Savior was. Before his hanging on **June 1, 1661,** he said to the hushed crowd,

> "I take God to record upon my soul, I would not exchange this scaffold with the palace and mitre of the greatest prelate in Britain. Blessed be God who has shown mercy to me such a wretch, and has revealed His Son in me. . . . Jesus Christ is my Life and my Light, my Righteousness, my Strength, and my Salvation and all my desire. Him! O Him, I do with all the strength of my soul commend to you. Bless Him, O my soul, from henceforth even forever. Lord, now lettest thy servant depart in peace for mine eyes have seen thy salvation."

And with those words he was with his Savior. His head was placed on a pike high above the Netherbrow Port of Edinburgh, where it remained for twenty-seven years.

Reflection

For what are you willing to die? What effect does that have on how you live your life? James Guthrie lived for twenty-three years with the knowledge that his stand to uphold the Reformed faith might cost him his life, yet he never wavered in his convictions. What is your attitude when God brings trials into your life?

I live in eager expectation and hope that I will never do anything that causes me shame, but that I will always be bold for Christ, as I have been in the past, and that my life will always honor Christ, whether I live or I die.
PHILIPPIANS 1:20

June 2

God changes lives in unexpected ways!

A GROUP of Jews in Jerusalem in A.D. 35 made false accusations against Stephen, a deacon in the church. They successfully stirred up the people into an angry mob that seized Stephen and dragged him away to appear before the Sanhedrin. There a young Pharisee by the name of Saul witnessed both the false accusations and Stephen's defense of his faith in Jesus the Messiah. Later when the Jewish mob dragged Stephen out of the city to stone him, they threw their coats at Saul's feet for safekeeping as they picked up their stones to throw at Stephen (Acts 6:8–8:1). Saul not only supported Stephen's murder but later became the chief persecutor of Christians.

Twenty-two years later, on **June 2, A.D. 57,** the tables were turned, and Saul was in Stephen's shoes. Saul, by then known as Paul, was the one falsely accused in Jerusalem by a group of Jews from the Roman province of Asia. Finding Paul in the temple, they shouted, "Men of Israel! Help! This is the man who teaches against our people and tells everybody to disobey the Jewish laws. He speaks against the Temple—and he even defiles it by bringing Gentiles in!" (Acts 21:27-28). This time it was Paul who was attacked by a Jewish mob, and he then must give his defense (Acts 21:30–22:21).

Paul began his defense with the same words Stephen had used:

"Brothers and esteemed fathers, listen to me" (Acts 22:1; cf. 7:2). Paul explained, "I am a Jew, born in Tarsus, a city in Cilicia, and I was brought up and educated here in Jerusalem under Gamaliel. At his feet I learned to follow our Jewish laws and customs very carefully. I became very zealous to honor God in everything I did, just as all of you are today. And I persecuted the followers of the Way, hounding some to death, binding and delivering both men and women to prison. The high priest and the whole council of leaders can testify that this is so. For I received letters from them to our Jewish brothers in Damascus, authorizing me to bring the Christians from there to Jerusalem, in chains, to be punished.

"As I was on the road, nearing Damascus, about noon a very bright light from heaven suddenly shone around me. I fell to the ground and heard a voice saying to me, 'Saul, Saul, why are you persecuting me?'

" 'Who are you, sir?' I asked. And he replied, 'I am Jesus of

FROM PERSECUTOR TO PERSECUTED

Nazareth, the one you are persecuting.' The people with me saw the light but didn't hear the voice.

"I said, 'What shall I do, Lord?' And the Lord told me, 'Get up and go into Damascus, and there you will be told all that you are to do.'

"I was blinded by the intense light and had to be led into Damascus by my companions" (Acts 22:3-11).

Just as Stephen's defense had caused a riot, so did the words of Paul. "The crowd . . . shouted, 'Away with such a fellow! Kill him! He isn't fit to live!' " (Acts 22:22). And just as the men of Jerusalem had thrown off their coats at Saul's feet before stoning Stephen, now they "threw off their coats, and tossed handfuls of dust into the air" in rage against Paul (Acts 22:23). Fortunately for Paul, the Roman soldiers saved him that day from being killed by the angry mob (Acts 22:24-30).

Paul's encounter with the Lord Jesus Christ changed him from Saul the persecutor into Paul the persecuted.[3]

Reflection

The change in Paul's life brought persecution upon him. Have you ever been persecuted for your faith? If you have, how did you react to it? When persecution comes, how precious it is to know that God blesses the persecuted.

∞◎∞

God blesses those who are persecuted because they live for God, for the Kingdom of Heaven is theirs.   MATTHEW 5:10

June 3

Knowing his adversary helped him control the situation.

YESTERDAY we learned that Paul caused a riot in Jerusalem on June 2, A.D. 57, when he defended himself against false charges brought by the Jews by telling how he met the risen Lord on the road to Damascus. The Roman army commander saved Paul from the mob and held him in custody to determine why he had been accused by the Jews (Acts 21:27–22:29).

Then on **June 3, A.D. 57,** the Roman commander decided to clarify the situation by having Paul appear before the Sanhedrin, the supreme court of Judaism (Acts 22:30). Paul began his defense by saying, "Brothers, I have always lived before God in all good conscience!" Then, just as Jesus had been struck in the face in his trial before the high priest (John 18:22), so now Ananias the high priest, known for his overbearing, insolent manner, ordered that Paul be struck in the mouth. And just as Jesus had challenged his attack (John 18:23), Paul retorted to the high priest, "God will slap you, you white-washed wall! What kind of judge are you to break the law yourself by ordering me struck like that?" (Acts 23:1-3).

Then, with that as a warm-up, Paul went on the offensive. Knowing that the Sanhedrin was composed of both Pharisees who believed vigorously in resurrection and Sadducees who just as vigorously did not, Paul set them up with, "Brothers, I am a Pharisee, as were all my ancestors! And I am on trial because my hope is in the resurrection of the dead!" (23:6). Then Paul stood back and let them have at each other!

A dispute over the resurrection immediately broke out between the Pharisees and Sadducees. The shouting escalated and the two opposing sides kept grabbing Paul away from the other. They got so aggressive that the Roman commander was afraid they would tear Paul apart, so he ordered his soldiers to take him back to the fortress (23:9-10).

Paul had feared such a reception in Jerusalem (21:13), and that night as he was being held in the Roman barracks in the fortress of Antonia, he felt that his worst fears might be realized. He no doubt wondered whether he would ever achieve his goal of going to Rome (Romans 15:23-29).

Suddenly, at Paul's lowest moment, the Lord himself stood before him and said, "Be encouraged, Paul. Just as you have told the people about me here in Jerusalem, you must preach the Good News in Rome" (Acts 23:11). The

THE PHARISEES VERSUS
THE SADDUCEES

Lord was not only giving his approval of Paul's testimony in Jerusalem, but also the assurance that he would testify in Rome.

To the Pharisees and Sadducees the doctrine of the resurrection was merely a hotly contested theological issue—something to fight about. But to Paul, the resurrection of Christ was what changed his life, and now the appearance of his resurrected Lord on this day sealed once again the verity of his faith.[4]

Reflection

What does Christ's resurrection mean to you? Is it just another Christian doctrine, or is it your living hope? Regardless of the tumult in Paul's life, he never questioned the reality of the Lord's resurrection because he had seen him personally after he had risen. His first-hand knowledge of the Resurrection gave him courage.

We know that the same God who raised our Lord Jesus will also raise us with Jesus and present us to himself.　　　2 CORINTHIANS 4:14

June 4

Do you remember the Bible story about the daring young nephew? Not many do.

ROMAN TROOPS had rescued Paul from a riot that ensued when he addressed the Sanhedrin the previous day. Fearing the continued violent reaction of the Jews to Paul, the Roman commander kept Paul under guard overnight in the Roman army barracks (Acts 22:30–23:10).

Meanwhile, since Jews from Asia Minor (21:27-31) and some of the members of the Sanhedrin had both been unsuccessful in their previous attempts to kill Paul (23:10), on **June 4, A.D. 57,** more than forty Jewish men devised a plot to murder Paul, binding themselves by an oath not to eat or drink until they had accomplished their mission. Telling the chief priests of the oath they had taken, they plotted with the priests and the elders to petition the Roman commander to bring Paul again before the Sanhedrin on the pretext of gaining more information about his case. Their plan was that the would-be assassins would kill Paul on the way (23:12-15).

But the most carefully laid plans of men are of no avail against God. In this case, God supernaturally intervened through Paul's nephew. The brave nephew learned of the plot and, in spite of the risk to himself personally, came to the Roman barracks to inform Paul of what he had heard. Paul then asked one of the centurions to take the young man to the commander, Lysias. Paul's nephew told him about the plot, and Lysias immediately ordered almost half of the troops in Jerusalem to take Paul safely to Governor Felix in Caesarea. Then he wrote a letter to the governor explaining that Paul was a Roman citizen and therefore he was transferring the case to him:

> From Claudius Lysias, to his Excellency, Governor Felix. Greetings!
> This man was seized by some Jews, and they were about to kill him
> when I arrived with the troops. When I learned that he was a Roman
> citizen, I removed him to safety. Then I took him to their high council
> to try to find out what he had done. I soon discovered it was something
> regarding their religious law—certainly nothing worthy of imprison-
> ment or death. But when I was informed of a plot to kill him, I immedi-
> ately sent him on to you. I have told his accusers to bring their charges
> before you. (23:26-30)

RESCUED IN THE NICK OF TIME

That same night the Roman troops left under cover of darkness and marched with Paul some thirty-five miles to the city of Antipatris to save him from those wishing to kill him.

God used Roman justice to thwart the Jewish opposition to Paul and the bravery of a young man to save his uncle Paul's life.[5]

Reflection

How have you experienced God's protection in your life? Did you see God's hand in it at the time or only later after reflection? As we consider this story, we see not only how God protects his children but also how he can use us in the lives of others. Whether we are on the giving end or the receiving end, it is wonderful to be a participant when God is protecting his own!

God is our refuge and strength, always ready to help in times of trouble. So we will not fear, even if earthquakes come and the mountains crumble into the sea. Let the oceans roar and foam. Let the mountains tremble as the waters surge! . . . The Lord Almighty is here among us; the God of Israel is our fortress.   PSALM 46:1-3, 7

June 5

When God decides a man and woman are meant for each other, he can use just about anything to bring them together!

GRADY WILSON and his boyhood friend Billy Graham attended Wheaton College together. On the "Senior Sneak," an annual outing at Muskegon, Michigan, for graduating seniors, Grady became enamored of a beautiful fellow student named Wilma Hardie. He had heard that she was engaged but that she had just broken up with her fiancé. During the retreat, with a lump in his throat and sweating palms, he asked her to go on a date—canoeing. After their ride, as they were pulling the canoe back up on shore, Wilma saw a small green water snake sunning itself on a nearby log. Reacting as if it were a boa constrictor, Wilma threw her arms around Grady's neck and held on for dear life. With great bravado, Grady grabbed the snake and threw it into the bushes, secretly thankful for the snake's strategic appearance. From that time on Grady was of the opinion that the snake had been part of God's perfect plan to get them together.

On the way back to Wheaton, the bus driver had to swerve suddenly to avoid an oncoming car, and the bus almost tipped over. Fortunately, the driver never lost control, and the students were all safe. However, the force of the swerve threw Wilma into Grady's arms once again as Grady prayed, "Oh, Lord, protect us!" Wilma was sure that it was Grady's prayer that kept the bus upright. Thus began their lifetime love story.

After they graduated from Wheaton, Grady and Wilma were married on **June 5, 1943.** The wedding was held at Wilma's home church, Cicero Bible Church in Cicero, Illinois, then one of the largest evangelical churches in the Chicago area.

Dr. William McCarrell, the pastor of the church and also the head of the evangelism department of Moody Bible Institute, performed the ceremony. Confusion was rampant as the wedding was about to begin. The best man had missed the rehearsal, and everyone arrived late for the ceremony. Dr. McCarrell had told Grady that the signal for him to kiss the bride would be the phrase "Let us pray." However, he forgot to tell Grady that he was going to pray three times during the ceremony, and the signal applied only to the third prayer.

At the start of the wedding he began the invocation by saying, "Let us pray." Grady, the conscientious bridegroom, lifted Wilma's veil and kissed her. The best man hissed, "Not now, you moron."

When Dr. McCarrell asked Grady to repeat the words, "With all my worldly goods I thee endow," the best man whispered, "There goes your shotgun and your rod and reel."

By the time they got to the end of the ceremony and Dr. McCarrell said, "You may now kiss the bride," Grady had already kissed her three times. This "kissingist" wedding launched a marriage filled with love and laughter. Grady and Wilma were blessed with two daughters and a rich life of serving the Lord together.

Grady Wilson went on to become an associate evangelist to Billy Graham[6] and one of his lifelong best friends.

Reflection

To what extent has your family life been filled with love and laughter? Can you laugh at the funny things that happen in life? Are you able to laugh at yourself? Think of ways in which you can inject a dose of holy hilarity into your family. You'll be amazed at the difference it makes!

A cheerful heart is good medicine.   PROVERBS 17:22

June 6

The seeds of evangelism bear fruit in God's time, not man's.

Pioneer missionary Adoniram Judson graduated from Brown University as valedictorian at the age of nineteen and in 1810 graduated in the first class of Andover Theological Seminary.[7] He and his wife journeyed from America to Burma (now Myanmar), arriving in 1813. Shortly thereafter they were joined by two other missionaries. However, after six years of labor not one Burmese had trusted in Christ.

Then on **June 6, 1819,** Judson received a letter from Moung Nau, a Burmese man who had shown great interest in the gospel but up to this point had not acted on it. The letter read:

> I, Moung Nau, the constant recipient of your excellent favor, approach your feet. Whereas my Lord's three [i.e., three missionaries] come to the country of Burma—not for the purposes of trade, but to preach the religion of Jesus Christ, the Son of the eternal God—I, having heard and understood, am, with a joyful mind, filled with love.
>
> I believe that the divine Son, Jesus Christ, suffered death, in the place of men, to atone for their sins. Like a heavy-laden man, I feel my sins are very many. The punishment of my sins I deserve to suffer. Since it is so, do you, sirs, consider that I, taking refuge in the merits of the Lord Jesus Christ, and receiving baptism, in order to become his disciple, shall dwell one with yourselves, a band of brothers, in the happiness of heaven, and therefore grant me the ordinance of baptism. It is through the grace of Jesus Christ that you, sirs, have come by ship from one country and continent to another and that we have met together. I pray the Lord's three that a suitable day may be appointed, and that I may receive the ordinance of baptism.
>
> Moreover, as it is only since I have met with you, sirs, that I have known about the eternal God, I venture to pray that you will still unfold to me the religion of God, that my old disposition may be destroyed, and my new disposition improved.

Three weeks later Moung Nau was baptized, and the barrier of unbelief was broken.

What enabled Adoniram Judson to faithfully labor so many years before seeing any fruit? We can see evidence of his motivation in the following lines, which he penciled on the inner cover of a book he used in his translation of the Bible into Burmese:

> *In joy or in pain,*
> *Our course be onward still;*
> *We sow on Burma's barren plain;*
> *We reap on Zion's hill.*

Today there are more than two million believers in Myanmar, and 40 percent of the Karen people to whom Adoniram Judson directed his ministry are now Christians.

Reflection

How do you think it would feel to be a missionary for six years and have no converts? It's easy to be discouraged when we do not see immediate results. Like Adoniram Judson, we need to see the big picture. We must remember that sowing is our responsibility; the results are God's.

My job was to plant the seed in your hearts, and Apollos watered it, but it was God, not we, who made it grow. 1 CORINTHIANS 3:6

June 7

Was the Israeli capture of the old city of Jerusalem predicted in the Bible?

On June 7, 1967, a date dear to the heart of every patriotic Israeli, the army of Israel captured the Old City of Jerusalem. The previous month the Egyptians had decided to attempt once more to conquer Israel. They poured one hundred thousand troops into the Sinai Peninsula, ordered the UN peacekeepers out, and made a military alliance with neighboring Jordan. Israel felt its only hope was to launch a preemptive strike, which it did on June 5. Jordan and Syria immediately entered the war. Two days later the Israelis captured the Old City of Jerusalem, which had been part of Jordan. As a result of this military victory in what is known as the Six-Day War, Israel once again possessed her ancient capital. It had been 1,897 years since the Romans conquered Jerusalem in A.D. 70.

Jesus had predicted that Jerusalem and its temple would be destroyed.[8]

> He said, "The time is coming when all these things will be so completely demolished that not one stone will be left on top of another" (Luke 21:6). When his disciples asked him, "When will all this take place? And will there be any sign ahead of time?" Jesus answered, "When you see Jerusalem surrounded by armies, then you will know that the time of its destruction has arrived. . . . There will be great distress in the land and wrath upon this people. They will be brutally killed by the sword or sent away as captives to all the nations of the world" (21:7, 20, 23-24).

From the beginning of Jesus' ministry he warned the Jews of God's coming wrath unless they repented (Matthew 3:8). In response to the Jews crucifying their Messiah, God sent the Roman armies to conquer Galilee and Samaria and then to surround and destroy Jerusalem (cf. 21:37–22:7). The attack began in A.D. 66 when the Jews rebelled following a theft from the temple treasury by the last Roman prefect. To quell the rebellion the Romans sent four legions, which arrived the following year. After a siege Jerusalem fell in A.D. 70. The Roman general Titus[9] completely destroyed the city and temple.

Jesus had also prophesied that following its defeat "Jerusalem will be . . . trampled down by the Gentiles until the age of the Gentiles comes to an end"

FULFILLMENT OF PROPHECY?

(Luke 21:24). Does this mean that "the age of the Gentiles," or as other translations put it, "the times of the Gentiles," ended on **June 7, 1967**, when the Jews gained control of Jerusalem?

Revelation 11:2 seems to answer no. It states that the Gentiles "will trample the holy city for forty-two months," apparently the three and a half years prior to the second coming of Christ, implying that the Jews will not be in control of Jerusalem at that time. If this explanation is correct, the times of the Gentiles did not end on **June 7, 1967**. They will end at the second coming of Christ.

June 7, 1967, was an extremely significant event in Jewish history, but it was not the fulfillment of prophecy.

Reflection

When you read the unfulfilled prophecies of the Bible, do you believe that they will be literally fulfilled? The first coming of Jesus Christ fulfilled many prophecies, and his second coming will fulfill many more.

We were not making up clever stories when we told you about the power of our Lord Jesus Christ and his coming again. We have seen his majestic splendor with our own eyes.　　　　2 PETER 1:16

June 8

He successfully invented a new religion.

MOHAMMED, the founder of Islam, the world's youngest major religion, was born in Mecca between 570 and 580. His father died before he was born and his mother when he was six. He was subsequently raised in relative poverty, first by his grandfather and then by an uncle.

At the age of twenty-five Mohammed entered the service of a wealthy widow, fifteen years his senior, named Khadija. His marriage to her shortly thereafter provided him with instant wealth. Her affluence provided him with the luxury to indulge in a life of religious contemplation.

When he was about forty, Mohammed claimed that he received a prophetic call from Allah through the angel Gabriel. He began preaching monotheism, a final judgment, alms, prayer, and surrender to the will of Allah. In the course of three years he attracted only twelve converts. Because he was persecuted in his hometown of Mecca, he fled to the city of Medina in 622. His flight to Medina is called the hegira and is traditionally dated to July 15, 622, which marks the beginning of the Muslim calendar.

During his time in Medina, Mohammed's revelations became more legalistic and secular. Islam, as his new religion was called, became both a community and a state with Mohammed being both its ruler and lawgiver.

Once his power was centralized in Medina, Mohammed was able to return to Mecca and conquer it in 630. By the time he died on **June 8, 632,** almost all of Arabia had embraced Islam, and in the hundred years following his death, Islam spread like wildfire.

The successors of Mohammed encouraged jihad, or holy war, against non-Muslims and within a century built an empire stretching from northern Spain all the way across North Africa to India. Many of the areas conquered, such as Iraq, Syria, Palestine, and North Africa, were formerly Christian strongholds where believers faced the choice of converting to Islam or dying by the sword. Even western Europe was threatened by the advance of Islam until Charles Martel of France finally halted expansion when he defeated the Muslims at the battle of Tours, France, in 732, exactly one hundred years after the death of Mohammed.

Islam has continued to expand today so that more than one-fifth of the world's population is Muslim. In 1900 only 12 percent of the world embraced Islam; by 2000 the percentage had grown to 21 percent. Today Islam is the

A MAN NAMED MOHAMMED

fastest growing major religion, in part due to a higher birthrate, numbering 1.3 billion in the year 2000. Most live in a belt stretching from West Africa to Southeast Asia. Islam is the majority religion in forty-two countries and territories. Most of these countries prohibit Christian evangelism and exclude Christian missionaries.

In spite of the fact that the followers of Mohammed have greatly increased their numbers and their political power, it is encouraging that more Muslims came to Christ between 1980 and 2000 than in any earlier period of history.

Reflection

Do you know any Muslims? Today in America there are more Muslims than Episcopalians. Think of how you can prepare yourself to share the gospel with them. It is a great opportunity to live in a time when there is so much intermingling of nationalities around the world. Most of us need look no further than our own community to find people from another culture with whom we can share our lives and our faith. God is bringing the mission field to us.

With my authority, take this message of repentance to all the nations, beginning in Jerusalem: "There is forgiveness of sins for all who turn to me."　　　　　　　　　　　　　　　　　　　　LUKE 24:47

June 9

Show respect for everyone. Love your Christian brothers and sisters. Fear God. Show respect for the king. (1 Peter 2:17)

WHEN PETER told Christians to "show respect for the king," do you know who the king was at that time? It was Nero, in the latter years of his reign.

Born in A.D. 37, Nero became emperor of the Roman Empire in 54. The first five years of his reign were known for their sound and orderly administration because Nero allowed the philosopher Seneca and Burrus, the commander of the Praetorian guard, to rule the empire for him. Able men, appointed no doubt by Seneca and Burrus, governed the provinces with wisdom.

Nero's troubles began in 58 when a devious woman named Poppaea set her sights on him, becoming his mistress. The Roman historian Tacitus described her as having every gift of nature except an honorable mind. Under her influence Nero gradually threw off all restraints, ignored the advice of his wise counselors, and plunged into immorality and crime.

Poppaea first induced Nero to murder his own mother. Then when Burrus died in 62, she forced Seneca to retire from the imperial court, thereby removing all traces of their formerly orderly rule. Poppaea next persuaded Nero to divorce his wife and marry her. Nero then had his first wife murdered and her head brought to Poppaea. However, Poppaea got a taste of her own medicine in 65, when Nero in a rage kicked her in her pregnant belly, killing her.

Nero's excesses exhausted the Roman treasury and were the beginning of the Roman Empire's decline into bankruptcy. He surrounded himself with greedy, arrogant men. The situation deteriorated rapidly in 64 when a fire destroyed over half of the city of Rome. In response to rumors that he had started the fire to free space for his megalomaniac building plans, Nero placed the blame instead on the Christians of Rome. Thus began the first systematic persecution of Christians. They were arrested in large numbers and subjected to unspeakable atrocities. The Roman historian Tacitus reported, "Some were covered with the skins of wild animals and then torn apart by dogs, some were crucified, some were burned as torches to light at night." These were the very Christians to whom Paul had written his epistle just seven years earlier. Evidence indicates that both the apostle Peter and the apostle Paul were martyred by Nero as part of this persecution.

As Nero became more and more consumed by his despotism, sensuality, and delusions of grandeur, the Roman provinces accelerated their demands that he be removed as caesar. His buffoonery hit new heights when he went to Greece to compete in the Greek games and because he was caesar was allowed to win every contest. In the end Nero lost his will to live and did nothing to stop the growing rebellion against him. He ended his own tragic life by committing suicide on **June 9, A.D. 68.**

In spite of Nero's despicable character, Peter commanded his fellow believers to honor and respect the king. Christians are to show respect for the king, regardless of how bad things get.

Reflection

How are you doing at honoring the elected officials with whom you disagree? Think of the elected official you like the least, and determine how you can apply the command to "show respect for the king" (1 Peter 2:17). As Christians we are to be responsible citizens of our community, state, and nation. To show respect for the king does not mean to condone everything elected officials do, but it does mean to respect the office they hold.

For the Lord's sake, accept all authority—the king as head of state, and the officials he has appointed. 1 PETER 2:13-14

June 10

Some people can never get enough of themselves.

ALEXANDER III of Macedon, whom we know as Alexander the Great, was born in 356 B.C. The most successful world conqueror of all time, Alexander was such an important figure in world history that chapters 2, 7, 8, and 11 of Daniel all contain prophecies of him and his kingdom. Daniel 11:3-4 prophesies this of Alexander: "Then a mighty king will rise to power who will rule a vast kingdom and accomplish everything he sets out to do. But at the height of his power, his kingdom will be broken apart and divided into four parts. It will not be ruled by the king's descendants, nor will the kingdom hold the authority it once had. For his empire will be uprooted and given to others."

Even as a boy Alexander was fearless. He tamed a beautiful, spirited horse named Bucephalus that no one else dared to touch. Bucephalus later carried his master all the way to India.

Tutored by Aristotle, Alexander at the age of sixteen became coregent of Macedon with his father, King Phillip of Macedon, who had been the first person to unite the cities of Greece into a political organization. Immediately the teenager was thrust into leadership of a military campaign. Two years later as commander of part of the Macedonian cavalry, he saved his father's life in battle.

When Alexander was twenty, his father died, and he became king. He likewise became the leader of the League of Corinth, founded by his father, uniting all of Greece under his authority.

Alexander immediately went on the offensive and first conquered Asia Minor, then the Mediterranean coast all the way to Egypt. There he founded the city of Alexandria, which soon became the greatest city in the Mediterranean. He named it after himself, as he did more than sixty other cities, apparently being quite pleased with his name.

Next Alexander's ambitions led him east. His greatest career accomplishment was when he defeated the Persians and as the prize controlled the splendid capitals of its empire.[10] He reached India on his faithful old horse Bucephalus in 327 B.C. At that point his weary soldiers refused to go any farther, and so Alexander turned back to the west. There he shocked his Greek compatriots by adopting the style of the Persian court, including the harem.

Alexander was so impressed with his own success that in the last year of his life he apparently believed that the appropriate way for his Greek subjects to recognize his greatness was to worship him as a god. However, he didn't have much time to enjoy this worship. Alexander died in Babylon on **June 10, 323 B.C.**, at the age of only thirty-three. In thirteen years he had conquered most of the known world, and his military triumphs spread a Greek influence over the Near East that would last for a thousand years. It is because of Alexander the Great that the New Testament was written in Greek.

But after his death the mighty kingdom Alexander had amassed was broken up and divided by his Greek generals into four parts: Macedon and Greece under Antipater and later Cassander, Thrace and Asia Minor under Lysimachus, Syria under Seleucus, and Egypt and Palestine under Ptolemy.

God had no tolerance for a world emperor who desired to be worshiped.

Reflection

God is not impressed by those who are impressed with themselves and give themselves the credit for their accomplishments. He is a jealous God who will not share his glory with another, be he king or emperor.

The Lord is a jealous God, filled with vengeance and wrath. He takes revenge on all who oppose him and furiously destroys his enemies! The Lord is slow to get angry, but his power is great, and he never lets the guilty go unpunished.　　　　NAHUM 1:2-3

June 11

Not many missionaries make the headlines, but these did.

IN JANUARY 1956 the news media told the world how five missionaries had been martyred by members of a primitive Ecuadorian tribe called the Aucas. The martyrs became known as the Auca Five.[11]

What happened to the Aucas after that fateful day? Rachel Saint, the sister of slain missionary Nate Saint, had already been learning the Auca language from Dayuma, an Auca woman who ten years prior to the murder of the missionaries had fled from her tribe because of all the killing among them. Rachel Saint had met her in 1955 when Dayuma worked at a hacienda near Auca territory.

In 1957 Rachel Saint brought Dayuma to the United States to what she thought was to be a missionary conference. Rachel took Dayuma to witness a live television program and was completely surprised to find herself featured on the popular network program *This Is Your Life*. Afterward Rachel took Dayuma to the seclusion of the Wycliffe Bible Translator Home in Sulphur Springs, Arkansas, for intensive language study.

As Rachel learned the language, Dayuma learned more and more of what Christ's death could mean for her personally. She finally confessed her faith in Christ and became the first Auca convert.

In November 1957 Betty Elliot, who had continued serving as a missionary in Ecuador even after her husband, Jim, was slain, learned that two Auca women had left their tribe and were staying in the fishing village of a neighboring tribe. Betty went immediately to meet the Auca women, Mankamu and Mintaka. They turned out to be two of the three women who had visited the five missionaries on the beach, where they were later killed. They had come looking for Dayuma who was still in the United States.

Betty Elliot was able to persuade the two women to come to her mission station, where she began a concentrated study of the Auca language. In the spring of 1958 Rachel Saint returned with Dayuma, and the two missionaries continued to learn the language. Some months later Mankamu and Mintaka decided that they wanted to return to their families. Dayuma, who had been away from her people for twelve years, decided to return with them. In September the three Auca women set out on the jungle trail with three puppies and food for the trip.

Three weeks later Betty was told by another Indian that the Auca women had returned to the mission station. Soon Betty heard someone singing "Jesus Loves Me" with an Auca accent. It was Dayuma. With her were Mankamu and Mintaka and seven other Aucas. They brought the good news that the Aucas wanted the two missionaries to visit them. In October Rachel Saint, Betty Elliot, and Betty's three-year-old daughter, Valerie, went to live in the Auca village.

Back in her own village, Dayuma shared the gospel with her fellow Aucas. One by one they began to put their trust in the Lord Jesus. Eventually all five men who had murdered the missionaries were converted and became leaders of the Auca church.

Rachel Saint began the translation of the New Testament into Waorani, the Auca's official tribal name, and it was completed by Catherine Peake and Rosi Jung. On **June 11, 1992,** the Aucas finally received the New Testament in their language. What a day of celebration! Present was Rachel Saint, who had retired from Wycliffe Bible Translators but had returned to live near the Aucas. All three translators saw the fruit of their labors completed, and today the new generation of Auca believers are reading God's Word in their own language.

The Auca Five did not die in vain.

Reflection

The death of the five missionaries was initially considered a tragedy by many. Yet in God's providence the goal the missionaries had set for themselves was achieved beyond their greatest expectations. It is thrilling to have a God who can bring victory out of what appears to be tragedy.

Blessed are those who die in the Lord. . . . They are blessed indeed, for they will rest from all their toils and trials; for their good deeds follow them! REVELATION 14:13

June 12

Founding the America we all take for granted was at times a depressing ordeal.

JOHN WINTHROP was a dedicated Puritan lawyer in England. We get a glimpse of his character from a statement he wrote at the age of twenty-four: "I do resolve first to give myself—my life, my wits, my health, my wealth—to the service of my God and Saviour who by giving Himself for me and to me, deserves whatsoever I am or can be, to be at His commandment and for his glory."

Winthrop had been elected governor of the Massachusetts Bay Company prior to departing from England on the *Arabella* with some seven hundred colonists. Two years earlier sixty-six English settlers led by John Endecott had settled at Salem, Massachusetts, and the next year two hundred more had followed.

On **June 12, 1630,** John Winthrop stood at the rail of the *Arabella* as it entered Salem harbor. For seventy-two days he had been at sea, and now he had finally arrived in New England, filled with anticipation for what God was going to do on these new shores.

As they approached, the sight that greeted Winthrop perplexed him. Where was Salem? All that was visible was a collection of huts and canvas shelters. Stepping on shore from the first boat, he realized to his great disappointment that this pathetic settlement was indeed Salem.

John Endecott, the acting governor, informed him that of the first two groups of settlers now eighty-five remained. More than eighty had died, and the rest had returned to England. And many of those remaining planned to do the same.

As Winthrop surveyed the disheartening sight, he thought of the words he had written the day before to spell out his goals for the new colony, which he titled "A Model of Christian Charity":

> Thus stands the cause between God and us: we are entered into covenant with Him for this work. . . .
>
> Now the only way . . . to provide for posterity, is to follow the counsel of Micah, to do justly, to love mercy, to walk humbly with our God . . . for this end, we must be knit together in this work as one man. . . . We must hold a familiar commerce together in all meekness,

gentleness, patience, and liberality. We must delight in each other, make one another's condition our own, rejoice together, mourn together, labor and suffer together, always having before our eyes our Commission and Community in his work, as members of the same body. So shall we keep the unity of the Spirit in the bond of peace. . . .

We shall find that the God of Israel is among us, when ten of us shall be able to resist a thousand of our enemies, when he shall make us a praise and glory, that men of succeeding plantations shall say, "The Lord make it like that of New England." For we must consider that we shall be as a City upon a hill." . . .

Rekindled in his vision, John Winthrop went on to serve as governor of Massachusetts almost continually until his death in 1649. He was instrumental in shaping Massachusetts into a Christian commonwealth that went on to have a profound effect on the rest of the developing new nation.

Reflection

John Winthrop was able to overcome his initial disappointment in Salem because God had given him a vision of the future. What vision has God given you for overcoming your disappointments? When we focus on only what is immediately in front of us, it is easy to miss the big picture. God's perspective includes today as well as the future, all as part of one master plan.

Hope deferred makes the heart sick, but when dreams come true, there is life and joy. PROVERBS 13:12

June 13

The message was the same but the results were quite different.

IN 1845 the Methodists in Vermont sent evangelist James Caughey to Europe
to minister for two years. He first went to Birmingham, England, where he had
a successful five-month ministry. From there he went by train to Nottingham,
England, where he had been invited to preach in Wesley Chapel, a large
church seating between two and three thousand.

When John Wesley,[12] the great Methodist evangelist, had first preached
in Nottingham 105 years earlier, he had described in his journal how disappointed he was by the people's response to the gospel: "Not one person who
came in used any prayer at all; but everyone immediately sat down, and began
talking to his neighbor, or looking to see who was there." Wesley said he "ex-
pounded with a heavy heart." But now things had started to change. On
Caughey's first Sunday in Nottingham, God began to pour out his Spirit on
the chapel, and 136 people put their faith in the Lord Jesus. As the weeks went
by there were daily meetings with many putting their trust in Christ each day.

On Monday evening a prayer meeting was held, and 47 more found salvation. On Tuesday night there were 24 more, on Wednesday 22, and so on,
day after day throughout the week.

One of the secrets to his success was the Methodists' organized follow-up
of new converts. The names and addresses of every new convert were immediately recorded. Then they were assigned to meet with a leader of the church,
and the day and time of the meeting were recorded. The converts were also assigned to one of the classes that were held at the chapel. In addition, the chapel secretary recorded whether the new converts had met as they had
promised. With such a system in place, no one slipped through the cracks or
was overlooked.

By **June 13, 1846,** the day Caughey left Nottingham, less than five weeks
after his arrival, he had seen 1,412 persons trust in Christ as their Lord and
Savior. More than a thousand of the new converts came to his last service to
bid him a tearful farewell.

One hundred and five years after John Wesley's discouraged journal entry about Nottingham, Caughey wrote in his journal:

> Glory be to the Father, and to the Son, and to the Holy Ghost for such
> a work—which only the Omnipotent God could perform. . . . Such a

TWO MESSENGERS, TWO RESULTS

work of God as this, in so short a time, I have never before witnessed. It has been, indeed, one of the great spring tides of the Spirit; the like of which one may never see again, unless viewed from our position in eternity, in the future triumphs of Emmanuel. . . . But why should it not have been accomplished in a short time if the people were willing to be saved? Seeing that it is written we are justified by faith, and sanctified by faith; and that God himself saith, "Behold, now is the accepted time; Behold, now is the day of salvation!"

Both John Wesley and James Caughey faithfully preached on their first visit to Nottingham, but the results were according to God's timing.

Reflection

Were the different results of Wesley's and Caughey's initial preaching in Nottingham any reflection on their faithfulness? What do the experiences of these two men teach us about focusing on results? Both men served God faithfully, and that is all that God requires of us. The rest is up to him.

The ones who do the planting or watering aren't important, but God is important because he is the one who makes the seed grow.

1 CORINTHIANS 3:7

June 14

Just because something appears to be supernatural doesn't mean it's from God.

THE YEAR was 1108, and the place was Antioch. For centuries pilgrims had journeyed freely from western Europe to visit the Holy Land. The Muslims who controlled Jerusalem from the seventh century did not interfere with these pilgrimages. However, by 1071 the fierce Seljuk Turks not only captured Jerusalem from their fellow Muslims but also defeated the Byzantine Empire. This led to Turkish control of Asia Minor (modern Turkey).

Rumors swirled through Europe of mistreatment of pilgrims by the Turks. In 1095 the Byzantine emperor sent Pope Urban II an urgent appeal for military assistance. Urban's response was to organize the First Crusade to regain the Holy Land from the infidels.[13] Offering the incentive of full forgiveness for past sins to those who joined the Crusade, Urban was able to raise an army of five thousand knights and infantry from France, Germany, and Italy.

On their way to Jerusalem, the crusaders were finally able to capture Antioch, but only after a bitter nine-month siege. However, no sooner had the crusaders taken possession of the city than a Turkish relief force arrived and surrounded the city, holding the very positions the crusaders had held a few days before. The crusaders were now near starvation. Not wanting to kill their horses for food, they drank the horses' blood to keep themselves alive. A crusader relief force approached the city, but when the commander saw the immense size of the army surrounding Antioch, he quickly fled with his army rather than try to save the starving crusaders.

At this pivotal moment a crusader named Peter Bartholomew, known more for his frequenting of taverns than his skill as a soldier, announced that the apostle Andrew had appeared to him in a vision and told him that the lance that had pierced Christ's side lay buried behind the altar of the church of St. Peter in Antioch and that if the Crusaders would raise the lance against their foes, they would be victorious.

The date was **June 14, 1098.** The Crusaders immediately began to dig behind the altar as directed by Bartholomew. After others had dug for a whole day, Peter Bartholomew jumped into the excavation, asking the bystanders to pray that the lance would be found. Then he furtively slipped an old Arab spear he had concealed under his garment into the dirt and began to dig himself. Clanging against the spear with his shovel, Bartholomew triumphantly pulled it out of the dirt. Holding it aloft, he shouted, "See, what heaven promised, the earth preserved, the apostle promised and the prayers of a contrite people obtained!" An awestruck chaplain kissed the lance. Hope and excitement filled the crusaders as they paraded through the city, singing and praising God for giving them the lance. Peter Bartholomew was dressed in gold and fine clothes and presented with expensive gifts.

Two weeks later the Crusaders, energized by the apostle Andrew's promise of victory and carrying their "holy" lance before them, confidently attacked the Turkish army and were victorious

Reflection

Have you personally been aware of things that appeared to be supernatural but that you doubted were really from God? How can we prevent ourselves from being deceived? Just because something is supernatural doesn't mean it is necessarily from God. Never forget that Satan is the great deceiver.

∼≈⌢

For false messiahs and false prophets will rise up and perform great miraculous signs and wonders so as to deceive, if possible, even God's chosen ones. See, I have warned you.   MATTHEW 24:24-25

June 15

Have you ever wondered how Bible scholars are able to assign dates to the events of the Old Testament?

THE MAJOR breakthrough came with the discovery of the tablets containing the Assyrian Eponym lists. (An eponym is a person from whom something gets its name.) They listed all the years from 892 to 648 B.C., naming each year after the prime minister, or *limmu*, of Assyria who was elected that year. In addition to these names, the tablets also recount the major events of each year.

The Eponym lists contain an unbroken chain of events relating not only to Assyria but also to other nations that were interacting with Assyria. Because the tablets list the years of battles between Assyria and Israel, Bible scholars have been able to date the reigns of the kings of Israel and Judah from these dates.

In the year of a prime minister named Bur-Sagale, the Assyrians recorded that there had been an eclipse of the sun. Modern astronomers are able to calculate the dates of eclipses with great precision and have determined that the eclipse of the sun described in the tablets occurred on **June 15, 763 B.C.**

Ninety years before this eclipse in the year 853 B.C., the lists report the battle of Qarqar in which the Assyrian emperor Shalmaneser III defeated a coalition of Syria and Israel under King Ahab. According to 1 Kings 22:1, the only period in which Israel was at peace with Syria was near the end of Ahab's reign, so it must have occurred during that time.

While that information was interesting, it did not conclusively link the Eponym lists to the Old Testament until the discovery of the Black Obelisk. The Black Obelisk is a pillar erected by Shalmaneser III of Assyria in 841 B.C. to commemorate his victory over his enemies, including King Jehu of Israel. Jehu is pictured on the Obelisk as kneeling in subjection to Shalmaneser in the eighteenth year of the Assyrian emperor's reign. This can then be dated from the Eponym lists since they give the dates of Shalmaneser's reign. The date of the Black Obelisk is 841 B.C., which apparently was the first year of Jehu's reign over Israel. According to 2 Kings 3:1; 9:1-8, 24, there were twelve years between the end of Ahab's reign and the beginning of Jehu's. Thus the date of 853 B.C. can be determined as the end of Ahab's reign over Israel.

Nailing down these two dates made the process of constructing the chronology of the Old Testament relatively easy. The books of 1 and 2 Kings give the lengths of the reigns of the kings of Israel and Judah before and after Ahab and Jehu. By adding the years of these reigns, the accession year of each king can be determined, as well as the dates of many associated events.

Reflection

Do you think God intends us to understand that the stories of the Bible are historical events? Why? Luke was one biblical author who explained the methodology he used in writing his Gospel. He wanted to make sure that his readers were aware of the accuracy of his research and truth of his account.

Many people have written accounts about the events that took place among us. They used as their source material the reports circulating among us from the early disciples and other eyewitnesses of what God has done in fulfillment of his promises. Having carefully investigated all of these accounts from the beginning, I have decided to write a careful summary for you, to reassure you of the truth of all you were taught.   LUKE 1:1-4

June 16

In times of battle men's thoughts often turn to prayer—and for good reason!

On June 16, 1775, a significant prayer meeting took place in Boston. The day before, the patriots had learned of English general Gage's plan to occupy the southern projection of Bunker Hill on the Charleston peninsula across the Charles River from Boston. In the twilight of June 16, twelve hundred patriot troops gathered on the Cambridge Common. There Samuel Langdon, the gray-haired president of Harvard College, led them in prayer concerning the awesome task before them. He prayed, "O may our camp be free from every accursed thing! May our land be purged from all its sins! May we truly be a holy people and all our towns cities of righteousness!"

After the prayer, the patriot commander William Prescott led the patriot troops to a rise near Bunker Hill overlooking the British army that occupied Boston. All through the night they worked to prepare fortifications to withstand the British soldiers the next day.

General Gage committed twenty-two hundred British soldiers, a third of all his troops, to the operation. At two in the afternoon the cannon fire from the British ships in Boston Harbor intensified against the patriot position as the British troops crossed the Charles River in small boats and then formed themselves into long lines. As the church bells tolled three o'clock, Gage's field commander, General William Howe, began leading his troops up the long hill. Behind him two rows of British soldiers stretching the complete width of the peninsula advanced up the open slope toward the patriot position.

It puzzled the British troops that the patriots did not fire a single shot at them as they advanced, even though they were well in range. Prescott, the patriot commander, had commanded his men with the now famous words "Don't fire until you see the whites of their eyes." The young soldiers bravely did as they were told and were victorious.[14] Seeing the piles of red-coated British soldiers all around them, they knew that they had not just won a battle but that God had given them the victory.

Amos Farnsworth, a corporal in the Massachusetts militia, wrote in his diary that night, "O the goodness of God in preserving my life, although they fell on my right hand and on my left! O may this act of deliverance of thine, O God, lead me never to distrust thee; but may I ever trust in thee and put

"DON'T FIRE UNTIL YOU SEE THE WHITES OF THEIR EYES"

confidence in no arm of the flesh!" Another soldier, Peter Jennings, wrote to his mother, "God, in His mercy to us, fought our battle for us, and although we were but few . . . we were preserved in a most wonderful way, far beyond expectation."

God answered the prayers of the previous night's prayer meeting.

Reflection

What "battles" are you facing where you need to trust God for the victory? Notice that Samuel Langdon didn't pray merely for physical deliverance from the battle but that they would be delivered from sin and be a holy people. As part of your prayer life, make a list of your requests, and then record the victories that God gives you.

I will call on God, and the Lord will rescue me. Morning, noon, and night I plead aloud in my distress, and the Lord hears my voice. He rescues me and keeps me safe from the battle waged against me, even though many still oppose me. God, who is king forever, will hear me and will humble them. PSALM 55:16-19

June 17

In the late nineteenth century, Anglo-American communications were difficult for everyone . . . and how! Yet God was in charge then, too.

On June 17, 1873, Dwight L. Moody[15] and his new inexperienced song leader, Ira Sankey,[16] arrived in Liverpool, England, with their wives and the Moody children to hold evangelistic meetings. They had come at the invitation of three Christian men, who had promised to pay for their travel expenses even though they had never actually met Moody. Having exhausted all his own funds for the steamship tickets, Moody arrived in England only to learn that two of the men had died, and the third had forgotten his promise. No arrangements had been made for any meetings, there was no sponsoring committee and no funds. They were stranded three thousand miles from home.

Moody said to Sankey, "God seems to have closed the doors. We'll not open any ourselves. If He opens the door, we'll go in. If He doesn't, we'll return to America."

At their hotel that night Moody remembered that the one specific invitation he had received from England was from George Bennett, a young chemist in York who was the founder/secretary of the local YMCA. Moody had only vaguely replied to Bennett's invitation when he first received it. Telling Sankey, "This door is only ajar," Moody now had the secretary of the Liverpool YMCA send Bennett a telegram: "Moody here—are you ready for him."

Since he had received no firm reply to his invitation, Bennett had not pursued the idea any further and had only told one person that he had sent the invitation. He was thus justifiably shocked when he received Moody's telegram saying he had arrived. He replied with a telegram to Moody: "Please fix date when you can come to York." Moody replied immediately, "I will be in York tonight ten o'clock—Make no arrangements till I come."

Bennett appeared dazed as he met Moody at the train station that evening. Over supper Moody suggested a course of action: "I propose we make arrangements tomorrow, Saturday, to commence meetings Sunday." As they ate, they came up with a plan to have posters printed and posted on Saturday as soon as Bennett could find a place for him to preach.

Starting that Sunday, Moody began holding services in local churches, including one pastored by F. B. Meyer. Initially the meetings were only moderately successful, but for Meyer the experience of having Moody preach in his church was life changing. In the small vestry room of Meyer's church, Moody and Meyer prayed many hours for England, kneeling together at the leather-covered table in the center of the room. Moody later referred to that little room as "the foundation from which the river of blessing for all England had sprung," for during the next two years, two and a half million people heard Moody preach throughout England. It was the greatest British revival since John Wesley's day.

Reflection

We all experience times when we are at the end of our resources and it seems as if God is not there. When this happens, the answers are to be found in our own prayer rooms, where God will in time reveal himself. His timing may not be our timing, but his plan is perfect if we are willing to wait and put our trust in him.

❧

I am confident that I will see the Lord's goodness while I am here in the land of the living. Wait patiently for the Lord. Be brave and courageous. Yes, wait patiently for the Lord. PSALM 27:13-14

June 18

Can you imagine William Tyndale on the "Ten Most Wanted" list?

WILLIAM TYNDALE was born about 1494 and educated first at Oxford, where he was ordained into the priesthood, and then at Cambridge, where he joined the Reformation. When he completed his education, he felt he needed to get away from the academic atmosphere of the university to be able to think, pray, and study the Greek New Testament on his own. His solution was to take a job as tutor for a wealthy family. During that time he became convinced that England would never be evangelized using Latin Bibles because "it was impossible to establish the lay people in any truth, except the Scripture were laid before their eyes in their mother tongue."

However, Tyndale's efforts to get permission from the bishop of London to translate the Bible into English were unsuccessful, so he left England, never to return.

Tyndale settled in Antwerp,[17] where sympathetic English merchants hid and protected him as he translated the Greek New Testament and parts of the Hebrew Old Testament into English. His first English New Testament was printed in Germany in 1525.

As Tyndale's English Bibles were smuggled into England, the archbishop of Canterbury and the bishop of London began attacking him fiercely. Finally on **June 18, 1528,** Thomas Wolsey, the English cardinal, ordered the ambassador to the Low Countries to demand from the Low Countries regent that Tyndale be arrested and extradited to England. It took his pursuers seven years to track him down, but Tyndale was finally arrested near Brussels in 1535. He was held in a cold castle dungeon nearby for eighteen months before his trial.

A long list of charges was drawn up against him, among them: He had maintained that faith alone justifies and that to believe in the forgiveness of sins and to embrace the mercy offered in the gospel was enough for salvation.

Tyndale, in his early forties, was found guilty at his trial and condemned to death as a heretic. Referring to the king's opposition to his English Bible, Tyndale said, "Lord, open the king of England's eyes." Then William Tyndale was strangled and his body burned.

The year that Tyndale died, there were two English Bibles containing his translation of the New Testament circulating in England, awaiting the approval of King Henry VIII.[18] When the first was presented to him, the king, not realizing it was Tyndale who had translated the New Testament, proclaimed, "In God's name let it go abroad among the people."

Two years later the king directed that every church in England display "one book of the whole Bible in English." Tyndale's dying prayer was answered.

Tyndale's Bible translations were his lasting legacy. They were so well done that they make up 90 percent of the wordings of the King James Version published nearly one hundred years later and 75 percent of the wordings of the Revised Standard Version of 1952.

Reflection

Some of our prayer requests may not be answered in our lifetime, but that doesn't mean they won't ever be. Which of your prayers are you afraid may fit into this category? Toward the end of his life the prophet Daniel prayed, "For your sake, Lord, smile again on your desolate sanctuary. . . . See how your city lies in ruins—for everyone knows that it is yours. . . . O Lord, listen and act!" (Daniel 9:17-19). Daniel did not live to see the rebuilding of the temple and the city of Jerusalem, but God answered Daniel's prayers according to his own timing. Don't despair! Keep on praying!

Every day I call to you, my God, but you do not answer. Every night you hear my voice, but I find no relief. Yet you are holy. The praises of Israel surround your throne. Our ancestors trusted in you, and you rescued them. You heard their cries for help and saved them. They put their trust in you and were never disappointed. PSALM 22:2-5

June 19

Some children seem to be born with an "I'll do it myself" attitude.

BLAISE PASCAL, one of the greatest intellects of the Western world, had an unquenchable thirst to learn. He was born into an upper-class family in central France on **June 19, 1623.** His father, Etienne, was an attorney, magistrate, and tax collector who loved languages and mathematics and was intensely interested in his children's education. Pascal's mother died when he was only three, and four years later, Etienne moved his family to Paris. There he homeschooled his three children, starting with the study of languages. He was of the opinion that it was best to withhold the study of geometry until they were proficient in languages so they wouldn't be preoccupied with the fascination of mathematics.

However, when young Blaise was only twelve, his father discovered that his precocious son had taught himself geometry. At age sixteen, Pascal attracted the attention of mathematician and philosopher René Descartes by writing a book on the geometry of cones. Concerned by the long hours his father would spend adding up figures at night, Pascal put his problem-solving ability to work and invented the first mechanical calculating machine when he was nineteen. Its principles have remained in use into modern times. Pascal also originated the theory of probability. In the field of physics he discovered a principle known as Pascal's Law, which is the foundation of modern hydraulics.

Pascal was interested in things of the Spirit as well as in science. Encouraged by his father to learn by observation and discovery, Pascal's inquiring mind devoured the Scriptures as well as scientific data. Just as he learned geometry on his own, so his spiritual journey to belief was a private one. On the night that he put his faith in Christ he wrote:

> God of Abraham, God of Isaac, God of Jacob, not of the philosophers and scholars. . . .
> He is to be found only by the ways taught in the Gospel. . . .
> "Righteous Father, the world has not known Thee, but I have known Thee." . . .
> Let me not be separated from Him eternally.
> "This is the eternal life, that they might know Thee, the only true God, and the one whom Thou has sent, Jesus Christ." . . .

Let me never be separated from Him.
We keep hold of Him only by the ways taught in the Gospel.

A few days after Pascal died, a servant of the house happened to notice a bulge in the lining of Pascal's coat. Carefully pulling out the stitches, he discovered two small pieces of parchment in Pascal's handwriting—one a copy of the other. Dated November 23, 1654, the document was a record of his intensely personal revelation on that night. It was apparently so important to Pascal that he made two copies and carefully sewed and unsewed the parchments into the coats he wore until his death eight years later.

Before he died Pascal wrote a classic defense of the Christian faith that was published posthumously under the title *Pensées*.

Reflection

When we read about the conversion of different people, it is tempting to try to generalize from them. It is important to remember that each person's journey to faith is unique. Blaise Pascal came to know God in the way that was best for him. Pascal found because he sought. Likewise, God sought Pascal and found him. Are you seeking God?

"If you look for me in earnest, you will find me when you seek me. I will be found by you," says the Lord.   JEREMIAH 29:13-14

June 20

Less than a century before, France was the ally of the colonists during the Revolutionary War, but now she was their worst enemy.

EVER SINCE William of Orange, a firm Protestant, became king of England in 1689,[19] the French attacks on the English colonies in America had been ferocious. In 1745 the New England forces successfully captured Louisbourg, Nova Scotia, from the French with the help of the English fleet. On **June 20, 1746,** the French angrily responded by dispatching half of their navy "to lay waste the whole seacoast from Nova Scotia to Georgia." When the New Englanders heard rumors of the impending attack, they weren't too concerned because they believed that the English navy was so powerful that it would prevent the French ships from even leaving the shores of France. Little did they know that the French had been able to slip out to sea without being detected.

As the Rev. Thomas Prince, pastor of the South Church in Boston, described it: "While we knew no thing of Danger, God beheld it and was working Salvation for us. And when we had none to help in America, He even prevented our Friends in Europe from coming to succour us; that we might see our Salvation as his Work alone, and that the Glory belongs entirely to Him."

The colonists may not have had the king of England to protect them with his navy, but they had the King of kings. As the seventy French ships headed for Halifax, God first sent a great calm that prevented their ships from sailing, and then he sent several severe storms in which many ships were lost. In addition, a deadly disease swept through the French navy, killing many.

Rev. Jonathan French, a New England pastor, wrote of the people's response when they saw the French ships approaching Halifax: "Never did the religion, for which the country was settled, appear more important, nor prayer more prevalent, than on this occasion. A prayer-hearing God, stretched forth the arm of His power, and destroyed that mighty Armament, in a manner almost as extraordinary as the drowning of Pharaoh and his host in the Red Sea."

Shortly after arriving in Halifax, the French admiral, appalled at the loss of most of his fleet and finding his few remaining ships damaged with many crewmen dead or dying, lapsed into a deep depression and died a few days later, his crew suspecting that it was at his own hand. A few more ships limped into port, but they also had so many sick crewmen and such low stocks of food that the commander who replaced the deceased admiral himself committed suicide.

Three days after the remaining French ships left Halifax to attack Annapolis, the citizens of New England held a day of prayer and fasting for God's deliverance. The Reverand Mr. French described it: "On this great emergency, and day of darkness and doubtful expectation, the 16th of October was observed as a day of fasting and prayer throughout the Province. And, wonderful to relate, that very night God sent upon them a more dreadful storm than either of the former, and completed their destruction. Some overset, some foundered, and a remnant only of this miserable fleet returned to France to carry the news. Thus New England stood still, and saw the salvation of God."

Reflection

How wonderful to know that God often begins to answer our prayers before we even pray. Has this ever happened to you? What does this tell you about God? Living a life of dependence on God means trusting him to protect us even when we don't know we are in danger!

I will answer them before they even call to me. While they are still talking to me about their needs, I will go ahead and answer their prayers!   ISAIAH 65:24

June 21

Five hundred years ago being ahead of the curve in science could put you on a collision course with the church.

GALILEO GALILEI was born in Pisa, Italy, the day Michelangelo died (February 18, 1564) and the same year that Shakespeare was born. He became the leading astronomer of his day and was given lifetime tenure as a professor at the University of Padua. In 1610, using his newly invented telescope that could magnify one thousand times, Galileo discovered four moons revolving around Jupiter. By analogy he reasoned that the planets revolved around the sun, agreeing with the view set forth by Copernicus a century earlier. The other professors at Padua refused to even look through his telescope. Galileo took this as his signal that he should leave Padua and go to Florence instead.

Galileo's conclusions brought to public attention the question of whether the earth circled the sun or the sun circled the earth. Soon Galileo was accused of contradicting the Bible. In 1615 a formal protest was lodged against Galileo before the Inquisition, a special tribunal set up in the medieval church to combat heresy. To answer his critics, Galileo went to Rome, hoping to convert the leaders of the church to his point of view. Galileo promoted his ideas so extensively in Rome that soon everyone in the city was discussing astronomy. However, the Inquisition directed Galileo to abandon his opinions and not discuss them further. In February 1616 the Inquisition published its edict: "The view that the sun stands motionless at the center of the universe is foolish, philosophically false, and utterly heretical." To avoid the threatened imprisonment, Galileo declared his submission to the decree.

Galileo was able to keep out of the public eye until 1632 when he published his major book on astronomy, which explained his understanding of the relationship between the earth and the sun. The book was widely acclaimed throughout the academic world, but the Inquisition immediately demanded that Galileo appear before it once again, accusing him of breaking his promise to obey the edict of 1616. Threatened with torture on **June 21, 1632,** Galileo agreed with the position of the church and declared the earth to be motionless with the sun moving around it. The next day, in spite of this denial of his convictions, the Inquisition found Galileo guilty of heresy and sentenced him to prison for an indefinite length of time. As penance, he was to recite seven penitential psalms daily for three years.

DOES THE SUN CIRCLE THE EARTH?

Fortunately for Galileo, after he had spent just three days in prison the pope allowed him to be kept as prisoner in his own villa. There he was free to pursue his studies, while his daughter, a nun, recited the penitential psalms for him.

Reflection

Since God is the author of both nature and the Bible, from his perspective there are no contradictions between the two. Christians need to study both science and the Bible to see how they fit together. We don't need to be afraid of what we will find, for the Bible is an absolute standard of truth. We just need to trust God to show us what the real facts are—even if the answer may be slow in coming!

୶

Fear of the Lord is the beginning of knowledge. Only fools despise wisdom and discipline.   PROVERBS 1:7

June 22

A truly great teacher lives on in the lives of his students.

EVERY STORE closed and all business was suspended on **June 22, 1878,** in Princeton, New Jersey. The occasion was a funeral—but not for a war hero or for a famous statesman, as one might presume. It was the funeral of Charles Hodge, the leading American theologian of the nineteenth century.[20]

Born in Philadelphia in 1797, the son of an army surgeon, Hodge attended Princeton College and while there made a public profession of faith in Christ in a revival that spread through the college in the winter of 1814–1815. After graduating, he went across the street to attend Princeton Seminary, receiving his degree in 1819. One year later Hodge became an instructor at the seminary at the age of twenty-three. He remained there for the rest of his life.

During his lifetime he taught more than three thousand students. His influence was spread further because thousands heard his sermons and tens of thousands read his writings. Hodge wrote over five thousand pages in *The Biblical Repertory,* later named *The Princeton Review,* a theological journal that he founded. In addition, he wrote a similar amount in articles published elsewhere and in his books. His three-volume *Systematic Theology* is still a standard today. Yet Hodge's greatest legacy was not his writings but the three thousand students he taught through the years. Most of them became pastors, missionaries, and church leaders.

Perhaps the best illustration of Hodge's impact on his students was the graduation tradition at the seminary that began about 1868 and continued every year until Hodge's death. After the benediction was pronounced, the graduating class made a circle around Charles Hodge at the middle of the front campus. They sang several verses of the hymn "All Hail the Power of Jesus' Name." Then, making a tighter circle with each graduate crossing his arms across his chest and grasping the hands of the students on either side, they sang together "Blest Be the Tie That Binds," followed by the doxology. After Hodge pronounced a benediction, he shook hands with each student, and all went their separate ways to minister the gospel.

When Charles Hodge died, the entire town of Princeton closed down to honor its most beloved son at his funeral on **June 22, 1878.** A former student who gave the funeral address said, "When due allowance is made for his intellect and his learning, . . . his chief power was in his goodness. Christ enshrined in his heart was the center of his theology and life. The world shall write upon his monument GREAT; but we, his students, will write upon it GOOD."

The funeral procession moved slowly down Witherspoon Street to the cemetery, where his sons laid him in the grave next to the wife of his youth. They read once more the inscription that Hodge, as a grieving husband years before, had placed on his wife's tombstone: "We lay you gently here, our best beloved, to gather strength and beauty for the coming of the Lord."

Reflection

Charles Hodge invested his life in his students. In so doing, he was following Jesus' example of investing his life in his disciples. Think of the people who are in your daily sphere of influence—your children, coworkers, neighbors and friends. Whom do you believe God has given to you in whom you can invest your life?

∽≈⌒

You have heard me teach many things that have been confirmed by many reliable witnesses. Teach these great truths to trustworthy people who are able to pass them on to others.   2 TIMOTHY 2:2

June 23

Even more important to Charles Hodge than his students were his own children.

YESTERDAY we read of the great ministry to students that theologian Charles Hodge had while teaching on the faculty at Princeton Seminary.[21] But even more important to Hodge than his students were his own children.

The Hodge children were an active and lively bunch who loved to play in their large house on the seminary grounds as well as on the campus. Whenever Hodge was not teaching a class, he was at his study in his home. From the summer of 1833 to the winter of 1836 Hodge even taught his classes in his home—either in the large back parlor or in his study. Hodge's study was also where the seminary faculty meetings were held and where college and seminary professors would gather for regular times of discussion and fellowship. Almost every night a colleague, pastor, or scholar stopped by, and the children looked on with interest as great debates and discussions took place.

Hodge's study had two doors. One was an outside door for students or other faculty members to use. The other door was into the main hall of the house so that he was always available to his children. One of his sons recalled how he led daily family prayers and taught his children at his knee with such tenderness that however naughty they may have been, their hearts melted at his touch. As part of their morning family worship they repeated a personal consecration to the Father, Son, and Holy Spirit that Hodge had written for his family. In such an atmosphere of openness and availability, the children followed their father's faith, and each made an early commitment to the Lord Jesus.

Many of the students became familiar to the family. When Hodge's ten-year-old son, Archibald, and daughter Mary Elizabeth heard that James Eckard, one of the seminary graduates, was soon to set sail as a missionary to Ceylon, the two children wrote a letter on **June 23, 1833,** to send with Eckard. It read:

Dear Heathen:
    The Lord Jesus Christ hath promised that the time shall come when all the ends of the earth shall be His kingdom. And God is not a man that He should lie nor the son of man that He should repent. And if this is promised by a Being who cannot lie, why do you not help it to come sooner by reading

the Bible, and attending the words of your teachers, and loving God, and renouncing your idols, take Christianity into your temples? And soon there will be not a Nation, no, not a space of ground as large as a footstep, that will not want a missionary. My sister and myself have, by small self-denials, procured two dollars which are enclosed in this letter to buy tracts and Bibles to teach you.

    Archibald Alexander Hodge and Mary Elizabeth Hodge
    Friends of the Heathen

Archibald Alexander Hodge grew up to succeed his father as professor of systematic theology at Princeton Seminary.

Reflection

We can see the priority that Charles Hodge placed on spending time with his children. Many of the most important lessons we can impart to children come about because we are in the right place at the right time to teach them. Can you think of ways that God can use you more in the lives of the children in your sphere of influence?

        ❧

Teach your children to choose the right path, and when they are older, they will remain upon it.   PROVERBS 22:6

June 24

Behold the power of prayer.

WILLIAM CAREY has been called the "Father of Modern Missions."[22] Born near Northampton, England, in 1761, Carey worked as a shoemaker from the age of fourteen to twenty-eight. Born again at eighteen, he began preaching in the evenings.

At the age of nineteen Carey married Dorothy Plackett, who was called Dolly. She was six years older than her husband and had very little in common with him. Whereas Carey had taught himself Latin by the age of twelve and went on to master Greek, Hebrew, French, and Dutch, Dolly was illiterate and signed her name with an X. As a journeyman shoemaker, Carey was never able to raise his family out of poverty.

As a young man Carey developed a great burden for unevangelized people in foreign lands. In 1792 he was instrumental in founding the first modern missionary society, the Particular Baptist Society for Propagating the Gospel among the Heathen, later known as the Baptist Missionary Society. The following year Carey went to India as the mission board's first missionary.

At first Dolly refused to accompany her husband to India, wanting to stay behind with her two youngest sons, Peter and Jabez. Carey insisted that at least his six-year-old son, William Jr., go with him. Finally Dolly was pressured into joining the venture, and the whole family went together to India.

Once there, five-year-old Peter died of dysentery, and Dolly was pushed over the edge into insanity. She had delusions that her husband was having affairs with other women and would follow him down the street berating him. Finally he had to keep her in a locked room. Their deeply troubled family life had a devastating effect on the children. Throughout their early years the boys never experienced a functional family. They basically raised themselves because their father, though he loved them dearly, was too busy and too mild mannered to discipline them.

Years later back in England on **June 24, 1812,** the Baptist Missionary Society met to celebrate its twentieth anniversary. John Ryland,[23] the pastor who had baptized William Carey years before, gave the evening sermon. As he was about to close his remarks, Ryland mentioned that he had gotten a letter from William Carey in which he wrote that one of his sons, nineteen-year-old Jabez, had brought much heartache to his father in India because he had never given his allegiance to Jesus. Carey had agonized in prayer for years over his son's lost condition and now was asking his English supporters to join him in prayer for him. As Ryland explained about the lost condition of Jabez, tears streamed down his face, and he pleaded, "Brethren, let us send up a united, universal and fervent prayer to God in solemn silence for the conversion of Jabez Carey." One of the men who had been in the room related that these words hit the audience like a clap of thunder, as nearly two thousand people bowed their heads in prayer for Jabez's salvation.

The next mail the mission society received from India contained a letter that reported that Jabez Carey had recently put his trust in Jesus.

Reflection

Are you praying for the salvation of unsaved friends or relatives? If not, start now. William Carey prayed for his son for years, even when it seemed hopeless. Ask God for whom you should pray, and then ask others to join with you to pray for their salvation. Then keep on praying regardless of the time that passes.

As for me, I will certainly not sin against the Lord by ending my prayers for you.　　　　　　　　　1 SAMUEL 12:23

June 25

It all began with King Saul.

IN THE fifth century B.C. all the Jews in the world lived under the rule of the Persian Empire that controlled the entire Near East. In 474 B.C. they were in a desperate situation. Xerxes was king of the empire, and his prime minister, Haman, hated the Jews. Incensed that a Jew named Mordecai refused to kneel down before him, Haman vindictively plotted to have not only Mordecai, but all the Jews in the empire put to death. As prime minister, he received permission from Xerxes to issue a decree setting a date for the extermination of the Jews eleven months later (Esther 3). Since virtually all Jews lived within the Persian Empire, this decree was a direct threat to God's program of redemption.

The key to understanding this confrontation can be found in the name of Haman's father, Hammedatha the Agagite (Esther 3:1). Haman's name indicates that he and his father descended from Agag, the king of Amalek (1 Samuel 15:20). Thus, Haman himself could be considered an Amalekite. The Amalekites had been the first nation to attack Israel after its exodus from Egypt, and as a result, God had declared, "I will blot out every trace of Amalek from under heaven" (Exodus 17:14). Later God commanded Israel, "Never forget what the Amalekites did to you as you came from Egypt. . . . Therefore, when the Lord your God has given you rest from all your enemies in the land he is giving you as a special possession, you are to destroy the Amalekites and erase their memory from under heaven. Never forget this!" (Deuteronomy 25:17, 19) Years later Saul, the first king of Israel, disobeyed God and spared Agag, king of the Amalekites, rather than killing him as God had commanded. Because of this disobedience, God rejected Saul as king (1 Samuel 15; cf. 30:1-18).

Mordecai is described as a descendant of Kish (Esther 2:5) who was the father of Saul (1 Samuel 9:1-2). And now, five hundred years after King Saul, Mordecai, Saul's descendant, continued to battle the Amalekites.

Mordecai persuaded his cousin Queen Esther to go uninvited to the court of King Xerxes at risk of her life to petition him to spare her people, the Jews, from Haman's decree. She found favor with the king, and he granted her an audience. The king listened to her petition and agreed to grant it; however, since a Persian law could not be revoked, he had to issue another decree. On **June 25, 474 B.C.**, King Xerxes issued a decree granting authority to the Jews

THE COST OF INCOMPLETE OBEDIENCE

to defend themselves against their enemies when the attack mandated by his first decree commenced (Esther 4:1–8:16).

The book of Esther thus describes the final chapter in God's holy war on the Amalekites.

Haman was hanged on the gallows he had prepared for Mordecai (Esther 7:1-10), and Mordecai replaced him as prime minister (Esther 8:2, 15). The following year when the Jews were attacked, they successfully defended themselves, killing seventy-five thousand of their enemies, including all the sons of Haman (Esther 9:1-17). God's command to exterminate the Amalekites (1 Samuel 15:2-3) was finally fulfilled.

Reflection

King Saul's incomplete obedience resulted in five hundred years of further conflict. What are examples in your life when you have been only partially obedient to God? What have been the results? We can't make a partial effort and expect a full result. God expects full obedience.

Teach these new disciples to obey all the commands I have given you.
MATTHEW 28:20

June 26

Have you ever wondered what it would be like to face imminent martyrdom?

ON JUNE 26, 1570, Anabaptist Joost Verkindert wrote the following letter to his brother and sister-in-law from an Antwerp prison before he was burned at the stake for his faith:

> Grace, joy and peace from God the heavenly Father, and our dear Lord Jesus Christ, who loved us and washed us from our sins in His own blood, and the consolation of the Holy Ghost, who is the comforter of them that are in any tribulation and sorrow. To Him be praise, honor, glory, dominion, power and majesty forever and ever. Amen. This I wish you for a friendly and cordial greeting, my very dear and beloved brother with your dear wife.
>
> Know further, that I am still tolerably well, according to the flesh, and as regards the spirit, I hope through God's great and unspeakable grace to finish this great and severe conflict with the help of the Most High—from whom we must expect help and comfort—to the praise of His holy name. . . . I also received a salutation from you together with the things that were sent to us, which much exhorted us, and was a great consolation in our tribulation, so that we rejoiced, and praised and thanked God, that there are still such good-hearted brethren, who remember us poor, weak prisoners.
>
> O dear brethren and sisters, always remember us in your prayers, that the Lord may strengthen us, so that we may put off our flesh with joy here upon earth; for it is sometimes much afraid of the gag and of being burnt alive, which is nevertheless very soon over. But when I think of the fire that shall burn and last forever, I thank the Lord, that He has made me worthy to confess His holy name among this evil and perverse generation. . . .
>
> Further, my dear brother, I commend to you my wife, whom I love from the heart; desiring and requesting of you that you will exercise Christian care over her, the more so because she desires to remain a widow; for the holy Scripture commands us to visit the widows and orphans in their affliction. James 1:27. Hence, be diligent to aid her in everything wherein she may need your counsel, in order to gain a livelihood for herself and my children; so that she may not become despondent.
>
> O my dear brethren, this I exhort you with tears, for if the Lord had not

taken me from them, I could have provided for them myself according to my weakness; but now the Lord has ordered it otherwise with me, since He knows best what we need, and what is for our best. Hence, I will also leave them for the Lord's sake; for, dear brother, my wife has been with me, and we ate together a parting meal, and thus took final adieu from each other. Think for yourself, how bitter a parting it was, for I know that she also loves me from the heart. . . .

Remember me, my dear brother and sister; I hope to wait for you under the altar, where all tears shall be wiped away from our eyes. Herewith I will commend you to the crucified Christ Jesus; may He strengthen our hearts and minds, and direct them into all that is acceptable before Him. Herewith I bid you adieu. Adieu, my beloved brother and sister.

Joost Verkindert

Reflection

We can be deeply touched by the stories of martyrs like Joost Verkindert yet still find their experiences somewhat irrelevant to our lives. But did you know that there were more martyrs in the twentieth century than in any other? We always think that martyrdom is something that happens to other people, but what if it isn't? What if it happens to us? The Scriptures that brought comfort to martyrs long ago are written for our comfort as well.

Even when I walk through the dark valley of death, I will not be afraid, for you are close beside me. PSALM 23:4

June 27

For eight long years the emperor had been Julian the Apostate, but things were about to change.

JUNE 27, 363, was a happy day for the Christians of the Roman Empire. For eight long years the emperor had been Julian the Apostate, but things were about to change.

Born in 331, Julian was the nephew of Constantine the Great, the first Christian emperor of the Roman Empire. Constantine the Great had legalized Christianity in the empire.[24] When Julian was six years old, Constantine died, and the empire was divided among his three sons, Constantine II, Constans, and Constantius, all Julian's cousins. After a series of wars between the sons, Constantius, also a Christian, emerged victorious as emperor.

Julian had received a Christian education, but he had secretly rejected it, seeing hypocrisy in the lives of his supposedly Christian teachers. He was baptized and even ordained to serve as a lector, one who read the Scriptures in worship services, but the austere Christianity that was forced on him made him a rebel. He went to study in Athens, where he enthusiastically embraced the teachings of Homer, Plato, and Aristotle. While in Athens he became a convert to ancient Greek idolatry. He told his private confidants that he was in daily communication with Jupiter, Minerva, Apollo, and Hercules, who assured him of their personal special protection. However, he publicly concealed his commitment to the Greek gods, for it was politically incorrect at the time since the Roman Empire had become Christian.

In 356 Emperor Constantius made Julian, his cousin, the governor of Gaul (modern France), where Julian had distinguished himself in battle. Meanwhile, Constantius was in Constantinople (modern Istanbul) and was threatened by the Persians. He ordered some of Julian's troops to come to his aid. Not wanting to march the two thousand miles to Constantinople, Julian's troops mutinied against Constantius's orders and proclaimed Julian emperor instead. This act of outright rebellion made civil war appear imminent, but Constantius died before it could occur, leaving Julian the undisputed emperor. It was not until just before Constantius died that Julian publicly revealed his allegiance to the Greek gods.

As emperor, Julian immediately set about restoring paganism, earning him the name of Julian the Apostate. In addition to levying heavy taxes on

A DECEITFUL EMPEROR

Christians, Julian also removed them from military and government offices and prohibited them from teaching school. He reopened the pagan temples and reinstituted the priesthood and the sacrifices.

In an effort to discredit the Christian holy places in Jerusalem, Julian decided to rebuild the Jewish temple. However, when the workers were laying the foundation, they struck underground deposits of gas that exploded and burned, ending the project.

After reigning eight years, Julian went to war against the Persians. The Christians dreaded his return and were relieved to hear that he had died of wounds he received in battle. The day after Julian's death, **June 27, 363**, the army elected a Christian general, Jovian, as the new emperor. When news arrived that Julian had died and that his replacement was a Christian, there was great rejoicing in the churches.

Reflection

Throughout history tyrants often arise unexpectedly. How do you think you would react to living under an anti-Christian dictator? The people in Julian's time were not expecting his return to paganism and the resulting persecution of Christians. What can you be doing to prepare for such a possibility? Faith needs strong roots if it is to stand firm in difficult times.

The Most High rules over the kingdoms of the world and gives them to anyone he chooses.   DANIEL 4:17

June 28

Have you ever noticed how God sometimes uses unlikely characters to play important roles in executing his plan?

A CASE in point is the four-hundred-pound founder of the Episcopal Church.

He was born on **June 28, 1491,** the second son of King Henry VII of England. Named after his father, young Henry was trained for a career in the church with a classical education since as second son he was not born to be king. However, when his older brother, Arthur, died in 1502, young Henry became the heir apparent to the throne.

Henry was just seventeen when his father died and he began to reign as King Henry VIII. Honoring his father's dying request, he married his brother's widow, Catherine of Aragon, thus maintaining the alliance between England and Spain. Two weeks after their wedding in 1509, they were crowned king and queen of England. Henry turned over the management of his realm to his ministers, in particular to Thomas Wolsey, his chaplain. In 1515 Wolsey was made a cardinal by the pope and lord chancellor by Henry.

In the early years of his reign, Henry was concerned with two issues: the spreading Reformation and his inability to sire a male heir. In ecclesiastical matters, Henry VIII was a strong supporter of the pope against the Reformation. In 1521 he coauthored a book, *Defense of the Seven Sacraments*, which became a best-seller throughout Europe.

As Henry VIII grew older and larger, his preoccupation with his lack of a male heir grew. Catherine of Aragon bore him six children, but only one, Mary Tudor, survived infancy.[25] To Henry, it was unthinkable that a girl would succeed him. This became especially frustrating for him in 1519 when his mistress Elizabeth Blount bore him a son who was ineligible to succeed him because of his illegitimacy. When Catherine turned forty in 1526, it was obvious to Henry that she would never bear him a son.

By 1527 Henry was "head over heels" in love with twenty-year-old Anne Boleyn, the younger sister of an earlier mistress. Cardinal Wolsey tried to arrange a divorce from Catherine through the pope, but the issue dragged on for years. Finally, Henry defiantly took things into his own hands and in a direct challenge to the pope's authority, made himself head of the Church of England. He felt it was the only way he could ever get a divorce from Catherine. Henry named Thomas Cranmer, who had been influenced by Lutheranism, archbishop of Canterbury, and Cranmer reciprocated by granting Henry VIII's divorce from Catherine of Aragon.[26] Henry secretly married Anne Boleyn,[27] the second of his six wives, before his divorce was final.

More important for the future, Henry enacted a series of laws that permanently separated the Church of England from the Roman Catholic Church. Today the Church of England is known in the United States as the Episcopal Church and elsewhere as the Anglican Church.

Henry himself may never have subscribed to any Protestant doctrines and his motives may have been self-serving, yet God used him to begin the Reformation in England. God uses whom he chooses to achieve his purposes.

Reflection

What person or experience has God used in your life in unexpected ways? Did his choice puzzle you? King Henry VIII may have had selfish reasons for forming the Anglican Church, but God used him for his purposes anyway. The wonder of God's sovereignty is that we don't have to understand why he does what he does. It is enough to know that it is all part of his greater plan for our good and his glory.

We know that God causes everything to work together for the good of those who love God and are called according to his purpose for them.

ROMANS 8:28

June 29

God began the American foreign missions movement in a very unlikely place.

Foreign missions organizations are common in America today, but in the early 1800s there was not a single foreign missions board in the United States. God was to begin the American foreign missions movement in a very unlikely place—a haystack!

Williams College in Williamstown, Massachusetts, was just twelve years old in 1805 when the Second Great Awakening reached the school. In the spring of 1806 Samuel Mills, the son of a Congregational minister, joined the freshman class with a passion to spread the gospel around the world. He began leading a prayer group of four other students who had been touched by the revival. They met three afternoons a week in the maple grove of nearby Sloan's Meadow.

One sultry day in August 1806 a violent thunderstorm interrupted their prayer time, and they took refuge on the sheltered side of a large haystack. There in the sanctuary of the haystack, Mills directed their prayers to their own personal missionary obligation. God spoke to them as they prayed, and four of the five committed themselves to serving God overseas if he so led. The Haystack Prayer Meeting was not only the beginning of the first American student mission society but was also the beginning of the American foreign missions movement itself. In two years their prayer group took the name The Society of the Brethren, with the motto "We can do it if we will."

Two years later many of the group enrolled at Andover Seminary in Andover, Massachusetts, where they were joined by Adoniram Judson[28] and others interested in foreign missions. There they continued to believe that God was calling them to the mission field, but there was no foreign missions board in America to send them.

The students took their problem to the seminary faculty and to pastors in the area. In response, the teachers and pastors met at the home of Moses Stuart, one of the Andover faculty. Their advice was that the students submit their case to the General Association, a body made up of the Congregational Churches of Massachusetts, which was to meet in Bradford, Massachusetts, beginning the following day.

Acting on this advice, the students wrote a letter explaining their plight and soliciting the association's help. The letter was signed by Adoniram Judson, Samuel Mills, and two others. Originally Luther Rice and James Richards also signed the letter but removed their names, lest the number of potential missionary candidates needing support scare the Association.

Two days later, on **June 29, 1810,** the association responded to their request by forming the American Board of Commissioners for Foreign Missions, the first foreign missions board in America. A year later the board sent out Adoniram Judson and three other men with their families as their first missionaries.

From that humble beginning the foreign missions force of the United States has grown to over sixty thousand missionaries sent out by hundreds of mission boards.

Reflection

God's plan for this age is to "make disciples of all the nations" (Matthew 28:19). What do you see as your role in fulfilling the great commission? The students in the Haystack Prayer Meeting prayed faithfully for the opportunity to be foreign missionaries. They did not let the lack of a mission board in America to send them stand in their way. We can learn much from their faithfulness. Not everyone can go, but all can pray and give.

My ambition has always been to preach the Good News where the name of Christ has never been heard, rather than where a church has already been started by someone else. I have been following the plan spoken of in the Scriptures, where it says, "Those who have never been told about him will see, and those who have never heard of him will understand."
ROMANS 15:20-21

June 30

If you can't change your husband, God can.

ROBERT E. LEE was born in Virginia in 1807, son of "Light-horse Harry" Lee, a famous Revolutionary War cavalry officer and governor of Virginia. In 1829 Robert graduated from West Point second in his class and was commissioned a second lieutenant in the army.

Mary Custis was the great-granddaughter of George Washington, Lee's hero, and grew up in Arlington House, which still stands today on a hill in Arlington National Cemetery overlooking Washington, D.C.

The Lee and Custis families were distantly related, and Robert spent much time at Arlington as he was growing up. He fell in love with Mary, the only child in the Custis family, and they chose **June 30, 1831,** for their wedding day.

Mary had recently put her trust in Christ, and as their wedding date approached, she was particularly concerned about Robert's spiritual condition. Not too long before, she had struggled with her own sinfulness until, in her own words, "I was made to feel willing to give up all for God, even my life if God should require it." Thereafter, she said, "came joy and peace." In her letters to Robert she described praying ceaselessly that God "may turn your heart to Him."

But unfortunately Robert brought no such change of heart to their wedding. He half-jokingly said that the sermon in their wedding service made him feel as if his death warrant was being read!

It wasn't until seventeen years later after hearing a remarkable sermon in Baltimore that Lee found the blessed assurance for which Mary yearned for him. He told her that he was now certain that only surrender to God was the answer to the problems of life. It thrilled Mary to hear him tell her, "My trust is in the mercy of Christ."

When the Civil War broke out, President Lincoln offered Lee the field command of the Union Army. However, though Lee opposed both slavery and secession and had freed all the slaves he had inherited, his loyalty was first and foremost to his beloved Virginia. He concluded that Virginia was fighting for the very freedom for which the Revolutionary War was fought and therefore joined the Confederate cause, seeing it as a second war of independence.

June 30, 1864, their thirty-third wedding anniversary, found Robert E. Lee defending Petersburg, Virginia, as the general of the Army of Northern Virginia at the beginning of what was to be a nine-month siege by Grant's Union army. Yet he took time to write his dear wife, who had been quite sick that summer, an anniversary note:

> *I was very glad to receive your letter yesterday, and to hear that you were better. I trust that you will continue to improve and soon be as well as usual. God grant that you may be entirely restored in His own good time. Do you recollect what a happy day thirty-three years ago this was? How many hopes and pleasures it gave birth to! God has been merciful and kind to us, and how thankless and sinful I have been. I pray that He may continue His mercies and blessings to us, and give us a little peace and rest together in this world, and finally gather us and all He has given us around His throne in the world to come. The President has just arrived and I must bring my letter to a close.*

Reflection

Are you praying for members of your family who have never put their trust in Jesus? Mary Lee prayed for seventeen years before her husband finally trusted in Jesus Christ as his Savior, so don't lose heart!

In the same way, you wives must accept the authority of your husbands, even those who refuse to accept the Good News. Your godly lives will speak to them better than any words. They will be won over by watching your pure, godly behavior.   1 PETER 3:1-2

July 1

Some go to Hawaii for more than the scenery.

TITUS COAN was converted at a Charles Finney revival in western New York State. After graduating from seminary in 1834, he went as a missionary to Hilo, Hawaii, then known as the Sandwich Islands. Having a burning desire to bring revival to Hawaii, he applied himself vigorously to learning the native languages of Kau and Puna and by 1836 was fluent enough to preach in both.

Coan's official responsibility was to train teachers and oversee about two dozen schools. But Titus Coan's vision went far beyond teacher training. His prayer was that Hawaiians would come to Christ, and he determined to take the gospel directly to the people himself. In November 1836 he gave his students a long Christmas vacation and went on a walking tour of the island, ostensibly to visit the schools for which he was responsible. Each time he came to a village, he preached. As he had hoped, crowds of people gathered to hear him, and he was able to preach in three to five villages a day.

When Coan reached the Puna region, large crowds gathered to hear him. In the largest city he preached ten times in two days. Many wept as they came to understand that Christ had paid the penalty for their sins on the cross. Each time Coan finished his message, the crowds, instead of leaving, would follow him to the house where he was staying. They would crowd in, hanging on his every word, until the house could hold no more. At eleven at night he would insist that everyone go home, but they would be back as soon as the cock crowed the next morning.

A particularly stunning conversion in Puna was that of the high priest of the volcano. In addition to the idolatry, drunkenness, and adultery associated with his priesthood, he also was a murderer. Yet upon his conversion, he became a man filled with zeal for God. His sister, the high priestess of the volcano, though initially hostile to the gospel, put her faith in Christ after seeing the change in her brother.

When Coan returned home to Hilo after a month, he found a heightened interest in the way of salvation. People who had heard him preach in their villages in Kau and Puna now came to Hilo to hear more. In some cases, whole villages would come. The population of Hilo grew to ten thousand as people moved there just to hear Coan preach. On Sundays the two hundred-by-eighty-five-foot building would be packed, with hundreds more listening outside. The Hawaiians decided on their own they needed a bigger church and in three weeks built a building large enought to hold two thousand.

On one occasion a young man came intending to disrupt the service by making people laugh during the prayers. Instead, he suddenly fell unconscious and had to be carried out. Several hours later when he came to, he confessed his sin. Before long he became a member of the church he had tried to disrupt.

A year into the revival tragedy struck. A tidal wave hit the island during an evening prayer service. About two hundred were swept out to sea. Only thirteen drowned, but the survivors lost almost all of their possessions. Yet after the tidal wave the church continued to grow.

In spite of thousands of conversions in 1836 and 1837, the church's membership didn't grow until 1838 and 1839. The slow growth reflected a flaw in missionary Coan's methodology, not disinterest on the part of the new converts. Coan would record the date of each conversion and then wait months before recontacting the person to ascertain if the conversion was real. Only then would the person be invited to join the church. It wasn't until **July 1, 1838,** that the first converts were finally baptized and received into the church. On that stirring day 1,705 were baptized. By 1853 fifty-six thousand of the seventy-one thousand native Hawaiians were professing Christians.

Reflection

Titus Coan's zeal for reaching the Hawaiians for Christ influenced everything he did. Do you have zeal for seeing those around you come to Christ? What can we learn from Titus Coan's life to help us reach our friends and relatives for Christ?

How can they believe in him if they have never heard about him?
ROMANS 10:14

July 2

When should Christians rebel?

In 1642 the Puritans of England thought that the time had come. Charles I had been king of England since 1625. In that year he had married the daughter of King Henry IV of France, a fervent Roman Catholic. Charles, as head of the Church of England, supported the High Church Party within the church with its tendencies toward Roman Catholicism and sought to crush his Puritan opposition.

His effort to force Puritans to conform strictly to the practices of the Anglican Prayer Book caused many to emigrate to America. Those who remained in England harbored a growing resentment against Charles.

Earlier, in 1637, Charles set up his own downfall by ineptly handling the Scottish Church. Having declared himself the head of the Church of Scotland, Charles imposed a book of prayer on the Scottish Church that was more Roman Catholic than the one used by the Church of England. The Scots responded by signing the National Covenant in 1638, which made the Scottish Church officially Presbyterian. The following year they revolted against Charles. Needing funds to fight the Scots, in 1640 Charles was forced to convene Parliament for the first time in eleven years to raise money. Unfortunately for Charles, most of the members of the House of Commons were Puritans.

Charles's fatal blunder came in 1642 when he attempted to arrest five leaders of Parliament for treason. The result was civil war. Charles I had the support of the Anglican clergy and the nobility, while Parliament had the support of the Puritans and the merchant class.

The crucial battle came in 1644. Oliver Cromwell, a godly Puritan, became the leading general of the Parliamentary army. In early summer he began a siege of the royalist city of York. From his headquarters in Oxford, Charles I ordered his son Prince Rupert with his army of twenty thousand to go to the relief of York. When Rupert arrived, the Parliamentary army retreated a few miles southwest to Marston Moor. On **July 2, 1644**, Prince Rupert, not content simply to relieve York, attacked the Parliamentary army as they were about to move south. Initially the right wing of the Parliamentary army was routed by the Royalists. But on the left, Cromwell's cavalry defeated the cavalry of Rupert and followed them in hot pursuit. When the rout was complete, they turned back to aid the Parliamentarian infantry. The result was a total victory for Cromwell. The king lost his army, and the queen escaped to France.

The Puritans' attitude in the civil war can be sensed in a letter that Cromwell wrote three days after the battle to the father of a soldier who had died at Marston Moor:

Dear Sir, It is our duty to sympathize in all mercies; and to praise the Lord together in chastisements or trials, that so we may sorrow together.

Truly England and the Church of God hath had a great favor from the Lord, in this great victory given unto us, such as the like never was since this War began. It had all the evidences of an absolute victory obtained by the Lord's blessing upon the Godly Party principally. We never charged but we routed the enemy. . . . The particulars I cannot relate now; but I believe, of twenty thousand the Prince hath not four thousand left. Give glory, all glory, to God.

Sir, God hath taken away your eldest son by a cannon shot. It broke his leg. We were necessitated to have it cut off, whereof he died. Sir, you know my own trials this way [his own son Oliver had been killed not long before]; but the Lord supported me in this, that the Lord took him into the happiness we all pant and long for. There is your precious child full of glory, never to know sin or sorrow anymore.

The Lord be your strength: so prays,
Your faithful and loving brother,
Oliver Cromwell

Reflection

If you had lived at the time of the English civil war, on which side do you think you might have been? Are there circumstances under which Christians have the right to overthrow their government? What would those circumstances be?

❧

Give to everyone what you owe them: Pay your taxes and import duties, and give respect and honor to all to whom it is due.

ROMANS 13:7

July 3

Not all faithful preachers end their years of ministry being appreciated outside their own congregation.

DEVEREUX JARRATT was born about twenty-five miles southeast of Richmond, Virginia, in 1733. There was a Church of England parish about three miles away, but the Jarratts attended infrequently.

When Jarratt was nineteen, he left home to become a schoolteacher in northwestern Virginia on the edge of the Appalachian Mountains, then considered the American frontier. There were no churches in the area.

After his initial teaching job, Jarratt was invited to stay at the home of a wealthy Virginian named John Cannon and took a job teaching at a nearby school. Mrs. Cannon was a supporter of the Great Awakening that had been sweeping through America under the preaching of George Whitefield.[1] She read sermons out loud every evening and invited Jarratt to come and listen. Although initially he just feigned interest, eventually the sermons touched his heart, and he determined to try to abandon his sins and to save his soul. Jarratt was the first person Mrs. Cannon had ever seen who seemed to be drawn to her faith, so she invited him to stay on in their home. Jarratt stayed for a year, teaching school during the day and listening to sermons in the evening.

After returning briefly to his first teaching position, Jarratt moved back into the Cannons' home to take a better paying position tutoring their son. At this time a Presbyterian minister began preaching nearby once a month. Although he was not a particularly gifted preacher, Jarratt attended every service. He spent time with the pastor, who introduced him to the writings of Richard Baxter[2] and the hymns of Isaac Watts.[3]

It was during his second stay at the Cannons' home that Jarratt finally met the Savior personally. He described his experience as follows:

> I was blessed with faith to believe, not one promise only, but all the promises of the gospel with joy unspeakable and full of glory. I saw a fullness of Christ to save to the uttermost, that, had I ten thousand souls as wretched and guilty as mine was, I could venture all on his blood and righteousness without one doubt or fear. . . . Such a bright manifestation of the Redeemer's all-sufficiency and willingness to save, and such a divine confidence to rely on him, I never had until that moment—it was a delightful little heaven on earth—so sweet, so

ravishing, so delightful, I uttered not a word, but silently rejoiced in God my Savior.

After his conversion, friends encouraged him to enter the ministry. Learning that both George Whitefield and John Wesley[4] were ordained in the Church of England, he decided to prepare for ordination there as well. However, in order to be ordained in the Church of England he had to go to England. Jarratt sold a piece of land that he had inherited and used the proceeds to finance his trip to England.

On **July 3, 1763,** Devereux Jarratt arrived back in America an ordained priest of the Church of England, which after the Revolutionary War became known in the United States as the Episcopal Church. He became pastor of the Bath parish in Dinwiddie County, Virginia, south of Petersburg, within thirty miles of where he was born.

Jarratt played a major role in the Southern Awakening. From 1764 to 1772 he led a revival among the Anglicans of Virginia and North Carolina. In 1773 he joined forces with the Methodists, a cooperation that climaxed in 1775 to 1776 in what is known as the Methodist phase of the Southern Awakening.

Jarratt was opposed by his fellow Anglican priests, who regarded him as a fanatic and "a Presbyterian," in their minds the ultimate insult. Hurt by their rejection, he eventually stopped attending denominational meetings. He became more and more isolated within the Church of England, yet he remained loyal to it, the denomination of his ordination.

Reflection

In Virginia in the 1700s those claiming to be Christians often had a hard time getting along with one another. Sadly, the same is true today. What do you feel are the causes? the cures? What can individual Christians do to bring unity to God's people?

~∾✇∽~

My prayer for all of them is that they will be one.   JOHN 17:21

July 4

What makes churches grow?

In 1928 the Sudan Interior Mission sent the first missionaries to the Wallamo tribe of Ethiopia. They faced a difficult task, for the Wallamos were Satan worshipers. On the first day of the year the tribe performed a ceremony resembling the Old Testament Passover but that was, in reality, a sacrifice to the devil. A bull was sacrificed, its blood was smeared on the doorposts of each house, and a drop of blood was placed on each family member. The ceremony ended with the head of the household on his knees praying to Satan. Then everyone ate the raw meat.

Wealthy Wallamos were slave owners. If a slave owner decided his slaves had had enough children, he would have all further babies born to them buried alive.

By 1930 the Ethiopian government was attempting to stop the infanticide and slavery among the Wallamos. In 1935 Emperor Haile Selassie I was in the process of trying to modernize his nation when Italian troops under Mussolini invaded. Italian troops had attacked once before in 1896, but that time Ethiopia had overpowered them. That humiliating defeat marked the first time in history that an African nation had defeated a European invader. Now Mussolini was determined to avenge that defeat.

This time the Ethiopians were no match for the well-equipped Italian army. They fought courageously, but in May 1936 the capital of Addis Ababa fell.

The Italian army advanced into the tribal areas, demanding that the missionaries leave. On April 16, 1937, the day before the missionaries to the Wallamo left, they shared the Lord's Supper with the believers. When the missionaries had first arrived, there were no believers in the tribe. Now, nine years later, there were forty-eight.

The next day Italian army trucks took the twenty-six missionaries and their children to Addis Ababa for evacuation. As the trucks pulled away, the missionaries wondered if they would ever be able to return and what they would find if they did.

With the missionaries gone, the Italians tried to stamp out the fledgling church. Many church leaders were given one hundred lashes, and one was given four hundred. After the lashings they could not lie on their backs for months, and three died.

Toro, a leader in the Wallamo church, was able to stay in hiding for six months before he was finally captured. He was given forty lashes. Then an Italian officer wearing hobnailed boots jumped up and down on his chest, nearly crushing his rib cage. Later as he lay immobile in his prison cell, he saw a vision of Jesus, who said to him, "Do not be afraid. You are my child."

After a slow recovery, Toro was released from prison, only to be arrested again when he resumed preaching. This time he and other church leaders were taken to the marketplace, stripped naked, and each given more than one hundred lashes. Back in jail, Toro's Italian captors taunted him saying, "Where is your God who can deliver you from us? You'll never get out of here alive." Hardly able to speak, Toro whispered that God could deliver him "if he chooses—and if not, he has promised to take me to heaven to be with him there."

Later, Toro and his fellow believers were praying when a fierce thunderstorm descended upon the prison. The gale-force winds literally blew the roof off. Torrents of water separated the mud walls from the foundation. Most of the non-Christian prisoners escaped. The frightened jailers were convinced the storm had come in answer to the prisoners' prayers. "Ask your God to withhold his anger," they begged Toro, "and we will release you." They kept their word and released him.

Finally on **July 4, 1943,** the missionaries were able to return to the Wallamo. During the six years that they were gone, the forty-eight believers had multiplied to eighteen thousand.

Reflection

In your judgment, what factors caused the growth of the church from forty-eight to eighteen thousand in just six years with no missionaries present? What can we learn from the experiences of the Wallamo about how God works?

∿

The Kingdom of Heaven is like a mustard seed planted in a field. It is the smallest of all seeds, but it becomes the largest of garden plants and grows into a tree. MATTHEW 13:31-32

July 5

You never know how God will bring fruit from your life.

GOD USED the influence of Robert and James Haldane, two Scottish brothers, to reach all the way to Africa. Converted in 1795, they began to preach throughout Scotland.

James Haldane preached in Edinburgh for years. After ministering in Scotland, Robert Haldane went to Geneva, Switzerland, and began a student Bible study. Most of the students attending became preachers used by God to bring a religious awakening to Switzerland and France. This revival gave birth in 1822 to the Paris Evangelical Missionary Society. As Robert Haldane lay dying in 1842, little did he know how the streams of his influence would converge on a little boy then tending turkeys on a French farm.

One of Robert Haldane's students in Geneva was Ami Bost, who became a pastor of a church in Asnieres, France, originally founded by John Calvin.[5] In the church was Mrs. Coillard, a poor widow with seven children. She had dedicated her youngest son, François, to the ministry, but as a six-year-old he had to herd turkeys to help support the family. When Ami Bost came to the church, his preaching kindled a passion for foreign missions in the impressionable young Francois.

At seventeen Francois was admitted to a training school for young men without means. The founder and director was Monsieur Jaquet, a man of great faith whose motto for the school was "The Lord will provide."

One Sunday, instead of his usual dry sermon, Jaquet read a tract that ended with the question "Wheat or chaff, which art thou?" Francois was tormented by the question, wondering what it meant. He struggled for days, unable to grasp the concept of belief. He later wrote that finally "a ray of light flashed into my night of anguish." He saw that to "believe" means to accept God's salvation through Jesus Christ without reservation. A peace previously unknown flooded his soul, and the experience colored the rest of his life.

After attending university, seminary, and missions school, Francois asked to be sent to a place where no missionary had gone before. The Paris Evangelical Mission Society assigned him to Basutoland, the modern kingdom of Lesotho, in South Africa.

Before leaving for Africa, Francois spoke at a mission meeting in Paris, and a young Scottish woman named Christina Mackintosh was in the audience. When she was a child, her family had attended the church of James

FRUITFUL MINISTRY

Haldane, and under his influence Christina's father became a minister himself. As Christina listened to the enthusiastic young missions recruit, a deep desire was awakened to do missionary work herself. When the two met after the meeting, it was love at first sight for Francois, but he was too shy to give any hint of his feelings.

When the young missionary arrived in Africa in 1857, clean-shaven and eager to begin, the Africans immediately informed him that no one would listen to a man without a beard and a wife. At once he began growing a beard, but securing a wife was a greater challenge. Right away he thought of the lovely Christina Mackintosh, and after much prayer, he followed the French custom of writing a mutual friend to propose marriage to her for him. Six anxious months later Francois received a letter saying that she didn't know him well enough.

He waited two long years before trying again. This time he wrote to Christina directly. When she received his letter, she experienced a peace from God that this was indeed his will for her life. On **July 5, 1860,** Francois received her reply. She sailed for Africa, and they were married in 1861.

Francois and Christina Coillard served together for thirty years until her death in 1891. The culmination of their fruitful years of service was the founding of mission stations along the Zambesi River in modern Zambia.

The fruit of the Haldane brothers reached halfway around the world. The more than two million evangelical Christians in Zambia today are part of the fruit of their labors.

Reflection

God has purposes of which we know nothing. If we are faithful to him, he may use us to accomplish purposes we never could have dreamed. Our responsibility is to trust and obey. The results are up to him.

❧

My ways are far beyond anything you could imagine.   Isaiah 55:8

July 6

Talk about not having a childhood.

IN 1534 King Henry VIII of England made himself the head of the Church of England.[6] His reason? He wanted to divorce his wife and remarry in hopes of having a male heir. Ultimately he went through a series of six wives resulting in but one surviving son.

Edward, Henry's son, was born in 1537. Henry VIII did Edward a great favor by providing him with Protestant tutors and by placing a Protestant majority on the Council of Regency, which would appoint a protector for Edward if he became king before adulthood.

Henry VIII died when Edward was just nine, and he was crowned Edward VI. Although initially healthy, as a youth Edward suffered from congenital syphilis.

Though young, Edward VI was a committed Christian. With Henry VIII's death, the English had buried an ogre and crowned a saint. The Council of Regency appointed the young king's Protestant uncle, Edward Seymour, soon to be made the duke of Somerset, as regent for him, giving him the title "Protector of the Realm."

Under Henry VIII England had rejected papal authority but retained medieval dogma. Now the child king and Protector Somerset set out to reform the Church of England. A statute was issued ordering that all services be conducted in English and that communicants be offered both the bread and the cup. Purgatory and Masses for the dead were repudiated.

Archbishop of Canterbury Thomas Cranmer[7] issued his first *Book of Common Prayer*, in which the Protestant faith was stated with solemn beauty. Cranmer was able to diplomatically transform the Mass into the Lord's Supper without creating a reaction. He submitted the book to Parliament, which ordered every church in England to adopt it. But complete religious freedom was yet to come.

The resulting improvement in the religious climate caused the Protestants who had fled England under Henry VIII to come streaming back, bringing with them the doctrines of Luther,[8] Calvin,[9] Zwingli,[10] and the Anabaptists.[11] A new day had dawned in England.

The English nobility was enraged by the duke of Somerset's sympathy for the poor. When the army had to put down a revolt of Roman Catholic peasants, Somerset was accused of having encouraged the uprising by his outspoken concern for the poor. He was arrested and imprisoned in the Tower of London.

Somerset's responsibilities were taken over by John Dudley, the head of the Privy Council, whom King Edward made duke of Northumberland. Among the adventurers drawn to Edward, Northumberland proved to be both the ablest and the worst. A Roman Catholic at heart, he espoused the Protestant cause only because that was where power currently resided.

In spite of Northumberland's corrupt and self-serving leadership, the Reformation accelerated in England. By 1553 England had abandoned most of what was distinctly medieval Catholicism. The prayer book was revised once more with very little left of the Mass and nothing of private confession. The Edwardian Reformation was noteworthy for its mildness. During his reign two were executed for their speculations about the deity of Christ, but these were exceptions, not the rule.

Edward then contracted tuberculosis in addition to his syphilis. Finally on **July 6, 1553,** at the age of just fifteen, Edward was dying. Three hours before his death, thinking that he was alone in the room, he prayed:

> Lord God, deliver me out of this miserable and wretched life, and take me among thy chosen: howbeit not my will but thy will be done. Lord, I commit my spirit to thee. O Lord, thou knowest how happy it were for me to be with thee; yet for thy chosen sake send me life and health that I may truly serve thee. O my Lord God, bless thy people and save thine inheritance. O Lord God, save thy chosen people of England. O my Lord God, defend this realm from papistry, and maintain thy true religion, that I and my people may praise thy holy name, for thy Son Jesus Christ's sake.

Reflection

For the Protestants of England, the reign of Edward VI was the high point of the sixteenth century. God may not have called you to earthly royalty, but where in your world do you think God wants you to make a difference?

Whatever you do, you must do all for the glory of God.

1 CORINTHIANS 10:31

July 7

When did democracy begin in America?

THE FOUNDER of American democracy was born on **July 7, 1586**, in Marfield, England. His name was Thomas Hooker. In 1608 he graduated from Emmanuel College, Cambridge, the quintessential Puritan college of its time. Three years later he received a master of arts degree and became a lecturer at the college until 1618. It was during this time that he experienced a transforming spiritual rebirth. He was so excited about what had happened to him that he preached a series of sermons at the college about his conversion.

Later, as a lecturer at the Church of St. Mary in Chelmsford, he attracted attention, both good and bad. Many were drawn to his preaching and became his committed followers. At the same time the hierarchy of the Anglican Church, which at that time was a halfway house between the Reformed Church and the Church of Rome, became his committed opponents. Forced to leave Chelmsford because of his Puritan views, he went to Little Baddow where he began a school with assistance from John Eliot, later the missionary to the American Indians.

In 1629 Hooker was called before the archbishop to answer for his evangelical preaching and nonconformity to the Anglican Church. He was released under a bond of fifty English pounds to force him to appear at a later date before the Court of High Commissioners. A Puritan farmer became surety for him, and a group of Hooker's friends paid off the farmer. Hooker abandoned the bond and escaped to Holland, where for two years he was an assistant pastor of the English Nonconformist church at Delft.

During this time a group of his former followers from Chelmsford had emigrated to the Massachusetts Bay Colony and were known as "Mr. Hooker's Company." They encouraged Hooker to follow them to New England. Hooker returned to England and decided to go to Massachusetts Bay, leaving on the same boat in 1633 as John Cotton, who would become teacher of the First Church of Boston and the father of New England Congregationalism.

Hooker became pastor of the church in Newtown (present-day Cambridge), Massachusetts. The church prospered, and its leading member, John Haynes, was elected governor of Massachusetts Bay.

Members of Hooker's church complained for years that they had insufficient land for farming. Therefore in 1635 they moved to a site along the Connecticut River and named their town Hartford.

THE FOUNDER OF AMERICAN DEMOCRACY

Since they were now outside the charter of Massachusetts Bay, they formed their own government, naming their settlement Connecticut. In 1638 the General Court of Connecticut was given the responsibility of drawing up a constitution for Connecticut. The document was called *The Fundamental Orders* and was the first written constitution in America. As the leader of the Connecticut settlers, Thomas Hooker preached a sermon to the framers of their constitution. He stated that "the foundation of all authority is laid . . . in the free consent of the people" and that "the privilege of election . . . belongs to the people." This concept was diametrically opposed to the principles undergirding Massachusetts. The leaders there were in total opposition to democracy, whereas Hooker was committed to it. In Massachusetts only church members could vote. In Connecticut suffrage was for all citizens. The seed of democracy had been planted in America.

In 1643 Hooker was a prime mover in organizing the United Colonies of New England, the earliest system of federal government in America. Although he had considerable political influence, above all Thomas Hooker was a faithful expositor of the Bible and one of the most powerful preachers of his generation.

Reflection

Do you believe Hooker or the leaders of Massachusetts were correct on the issue of democracy? America's founding fathers largely feared democracy and out of that fear created a republic in which final authority rests with democratically elected officials. Does the Bible shed any light as to which is preferable, a pure democracy or a federal (representative) form of government?

Hallelujah! For the Lord our God, the Almighty, reigns. Let us be glad and rejoice and honor him. REVELATION 19:6-7

July 8

It was the most famous sermon ever preached in America.

THE PREACHER was Jonathan Edwards, pastor of the Congregational church in Northhampton, Massachusetts, and a future president of Princeton College.[12] The date was Saturday, **July 8, 1741,** and the place was Enfield, Connecticut, where Edwards had been invited to speak.

Enfield was not a religious place. The Great Awakening had touched surrounding towns but not Enfield. In fact, Christians nearby feared that God would pass them by because of the lethargy of the folk of Enfield. As the crowd entered the meetinghouse to hear Edwards speak, it was with curiosity and nonchalance.

Then Edwards began to speak. He did not sound like the evangelists of today. He wrote out his sermons word for word and then usually read them. Listening to Edwards was like listening to a lecturer who made his case in an even-tempered, intellectually demanding style in which he tried to develop each step of his argument logically.

The title of Edwards's sermon was "Sinners in the Hands of an Angry God," and his text was Deuteronomy 32:35: "Their foot shall slide in due time" (KJV).

Edwards explained his text:

As he that walks in slippery places is every moment liable to fall, he cannot foresee one moment whether he shall stand or fall the next; and when he does fall, he falls at once without warning: Which is also expressed in Psalm 73:18, 19. "Surely thou didst set them in slippery places: thou castedst them down into destruction: How are they brought into desolation as in a moment!" . . .

The bow of God's wrath is bent, and the arrow made ready on the string, and justice bends the arrow at your heart, and strains the bow, and it is nothing but the mere pleasure of God, and that of an angry God, without any promise or obligation at all, that keeps the arrow one moment from being made drunk with your blood. Thus all you that have never passed under a great change of heart, by the mighty power of the Spirit of God upon your souls; all you that were never born again, and made new creatures, and raised from being dead in sin, to a state of new, and before altogether unexperienced light and life, are in the hands of an angry God. . . .

SINNERS IN THE HANDS OF AN ANGRY GOD

And now you have an extraordinary opportunity, a day wherein Christ has thrown the door of mercy wide open, and stands calling, and crying with a loud voice to poor sinners; a day wherein many are flocking to him, and pressing into the kingdom of God. Many are daily coming from the east, west, north, and south; many that were very lately in the same miserable condition that you are in, are now in a happy state, with their hearts filled with love to him who has loved them, and washed them from their sins in his own blood, and rejoicing in the hope of the glory of God.

As Edwards preached, members of the audience cried out, "What shall I do to be saved? O, I am going to hell!" Some crowded toward the pulpit begging him to stop. At one point during the sermon there was so much noise that Edwards asked everyone to be quiet so that he could be heard.

He ended the sermon by saying, "Let everyone that is out of Christ now awake and fly from the wrath to come. The wrath of Almighty God is now undoubtedly hanging over a great part of this congregation. Let everyone fly out of Sodom: 'Haste and escape for your lives, look not behind you, escape to the mountain, lest you be consumed.' "

The little town of Enfield was never the same.

Reflection

Why do you think this sermon is so well known? Do you believe that God is angry with you, or are you among those whose sins have been washed away in his blood? We all need to flee to Jesus from the coming wrath.

∽◦⌇◦∼

They cried to the mountains and the rocks, "Fall on us and hide us from the face of the one who sits on the throne and from the wrath of the Lamb. For the great day of their wrath has come, and who will be able to survive?" REVELATION 6:16

July 9

Some men are afraid to show their feelings.

ALEXANDER DUFF was born in Scotland in 1806, the son of a godly Gaelic-speaking farmer. He was raised on a spiritual diet of *Foxe's Book of Martyrs* and the Gaelic poetry of Dugald Buchanan.

Buchanan's best known poem, "The Day of Judgment," so alarmed young Alexander that he had a terrifying dream of humanity's being summoned before God's judgment seat. He watched terror stricken as God's sentence was pronounced on one person after another, wondering what God's pronouncement on him would be. He awoke trembling, but it was out of that experience that he came to an assurance of his acceptance by God through the redeeming blood of Christ.

While at St. Andrews University, Duff became interested in foreign missions and accepted the call to be the Church of Scotland's first missionary to India.

Duff had given no thought to marriage during his university years or even after accepting his missionary call. After hearing Duff explain this, an elderly Christian gentleman replied: "Well . . . my advice to you is, be quietly on the look-out; and if, in God's providence, you make the acquaintance of one of the daughters of Zion, traversing, like yourself, the wilderness of this world, her face set thitherward, get into friendly converse with her. If you find that in mind, in heart, in temper and disposition, you congenialise, and if God puts it into her heart to be willing to forsake father and mother and cast in her lot with you, regard it as a token from the God of providence that you should use the proper means to secure her Christian society."

Somehow Duff grasped the meaning of this advice and on **July 9, 1827,** married Anne Scott Drysdale. They "congenialised" for nearly fifty years.

Duff was ordained in August 1829 and sailed with Anne for Calcutta in October. During the voyage they survived two shipwrecks, including one in which he lost his personal library—a tremendous loss for a missionary educator.

Upon arriving, Duff set about to reach the upper castes by means of higher education. His plan was to teach Western arts and sciences along with the Bible to the elite of India, and within a few months he opened his school with five students. News of the school spread like wildfire, and by the end of the week three hundred more had applied. In the school's first decade attendance averaged eight hundred. Duff's College, as it was known, became the largest mission school in India.

UNDEMONSTRATIVE LOVE

Duff was more successful educationally than evangelistically. Only thirty-three conversions were recorded among his students. Yet almost all of the converts became influential Christians in India. He also was a great missionary statesman and orator, who influenced hundreds to volunteer for missionary work and tens of thousands to contribute to their support.

Duff was a sober, humorless Presbyterian, whose achievements were made through great sacrifices by his wife and family. Yet a missionary never had a more dedicated wife than Anne. She was the family's source of affection and joy.

We get a glimpse into the family dynamics when we read their youngest son's description of being left behind in England as a teenager when his parents were returning to India: "I . . . well remember how my mother's and my own heart were well nigh breaking, and how at London Bridge my father possessed himself of the morning's *Times* and left us to cry our hearts out in sorrow."

Anne Duff died in England after a brief illness in 1865. With uncharacteristic warmth, Duff wrote his son in India of his mother's death: "The most loving, lovable, and beloved of wives and mothers is now one of the bright spirits that shines in white array in the realms above."

Reflection

Alexander Duff was blessed with a wife who complemented his own emotional shortcomings. But had he been able to more freely express his feelings to his wife and children, family life may have been more rewarding for all of them. Do you ever have trouble showing your love? God wants us to communicate our love for one another. He sent his Son as the ultimate demonstration of his love for us.

◦◦◦

Let us stop just saying we love each other; let us really show it by our actions. 1 JOHN 3:18

July 10

Imagine leaving your children, realizing you would probably never see them again.

ADONIRAM JUDSON, born in 1788, had been part of the first American missionary contingent that sailed for Asia in 1812.[13] His missionary career in Burma had been painful yet rewarding. He had undergone a horrendous seventeen-month imprisonment and had lost his first wife, Ann, and three children. Yet he had translated the Bible into Burmese and seen many come to Christ.

In 1845 Adoniram, in poor health, left with his second wife, Sarah,[14] and their three oldest children. The plan was to leave the children in America for their education. During the voyage Sarah died, and Adoniram arrived in America a widower for the second time.

While there, Judson traveled from Boston to Philadelphia with a Dr. Gillette, who gave him a book of short stories called *Trippings* by Fanny Forester. Judson read portions of the book and remarked that it was regrettable that a person with such intellectual gifts would waste her talents on popular fiction and he would like to tell her so.

Dr. Gillette replied that Judson would meet her since she was staying at his home in Philadelphia. Her real name was Emily Chubbuck.

When they met Judson was humbled to learn that she had been forced to write fiction to escape poverty. He asked her if she would write a book about his recently deceased wife. Emily agreed, and they spent much time together on the project. As they talked, Emily revealed how as a child she had read a book about Judson's first wife, Ann, and had felt ever since that she would be a missionary someday.

Romance grew out of their camaraderie, and Adoniram and Emily were married in June of 1846. With his burden for the work in Burma and his health failing, Adoniram made preparations to return after just nine months. Aware that he would probably never see his children again, on **July 10, 1846,** he wrote them all letters:

> *My Dear Sons:*
> *Farewell. We embark tomorrow about noon. Many a time I shall look at your likenesses, and weep over them, and pray that you may early become true Christians. Love your brother George [Boardman, their eighteen-year-*

old half brother] and your uncle and aunt Newton. Pray every morning and evening. Your new mama sends you her best love. Forget not
 Your affectionate father,
 A. Judson

My Dear Daughter:
 Farewell. We embark tomorrow about noon. I think the likenesses taken of your face very good. I shall take one with me, and shall many a time look at it and weep over it, and pray that you may early become a Christian. . . .
 Love your dear aunts and cousins, with whom you live; pray every morning and evening, and may we meet again on earth, and if not, O may we meet in heaven, and be happy together. Your new mama sends her best love.
 Your affectionate father,
 A. Judson

Judson lived just four more years but he left behind a church of seven thousand Burmese and more than one hundred native pastors.

Reflection

Life was harsh and the sacrifices great for early missionaries like Adoniram Judson. Has God called upon you to give up anything for him?

If you love your son or daughter more than me, you are not worthy of being mine. If you refuse to take up your cross and follow me, you are not worthy of being mine.

MATTHEW 10:37-38

July 11

In Tientsin, China, in 1902 a baby boy was born to Scottish missionaries James and Mary Liddell. They named him Eric.

WHEN ERIC was four, his father read in the newspaper how a Scotsman, Wyndham Halswelle, had won second place in the four hundred-meter race in the Olympics, the first Scot ever to win an Olympic medal in track. When his father tried to explain this to Eric and his older brother, Eric asked whether that meant that no Scotsman had ever finished first. The answer was yes.

Eric's parents took him and his older brother to a boarding school for sons of missionaries in England, and then they returned to China. At school both boys excelled in rugby, cricket, and track. Eric set a school record of 10.2 seconds in the one hundred-meter dash.

Eric attended the University of Edinburgh, where he continued to excel in track. He quickly emerged as the fastest sprinter in Scotland and became a national hero.

In college his older brother was active with other Christian college students in holding evangelistic meetings throughout Scotland. When Eric was invited to speak at one of these rallies in 1923, he accepted. The next morning every newspaper in Scotland announced that Eric Liddell had preached at an evangelistic service. The experience stirred Eric's soul. It gave him a desire to share the gospel with whomever would listen. Over the next two years he spoke to thousands throughout the British Isles, men and women who came to hear the famous athlete but who returned to hear his message of salvation. Yet newspapers questioned Eric's commitment to running since he was spending so much time preaching.

The Olympics were to be held in Paris in 1924, and the hopes of England were now pinned on the young Scot as the nation's champion sprinter. Eric's best event was the one hundred-meter dash, but when the schedule for the Olympic races was published, the first heats for the one hundred-meters were on a Sunday. Eric held the conviction that he was never to race on Sunday and refused to do so. The English Olympic committee tried to have the date for the first heats changed but to no avail.

As a result, Eric was entered in the two hundred- and four hundred-meter races, events in which he was not at all as dominant as the one hundred meters. The British press attacked him mercilessly. "A traitor to Scottish sporting, to all that Wyndham Halswelle stood for!" announced one newspaper.

THE FLYING SCOTSMAN

On the Sunday of the one hundred-meter trial in Paris, Eric preached in the Scots Kirk, the Scottish Presbyterian church in Paris. In the one hundred-meter trials, Harold Abrahams was the one English sprinter to qualify for the finals the next day.

Harold Abrahams won the one hundred-meter race, the first British runner to win a gold medal in the Olympics. Eric saw that this was just part of God's plan.

On Wednesday Eric finished second in the two hundred-meter dash, the first Scot ever to win a medal in the 200 meters. But there was still one race to go.

Eric qualified on Thursday for the four hundred-meter finals. But he was far from being the favorite. The finals were held on Friday, **July 11, 1924.** As he prepared to go to the stadium, the team masseur handed Eric a small folded piece of paper. It read "He that honors me I will honor," quoting 1 Samuel 2:30. Eric Liddell won the four hundred-meter race, setting a new world record of 47.6 seconds. He was the first Scot to win Olympic gold in track.

The next year Eric Liddell returned to China as a missionary and during World War II died in a Japanese prisoner of war camp.[15] *Chariots of Fire,* the movie about his athletic career, won the Academy Award for best picture in 1981.

Reflection

Eric Liddell stood up for his conviction even though all England opposed him. Have you ever had to take a public stand for your convictions? When you take a stand for God, you are never alone.

∽∾∾

No one will be able to stand their ground against you as long as you live. For I will be with you as I was with Moses. I will not fail you or abandon you.   JOSHUA 1:5

July 12

Was his desire to be a minister a commitment to God or a yearning to be like his brother?

DAVID BRAINERD was the sixth of ten children of Hezekiah Brainerd, a Puritan legislator from Haddam, Connecticut.[16] His was not to be a carefree childhood. When David was nine, his father died, and when he was thirteen, his mother passed away.

After his mother's death David continued to live at the homestead, now headed by his oldest brother, Hezekiah Jr., and his wife. A year later when his sister Jerusha married a farmer in East Haddam, he moved in with them.

David had inherited a farm from his father about ten miles from Haddam. When he turned nineteen, he decided to try his hand at farming. However, he soon discovered that he was not destined to be a farmer. Instead he made a pledge to God to become a minister. David greatly admired his older brother Nehemiah, who had become a minister after graduating from Yale, and he longed to follow in his footsteps.

Even though he wanted to go into the ministry, Brainerd had his disagreements with God. He rebelled against the doctrines of original sin and the sovereignty of God. Divine law was too strict for him. He also disliked the idea that there was nothing he could do through his own strength to commend himself to God.

After his trial year on the farm, Brainerd returned to Haddam to live and study with his pastor, Phineas Fiske, in preparation for attending Yale. After six months Fiske died, and Brainerd continued his studies under his brother Nathaniel.

In spite of his plans for the ministry, Brainerd was not yet a church member. To join the church one needed to have an assurance of salvation, and Brainerd didn't.

On a Friday morning in July 1739, as Brainerd was walking in the forest, he came to the realization that he was spiritually lost. He saw that all of his religious endeavors in no way obligated God to bestow his grace.

The turning point in David Brainerd's life came two days later on **July 12, 1739.** In his diary Brainerd wrote:

> When I was again walking in the same solitary place . . . unspeakable glory seemed to open to the view and apprehension of my soul. I do

not mean any external brightness, for I saw no such thing. . . . It was a new inward apprehension or view that I had of God, such as I never had before; nor anything which had the least resemblance of it. . . .

I felt myself in a new world. . . . At this time the way of salvation opened to me with such infinite wisdom, suitableness, and excellency, that I wondered I should ever think of any other way of salvation; was amazed that I had not dropped my own contrivances, and complied with this lovely, blessed, and excellent way before. If I could have been saved by my own duties, or any other way that I had formerly contrived, my whole soul would now have refused it. I wondered that all the world did not see and comply with this way of salvation, entirely by the righteousness of Christ.

Two months after writing the above entry in his diary, David Brainerd entered Yale and went on to become a missionary to the Indians of Massachusetts, New Jersey, and Pennsylvania. He died in the home of Jonathan Edwards at the age of twenty-nine. His diary became a devotional classic, influencing hundreds to follow him into missionary service.

After Brainerd's death, when Jonathan Edwards[17] edited his diary, he wrote at the top of the page for this day, "Lord's day, July 12th 1739 forever to be remembered by D.B."

Reflection

Can you identify with any of the details of David Brainerd's conversion? Have you found yourself quarreling with God or trying to merit God's grace through your own efforts? What a wonderful salvation it is that can't be earned but only be received through faith.

◦≈◦

It is clear that no one can ever be right with God by trying to keep the law. For the Scriptures say, "It is through faith that a righteous person has life."　　　　GALATIANS 3:11

July 13

He was regarded by the class-conscious English missionaries as inferior in background and education.

Hudson Taylor arrived in China as a missionary in 1854 at the age of twenty-one.[18] Son of a pharmacist in Yorkshire, he was regarded by the class-conscious English missionaries as inferior in background and education. To make matters worse, Hudson chose to adopt Chinese dress.

In 1857 Taylor came to the coastal city of Ningpo, where the Anglican, American Baptist, and American Presbyterian missions had separate compounds. Into this society of precisely graded ranks of seniority and social background came short Hudson Taylor with his native dress and Chinese pigtail.

Once a week Miss Aldersey, the first woman missionary to China, hosted a meal for all the missionaries of Ningpo, including Hudson. Miss Aldersey had a rigid sense of what was proper and ruled her two young assistants, Burella and Maria Dyer, with an iron hand.

The Dyer sisters had an uncle in England who was their closest relative since their missionary parents were deceased. Burella was engaged to a missionary in Shanghai and Maria was, as Hudson described in a letter home, "a good-looking girl with a squint." She was reported to be the second-best Chinese-speaking missionary in the city and was completely dedicated to her work, having already turned down two marriage proposals.

After meeting Hudson, Maria wrote to her brother in London, "I met a gentleman and, I cannot say I loved him at once, but I felt interested in him and could not forget him. I saw him from time to time and still the interest continued. I had no good reason to think it was reciprocated."

Hudson had similar feelings but told no one. Finally, in March of 1858 he wrote to Maria expressing his love for her and proposing marriage. Before opening the letter, Maria prayed over it, hoping it was from Hudson.

The next morning Maria went to tell Miss Aldersey the good news. To Miss Aldersey, however, this was not good news. She ranted, "That young, poor, unconnected nobody! . . . He is not a gentleman. He is without education, without position. . . . He is short, you are tall. And he wears Chinese clothes!" Miss Aldersey then dictated a letter for Maria to write to Hudson, undiplomatically refusing his proposal.

Maria was heartbroken but incapable of crossing Miss Aldersey. When Hudson received her reply, he suspected that Miss Aldersey was behind it.

On **July 13, 1857,** Hudson went to meet personally with Miss Aldersey and learned that she had dictated the letter. He also discovered that the uncle, not Miss Aldersey, was Maria's legal guardian. Miss Aldersey reported that she had written Maria's uncle describing the scandalous situation. Maria wrote to her uncle explaining her side.

Hudson knew that he had to get Maria's permission to write her uncle asking for her hand. Later that month the opportunity came. During a ladies prayer meeting at the missionary home where Hudson lived, a water spout from a tornado swept in from the sea and flooded the streets. As a result, some of the coolies were late in bringing the sedan chairs to take the ladies home. When Hudson returned, Maria was still there. Hudson had the man of the house ask Maria for permission to meet with her. As they met and shook hands in greeting, they knew their love was mutual, and Maria gave Hudson permission to write her uncle asking for her hand in marriage.

Finally in December, Hudson received a note from Maria saying that her uncle had given permission for her to marry as soon as she was twenty-one.

Hudson and Maria were married on January 20, 1858, four days after her twenty-first birthday. Maria went on to play a crucial role in shaping the ministry of the Yorkshire lad who was to change forever the way missionaries work. Their four surviving children all became missionaries to China.

Reflection

The most important decision in life after choosing to become a Christian is whether to remain single or be married. How should we decide whether to marry and whom to marry? To what extent should we regard the counsel of others?

❧

Let the peace that comes from Christ rule in your hearts.

COLOSSIANS 3:15

July 14

Does it make a difference if the president of the United States is a Christian?

JIMMY CARTER was born in Plains, Georgia, in 1924 and grew up on a farm just outside of town. As a child, Jimmy had only one white friend outside of school, the rest being the children of the local black sharecroppers. He attended the white segregated school in Plains. There every school day began with a half-hour chapel service for all the students. After the pledge of allegiance, a hymn such as "He Leadeth Me" or "Onward Christian Soldiers," was sung, and the singing of "America" or "Dixie" followed. Bible verses were recited, and sometimes there was an outside speaker, usually one of the white ministers from the town.

The three white churches in Plains were Southern Baptist, Methodist, and Lutheran. All three were too small to support a full-time pastor. Often the Baptists and Methodists would hold services on alternate Sundays so their congregations could visit back and forth. Black and white Baptists had worshiped together at the Lebanon Baptist Church until the Civil War, when emancipation led to the formation of a white church, Plains Baptist Church. The black Lebanon Baptist Church was the largest church in town.

The high points of the church year in Plains were the weeks of revival meetings. The Baptist and Methodist churches would schedule their revivals at different times so that their congregations could attend both. In the weeks leading up to each revival, the pastor and deacons would visit the members of every white family in Plains who had not yet trusted Jesus Christ as their Lord and Savior. An outside preacher would be invited in for the week, and there would be two services each day, one in the morning especially for housewives and one in the evening for everyone. It was at one of these revival services when Jimmy was eleven that he put his trust in Jesus Christ.

Jimmy received an appointment to the U.S. Naval Academy, graduating in 1946. He then married his high school sweetheart, Rosalynn Smith, and spent the next seven years in the navy. However, when his father died in 1953, he resigned his commission to return home to run the family farm and peanut business.

In addition to successfully taking over the family business, Carter was elected to the state legislature as a Democrat in 1962 and 1964. Carter then ran unsuccessfully for governor of Georgia in 1966 and was very discouraged by his defeat. He asked his sister, Ruth Carter Stapleton, to go for a walk with him in the woods. As they talked, Ruth convinced him that he would never be really happy until he made Jesus Christ the most important thing in his life.

The following year, 1967, proved to be the spiritual turning point. As he later said, "I began to realize that my Christian life, which I had always professed to be preeminent, had really been a secondary interest in my life, and I formed a very close, personal intimate relationship with God through Christ."

Carter was elected governor of Georgia in 1970. After completing his term, he launched a campaign for president and on **July 14, 1976,** he received the Democratic nomination for president of the United States. In the election he soundly defeated President Gerald Ford, the Republican candidate.

Carter's administration produced mixed reviews. He persuaded Israel and Egypt to agree to the Camp David peace accord, but his White House years were also plagued with inflation, unemployment, and above all, the Iran hostage crisis.

In Carter's run for reelection in 1980, Ronald Reagan won a landslide victory, criticizing Carter for ineptitude and a lack of leadership.

In spite of the challenges he faced as president, Jimmy Carter was perhaps the most dedicated Christian ever to occupy the White House.

Reflection

Should a person vote for a candidate just because he is a Christian? Many voters did so in voting for Jimmy Carter in 1976 and then abandoned him for Ronald Reagan in 1980. To what extent should a candidate's religious beliefs influence our vote?

Let us follow the Holy Spirit's leading in every part of our lives.
GALATIANS 5:25

July 15

He went against the grain.

JULINS PALMER was the son of the mayor of Coventry, England. He went to Magdalen College, Oxford, distinguishing himself as a student. He spoke Latin with great facility and excelled in Greek as well. He loved to stay up all night debating philosophy with other students. After receiving his bachelor of arts degree in 1550, he began teaching logic at Magdalen College.

But it wasn't his teaching that attracted the most attention; it was his religious views. Palmer was a committed Roman Catholic in what had become a largely Protestant university. Edward VI, the teenaged king of England, was a committed Christian and firm supporter of the Reformation.[19] During Edward's brief reign, the Reformation accelerated throughout England, and so Palmer's views were not popular. Palmer was not bashful about his beliefs. As a result, he was often called before the officers of the university and disciplined for his aggressive Catholicism.

Shortly before the death of Edward VI in 1553, anti-Protestant signs attacking the college president were put on the walls and doors. Julins Palmer was the prime suspect. When questioned by the college officers, he denied that he was responsible. Yet in the interviews he attacked the college leadership so aggressively that he was removed from the faculty. Palmer was forced to take employment as a tutor for a wealthy family.

Then Edward VI died, and the new queen, Mary Tudor, was an ardent Roman Catholic.[20] She sent representatives to Oxford to get rid of the Protestant professors and to replace them with Roman Catholics. Julins Palmer promptly got his job back at Magdalen College.

Back at his teaching, Palmer became fascinated by the behavior of the many Protestants who were being burned at the stake by Queen Mary, who was earning her name "Bloody Mary." Under Edward VI, he had often said that the Protestants would never die for their faith, but now they were. He investigated in great detail how they were arrested, what beliefs they held, and how they died. He learned how brutally the martyrs were treated and how valiant they were in death. When the burnings started in Oxford, he went to see for himself.

Palmer was present when Latimer and Ridley were burned at the stake.[21] God used that experience to begin to change his heart. Then as he earnestly began to study the Scriptures, God completed Palmer's change of heart.

394

AN ABOUT-FACE

Realizing he could no longer teach at Oxford, he resigned and became the schoolmaster of a grammar school in the town of Reading. Roman Catholics in the town, suspecting he might have become a Protestant, entered his study and found documents he had written against the Catholic Church. They threatened to expose him if he would not leave Reading.

Leave he did, not being able to take with him his belongings or his last payment for his work. He returned home to his mother to request the funds his father had left him in his will. His mother told him, "Thy father bequeathed nought for heretics."

Returning to Reading to try to reclaim his belongings, he was arrested. On **July 15, 1556,** Julins Palmer was condemned to death for his faith. The sheriff gave him one last chance to recant, telling him that if he did, the sheriff would see that he had financial support for life. He even offered to find Palmer a wife. Palmer very graciously declined, saying that he had already given up two positions for Christ's sake and was now willing to give up his life.

The next day at 5:00 P.M., Palmer and two other martyrs were brought to the place of execution. The three dropped to their knees, and Palmer prayed Psalm 31, ending with the words, "Be strong and take courage, all you who put your hope in the Lord!" As the flames engulfed them, the three lifted their hands to heaven crying out, "Lord Jesus, strengthen us; Lord Jesus, receive our souls."

Reflection

Tertullian said, "The blood of the martyrs is the seed of the church." The death of the English martyrs is what led to Julins Palmer's conversion. Have you been affected by the death of a Christian you have observed or read about?

Saul was one of the official witnesses at the killing of Stephen.

ACTS 8:1

July 16

He had to decide whom to evangelize—the rich or the poor.

ON JULY 16, 1838, John Clough was born in western New York, and his family later moved to Iowa. While in college, John gave his life to Christ and felt God calling him to spread the gospel to those who had never heard it. He was ordained as a Baptist minister in 1864, and he and his wife arrived in southern India as missionaries to the Telugu people in 1865.

Eleven years earlier at a predawn prayer meeting on a hill overlooking the city of Ongole, two missionaries and three Telugu Christian women had asked God to send a missionary to that city. The Cloughs' arrival was the answer to that prayer. In 1866 Clough founded the mission station at Ongole, and immediately the gospel began to spread. A church was organized, and soon they had twenty-eight new converts. Most of them were Madigas, who were outcastes. This presented Clough with a problem. Up to this point all of the Christians in Ongole were of the higher castes and did not associate with outcastes. If Clough continued to accept outcastes into the church, he would lose the higher castes. He and his wife sought the Lord's guidance separately on this issue, and both were led to 1 Corinthians 1—that God calls the lowly, weak, and ignorant rather than the noble, strong, and wise.

From that point forward, Clough's evangelistic efforts concentrated on the outcastes. He endured insults and attempts upon his life by the higher castes for this decision. However, he persisted, and at the end of five years of working at the Ongole station, the Madigas church had fifteen hundred members.

Clough's approach to foreign missions was philosophically different from that of his time. He required converts to live by a few principles that he considered essential but was lenient when it came to matters of cultural practice. He was careful not to impose Western culture upon the Telugus unnecessarily. He felt the gospel would have the longest lasting effect and reach the most people if it was culturally relevant to the systems already in place.

For example, Clough allowed his preachers to follow the Hindu guru model, like the spiritual teachers the people already respected. He placed heavy emphasis on the work of these indigenous preachers, for he felt the gospel would carry the greatest weight when it came from one of their own. He encouraged new converts to return to their social groups, rather than removing them from their pagan environments as other missionaries attempted to get their converts to do. Churches were organized in the villages in accordance with indigenous social structures. He made the village elder a deacon in the church, which united community and church leadership in an effort to Christianize the village leadership.

Beginning in 1876, India suffered through three years of terrible famine and cholera. Clough worked tirelessly during this time to obtain food, supplies, and health care for all, regardless of caste. By participating in a government relief project, he obtained the contract to oversee construction of four miles of the Buckingham Canal. He was able to employ many starving people, mostly Madigas, at good wages. During this time he refused to accept new church members or baptize new converts because he didn't want people converting for the wrong motives. After the famine was over Clough offered baptism to all who really believed. During a three-week period in 1878 almost 9,000 were baptized upon their profession of faith, with 2,222 on one day! By the end of 1878, church membership at Ongole had reached 12,000!

John Clough worked with the Telugus for the next three decades, embracing the outcastes, working for their social good, and honoring the indigenous cultural structures. When Clough left India shortly before his death in 1910, he left behind a church of 60,000 members!

Reflection

How important is it in world missions to embrace local cultural principles and customs rather than to impose one's own? To what extent should churches on the mission field resemble the churches from which the missionaries came? Do you feel the Cloughs made the right decision to evangelize the poor instead of the rich?

∽◦✦◦∽

God chose things despised by the world, things counted as nothing at all.
1 CORINTHIANS 1:28

July 17

He was an adventurer with the heart of a poet.

War broke out between England and France in 1755, and a sixteen-year-old named Samuel Medley fulfilled his dream by becoming a midshipman in the Royal British Navy. During the battle of Cape Lagos in 1759, Medley's leg was severely wounded when most of his calf was shot away. The wound would not heal, and the ship's surgeon informed him that gangrene had set in and the leg would have to be amputated. Medley protested, and the surgeon granted him one more day before removing the leg. Medley had a Bible in his trunk and spent the whole night reading it and praying. The next day the surgeon reported that healing had begun and surgery would not be necessary. Did this lead Medley to God? No, he rejoiced in his good fortune and packed away his Bible.

When the ship returned to London, Medley was carried to the home of his grandfather to recuperate. Medley's grandfather was a godly man and was concerned about the spiritual state of his wild and worldly grandson and repeatedly shared the gospel with him to no avail until one Sunday evening when he read Medley a sermon by Isaac Watts.[22] God used the sermon to convict Medley of his sin and to transform his life. He started reading the Christian books in his grandfather's library and was baptized in December 1760.

Medley soon resigned from the navy and began preparing for the ministry, learning both Greek and Hebrew. In 1767 he became pastor of the Baptist church in Watford, Hertfordshire. The next four and a half years were very difficult since the church was small and unable to support him fully. However, in 1772 Medley was called as pastor of the Particular Baptist Church in Liverpool (Particular Baptist meant Calvinistic Baptist). He served there for the rest of his life. He especially enjoyed ministering to the sailors of this seaport city.

Samuel Medley is best remembered for the hymns he wrote. Most familiar is "O Could I Speak the Matchless Worth":

> *O, could I speak the matchless worth,*
> *O, could I sound the glories forth*
> *Which in my Saviour shine,*
> *I'd soar and touch the heavenly strings*
> *And vie with Gabriel while he sings*
> *In notes almost divine.*

THE STORY OF A SEAMAN

I'd sing the precious blood he spilt,
My ransom from the dreadful guilt
Of sin and wrath divine!
I'd sing his glorious righteousness,
In which all-perfect heavenly dress
My soul shall ever shine.

Samuel Medley died on **July 17, 1799**. Ever the seaman, he said from his deathbed, "I am now a poor shattered bark, just about to enter the blissful harbor; and O, how sweet will be the port after the storm." He could then experience the reality of what he had written:

Soon the delightful day will come
When my dear Lord will bring me home,
And I shall see his face;
Then with my Saviour, Brother, Friend,
A blest eternity I'll spend,
Triumphant in his grace.

Reflection

Samuel Medley longed for heaven. He knew he was going there because he trusted "the precious blood he spilt, / my ransom from the dreadful guilt / of sin and wrath divine." What are you trusting to get you there?

∽≪✦≫∼

After this I saw a vast crowd, too great to count, from every nation and tribe and people and language, standing in front of the throne and before the Lamb. They were clothed in white and held palm branches in their hands. And they were shouting with a mighty shout, "Salvation comes from our God on the throne and from the Lamb!"

REVELATION 7:9-10

July 18

The kingdom of Judah was in trouble.

THE YEAR was 586 B.C. It was almost five hundred years since Israel had become a kingdom under Saul in about 1050 B.C. David had begun his reign in approximately 1010 B.C., and then in 930 B.C. the kingdom had been divided between the northern kingdom of Israel and the southern kingdom of Judah. Israel, the northern kingdom, never had a godly king, and so God's judgment fell in 722 B.C. when he sent Assyria to defeat Israel and take its citizens away captive.

The southern kingdom of Judah had the Davidic dynasty, and some of its kings were good, but unfortunately most weren't. King Zedekiah fell into the latter category. God sent prophets to his people throughout their history to try to persuade them to return to the stipulations of his covenant with them and to warn them of the judgments that would fall if they persisted in their disobedience and rebellion. The prophets were largely ignored.

In the very first prophecy that the prophet Jeremiah gave, the Lord said through him, "Listen! I am calling the armies of the kingdoms of the north to come to Jerusalem. They will set their thrones at the gates of the city. They will attack its walls and all the other towns of Judah. I will pronounce judgment on my people for all their evil—for deserting me and worshiping other gods. Yes, they worship idols that they themselves have made!" (Jeremiah 1:15-16). Later, the Lord was even more specific: "This entire land will become a desolate wasteland, Israel and her neighboring lands will serve the king of Babylon for seventy years" (25:11).

Finally in 588 B.C., Nebuchadnezzar began his final siege of Jerusalem. Two and a half years later, on **July 18, 586 B.C.**, the Babylonians broke through the wall, and the city fell. Jeremiah records that "all the officers of the Babylonian army came in and sat in triumph at the Middle Gate" (Jeremiah 39:23), thus fulfilling the prophecy of Jeremiah 1:15 that the enemies from the north would set their thrones at the gate of the city.

When King Zedekiah and his royal guard saw the Babylonians in the city gate, they fled as soon as darkness fell:

> They went out through a gate between the two walls behind the king's garden and headed toward the Jordan Valley. But the Babylonians chased the king and caught him on the plains of Jericho. They took

him to King Nebuchadnezzar of Babylon, who was at Riblah in the land of Hamah. There the king of Babylon pronounced judgment upon Zedekiah. He made Zedekiah watch as they killed his sons and all the nobles of Judah. Then he gouged out Zedekiah's eyes, bound him in chains, and sent him away to exile in Babylon.

Meanwhile, the Babylonians burned Jerusalem, including the palace, and tore down the walls of the city. (Jeremiah 39:4-8)

Then the captain of the Babylonian guard took the remnant of the population captive to Babylon. The captivity of the Jews lasted for seventy years just as God had decreed.[23] God had judged his own people for their sin.

Reflection

God judged the sins of his people with catastrophic results. Who are God's people today? Do you believe that they are sinning in ways that will bring a similar catastrophic judgment? How about you personally? Are there sins in your life that will bring his chastening?

Our earthly fathers disciplined us for a few years, doing the best they knew how. But God's discipline is always right and good for us because it means we will share in his holiness. No discipline is enjoyable while it is happening—it is painful! But afterward there will be a quiet harvest of right living for those who are trained in this way.

HEBREWS 12:10-11

July 19

It's an old familiar story—people couldn't get along with one another.

COUNT NICOLAUS Ludwig von Zinzendorf was born in Dresden, Germany, in a Pietist noble family in 1700. The Pietists were Lutherans who sought to know Jesus personally and to live a godly life.

At the age of six Zinzendorf committed his life to Jesus. In childlike simplicity he wrote love letters to Jesus and threw them out the windows of the castle. At ten he was sent to school in Halle, the center of German Pietism.

He completed his education at the University of Wittenberg, and in 1721 purchased his grandmother's estate containing the village of Berthelsdorf. Soon thereafter a leader of the Moravians, the spiritual descendants of Jan Hus,[24] came and asked him if oppressed Moravians could take refuge on his estate. Zinzendorf agreed, and in December 1722 the first ten Moravians arrived. They were given a plot of land that was named Herrnhut, meaning "The Lord's Watch."

Because the Pietist pastor of the Lutheran church in Berthelsdorf shared the Moravians' vision in his preaching, Lutheran Pietists soon became part of Herrnhut, as did Reformed and Anabaptists. By 1727 the population had reached three hundred, but divisions were arising.

There were language barriers as well as squabbles between the Moravians and the Lutherans over the church liturgy. Zinzendorf, determined not to let Herrnhut destroy itself, moved there himself, going house to house trying to bring unity to the community.

On **July 19, 1727,** Zinzendorf organized all the adults into spiritual "bands" of two or three. He grouped people with a natural affinity for one another and appointed one of them as leader. They began to meet together regularly to pray, exhort, and share one another's burdens.

The people in Herrnhut saw their differences start to fade as they focused on one another. On Sunday, August 13, the pastor of the Lutheran church gave an early morning address at Herrnhut to prepare them for the Lord's Supper. The people then walked to the church in Berthelsdorf. The service began with the singing of the hymn "Deliver Me, O God, from All My Bonds and Fetters." Then everyone knelt and sang,

My soul before Thee prostrate falls
To thee, its source, my spirit flies.

THE ANTIDOTE TO DISUNITY

The congregation became gripped with such emotion that the sound of weeping nearly drowned out the singing. Several men prayed with great fervor. Zinzendorf led the congregation in a prayer of confession for their earlier broken fellowship. Then they partook of the Lord's Supper together. After the service people who had previously been fighting embraced one another, pledging to love one another from that time on.

The residents of Herrnhut saw that day as their Pentecost. Soon an around-the-clock prayer ministry began at Herrnhut and continued for one hundred years.

The Moravians became the first missionary-sending Protestant church. When Zinzendorf died thirty-three years later, 226 missionaries had been sent out from Herrnhut to St. Croix, Greenland, Lapland, Georgia, Suriname, Guinea, South Africa, Algeria, Ceylon, Romania, and Constantinople. One of every sixty of the early Moravians became a missionary.

The day before he died, Zinzendorf asked a Moravian friend, "Did you ever suppose in the beginning that the Savior would do as we now really see in the various Moravian settlements . . . amongst the heathen?. . . What a formidable caravan from our church already stands around the Lamb."

The next day Count von Zinzendorf joined that caravan adoring the Lamb upon his throne.

Reflection

It wasn't a coincidence that the Moravian "Pentecost" was preceded by weeks of earnest prayer or that the first Protestant church to emphasize missions was the church with the hundred-year prayer meeting. What is God's prayer role for you in reaching the world for Christ?

The harvest is so great, but the workers are so few. So pray to the Lord who is in charge of the harvest; ask him to send out more workers for his fields.　　　　MATTHEW 9:37-38

July 20

One plants, another waters, but God gives the increase.

JAMES TAYLOR had a pharmacy in Yorkshire, England. In early 1832 he knelt in the back of his shop beside his pregnant wife, Amelia, and prayed, "Dear God, if you should give us a son, grant that he may work for you in China."

God gave them a son a few months later, and they named him James Hudson Taylor.[25] Although his parents did not tell him of their prayer for him for years, as a boy he would often say, "When I am a man, I mean to be a missionary and go to China."

But by the time Hudson was seventeen, he was a typical rebellious teenager and had no interest in being a missionary. But his family continued to pray. That summer when his mother was visiting her sister forty miles away, she felt led to lock herself in a room to pray for Hudson's salvation and not come out until she had the assurance that her prayer had been answered. Back home, Hudson picked up a gospel tract that afternoon on Christ's death on the cross for sinners and accepted the Savior.

Within a few months after Hudson experienced his new birth, his call to China was reconfirmed during a night of prayer, which he described as filled "with unspeakable awe and unspeakable joy."

With a sense of urgency, Hudson finished his schooling and sailed for China at the age of twenty-one. At that time there were 350 baptized Chinese believers. During his first term he married and made several evangelistic trips into the closed interior of China but was forced to return to England because of illness.

There he regained his health and felt an increasing burden for the millions in the interior of China. When the interior was opened to Westerners, Hudson could find no mission willing to back him, so he founded the China Inland Mission (CIM) in 1865. The CIM had several unique distinctives. It was interdenominational and missionaries were recruited from the working class rather than from the universities. Direct appeals for funds were forbidden, with missionaries depending directly upon God for their support.

Initially Hudson prayed for twenty-four workers, two for each unreached province of China. The first fifteen sailed in May 1866, and by 1882 the China Inland Mission had workers in every province. By 1895 it had 641 missionaries, and by 1914 the China Inland Mission was the largest missionary organization, reaching its peak in 1934 with 1,368 missionaries. There were now five hundred thousand baptized believers in China. Then civil war broke out between the Chinese Nationalists and the Communists. The two enemies joined forces to fight Japan; but after the war they went back to fighting each other. By September 1949 the Chinese Communists had won, and the Nationalists retreated to the island of Taiwan. The last CIM workers left China on **July 20, 1953,** leaving behind about one million believers.

The first two decades under Communism were ones of intense persecution. In reaction the church went underground, and many Christians stopped attending church. Yet by 1980 there were two million believers.

Since the early 1980s the growth of the church in China has no parallels in history. In 2000 there were approximately seventy-five million Christians in China. The church of the Lord Jesus Christ in China is larger than the Communist Party.

The sacrificial seed sown by the missionaries of CIM and other missions bore fruit a thousandfold, yet God chose to have the missionaries removed before the harvest that he alone might receive the glory.

Reflection

How would you account for the explosive growth of the church in China since the 1980s? Do you get discouraged when you share your faith with little or no results? The story of the Chinese church should encourage all of us that once the seed of the gospel has been planted it is God who gives the increase.

The rain and the snow come down from the heavens and stay on the ground to water the earth. They cause the grain to grow, producing seed for the farmer and bread for the hungry. It is the same with my word. I send it out, and it always produces fruit. It will accomplish all I want it to, and it will prosper everywhere I send it. Isaiah 55:10-11

July 21

At the Scopes "Monkey" Trial, was Scopes found guilty or innocent?

THE ISSUE of evolution had become more and more divisive ever since Charles Darwin published his *Origin of Species by Means of Natural Selection* in 1859. Initially, conservative Christians were divided over the question as to whether evolution contradicted the biblical account of Creation. Some who held to the inerrancy of the Scriptures believed that God may have used limited means of evolution in his creative activity. Others argued that evolution was diametrically opposed to the biblical account of Creation.

Following World War I, many prominent members of the emerging Fundamentalist movement went aggressively on the attack against evolution, believing that it undermined the authority of the Scriptures. One of the leading critics of evolution was William Jennings Bryan. Bryan had become a national figure as a politician. Three times he was the Democratic nominee for president. In 1896 he was defeated by William McKinley and in 1900 and 1904 by Theodore Roosevelt. In 1912 when Woodrow Wilson[26] was elected president, he made William Jennings Bryan his secretary of state.

When Bryan resigned as secretary of state in 1915, he threw himself into leadership of the Christian movement in America. As Bryan saw the moral standards of America crumbling around him, he became convinced that a prime cause was Darwin's view of the origin of man.

Beginning in 1921, Bryan began actively attacking evolution. In his popular lecture "The Menace of Darwinism," he argued that evolution robbed man of the stimulus for moral living.

Due in large measure to Bryan's efforts, the opposition to evolution became a national movement in the 1920s. A number of Southern states passed laws outlawing the teaching of evolution in the public schools. The law passed in Tennessee was one of the strongest. It made it illegal "to teach any theory that denies the story of Divine Creation of man as taught in the Bible, and to teach instead that man has descended from a lower order of animal."

Within two weeks of the Tennessee governor's signing the bill into law, the American Civil Liberties Union (ACLU) announced that they would test the law. They promised to provide counsel to any teacher in Tennessee willing to be the defendant in the case. Some prominent citizens of Dayton, Tennessee, persuaded John Scopes, a young science teacher, to break the law and allow himself to be arrested. The ACLU provided him with a star-studded defense team headed by Clarence Darrow, a religious skeptic and the nation's most famous trial attorney. The attorneys for the prosecution asked William Jennings Bryan to become their lead attorney.

The resulting Monkey Trial, as the Scopes trial came to be known, proved to be one of the first great media events in history, with reporters packing the little town of Dayton and wiring their stories around the world. There was even a nationwide radio hookup. The reporters particularly delighted in portraying the Christians of Tennessee as backward hillbillies.

Bryan gave an impassioned speech for the prosecution, and then the drama of the trial reached its crescendo when Darrow called Bryan as an expert witness on the Bible for the defense. Bryan's difficulty in answering many of Darrow's questions brought him ridicule from the press. A tired old man at this point, Bryan's testimony consisted of more fervor than fact. The following day the judge struck all of Bryan's testimony as a defense witness from the record.

On **July 21, 1925,** the jury found Scopes guilty in just a few minutes. He was fined $100, but the Tennessee Supreme Court later threw out the conviction on a technicality. The big story nationally, however, was that the most famous trial lawyer of the day had humiliated the nation's greatest orator. The Bible had won in Dayton, but in the eyes of the nation's press evolution had won.

William Jennings Bryan died in his sleep the following Sunday.

Reflection

The world is most interested in who wins and who loses. Ultimately, who do you think were the real winners and losers of the Scopes trial? Why do you think the press was so quick to ridicule Christians? If you could rewrite this chapter of history, how would you do it?

If you are asked about your Christian hope, always be ready to explain it.   1 PETER 3:15

July 22

What is worth dying for?

IN THE late 1640s Alan Cameron, a Scottish merchant, had three sons. The oldest was Richard, followed by Michael and Alexander. Richard attended St. Andrews University, receiving a master of arts degree in 1665. He became a schoolteacher, indifferent to matters of faith. Then he began going to listen to the field preachers, men who went from town to town preaching the gospel outdoors. One day the message of mercy and grace suddenly became real to Richard Cameron, and he gave his life to Christ, soon becoming a field preacher himself.

By the end of 1678 Richard Cameron had joined the Covenanters—Presbyterians who challenged the government's authority not only in spiritual matters but also in the realm of civil government.

In 1679 he went to Holland, where he was ordained. There an exiled Scottish pastor laid his hands on Cameron's head and said, "Here is the head of a faithful minister and servant of Jesus Christ who shall lose the same for his Master's interest, and it shall be set up before sun and moon in the public view of the world."

Returning to Scotland, Cameron could find no one willing to join him in preaching in the fields because the laws had become so restrictive. Eventually Donald Cargill[27] joined him in holding field meetings in the inaccessible parts of the country. By 1680 thousands were attending.

Cameron and the other Covenanters felt that the character of a ruler determines the extent of the subjects' obedience. Therefore they believed that King Charles II must be rejected because he was a tyrant who rejected both covenants he had earlier signed: the 1638 National Covenant, which preserved the Reformed faith in Scotland and guaranteed the church's freedom from civil control and the 1643 Solemn League and Covenant, which again preserved the Reformed faith and Presbyterian government in the Church of Scotland. In fact, Charles II had sworn to establish Presbyterianism throughout his realm. Instead he reestablished the Anglican Church in Scotland and outlawed the covenants.

In response, Richard Cameron rode into the city of Sanquhar with twenty horsemen on the first anniversary of the Battle of Bothwell Bridge[28] and delivered what became known as the Sanquhar Declaration. The declaration rejected Charles II as king and declared war on him as a tyrant. It also rejected his brother, the duke of York, as heir apparent because he was a Roman Catholic. Although regarded at the time as a futile protest by a small minority, it became the position of Britain as a whole within nine years .

As a result of the Sanquhar Declaration, Richard Cameron was declared a traitor and a reward was placed on his head.

A month later he preached what was to be his last sermon. Cameron spent that night at the home of William Mitchell, a Covenanter. The next morning, **July 22, 1680,** as he washed his hands he placed them on his face and said, "This is their last washing." Mrs. Mitchell wept.

About four that afternoon, Cameron and about sixty Covenanters were at Arysmoss, a moor in Ayrshire. Suddenly they were surrounded by government troops. Richard Cameron led the Covenanters in prayer. Then to his brother he said, "Come Michael, let us fight it out to the last; for this is the day that I have longed for, to die fighting against our Lord's avowed enemies; and this is the day that we shall get the crown." To the rest he said, "Be encouraged all of you, to fight it out valiantly, for all of you who fall this day I see heaven's gates cast wide open to receive them."

In the ensuing battle, twenty-eight government troops and nine Covenanters fell. One of the nine was Richard Cameron. His head and hands were taken to Edinburgh, where they were displayed on the Netherbow Port.

The next Sunday Donald Cargill preached on the passage "Know ye not that there is a prince and great man fallen this day in Israel?" (2 Samuel 3:38, KJV).

Reflection

If you had been living in Scotland in 1680, would you have been a Covenanter? Is it ever right to rebel against one's government? If so, under what circumstances?

～❧～

Give to Caesar what belongs to him. But everything that belongs to God must be given to God. MATTHEW 22:21

July 23

Her marriage was very happy but short lived.

MARIA DYER was born in 1837 in China, the youngest of three children of Anglican missionaries. Both parents died by the time she was ten, and the children were raised by an uncle in England. But China was home, and so when Maria turned eighteen, she and her older sister went to Ningpo, China, to teach in a girls school directed by Mary Ann Aldersey.

In Ningpo, Maria met and married Hudson Taylor,[29] much against the wishes of Miss Aldersey. Maria was better educated than her husband and was just the companion and helper that he needed. She polished his rough edges and helped him focus his enthusiasm. Their marriage was a true partnership. Having spoken Chinese from childhood, she immediately started a primary school. When Hudson founded the China Inland Mission, Maria was the ideal person to train the women missionaries in the language and customs of China.

In January 1870 the Taylors began making preparations to send their four oldest children to England for their education. A close friend of the family agreed to return to England with the children and to care for them there. Fear of parting was too traumatic for five-year-old Sammy, who died in February. A month later Hudson and Maria tearfully bid farewell to their children.

Maria suffered from tuberculosis and was now pregnant with their eighth child, due in July. Hudson, who had medical training, knew his wife would not survive to old age.

A missionary couple came to visit the Taylors. To accommodate the new arrivals, a curtain was hung in the Taylors' bedroom so that Maria could share the room with another woman missionary yet both could have privacy.

During the night of July 5, Maria came down with a severe case of cholera, and the curtain prevented her roommate from seeing how sick she was. When Hudson saw her the next morning, he was shocked at how she had deteriorated overnight.

On July 7 Hudson went out to buy some brandy that he thought might help her. When he returned, he was stunned to learn that in his short absence a son, Noel, had been born. Later that evening Maria began to hemorrhage internally. Hudson felt that if he had not been there at that moment or had not had the brandy, he would have lost her.

They bottle-fed the baby for a week, then his throat developed thrush, and his little body grew weaker and weaker. They searched for a wet nurse, but none was found until July 20. By then it was too late. Little Noel died that afternoon. Maria felt well enough to pick the hymns for his funeral.

On the morning of **July 23, 1870,** Hudson could see that Maria was dying. He said to her, "You are going home. You will soon be with Jesus."

"I am so sorry," she replied.

"You are not sorry to be with Jesus?"

"Oh no!" she exclaimed, looking right into Hudson's eyes. "That is not it. You know, Darling, that for ten years past there has not been a cloud between me and my Savior. I cannot be sorry to go to him. But it does grieve me to leave you alone at such a time. Yet . . . he will be with you and meet all your needs."

She kissed him many times in tender parting. Just before she died, Hudson knelt beside her and prayed, committing her to the Lord and thanking God for the twelve and a half years of happiness they had shared. He thanked God for taking her to his presence and solemnly rededicated his life to his service.

Maria was just thirty-three.

Reflection

How do you feel when you hear of a person dying at a young age? Are you ever tempted to blame God or ask, *why*? Maria Taylor died at about the same age as Jesus. If we belong to him as Maria Taylor did, we can share her assurance that God doesn't make mistakes.

∽≪∾

Should the thing that was created say to the one who made it, "Why have you made me like this?"   ROMANS 9:20

July 24

Does God give special revelations to some of his children?

As a boy Robert Annan was such a natural swimmer that his friends called him "Water Dog." But life in Dundee, Scotland, in the 1840s was not all fun and games. While learning masonry from his father, Robert fell in with the wrong crowd and at the age of fourteen spent three months in prison.

After Robert was released, his father decided to help him start a new life and gave him money to go to America. However, America was not the land of opportunity for young Robert, and soon his money was gone. He went to Canada, joined the British army, and ended up back in England, where he deserted. When he finally turned himself in, he was severely punished.

After the fiasco of his military experience, he returned to Dundee. Robert was sure that he had turned over a new leaf but got drunk with his old buddies. Waking up with a hangover the next morning, he realized he couldn't reform himself.

From 1860 to 1861 gospel meetings were held in a large hall in Dundee. Since not much else was happening in town, Robert decided to go. But the message he heard only made him feel more desperate. As he was leaving, he paused on the steps. Others had stayed behind to learn the way of salvation. Should he go back and join them? He finally decided he would, but as he walked back up the steps, the door to the hall slammed in his face. Did this mean he was shut out of salvation forever?

Tortured by that question, Robert knocked on a minister's door at midnight. "What must I do to be saved?" he asked. The pastor pointed him to salvation in Jesus Christ, but Robert wasn't ready.

He fled to his father's hayloft and spent the night praying for mercy. His family found him there the next day and persuaded him to come into the house. But for three days he didn't eat or sleep as he waited to hear God's voice from heaven.

Two ministers came to visit him and said, "You think that if you heard a voice assuring you of salvation or felt some strange thing within you, you would believe and rest on Jesus? God gives you his word; will you rest on that? 'Believe on the Lord Jesus Christ and thou shalt be saved.' Jesus said, 'Him that cometh to me I will in no wise cast out.' "

Three days later Robert gave up listening for God's audible voice and simply believed in Jesus Christ as his Savior and Lord.

Robert worked days as a mason but became the leader of a group of young men who preached regularly on street corners. Many of his hearers came to know Jesus personally as he had.

On **July 24, 1867,** while Robert Annan was relaxing on a raft in Dundee Harbor, he experienced his Savior's presence in such a real way that he wondered if he was in heaven.

The next Sunday as Robert preached on the street, he said, "I cannot tell you how happy I was last Wednesday morning down there upon the water, when the Lord showed me His glory. . . . I may never have another opportunity of speaking to you. I may be in heaven before the next Sabbath."

The next Wednesday Robert rose at four o'clock to pray. As he left his house, with a piece of chalk he wrote "DEATH" on the gate and "ETERNITY" on the pavement in front of his house. Then he went off to work at the harbor.

About noon a young boy fell into the water and was drowning. Robert, the "water dog," had rescued others before and quickly jumped into the water to save him. But this day was different. As Robert handed the boy to other rescuers in a boat, he slid beneath the waves, passing through the gate of Death into Eternity.

Reflection

Why did God reveal himself to Robert Annan that day on the raft and not during the night in the hayloft? Is it ever appropriate to entreat God for a special revelation?

∽≈∾

Blessed are those who haven't seen me and believe anyway.

JOHN 20:29

July 25

There is neither slave nor free man.

IN 1812 a slave Baptist preacher died on the plantation of the Peachy family in Virginia, leaving a pregnant wife. The young widow dedicated her unborn child to the Lord. Her continual prayer was, "Lord, if dis chile you's sendin' me is a boy, doan' let him do nuthin' else but sing de praises of Jesus." When the child was born, she named him John after John the Baptist.

John Jasper grew up as a prodigal son, but his mother persevered in prayer for him. John was eventually purchased by Samuel Hargrove, a deacon at the First Baptist Church in Richmond, Virginia.

Hargrove put John to work in his tobacco factory, and on **July 25, 1839,** God answered his mother's prayers. John Jasper loved to tell the story of what happened that day:

One July mornin' somethin' happen'd. . . . Fac' is, bruthr'n, de darkness of death was in my soul dat mornin'. My sins was piled on me like mount'ns; my feet was sinkin' down to de reguns of despar, an' I felt dat of all sinners I was de wust. I tho't dat I would die right den, an' wid what I supposed was my lars breath I flung up to heav'n a cry for mercy. 'Fore I kno'd it, de light broke; I was light as a feather; my feet was on de mount'n; salvation rol'd like a flood thru my soul, an' I felt as if I could 'nock off de fact'ry roof wid my shouts. . . .

'Twan' long 'fore I looked up de line agin, an' dar was a good ol' woman dar dat know all my sorrers, an' had been prayin' fur me all de time. I had to tell her, an' so I skip along up quiet as a breeze, an' start'd to whisper in her ear, but just den de holin-back straps of Jasper's breachin' broke, an' what I tho't would be a whisper was loud enuf to be hearn clean 'cross Jeems River. . . . All I know'd I had raise my fust shout to de glory of my Redeemer.

But for one thing thar would er been a jin'ral revival in de fact'ry dat mornin'. Dat one thing was de overseer. He bulg'd into de room, an' wid a voice dat sounded like he had his breakfus dat mornin' on rasps an' files, bellowed out: "What's all dis row 'bout?" Somebody shouted out dat John Jasper dun got religun, but dat didn't work 'tall wid de boss. He tell me to git back to my table . . . so I sed: "Yes, sir,

FREED TO PREACH

I will; I ain't meant no harm; de fus taste of salvation got de better un me, but I'll git back to my work." An' I tell you I got back quick.

Bout dat time Mars Sam he come out'n his orfis, an' he say: "What's de matter out here?" An' I hear de overseer tellin' him: "John Jasper kick up a fuss, an' say he dun got religun."

Little aft'r I hear Mars Sam tell de overseer he want to see Jasper. . . I sez to him: " . . . Jes' now out dar at de table God tuk my sins away, an' set my feet on a rock. I didn't mean to make no noise, Mars Sam, but 'fore I know'd it de fires broke out in my soul, an' I jes' let go one shout to de glory of my Saviour." Mars Sam's face was rainin' tears.

Hargrove gave John Jasper his freedom so that he could preach, and preach he did. He founded the Sixth Mount Zion Baptist Church in Richmond with nine members. At the time of his death in 1901, it had grown to over two thousand.

Reflection

Could just any pastor build a church of two thousand slaves and former slaves? Probably not. God called and used John Jasper because he was uniquely equipped to fulfill God's purpose for him. What is God's purpose for your life? He can use you just as he used John Jasper.

For we are God's masterpiece. He has created us anew in Christ Jesus, so that we can do the good things he planned for us long ago.
EPHESIANS 2:10

July 26

He never gave up.

WILLIAM WILBERFORCE was born to affluence in Hull, England, in 1759. His schooling began at the Hull Grammar School, where he came under the influence of two brothers, headmaster Joseph Milner, and teacher Isaac Milner. Isaac used to lift the small boy onto a table so that the other students could listen to him read. After just two years in school William lost his father and was sent to live with his aunt, a staunch Methodist.

By fourteen, Wilberforce had already developed a social conscience, and he wrote a letter to the local newspaper on the evils of the slave trade. He completed his education at St. John's College, Cambridge, where he largely wasted his time. However, in 1780 he was elected to Parliament, where he became a supporter and confidant of William Pitt the Younger, the British prime minister. Pitt persuaded Wilberforce to focus his efforts on the abolition of slavery.

In 1785 Wilberforce was looking for someone with whom to tour Europe when he ran into Isaac Milner, now a tutor at Cambridge. On impulse he invited Milner on the expense-paid trip. Had Wilberforce known that Milner was a committed Christian, he would not have extended the invitation.

As Wilberforce and Milner traveled together, they began arguing about religion. The arguments started to dissipate as they read together *The Rise and Fall of Religion in the Soul* by Philip Doddridge, an evangelical English pastor. By the end of their trip Wilberforce had given intellectual assent to many of the teachings of the Bible, but once back home he returned to politics and put religion on a back burner.

The next year Wilberforce took Isaac Milner on another tour of Europe. This time they studied the Greek New Testament together. Wilberforce later said, "I now fully believed the gospel and was persuaded that if I died at anytime I should perish everlastingly."

Wilberforce was miserable, realizing that he must choose between Christ and the world, but he wanted both. Needing someone to talk to, he went to see his boyhood hero John Newton,[30] the former slave trader, who now at sixty was a London pastor and the author of "Amazing Grace." On December 7, 1785, he left John Newton's home with the decision settled. He had chosen Christ and committed himself to being God's man in politics.

Wilberforce became the leader of a group of wealthy Anglican evangelicals who lived mainly in the hamlet of Clapham, three miles from London.

DEDICATION TO A CAUSE

They became known as the Clapham Sect, although they were in no sense a sect. They were more like a close family determined to change the world for Jesus. The group included an amazing galaxy of talent: the governor general of India, the chairman of the East India Company, the undersecretary for the colonies, and a leading attorney. Intimates of the group who did not live in Clapham included Isaac Milner, Grenville Sharp, and Charles Simeon. Together they formed a remarkable fraternity, unique in British history. They determined which wrongs needed to be righted and then delegated to each person the work he could best perform for their mutual goals.

The first great achievement of Wilberforce and his friends was the abolition of the slave trade in 1807. But the abolition of slavery itself proved a tougher goal to achieve.

On **July 26, 1833,** at the age of seventy-three, Wilberforce was on his deathbed. Late that evening he received word that the Emancipation Act freeing the slaves of the British Empire was assured of passing. His final political goal had been reached. Three days later he died.

If the United States had not declared its independence from England in the Revolutionary War, slavery would have ended in America in 1833 without the Civil War.

Reflection

It took forty-six years for William Wilberforce to achieve his goal of abolishing slavery in the British Empire. Has God called you to a cause? If you feel discouraged because things seem to be moving slowly in spite of your efforts, remember Wilberforce and don't give up!

Don't get discouraged and give up, for we will reap a harvest of blessing at the appropriate time. GALATIANS 6:9

July 27

One seldom meets a literal prophet of doom.

DONALD CARGILL, by nature a shy, troubled person, was born in Scotland in the early 1600s. During his theological studies at St. Andrews University, he was so troubled by various temptations that he decided suicide was the only escape. More than once he went to the Clyde River to drown himself, but each time a passerby dissuaded him. On another occasion as he was about to throw himself into an abandoned coal pit, God gave him the words "Son, be of good cheer, thy sins are forgiven." Immediately his fears and doubts disappeared, and all thoughts of suicide vanished.

After completing his studies at St. Andrews, he was ordained as the minister of the Barony Church of Glasgow in 1655. Things went well until 1660 when Charles II was restored to the throne after the Commonwealth and the Protectorate ended. In 1662 the king went back on his earlier promises, restoring Episcopal government to the Church of Scotland, which was Presbyterian. This forced 270 Presbyterian pastors, called Covenanters, out of their churches. Donald Cargill was banished to the area north of Scotland's Tay River. Meanwhile the Presbyterians who had been forced from their churches met together in fields.

In 1669 when the banishment order was relaxed, Cargill began to preach in the fields. As the persecution of the Covenanters escalated, Cargill became increasingly prominent as a leader, and thousands went to hear him preach.

In May 1679 Cargill was one of the leaders of a Covenanter army of four thousand attacked by a government army of ten thousand at Bothwell Bridge. More than four hundred Covenanters were killed and twelve hundred taken prisoner, including a wounded Donald Cargill. Yet when his captors learned he was a minister, they let him go.

Cargill joined Richard Cameron in preaching in the fields until Cameron's death at Ayrsmoss.[31] Then in September 1680 Donald Cargill publicly excommunicated King Charles II and other leading persecutors of the church. This action infuriated the authorities, and they offered a reward for his capture.

Cargill was finally arrested in May of 1681. As one of his captors was tying him on his horse, Cargill said to him, "Your wickedness is great: You will not escape the just judgment of God; and if I am not mistaken, it will seize you in this very place." A year later the man was murdered on the same exact spot.

Coming to Glasgow, an assistant to the Anglican archbishop made fun of

Cargill, repeatedly saying, "Will you give us one word more?" quoting an expression Cargill often used in his sermons. Cargill replied, "The day is coming, when you will not have one word to say, though you would." A few days later the man's tongue swelled so that he could not speak, and he died.

Cargill was taken to Edinburgh to appear before the council. There Chancellor Rothes, one of those he had excommunicated, raged against him. Cargill replied, "My Lord Rothes, forbear to threaten me, for die what death I will, your eyes shall not see it." Chancellor Rothes died the morning of **July 27, 1681,** and Donald Cargill was executed that afternoon.

On the scaffold before he was hanged, Cargill called out, "Farewell, all created enjoyments, pleasures, and delights; farewell sinning and suffering; farewell praying and believing; and welcome heaven and singing. Welcome, joy in the Holy Ghost; welcome, Father, Son, and Holy Ghost; into thy hands I commend my spirit."

After he died, the hangman cut off his head with an ax and set it on the Netherbow Port.

Reflection

Acts 5 tells of Ananias and his wife, Sapphira, who lied to Peter and to the church after which God struck Ananias dead. Later Peter asked Sapphira, "How could the two of you even think of doing a thing like this—conspiring together to test the Spirit of the Lord? Just outside that door are the young men who buried your husband, and they will carry you out, too." Instantly she died (Acts 5:9). Do you believe that Donald Cargill's prophecies of the death of his enemies was similar to what occurred in Acts 5? What lessons can you learn from Cargill's life?

Great fear gripped the entire church and all others who heard what had happened.
                                                              ACTS 5:11

July 28

In heaven we'll understand why.

KEITH GREEN was a struggling Hollywood nightclub singer, but at the same time he was fascinated with Jesus. A Christian friend invited Keith and his wife, Melody, to a Bible study of his Vineyard Christian Fellowship at a home in Beverly Hills. The leader spoke about how God sent his Son to earth to show the way to the Father. He explained, "You need to open your heart to Jesus and let him come into your life."

As he ended his talk, he asked those wanting to receive Jesus to raise their hands. Keith raised his hand, but Melody couldn't get her hand to move. The leader had those who raised their hands repeat a prayer, and then they were dismissed.

Keith had a gig that night at a bar, but during one of his breaks, he told Melody, "I just can't do this anymore."

The next week seemed to go on forever for Melody. She kept thinking, *I want to go back to the Vineyard. I hope he asks us to raise our hands again.*

They returned to the Bible study the next Friday night. At last the leader got to the hand-raising part. Melody raised her hand and a rush of peace greater than anything she had ever experienced filled her heart.

Keith Green quickly became one of the most popular Christian singer-songwriters. His debut album set a record for sales in the Christian recording industry. As a result, requests for concert bookings came flooding in.

Not only did God give Keith success in his music and speaking ministry, but in the next years he blessed them with three children: Josiah, Bethany, and Rebekah.

On **July 28, 1981,** the Greens and their children were at the Youth With A Mission base in Cimmaron, Colorado. Melody was rejoicing because she had just learned she was pregnant again. While leading a worship time for the staff, Keith surprised Melody by announcing to the group, "God is going to raise my wife up! She is going to speak against abortion—but that is not all. The Lord is going to use Melody in a mighty way, and she's going to speak about many different things in many different places."

After dinner the pilot who had flown their family to Colorado offered to take Keith, his children, and another family on a plane ride to see the area from the air. Keith took their two oldest children, Josiah and Bethany, with him for the plane ride. As he was leaving he called to Melody in an offhand way, "If I don't come back, raise Rebekah to be a woman of God." Keith jumped in the car and drove to the airstrip.

In a short while Melody received a phone call that the plane had crashed. Rushing to the crash site, she learned that there were no survivors. Keith Green was just twenty-eight.

That night a close friend called Melody with a word she had received from the Lord for her. Melody quickly got a pencil and wrote as her friend spoke:"They are with me. My glory is revealed to them. They are in my arms."

The following winter Melody gave birth to Rachel. In the next two years Melody traveled to 110 cities and spoke to three hundred thousand people at Keith Green Memorial Concerts. She served as president of Last Days Ministries and its sister organization, Americans against Abortion.

Years after his death Keith Green is still considered to be among the most popular Christian recording artists.

Reflection

When someone we care about dies, our natural reaction is to ask God *why*. What should our reaction be when negative events occur in our lives? It is significant that in the book of Job, Job himself never knew about the spiritual contest that was the cause of his sufferings and the death of his children (Job 1:16-19).

Job stood up and tore his robe in grief. . . . He said, "I came naked from my mother's womb, and I will be stripped of everything when I die. The Lord gave me everything I had, and the Lord has taken it away. Praise the name of the Lord!" In all of this, Job did not sin by blaming God.
JOB 1:20-22

July 29

Why is England largely Protestant and not Catholic?

In 1558 Elizabeth I, a Protestant, succeeded her half sister Mary Tudor,[32] a Roman Catholic, as queen of England. Mary had done everything she could to make England Catholic and had earned her name "Bloody Mary" by burning many Protestants at the stake. On the other hand, the pragmatic Elizabeth realized that her subjects were largely Protestants, and she adamantly opposed allowing the pope to rule her country.

England's arch rival at the time was Spain, which was Catholic. The Spanish king Philip II was Europe's most powerful monarch. The pope, Emperor Ferdinand I of the Holy Roman Empire, and the Catholic Mary Queen of Scots all encouraged Philip to invade England to restore Catholicism.

Queen Elizabeth cleverly toyed with King Philip, letting him think she might marry him or his son. King Philip, hoping that he might be able to win England with a wedding ring, patiently waited to see what would happen.

Meanwhile, English pirates under the direction of Francis Drake plundered Spanish merchant ships with Elizabeth's tacit approval.

At this time the Netherlands were in revolt against Spain. Elizabeth knew that as long as Philip was fighting in the Netherlands, he was less likely to invade England. Therefore she secretly helped the Dutch rebels so that they would not surrender to Spain.

Then Elizabeth received a financial windfall. Spanish ships carrying the payroll for their troops in the Netherlands were driven into England's ports by English pirates. Philip kept his temper, and Elizabeth kept the money.

But when she imprisoned Mary Queen of Scots, Philip's patience ran out, and he became involved in a plot to assassinate Elizabeth. When Elizabeth found out, she expelled the Spanish ambassador and began openly aiding the Netherlands. The lines were drawn. Both Elizabeth and Philip put all their resources into preparing for the war that would determine the mastery of the seas and the religion of England.

Queen Elizabeth assembled her fleet of 34 royal warships. In addition, she induced the owners of 170 merchant ships to equip their vessels with armaments. Philip's Spanish Armada consisted of 130 ships, the most powerful navy the world had ever seen. Hundreds of monks accompanied the Armada to help restore Catholicism to England. A profound religious spirit pervaded the Spanish sailors. On the morning the armada sailed, every sailor took the

A POWER STRUGGLE OR A HOLY WAR?

Eucharist, and all Spain prayed. The plan was to defeat the English navy and then to invade England.

The winds favored the English. The armada immediately ran into a destructive storm and had to retreat to a harbor to heal its wounds.

The battle's main action occurred off the coast of France. Shortly after midnight on July 28, Francis Drake set fire to several small boats and placed them in the wind to drift into the Spanish fleet. Panic seized the Spaniards as two ships caught fire and several of the largest became entangled with one another trying to escape the burning boats. Beginning at noon, the full English fleet poured its artillery into the armada. Some ships sank, and many that survived had difficulty staying afloat.

The coup de grace for the Spanish came the following day, **July 29, 1588.** The wind carried the broken armada off into the North Sea, where heavy winds wrecked many of the remaining ships off the coast of Ireland. One Irish city saw the bodies of eleven hundred Spanish sailors wash ashore.

Of the 130 ships that had left Spain, just 53 returned, and they were so badly damaged that they were worthless. Of the twenty-seven thousand men who left, ten thousand returned, most of them wounded or sick.

England lost just sixty men and not one ship and would remain Protestant.

Reflection

What role, if any, do you feel that God had in the defeat of the Spanish Armada? Did the English have God to thank for the victory? Do you believe that God has a plan for history that he is working out, or are such events ruled by chance?

All things happen just as he decided long ago.   EPHESIANS 1:11

July 30

God's will includes the past, present, and future.

In 1854 Hudson Taylor[33] went as a missionary to China, where he married Maria Dyer. They were forced to return home to England in 1860 because of illness. When inland China was officially opened to foreigners, Taylor, finding no mission board to back him, founded the interdenominational China Inland Mission (CIM) in 1865, now the Overseas Missionary Fellowship.

Burdened for inland China, Hudson prayed for twenty-four missionaries, two for each of the unreached provinces of China. By 1866 he had his twenty-four, and he and his family sailed for China with the first fifteen of them. One of the new missionaries was twenty-two-year-old Jane Faulding, who went by the name of "Jennie." She was a Baptist and the daughter of a well-to-do London couple who were friends of the Taylors. On the leisurely voyage, Jennie found that she had much in common with Maria Taylor, and the two women became best friends.

With their arrival, the Taylors and their fifteen new recruits increased the number of Protestant missionaries in China by approximately one quarter.

At that time there were only fourteen single European women in all of China, all in Hong Kong or treaty ports. Taylor decided to make the port city of Hangchow his headquarters and from there send out his missionaries two by two into the inland provinces. The international community in China thought it unwise for Taylor to send single women into the interior, but Taylor found it to be an effective strategy. Jennie, however, chose to remain in Hangchow.

Before they had been there a week, many Chinese were dropping in to meet them, and soon, more than two hundred were attending their Sunday services. One woman was openly interested in the gospel, and Jennie, who was learning Chinese quickly, visited her daily.

The Chinese character sounding most similar to her last name, Faulding, is *Fuh,* which means "happiness." Soon Jennie became known as Miss Happiness, an apt description for the young, bright-faced girl. Jennie as well as the other CIM missionaries followed Hudson's example of wearing Chinese clothing, finding that it often opened up opportunities to meet the Chinese. "Miss Happiness" was continually being invited into the homes of Chinese women.

Tragedy struck the following year when Maria Taylor died of cholera soon after giving birth to her eighth child, Noel, who lived only a week. After

Maria's death Hudson Taylor visited the CIM headquarters at Hangchow, spending a time of healing with Jennie and the other missionaries.

In 1872 Jennie was scheduled to go home to England for a furlough. She made reservations that fell through at the last moment, and she ended up booked on the same steamer to England as Hudson Taylor. On the boat their friendship developed into something more, and while in England they were married in her parents' London home.

Jennie had all along been the most effective women's worker in the mission. Now as Hudson's wife, she became a mentor to the other women CIM missionaries. Partners in marriage and ministry, Hudson and Jennie joyously labored together in their beloved China.

In 1902 Hudson Taylor resigned as director of the China Inland Mission, and as Jennie's health deteriorated, they went to live in Switzerland. Her strength continued to decline, and on **July 30, 1904,** she was having extreme difficulty breathing. Towards morning, she whispered to Hudson, "Ask him to take me quickly."

Never had a husband a more difficult prayer to pray, but for her sake he cried out to God to free her spirit. Five minutes later Jennie's breathing became quiet, and in a short time there was peace. Her last words were "His grace is sufficient" and then "He will not fail."

Reflection

Jennie Faulding Taylor always rejoiced in the will of God. After her death Hudson frequently reminisced that Jennie never thought anything could be better than God's will. Do you rejoice in God's will, or are you afraid of what it might hold for you? God's will is perfect, and anything else we might choose for ourselves will be second best.

I want your will, not mine. MARK 14:36

July 31

When God called Ezekiel to be a prophet, he knew he was called.

In 605 B.C. Nebuchadnezzar became king of Babylon and King Jehoiakim of Judah became his vassal. However, after three years Jehoiakim switched his allegiance from Babylon to Egypt and became the vassal of the pharaoh (2 Kings 24:1-2), ignoring the warnings of the prophet Jeremiah (Jeremiah 27:8-11). In response, Nebuchadnezzar declared war on Judah and in 597 B.C. conquered Jerusalem. He took Jehoiakim's son and successor, King Jehoiachin, captive to Babylon along with ten thousand of Judah's leading citizens (2 Kings 24:10-16). Nebuchadnezzar then made Johoiachin's uncle, Mattaniah, king of Judah in his place and changed his name to Zedekiah (2 Kings 24:17).

Among the captives taken to Babylon was a priest named Ezekiel who had been looking forward to serving in the temple when he reached his thirtieth birthday (cf. Numbers 4:3). However, his thirtieth birthday found him a long way from the temple in Jerusalem; he was by the Kebar River, a canal near the city of Tel Abib, Babylon, which made a loop off of the Euphrates River (Ezekiel 1:1).

There by the Kebar River on **July 31, 593 B.C.**, Ezekiel received a vision that would change his life (chapters 1–3).[34] Ezekiel

> saw a great storm coming toward him from the north, driving before it a huge cloud that flashed with lightening and shone with brilliant light. The fire inside the cloud glowed like gleaming amber. From the center of the cloud came four living beings that looked human, except that each had four faces and two pairs of wings. . . . There was a surface spread out above them like the sky. . . . Above this surface over their heads was what looked like a throne made of blue sapphire. And high above this throne was a figure whose appearance was like that of a man. From his waist up, he looked like gleaming amber. . . . All around him was a glowing halo, like a rainbow shining through the clouds. (Ezekiel 1:4-28)

The Lord was appearing to Ezekiel in his glory. Ezekiel fell down and the Lord said to him, "Stand up, I want to speak to you." As the Lord spoke, the Holy Spirit entered Ezekiel and enabled him to stand. "Son of man," the Lord said, "I am sending you to the nation of Israel, a nation that is rebelling against me. Their ancestors have rebelled against me from the beginning, and they are still in revolt to this very day. They are a hard-hearted and stubborn people. But I am sending you to say to them, 'This is what the Sovereign Lord says!' And whether they listen or not—for remember, they are rebels—at least they will know they have had a prophet among them" (Ezekiel 2:1-5).

The Lord continued,

> "I am sending you to the people of Israel, but they won't listen to you any more than they listen to me! For the whole lot of them are hard-hearted and stubborn. But look, I have made you as hard and stubborn as they are. I have made you as hard as rock! So don't be afraid of them or fear their angry looks, even though they are such rebels."
>
> Then he added, "Son of man, let all my words sink deep into your own heart first. Listen to them carefully for yourself. Then go to your people in exile and say to them, 'This is what the Sovereign Lord says!' Do this whether they listen to you or not." (Ezekiel 3:7-11)

Then the Holy Spirit returned Ezekiel to the colony of exiles at Tel Abib beside the Kebar River. He was so overwhelmed by his experience that for seven days he just sat among his fellow exiles, meditating on what he had seen and heard and letting it sink deep into his heart.

God had taken Ezekiel the priest and made him into a prophet.

Reflection

How do you feel when others reject spiritual truths you share with them? Why do you think God told Ezekiel to give his message to the Israelites whether they listened to him or not? What does that tell us about where the responsibility for results resides?

You must give them my messages whether they listen or not.

EZEKIEL 2:7

August 1

There was more to Francis Scott Key than just one song.

FRANCIS SCOTT KEY was born in Maryland on **August 1, 1779,** the son of an army officer in the Revolutionary War. He received his law degree and opened his first practice in Frederick, Maryland, in 1801. In 1802 he married and then moved to Georgetown, Washington, D.C., to enter legal practice with his uncle. He worked in Washington for the rest of his life and served as the United States district attorney for three terms, until his death in 1843.

During the War of 1812 the British occupied Washington, D.C., and set fire to the Capitol and the White House. The British then began advancing on Baltimore. Key was authorized by President James Madison to help negotiate the release of a Washington physician, William Beanes, who had been taken prisoner by the British and was being held aboard the ship *Tonnant* in the Potomac.

Key went by sloop, the *Minden*, out to the *Tonnant* and negotiated successfully for the release of Dr. Beanes, but they were not allowed to return to land because the British fleet was preparing an imminent attack on Baltimore. Key and the others on the ship watched the British naval bombardment of Fort McHenry in Baltimore. Throughout the night of September 13, 1814, Key stayed on deck, watching "the rockets red glare, the bombs bursting in air," hoping and praying the American fort would stand. At "dawn's early light," Key saw the American flag still flying and was overcome with joy—"the flag was still there!" He began writing "The Star-Spangled Banner" on an envelope on his way to shore and edited it in his hotel room that night.

The poem was printed in the *Baltimore American* on September 21, 1814. Set to the tune of a well-known British drinking song, it soon gained nationwide popularity. But it was not until 1931 that Congress officially adopted it as the national anthem of the United States of America.

This song and story are familiar to most Americans. Less well known is the fact that Francis Scott Key was a dedicated Christian. He seriously considered becoming a clergyman in the Episcopal Church. He was a lay reader in the church and a faithful visitor of the sick. Key was one of the founders of the American Sunday School Union and served on its board for many years. While he was on the board, they launched the 1830 Mississippi Valley Campaign, which sought to establish a Sunday school in every town in a 1.3 million-square-mile area within two years. Key worked actively in Washington to publicize the Mississippi campaign and raise funds for it. The campaign actually took fifty years to complete—with 61,297 Sunday schools started, reaching 2,650,784 pupils.

THE STAR-SPANGLED BANNER

Francis Scott Key also wrote the hymn "Lord, with Glowing Heart I'd Praise Thee":

Lord, with glowing heart I'd praise Thee,
For the bliss Thy love bestows,
For the pardoning grace that saves me,
And the peace that from it flows;
Help O God, My weak endeavor;
This dull soul to rapture raise;
Thou must light the flame, or never
Can my love be warmed to praise.

Praise, my soul, the God that sought thee,
Wretched wanderer, far astray;
Found thee lost, and kindly brought thee
From the paths of death away.
Praise, with love's devoutest feeling,
Him who saw thy guilt-born fear,
And, the light of hope revealing,
Bade the blood-stained Cross appear.

Reflection

Francis Scott Key was deeply committed to God and country both in word and in action. Do you take seriously your responsibilities as both a citizen and church member?

Love the Lord your God, walk in all his ways, obey his commands, be faithful to him, and serve him with all your heart and all your soul.

JOSHUA 22:5

August 2

In 1492 Columbus sailed the ocean blue—but another departure from Spain in 1492 was more momentous for some than the voyage of Columbus.

AT THE END of the fifteenth century Spain emerged as the greatest empire since antiquity. In 1469 Ferdinand, son of the king of Aragon, married his cousin Isabella, daughter of the king of Castile. In 1474 Isabella became queen of Castile, and in 1479 Ferdinand became king of Aragon. Together they ruled a united Spain and defeated the Muslim Moors, ending the presence of Islam in Europe.

In 1479 Ferdinand and Isabella introduced the Inquisition in Spain, a tribunal to identify and remove heresy. The Jews of Spain were a particular target. In the early Middle Ages Spain had been the safest Latin area for Jews to live and thus became a center of Jewish learning and finance. But by the thirteenth and fourteenth centuries anti-Semitism was on the rise. In Seville in 1391 four thousand Jews were massacred. Others, while secretly adhering to Judaism, outwardly professed Christianity and were baptized to save their lives. The Spaniards derisively referred to them as *marranos,* from the word for "swine." The *marranos* had the legal rights of Catholic citizens, yet it was well known that privately many were still practicing Jews.

The Spanish Inquisition targeted all kinds of suspected enemies of the church, but the majority were Jews. Torture was a primary means of interrogation. In twelve years the Inquisition had condemned 13,000 *marranos* for the secret practice of Judaism. In total, the Spanish Inquisition punished 341,000 people, more than 32,000 of whom were burned to death. Ferdinand and Isabella seized the assets of all those convicted in the Inquisition.

The final indignity forced on the Jews was the Edict of Expulsion signed by Ferdinand and Isabella. It decreed that every Jew who would not immediately be baptized had to leave Spain within three months of the deadline of **August 2, 1492.**

At this time there were still two hundred thousand Jews living in Spain. Many decided to be baptized, including the senior rabbi and a majority of the leading families. Approximately one hundred thousand fled to Portugal only to be expelled four years later. Another fifty thousand crossed the straits to North Africa or went by ship to Turkey, leaving the land that had been their home for nearly fifteen hundred years. Others went to the Netherlands, the only Christian country that would receive them.

The reason that Columbus[1] chose to disembark from the smaller port of Palos was that the larger port of Cadiz had been designated as the embarkation place for Jews and was filled with thousands fleeing the country by ship. Some eight thousand Jewish families sailed from Cadiz during the summer of 1492.

Columbus set sail from Spain half an hour before the sunrise deadline on August 3 with his Jewish secretary Luis Torres, who had recently been baptized. Columbus always signed his name Colon, a common name among the *marranos* of Genoa, his home, evidence that he may have been a Hebrew Christian himself.

August 2, 1492, in the Hebrew calendar, was the ninth day of the month Ab. This was the same day as the destruction of the Jewish temple in 586 B.C., beginning the exile among the Babylonians, and the same day as the destruction of the temple in A.D. 70 by the Romans, beginning the exile among the Gentiles. It was also the same day in the Jewish calendar that the Jews were expelled from England in 1290.

The persecution and exile of the Jews from Spain was the most momentous event for Judaism between the middle of the second century A.D. and the holocaust. The Spanish Jews have become known as the *Sephardi* Jews (a corruption of an old word for Spain). They remained dispersed until the creation of the state of Israel in 1948.

Reflection

Why do you believe the Jews suffered such persecution in Spain? Is there any possible defense for their persecutors who called themselves Christians? Do you believe that God was involved in the situation? Why did God threaten Israel with dispersion?

If you do not fear the glorious and awesome name of the Lord your God . . . the Lord will scatter you among all the nations.

DEUTERONOMY 28:58, 64

August 3

This was not a boxing match; it was a struggle of life and death.

IN THE latter half of the nineteenth century China had opened itself to foreign missions because of Western political and military pressure. The results, however, were not all positive. Disease accompanied the missionaries, and life expectancy dropped to forty. There was much violence and frequent rebellions.

By 1898 the young emperor of China, Kuang-hsu, determined that the only hope for his nation was Christian moral and social reform. He invited an influential Baptist missionary to the palace to help him draw up his plans, but the very day the missionary arrived at the palace, the emperor was overthrown by a secret Chinese society that feared he would sell out to foreigners.

The secret society called itself "Righteous and Harmonious Fists," but Westerners nicknamed these Chinese the "Boxers."[2] The Boxers were desperate to retain the old pagan Chinese religions. Forming secret cells across China, they performed black-magic rituals and even human sacrifices to temple idols.

Following the coup, the Boxers installed the emperor's mentally ill aunt as empress. They persuaded her that foreign missionaries were gouging out the eyes of Chinese children to use in the making of their medicine. At the urging of the Boxers, the new empress sent a secret decree to officials in the provinces calling on them to kill all foreigners and to exterminate Christianity. The messengers to southern China altered one Chinese character in the decree to make it read "protect" instead of "kill" foreigners. So the bloodletting was confined to the north. When the disobedience of the messengers was discovered, their bodies were cut in half.

Most local Chinese officials sought to protect the missionaries. The magistrate at Fenchow in north Shandi was particularly friendly to missionaries, and a missionary couple living there invited five missionaries from other areas to stay with them in July when the mob violence was at its peak. However, no sooner had the missionaries arrived than the vindictive provincial governor appointed a new magistrate for Fenchow. The new official ordered the missionaries out of Fenchow and gave them armed guards, supposedly for their protection.

The missionaries apparently could read the handwriting on the wall. On **August 3, 1900,** Lizzie Atwater, an American missionary wife and mother wrote to her family:

THE BOXERS

Dear ones, I long for a sight of your dear faces, but I fear we shall not meet on earth. They beheaded thirty-three of us last week in Taiwan. I am preparing for the end very quietly and calmly. The Lord is wonderfully near, and He will not fail me. I was being restless and excited while there seemed to be a chance of life, but God has taken away that feeling, and now I just pray for grace to meet the terrible end bravely. The pain will soon be over, and oh the sweetness of the welcome above!

My little baby will go with me. I think God will give it to me in heaven, and my dear mother will be so glad to see us. I cannot imagine the Savior's welcome. Oh, that will compensate for all these days of suspense. Dear ones, live near to God and cling less closely to earth. There is no other way in which we can receive that peace from God that passeth understanding. . . . I must keep calm and still these hours. I do not regret coming to China but am sorry I have done so little. My married life, two precious years, has been so very full of happiness. We will die together, my dear husband and I.

Twelve days later the guards assigned to them by the magistrate murdered the seven missionaries and their children.

Reflection

How would you react if you were in a similar situation to that of Lizzie Atwater? We all know that we are going to die someday. It is just a question of when and how. Do you share Lizzie's assurance of going to heaven?

∽◦≈

Just as it is destined that each person dies only once and after that comes judgment, so also Christ died only once as a sacrifice to take away the sins of many people. HEBREWS 9:27-28

August 4

Imagine walking nine hundred miles.

EZRA APPARENTLY was the commissioner for Jewish affairs under Artaxerxes I, king of the Persian Empire.[3] In 458 B.C. the king sent Ezra to Judah to investigate the situation there. The first return from the Babylonian captivity had occurred seventy-nine years earlier, under Sheshbezzar, when work to rebuild the altar and the temple began. The temple was finally completed in 516 B.C. Ezra was sent to enforce the Jewish laws and had authority to appoint magistrates and judges in Israel.

As many as five thousand Jewish exiles from the Babylonian captivity accompanied Ezra, and they brought with them valuable gifts for the temple in Jerusalem from King Artaxerxes and from the Jewish exiles who remained in Babylon (Ezra 7:1-26).

Ezra, however, was much more than a Persian government official. He was both a priest and a scribe. As a priest, he could trace his lineage back to Aaron (7:1-5). He also was a scribe, one who studied and interpreted the Scriptures (7:6). He was a teacher of the Jews of Babylon and was coming now to teach the Jews of Judah.

Ezra and his fellow travelers left their homes in Babylon on April 8, 458 B.C., and assembled along the Ahava Canal off the Euphrates (7:9; 8:15).

On April 19 they broke camp and started off for Jerusalem (8:31). The caravan arrived in Jerusalem four months later, on **August 4, 458 B.C.** (7:8-9). The distance from where the Jews lived in Babylon along the Euphrates River to Jerusalem was approximately five hundred miles if one traveled in a straight line. However, because it was desert all the way, the route traders took from Babylon and Persia went northwest along the Euphrates and then southwest to Jerusalem, making it a nine-hundred-mile trip. The terrain surrounding the Euphrates was very lush, especially in the spring when Ezra and the exiles traveled. They were traversing what we today call the Fertile Crescent. Resting on each Sabbath, they averaged about ten miles a day. Since their entourage included both young children and the elderly, this was a realistic pace everyone could maintain.

Such a trip was by nature dangerous, but God protected them from enemies and bandits along the way. In describing God's protection, Ezra explains that "the gracious hand of our God protected us" (8:31). This is the same hand of our heavenly Father from which none of his people can be snatched (John 10:29).

God put his gracious hand on Ezra because Ezra had determined to study and obey the law of the Lord and to teach it to the people of Israel (7:9-10). God's hand was upon Ezra because he put study, conduct, and teaching in their proper order. He taught what he had first lived, and what he lived was based on his study of the Scriptures. God keeps his hand upon such a person.

Reflection

Do you want God's gracious hand to protect and direct you? God is looking for new Ezras. He may not ask you to teach a nation as he did Ezra, but we can all teach those in our sphere of influence. The first step is to study God's Word so that we understand it and hear him speaking to us through it. The second step is to apply to our lives what God has revealed. Once we have lived out God's truths in our lives, we can share them with others and God's hand will be upon us.

Be a good worker, one who does not need to be ashamed and who correctly explains the word of truth. 2 TIMOTHY 2:15

August 5

They abandoned their war hero.

CHARLES GORDON was born in 1833 to a large military family in Victorian England. At the age of sixteen he went to military school. Although he showed promise as a soldier, he was also independent and rebellious, often exhibiting a short fuse toward authority figures.

Consistent with his fiercely independent personality, young Gordon was not a fan of organized religion and refused to be confirmed. However, from the time he was a boy he always believed that the Bible was true and that every human event was preordained by God. These two beliefs were to be foundational for him throughout life.

In 1854 during his second military assignment after becoming a second lieutenant in the Royal Engineers, he became friends with his captain, who was a Christian. Captain Drew gave him Andrew Bonar's *Memoir of Robert Murray M'Cheyne* and other Christian books. Through Captain Drew and the books he read, Charles Gordon passed from death to life.

For thirty years he dedicated his life to serving his country, working his way up to general. Gordon possessed bravery, wisdom, and an intensity unlike others. He was widely decorated for his role in military operations in Armenia, the Crimea, China, and throughout central Africa.

Gordon's next spiritual step came in the mid-1860s. His good friend Mrs. Freese recalls how he discovered what he called "the secret": "While dressing rather listlessly before dinner his eye fell on an opened Bible on the table and on these words: 'Whosoever confesseth that Jesus is the Son of God, God dwelleth in him and he in God.' Suddenly it flashed upon him that he had found a jewel of priceless value—he had found what alone could satisfy him, oneness with God: Henceforth that was the key to his whole after life, and he wondered he had never seen it before. He wondered far more that anyone could read such words and be indifferent to them, and he now tried to make them known to as many as he could."

Gordon had always had a burden for the poor. But after realizing his "secret," he spent as much time as he could with the poor and the sick. He shared the gospel with as many people as would listen.[4]

In April of 1884 while in the Sudan defending the city of Khartoum against the Mahdi Muslims, Gordon found himself surrounded by the enemy. His repeated requests for reinforcements fell on deaf ears. With few men or resources, he masterfully maintained the morale of his troops while holding off the enemy.

Back in Britain, popular opinion was that the government should send Gordon more reinforcements. Finally, on **August 5, 1884,** Prime Minister Gladstone authorized a little money for a relief operation for General Gordon. When the relief force finally arrived in Khartoum in January, they were sixty hours too late. After a 317-day siege Khartoum had fallen, and Gordon was dead.

Gordon's last letter to his sister said, "I am quite happy, thank God . . . I have tried to do my duty." His diary ended on the same day with "I have done the best for the honour of my country. Good-bye."

When the news of Gordon's death reached England, there was an outburst of public grief. It was internationally acknowledged that the world had lost a hero. A national day of mourning was held for him and a monument erected.

Loved and respected not only for his military accomplishments but also for his unique character, Gordon was dominated by his simple yet unshakable Christian faith.

Lord Tennyson wrote his epitaph:

> *Warrior of God, man's friend, not here below,*
> *But somewhere dead far in the waste Sudan,*
> *Thou livest in all hearts, for all men know*
> *This earth hath borne no simpler, nobler man.*

Reflection

General Charles Gordon trusted God in every circumstance—no matter how hopeless. He was able to rest in the knowledge that God was in control and could be trusted implicitly. To what extent do circumstances affect your faith in God?

Love never gives up, never loses faith, is always hopeful, and endures through every circumstance.   1 CORINTHIANS 13:7

August 6

Some called it America's Pentecost.

THE STATE of the American frontier in the late 1700s was one of growing religious indifference. Christianity was on the decline as settlers began to experience economic success.

Settlers went to the frontier to get land, not religion. Referring to Lexington, Kentucky, in 1795, Methodist James Smith feared that "the Universalists, joining with the Deists, had given Christianity a deadly stab hereabouts."

James McGready arrived in Kentucky in 1798 to pastor three small frontier Presbyterian churches. His fiery preaching, with its vivid descriptions of heaven and hell, shook the apathy from his congregation. When the Red River church started to plan its annual Communion service in 1800, it decided to invite other local Presbyterian and Methodist churches to participate. The typically reverent, quiet Communion service of Presbyterianism turned surprisingly emotional and ecstatic. The ministers and parishioners alike were amazed at how God worked in their midst. Although somewhat wary of emotionalism, the Presbyterian and Methodist ministers began to plan a larger Communion service weekend for the following summer at Cane Ridge.

Word of the upcoming camp meeting spread throughout the frontier, and on **August 6, 1801,** the Cane Ridge Revival began. For seven days thousands of people descended on the Cane Ridge meetinghouse in Bourbon County, Kentucky, about 20 miles west of Lexington. They gathered together to worship, fellowship, and celebrate the Lord's Supper.

Friday and Saturday were solemnly observed, devoted to fasting and praying in preparation for Sunday's Communion. But as thousands more than expected arrived, the crowds grew restless and sabotaged the traditional Presbyterian routine. Preachers began to take the stage one after the other, with the large crowd growing into a frenzy on occasion. Some ministers were encouraging ecstasy and emotionalism, while others were fighting to maintain control of their audience and to return the focus to the solemnity of the Lord's Supper.

The excitement of the crowd won out. Large numbers of people were crying, shrieking, fainting, and convulsing in religious ecstasy. This went on for days. Although all of the ministers were pleased that so many had turned out and that apathy wasn't an issue, there were heated disagreements over whether the preachers should be trying to stir up emotionalism with their preaching.

THE CANE RIDGE REVIVAL

The Cane Ridge meeting was both a beginning and an end. It was the end of the long-preserved Scotch-Irish Presbyterian tradition of lengthy, highly ritualized large-group Communion services. This was the first of such services in the New World, and the emotional events of Cane Ridge served to force the end of that tradition. The Cane Ridge meeting was also the beginning of a new institution, organized camp meetings and revivals that turned the American frontier from apathy back to Christianity.

Estimates of attendance at Cane Ridge vary widely from ten thousand to twenty-five thousand with from one thousand to three thousand reported conversions. The banner year for camp meetings was 1811 when as many as one-third of all Americans attended at least one such meeting.

Reflection

How do you think you would have reacted to the Cane Ridge Revival if you had been there? Does the outward display of emotions in worship services make you feel ill at ease, or does it enhance your worship experience?

Shout with joy to the Lord, O earth!
Worship the Lord with gladness.
Come before him, singing with joy.
Acknowledge that the Lord is God!
He made us, and we are his.
We are his people, the sheep of his pasture.
Enter his gates with thanksgiving;
Go into his courts with praise.
Give thanks to him and bless his name.
For the Lord is good.
His unfailing love continues forever,
And his faithfulness continues to each generation.

PSALM 100

August 7

His life was an example of what God can do with one man.

FRANCIS ASBURY was born to a poor family near Birmingham, England, in 1745. His parents had been among the early converts of John Wesley, the founder of Methodism.[5] They had found God while grieving the death of their infant daughter, Francis's only sibling.

Asbury's mother surrounded him with prayer, Scripture, and hymns when he was a boy. She invited everyone whom she met who seemed "religious" to stay at her house. Young Asbury was a good boy. "I abhorred mischief and wickedness, although my mates were among the vilest of the vile for lying, swearing, fighting, and whatever else boys of their age and evil habits were likely to be guilty of. From such society I very often returned home uneasy and melancholy." His peers often ridiculed him for his principles and because of the constant stream of religious folk at his home. They jeeringly called him "Methodist Parson," which was a cutting insult because Methodism at that time was seen as a crazy new religion, and its advocates were often persecuted.

At the age of thirteen young Asbury began asking his mother questions about the Methodists. She arranged for a friend of hers to take him to a Methodist service in the town of Wednesbury[6] so that he could see for himself. He was particularly impressed with the spontaneity and afterward said, "This was not the Church but it was better. The people were so devout, men and women kneeling down, saying 'Amen.' Now, behold! They were singing hymns, sweet sound! Why, strange to tell! The preacher had no prayer book, and yet he prayed wonderfully! What was yet more extraordinary, the man took his text and had no sermon book: thought I, this is wonderful indeed! It is certainly a strange way, but the best way."

Soon thereafter, when Asbury and a Christian friend were in his father's barn loft praying together, he trusted the Savior he had heard about for so long.

He was so excited about his salvation that he became a local traveling preacher at the age of seventeen, while also continuing his work as a blacksmith's apprentice. By the age of twenty he was ministering full-time in various Methodist preaching circuits throughout England.

On **August 7, 1771**, at the age of 21, he answered John Wesley's call for Methodist preachers to go to America. When Wesley announced, "Our brethren in America call aloud for help," Asbury answered, "Here am I, send me."

THE METHODIST PARSON

Once in America Asbury was chosen to be one of the first two Methodist superintendents in what under his leadership became a new denomination, the Methodist Episcopal Church. He subsequently changed the title to "bishop."

Asbury defined the role of an itinerant minister. His motto was, "Go into every kitchen and shop; address all, aged and young, on the salvation of their souls." He urged all Methodist ministers to do the same. He became a "circuit rider," visiting camp meetings, revivals, and conventions on horseback.

Asbury traveled constantly for forty-five years, covering about three hundred thousand miles, mostly on horseback, and crossing the Appalachians more than sixty times. He literally had no home of his own in America but found shelter wherever he could.

When Asbury came to America in 1771, there were about 300 Methodists and four ministers, all on the Atlantic seaboard. At the time of his death in 1816, Methodism had spread into every state, and more than 214,000 people in America called themselves Methodists. Asbury himself had ordained more than 4,000 Methodist ministers and preached more than 16,000 sermons.

Reflection

Francis Asbury gave his entire life to his ministry, forgoing a home and a family in order to spread the gospel on horseback. To what ministry have you been called? What sacrifices is God calling you to make?

I will gladly spend myself and all I have for your spiritual good.

2 CORINTHIANS 12:15

August 8

Being God's representative is an awesome responsibility.

WHEN EZEKIEL was thirty years old, God gave him a vision, calling him to be a prophet.[7] At the time he was an exile living in Tel Abib (Hebrew spelling Tel Aviv), Babylon, during the Babylonian captivity. For seven days after receiving the vision, Ezekiel just sat among his fellow Jews, overwhelmed at what God had revealed to him (Ezekiel 1:1–3:15).

Throughout the Old Testament when God called someone to be a prophet, typically that individual was disturbed by the prospect of his new role. Ezekiel was no exception. During those seven days he was in bitterness and turmoil as he considered the prospect that his mission in life would be to deliver an unpopular message to an unreceptive audience. It was hardly a role he would have chosen for himself. Yet in spite of his understandable trepidation, the Lord's hold on him remained strong.

The fact that Ezekiel sat for seven days considering his vision and what lay before him is significant because he was a priest (1:3) and a priest entered his priestly ministry at the age of thirty (Numbers 4:3) through a seven-day consecration (Leviticus 8:33). Since Ezekiel was thirty (Ezekiel 1:1), this served as his seven-day consecration (3:15) as both a priest and a prophet.

At the end of the seven days, on **August 8, 593 B.C.**, the Lord gave Ezekiel a message of what his specific role was to be. Ezekiel was to be "a watchman for Israel." In Old Testament times the watchmen would stand as sentries on the wall of a city, looking for any threat to the city from without or from within. If a watchman saw an invading army on the horizon or any danger within the city such as a fire or a riot, his role was to sound the alarm to warn the people. God said to Ezekiel,

> Son of man, I have appointed you as a watchman for Israel. Whenever you receive a message from me, pass it on to the people immediately. If I warn the wicked, saying, "You are under the penalty of death," but you fail to deliver the warning, they will die in their sins. And I will hold you responsible, demanding your blood for theirs. If you warn them and they keep on sinning and refuse to repent, they will die in their sins. But you will have saved your life because you did what you were told to do. If good people turn bad and don't listen to my warning, they will die. If you did not warn them of the consequences,

then they will die in their sins. Their previous good deeds won't help them, and I will hold you responsible, demanding your blood for theirs. But if you warn them and they repent, they will live, and you will have saved your own life, too. (Ezekiel 3:17-21)

Reflection

Ezekiel was given the awesome responsibility to be a watchman for Israel. Do you feel that God's charge to Ezekiel has any application to you? What would it mean to you to be a watchman? Our message is the news of salvation that is available through trusting Jesus, God's Son. Do you feel a responsibility to share that message with those around you?

If the watchman sees the enemy coming and doesn't sound the alarm to warn the people, he is responsible for their deaths. They will die in their sins, but I will hold the watchman accountable. EZEKIEL 33:6

August 9

The measure of a man is how he lives his daily life.

In 1604 Jonathan Burr was born to a Christian family in Suffolk, England. He trusted Jesus as his Savior at a young age and as a boy was known for his knowledge of the Scriptures.

As a young man he became a pastor in Suffolk. He was very knowledgeable, but more important he was known for his humility. He liked to say, "I preach not what I am, but what I ought to be." Generous to a fault and a tireless worker for the Lord, Burr often repeated the phrases "He that soweth sparingly, shall reap sparingly," and "It is better to wear out with work, than be eaten out with rust."

Because Burr did not conform to the Church of England, he eventually was suspended from his church and not allowed to preach. In his growing despair he said, "My preaching is my life. If I be laid aside from that, I shall quickly die." As they prayerfully considered what to do, Burr and his family decided that their best option was to go to New England to obtain religious freedom.

Shortly after his arrival in the colonies, Burr became severely ill with smallpox. The Lord was gracious and spared his life. In the aftermath of his recovery, he made the following covenant with the Lord:

> I, Jonathan Burr, being brought in the arms of Almighty God over the vast ocean, with my family and friends, and graciously provided for in a wilderness; and being sensible of my own unworthiness and self-seeking; yet of infinite mercy, being called to the tremendous work of feeding souls; and being of late with my family, delivered out of a great affliction of the small-pox: and found the fruit of that affliction, God tempering, ordering, and mitigating of evil thereof; so that I have been graciously and speedily delivered; I do promise and vow to Him, who has done all these things for me:
>
> 1. That I will aim only at his glory and the good of souls, and not my own glory.
> 2. That I will walk humbly, with lower thoughts of myself, considering that I am a puff of breath sustained by the power of his grace alone.
> 3. That I will be more watchful over my heart, to keep it in a due

frame of holy obedience, without running so far after the creature: for I have seen that he is my only help in time of need.

4. That I will put more weight in that firm promise, and sure truth, that he is a God hearing prayer.

5. That I will set up God more in my family, more in myself, wife, children, and servants, conversing with them in a more serious manner. For this God aimed at by sending this affliction into my family. I will remember death. In myself I am nothing, in Christ all things.

God blessed Burr's ministry in Dorchester, Massachusetts, and he was greatly admired both for his preaching and for his fervent inner pursuit of holiness.

One Sunday after preaching a sermon on "redeeming the time," he was suddenly taken very ill. As his wife cared for him tenderly over the next week, he slipped closer and closer to death. Finally realizing that only death would offer relief from his pain, his grieving wife asked him whether he wished to leave her and the children. He quickly replied, "Do not mistake me. I am not desirous of that. But, I bless God, that now my will is the Lord's will. If he will have me yet to live with my dear wife and children, I am willing. It is better for you that I abide with you; but it is better for me to be dissolved and to be with Christ. . . . Our parting is but for a time." His last words to his wife were, "Cast thy care upon God; for he careth for thee. Hold fast, hold fast."

Jonathan Burr died on **August 9, 1641,** at the age of thirty-seven.

Reflection

Although written over 350 years ago, the covenant that Jonathan Burr made with God is remarkably relevant to the Christian walk today. What can you learn from it?

∼✑∼

He must become greater and greater, and I must become less and less.
JOHN 3:30

August 10

God can be trusted to work out the details.

CAMERON "CAM" TOWNSEND was born in California in 1896. At the age of twelve he joined the Presbyterian church in which he was raised. Afterward his father, who was deaf, took him out into the barn and questioned him about his faith. Cam wrote out the answers so his father could be satisfied that his son had a personal faith in Jesus Christ as Lord and Savior.

In 1917 Townsend went to Guatemala to sell Spanish Bibles to the Cakchiquel Indians. But Townsend soon realized that the Cakchiquel Indians had no use for Spanish Bibles and were often offended by his efforts to sell them. One day an Indian asked him, "If your God is so smart, why hasn't he learned our language?"

That question burned in his mind until he determined to translate the gospel of Mark into Cakchiquel himself. With that task completed, Townsend proceeded to translate the rest of the New Testament. Upon its completion in 1929, the Cakchiquels exclaimed, "Now God speaks our language." This gave Cam the motivation to translate the Bible into yet another language.

A prominent Mexican educator visited Townsend and was impressed by what he had done for the Indians. After returning to Mexico, he wrote to Townsend saying, "Come to Mexico. Our revolutionary leaders will help you."

But illness interrupted—Cam contraced tuberculosis, and his wife developed a life-threatening heart condition. They returned to California to recuperate.

Once Townsend had recovered, L. L. Legters, a missionary friend, urged him to go to Mexico, where at least fifty Indian tribes had no Bible in their language. Then news came from Mexico that a new Socialist president had confiscated all religious property and ordered all foreign missionaries to leave the country.

Legters traveled to New Jersey to America's Keswick, a Bible conference, where on **August 10, 1933,** there was a day of prayer for Mexico and Townsend's vision for translating the Bible into tribal languages there. When Addison Raws, Keswick's director, announced that the leaders would be fasting for the day, no one went to the dining hall. Legters and his wife prayed all night in the auditorium.

Those at Keswick were so sure that God would answer their prayers that they encouraged Townsend and Legters to go immediately to Mexico and ask permission to do their Bible translation work. They later learned that at the same time, a group at Keswick in England was praying for the Indians of Mexico.

Cam sent his wife to stay with her parents while he and Legters headed for the Mexican border. When they were denied entry, Townsend brought out the letter from the Mexican educator, and they were allowed to enter.

Through an amazing series of contacts Townsend met Mexico's director of rural education in Mexico City, who gave Townsend permission to study Mexico's rural education system for six weeks and was pleased with the analysis Cam wrote.

So sure were Townsend and Legters that Mexico would be open to them that they organized a three-month translation school in a barn in Arkansas for training Bible translators. They called it "Camp Wycliffe," naming it after John Wycliffe, the first translator of the Bible into English. The three students and four faculty members sat in the barn on nail kegs.

The Townsends went to Mexico in 1935 with their students and began to translate the Bible into tribal languages. Wycliffe Bible Translators grew to become the largest independent Protestant mission agency in the world. At the time of Townsend's death in 1982 half of the world's five thousand languages still did not have any portion of Scripture, but half did—because of Cameron Townsend.

Reflection

Do you think it is important for people to be able to read the Bible in their mother tongue? Children from immigrant homes often pray for the rest of their lives in the language of their land of origin. One's first language is the language of the heart.

≈≈≈

We all hear these people speaking in our own languages about the wonderful things God has done! ACTS 2:11

August 11

The hymn "Rock of Ages" was written by someone who knew he would soon die.

AUGUSTUS TOPLADY was born in Farnham in Surrey, England, in 1740, the only child of a major in the English army, who was killed in battle before ever seeing his son. His mother sent him to Westminster School in London, where hymn writers Charles Wesley[8] and William Cowper[9] had attended.

After he and his mother moved to Ireland, sixteen-year-old Augustus went to hear a Methodist layman preach to a small group assembled in a barn. The text was Ephesians 2:13: "Ye who sometimes were far off are made nigh by the blood of Christ" (KJV). That night Augustus himself was "brought nigh" to God by putting his faith in Christ and the blood he shed for him.

Toplady later reminisced about that night: "Strange that I, who had so long sat under the means of grace in England, should be brought nigh to God in an obscure part of Ireland, amidst a handful of God's people met together in a barn, and under the ministry of one who could hardly spell his name! Surely it was God's doing and is marvelous! The excellency of such power must be of God and cannot be of man. The regenerating Spirit breathes not only on whom, but like and when, where, and as he listeth."

Toplady graduated from Trinity College in Dublin in 1760 and two years later was ordained as a minister of the Church of England. He pastored several churches, including the French Calvinist Chapel in London.

Always frail in body, he contracted tuberculosis as a young man. As he fought the ravages of the disease, he wrote "Rock of Ages." It is considered the most popular hymn in the English language.

> *Rock of Ages, cleft for me,*
> *Let me hide myself in Thee;*
> *Let the water and the blood,*
> *From Thy riven side which flowed,*
> *Be of sin the double cure,*
> *Cleanse me from its guilt and power.*
>
> *Not the labors of my hands*
> *Can fulfill Thy law's demands;*
> *Could my zeal no respite know,*
> *Could my tears forever flow,*

All for sin could not atone;
Thou must save, and Thou alone.

Nothing in my hand I bring,
Simply to Thy cross I cling;
Naked, come to Thee for dress;
Helpless, look to Thee for grace;
Foul, I to the fountain fly,
Wash me, Saviour, or I die!

When I draw this fleeting breath,
When my eyes shall close in death,
When I rise to worlds unknown,
And behold Thee on Thy throne,
Rock of Ages, cleft for me,
Let me hide myself in Thee.

Two years later Augustus Toplady drew his last fleeting breath and closed his eyes in death on **August 11, 1778.** In his final hour he said to his friends, "No mortal can live having seen the glories which God has manifested to my soul!" He was just thirty-eight years old.

Reflection

The strength of the hymn "Rock of Ages" lies in its simplicity in setting forth the message that salvation is by grace alone on the merits of Christ's sacrifice on the cross and not by anything that we can do. Even a child can understand the familiar yet powerful words. Let your meditation today be the words of Augustus Toplady's great hymn, "Rock of Ages." Either sing it or read it as your heart's prayer to God.

◦◦◦

You will keep in perfect peace all who trust in you, whose thoughts are fixed on you! Trust in the Lord always, for the Lord God is the eternal Rock.   ISAIAH 26:3-4

August 12

God's dealings with us may be a painful process.

AFTER SERVING in the marines and completing law school, Charles Colson became a senior partner in a prestigious Washington, D.C., law firm. Then in 1969 he received a phone call that changed the course of his life: President Richard Nixon[10] needed him. A *Wall Street Journal* headline summed up his role as special counsel to the president: "Nixon Hatchet Man. Call It What You Will, Chuck Colson Handles President's Dirty Work." Then came the Watergate scandal, and Colson resigned his position to form his own law firm.

In March of 1973 he went to visit Tom Phillips, president of the Raytheon Company and his client before Colson had served in the White House. Warned by the executive vice president that Phillips had changed because of a religious experience, Colson mentioned that he had heard that Phillips had become involved in some religious activities. Phillips replied, "Yes, that's true, Chuck, I have accepted Jesus Christ. I have committed my life to him, and it has been the most marvelous experience of my whole life."

Colson was stunned and turned the conversation back to more comfortable subjects. As Phillips later walked him to the door, he added, "I'd like to tell you the whole story someday, Chuck. I had gotten to the point where I didn't think my life was worth living. Now everything has changed." The reference to an empty life struck a raw nerve with Chuck.

That summer while on vacation with his wife in the Boston area to get away from the Watergate hearings, Chuck found himself calling Tom Phillips, who invited him to his home the evening of **August 12, 1973.** Phillips straightforwardly told Chuck about Jesus and read to him from C. S. Lewis's book *Mere Christianity*.[11] Lewis's description of pride as a cancer that prevents a person from knowing God hit Chuck like a torpedo. Phillips gave Chuck a copy of the book and invited him back.

Back in his car, Chuck began crying uncontrollably and prayed to God over and over through tears, "Take me! Take me!"

Chuck's heart had been pierced, but his mind still needed to be persuaded. He studied *Mere Christianity* until a short time later words that he initially hadn't understood fell easily from his lips: "Lord Jesus, I believe you. I accept you. Please come into my life. I commit it to you."

Colson soon became part of a small prayer group of five, including Democratic senator Harold Hughes of Iowa and Republican congressman Al Quie of Minnesota. Supported by these new brothers in Christ, Colson decided to plead guilty to a Watergate crime of which he had not been charged—passing derogatory information to the press about Daniel Ellsberg, an antiwar activist. He was sentenced to a prison term of one to three years. The former special counsel to the president was put in charge of the washing machine at Maxwell Federal Prison in Alabama. After Chuck had been in prison for nearly seven months, his family began falling apart. His wife was near the breaking point, and his son was in jail for narcotics possession.

At this point Al Quie called and said, "There's an old statute someone told me about. I'm going to ask the president if I can serve the rest of your term for you." That night, overwhelmed, Chuck Colson completely surrendered himself to God. Two days later the judge at his trial released him from prison because of his family problems. As he left prison a Christian federal marshal told him that he had felt God would set him free that day. Colson replied, "Thank you, brother, but he did it two nights ago."

In 1976 Chuck Colson founded Prison Fellowship, which ministers in six hundred prisons in eighty-eight countries with fifty thousand volunteers. Colson was prepared for this role in God's kingdom through a painful process.

Reflection

What do you believe your role is in God's kingdom? Have you experienced painful periods of preparation? Can you see God's hand through it all?

I want you to know, dear brothers and sisters, that everything that has happened to me here has helped to spread the Good News. . . . And because of my imprisonment, many of the Christians here have gained confidence and became more bold in telling others about Christ.

PHILIPPIANS 1:12-14

August 13

God often uses the weak and infirm in mighty ways.

ELIZABETH PAYSON PRENTISS was born in 1818 in Portland, Maine, where her father, Edward Payson,[12] served as a pastor. Edward, a godly man, was frail throughout his life, and Elizabeth inherited his physical weakness. She was frequently an invalid and almost never without pain.

When Elizabeth was twenty-one, she began to realize that in spite of her Christian home she herself was not a believer. Her realization of her sin became more and more intense. Then she heard a sermon on Christ's ability to save "unto the uttermost." Affected deeply, she later wrote, "While listening to it my weary soul rested itself, and I thought, 'Surely it cannot be wrong to think of the Savior, although He is not mine.' With this conclusion I gave myself up to admire, to love and to praise Him, to wonder why I had never done so before, and to hope that all the great congregation around me were joining with me in acknowledging Him to be chief among ten thousand and the One altogether lovely." On her way home from church she could hardly believe the peace she was experiencing, which was so unlike the negative emotions that had long troubled her soul.

In 1845 she married George L. Prentiss, a Presbyterian pastor. Six years later the family moved to New York City with their two children. Soon thereafter their son died,[13] and the following year Elizabeth gave birth to their third child, who also died rather suddenly.

One night as the grief-stricken parents returned from visiting the graves of their children, Elizabeth's emotions reached the breaking point. In despair she cried to her husband, "Our home is broken up, our lives wrecked, our hopes shattered, our dreams dissolved."

Her husband's wise counsel to her was, "But it is in times like these that God loves us all the more, just as we love our own children more when they are sick or troubled in distress."

Elizabeth immediately took her Bible and began reading. Then she searched her hymnal for comfort. She came to "Nearer My God to Thee." As she meditated on the words of the hymn and on the words her husband had shared with her, she began composing a poem in the same metrical pattern as "Nearer My God to Thee."

Elizabeth went on to write many poems, publishing a volume containing 123.

Elizabeth Prentiss died on **August 13, 1878,** in Dorset, Vermont. The pastor of the local Congregational church conducted the funeral on the following day. In his hand he held a small well-worn volume in which Elizabeth had written down special anniversaries and memorable events with a Bible verse for each day of the year. The pastor first read the verse for August 13: "I heard a voice from heaven saying unto me, 'Write, Blessed are the dead which die in the Lord, from henceforth: Yea, saith the Spirit, that they may rest from their labors; and their works do follow them'" (Revelation 14:13).

Then he read the verse for August 14, the day of the funeral: "For God is not unrighteous to forget your work and your labor of love, which ye have showed toward his name, in that ye have ministered to the saints" (Hebrews 6:10, KJV).

The graveside service closed with the singing of Elizabeth's hymn "More Love to Thee," ending with these words:

> Then shall my latest breath
> Whisper Thy praise;
> This be the parting cry
> My heart shall raise;
> This still its prayer shall be:
> More love, O Christ, to Thee,
> More love to Thee!

Reflection

Elizabeth Prentiss discovered that the greater her need, the greater God's love was to her. How do you respond to Christ in love? How can you love him more?

∼✎∽

Those who obey my commandments are the ones who love me. And because they love me, my Father will love them, and I will love them. And I will reveal myself to each one of them.　　　JOHN 14:21

August 14

How does it feel to have God confront you with your sin?

EZEKIEL the prophet[14] had come as a captive to Babylon in 597 B.C. with ten thousand other Jews in the second deportation of the Babylonian captivity.

In those days when the leaders of Israel wanted to hear from God, they would request an audience with a prophet. Thus, on **August 14, 591** B.C., some of the elders of the exiled Jews came to Ezekiel to see whether he had any message from the Lord. They then sat down in front of him to await his reply (Ezekiel 20:1).

But the message they received was not what they wanted to hear. This message came to Ezekiel from the Lord:

> "Son of man, give the leaders of Israel this message from the Sovereign Lord. How dare you come to ask for my help? As surely as I live, I will tell you nothing. This is the word of the Sovereign Lord!" (v. 3).
>
> Then the Lord gave Ezekiel further words to say to these leaders: "Make them realize how loathsome the actions of their ancestors really were. . . . I promised that I would bring [Israel] and her descendants out of Egypt to a land . . . flowing with milk and honey, the best of all lands anywhere. Then I said to them, 'Each of you, get rid of your idols. Do not defile yourselves with the Egyptian gods' (vv. 4-7).
>
> "But they rebelled against me and would not listen. They did not get rid of their idols or forsake the gods of Egypt. . . . So I brought my people out of Egypt and led them into the wilderness. There I gave them my laws. . . .
>
> "But the people of Israel rebelled against me, and they refused to obey my laws. . . . I took a solemn oath against them while they were in the wilderness. I vowed I would scatter them among all the nations because they did not obey my laws" (vv. 8-24).
>
> "Therefore, give the people of Israel this message from the Sovereign Lord. . . . When you give your little children to be burned as sacrifices, you continue to pollute yourselves to this day. Should I listen to you or help you, O people of Israel? As surely as I live, says the Sovereign Lord, I will not give you a message even though you come to me requesting one" (vv. 30-31).
>
> "I will rule you with an iron fist in great anger and with awesome

power. With might and fury I will bring you out from the lands where you are scattered. I will bring you into the wilderness of the nations, and there I will judge you face to face . . . just as I did your ancestors in the wilderness after bringing them out of Egypt, says the Sovereign Lord. . . . I will purge you of all those who rebel and sin against me. I will bring them out of the countries where they are in exile, but they will never enter the land of Israel" (vv. 33-38).

"As for you, O people of Israel . . . if you insist, go right ahead and worship your idols, but then don't turn around and bring gifts to me. Such desecration of my holy name must stop! For on my holy mountain . . . the people of Israel will someday worship me, and I will accept them. . . I will display my holiness in you as all the nations watch. Then when I have brought you home to the land I promised your ancestors, you will know that I am the Lord" (vv. 39-42).

Reflection

In Ezekiel's day God prophesied a future wilderness judgment for Israel. Do you think that wilderness judgment has happened yet? If not, when do you think it will? What lessons can you learn from how God dealt with the sins of Israel?

In the last days, the Temple of the Lord in Jerusalem will become the most important place on earth. . . . Many nations will come, and say, "Come let us go up to the mountain of the Lord, to the Temple of the God of Israel."   ISAIAH 2:2-3

August 15

"No one can come to me, unless the Father who sent me draws him."

GUIDO SCALZI grew up in a hamlet of Mesoraca, Italy. Nearby on a beautiful hill was a monastery of the Franciscan friars, where he went to Mass weekly with his family. One balmy spring day Guido was particularly moved by the beautiful strains of the organ. He thought of how inspiring it would be to spend his life in a monastery in close communion with God and nature. He announced to his mother, "Mama, how wonderful it would be if I could become a priest"—words to thrill the heart of any Italian mother.

Guido attended seminary from 1928 to 1932, and they were four difficult years. The seminary had no heat and no running water. In the winter, ice was broken into pieces and used as soap. He had no friends and no one in whom he could confide. Yet he persevered toward his goal.

In July 1940 Guido was ordained as a priest. He became part of a monastery in Reggio di Calabria. There on **August 15, 1945,** as he was passing by the local Baptist church, he suddenly had an unexplained desire to meet its pastor. As they talked, the pastor encouraged Guido to read the Bible.

Guido returned to the monastery and began to read the Bible in Italian. He was amazed by its contents. Every page brought new surprises. He kept asking himself how it was possible that he had lived so many years without ever knowing all the marvelous things he was learning from its pages.

Not long after this encounter, Guido was transferred to a monastery at Staletti, Italy. One day a local peasant farmer stopped him and said that he had heard of his meeting with the Baptist pastor in Reggio di Calabria and said that his own pastor would like to meet him.

Several nights later he went to the pastor's home. The pastor was himself a simple peasant and did not make a very good first impression on the well-educated Guido. The pastor said to him, "By now you know everything there is to know about the Word of God. What you need now is salvation. Jesus wants to save you. He died on the cross to save your soul." As the pastor told the story of Jesus and Nicodemus from John 3, Guido listened intently and thought to himself, *Born again, if I could only be born again.*

As their discussion ended, the pastor asked if he could pray. He knelt, raised his hands toward heaven, and closed his eyes. Guido kept his eyes open. The pastor prayed that God would purify Guido's heart from sin and wash him in the blood of Jesus, who had died to pay the price to redeem him.

FROM RELIGION TO SALVATION

Guido had never heard anyone pray like this before. The pastor was imploring God with his whole being.

Guido finally closed his eyes, and suddenly all of his sins passed before him. In anguish he wondered how he could free himself from this oppression. Then words from the pastor's prayer flashed through his mind, "The blood of Jesus purifies us from all sin." It was then that Guido abandoned himself to Jesus, crying, "Lord, have mercy on me, a sinner. Save my soul."

Peace flooded into his heart, and for the first time in his life he felt the presence of Christ. It was so real that Guido felt that had he stretched out his hand, he would have touched the hem of Christ's garment. With eyes filled with tears, he embraced the pastor and told him, "Brother, I have decided to serve the Lord for life or death."

Guido Scalzi left the monastery and served the Lord as director of *La Voce Della Speranza* (The Voice of Hope), a radio broadcast carried on stations in the United States and throughout Europe.

Reflection

Like Guido Scalzi, many people are very religious, trusting their church involvement to get them to heaven. Does that describe you? It wasn't until Guido personally trusted in Christ to cleanse him from his sin that he found peace and salvation.

Believe on the Lord Jesus and you will be saved.   ACTS 16:31

August 16

Would your church call a nineteen-year-old pastor?

On a Saturday afternoon in December 1853 a nineteen-year-old lad came to London from Cambridge on the Eastern Counties Railway and then went to the boardinghouse that was expecting him. It was his first trip to London and he stared wide-eyed at the sights around him. No one observing him would have guessed that this young fellow was about to begin a ministry to the influential city of London that would last thirty-eight years, a ministry unparalleled in the history of the church to that time.

His name was Charles Haddon Spurgeon.[15] His father and grandfather were Congregational pastors. His grandfather had been the pastor of the Independent Church in Essex for fifty-four years, and his father pastored a number of independent churches throughout England. The family had descended from Huguenots, who had fled France after the revocation of the Edict of Nantes[16] and had settled in Essex.

When Charles was just ten years old and vacationing at his grandfather's, a pastor friend of his grandfather's heard him read a chapter from the Bible in the Sunday service and was extremely impressed at how well he read. The next day, the pastor told the family that he had a conviction that someday Charles would preach the gospel to thousands. He said, "So sure am I of this, that when my little man preaches in Rowland Hill's Chapel [Surrey Chapel, the largest independent church in London], as he will do one day, I would like him to promise me that he will give out the hymn commencing 'God moves in a mysterious way his wonders to perform.' " The promise was made, and the prophecy was later fulfilled. Spurgeon did preach in Rowland Hill's Surrey Chapel, and the hymn was sung.

After being converted at a Primitive Methodist chapel at the age of sixteen, he began to study the issue of baptism. He became convinced that the New Testament taught that baptism was to be for believers and by immersion. In spite of their belief in infant baptism, his parents encouraged him to follow his own convictions, and so he was baptized. Shortly thereafter Charles joined a Baptist church in Cambridge.

He soon discovered his gift of preaching, and in spite of his young age he was in much demand. After taking a brief pastorate at the age of eighteen near Cambridge, Spurgeon was called the following year to the pastorate of the New Park Street Baptist Chapel in London. It was a small church, but within a few weeks of his arrival he was attracting great crowds. The chapel soon proved to be too small, so the church decided to enlarge the building. During construction the church moved to a large hall, but once again the crowds surpassed what the hall could accommodate. When Spurgeon resumed preaching in the enlarged chapel on New Park Street, it once again proved to be too small.

The decision was finally made to build a tabernacle sufficiently large to accommodate the crowds coming to hear the twenty-five-year-old preacher. On **August 16, 1859**, the cornerstone of the Metropolitan Tabernacle was laid. The church was built to hold sixty-five hundred, and it was Spurgeon's prayer that it open debt-free. Metropolitan Tabernacle opened in May 1861, with no outstanding debt. Spurgeon preached there until shortly before his death in 1892.

The Metropolitan Tabernacle was more than just a preaching station. It was an educational and social center. Spurgeon founded a pastor's college and an orphanage, both of which continue to minister to this day. He also began a literature ministry and provided many services to the nearby slums. Spurgeon's Metropolitan Tabernacle was one of the great churches of all time.

Reflection

What do you value more in a church—the bricks and mortar or the message that is preached there? Spurgeon's Metropolitan Tabernacle had both architectural beauty and powerful preaching. But breathtaking sanctuaries have never changed any lives. It is the gospel of Jesus Christ that is the power of God unto salvation.

When we preach that Christ was crucified, the Jews are offended, and the Gentiles say it's all nonsense. But to those called by God to salvation, both Jews and Gentiles, Christ is the mighty power of God and the wonderful wisdom of God. 1 CORINTHIANS 1:23-24

August 17

God works in mysterious ways.

THE LAND of southern Minnesota belonged to the Sioux Indians, but the pioneers wanted it for themselves. Therefore, in 1851 the government purchased the land for several hundred thousand dollars down, with the rest to be paid to the individual Indians as an annual annuity.

The Sioux barely survived the winter of 1861–1862 because of a poor corn crop the previous summer. When they came to the Indian agency to receive their annual annuities, they were told that the funds hadn't arrived. With no funds, the Indians could not buy the food and goods that had arrived. The delay continued for weeks. Finally on Friday, August 15, one of the traders was heard to say, "So far as I am concerned, if they are hungry, let them eat grass." The Sioux were enraged.

The annuity money arrived in St. Paul the next day, but it didn't get to the first Indian agency until the following Monday. By then it was too late.

On Sunday, **August 17, 1862,** four Indians entered a home in Acton, Minnesota, and shot and killed four white settlers. The four Indians then ran to their chief, Little Crow, and asked him to lead them in a war against the white man. Little Crow agreed, not because he thought they could win, but because of the Sioux hatred of the white man and his Christianity.

Within four weeks the Indians had killed hundreds of whites throughout Minnesota while thousands more fled to the safety of the forts. The governor of Minnesota raised an army to put down the revolt.

About seventeen hundred Sioux warriors were imprisoned, and initially an order was given to hang three hundred of them. However, President Abraham Lincoln reduced this number to thirty-eight. They were hung on the day after Christmas 1862, in Mankato, Minnesota, while the other Sioux prisoners watched. It was the largest mass execution in American history.

Up to this point a few Sioux had become Christians, but the majority hated the white man's religion. The Sunday following the execution, Dr. Thomas Williamson, a Presbyterian missionary to the Sioux, held an outdoor service in the yard of the Mankato prison as the prisoners stood in foot-deep snow. He preached about God's plan for saving men from eternal death. That day a marvelous work of grace began in the prison.

Dr. Williamson spent the winter teaching and preaching to the Sioux prisoners. Soon the prisoners began to sing and pray together every morning and evening. Hundreds who had refused to listen to the gospel before eagerly listened. The work of God's Spirit continued throughout the winter. At the first baptismal service in the spring, three hundred were baptized.

Another group of prisoners were imprisoned in Fort Snelling near Minneapolis, with their wives and children and additional Sioux families camped outside the fort. Dr. Williamson's son John, another Presbyterian missionary, began meeting with interested Sioux in a tepee among the families camped there. Within a few months the group grew to hundreds who met together in the garret of a warehouse to learn more about Jesus. A similar awakening occurred within the Fort Snelling prison itself.

In the spring of 1863 the Mankato prisoners were taken to a prison in Davenport, Iowa. With only a few exceptions all professed to be Christians. Every morning and evening they sang and prayed together.

In 1866 the prisoners at Davenport were released and taken along with the Sioux from Fort Snelling to settle in Niobrara, Nebraska. They had prayed that God would remove their chains, and God had answered. John Williamson accompanied the Sioux to Niobrara, and every morning and evening they continued to meet for prayer and praise, reading the Bible and rejoicing in what God had done for them.

Reflection

The Sioux Uprising was the culmination of the hatred of the white man and his Christianity. But God in his infinite wisdom made the uprising the means of their salvation. The uprising is a picture of how everyone comes to God. By nature we are his enemies—until he brings us to himself.

For since we were restored to friendship with God by the death of his Son while we were still his enemies, we will certainly be delivered from eternal punishment by his life. ROMANS 5:10

August 18

He didn't expect his theological training to include a stint in a mental institution.

JOHN SUNG was born in 1901, the son of a Methodist minister in southeast China. When he was nine, a great revival swept through the city of Hinghwa, and John gave his life to Jesus. He immediately began assisting his father in his ministry. Throughout his teenage years, he gave himself completely to evangelism and study.

In 1919 Sung had a dream that he would one day become a great evangelist. He came to America to escape the political climate of China, which he felt would restrict his academic pursuits. Once in America, he threw himself into studying physics and chemistry at Ohio Wesleyan University and then at Ohio State University, where he earned a Ph.D. in chemistry in just twenty-one months. He started to pursue a degree at Union Theological Seminary in New York City, but he felt his faith in Jesus slipping away as his studies of rationalism, Taoism, and Buddism influenced his thinking.

Then in February of 1927 he attended an evangelistic service at a local Baptist church, where he heard a fifteen-year-old girl read from the Scriptures and speak of the gospel with incredible conviction and passion. It touched him profoundly. He deeply desired the faith and power he saw in the girl, a faith he had once had. Later as he read the story of the death of Christ in Luke 23, he experienced deep repentance as he realized that his sins were indeed forgiven. He could not contain his joy and newfound peace, and he ran throughout the campus shouting for joy and singing the praises of his Savior.

Sung's enthusiasm for his reclaimed faith was not seen as positive by all at the seminary. Because he had previously been an intensely serious student and now was running around jumping for joy and telling everyone of his spiritual experience, the president of the seminary thought that Sung had lost his mind and had him committed to a mental institution. It was only due to the intervention of the Chinese consul and a professor friend at Ohio Wesleyan that he was released from the mental hospital after six months on the condition that he would return to China.

Back in China John Sung's driving passion was to proclaim to everyone the joy of the gospel of Christ Jesus. During the next fifteen years he was a highly effective evangelist, leading many thousands to Christ throughout

CHINA'S GREATEST EVANGELIST

China and Southeast Asia. His two-hour sermons focused on the need for repentance, with the Cross as the remedy. His unique preaching style and his scathing reproaches of lukewarm leaders and missionaries created a stir wherever he went.

Finally Sung's long neglected health began to deteriorate, and in 1940 he was diagnosed with cancer and tuberculosis. Over the next three years he underwent multiple surgeries, still preaching whenever possible. In June of 1944 his condition worsened. No longer strong enough to preach, his days were spent reading the Bible, singing, and praying with family and friends.

On August 16 he told his wife that God had shown him he would die. He fell into a coma but recovered enough to sing verses of three hymns the next day: "Sweet By and By," "Jesus, Keep Me Near the Cross," and "Jesus Is All the World to Me." His last words to his wife were "Don't be afraid! The Lord Jesus is at the door. What is there to fear?"

John Sung died the morning of **August 18, 1944**, at the age of forty-two. As he was carried to his grave, the crowd sang many of his favorite hymns, a fitting tribute to a life characterized by singing praise to Jesus.

Reflection

John Sung was so passionate and joyful about the forgiveness he had found in Jesus Christ that some thought he was crazy. Do you experience joy in serving Jesus? Do you share that joy with others?

I was chosen for this special joy of telling the Gentiles about the endless treasures available to them in Christ. EPHESIANS 3:8

August 19

Samuel Miller lived a life of hope.

H E WAS born in 1769 near Dover, Delaware, where his father was a Presbyterian minister. Miller was a descendant of Pilgrims John Alden and Priscilla Mullens, the hero and heroine of Longfellow's poem "The Courtship of Miles Standish." He went to Philadelphia in 1788 and entered the University of Pennsylvania a year after the Constitutional Congress began its deliberations there. After graduating he studied theology at Dickinson College and then became a prominent Presbyterian minister in New York City. Miller also achieved fame as an author.

In 1812 Miller and several others cofounded Princeton Theological Seminary. The following year he left his congregation in New York and went to Princeton to become the seminary's second professor. He taught church history and church government.

Miller spent the next thirty-six years at Princeton, teaching and preaching with equal passion. He reveled in educating future Presbyterian ministers, watching them grow into theologically knowledgeable and godly pastors. During the early 1840s his health began to deteriorate, but he was able to continue his work. In August 1849 it was clear that he was too weak to carry out his teaching duties. Students continued to visit him for prayer and guidance, but he did not return to his seminary classroom.

On Sunday, **August 19, 1849,** although very weak, Samuel Miller preached at the Dutch Neck Presbyterian Church five miles from Princeton, where for ten years he and Archibald Alexander[17] had served while the church was without a pastor. He spoke on "Hope as the Anchor of the Soul" (Hebrews 6:19), emphasizing the differences between the anchor of a ship and the anchor of the soul. Whereas an anchor on a ship takes hold of things below, the believer's hope takes hold of things above. He told the congregation, "Whether or not this may be the last time that I shall address you, is a matter of small importance. But you may inquire how does this 'hope' appear to an old man standing just upon the verge of the grave?" Then he lifted up his hands and exclaimed in a faltering voice, "Oh! Inexpressibly delightful!" This was Samuel Miller's last sermon. He was eighty years old.

Although homebound and gravely ill, Samuel Miller continued to accept visitors. He was aware of his imminent death and spoke of it welcomingly and hopefully. When his visitors were leaving, he would say that since it would be their last encounter on earth, "it would be well to close it with prayer."

Miller's life was marked by humility and fervent prayer, nowhere better demonstrated than in a last prayer for a former student and beloved friend:

> And now, Lord, seeing that thine aged, imperfect servant is about to be gathered to his fathers . . . let the years of thy young servant be as the years of his dying teacher; let his ministry be more devoted, more holy, more useful; and when he comes to die, may he have fewer regrets to feel in reference of his past ministrations. We are to meet no more on earth; but when thy servant shall follow his aged father to the grave, may we meet in Heaven, there to sit, and shine, and sing, with those who have turned many to righteousness, who have washed their robes and made them white in the blood of the Lamb. Amen.

Samuel Miller's epitaph reads: "He lived esteemed by thousands, and died amidst light and joy from the Lord Jesus Christ, in whom was all his hope."

Reflection

Do you have the kind of hope in Jesus Christ that Samuel Miller experienced, even on the verge of death? Is your hope anchored to things on this earth or on things above?

We who have fled to him for refuge can take new courage, for we can hold on to his promise with confidence. This confidence is like a strong and trustworthy anchor for our souls. It leads us through the curtain of heaven into God's inner sanctuary. Jesus has already gone in there for us. HEBREWS 6:18-20

August 20

Little did he know what lay ahead.

AFTER finishing high school, Haralan Popov left his village in Bulgaria and went to the city of Ruse looking for work. There he lived in a tiny room with Christo, a friend from his village.

One evening Christo invited Haralan to a Baptist church, even though he knew Haralan was a convinced atheist. Haralan was impressed by the beautiful music and the intelligence of the speaker. All he could think about when he returned home that night was the question "Is there a God?" To help Haralan find the answer, Christo introduced him to his friend Petroff. When Petroff explained what Christ meant to him, his face seemed to reflect God's love, and it became obvious to Haralan that God existed.

As he spent more time with Petroff, Haralan came to understand that he wasn't seeking God, God was seeking him. He received Jesus Christ as his Savior, and his life was changed!

To prepare himself for Christian service, Haralan attended Bible institutes in both Germany and England. He fell in love and married a Swedish Christian woman. Returning to Bulgaria, he pastored a church and served as an evangelist. Then in 1944 the Russian army invaded, and by 1947 Bulgaria was under a Communist dictatorship.

At 4:00 A.M. on July 24, 1948, Popov's doorbell rang, and he was snatched from his wife and two children by the police and sent to prison.

At first, Popov was made to stand facing a wall all night without moving while being constantly questioned and berated. Then on August 5 he was put into solitary confinement and subjected to "the wall" twenty-four hours a day. For fourteen days he faced the wall, not allowed to move or eat or drink, and was constantly interrogated and beaten.

When the guards realized he was about to die, they gave him food and water and let him lie down. Popov thought that the worst was over. However, the next day, **August 20, 1948,** the guard pointed a gun to his head and said he had five seconds to admit he was a spy. At this point Popov was gladly anticipating death so he could be with Jesus. When the officer paused after counting to four, Popov, strengthened by the Holy Spirit, shouted, "Don't wait! Shoot me straight in the head!" The guard, who had been bluffing to extract a confession, was shocked by Haralan's bravery. Feeling like a puppet on a string, Popov, cried out to God, "I was faithful to the death, but death didn't come."

TORTURED FOR HIS FAITH

Popov's imprisonment continued, and despite the pain and suffering, he had the joy of leading many prisoners to Christ. He was released thirteen years and two months after his arrest.

After his release he longed to be reunited with his family. They had fled to Sweden during his imprisonment, seeking religious and political freedom. Not sure if he would ever see them again in this life, Popov worked tirelessly organizing underground churches and helping produce Bibles for them.

Finally, Popov and his friends decided that he should attempt to leave Bulgaria and join his family in Sweden, where he could serve as the outside source for Bible smuggling. They knew it would take a miracle for the Communists to grant Popov a passport. With hundreds praying fervently, Popov's attempts to obtain a passport were repeatedly rejected. Then inexplicably he received a letter saying that he was free to go!

On December 31, 1962, Haralan Popov was reunited with his wife and family. It had been fourteen and a half years, and now they were together in a free country! Haralan Popov became a world spokesman for oppressed Christians behind the Iron Curtain.

Reflection

Over and over Haralan Popov was given strength and courage when he prayed for it. Do you ask for strength and courage when you need it? Do you expect it to come? How would your faith hold up under similar circumstances?

❧

Can anything ever separate us from Christ's love? Does it mean he no longer loves us if we have trouble or calamity, or are persecuted, or are hungry or cold or in danger or threatened with death? . . . No, despite all these things, overwhelming victory is ours through Christ, who loved us. ROMANS 8:35-37

August 21

God is our only refuge and our strength. Let us humble ourselves before him.

Reverend J. W. Jones was a chaplain in the Army of Northern Virginia during the Civil War. In his book, *Christ in the Camp,* he related how God worked among the Confederate Army troops.[18] Jones attributed thousands of conversions directly and indirectly to a day of prayer and fasting that Jefferson Davis, president of the Confederacy, called for on **August 21, 1863.**

Robert E. Lee gave the following order in response to President Davis's request:

> The President of the Confederate States has, in the name of the people, appointed the 21st day of August as a day of fasting, humiliation and prayer. A strict observance of the day is enjoined upon the officers and soldiers of this army. All military duties, except such as are absolutely necessary, will be suspended. . . . Soldiers! We have sinned against Almighty God. We have forgotten His signal mercies, and have cultivated a revengeful, haughty, and boastful spirit. We have not remembered that the defenders of a just cause should be pure in His eyes; that "our times are in His hands;" and we have relied too much on our own arms for the achievement of our independence. God is our only refuge and our strength. Let us humble ourselves before Him. Let us confess our many sins, and beseech Him to give us a higher courage, a purer patriotism, and more determined will; that He will convert the hearts of our enemies; that He will hasten the time when war, with its sorrows and sufferings, shall cease, and that He will give us a name and place among the nations of the earth. R. E. Lee, General

The day of fasting was almost universally observed within the army. The troops were deeply affected by the Christian influence of General Lee.[19] A revival of sorts had recently begun, and the soldiers were open and receptive to a day of fasting, preaching, and prayer. The services were well attended that day, and many miraculous events were attributed to the day's observance. The following excerpts are from letters written in the days surrounding **August 21, 1863.**

Rev. Haley wrote, "It has been my pleasure recently to spend a week with

REVIVAL IN THE ARMY

Smith's Brigade, Early's Division. I preached every day while I was with them.
. . . There are religious revivals all over the army. Many are turning to God."

Chaplain Tomkies of the Seventh Florida Regiment wrote, "On last evening fifteen were buried with Christ in Baptism. . . . Each evening scores of soldiers are inquiring, 'What shall we do to be saved?' "

The chaplain of the Tenth Alabama Regiment wrote, "I believe that 100 anxious souls presented themselves for prayer last night after the sermon."

The revival began spreading at home, also. The *Richmond Christian Advocate* reported:

Not for years has such a revival prevailed in the Confederate States. . .
The Pentecostal fire lights the camp, and the hosts of armed men sleep
beneath the wings of angels rejoicing over the many sinners that have
repented. The people at home are beginning to feel the kindling of the
same grace in their hearts. It is inspiring to read the correspondence,
now, between converts in the camp and friends at home, and to hear
parents praise God for tidings from their absent sons who have lately
given their hearts to the Lord. "Father is converted," says a bright-faced
child of twelve years; "Mamma got a letter to-day, and father says that
there is a great revival in his regiment." What glorious news from the
army is this! It is the best evidence that prayer is heard, and that the
Lord is with us. Let us show ourselves grateful for such grace and "walk
worthy of God, who has called us to His kingdom and glory."

Reflection

When God's people pray, he listens and will answer regardless of their politics. Recommit yourself today to pray without ceasing, and he will listen!

∽೦೧∽

When you pray, I will listen.   JEREMIAH 29:12-13

August 22

"Thou wilt show me the path of life."

MARIANNA SLOCUM, born in Philadelphia in 1917, was the daughter of Stephen Slocum, a university professor. Hers was a godly home. She recalls, "I cannot remember ever *not* believing in Christ as my Savior. We were a church-going . . . family. Father asked the blessing at every meal, and each night we had family worship."

During her junior year of college Marianna felt God calling her to be a missionary Bible translator. After completing her education, she began linguistic training in 1940 at the Summer Institute of Linguistics and joined the Wycliffe Bible Translators.[20]

At the Summer Institute of Linguistics, Marianna met Bill Bentley, a Wycliffe translator who had been working among the Tzeltal Indians of Mexico since 1938. He was a college graduate who had initially planned to go to medical school but had gone to Moody Bible Institute instead. At Moody he had heard L. L. Legters describe the need of unreached tribes to have the Bible translated into their native languages. Responding to the need, he had joined Wycliffe and gone to the Tzeltals. Marianna felt herself falling in love with him, but he didn't single her out for any special attention.

Marianna and a coworker were assigned to the Chol tribe and took up residence at a coffee plantation just a day's hike from Bill Bentley's headquarters among the Tzeltals. Since Chol was a Mayan language similar to Tzeltal, Bill made the long day's hike frequently to help the two women with their translating.

On one trip Bill brought a large box of cookies for the girls, and at the bottom of the box was a large heart-shaped cookie for Marianna. The love was mutual!

In February 1941 Bill proposed, and Marianna accepted. They set their wedding date for August 30 and planned to hold the ceremony in the Slocum home in Philadelphia.

That summer Bill and Marianna returned to the U.S. for the final week of busy wedding activities. On **August 22, 1941,** they drove from Philadelphia to America's Keswick near Tom's River, New Jersey, where Bill spoke at the evening service. The next morning they went up to New York City, where they enjoyed a day of sight-seeing hand in hand. That night on the trip back to

A NEW TESTAMENT FOR
THE TZELTALS

Philadelphia, both were exhausted but jubilant in spirit as they talked about their wedding exactly a week away.

The next morning at the Slocum home, Bill was late for breakfast. Marianna's father went up to call him but came back alone. Bill had died during the night of an undetected congenital heart condition. He was just twenty-seven.

Marianna's parents immediately called Cameron Townsend, the head of Wycliffe. In a daze Marianna asked if she could speak to him. Her voice barely audible she asked, "May I return to the Tzeltals in Bill's place?" The answer was a resounding yes!

Bill was buried in Topeka, and Marianna went on alone to the Summer Institute of Linguistics, arriving on August 30, the date she and Bill were to have been married. The verse that sustained her was Psalm 16:11: "Thou wilt show me the path of life: in thy presence is fullness of joy; at thy right hand there are pleasures for evermore" (KJV). She returned to Mexico alone.

Marianna and her coworkers completed the translation of the first Tzeltal New Testament in 1956 and of the second in 1965. A leading Mexican magazine wrote that "she had lifted an entire Indian nation from barbarism to civilization." Marianna could only say, "Thank you, Lord!"

Reflection

How do you respond to tragedy? In spite of her incredible heartache Marianna Slocum was able to continue on by holding on to God. Jesus was her Savior, and the Holy Spirit was her Comforter. They are there for all who believe.

∼✦∼

I will turn their mourning into joy. I will comfort them and exchange their sorrow for rejoicing.   JEREMIAH 31:13

August 23

Every war has casualties.

In 1935 Italy invaded Ethiopia and two years later expelled the missionaries of the Sudan Interior Mission (SIM).

SIM was founded in 1839 when Rowland Bingham of Canada and two other missionaries arrived in Africa to evangelize its unreached inland tribes. All of north central Africa was called the Sudan at the time, and therefore Bingham named his mission Sudan Interior Mission (changed in the 1980s to the Society for International Ministries).

After being forced out of Ethiopia, SIM missionaries moved to southern Anglo-Egyptian Sudan. There they found the people trapped in demonism. Whenever twins were born, they were buried alive because they were believed to have the evil eye. An SIM missionary couple helped protect the first Uduk tribe twins ever allowed to live. They named the infants Borgay meaning "praise" and Thoiya meaning "prayer."

In June 1940 two airplanes flew over the Doro mission station. The five SIM missionaries there did not know whether the planes were lost or on a bombing raid. Mrs. Kenneth Oglesby, one of the missionaries, wrote, "We don't know what is ahead of us, but we do know our God is above us and He will watch over us."

A month later an Italian Air Force plane bombed a Sudanese town near the Ethiopian border. Nick Simponis, an SIM missionary, was hit in the stomach by shrapnel but was able to return to his mission station at Chali. Dr. Robert Grieve, a new SIM physician stationed at Doro, walked thirty-five miles to Chali to treat Simponis's wound.

On the morning of **August 23, 1940,** the Grieves, Oglesbys, and Miss Zillah Walsh watched as planes flew over Doro.

Suddenly bombs began exploding everywhere. "Oh, Bob, I'm dying!" Claire Grieve called out. The doctor didn't answer. Kenneth Oglesby reached him and found him dying.

The planes circled back again. Blanche Oglesby ran and one of the planes tried to follow her. She and Zillah Walsh hid in tall grass as bombs fell around them. Kenneth Oglesby took refuge under a large tree.

Then the planes were gone. Zillah Walsh and some Africans carried Claire Grieve into the clinic while Kenneth Oglesby and others brought in the doctor. He had been hit in eight places and was dead. Claire Grieve was bleeding pro-

THE RESCUE OF PRAISE AND PRAYER

fusely and appeared to have a severed spinal cord. They couldn't stop the bleeding. "Let me go be with Bob," she pleaded. When asked if she had any message to give to her loved ones, she whispered, "Tell them my choice is to see him [Jesus] face-to-face." A little while later she asked that the hymn "Face to Face" be sung at her husband's funeral. Then she too slipped away to see her Savior.

Only Zillah Walsh was uninjured. Kenneth Oglesby was hit in the back, and his wife, Blanche, had thirty-five shrapnel wounds. The Italians had dropped eighty-nine bombs on their mission station.

The Oglesbys both recovered, but the following February Blanche came down with yellow fever. After five days her heart gave out and she joined the Grieves in heaven.

There were no further bombings after that fateful day, and the Sudanese churches grew rapidly. By the time Sudan achieved independence in 1955, SIM had established many schools and dispensaries and an orphanage for unwanted twins. Two of the most promising young adults were "Praise" and "Prayer," the first twins they had rescued.

Today SIM has over eighteen hundred missionaries in twenty-five nations and over a million Africans attend the more than twenty-five hundred churches they have established.

Reflection

Have you ever seen God turn initial tragedy into blessing? Maybe you have experienced the tragedy but have yet to see the blessing. In some cases we won't understand until we get to heaven, but God is working all things for his glory and for his children's best.

God blesses the people who patiently endure testing. Afterward they will receive the crown of life that God has promised to those who love him. JAMES 1:12

August 24

"The time is coming when those who kill you will think they are doing God a service. This is because they have never known the Father or me" (John 16:2-3).

IN PARIS on August 18, 1572, there were hopes for peace between the warring Catholics and Protestants. On this day a royal wedding between the Protestant king Henry of Navarre[21] and the Catholic Margaret of Valois brought together the two hostile factions. Margaret was the sister of young King Charles IX of France and the daughter of Catherine de Medici, the powerful Queen Mother. Protestant and Catholic nobles who had fought each other for ten years turned out for the celebration. Thousands of Protestants came to Paris for the wedding. The festivities lasted for days.

Calvinism had come to France in 1555. Soon there were two thousand French Reformed Churches, and nearly half of the population had embraced the Reformed faith. French Protestants became known as Huguenots.

Fighting broke out in 1562 with the massacre of Vassy, in which twenty-three Huguenots were killed and one hundred wounded. The Huguenots fought back in three successive "wars of religion." Between 1562 and 1572 there were eighteen massacres of Huguenots, five of Roman Catholics, and thirty assassinations.

While Catherine the Queen Mother was planning her daughter's wedding, she had also been plotting the assassination of Admiral Gaspard de Coligny, a popular French war hero who had become a leader of the Huguenots.

On August 22 the assassination attempt failed. This ignominious plot so soon after the royal wedding threatened to embarrass the royal family. Near midnight the following night the twenty-two-year-old French king, brother of the bride, shouted to his mother in a fit of rage, "If you are going to kill Coligny, why don't you kill all the Huguenots in France, so that there will be no one left to hate me."

Following this impetuous directive, Catherine ordered the murder of all the Huguenot leaders currently in Paris, including those who had attended the wedding. The massacre began **August 24, 1572,** which was St. Bartholomew's Day. The gates of the city were closed so that no Huguenot could escape. Admiral Coligny was murdered first as he knelt in prayer.

ST. BARTHOLOMEW'S DAY

Many of the Huguenot nobles who were guests at the royal wedding were lodged at the Louvre. They were called into the courtyard and shot one by one as they appeared. King Charles IX watched approvingly.

During the night the homes of Paris Huguenots had each been marked with white crosses. Before daybreak messengers were sent throughout the city screaming, "Kill! Kill! The king commands it." A murdering frenzy fell on the whole city. Whole Huguenot families were taken into the streets and murdered. Unborn children were cut from their dead mothers' bellies and smashed on the pavement. The dawn of St. Bartholomew's Day revealed thousands of martyred Huguenots.

But the savagery was not without cost to the king. Charles IX soon began having nightmares about the massacre. In less than two years at the age of just twenty-four he was dying. His last days were plagued with visions of his victims. "What bloodshed, what murders!" he cried to his nurse. "What evil counsel have I followed? O my God, forgive me! . . . I am lost!"

Reflection

The St. Bartholomew's Day Massacre was one of the most horrible days that God's people have ever experienced. But Jesus said that the worst is still to come. How can you prepare yourself for even worse persecution if you live to experience that future awful day?

For that will be a time of greater horror than anything the world has ever seen or will ever see again.   MATTHEW 24:21

August 25

It was a meeting he never forgot.

ASAHEL NETTLETON was a young farmer, born in Killingworth, Connecticut, in 1783. His contentment with his life was shaken when he heard a sermon on regeneration that awakened him to his need for repentance. He thought of himself as a good person and was having difficulty feeling guilty for his sin. "I tried to repent, but I could not feel the least sorrow for my innumerable sins. By endeavouring to repent, I saw my heart still remained impenitent." Over a period of ten months he wrestled with God daily, praying, crying, and feeling hopeless as he began wonder if he was not one of the elect because his heart was so hard toward God.

One day while contemplating his despair in a field, he was suddenly filled with a calmness he had never felt before. As he examined himself he realized that his resistance to certain Christian doctrines had suddenly passed away and that he had truly repented for the first time—not because he was afraid of the consequences of sin but because his sins were an affront to his Holy God. He experienced joy for the first time in ten months as he suddenly was sure of his salvation.

After his conversion Nettleton left farming to attend Yale. During his postgraduate studies he developed a strong interest in evangelism. He was ordained in 1811 in the Congregational Church and served for over a decade as an itinerant revivalist throughout New England.

The early 1800s were important years in American church history. Revivals had started on the frontiers in 1801[22] and had spread throughout the nation. Nettleton was an important figure in bringing spiritual revival to New England.[23] Part of his success in convicting sinners was due to the fact he had wrestled so deeply with his own sin and repentance, which gave him uncommon knowledge of the human heart.

During the summer and fall of 1820, Nettleton preached in New Haven and at Yale College at the request of local pastors. A revival was taking place throughout the city, and Nettleton was involved in preaching and visiting with new converts and with those who were still searching. Of the hundreds of meetings he attended, he recalled a particular visit on **August 25, 1820,** at 2:00 P.M. as "one which will never be forgotten."

It was a meeting of twenty women, all of whom were distressed about the lack of purpose in their lives. Sensing their spiritual need, Nettleton spoke to them, appealing to their consciences and urging them to repent. Suddenly one named Emily spontaneously interrupted and said, as though talking to herself, "Oh! I can submit, I can love Christ. How easy it is! Why did I not do it before?" The other women were deeply struck by her words. Emily jumped to her feet and began to entreat her friends to immediately repent and submit themselves to God, telling them that their burdens would be lifted just as hers had been. Nettleton remained silent, praying for the women, knowing that at that moment, Emily was the more powerful preacher.

One by one the women either repented and found salvation or left the room. At the end of three hours nine women had given their lives to Christ—their former lack of purpose replaced by unspeakable joy.

Nettleton later recounted the experience: "Suffice it to say, I never saw or heard of such an afternoon visit before. . . . At the close, we began to look about us to see and inquire, What hath God wrought? . . . I said: Is it possible? This is too much! Had I not seen it, I could not have believed it. For nine of those who entered the room in deep distress were now rejoicing in hope."

Reflection

At the beginning of the meeting the women were experiencing anxiety over their spiritual state. Their misery led them to repentance and then to peace and joy. Have you ever had a similar experience? Are you despairing over your sinfulness? Repentance means turning to God from your sins. If you have never repented of your sins, turn to God and let him bring you his peace and joy.

ᗡ

Now turn from your sins and turn to God, so you can be cleansed of your sins. Then wonderful times of refreshment will come from the presence of the Lord. ACTS 3:19-20

August 26

Baptism didn't do him any good.

KARL MARX was born on May 5, 1818, in Trier, Prussia, descending from a distinguished line of Jewish scholars. His father was an attorney, and when in 1816 a Prussian decree prohibited Jews from prestigious positions in law, Marx's father became a Lutheran. On **August 26, 1824**, Karl and his siblings were baptized.

Karl was confirmed at fifteen and for a while appeared to be a committed Christian. However, as he continued his education, all appearances of Christianity faded away. He received a doctorate in philosophy from Jena University. He worked as an editor in Paris and Brussels before settling in 1849 in London where he remained for the rest of his life. There he became involved in revolutionary politics but spent most of his time studying at the British Museum.

Marx was a poet. As a boy his poetry revolved around two themes: his love for Jenny von Westphalen, the girl next door whom he married in 1841, and the destruction of the world. His poems were filled with savagery, hatred, suicide pacts, and pacts with Satan. In one poem he wrote, "We are the apes of a cold God." One of his favorite phrases was from Faust, "Everything that exists deserves to perish." The theme of a coming apocalyptic conflagration occupied his thinking throughout his life. He wrote of the "Day of Judgment" when "the reflections of burning cities are seen in the heavens." In a speech in 1856 he said, "History is the judge, its executioner the proletariat." This vision of doomsday was an artistic notion in Marx's mind, not a scientific conclusion. It was a conclusion from which he as a political scientist worked backward.

Many of his favorite phrases showed his disdain for religion: "Religion is the opiate of the people"; "Religion is only the illusionary sun around which man revolves, until he begins to revolve around himself." An acquaintance concluded, "Marx does not believe in God, but he believes much in himself and makes everyone serve himself. His heart is not full of love but of bitterness, and he has little sympathy for the human race."

What kind of fruit would attitudes like these produce in a man's life? Marx had a very unhealthy lifestyle. He smoked and drank heavily. He seldom bathed or washed. He was totally incompetent at handling money. He never seriously tried to get a job but instead lived off loans from family and friends that were never repaid. His mother once expressed her wish that Karl would "accumulate capital instead of just writing about it."

Marx was saved financially by substantial inheritances that provided an annual income equal to three times the earnings of a skilled workman at that time. Even with this generous inheritance, all Marx and his wife knew how to do was to spend and borrow. The family's silver service was often at the pawnbrokers, as were their clothes. At one point only Karl had enough clothing left to leave the house, and he was down to his last pair of pants.

His family life was also disastrous. One daughter died of an opium overdose and another in a suicide pact.

In spite of his writings regarding the struggle of the working class, Marx only knew one member of the working class personally. She was called "Lenchen" and was the Marx family's servant from 1845 until her death in 1890. Although Marx collected reports of many low-paid workers, he never found evidence of a worker who was paid no wages at all. Yet one such person lived in his own house. Lenchen never received a cent from Marx for her labors, only room and board. Marx fathered a son, Freddy, by her but convinced his protégé Friedrich Engels to claim paternity in his stead. Freddy was allowed to visit Lenchen only by coming to the back door. Marx met his son once, at the back door, but Freddy never realized that the radical philosopher was his father.

Reflection

Do you think that Karl Marx's baptism and confirmation had any effect on his later life? What do you feel were the primary factors making Marx the man he turned out to be?

∽᙭∾

These people left our churches because they never really belonged with us; otherwise they would have stayed with us.   1 JOHN 2:19

August 27

He was a man of conviction, and it cost him his job.

THE LORD gave me an attentive ear and heart to understand preaching. . . . The Lord showed me my sins and reconciliation by Christ . . . and this word was more sweet to me than anything else in the world." So reads the testimony of Henry Dunster, born in 1609 in Bury, England. After receiving bachelor and master degrees at Cambridge University, he was ordained as a minister in the Church of England. As he served in his church, Dunster became increasingly disheartened by the corruption in the church and by its persecution of Christians who didn't conform to the Church of England. As a result, he fled to America in 1640.

Dunster's scholarly reputation, especially his expertise in Oriental languages and Latin, had preceded him to America. On **August 27, 1640,** shortly after arriving in Boston, Dunster was unanimously elected as the first president of America's first college, Harvard, in Cambridge, Massachusetts. The college had been struggling without a president for four years since its founding, but during the years of Dunster's administration the college flourished. He established the rules of administration and admission, set degree requirements, strengthened the curriculum, erected buildings, attracted students, and taught full-time. He was a tireless fund-raiser for the school, and although he himself was poor, he gave one hundred acres of his own land to the college.

The Baptist movement was making slow progress throughout New England at the time, and those who were leading the movement endured persecution in the Massachusetts Bay Colony. Dunster was troubled by this intolerance and began to investigate their arguments in support of believer's baptism. The more he studied, the more convinced he became of the Baptists' position. By 1653 he was so strongly opposed to infant baptism that he refused to have his fourth child baptized. This caused quite a stir within the Harvard community. Because of the controversy, he offered his resignation, but it was refused.

Dunster was such a beloved and respected figure within the Harvard community that if he had been willing to keep silent regarding his view of baptism, he would have been able to keep his position at Harvard indefinitely. But he was a man of conviction and became so thoroughly convinced of the truth of believer's baptism that he preached a series of sermons against infant baptism. On one occasion he even disrupted a baptismal service in the church at Cambridge. For this latter incident he was indicted by the grand jury, found guilty of disturbing public worship, and was sentenced to receive a public admonition.

Under these circumstances Harvard was too embarrassed to have Dunster remain as president, and so on October 24, 1654, they accepted the resignation they had previously rejected. He had served Harvard as president for fourteen years.

Dunster spent the last five years of his life as pastor of the church at Scituate in the Plymouth Colony. The church's previous pastor, Charles Chauncy, succeeded him as president of Harvard.

Dunster held no animosities from this experience. At his death he bequeathed legacies to several of the people at Harvard who had called for his resignation.

Reflection

Henry Dunster realized it was a great honor to be the first president of the first college in America. Yet when he was removed because of his convictions, he didn't bear a grudge against his opponents. How prone are you to holding grudges? How do you feel about those who have wronged you? Can you graciously forgive them?

∽◎∾

Never seek revenge or bear a grudge against anyone, but love your neighbor as yourself.   LEVITICUS 19:18

August 28

His mother's prayers had far-reaching effects!

Iɴ Coᴡᴇᴛᴀ, Oklahoma, in 1921 a young mother prayed over her yet unborn son, dedicating him to the Lord's service. When the baby was born, his parents named him William Bright. As a child he showed little interest in spiritual things, but his mother continued to pray for him tirelessly.

Bill Bright graduated from college in 1943 and went west to Los Angeles to seek his fortune in business. On his first evening there, he picked up a hitchhiker who invited him to spend the night at the home where he was living. The young man worked for the Navigators, an evangelical ministry, and the home happened to be that of Dawson Trotman, the founder and director of the Navigators![24] Bright was impressed by the hospitality and stimulating conversation of the Trotmans and the other Navigators he met that night, but he quickly forgot them as he went on his way the next morning to pursue his financial goals. Meanwhile his mother was still praying.

The business he started was Bright's California Confections, which marketed gourmet foods in upscale shops and department stores. He was quickly achieving his dream of financial success.

After repeated invitations from his landlords, Bright began attending meetings for college students and young professionals led by Dr. Henrietta Mears at Hollywood Presbyterian Church. He was very impressed by her and other members of the group, finding them intellectually stimulating and successful yet not materialistic and selfish as he was. He began to realize that something was missing in his own life.

After a particularly challenging teaching by Dr. Mears on finding happiness at the "center of God's will," Bill went home yearning for this inner happiness. He later recalled:

> I knelt down beside my bed that night and asked the questions which Dr. Mears had challenged us to pray, "Who art Thou, Lord? What wilt Thou have me to do?"
>
> In a sense this was my prayer for salvation. It wasn't very profound theologically, but God knew my heart and He interpreted what was going on inside of me. Through my study I now believed Jesus Christ was the Son of God, that He died for my sin, and that, as Dr. Mears had shared with us, if I invited Him into my life as Savior and Lord, He would come in.

FULFILLING THE VISION

Bright enrolled at Fuller Theological Seminary in Pasadena. In 1948 he married his wife, Vonette, who had also been led to Christ by Henrietta Mears. Meanwhile he was constantly torn between business, evangelism, and seminary pursuits.

Late one night in 1951 while studying for an exam, he had a powerful vision of helping to fulfill the great commission in his lifetime by evangelizing college campuses. Greatly affected by the vision, he shared it the next morning with Dr. Wilbur Smith, his professor and mentor. Smith responded, "This is of God! This is of God!" The next day Smith told him, "I believe God has given me the name for your vision—Campus Crusade for Christ."

After much prayer Bill and Vonette decided that he should leave seminary to pursue his vision of bringing the gospel to college students and training them to evangelize their peers. Bright sold his confection business and rented a house one block from the campus of UCLA, and within a few months 250 students, including the president of the student body, the editor of the school newspaper, and several top athletes had given their lives to Jesus.

Campus Crusade quickly spread to other campuses, and on **August 28, 1953**, Campus Crusade for Christ was officially incorporated.

Bill Bright's vision and ministry have shaped Campus Crusade into one of the largest interdenominational mission agencies in the world. Its most substantial mark on world missions is the *JESUS* film, which has been viewed by more than 4 billion people in more than 650 languages, with 121 million reported conversions since 1979!

Reflection

The prayer of Bill Bright's mother was answered beyond her wildest imagination. Do you think God could use your life in an amazing way? Have you asked him to?

With God's help we will do mighty things.   PSALM 60:12

August 29

"What a doctor you will make!"

W. A. CRISWELL heard these words hundreds of times from his mother while growing up in rural Texas in the 1910s.

When Criswell was ten years old, the Southern Baptist church the family attended held a Wednesday morning service during its annual revival. Sitting next to his mother, he realized that this would be the day he would accept Jesus Christ as his Lord and Savior. Tears streamed down his cheeks as his mother leaned over and asked him, "W. A., will you give your heart to Jesus today?"

"Yes, Mother," he answered, "I will." And when the evangelist invited those who would put their faith in Jesus to come forward, young Criswell did.

Criswell's mother willingly sacrificed her own life in order to guarantee a good education for her son. Three different times she temporarily left her husband and moved with her son to further his education—first, to be closer to his elementary school, then to be sure that he graduated from an accredited high school, and then to oversee his education at Baylor University.

Criswell felt called to the ministry. Although his mother was a committed Christian, her lifelong dream was that her son would rise out of poverty by becoming a doctor. She kept hoping that he would outgrow his interest in becoming a preacher. At Baylor he spent every spare minute evangelizing, making his mother very concerned about his "preoccupation." When he received four A's and a B+ his first semester, his mother replied sternly, "It isn't easy getting into medical school. Every B+ is a mark against us."

Criswell and his mother returned home to Amarillo for the summer. Although she realized her dream was slowly dying, she still occasionally brought up the subject of his becoming a doctor. "There's plenty of time to choose a premed major, and you could preach on the side. A doctor with a gift for preaching would be quite unique, you know."

Finally Criswell replied firmly, "I love you, Mother, but God has called me to preach, and I have to answer that call."

At the end of that first summer at home from Baylor, Criswell was ordained into the Southern Baptist ministry. On **August 29, 1928,** after being questioned by six Baptist leaders to determine that his conversion was genuine, that he was called to the ministry, and that he was well versed in Baptist doctrine, he was ordained. He eagerly scanned the crowd for his parents but did not see them. Then the pastors and deacons laid hands on Criswell and prayed for him. As the congregation echoed their last amen, he was relieved to catch a quick glimpse of his parents. His mother was smiling through her tears, and his father was looking pleased and proud. Criswell was overjoyed.

The next morning W. A. Criswell boarded the train alone for Baylor. His mother had devoted thirteen years of her life to her son's education, all with the dream of his becoming a doctor. She finally realized that God's call on his life was stronger than her dream, and it was time for her to step aside.

W. A. Criswell graduated from Baylor University and then received a Th.M. and Ph.D. from Southern Baptist Theological Seminary. He pastored for a few years in Oklahoma before accepting a call from First Baptist Church of Dallas in 1944, where he served for almost fifty years. Under Criswell's ministry the church became the largest Southern Baptist congregation in the nation with nearly twenty-six thousand members. He wrote more than fifty books and was considered one of the great preachers of America.

W. A. Criswell died on January 10, 2002, at the age of ninety-two.

Reflection

If you have children, have you ever found yourself imposing your ambitions on them? Have you personally had someone try to point your life in a direction you did not want to go? We all have to be careful about imposing our will on those around us.

That does not mean we want to tell you exactly how to put your faith into practice. We want to work together with you so you will be full of joy as you stand firm in your faith.   2 CORINTHIANS 1:24

August 30

It was the Boxers versus the Christians.

THE YEAR 1900 found China increasingly embroiled in political conflict. Foreign powers were asserting their influence on China, polarizing the Chinese into two warring factions: those in favor of westernization and those opposed to it. A particularly conservative Chinese group called "The Righteous and Harmonious Fists," known as "Boxers," did everything in their power to fight westernization.[25] Their goals were to preserve old pagan religions and to keep foreigners out of China. Organized and active throughout all of the Chinese provinces, the Boxers had a particular stronghold in the Shansi Province, where they were able to get one of their own appointed governor. Their movement was called the Boxer Rebellion.

Because of the Boxers, no missionary was safe in Shansi Province. The China Inland Mission's (CIM) Emily Whitchurch from England and Edith Searell from New Zealand were two of the many single women teams stationed in isolated towns. In their town of Hsiao-i, in south central Shansi Province, they worked with opium addicts. In the midst of the Boxer reign of terror Miss Searell wrote to a friend, "From the human standpoint [all missionaries in Shansi Province] are equally unsafe. From the point of view of those whose lives are hid with Christ in God all are equally safe! His children shall have a place of refuge, and that place is the secret place of the Most High."

Two days after the letter was written a Boxer mob stormed their house and brutally killed the two women. The local Christians risked their lives to rescue their bodies and bury them properly, covering them with flowers from Miss Searell's garden.

Another group of CIM missionaries, Willie and Helen Peat, their two daughters, and two single women missionaries, were hidden by Chinese Christians in caves for three weeks before being discovered by the Boxers. "We are in God's hands," Willie Peat wrote. "I can say, 'I will fear no evil, for thou art with me.' " Edith Dodson, one of the single women, wrote in her last letter, "We know naught can come to us without His permission. So we have no need to be troubled: it is not my nature to fear physical harm, but I trust, if it come, His grace will be all-sufficient."

They were temporarily spared when a magistrate intervened and ordered that they be delivered to a nearby city. But threatened by a mob, they were forced to flee again to the mountains. While hiding in a cave, Willie Peat wrote his final letter to his mother and uncle:

> *The soldiers are just on us, and I have only time to say "Good-bye" to you all. We shall soon be with Christ, which is very far better for us. We can only now be sorry for you who are left behind and our dear native Christians. Good-bye! At longest it is only "til He come." We rejoice that we are made partakers of the sufferings of Christ, that when His glory shall be revealed we may "rejoice also with exceeding joy."*

Helen Peat added: "Our Father is with us and we go to Him, and trust to see you all before His face, to be forever together with Him."

On **August 30, 1900,** Willie and Helen Peat, their two daughters, and the two women with them were martyred.

Throughout China, 188 missionaries and missionary children were killed during the Boxer Rebellion. Of these, 159 were martyred in Shansi Province.

Reflection

The missionaries in China during the summer of 1900 experienced incredible sufferings. Are you willing to share in Christ's sufferings as they did? Can you rejoice like the Peats when you are made to suffer for him? What do you think you would write in a final letter to your family?

And they were not afraid to die.   REVELATION 12:11

August 31

He loved God, his congregation, and his wife.

AFTER THE death of the godly teenage king Edward VI[26] and the nine-day reign of the likewise godly teenager Lady Jane Grey[27] in 1553, Mary Tudor,[28] the Roman Catholic daughter of King Henry VIII,[29] became queen of England. She insisted on restoring Catholicism as the state religion of England and in 1555 gave the courts of the Roman Catholic Church the power to burn heretics. All Protestants were considered heretics, and the burning began—thus earning the queen her name "Bloody Mary." Robert Samuel found himself among the ranks of the heretics.

Robert Samuel was the pastor at Barfolde, England, where he was known during the reign of King Edward VI for his sincere faith, holy life, and dedication to preaching the Word of God. As part of Queen Mary's quest to eliminate Protestantism, Samuel and the other Protestant ministers were removed from their parishes and forbidden to preach. Putting his commitment to serve God above his personal safety, Samuel decided to continue to minister to his congregation secretly.

The English clergy under the Roman Catholic Church had been celibate but under the influence of the Reformation had been allowed to marry. Now, adding insult to injury, the queen ordered all married clergymen to leave their wives and return to celibacy. Samuel was not willing to leave his wife. In his judgment he would be breaking God's law if he left her, and he was not willing to break God's law for man's tradition. As a result, he risked arrest and refused to leave his wife.

One night when he returned home to his wife, the authorities were waiting for him and arrested him. He was immediately taken to prison, never to see his wife again.

While in prison the bishop ordered that he be tortured with the cruelest techniques of the times. Many prisoners succumbed to such torture and either renounced their faith or lost their minds. Samuel was chained upright to a post, so that he had to support his weight with only the tips of his toes. At the same time, he was deprived of food and drink, given only two or three mouthfuls of food and a few sips of water each day, just enough to keep him alive to endure more pain. But Samuel showed great tenacity in enduring the pain, and he remained true to his faith.

On **August 31, 1555,** Samuel was taken from prison to be burned at the stake. He was eager to put an end to his torment and to be with his Savior. Before his execution he told the assembled crowd how, after he had been deprived of food and water for a few days, he had fallen asleep and a man dressed all in white appeared to him and said, "Samuel, take a good heart unto thee; for after this day shalt thou never be hungry or thirsty." He reported that after he awoke, he did not suffer from hunger or thirst during the rest of his imprisonment and torture!

Robert Samuel was burned at the stake and went to meet his Savior.

Reflection

Although many of God's people have suffered and died under similar circumstances without having a divine visitation like Robert Samuel had, his experience demonstrates how God is concerned for the sufferings of his people. If we are ever called upon to suffer in a similar way, let us remain faithful unto death, whether or not we have a visit from heaven.

∾⟐∾

Everyone will hate you because of your allegiance to me. But those who endure to the end will be saved. MATTHEW 10:22

September 1

There can be a cost to following Jesus.

In 1803 in New Hampshire, Ralph and Abiah Hall welcomed their first child into the world. From an early age Sarah Hall showed a keen interest in foreign missions. At the age of thirteen she wrote a poem on the death of Roger Judson, the infant son of Adoniram and Ann Judson, pioneer missionaries to Burma. Little did she know that one day she would take the place of her childhood heroine, Ann Judson.

In 1825 Sarah married Rev. George Boardman, and they left immediately to work with Adoniram and Ann Judson in the jungles of Burma. They went to work among the tribal Karen people.

Their early years in Burma were busy and blessed. In addition to having a fruitful ministry among the Karens, the Boardmans were blessed with three children in rapid succession. Then just as quickly, sorrows descended upon the Boardman home. They first lost their oldest daughter, Sarah, at the age of two and a few months later, their youngest son, at eight months of age.

The great blow came in 1831. Everyday life was increasingly stressful for the Boardmans because of an uprising of Burmese workers against their masters in the city of Tavoy, and George's health began to decline rapidly. Accompanied by Sarah, he went into the jungle to baptize recent Karen converts. Boardman was so weak that he had to be carried on a litter, yet to his great joy he watched as thirty-eight new believers were baptized in a river.

Realizing that he was dying, Boardman spoke to his beloved Karen people: "I am about to die and shall soon be inconceivably happy in heaven. When I am gone, remember what I have taught you; and O, be careful to persevere unto the end, that when you die, we may meet one another in the presence of God, never to part." The next day God called him home.

Sarah's good friend Adoniram Judson, who had lost his own wife, Ann, five years earlier, wrote to her, "As to your beloved, you know that all his tears are wiped away, and that the diadem that encircles his brow outshines the sun. Little Sarah and the others have again found their father, not the frail, sinful mortal that they left on earth, but an immortal saint, a magnificent, majestic king. What more can you desire for him? While, therefore, your tears flow, let a due proportion be tears of joy."

Drawn together by their shared losses and their mutual desire to win the Karen people to Jesus, Adoniram Judson and Sarah Boardman fell in love.[1]

THE AGONY AND THE ECSTASY

Three years after George's death they were married. They had eight children, two of whom died in infancy. After the birth of her last child, Sarah's health began to deteriorate. Determining that only a total change of climate could save her life, Adoniram and Sarah sailed for America with their three oldest children in April of 1845. Their three youngest were left in the loving care of their fellow missionaries in Burma.

While their ship was in port on the English island of St. Helena off the coast of Africa, the end drew near. Early in the morning of **September 1, 1845,** Adoniram asked Sarah, "Do you still love the Savior?"

"Oh yes," she said. "I ever love the Lord Jesus Christ."

Then Adoniram asked, "Do you still love me?" She answered with a kiss, and an hour later she was gone. She was buried the same day on the island of St. Helena.

After reaching America, Adoniram learned that little Charlie, one of his children left behind in Burma, had died twenty-six days before his mother and was there to welcome her into heaven.

Reflection

When we ponder the life of someone like Sarah Boardman Judson, our own problems seem to pale into insignificance. The cost of serving Christ may be great, but God promises to give us grace sufficient for any circumstance in which He places us.

Although he died on the cross in weakness, he now lives by the mighty power of God. We, too, are weak, but we live in him and have God's power.   2 CORINTHIANS 13:4

September 2

What was to become of the temple in Jerusalem?

ONE DAY when Jesus and his disciples were talking about the beautiful stonework of the temple, Jesus surprised them by prophesying of its future destruction.[2] He said, "The time is coming when all these things will be so completely demolished that not one stone will be left on top of another" (Luke 21:6).

"Teacher," they asked, "when will all these things take place? And will there be any sign ahead of time?" (v. 7).

After telling about future wars and persecutions he said, "And when you see Jerusalem surrounded by armies, then you will know that the time of the desolation has arrived" (v. 20). Jesus went on to say, "For there will be great distress in the land and wrath upon this people" (v. 28). Wrath is an expression used throughout the Bible for God's judgment on those who have broken his covenant. The Jews had broken God's covenant by rejecting their Messiah.

Jesus ends his prophesy of the destruction of Jerusalem by saying, "They will be brutally killed by the sword or sent away as captives to all the nations of the world. And Jerusalem will be conquered and trampled down by the Gentiles until the age of the Gentiles comes to an end" (v. 24).

Approximately thirty-three years later the events leading up to fulfillment of Jesus' prophecy began to unfold. In A.D. 66 a Jewish revolt against the Romans was triggered when a Roman official stole money from the temple treasury. Fighting broke out in Jerusalem, and soon a full-scale revolt was under way. Jewish extremists took control of Jerusalem and massacred the Romans there. The Roman legate in Syria learned of the massacre and assembled an army. His attempt to storm Jerusalem was thwarted, so he ordered a retreat that soon turned into a rout.

When news of the Jewish uprising reached Rome, one of Rome's most experienced generals, Vespasian, was dispatched to Judea to deal with the revolt. Accompanied by his son Titus[3] and three Roman legions, Vespasian conquered Galilee in 67. In the early summer of 68 as he marched toward Jerusalem, word came of the death of Nero, the emperor. Vespasian then withdrew to Caesarea to wait for news of who would emerge as emperor.

In July 69 Vespasian himself was proclaimed emperor, and he turned over his army to Titus. By the end of 69 Titus had subdued all of Judea except for Jerusalem and three outposts overlooking the Dead Sea. In the spring of 70

NOT ONE STONE UPON ANOTHER

Titus began his siege of Jerusalem. The Jews from outside the city were so confident of their eventual victory that just prior to the siege, great numbers of pilgrims entered Jerusalem for the Feast of Passover.

The city was full when the siege began in earnest. The Romans broke through the walls of the city and fought the Jews house by house, destroying the city as they went. On **September 2,** A.D. **70,** the conquest was complete. The temple had been burned, and not one of its stones was left standing on another. Historian Josephus reported that over a million Jewish lives were lost in the siege. Ninety-seven thousand were taken away captive. The Jews had paid a fearful price for rejecting their Messiah.

Reflection

The disciples might have been surprised by the harsh things that Jesus told them were going to happen to their temple and their people, the Jews. But God's covenants contain both blessings and curses. The Jews experienced God's curse in A.D. 70 for breaking God's covenant by rejecting their Messiah. Today we are under the New Covenant. Those who commit their lives to Jesus the Messiah receive the blessings of the covenant, forgiveness of sin, and eternal life, and those who do not, receive its curses.

For we know the one who said, "I will take vengeance. I will repay those who deserve it." He also said, "The Lord will judge his own people."　　　　　　　　　　　　　　　HEBREWS 10:30

September 3

Just one thing was missing.

ONE OF the most famous mothers of all time was Susanna Wesley. Among her nineteen children were John and Charles Wesley, the founders of the Methodist Church.[4] Susanna was born in 1669 or 1670, the twenty-fifth and youngest child of Dr. Samuel Annesley, a magazine editor and pastor in London who was a leader of the Dissenters (those who refused to conform to the Anglican Church).

Young Susanna was very bright and educated herself reading the many books in her father's house. She listened to many debates in her home on the differences between the Church of England and dissenting churches like her father's. Always of her own opinion, Susanna became convinced that dissent was wrong, and to her family's great surprise she left her father's church at the age of thirteen and joined the Church of England.

It was also at the age of thirteen that Susanna met her future husband, Samuel Wesley. Like Susanna, Samuel had grown up in a dissenting family but had disagreed with them and joined the Church of England. Samuel married Susanna a few months after he graduated from Oxford. He was twenty-six, and Susanna was nineteen.

Samuel was ordained in the Anglican Church and eventually became pastor in the parish of Epworth. Susanna gave birth to a baby a year, but by early 1702 the Wesleys had but one surviving son and five daughters. Eight children had died.

Both Samuel and Susanna were dogmatic, stubborn, and strong willed, with deeply held political allegiances. Both were Tories, but Samuel was an enthusiastic supporter of King William III while Susanna's sympathies were with James II who was in exile in France. When Samuel interceded for "our sovereign lord, King William" in evening prayers, Susanna apparently silently substituted James for William.

When word came that James II had died in France, Susanna stopped saying amen at the end of the prayer. When Samuel learned the reason why, he told her, "You and I must part: for if we have two kings, we must have two beds." He moved into another room of the house and finally went to London, saying he would never return.

That could have been the end of their family except for another change in royalty. King William died in March and was succeeded by Queen Anne, who had the loyalty of both Wesleys. Samuel then returned from London, but they continued to sleep in separate rooms. It took a fire in July 1702 that burned three quarters of their home to bring Samuel back to his senses and to his wife. They began sharing the same bed in August, and on June 17, 1703, John Wesley, their fifteenth child, was born. He owed his very existence to a fire and to the crowning of Queen Anne. Charles Wesley was born four years later, the eighteenth child.

Susanna Wesley's sons, John and Charles, both personally trusted Christ in 1738 and went on to found what became the Methodist Church. Susanna, however, was critical of their conversions.

Then on **September 3, 1739,** John Wesley had a conversation with his mother that both surprised and thrilled him. She told him that until recently she had never understood that a person could experience the forgiveness of sins in this life or that God's Spirit could witness with our spirit that we are children of God. Then she said, "Two or three weeks ago, while my son Hall was pronouncing those words in delivering the cup to me, 'The blood of our Lord Jesus Christ, which was given for thee,' the words struck through my heart, and I knew God for Christ's sake, had forgiven me all my sins."

Three years later Susanna Wesley died, sharing the same assurance of sins forgiven as her sons.

Reflection

All of Susanna Wesley's family and friends assumed that she was a Christian, but in fact, until near the end of her life, she had been very religious but had never experienced the personal forgiveness of sins. Have you personally committed your life to Jesus Christ, or are you just being religious, as Susanna was for so many years?

∽◈∾

His Holy Spirit speaks to us deep in our hearts and tells us that we are God's children. ROMANS 8:16

September 4

He discovered what he was looking for.

THE MOST widely circulated book about Hudson Taylor, pioneer missionary to inland China, is *Hudson Taylor's Spiritual Secret.*

Hudson Taylor was born in Yorkshire, England, in 1832, the son of a pharmacist and lay Methodist preacher.[5] Experiencing a dramatic conversion to Jesus Christ at the age of seventeen, Hudson soon became interested in becoming a missionary to the then almost closed country of China. He first went to China in 1854 with the China Evangelization Society, a short-lived mission group. While there he married another missionary, Maria Dyer, although many fellow missionaries discouraged her from marrying him.

Forced to return to England because of his health, he could find no mission society to back him when China was opened to Westerners. As a result, in 1865 he founded the interdenominational China Inland Mission, now the Overseas Missionary Fellowship. The following year he sailed for China with his first brigade of missionaries.

Supervising multiple mission stations throughout the expanse of China became a daunting and often frustrating task. In 1869 Taylor sank into deep depression, even contemplating suicide. His inner conflict increased as the summer months passed. He prayed, made resolutions, fasted, read his Bible—to no apparent avail. He prayed for faith, for holiness, for peace, but only felt more conflicted.

In August Hudson Taylor visited the mission station in Hangchow, where a volatile Irishman, John McCarthy, was in charge. Taylor shared his personal spiritual frustrations, and McCarthy told of his own continual feelings of failure and unrest. He, too, desperately desired the satisfaction of an ongoing fellowship with God.

Taylor left Hangchow and visited other mission stations on his way back to his own mission compound, all the while wrestling with his own spiritual despair. He arrived home in Chinkiang on **September 4, 1869.** After being greeted by his wife and children, he immediately hurried to his room to get caught up with his correspondence.

One of the letters he opened and read was from John McCarthy and had been written a day or two after Taylor's visit. McCarthy wrote, "I seem as if the first glimmers of the dawn of a glorious day has risen upon me. . . . I seem to have supped only that which can fully satisfy."

A SPIRITUAL SECRET

As he read on, Hudson Taylor became convinced that McCarthy had discovered the secret for which they had been searching. "To let my loving Saviour work in me His will . . . abiding, not striving or struggling; looking off unto Him; trusting Him for present power . . . resting in the love of an almighty Saviour in the joy of a complete salvation." Taylor read the final paragraph: "Not striving to have faith, or to increase my faith but a looking at the faithful one seems all we need. A resting in the Loved One entirely, for time, for eternity. It does not appear to me as anything new, only formerly misunderstood."

Hudson Taylor's long spiritual struggle was resolved in an instant! He later wrote, "As I read, I saw it all. I looked to Jesus, and when I saw—oh how joy flowed."

A colleague reported:

> He was a joyous man now, a bright, happy Christian. He had been a toiling, burdened one before, with latterly not much rest of soul. It was resting in Jesus now, and letting him do the work—which makes all the difference. Whenever he spoke at meetings after that, a new power seemed to flow from him, and in the practiced things of life, a new peace possessed him. Troubles did not worry him as before. He cast everything on God in a new way and gave more time to prayer.

Hudson Taylor had found his spiritual secret. It was the exchanged life—no longer I but Christ living in me.

Reflection

All of us can identify with Hudson Taylor's frustration at trying to live the Christian life by our own efforts. What is most helpful to you in the "secret" that Taylor discovered? What can you do to apply this truth to your life?

I have been crucified with Christ. I myself no longer live, but Christ lives in me. So I live my life in this earthly body by trusting in the Son of God, who loved me and gave himself for me. GALATIANS 2:19-20

September 5

What should the Christian's strategy be in dealing with pagans?

THE FIRST major step in the Christianization of the Roman Empire came in 312 when Constantine the Great,[6] just prior to the determinative battle for control of the western Roman Empire, saw in a dream a cross in the sky and the words "In this sign conquer." The next day Constantine was victorious over his rival Maxentius at the Battle of Milvian Bridge and credited his victory to the power of Christ.

Constantine immediately began favoring Christianity openly and the following year issued the Edict of Milan, which granted Christians freedom of religion. Yet Constantine had a major problem in promoting Christianity. Virtually the entire imperial bureaucracy was pagan as well as a majority of the population. Roman religion at that time was polytheistic, and gods of other nations were added to the Roman pantheon.

At this time Christians were a majority only in the Roman provinces of Asia, Bithynia and Pontus (present-day western Turkey), a portion of Armenia, and part of the seacoast of North Africa, which is now Tunisia. Vast areas, such as western Europe and the Balkans, were home to few, if any, Christians.

To deal with this situation, Constantine made a wise decision. He refused to attempt to destroy the pagans, as earlier caesars had tried to eradicate Christianity. Instead, he took a positive approach, promoting the precepts of Christianity in a way that made them socially preferable. He created an atmosphere where over time the zeal of the Christian population would win the day.

His successors continued his policies until 355, when Emperor Julian the Apostate attempted to restore paganism.[7] After his death in 363 he was succeeded by another Christian.

The Christian emperors of the second half of the fourth century became more ruthless in their treatment of paganism, the traditional Roman religion. Emperor Gratian ceased using the traditional title Pontifex Maximus (senior priest of the Roman religion) and cut off all subsidies to Roman cults.

The final victory over paganism was led by Theodosius I, the emperor of the eastern Roman Empire, from his capital in Constantinople, now Istanbul. He is called Theodosius the Great because of his enthusiastic, though often cruel, brand of Christianity. Beginning in 379 at the prompting of Ambrose, the bishop of Milan, Theodosius passed harsh laws making it treason to offer any kind of a sacrifice, removing all idols, and fining anyone who visited a pagan temple.

But paganism wasn't about to quietly fade away. In 392 in Rome, Eugenius, a supposed Christian, was made emperor of the western Roman Empire. When Theodosius refused to recognize him as emperor of the west, Eugenius defiantly restored traditional Roman religion to Rome. Then he rode off with his general to do battle against Theodosius and Christianity in the name of the Roman gods.

Eugenius and his general decided to try to ambush Theodosius at a pass near the Frigidus River on the southern end of the Alps. On **September 5, 394,** Theodosius and his troops reached the pass and found Eugenius and his troops prepared for battle with their pagan banners displaying Hercules waving in the wind.

Theodosius ordered an immediate head-on assault, and a fierce battle ensued. By the end of the day Theodosius had lost ten thousand men, and Eugenius, thinking he was victorious, ordered victory celebrations. Theodosius, however, refused to retreat, and the following day the battle reconvened with a terrible toll on both sides. The battle was again a standoff until a reported great gust of wind blasted down from the Alps through the pass, blinding Eugenius's soldiers. With that the battle was won by the Christian army of Theodosius. The Battle of Frigidus was the final victory of Christianity over the old Roman gods.

Reflection

Obviously we don't want to adopt Theodosius's methodology of head-on assault toward the pagans that we know. Yet we should have a strategy for bringing them into the kingdom. Ask God to show you how to reach each one of your friends who are in the same spiritual category as the pagans of Theodosius's day.

It is not by force nor by strength, but by my Spirit, says the Lord Almighty.   ZECHARIAH 4:6

September 6

Who was the first to baptize believers in modern times?

HIS REAL name was Jorg Cajakog, but we know him as Georg Blaurock. *Blaurock* means "blue coat" after the coat he always wore. Born about 1491, Blaurock was a Catholic priest from Chur, Switzerland, who came to saving faith in Jesus Christ through the preaching of Ulrich Zwingli[8] in Zurich sometime before 1523. Devoting himself to personal Bible study, Blaurock became convinced that baptism was for believers in Christ, not infants, thus disagreeing with Zwingli's position. In Zurich he met a group who, led by Conrad Grebel and Felix Manz, shared his views. They were given the nickname "Anabaptists," meaning "rebaptizers."

In early January 1525 the Zurich City Council, following the lead of Zwingli, the pastor of the Great Minster, the largest church in the city, warned all parents in Zurich that they must have their children baptized within eight days of their birth or face banishment from Zurich.

On January 21, 1525, the leaders of the Anabaptist movement in Zurich met at the home of Felix Manz to determine what to do. They began the meeting with earnest prayer, which was followed by a significant event in church history. Georg Blaurock asked Conrad Grebel to baptize him upon his confession of Jesus Christ as Lord and Savior. Grebel baptized him immediately, the first time in centuries an adult believer had been baptized solely on his confession of faith. Blaurock then baptized everyone else who was present. The Anabaptist movement had begun.

Just two weeks later Blaurock was arrested along with Manz and twenty-four others who refused to have their infants baptized. However, after a week, Blaurock was released.

In the midst of all this persecution Blaurock founded an Anabaptist church in nearby Zollikon, where he won over 150 converts through his powerful preaching.

That November Blaurock, Grebel, and Manz were arrested again and sentenced to an indefinite prison term on bread and water. As part of their sentence they were allowed no visitors. Finally, on January 5, 1527, Manz was drowned for his Anabaptist views, and Blaurock was stripped to the waist and paraded through the cold winter streets of Zurich with his hands bound as he was beaten until blood flowed from his wounds. He was taken to the city gate, and there the city officers offered to release him if he would take a vow never to return to Zurich. He refused, answering that oath taking was forbidden by God. As a result, he was taken back to prison. Finally he agreed to take the oath and was exiled from Zurich.

In the next two years Blaurock had an extremely fruitful ministry as an itinerant evangelist, winning thousands of people to Christ throughout central Europe. In particular, he established many congregations in the Tyrol region of what is today Austria and Italy.

He then became pastor of a small Tyrolean church whose pastor had been burned at the stake just three months earlier. This time the persecution was not from the followers of Zwingli but from the Roman Catholic Church. The persecution continued, and on **September 6, 1529**, Georg Blaurock himself was arrested for heresy and burned at the stake.

Thus ended the short but fruitful life of the first Baptist of modern times.

Reflection

We all hope that we will not be called upon to suffer like Georg Blaurock, but if we are, we should not be surprised. The Bible characterizes the Christian life as a life of suffering. Many Christians, Americans in particular, have had a suffering free Christian experience quite unlike that of believers in other countries and other times. So don't be surprised when suffering comes.

∽◉◞

This suffering is all part of what God has called you to. Christ, who suffered for you, is your example. Follow in his steps.   1 PETER 2:21

September 7

The most hurtful persecution is that which comes from God's people.

THE PURITANS of New England were great men and women of God, but they had blind spots when it came to accepting fellow Christians whose doctrine differed from theirs: In 1651 three Baptists, Obadiah Holmes, John Clarke, and John Crandall, walked eighty miles to visit an elderly friend, William Witter. At Witter's home the four men had a worship service together. In the midst of it, a marshal and his deputies broke in, arrested the three visitors, and escorted them to the Boston jail. They were charged with holding a private church service and rebaptizing persons who had already been baptized as infants.

After ten days the three were brought to trial. The prosecutor was none other than John Cotton, the leading Puritan minister in Boston. The accused sat in the prisoner's box and heard Cotton in his misguided zeal declare them to be soul murderers since they denied the saving power of infant baptism. Cotton then declared that this offense demanded the death penalty, as would any other murder.

The judge, Governor John Endecott, agreed that the three should be put to death. However, he also challenged the three defendants to debate their Baptistic views with Puritan ministers. They were then returned to jail. John Clarke immediately wrote Governor Endecott and offered to debate any Puritan minister. For a while it appeared that John Cotton might debate him, but in the end he declined.

Finally, although Governor Endecott felt that the three deserved to die, he agreed to let them off with a fine. However, he declared that if they did not pay the fine and leave Massachusetts immediately, they would be whipped. Friends of the three raised the money to pay their fines. John Crandall was released from jail without a fine, but Clarke and Holmes refused to let others pay their fines because they thought that would be an admission of guilt. As Clarke was being led to the whipping post, a friend handed money to an official to pay the fines. Clarke was thus released, but Holmes continued to refuse to let anyone pay his fine. Holmes was then stripped to the waist and given thirty lashes.

Immediately after the whipping, two Baptists, John Hazel and John Spur, shook Holmes's hand in a gesture of comfort. For their small kindness, Hazel and Spur were arrested. John Spur was sentenced to pay a fine of forty shillings or receive a whipping. Although he refused a friend's offer to pay the fine, the court accepted it anyway and freed Spur.

INJUSTICE FROM WITHIN

John Hazel's trial was held the next day. Hazel, a frail elderly man, was asked whether he agreed with the actions of Obadiah Holmes in holding a private church service. Hazel answered that he would not be questioned about the actions of another and demanded to know what law he had broken. Not knowing how to respond, Governor Endecott, returned him to jail for the night.

The next day, **September 7, 1651,** when John Hazel returned to court, Governor Endecott announced his sentence: a forty-shilling fine or a whipping. Again Hazel demanded to know what law he had broken. He was told that his crime was comforting a criminal. Hazel responded that he had comforted Holmes only after the whipping had satisfied the law and at that point Holmes was no longer a criminal. Nevertheless Hazel was told that he must return to jail until he either paid the fine or was whipped, although the number of stripes was reduced to ten because of his age.

Hazel continued to refuse to pay the fine, and day after day he was threatened with a whipping "tomorrow." Finally, because he refused to pay the fine and because the court did not want the embarrassment of whipping a frail old man, he was released, but died a few days later.

Reflection

Have you ever encountered gross injustice at the hand of other Christians? Have you been able to forgive them? Somehow it seems even more painful when it comes from fellow believers. Think how Jesus must have felt when he came unto his own but his own received him not.

Jesus said, *"Father, forgive these people, because they don't know what they are doing."*   LUKE 23:34

September 8

Does being born into a Christian family make one a Christian?

JOHN RYLAND JR. was born in 1753 to an English family with a noteworthy Christian heritage. He was from a long line of Dissenters, evangelicals who refused to conform to the Church of England. His great-grandfather, also named John Ryland, had been a member of a Baptist church in Oxfordshire, and all of his children had been believers, including John's grandfather, Joseph.

After Joseph's first wife died childless, he married Freelove Collett, a member of a Baptist church in Gloucestershire. Their oldest child, John, was John Ryland Jr.'s father.

John Ryland, Sr. was converted to Christ in a revival that swept through the Baptist community of Bourton-on-the-Water, England, when he was eighteen. Along with John Sr., forty others personally trusted Christ for their salvation and joined the Baptist church there.

John Sr. studied for the ministry and became pastor of the Baptist Church of Northhampton, England, where he had twenty years of fruitful ministry. His friends included George Whitefield,[9] the great evangelist; Augustus Toplady,[10] the author of "Rock of Ages"; and John Newton,[11] the author of "Amazing Grace."

John Ryland Jr., his son, grew up in a home of spiritual privilege since from his earliest years he was able to observe some of the world's most well-known Christians in his home. One of John Jr.'s earliest memories was of visiting an Anglican rector friend of his father's at the age of five and reading him the Twenty-third Psalm—in Hebrew!

At the age of thirteen John Jr. began to think seriously about spiritual things. In addition to pastoring the church, his father also ran a boys boarding school. One autumn evening young Ryland was talking to one of his friends from the school, a boy who had recently found salvation in Christ. The friend had begun meeting regularly with two other boys in the evenings for prayer and fellowship. During his conversation with John Jr. he suddenly realized that it was time to meet his two friends for prayer and quickly excused himself. Ryland was deeply hurt by this, thinking his friend was rejecting him.

The next day Ryland avoided him and later gave as his reason the friend's sudden departure the night before. The boy then explained why he had felt compelled to leave so quickly. He said that he and his prayer partners were "talking of something better." That phrase, "something better," stuck in

THE NECESSITY OF PERSONAL FAITH

Ryland's mind. From his evangelical upbringing he knew that phrase meant "Jesus Christ and the salvation of their souls." The more that Ryland thought about it, the more he wondered, would his friends go to heaven and he be left behind?

This encounter triggered a period of spiritual turmoil for young Ryland. One day he would feel that he had the joy of salvation; the next day he would have terrible doubts. It was during this period of personal struggle that George Whitefield, the great Anglican evangelist, came on a Saturday to visit Ryland Sr. Whitefield preached the next day, **September 8, 1767,** at the Castle Hill Church in Northhampton, and young Ryland went to hear him. At that service he personally gave his allegience to the Lord Jesus Christ.

Five days later Ryland was baptized by his father in the River Nene just down from where the Castle Hill Church stood.

In spite of his godly lineage, John Ryland Jr. needed to trust Christ personally himself. He became a Baptist pastor like his father, and in 1783 at the same place in the River Nene where he himself had been baptized he baptized William Carey,[12] the father of modern missions.

Reflection

Do you know people who assume that they are Christians because they have grown up in a Christian family? How about you? Have you ever made that assumption about yourself? Being born in a Christian family no more makes a person a Christian than being born in a garage makes one an automobile. Becoming a Christian is a personal decision. We all must make our own commitment to Jesus Christ as our Lord and Savior.

God so loved the world that he gave his only Son, so that everyone who believes in him will not perish but have eternal life.   JOHN 3:16

September 9

Prayer can change history.

NO ONE would have expected Rees Howells to make a worldwide impact. Born in a village in Wales in 1879, he went to school until he was twelve and for the next ten years worked in the local tin mill. After several of his friends went to America, Howells determined he would go, too. A cousin of his had settled in Pennsylvania, so Rees decided to join him, finding a job in a tin mill.

While in Pennsylvania, Rees went one night to a little Methodist chapel to hear a Hebrew Christian, Maurice Reuben, tell the story of his conversion. Later he recounted that as he listened, he "saw the cross. It seemed as if I had spent ages at the Savior's feet, and I wept and wept. I felt as if He had died just for me. . . . Then He spoke to me and said, 'Behold, I stand at the door and knock. May I come in to you as I came in to Reuben . . . ? Will you accept me?' 'Yes,' I replied and He came in and that moment I changed. I was born into another world."

In 1904 Howells returned to Wales a changed man and found work in the local coal mine. It was a time of change for Wales as well. Beginning in 1904 the fires of revival began springing up throughout Wales, and Howells spent his spare time enthusiastically participating in the revival. He married, and then to his surprise God called him, a coal miner, as a missionary to South Africa. There God used him to spread the Welsh Revival.

In 1920 God brought the Howells back to Wales and called Rees to start a Bible college, relying on prayer and faith alone. In 1924 as a result of miracle after miracle of God's provision, Rees Howells opened the Bible College of Wales. Not only was prayer central to the running of the school, but Howells felt it imperative to make it central in the students' lives as well.

When World War II began in Europe, Howells called collegewide prayer meetings, and time after time God answered the students' prayers for the war.

On **September 9, 1943,** the students met for an early evening prayer meeting and then again for a second one at 9:45 P.M. At the latter meeting Howells announced, "The Lord has burdened me between the meetings with the invasion of Salerno. I believe our men are in great difficulties, and the Lord has told me that unless we can pray through, they are in danger of losing their hold."

Soon everyone was on their knees imploring God to intervene. Suddenly at 11 P.M. they broke into spontaneous singing and rejoicing, believing that God had wrought a miraculous intervention at Salerno, Italy.

THE POWER OF PRAYER

Then they all listened expectantly to the midnight news. The radio announcer said that unless some miracle happened, the Allies would be pushed back into the sea—exactly the warning Rees Howells had heard from the Lord.

The next day the newspaper headline read, "The Miracle of Salerno." It reported that the pounding by the Nazi artillery on the first day was so heavy that it was obvious that unless a miracle occurred the beachhead could not be established. Then suddenly, for no accountable reason, the enemy artillery ceased firing—at eleven o'clock. The Salerno beachhead was established.

Reflection

God as the author of history ordains the means as well as the ends. At Salerno, God's end purpose was the victory of the Allies. One of the means that he used was the prayers of Rees Howells and his students. Have you ever hesitated to pray for something because you thought you were asking for too much? God can answer a prayer request for a military victory as easily as he can one for a parking space.

∼✑∽

The reason you don't have what you want is that you don't ask God for it.
JAMES 4:2

September 10

Do you know what the Feast of Tabernacles is all about?

In A.D. **32** the Feast of Tabernacles would begin on **September 10.** Jesus, like every faithful Jewish man, would make the journey to Jerusalem to attend.[13] The Feast of Tabernacles was the most popular of the three annual feasts requiring attendance in Jerusalem of every Jewish male.

The purpose of the Feast of Tabernacles was to remind the Jewish people of God's blessings on them during their forty years of wandering in the wilderness during which God had been present in their midst in the tabernacle. There in the wilderness he had provided them water from a rock when they were thirsty (Exodus 17:1-7) and manna from heaven when they were hungry (Exodus 16:4).

As an annual reminder of God's provision in the wilderness, every Jewish family was to build a small booth out of tree boughs and palm branches and live in it during the seven days of the feast (Leviticus 23:39-43).

Jesus' anticipated trip to Jerusalem was filled with absurdities. For the past months Jesus had been spending his time in Galilee because the Jews of Jerusalem and Judea were seeking to kill him (John 7:1). Now that the time had come for the Feast of Tabernacles (v. 2), Jesus was expected to go to Jerusalem, but he had to be careful how he went lest he be murdered before God's appointed time for his death on the cross.

The instruction for observance of the Feast of Tabernacles was that "every man in Israel must appear before the Sovereign Lord" (Exodus 23:17), yet here the Sovereign Lord, Jesus, was personally present but many in Israel were trying to kill him. Indeed, just a few months later they would crucify their Sovereign Lord.

In the first chapter of his Gospel, the apostle John used a verb related to the Greek word for tabernacle to introduce Jesus: "The Word became flesh and [literally] 'tabernacled' among us." In other words, just as God had been present in the midst of his people in the Old Testament tabernacle in the wilderness and later in the temple, God was now present in Jesus. The Jews were seeking to kill Jesus at the feast of which he was the fulfillment—he was the "tabernacle of God with men."

A daily highlight of each of the feast's seven days was the water-drawing ceremony. At daybreak priests went from the temple to the pool of Siloam. There they filled a golden pitcher with water and carried it back to the temple.

AN UNRECOGNIZED FULFILLMENT

As they approached the south side of the temple, trumpets sounded three times. The priests bearing the pitcher then proceeded around the altar while the temple choir sang the Hallel (Psalms 113–18). When the choir reached the opening words of Psalm 118, every male shouted with them three times, "Give thanks to the Lord." Then as the chosen priest mounted the altar, he poured the wine and water offerings into the two silver bowls. As he poured, the choir sang the words of Psalm 118: "The stone rejected by the builders has now become the cornerstone" (v. 22). On the seventh day of the feast, the priests circled the altar not once but seven times.

Of this particular Feast of Tabernacles John records, "On the last day, the climax of the festival, Jesus stood and shouted to the crowds, 'If you are thirsty, come to me! If you believe in me, come and drink! For the Scriptures declare that rivers of living water will flow out from within'" (John 7:37-38). Jesus used "living water" to refer to the Holy Spirit who would be "poured out" on believers after he had ascended into glory (John 7:39; Acts 2:17-18). Jesus, "the stone rejected by the builders," was the fulfillment of the Feast of Tabernacles.

Reflection

Have you come to Jesus and drunk the living water of his Spirit? The Spirit indwells all those who believe in Jesus, and the water that he offers satisfies their deepest longings.

For I will give you abundant water to quench your thirst and to moisten your parched fields. And I will pour out my Spirit and my blessings on your children.   ISAIAH 44:3

September 11

Setting dates for the return of Jesus Christ can be embarrassing.

In 1988 Edgar Whisenant, a retired NASA engineer living in Little Rock, Arkansas, suddenly became a best-selling author. He wrote two books that were bound together: *The Rapture Rosh Hash Ana 1988 and 88 Reasons Why* and *On Borrowed Time: The Bible Dates of the 70th Week of Daniel, Armageddon and the Millennium.* In these books Whisenant made the startling prediction that Jesus Christ would return to take Christians to heaven between sunset on **September 11, 1988,** and sunset on September 13, 1988.

This event, popularly referred to as the rapture of the church, is described in 1 Thessalonians 4:16-17: "For the Lord himself will come down from heaven with a commanding shout, with the call of the archangel, and with the trumpet call of God. First, all the Christians who have died will rise from their graves. Then, together with them, we who are still alive and remain on the earth will be caught up in the clouds to meet the Lord in the air and remain with him forever."

By the time **September 11** arrived, more than 4.5 million copies of his *88 Reasons* book had been sold, and another 300,000 free copies had been sent to the pastors of America. Christian bookstores had a difficult time keeping the book in stock. The effect of the book was dramatic. The media reported people putting their pets to sleep, selling their belongings, and going to hilltops to await the Rapture.

Some enterprising individuals promoted a Holy Land tour that offered the possibility of being raptured from the Holy Land. Part of the pitch for the tour read, "We stay at the Intercontinental Hotel right on the Mount of Olives where you can get the beautiful view of the Eastern Gate and the Temple Mount. And if this is the year of the Lord's return, as we anticipate, you may even ascend to Glory from within a few feet of His ascension." The price for the trip was quoted as "only $1,975 from Los Angeles or $1,805 from New York (and return if necessary)."

One Christian broadcasting network altered its telecasting schedule for September 11 to 13. The hosts of one program cancelled their regular live broadcast and instead ran videotapes on the Rapture, instructing unbelievers what to do if they found their Christian friends and relatives missing.

Apparently many Christians reasoned that if Whisenant knew eighty-

SETTING DATES FOR THE RAPTURE CAN BACKFIRE

eight reasons why Christ would return between September 11 and 13, 1988, at least one of them must be correct. Unfortunately none was.

So what happened when Christ did not return when Whisenant believed he would? Rather than learn from his mistakes, he went ahead and set another date, October 3, 1988. When once again Christ did not appear, Whisenant decided that his calculations were off by a year and wrote another book, *The Final Shout Rapture Report 1989, 1990, 1991, 1992, 1993.* In it he explained his mathematical error and predicted that the most likely date for the rapture was September 1, 1989, plus or minus one day. And once again he was mistaken.

Whereas Whisenant quoted many Scripture verses in his writings, he neglected to take seriously the words of Matthew 24:36: "No one knows the day or the hour when these things will happen, not even the angels in heaven or the Son himself."

Reflection

Have you ever been asked, "Do you think we are living in the last days?" How should we answer that question? It is important to remember Jesus' statement in Matthew 24:36 that from the long-distance perspective, no one knows the date of his second coming. Yet at the same time, Christians of every age are to live expectantly, looking for his return.

So stay awake and be prepared, because you do not know the day or hour of my return.   MATTHEW 25:13

September 12

Its membership was relatively small, but its influence continues today.

ON SEPTEMBER 12, 1905, approximately one hundred people met in a loft over Peck's Restaurant, at 140 Fulton Street in lower Manhattan. The purpose of the meeting was to strategize the overthrow of the Christian worldview that still pervaded much of American culture and to replace it with the ideas of a then rather unknown writer by the name of Karl Marx.[14] They called the organization they formed that day the Intercollegiate Socialist Society.

The godfather of the organization was a twenty-seven-year-old author named Upton Sinclair. The first president chosen was the author Jack London, age twenty-nine. Also present was Clarence Darrow, the attorney.[15]

The strategy of the organization was to infiltrate their ideas into academia by organizing chapters in as many colleges and universities as possible. And organize they did. Walter Lippmann, later author and director of the Council on Foreign Relations, was the president of the Harvard chapter. Walter Reuther, the future president of the United Auto Workers, headed the Wayne State chapter; and Eugene Debs, who went on to become the five-time Socialist candidate for president, was a leader at Columbia.

The society grew. The first annual convention was held in 1910, and by 1917 they were active on sixty-one campuses and a dozen graduate schools. Other early activists included W. E. B. DuBois, who would become an official of the NAACP and later a Communist Party member, and Victor L. Berger of Wisconsin, who became the first Socialist elected to Congress.

In 1921 the Intercollegiate Socialist Society took its next organizational step, changing its name to the League for Industrial Democracy. Its purpose was "education for a new social order based on production for use and not for profit." Norman Thomas, another perennial Socialist candidate for president, was the leader behind the scenes. The renamed organization's first president was Robert Lovett, editor of the *New Republic,* and the field secretary was Paul Blanshard, who later became an author.

The college chapters of the Intercollegiate Socialist Society now became the Student League for Industrial Democracy. As members graduated from college, some entered the pulpit, others the classroom; some wrote textbooks while others entered the labor movement and both political parties. When the New Deal began in 1933, they were prepared. At the time the league had only 5,652 members, but they were in positions of leadership everywhere.

A CASE STUDY IN CHANGING A
NATION'S CULTURE

By 1941 John Dewey, the founder of progressive education and the league vice president in the 1930s, was its honorary president, and Reinhold Niebuhr, the theologian, its treasurer. Dewey had already organized the Progressive Education Association and the American Association of University Professors.

The League for Industrial Democracy was so successful that those who held membership in the movement or were cooperating with it could have been a list for *Who's Who in America*: Robert N. Baldwin, founder of the American Civil Liberties Union; Charles Beard, the historian; Carroll Binder, editor of the *Minneapolis Tribune*; Helen Gahagan Douglas, the congresswoman who was defeated by Richard Nixon for the U.S. Senate; Felix Frankfurter, Supreme Court justice; Sidney Hook, the educational social philosopher; Edna St. Vincent Millay, the poet; Henry Morgenthau Jr., one of Franklin Delano Roosevelt's most trusted economic advisers; Walter and Victor Reuther, United Auto Workers; Will Rogers Jr., humorist; Franklin Roosevelt Jr., the president's son; and Arthur Schlesinger Jr., the historian.

The obscure loft in Manhattan where they organized has long been forgotten, but what began there that night permeates America's institutions and culture, having replaced the Bible-based values of the nineteenth century with a liberalism based on Marxism.

Reflection

To what extent do you feel that you have been influenced by the anti-Christian forces of modern culture? Do you think you have picked up any of the values of the League for Industrial Democracy? Unfortunately, all of us are the products of our own backgrounds. Even after we become Christians, we still are influenced by our culture. We need to evaluate our presuppositions against the truth revealed in God's Word.

∽୧୨∼

Fix your thoughts on what is true and honorable and right. Think about things that are pure and lovely and admirable. Think about things that are excellent and worthy of praise. Keep putting into practice all you learned from me and heard from me and saw me doing, and the God of peace will be with you. PHILIPPIANS 4:8-9

September 13

Can you imagine what it would be like to be someone's nineteenth wife?

CHAUNCEY WEBB and his parents were among Joseph Smith's earliest converts.[16] They first heard Smith in upstate New York in 1833 shortly after he had produced the *Book of Mormon* and presented himself as a new messiah who would restore true religion to the world. They followed Smith to Kirtland, Ohio, where Chauncey met and married Eliza Churchill, a Mormon girl of seventeen.

The Webbs next followed Smith to Nauvoo, Illinois, where they lived next door to Brigham Young and his family. In the summer of 1844 Joseph Smith was lynched by an anti-Mormon mob while in jail. Following his death, Brigham Young became leader of the movement. It was during their time in Nauvoo that Chauncey and Eliza's daughter, Ann-Eliza, was born on **September 13, 1844,** and Chauncey added a second wife.

Two years later the Mormons, having worn out their welcome in Illinois, started west and in 1848 reached Salt Lake City. There at the age of eight Ann-Eliza was baptized as a bishop carried her to a pond and threw her into the water. Four years later her father began receiving proposals from church dignitaries for her hand in marriage.

When Ann-Eliza turned seventeen, Brigham Young began to notice her. More and more she was aware of his staring at her, but that didn't stop her from falling in love with an Englishman named James Dee. When Ann-Eliza was eighteen, they were married. But all was not well, and within a month Ann-Eliza realized that the marriage had been a great mistake. Two years and two children later they were divorced.

Some time later at a Sunday service Ann-Eliza realized that Brigham Young was looking at her almost sensuously while he was preaching. After the service he walked her home and asked her parents for permission to marry her.

Ann-Eliza was shocked at the thought of marrying someone older than her father, yet she felt duty bound to yield to his wishes. On April 7, 1869, Ann-Eliza became the nineteenth wife of the head of the Mormon Church. He was sixty-eight; she, twenty-four. Young kept the wedding a secret, fearing the jealousy of his favorite wife.

After the wedding, Young returned Ann-Eliza to her parents for a while and then put her in a run-down little house of her own. She, like all but the favorite wife, lived poorly, receiving a monthly allowance of five pounds of sugar, some candles, a bar of soap, and a box of matches. She also received bread from a Mormon bakery and a supply of pork.

After a year of marriage, Young decided that Ann-Eliza should live at "The Farm," which supplied his families with food. After three and a half years on the farm, Young moved her to Salt Lake City.

There Ann-Eliza met the pastor of the Methodist church. She began to spend time with him and his wife, and for the first time in her life she had the opportunity to observe a monogamous family. She found herself drawn to the world they represented. Ann-Eliza soon decided that her only hope of happiness was to leave Mormonism and divorce Brigham Young. She went to court and was granted a divorce in 1874 amidst much publicity and had to sneak out of Salt Lake City at night, fearing for her life.

Once out of Utah she began lecturing against polygamy. A few weeks after her escape, Ann-Eliza was invited to the Methodist Female College of Delaware, Ohio. There the president carefully explained the gospel to her. It was like a new dawn breaking. Ann-Eliza left the darkness of her past and started a new life in the light of God's saving grace.

Reflection

When Mormon missionaries knock on your door, what should you do? If you are comfortable doing so, make sure they agree to give you equal time and then share your testimony with them. If you are unsure of what to say, it's best not to let them in.

If anyone tells you, "Look, here is the Messiah," or "There he is," don't pay any attention.   MATTHEW 24:23

September 14

He wrote some of the world's most beautiful music in an amazingly short period of time.

GEORGE FRIDERIC HANDEL was born in 1685, the same year as Johann Sebastian Bach. Handel's father was the town surgeon in a suburb of Halle, Germany, and his mother was the daughter of the pastor. George was the second child and received Lutheran baptism the day after he was born.

Handel was sent at a very young age to the local classical school, the head of which was an accomplished musician. However, when Handel began showing an interest in music, his father, determined that his son be a lawyer, forbade him to have anything to do with music, going as far as to burn all the musical instruments in the house. A sympathetic relative, however, secretly gave young Handel access to a clavichord away from his father's hearing, and Handel taught himself to play.

Handel's father was appointed surgeon to a duke. At the age of six when accompanying his father to the duke's court, Handel went up and played the organ after a Sunday worship service. Hearing the lad play, the duke was so impressed that he urged the father to give his son a formal music education. As a result, Handel was allowed to study under the organist of the Liebfrauenckirche in Halle. By the time he was twelve, Handel had written his first composition and was so proficient at the organ that he served as the substitute for his teacher.

In 1702, out of respect for his father's wishes, Handel studied law at the University of Halle. Soon, however, he switched his concentration solely to music.

In 1712 Handel moved to England but life there as a composer and musician was not easy. Between falling in and out of favor with various monarchs and competing with other English composers, Handel struggled financially. The Church of England attacked him for performing oratorios such as *Esther* and *Israel in Egypt* in secular theaters. In 1741 his health began to fail, and he was facing debtor's prison.

Then two events turned Handel's life around: A friend gave him a libretto for an oratorio on the life of Christ, with the words taken from the Bible, and three Dublin charities commissioned him to compose a work for a fund-raising benefit.

HANDEL'S MESSIAH

On August 22, 1741, Handel sat down to begin composing. He became so absorbed in his work that he hardly took time to eat. On **September 14, 1741,** he finished his composition and named it simply *Messiah*. In just twenty-four days he had written 260 pages of music. Considering the short time involved, it was the greatest feat in the history of musical composition. In those three weeks Handel never left his house. A friend who visited him found him sobbing with emotion. Later, in describing his experience, he alluded to the apostle Paul and said, "Whether I was in the body or out of my body when I wrote it, I know not."

The premier performance of *Messiah* was April 13, 1742, in Dublin. The benefit freed 142 persons from debtor's prison. A year later it was performed for the first time in London with the king in attendance. As the choir began to sing the "Halleluiah Chorus" the king rose to his feet and the whole audience followed his lead, beginning a tradition that continues to this day.

In all, Handel conducted thirty performances of *Messiah*. Of these only one was in a church, and John Wesley[17] was in attendance at the performance.

Handel's last public performance was of *Messiah* on April 6, 1759. At the end he fainted by the organ and died just eight days later. He was buried in Westminster Abbey, where his statue shows him holding the manuscript from *Messiah*, opened to "I Know That My Redeemer Liveth."

Reflection

Listen to *Messiah* today if you can. How do you think Handel was able to write this in just twenty-four days? How do the words and music minister to you?

❧

Let the words of Christ, in all their richness, live in your hearts and make you wise. Use his words to teach and counsel each other. Sing psalms and hymns and spiritual songs to God with thankful hearts.

COLOSSIANS 3:16

September 15

Apologies are difficult, especially when they are not accepted.

DAVID BRAINERD was born in Connecticut in 1718.[18] Shortly before he entered Yale in 1739, he experienced a profound conversion to Jesus Christ.[19]

Brainerd's years at Yale were difficult. Yale had been founded because Harvard had become Unitarian, yet the many religious activities there appeared to have little effect on the student body. The main diversions of the students were drinking parties, gambling, and harassment of the townspeople.

In August 1740 Brainerd's tutor noticed that he was spitting up blood, the first sign of tuberculosis. His tutor recommended that he return home to recuperate.

While Brainerd was at home, George Whitefield,[20] the twenty-five-year-old Anglican evangelist, preached at Yale. Brainerd returned to Yale in November, and by the following February the fruit of George Whitefield's preaching was beginning to manifest itself.

In March, Gilbert Tennant, an Irish American evangelist, preached at Yale and had a great impact upon the students. However, by September of 1741 Thomas Clap, the rector and president, and the college trustees took a stand against the revivalists. They condemned the students who were in support of what became known as the Great Awakening and passed a resolution stating "that if any student of this college shall indirectly state that the rector . . . the trustees or tutors are hypocrites, carnal or unconverted men, he shall for his first offense make a public confession in the Hall, and for the second offense be expelled."

David Brainerd, now a junior, spent many hours discussing spiritual things with his fellow students. One day the discussion was about a certain tutor. When one of Brainerd's friends asked him what he thought of the tutor he replied, "He has no more grace than this chair." A freshman overhead Brainerd's remark, and soon President Clap learned of it and summoned Brainerd. David admitted making the comment, and the president told him that he must make a public apology to the student body. Brainerd refused, believing that a public confession was inappropriate since it had been a private remark. To President Clap this was an act of rebellion, and he immediately expelled Brainerd.

A law recently passed in Connecticut stated that no minister could be installed in a church unless he was a graduate of Yale, Harvard, or a European

OUR NEGATIVES ARE SOMETIMES
GOD'S POSITIVES

university. Because of his expulsion David Brainerd was now cut off from his calling. On **September 15, 1743,** Brainerd wrote a letter to President Clap and the trustees of Yale confessing his sin in his handling of the situation and offering to make a public apology to the student body. His appeal was rejected.

Yet God worked the situation out for his glory and for Brainerd's good. A group of ministers sympathetic to the Great Awakening licensed Brainerd to preach and appointed him as a missionary to the American Indians. In the few remaining years before his death he brought the Great Awakening to the Indians of Massachusetts, New Jersey, and Pennsylvania.

But the results of Brainerd's expulsion from Yale went far beyond his ministry to the Indians. Jonathan Dickinson and Aaron Burr Sr.,[21] both graduates of Yale and Presbyterian pastors, took an interest in Brainerd's efforts to be readmitted to Yale and were disillusioned with the college's refusal to re-admit him.

Brainerd's expulsion brought to a head the Presbyterians' dissatisfaction with Yale and solidified their resolve to begin a college of their own. The College of New Jersey, later Princeton University, began in 1741 in Jonathan Dickinson's home, where David Brainerd, now twenty-nine, was living in his final months. Brainerd is thus considered to be the college's first student. Brainerd's expulsion from Yale precipitated the founding of Princeton.

Reflection

Have you experienced situations where God made something good out of something bad? Joseph in the Old Testament was sold as a slave by his brothers, yet he ended up becoming second in command in Egypt. Maybe the bad experience in your life hasn't yet resulted in something good. Make it a matter of prayer to ask God to glorify himself in your situation.

༚

Joseph told them, ". . . As far as I am concerned, God turned into good what you meant for evil."
GENESIS 50:19-20

September 16

What makes a religious person cruel?

Tomás de Torquemada had good religious genes. Born in Spain in 1420, he was the nephew of a prominent cardinal. After entering a Dominican monastery, Torquemada was made prior of another monastery and subsequently was appointed confessor to King Ferdinand II and Queen Isabella, best known for sponsoring Christopher Columbus.[22]

In 1163 Pope Alexander IV had encouraged princes and bishops to imprison heretics and confiscate their property. It was Pope Gregory IX who, beginning in 1231, set up a special church tribunal, called the Inquisition, for combating heresy.

No nation during this period was more interested in keeping the Catholic faith pure than Spain. Prodded by Queen Isabella, Pope Sixtus IV authorized the Spanish Inquisition in 1478. In 1483 Torquemada was appointed the Spanish grand inquisitor. He set up tribunals with such effectiveness that they lasted for three centuries. Torquemada became the most powerful person in Spain after the king and queen. In 1487 persecution was leveled against the Spanish Muslims, called Moors, and Jewish and Muslim converts to Christianity who were suspected of duplicity. The conversion of the Muslims and the Jews to Christianity had been forced in almost all cases.

The Inquisition in Spain began by offering heretics the Edict of Grace, a period of thirty to forty days in which heretics could identify themselves and, on their confession, be assured of a pardon. The catch was that those who confessed their heresies, called *penitentes*, were forced to take a vow to reveal other heretics.

The grounds for arrest was accusation by another or even mere rumor. A person was assumed to be guilty until proven innocent. Once arrested, prisoners were placed in a secret prison and allowed no contact with the outside world. They could not know their accusers' or witnesses' names, nor were they given access to documents relating to the case. Witnesses for the accused could be only orthodox Catholics, and no relative up to the fourth generation was allowed to testify. The charges could be for the slightest deviation from Catholic practice—even saying that the Virgin Mary herself and not her images effected cures.

Even when there was sufficient testimony from others to convict the accused, the victims were still tortured to extract a confession and to gain names of additional heretics.

The two primary tortures were water torture and the *garruche*. In the first, prisoners were tied to a rack, their jaws held open, linen cloth forced down their throat, and then up to eight quarts of water slowly poured down their throat. In the *garruche* weights were attached to the feet and the person was suspended so that only the toes touched the ground.

From the beginning the primary means of execution was burning. The tribunal established at Ciudad Real in 1483 burned 52 heretics in two years. When the Inquisition moved to Toledo in 1485, 750 *penitentes* were marched into the cathedral to be told that one-fifth of their property had been confiscated. Next the tribunal went to Avila, where 75 were burned at the stake and 26 corpses were exhumed and burned. And so it went.

King Ferdinand was the greatest supporter of Torquemada. It was with great delight that he witnessed many of the burnings, seeing each as an advancement of his Catholic faith.

In 1492 the conquest of the Muslim Moors in Spain became almost complete with the fall of Granada. Six months later King Ferdinand ordered all Jews to leave Spain,[23] but nearly half remained as forced converts.

By the time of Torquemada's death on **September 16, 1498,** two thousand heretics had been executed under his authority. The great irony is that Torquemada died hiding the fact that he himself had Jewish blood.

Reflection

The Spanish Inquisition was one of the cruelest institutions in human history. It tortured and murdered in the name of Jesus. How do you explain that? What does it teach about human nature? about religious commitment? What can you personally learn from these sordid events?

The human heart is most deceitful and desperately wicked. Who really knows how bad it is?   JEREMIAH 17:9

September 17

What does the Bible mean when it says that God is a jealous God?

On **September 17, 592 B.C.**, the prophet Ezekiel was sitting in his home in southern Babylonia with the elders of Judah.[24] It had been five years since Nebuchadnezzar had conquered Jerusalem for the second time and taken the Jews into exile.[25]

Suddenly Ezekiel had a vision in which the Spirit took him to the temple in Jerusalem (Ezekiel 8:1-4). There God appeared to Ezekiel and showed him the idolatry was being practiced in the temple. An idol had been erected at the entrance to the altar. Seventy elders of Judah were worshiping engraved animals in the dark, thinking that God would not see them. Women were weeping at the temple gate for the heathen god Tammuz. Twenty-five men with their backs to the altar were worshiping the sun (vv. 5-17).

God asked Ezekiel, "Is it nothing to the people of Judah that they commit these terrible sins, leading the whole nation into violence, thumbing their noses at me, and rousing my fury against them? Therefore, I will deal with them in fury. I will neither pity nor spare them. And though they scream for mercy, I will not listen" (vv. 17-18).

God commanded, "Bring on the men appointed to punish the city!" Six men appeared, each carrying a battle club. With them was a seventh man with a writing kit. To this man God said, "Walk through the streets of Jerusalem and put a mark on the foreheads of all those who weep and sigh because of the sins they see around them." To the other six God said, "Follow him through the city and kill everyone whose forehead is not marked" (9:1-5). The seven then carried out their respective orders.

The glory of God rose up and went to the entrance of the temple (10:4) and then to the eastern gate (v. 19). Ezekiel was taken to the eastern gate, where God told him the meaning of the vision. Speaking to the inhabitants of Jerusalem, he said, "I will drive you out of Jerusalem and hand you over to foreigners who will carry out my judgments against you. You will be slaughtered all the way to the borders of Israel" (11:9-10).

Ezekiel fell facedown in the dust and cried out, "O Sovereign Lord, are you going to kill everyone in Israel?" (v. 13).

The Lord answered:

> Give the exiles this message from the Sovereign Lord: Although I have scattered you in the countries of the world, I will be a sanctuary to you

during your time in exile. I, the Sovereign Lord, will gather you back from the nations where you are scattered, and I will give you the land of Israel once again. . . . And I will give them singleness of heart and put a new spirit within them. I will take away their hearts of stone and give them tender hearts instead, so they will obey my laws and regulations. Then they will truly be my people, and I will be their God. But as for those who long for idols, I will repay them fully for their sins." (vv. 16-21)

Then the presence of the Lord left Jerusalem and Ezekiel was taken back in the Spirit to Babylonia, where he told his fellow exiles everything he had seen and heard in his vision.

The prophet Malachi said that God's presence would not return to the temple until it did so in the person of Jesus: "Then the Lord you are seeking will suddenly come to his Temple" (Malachi 3:1).

God is a jealous God who will not share his worship with rivals. Ezekiel's vision was fulfilled six years later when God sent the Babylonian armies under Nebuchadnezzar to conquer Jerusalem a third and final time, destroying the temple, killing thousands of Jews, and taking the remainder captive to Babylonia.[26]

Reflection

What can we learn from this for our own lives? What modern gods are competing for the allegiance of God's people today? How about your allegiance?

࿐

I, the Lord your God, am a jealous God who will not share your affection with any other god! I do not leave unpunished the sins of those who hate me.　　　　　　　　　　　　　　　EXODUS 20:5

September 18

What was the apostle John doing on the island of Patmos?

JOHN WAS there because of a man named Domitian. Domitian was the second son of Vespasian, who commanded the Roman army sent in February A.D. 67, to put down the rebellion in Judea. Vespasian's army was so successful that by June A.D. 68, only Jerusalem was left to be conquered. Then on June 9 Nero, the emperor, committed suicide, and Vespasian halted military operations to see what would happen next in Rome.

The following year, 69, was a year of civil war with a succession of four caesars. Galba succeeded Nero and then was followed by Otho, Vitellius, and finally Vespasian. Vespasian turned the war against the Jews over to his oldest son, Titus,[27] and concentrated his energy on defeating Vitellius. To stem the revolt of Vespasian's legions, Vitellius tried to take Domitian as a hostage. However, after two daring escapes, Domitian was able to reach his father's legions. After the death of Vitellus in December, the Roman Senate proclaimed Vespasian as caesar, and Domitian returned in triumph to Rome.

Vespasian did not come to Rome for ten months. During that time the nineteen-year-old Domitian got a taste of ruling the empire. However, he became embroiled in arguments with a representative of his father and exercising power became a frustrating experience.

During Vespasian's reign Domitian was given only minor roles while his older brother Titus functioned as his father's aide and heir apparent.

When Vespasian died in 79, he was succeeded by Titus. Since Titus was only forty at the time, Domitian again received no positions of authority as it was assumed that Titus would rule for years to come.

However, this was not to be the case. Just two years later Titus took ill suddenly and died. Domitian, his brother, became caesar.

As caesar, Domitian was both autocratic and cruel. He declared himself "Lord and God" and demanded to be worshiped. Those refusing to acknowledge his deity were persecuted.

Pliny the Younger, a government official under Domitian, writes that the emperor persecuted all classes of Christians, Roman citizens and noncitizens, male and female, slave and free. It was as part of this persecution of Christians by Domitian that the apostle John, who had been living at Ephesus, was exiled to the island of Patmos. John tells us, "In Jesus we are partners in suffering and in the Kingdom and in patient endurance. I was exiled to the island of Patmos for preaching the word of God and speaking about Jesus" (Revelation 1:9).

Patmos is a desolate volcanic island ten miles long and six miles wide, thirty-seven miles off the coast of Asia Minor. In the Roman Empire prisoners were commonly exiled to islands.

Irenaeus, the bishop of Lyons, France, in approximately 175 to 195, writes about the apostle John, "who beheld the Apocalypse. For it was seen not very long ago, but almost in our day, toward the end of Domitian's reign." Irenaeus is a very credible witness since he was a disciple of Polycarp, who had been a disciple of John. In other words, Irenaeus knew someone who knew John personally.

If John was exiled to Patmos toward the end of Domitian's reign, that means he was there about the year 95. Domitian's behavior became so intolerable in his latter years—even to other pagans—that a conspiracy was formed against him that included even Domitian's wife. He was assassinated on **September 18, 96,** a few weeks before his forty-fifth birthday.

Nerva, the next caesar, proclaimed a recall of all of Domitian's exiles in 96, and John returned to Ephesus.

Reflection

Have you ever experienced persecution? In much of the world to be a Christian is to suffer persecution. In many nations persecution is from the government, as John experienced. We should not be surprised when we are persecuted; we should be surprised when we are not.

∽◈∾

God blesses those who are persecuted because they live for God, for the Kingdom of Heaven is theirs. God blesses you when you are mocked and persecuted and lied about because you are my followers. Be happy about it! Be very glad! For a great reward awaits you in heaven. And remember, the ancient prophets were persecuted, too.

MATTHEW 5:11-12

September 19

Some are overcome by challenges, while others are able to triumph over them.

Edward Payson was such a person. He was born in 1783 in Rindge, New Hampshire, where his father was pastor. Payson matriculated at Harvard in 1800 and quickly distinguished himself among his peers. He graduated in 1803 and took charge of the newly formed Portland Academy in Portland, Maine.

In his first year at the school, Payson was shaken by the death of a younger brother. He felt that God was somehow chastening him through his brother's death. He plunged into a yearlong period of conviction of sin, desire for holiness, and grief over his shortcomings. He finally realized that despite his intellectual assent to the doctrine of justification by faith alone, he had been trying to earn merit with God through his own efforts. As a result, his twenty-second birthday was a spiritual milestone in his life as he covenanted with God to give him his total allegiance.

In 1806 he resigned his position at the academy and returned home to study for the ministry. In spite of his new spiritual direction, he still battled his emotions. Today he would be diagnosed as having bipolar disorder. One minute he was supremely happy, and the next moment he was in the depths of despair.

In addition to his mood swings, Payson had physical problems. Throughout his life he was afflicted with migraine headaches that often left him prostrate in pain for days at a time. In later years insomnia afflicted him. A fall from a horse in 1807 dislocated his arm, leading eventually to its paralysis.

In August 1807 Payson was back in Portland preaching at the Second Congregational Church. He accepted the call as assistant pastor and stayed at the church for the rest of his life. In his first year at the church, he married Louisa Shipman. They had eight children, including Elizabeth Payson Prentiss[28] who became a hymn writer, authoring "More Love to Thee, O Christ" and many others.

Soon after Payson began his work at the church, he developed tuberculosis and nearly died. But he recuperated enough to continue his ministry, and almost immediately revival began at the church. His first year twenty-nine came to Christ, then forty-two for two years in a row. In 1811 the senior pastor retired, and Payson, then twenty-eight, became pastor. God richly blessed his ministry, and for the rest of his life the church averaged thirty-five conversions a year, with seventy-nine in the year of his death.

TRIUMPH IN THE FACE OF TRIAL

At the age of forty-four Payson's body gave out. His paralysis spread to other parts of his body, and he was often in acute pain. He and those around him knew he was dying, yet in spite of the discomfort, his joy was intense.

On **September 19, 1827,** a month before his death, he dictated a letter to his sister:

Dear Sister,

Were I to adopt the figurative language of Bunyan, I might date this letter, "from the land of Beulah" of which I have been for some weeks a happy inhabitant. The celestial city is in full view. Its glories beam upon me, its breezes fan me . . . and its spirit is breathed into my heart. Nothing separates me from it but the river of death, which now appears but an insignificant rill, that may be crossed at a single step, whenever God shall give permission. The Son of Righteousness has been gradually drawing nearer and nearer, appearing larger and brighter as he approached, and now he fills the whole hemisphere; pouring forth a flood of glory. . . .

And now my dear sister, farewell. Hold in your Christian course but a few days longer, and you will meet in heaven

Your happy and affectionate brother,
Edward Payson

Reflection

Do you have physical problems? mental problems? emotional problems? If you haven't experienced any of them yet, you probably will in the future. God doesn't grant us exemption from problems any more than he did Edward Payson, but he can enable us to look past them to the glory that lies ahead for the believer.

⌒◯⌒

Yet what we suffer now is nothing compared to the glory he will give us later. ROMANS 8:18

September 20

One of life's saddest experiences is to lose a child in death.

MARTIN LUTHER, the father of the Reformation,[29] married Katharina Von Bora, a former nun, in 1525. Luther and Katie, as he called her, had six children, Hans, Elizabeth, Magdalena, Martin, Paul, and Margaretha.

In 1542 when Hans was sixteen, the Luthers sent him to Torgau to school because Wittenburg did not have an appropriate school for his education. Scarcely had he arrived there than his thirteen-year-old sister, Magdalena, became deathly ill. Martin Luther wrote to Hans's teacher:

> *My daughter Magdalena is nearing her end and will soon go to her true Father in heaven unless he sees fit to spare her. She longs so much to see her brother, for they were very close, so I am sending a carriage for him, in the hope that a sight of him will revive her. I'm doing all I can lest afterwards the thought of having neglected anything should torment me. Please ask him to come at once, without telling him why. I shall send him back as soon as she has either fallen asleep in the Lord or been restored to health. Farewell in the Lord.*

Hans returned home, but Magdalena's health continued to deteriorate. Luther prayed, "Oh, God, I love her dearly, but thy will be done." Then he asked her, "Magdalena, my little girl, would you like to stay with your father here and would you just as gladly go to your Father in heaven?"

She answered, "Yes, dearest father, as God wills."

It grieved Luther that in spite of all the blessings he had received from God, he found himself unable in this situation to give thanks.

On **September 20, 1542,** as Magdalena's death drew near, Luther knelt at her bedside, praying through his tears that God would receive his little one. Katie stood at the end of the room, unable to watch as Magdalena died in her father's arms. Turning to his grieving wife, Luther said with compassion, "Dearest Katie, let us think of the home our daughter has gone to; there she is happy and at peace."

As Magdalena was laid in her coffin, Luther remarked, "My darling, you will rise and shine like the stars and the sun." Then he said to Katie, "How strange to know that she is at peace and all is well and yet to be sorrowful."

To his friends who came to mourn with him he said, "Let us not be sad. I have sent a saint to heaven. If mine could be like hers, I would gladly welcome death at this very hour."

SORROW IS PART OF LIFE

Luther wrote the epitaph for her grave:

> *Here, I, Magdalena,*
> *Doctor Luther's little maid*
> *Resting with the saints*
> *Sleep in my narrow bed.*
> *I was a child of death*
> *For I was born in sin*
> *But now I live, redeemed, Lord Christ,*
> *By the blood you shed for me.*

Three days after her death, Luther wrote a letter to his friend Justus Jonas:

I expect you have heard that my beloved Magdalena has been born again into Christ's everlasting kingdom. Although my wife and I ought to rejoice because of her happy end, yet such is the strength of natural affection that we cannot think of it without sobs and groans which tear the heart apart. The memory of her face, her words, her expression in life and in death—everything about our most obedient and loving daughter lingers in our hearts so that even the death of Christ (and what are all deaths compared to his?) is almost powerless to lift our minds above our loss. So would you give thanks to God in our stead? For hasn't he honored us greatly in glorifying our child?

Reflection

The death of a loved one brings sorrow to everyone. It is important not to deny these feelings. Jesus wept at the tomb of Lazarus even though he knew he was going to raise him from the dead. God intends that we mourn.

And now, brothers and sisters, I want you to know what will happen . . . so you will not be full of sorrow like people who have no hope.

1 THESSALONIANS 4:13

September 21

How do you get back up once you are down?

BECAUSE OF the heinous sins and idolatry of the Jewish people, God had sent Nebuchadnezzar and the Babylonian army three times to attack Judah and to take the Jews away captive. The final time in 586 B.C. the Babylonians destroyed Jerusalem and its temple. The prophet Jeremiah had prophesied that at the end of the Babylonian captivity God would return his people to Jerusalem (Jeremiah 29:10). This began in 538 B.C. when Cyrus, the Persian conqueror of Babylon, issued a decree allowing the Jews to return to Jerusalem and rebuild their temple (Ezra 1:2-4). Under the leadership of Zerubbabel about fifty thousand Jews returned and began to rebuild the temple. The Samaritans and other neighbors so vigorously opposed the rebuilding project that fear gripped the Jews and work on the temple stopped (4:4-24).

Then God sent his prophet Haggai with a message for the people of Jerusalem.[30] In Hebrew the message is just four words long. In English it is seven words, "I am with you, says the Lord!" (Haggai 1:13)

Often in the Bible when God declares, "I am with you," he precedes it by saying, "Do not be afraid" (Genesis 26:24). Although those words are omitted here, the message is the same. The answer to the Jews' fear was the knowledge that God was with them.

Often when God calls people to a particular task, part of the call is the promise of God's presence with them. God had promised his presence in his call of Moses (Exodus 3:12), Gideon (Judges 6:16), and Jeremiah (Jeremiah 1:8). Here the promise is directed to all of God's people in Jerusalem (Haggai 1:13).

God not only calmed their fears by the promise of his presence but also "sparked the enthusiasm" (v. 14). The Hebrew word translated "sparked" is used throughout the Old Testament for how God stirs the hearts of heads of state to accomplish his purposes (Ezra 1:1; Jeremiah 51:11; etc.). Here he sparks the enthusiasm of Zerubbabel, the Jewish governor of Judah, and Jeshua, the high priest, as well as the whole remnant of God's people in Jerusalem. He had stirred their hearts to return from Babylon and now was doing so again to rebuild his temple (Ezra 5:2).

From God's perspective, it required the enthusiastic support of both the governmental leader Zerubbabel and the religious leader Jeshua, the high priest, for the temple to be rebuilt. Zerubbabel was the grandson of King

A PEP TALK AND A PROMISE

Jehoiachin of Judah and an ancestor of Joseph, the stepfather of Jesus Christ (Matthew 1:12-17). Little did Zerubbabel know that the temple he was rebuilding would, after Herod's remodeling, be visited by the Messiah, whose right to the throne of David would come through Zerubbabel's own genealogy.

It is significant that God energized not only the leadership of the Jews but also the whole remnant of God's people. The result was that on **September 21, 520** B.C., the people "came and began their work on the house of the Lord" (Haggai 1:14).

The New Testament tells believers, "God is working in you, giving you the desire to obey him and the power to do what pleases him" (Philippians 2:13). That is how God works. First he gave his people the desire by sparking their enthusiasm. Then he gave them the power to begin to rebuild the temple.

Reflection

Has fear stifled your ministry for God? It could be fear of people, fear of rejection, fear of failure, even fear of success. It is significant that in the last chapter of Matthew's Gospel believers are twice told, "Don't be afraid" (Matthew 28:5, 10). Then the Gospel ends with "And be sure of this: I am with you always, even to the end of the age" (v. 20).

I will never fail you. I will never forsake you. HEBREWS 13:5

September 22

It became a literal witch-hunt.

IT ALL BEGAN in 1692 when the young daughter of Samuel Parris, the pastor of the Salem, Massachusetts, church, exhibited strange, psychotic symptoms. She experienced violent convulsions, hallucinations, and trancelike states. Shortly thereafter her cousin appeared to be similarly afflicted, and soon the hysteria spread to several other teenage girls within their social sphere. Parris's own slave, Tituba, had entertained these impressionable children with spellbinding tales of the occult recalled from her childhood in the West Indies.

Parris was at first ashamed and then alarmed by these manifestations in his daughter and her friends. When pressed, the girls blamed witches for their torment. In a sermon Parris told his parishioners that witches were everywhere, including in their church. He warned ominously, "God knows how many devils there are."

The ensuing witch-hunt was organized in a meeting held at the Parris home. Eventually approximately 150 suspected witches were imprisoned and 19 were hanged. Most of the victims were either social outcasts or members of families who had opposed the ministry of Samuel Parris. Many were middle-aged women with no male relatives to defend them, making them particularly vulnerable. Parris's own slave, Tituba, was one of the first to be accused. In the midst of the hysteria, neighbor accused neighbor of witchcraft over the slightest pretext, such as the death of a cow or the failure of bread to rise.

The final executions occurred on the morning of **September 22, 1692,** on Witches Hill in Salem. Eight middle-aged New Englanders, seven women and one man, were hanged.

Gathered at the foot of the scaffold were people representing every age group. Eighty-nine-year-old Simon Bradstreet, recently governor of Massachusetts Bay Colony, and other original Puritans still alive, had left England over a half century earlier to create a Christian commonwealth in the new world. They viewed their own children as unfaithful to their Puritan upbringing and felt their utopia was being judged because of their wayward progeny. In their minds, by purging the witches they hoped to put an end to these tribulations and bring God's blessing on them once again.

Also present at the gallows was sixty-one-year-old William Stoughton, the judge at the witch trials. His generation watched the execution with resignation. The condemned as well as the magistrates were all of their age. Stoughton's contemporaries didn't share the passion of their parents, having been repeatedly told by them that theirs was a lost and unconverted generation.

Representative of the younger generation was twenty-nine-year-old Cotton Mather, a brilliant young clergyman. Mather himself had been one of those who had examined the witches. Mather and his fellows considered the accused witches threats to their future and sought to get rid of them. Mather, a hardened witch-baiter in his youth, was to become a leading minister and theologian of his day. He was one of the founders of Yale College, organized to prepare ministers of the gospel.

The young girls who had been the accusers of the witches were also present. Their shrieking and twitching reminded everyone what the witches had done.

From the last of the original Puritans who had helped create Massachusetts as God's "City on a Hill"[31] to the youngest children who would someday be citizens of the future United States of America, this crowd at the final witch hanging witnessed a unique moment in American history.

After the executions the neighboring ministers took action to end the witch trials. A year later Samuel Parris, by then realizing his own responsibility for these shameful events, described his remorse for the executions in a sermon. He acknowledged that the wounds of their victims "accuseth *us* as the vile actors."

Reflection

Do you feel guilt over the darkest deeds of your life, even though they may have occurred long ago? Christ will forgive the most heinous of sins if we truly repent, confessing our sins and trusting him as the one who paid the penalty for all our sins on the cross. King David committed adultery and murder, but because he truly repented, God forgave him, and he is referred to as "a man after [God's] own heart" (Acts 13:22).

∽✑

If we confess our sins to him, he is faithful and just to forgive us and to cleanse us from every wrong. 1 John 1:9

September 23

What do you do if you announce a prayer meeting but no one comes?

THE SUMMER of 1857 was a frustrating time to be a Christian in New York City. In the commercial district wealthy bankers and real estate speculators conspicuously thanked God for their profitable deals. Yet in the vast slums poverty was inescapable. The revival fires of the Second Great Awakening had been dampened twenty years earlier by the financial panic of 1837.

Jeremiah Lanphier was a man who wanted to make a difference. Born south of Albany, he had come to New York City to enter the mercantile business. Then at the age of thirty-three he unexpectedly discovered that Jesus Christ was real and that he had paid the penalty for his sins. Lanphier gave his life to Jesus and joined the Brick Presbyterian Church, spending much of his spare time as a street evangelist. Then in the summer of 1857 the North Dutch (Reformed) Church on Fulton Street decided to hire a full-time lay evangelist to reach the immigrants living around their church. They chose the energetic fellow from Brick Presbyterian, Jeremiah Lanphier.

Lanphier immediately started passing out invitations to the church to all who lived within walking distance, but found few takers. He began praying, *Lord, what do you want me to do?* The answer he received was that God wanted people to pray. As he mulled this over in his mind, an idea started to take form. He would have a prayer meeting for businessmen from noon to 1:00 P.M. It would be simple and flexible. Businessmen could come for a few minutes or for the whole hour. It would include singing, prayer, and exhortation, and a bell would ring if anyone spoke over five minutes.

Lanphier printed up a handbill inviting the public to a weekly prayer meeting at noon on Wednesdays in the third-floor meeting room of the North Dutch Church on Fulton Street. The first prayer meeting would be held **September 23, 1857**.

The appointed day arrived and at noon Lanphier went to the room and knelt to pray. Ten minutes passed, and no one came. Twenty minutes passed, and still he was all alone. Finally at 12:30 he heard the door open from the street and the sound of footsteps coming up the stairway. One man entered the room and without saying a word knelt down next to Lanphier. Then another man came, followed by another until by one o'clock there were six.

But the following week there were twenty. Then in the first week of October the meetings were held daily, and the number gathered increased to forty.

THE FULTON STREET PRAYER MEETING

The fourth week attendance averaged over one hundred with many under conviction and inquiring how they might be saved.

New York City was to see a great need for God when on October 18 a financial panic seized the city, collapsing the economy into a brief but steep recession. "The Fulton Street Meetings," as they became known, soon filled all the rooms at the North Dutch Church and spilled over into the nearby John Street Methodist Church. Soon many other churches were opening their doors both at noon and before work in the morning. Even police stations and firehouses opened their doors to meet the need for places to pray. Within six months, ten thousand businessmen were gathering for prayer daily.

Although the revival was the most spectacular in New York City, businessmen's prayer meetings sprang up in many cities around the country. Within the next two years approximately one million converts were added to the churches of America.

Reflection

Have you ever felt prompted by God to plan an event only to have very few attend? It would have been easy for Jeremiah Lanphier to feel discouraged even after the five others finally showed up at his first prayer meeting, but he persevered. In similar situations we must remember that our responsibility is to be faithful to what God directs us to do and the results are up to him.

∽≫

The master was full of praise. "Well done, my good and faithful
servant. You have been faithful in handling this small amount, so now
I will give you many more responsibilities. Let's celebrate together!"
MATTHEW 25:21

September 24

The impact of a life matters more than its length.

AARON BURR SR. was born in Connecticut and graduated from Yale in 1735, first in his class. He then became pastor of the Presbyterian Church of Newark, New Jersey.

When a student named David Brainerd[32] was expelled from Yale in connection with his involvement in the Great Awakening, Aaron Burr and Jonathan Dickinson, pastor of the Presbyterian church in Elizabethtown, New Jersey, took an active interest in his case.[33] The two pastors were particularly upset when their alma mater refused to readmit Brainerd after he apologized for offhand comments that had led to his expulsion. Yale's action confirmed the conviction of the Presbyterian synods of New Jersey and New York that they should found their own college to prepare men for the ministry.

The College of New Jersey, which was to become Princeton University, received its charter from the governor of the state in 1746. Of the organizing seven trustees, all but one were graduates of Yale. Aaron Burr was the youngest. Four of the next five were graduates of the Log College.[34]

The college began in May 1747 in Jonathan Dickinson's home in Elizabethtown, New Jersey, with David Brainerd, the student initially expelled, as its first official student. The original students studied in Dickinson's library, had their classes in the parlor, and ate their meals in the dining room with the family. When Dickinson died, they accompanied the family to the funeral and burial.

Aaron Burr was persuaded to take charge of the college at that point, so the students packed up, bid farewell to the grieving Dickinson family, and moved six miles to Newark. They boarded in the town and held their classes at the Burr parsonage. Burr did all the teaching with the assistance of one tutor. A year later Aaron Burr was formally elected the college's second president, just thirteen years after his own graduation from college.

When Burr became president, he was still a bachelor. Some years earlier he had met fifteen-year-old Esther Edwards, a daughter of pastor and theologian Jonathan Edwards.[35] Unable to forget about fair Esther, Burr made a three-day courting visit to the Edwards's home. Esther accepted his declaration of love, and they were married at Burr's church in Newark. Burr was thirty-six and Esther twenty-one.

Burr filled the offices of both college president and pastor until 1755 when he resigned his pastorate to devote all his time to the college. He supervised the erection of the college's first building in Princeton, New Jersey. The trustees wanted to name it Belcher Hall in honor of Governor Belcher, but Burr insisted that it be named Nassau Hall in memory of King William III of the House of Nassau, whose monarchy restored Protestantism to England.[36] In 1756 Burr, the seventy students, and two tutors moved into glorious Nassau Hall, the largest stone building in the colonies.

The following year Governor Belcher died, and though ill, Burr traveled to Elizabethtown to deliver the funeral sermon. Returning to Princeton, Aaron Burr died on **September 24, 1757,** at the age of only forty-one.

The grieving Esther wrote to her mother, "I think I have been enabled to cast my care upon him and have found great peace and calmness in my mind, such as this world cannot give or take. . . . Give me leave to entreat you both, to request earnestly of the Lord, that I may never despise his chastenings, nor faint under this, his severe stroke."

Five days later her father, Jonathan Edwards, was chosen to follow his son-in-law as the college's next president.

Reflection

Even though the life of Aaron Burr Sr. was short, he accomplished much. We don't know how long we will live, but God has a purpose for each of us, and with his help we can accomplish it, regardless of the length of our lives.

All of us must quickly carry out the tasks assigned us by the one who sent me, because there is little time left before the night falls and all work comes to an end.   JOHN 9:4

September 25

John Oldcastle was part of the nobility, but more important, he was truly noble.

Prior to the Reformation the leading English reformer was John Wycliffe, born about 1329. He received a doctorate in theology from Oxford and served as a lecturer at the university and as a rector of local churches. Wycliffe taught that the Bible was the sole authority for faith and practice. He denied the Roman Catholic teaching of transubstantiation that claims that the bread and wine of Communion in the Mass actually becomes the body and blood of Christ. He repudiated the Catholic Church teaching that the sinner, unable to do sufficient penance to atone for his sins, is able to draw on the spiritual treasury of the surplus merits of Jesus Christ, the Virgin Mary, and the saints, called indulgences. He attacked the infallibility of the papacy and tried to have religious orders abolished.

Although Wycliffe died in 1384, his influence continued. His followers were called Lollards by their enemies, a term that seems to have meant "mumblers." By 1395 they had become an organized church with ordained ministers and spokesmen in Parliament. Their following was strongest among the middle and artisan classes. To contain the growing influence of the Lollards, Parliament passed a statute in 1407, "On the Burning of a Heretic," aimed specifically at the followers of Wycliffe. It stated that any heretic convicted by a church court could be turned over to the state to be burned.

After the death of Wycliffe the Lollards were leaderless until in 1410 Sir John Oldcastle stepped forward. Up to that time only a few nobles had been followers of Wycliffe, but they had drawn back when persecution arose. John Oldcastle was different. He had been a soldier who had fought for England. During the Welsh Wars he had become a friend of King Henry IV's son, Henry, the prince of Wales. (Shakespeare's character Falstaff in *Henry IV* is modeled after John Oldcastle, though Shakespeare made him more boisterous than he was in real life.) When Oldcastle married Jan, heiress of John, the third Lord Cobham, he became part of the nobility and in 1409 was made a member of the House of Lords as a baron.

In 1413 Oldcastle's friend, the prince of Wales, became King Henry V. Soon after the archbishop of Canterbury called a synod of the English clergy to bring charges against Oldcastle for being the leader of the Lollards. Realizing that Oldcastle was a friend of the new king, the archbishop and his bishops went to the king to present their case. The king indicated that he would speak to Oldcastle himself. Hearing firsthand Oldcastle's vigorous opposition to the Catholic Church, the king turned against his friend and gave the archbishop permission to bring his charges against him.

John Oldcastle was arrested and on **September 25, 1413**, was brought to trial before the archbishop and his bishops. The archbishop addressed him by his title, saying, "Lord Cobham, we once again require you to have none other opinion than the universal belief of the Holy Church of Rome." Oldcastle answered, "I will none otherwise believe in these points than I told you afore. Do with me what ye will . . . though ye judge my body . . . yet am I certain that ye can do no harm to my soul. He that created that will of his infinite mercy save it; I have therein no manner of doubt. Concerning these articles, I will stand to them to the very death by the grace of my God."

Oldcastle was sentenced to death, but the outcome was not what the archbishop had planned. Oldcastle escaped from the Tower of London, and soon it was the archbishop who felt the stroke of death rather than Oldcastle. Four years later Oldcastle was arrested a second time and hanged and then burned.

The condemned outlived the condemner by several years.

Reflection

When we are betrayed like John Oldcastle was by his friend King Henry, our natural reaction is to want revenge. But God is a righteous judge, and we must place our case in his hands. He will do what is right and ultimately vindicate his people.

∽◌↩

Dear friends, never avenge yourselves. Leave that to God. For it is written, "I will take vengeance; I will repay those who deserve it," says the Lord.　　　ROMANS 12:19

September 26

The more he drank, the rowdier he became.

LIFE ON the farm in 1887 was tough in Fentress County, Tennessee, where a boy named Alvin York was born. His father, William, needed to farm, hunt, and blacksmith to support a family that eventually included eleven children.

Alvin worked with his father on the farm. He especially enjoyed hunting with him and became a crack shot at an early age. But in 1911 Alvin's father died from a kick by a mule, leaving Alvin as chief provider for the family since his two older brothers had already moved away.

Floundering under the responsibility of caring for his family, Alvin began drinking the local moonshine. The more he drank, the rowdier he became, often ending his evenings in bloody fights. After every binge he would stumble home to his mother's two-room cabin where night after night she faithfully prayed for him.

One night about midnight when Alvin lurched home from a night of drinking and fighting, his mother plaintively asked him, "When are you going to be a man like your father and grandfather?"

She had nagged him for years about his drunkenness but had never before compared him to his father and grandfather. Neither of them had drunk, and both were legendary for their fairness and honesty.

His mother's words made Alvin suddenly realize that his life was hopeless and that all he deserved was God's wrath. Of that moment he later said, "God just took ahold of my life. My little old mother had been praying for me for so long, and I guess the Lord finally decided to answer her." He fell to his knees and shed tears of repentance in his mother's lap. As his tears turned to joy, he said, "Mother, I promise you tonight that I will never drink again as long as I live. I will never smoke or chew again. I will never gamble again. I will never cuss or fight again. I will live the life God wants me to live." It was the wee hours of New Year's Day, 1915, the dawn of a new day for Alvin York.

At the next revival at a nearby church, Alvin York walked down the aisle and to his neighbors' amazement publicly dedicated his life to God. He soon became an elder and song leader in his church.

Things were going well for Alvin until in 1917 the United States declared war on Germany. Joining the army was the last thing that York wanted to do because his church opposed war as a violation of the commandment "Thou shalt not kill." Then he received a notice requiring him to register with his

FROM CONSCIENTIOUS OBJECTOR
TO WAR HERO

draft board, the head of which was his pastor. He was in a quandary as was his pastor. He applied to be a conscientious objector but was turned down. He had no choice but to go to war.

On **September 26, 1918,** the battle for the Argonne Forest began. The great achievement of the battle, in fact the greatest single military achievement of the war, was performed by a corporal from Tennessee named Alvin York. As a member of a patrol sent to silence a group of German machine-gun nests, York personally killed more than twenty Germans and took 132 prisoners all by himself. He forced a German major to order all his soldiers to surrender. It all took place within three hours and fifteen minutes.

That night after recounting the day's events in his diary, he wrote, "So you can see here in this case of mine where God helped me out. I had bin living for God and working in the church some time before I came to the army. So I am a witness to the fact that God did help me out of that hard battle; for the bushes were shot up all around me, and I never got a scratch."

For his heroism Corporal York, soon to be Sergeant York, received the Congressional Medal of Honor. General Pershing called him "the greatest civilian soldier of the war."

Reflection

Was it just coincidence that a Christian won this amazing personal victory? Do you think that Alvin York would have accomplished this feat if he had not become a Christian? Why or why not?

The horses are prepared for battle, but the victory belongs to the Lord.

PROVERBS 21:31

September 27

She asked him what his name was, and he answered, "Charlie Manson."

SUSAN ATKINS had met the savior of the world—or so she thought. When she asked his name, he answered, "Charlie Manson."

Soon Susan, just eighteen, had joined Manson's "family" in a life of drugs and sex, and life took an ugly turn. Charlie told her that a friend, Gary Hinman, had inherited twenty-one thousand dollars. He said, "If you want to do something important, why don't you kill Gary and get his money?"

A few days later Charlie sent Susan with Bobby and Mary, two of his other followers, to get Gary's money. They were unsuccessful, but in the process Bobby killed Gary. To confuse the police, he wrote "Political Piggy" in Gary's blood on the living-room wall. Bobby was arrested a few days later. Obsessed with getting Bobby out of jail, Manson decided to stage "copy cat" murders to make the police believe that the real murderer was still at large.

A few nights later Susan and three others were sent to a house in Beverly Hills, where they were to kill everyone they found. One man was killed in the driveway, and inside the house they found Wojiciech Frykowski, a Polish playboy; Sharon Tate, an actress; Jay Sebring, an internationally known hairstylist; and Abigail Folger, heiress to the Folgers coffee fortune. After a bloody struggle all four were murdered. Susan wrote the word *Pig* on the front door in blood to convince the police that the murderer of Gary Hinman was still on the loose.

Susan was later convicted of multiple counts of murder and sentenced to death. As she sat defiantly on death row at the California Institute for Women, she received a Bible from an unknown benefactor. It was inscribed, "Jesus, my prayer is that you reveal yourself to Susan Atkins."

One day Susan heard on the radio that the California Supreme Court had voted six to one to abolish the death penalty. Susan dropped to her knees sobbing uncontrollably. For the first time in years she prayed, "Thanks, God. I want to thank you for letting me live—and all the others too."

In the succeeding months a member of the Manson family, "Old Bruce," serving a life sentence in Folsom Prison, began writing her letters about God and recommended that she read Hal Lindsey's *Late Great Planet Earth* and enroll in a Bible correspondence course. She took Old Bruce's advice.

On the night of **September 27, 1974,** as Susan lay on her prison bed, thinking about her numerous sins, she found herself saying, "I want to be forgiven."

FROM DEATH TO LIFE

The words came to her, *You have to decide.* She felt that if she didn't give her life to Jesus Christ at that moment, the opportunity would never come again. She recalled these words from the Bible: "Behold, I stand at the door and knock" (Revelation 2:20, KJV).

Her response was, "Okay. If you're there, come in."

Total silence. Then, *All right, I'll come in, but you have to open the door.*

She talked back to the voice, "What door?"

You know what door and where it is, Susan. Just turn around and open it, and I'll come in.

Suddenly she saw a door with a handle. She pulled on it, and it opened. The brightest light poured in upon her. Vaguely there was the form of a man, whom she knew to be Jesus. He spoke to her, *Susan, I am really here. I'm really coming into your heart to stay. Right now you are being born again, and you will live with me in heaven for all eternity, forever and ever. This is really happening. It is not a dream. You are now a child of God. You are washed clean, and your sins have all been forgiven.*

For the first time Susan Atkins felt clean inside and out.

Reflection

Do you really believe that God can save even the worst criminal? The apostle Paul was an accessory to the murder of Stephen, and we are all by nature desperately wicked and in need of forgiveness.

This is a true saying, and everyone should believe it: Christ Jesus came into the world to save sinners—and I was the worst of them all.

1 TIMOTHY 1:15

September 28

It all began with people praying.

In 1860 Christians in Jamaica heard about the prayer revival that was sweeping the world. Wanting to become a part of it, they began "peep of day" (dawn) prayer meetings. Most were held on plantations so that people could meet for prayer before they went to work in the fields.

Their prayers for revival were first answered in a Moravian chapel. The Moravians were the spiritual descendants of Jan Hus,[37] the Czech Reformer martyred in 1415. They had settled at Herrnhut, Germany, and had become a major missionary-sending movement.[38] A Moravian missionary from Germany, Theodor Sonderman, regularly visited the town of Clifton, Jamaica, as part of his ministry.

On **September 28, 1860,** Sonderman began what he expected to be a regular Moravian service. A hymn was sung, followed by an opening prayer. Then someone else prayed, and another and another. Even children led in prayer. One boy poured out his soul to God, and Sonderman saw tears streaming down everyone's cheeks as they cried to God for mercy. Even notorious sinners groaned to God in prayer. So many people were weeping that Sonderman became concerned about maintaining order. The meeting finally broke up after three hours so that Sonderman could deal with those who were in greatest distress. But many others went to a nearby schoolhouse to continue praying.

More prayer meetings sprang up in adjacent communities. Many genuinely put their faith in Jesus Christ while others were just frightened into temporary conformity to Christian living. One believer confessed, "Minister, we been praying for revival of religion. And now God poured out his Spirit, we all 'fraid for it."

After four weeks Theodor Sonderman was dealing with more than three hundred inquirers, and the revival was spilling into other denominations, the Anglicans, Baptists, Congregationalists, Methodists, and Presbyterians.

In early November when a minister from Clifton went to Montego Bay to preach, he found the whole city talking about the revival. The minister dealt with many inquirers even before he had a chance to preach.

In Bethel Town a missionary proposed a dawn prayer meeting the following morning, and five hundred came to pray. The missionary had to leave during the day, so the local pastor called for another meeting in the evening. At the conclusion of the service, the people felt the Spirit being poured out upon them so intently that they refused to leave the chapel. The missionary returned two days later for a service in which a hundred hardened sinners fell to their knees and a dozen unwed couples who were living together asked to be married.

The Mount Carey Chapel had no pastor, so the local justice of the peace presided over the Sunday morning service with twelve hundred crowded into the chapel. In three smaller communities, three thousand were awakened to faith in Christ with no pastor preaching.

Among the Methodists of Montego Bay, the chapel of 800 members saw 547 people come to Christ. The eighty Baptist churches of Jamaica reported 12,000 conversions during the revival. The Congregational churches grew so much that the missionary board was able to withdraw all its missionaries, leaving the church in able local hands. The Presbyterian churches of Jamaica saw more than 3,000 conversions in 1860 and another 1,700 the following year.

A Congregational minister summarized the results of the revival: "It closed the rum shop and the gambling houses, reconciled long-separated husbands and wives, restored prodigal children, produced scores of bans to be read for marriage, crowded every place of worship, quickened the zeal of ministers, purified the churches, and brought many sinners to repentance. It also excited the rage of those ungodly people whom it had not humbled."

And it all began with prayer.

Reflection

Have you ever had the privilege of being part of a revival? Whether you have or are still waiting for the experience, it is important to remember that they begin through prayer.

∾⟨᠎⟩⟩

I have heard all about you, Lord, and I am filled with awe by the amazing things you have done. In this time of our deep need, begin again to help us, as you did in years gone by. Show us your power to save us. And in your anger, remember your mercy. HABAKKUK 3:2

September 29

Some people just keep going—no matter what.

GEORGE WHITEFIELD was the greatest preacher of the eighteenth century and one of the best-known and best-loved individuals in America.[39] Born in England, he entered Oxford in 1734. He devoted his whole life to preaching. When the churches refused to let him use their pulpits, he preached outdoors. He traveled the English-speaking world making fourteen trips to Scotland and seven to America. He regularly delivered as many as twenty sermons a week.

On **September 29, 1770,** Whitefield preached his last sermon in the fields. Though feeling ill, he set out in the morning by horseback from Portsmouth, New Hampshire, to preach at Newburyport, Massachusetts, the next day. On the way he passed through Exeter, New Hampshire, not intending to stop. However, people were aware he would be passing through and had gathered, hoping that they could hear him preach. They had even erected a platform for him in a field. The crowd was insistent, and Whitefield agreed to speak.

As Whitefield approached the platform, an elderly gentleman said to him, "Sir, you are more fit to go to bed than to preach."

"True, sir," Whitefield replied, looking up to heaven. Then he said, "Lord Jesus, I am weary in thy work, but not weary of it. If I have not yet finished my course, let me go and speak for thee once more on the fields, seal thy truth, and come home and die."

When Whitefield mounted the platform, he stood for several minutes unable to speak. An observer noted that his spirit was willing but his flesh was dying. He finally said, "I will wait for the gracious assistance of God, for he will I am certain assist me once more to speak in his name." He then preached for two hours on the verse "Examine yourselves whether ye be in the faith." Toward the end of the message he said, "I go; I go to a rest prepared: my sun has given light to many, but now it must set—no, to rise to the zenith of immortal glory. I have outlived many on earth, but they cannot outlive me in heaven. Many shall outlive me on earth and live when this body is no more, but there—oh, thought divine! I shall be in a world where time, age, sickness, and sorrow are unknown. My body fails, but my spirit expands. How willingly would I live forever to preach Christ. But I die to be with him." Many of his hearers said that it was the best sermon that Whitefield had ever delivered.

After he was through, the exhausted Whitefield rode off to the home of

FAITHFUL TO THE END

Reverend Jonathan Parsons, pastor of the Old South Presbyterian Church in Newburyport. Arriving tired and sick, Whitefield ate early. As he was going up the stairs to bed with a candle in his hand, the front door was opened to let in a crowd that had gathered outside the house. They begged him to preach, and he did until the candle in his hand burned out.

At 2:00 A.M. Whitefield awoke panting for breath. The young man who was traveling with him gently chided him for preaching so often. To this Whitefield replied, "I had rather wear out than rust out."

He awoke again at 4:00 A.M. Getting out of bed, he went to the window, saying, "I can scarce breathe," at which point the young man went out to get a doctor.

At 7:00 that Sunday morning Whitefield entered the land for which he had been prepared by sovereign grace, the land to which he had pointed tens of thousands, and the land that would be his home for all eternity.

Reflection

Is it your purpose to serve God until you take your last breath? Some look forward to retiring not only from their day-to-day occupation but also from their work for the Lord. May we, like George Whitefield, be faithful to the end.

Remain faithful even when facing death, and I will give you the crown of life.
REVELATION 2:10

September 30

Why do Roman Catholic Bibles have more books in them than Protestant Bibles?

THE ANSWER comes from the work of a man who died on **September 30, 420.** His name was Sophronius Eusebius Hieronymus, but history knows him as Jerome. Born of Christian parents somewhere in what is now Yugoslavia, he went to Rome at the age of twelve to study. He was baptized there at the age of nineteen and resolved to devote himself single-mindedly to the service of his Lord.

Jerome became attracted to monasticism, spending time in both Gaul (modern-day France) and Syria. He lived a life of self-denial in the desert near the ancient town of Chalcis, Syria. During this time he began mastering Hebrew and perfecting his Greek. He was ordained in Antioch and recognized as a bishop without pastoral responsibilities. He next studied in Constantinople under Gregory of Nazianzus, one of the Cappadocian fathers who had a profound influence on Christian theology in general and on the doctrine of the Trinity in particular.

In 386 Jerome moved to Bethlehem and spent the rest of his life there. He was the overseer of a monastery and the spiritual adviser to a local convent.

Jerome spent most of his time writing. His linguistic ability and scholarship were unsurpassed in the early church. He carried on a voluminous correspondence, compiled a bibliography of Christian authors, and wrote a commentary on virtually every book of the Bible.

But Jerome's greatest contribution to the Christian world was his translation of the Bible. In 382 Pope Damasus commissioned Jerome, then no more than thirty-five years of age, to produce a uniform text of the Latin Bible. He was to standardize the texts then in circulation. This was a daunting task, for according to Jerome, there were almost as many Latin texts as there were manuscripts.

Jerome first translated the Gospels and then the rest of the New Testament, although others may have had a hand in the translation of Acts to Revelation. Jerome next turned to the Psalms, producing three successive translations. The second one was based on the Greek translation of the Hebrew Old Testament called the Septuagint. This translation of the Psalms became the standard Latin version from Jerome's day to the present.

Between 390 and 404 Jerome translated the rest of the Old Testament into

THE RESULTS OF A DECISION
LONG AGO

Latin. In addition to the thirty-nine books of the Hebrew Old Testament, Jerome also translated fourteen Jewish religious books that the translators of the Septuagint had also included. These fourteen books were never part of the Jewish Bible and were called the Apocrypha, which came to mean "spurious" or "not genuine." Even though Jerome included the Apocrypha with the Old Testament as the Septuagint had done, in speaking of the thirty-nine books of the Old Testament, he wrote, "Anything outside of these must be placed within the Apocrypha," the noncanonical books. In other words, Jerome saw a definite distinction between the thirty-nine inspired books and the Apocrypha.

Jerome's translation became known as the Vulgate. At the time of the Reformation, the pope called the Council of Trent to attempt to stem the tide of Protestantism. There in an attempt to differentiate the Roman Catholic Church from the Reformers, the Council declared the Latin Vulgate, including the Apocrypha, to be the authoritative Bible in matters of doctrine, while the Reformers recognized only the New Testament and the original thirty-nine books of the Old Testament.

Whereas Jerome had included the Apocrypha in the Vulgate as uninspired books, the Council of Trent declared them to be inspired. And so the difference between the Roman Catholic and the Protestant Bible was born.

Reflection

What difference does it make which books are in the Bible? How important is it that our Old Testament is the same as that of the Jews? When Jesus and the New Testament writers spoke of the Old Testament as authoritative, why is it important to know to which books they were referring?

All Scripture is inspired by God and is useful to teach us what is true and to make us realize what is wrong in our lives. It straightens us out and teaches us to do what is right. 2 TIMOTHY 3:16

October 1

What determines how long an empire will last?

IN 539 B.C., Cyrus II, the Persian king of the Medes and the Persians, conquered Babylon.[1] God had referred to Cyrus as his anointed who would fulfill his purposes (Isaiah 45:1-6). God had prophesied of Cyrus: "Before him, mighty kings will be paralyzed with fear. Their fortress gates will be opened, never again to shut against him" (Isaiah 45:1). To Cyrus himself the Lord said, "I will go before you, Cyrus. . . . I will smash down the gates of bronze and cut through bars of iron" (v. 2).

That is exactly what happened. The first step in Cyrus II's ascendancy to power was a successful rebellion against his Median overlord, who was also his grandfather. As a result, the entire Median army defected from his grandfather to him. The resulting nation is often referred to as "Medo-Persia" since the two former nations were combined into one. Then Cyrus conquered Babylon, and for the next two centuries the Medo-Persian Empire dominated the civilized world.

In the vision of the four beasts recorded in Daniel 7, Daniel writes, "Then I saw a second beast, and it looked like a bear. It was rearing up on one side, and it had three ribs in its mouth between its teeth. And I heard a voice saying to it, 'Get up! Devour many people!' " (v. 5). Here "rearing up on one side" is a reference to the ascendancy of the Persians over the Medes, and the three ribs in its mouth is most likely a prophecy of the three major victories of Medo-Persia over Lydia (546 B.C.), Babylon (539 B.C.), and Egypt (525 B.C.).

The end of the Medo-Persian Empire is prophesied in Daniel 8. Here Medo-Persia is symbolized by a ram with two horns representing Media and Persia: "One of the horns was longer than the other, even though it had begun to grow later than the shorter one" (v. 3), referring to the fact that Persia developed later as a power than Media but became the more powerful of the two. In the vision Daniel says that Medo-Persia "did as it pleased and became very great" (v. 4).

Daniel also relates that "suddenly a male goat [Greece] appeared from the west. . . . This goat . . . had one very large horn between its eyes [Alexander the Great]" (v. 5). The nation that was to defeat Medo-Persia and become the next world empire was Greece, under the leadership of Alexander the Great.[2] Becoming king of Macedon at the age of twenty, Alexander led a confederacy of Greek states to conquer Medo-Persia.

THE END OF AN EMPIRE

The first battle against Persia was at Issus in modern-day Turkey. There Alexander defeated Darius III on a narrow plain, where the Persians lost the advantage of their superior numbers.

Alexander then marched south toward Egypt. On the way he visited the temple in Jerusalem, where he offered sacrifices to God under the supervision of the high priest Jaddua. Then the high priest showed Alexander the prophecy of Daniel 8 that he was the one who was to conquer Persia. Alexander accepted the prophecy and as a result became favorably disposed toward the Jews, allowing them to continue to follow their religious practices and exempting them from paying tribute in sabbatical years when their fields lay fallow.

Alexander's fateful battle with Persia occurred on **October 1, 331** B.C., at Gaugamela in present-day northern Iraq when he was just twenty-five years old. There the Persians were decisively defeated. Daniel's vision described it: "The goat [Greece] charged furiously at the ram [Medo-Persia] and struck it, breaking off both its horns [Media and Persia]. Now the ram was helpless, and the goat knocked it down and trampled it. There was no one who could rescue the ram from the goat's power" (v. 7).

An empire that "did as it pleased" (v. 4) brought God's judgment upon itself.

Reflection

When you listen to the news, do you think about the role that God's hand plays in the affairs of nations? What are some examples? What does that tell us about God?

❧

Praise the name of God forever and ever, for he alone has all wisdom and power. He determines the course of world events; he removes kings and sets others on the throne. DANIEL 2:20-21

October 2

It's remarkable what can be accomplished with God's help.

THE JEWS had been back in Jerusalem for over ninety years since the Babylonian captivity. Back in Persia, Nehemiah, a Jew, was the cupbearer to King Artaxerxes (c. 465–424 B.C.). The cupbearer was an official of high rank whose duty was to serve the king his wine, often tasting it first to ensure it wasn't poisoned. Nehemiah received a report from Jerusalem that the walls and gates of Jerusalem were broken down, making the city impossible to defend (Nehemiah 1:1-3). After fasting and praying, Nehemiah asked the Persian king whether he could go to Jerusalem to rebuild its walls. Artaxerxes agreed, appointed Nehemiah governor of Judah, and sent him to Jerusalem (1:4–2:9; 5:14).

Upon arriving in Jerusalem, Nehemiah enlisted the help of everyone in the project, and they responded enthusiastically. When the news got out that the Jews were rebuilding the wall, Israel's enemies became alarmed. Sanballat, the governor of Samaria, Tobiah, from a powerful family in Ammon, and Geshem, the king of Kedar, an Arabian tribe, accused the Jews of rebelling against Persia. Nehemiah's reply was, "The God of heaven will help us succeed" (2:20).

The key to Nehemiah's success was that he had a plan and worked his plan. People were assigned to repair a particular portion of the wall, usually the section closest to their home. Eliashib the high priest set the example. He and his fellow priests rebuilt the Sheep Gate and its adjoining walls.

Once the building commenced, Sanballat became angry. Parading his Samaritan army past Jerusalem, he asked, "What does this bunch of poor, feeble Jews think they are doing?" (4:2).

Tobiah the Ammonite taunted, "That stone wall would collapse if even a fox walked along the top of it!" (v. 3).

What was Nehemiah's response? He prayed, "Hear us, O our God, for we are being mocked. May their scoffing fall back on their own heads, and may they themselves become captives in a foreign land! Do not ignore their guilt. Do not blot out their sins, for they have provoked you to anger here in the presence of the builders" (v. 4).

When Sanballat, Tobiah, and other enemies of the Jews learned that the wall was half built, they made plans to attack Jerusalem. In response, Nehemiah called together the exhausted workers and told them, "Don't be afraid of

AN AMAZING ACCOMPLISHMENT

the enemy! Remember the Lord, who is great and glorious, and fight for your friends, your families, and your homes!" He then posted half of his men on guard around the city while the other half worked on the wall. Everyone carried a weapon, and the city was guarded day and night (vv. 6-23).

When the walls were completely restored and all that remained was to hang the doors in the gates, Sanballat, Tobiah, and Geshem made four requests for a meeting with Nehemiah in a village half way between Samaria and Jerusalem. Nehemiah, realizing it was a trap, declined (6:1-4).

Then Sanballat sent a letter to Nehemiah saying, "Geshem tells me that everywhere he goes he hears that you and the Jews are planning to rebel and that is why you are building the wall. According to his reports, you plan to be their king. . . . You can be very sure that this report will get back to the king so I suggest that you come and talk it over with me" (vv. 5-7).

Nehemiah replied simply, "You know you are lying" (v. 8).

The project was finally completed on **October 2, 445 B.C.** The walls were rebuilt and the gates restored. This gigantic task had been completed in just fifty-two days! When the news reached their enemies, they were frightened and humiliated because even they realized that this had only been accomplished with God's help (vv. 15-16).[3]

Reflection

Have you faced projects that humanly speaking were too great to accomplish? Maybe you are facing one right now. Study Nehemiah's methodology to learn how you can succeed in spite of opposition. Remember, Nehemiah's God is your God too.

∽❧∾

Nothing is impossible with God.   LUKE 1:37

October 3

Some people are destined to write.

On October 3, 1832, a baby girl was born in the home of the pastor of the church in Froderyd, Sweden. She was named Carolina Sandell, but everyone called her Lina. A frail child from an early age, she preferred spending time in her father's study to playing with the other children outside.

At the age of twelve she was struck by a mysterious illness that left her paralyzed. One Sunday morning when everyone else had gone to church, she asked the Lord to help her get out of bed—and he did! In awe, she dressed herself and walked slowly across the room. She could hardly wait to tell her parents how God had answered her prayer and healed her.

A sensitive and expressive child, Lina started journaling at an early age. As she wrote down her thoughts, she discovered that they often came in poetry, and at the age of sixteen Lina published a small book of her poems.

When she was twenty-six, she left with her father on a trip to Gothenberg that changed her life. What started as a pleasant adventure resulted in tragedy. As they crossed Lake Vattern, the small boat lurched, throwing her father overboard, and before her horrified eyes, he drowned.

The next three years were a time of anguish and soul-searching for Lina. The only thing that brought her comfort was the writing of hymns that seemed to flow from her broken heart. Within a year of her father's death, fourteen of her hymns were published anonymously in the Christian periodical *Budbararen*. Those first fourteen remained the most popular of the 650 hymns she went on to write. Among the initial fourteen were "Children of the Heavenly Father" and "Day by Day."

At the age of thirty-five, Lina married C. O. Berg, a Stockholm merchant, but continued to write hymns under the initials "L. S." from her maiden name.

Her hymns were set to music by Oskar Ahnfelt, a former member of the Royal Opera who became known as the "Swedish troubadour." In a time of revival led by lay preacher Carl Rosenius, who also wrote hymns, Anhfelt traveled throughout Sweden singing Lina's songs, accompanying himself on his ten-stringed guitar. Lina once said, "Ahnfelt has sung my songs into the hearts of the people."

The other person who helped to make Lina's hymns known was Jenny Lind, the "Swedish Nightingale." Considered to be the greatest soprano of her day, Lind was a committed Christian who loved Rosenius's preaching and

WITH A SONG IN HER HEART

Ahnfelt's singing. Lind provided the funds for printing the first edition of *Ahnfelt's Songs,* which consisted primarily of the hymns of Lina Sandell and Carl Rosenius.

Jenny Lind not only was responsible for getting Lina's hymns into print but also popularizing them by singing them at many revival meetings. After giving up her operatic career, Jenny Lind's testimony to the Lord was largely known through her singing of Lina's hymns.

Lina died at the age of seventy-one. At her funeral the choir sang "Children of the Heavenly Father," and the congregation spontaneously joined in singing the beloved and familiar hymn:

> *Children of the heavenly Father*
> *Safely in his bosom gather;*
> *Nestling bird nor star in heaven*
> *Such a refuge e'er was given.*
>
> *God his own doth tend and nourish;*
> *In his holy courts they flourish;*
> *From all evil things he spares them;*
> *In his mighty arms he bears them.*

For many the emotional tug of those beautiful words continues to this day.

Reflection

Do you have a favorite hymn? What makes it special to you? Is it the words or a memory you associate with it? All too often we pay little attention to the words of our favorite hymns. Identify your favorite hymn, and carefully think through the words, line by line. Let it be God's message to you today.

I think how much you have helped me; I sing for joy in the shadow of your protecting wings.   PSALM 63:7

October 4

This match made in heaven had to wait until heaven.

DAVID BRAINERD was born in 1718 in Connecticut.[4] He entered Yale in 1739, shortly after his conversion to Christ. During his second year George Whitefield brought the Great Awakening to Yale, and tensions arose between students who were awakened and faculty members who weren't.

Jonathan Edwards[5] was invited to preach at the 1741 commencement in hopes that he would dampen the students' enthusiasm for the revival. But his sermon was not what the faculty wanted to hear. He sided with the students and argued that the Great Awakening was a genuine work of God. That very morning the trustees had voted that a student could be expelled for accusing a faculty member of being unconverted. In his address that afternoon Edwards stated, "It is no evidence that a work is not a work of God, if many that are subjects of it . . . are guilty of [so] great forwardness to censure others as unconverted." This also was the first meeting of David Brainerd and Jonathan Edwards, and they soon realized that they had much in common and saw each other often.

One wonders if Jonathan Edwards felt partly responsible when the following year David Brainerd, though first in his class, was expelled from Yale for being overheard saying that a certain tutor "had no more grace than a chair."

Brainerd found his life calling as a missionary to the Indians. His first assignment was to work among the Mohican Indians at Kaunaumeek, Massachusetts, about twenty miles northwest of Stockbridge, where Jonathan Edwards later served as a missionary.

During this time Brainerd took many trips to Northampton, Massachusetts, where Jonathan Edwards pastored. One of the benefits of visiting his mentor was getting to know Jerusha, Edwards's second daughter. They fell in love and eventually became engaged. She sometimes accompanied him when he preached in New England churches, and they corresponded throughout his missionary work among the Indians.

After a year in Massachusetts, Brainerd was reassigned to work among the Indians of Crossweeksung, New Jersey. There Brainerd saw 130 Indians come to Christ. Stricken with tuberculosis, he finally became too weak to minister, and in May of 1747 Jonathan Edwards invited him to stay at his home. Jerusha served as his very attentive nurse. Brainerd wrote, "It is a little piece of heaven to be in her presence."

A MATCH MADE IN HEAVEN

On Sunday, **October 4, 1747,** Brainerd knew he was about to die. As Jerusha entered his room that morning he said, "Dear Jerusha, are you willing to part with me? I am willing to part with you; I am willing to part with all my friends; I am willing to part with my dear brother John. . . . I have committed him and all my friends to God and can leave them with God. Though, if I had thought I should not see you and be happy with you in another world, I could not bear to part with you. But we shall spend a happy eternity together."

Five days later David Brainerd was dead at the age of twenty-nine. Jerusha Edwards came down with tuberculosis as well and died the following Valentine's Day at the age of eighteen, joining her beloved in eternity. Her family buried her next to David.

In 1749 Jonathan Edwards published the diaries of Brainerd, the one who was to have been his son-in-law. He called it *The Life of Brainerd*. It has been in print continuously to this day and has been used by God to shape the lives of John Wesley,[6] Henry Martyn, William Carey,[7] Robert Morrison, Robert Murray McCheyne,[8] David Livingston, Andrew Murray, Jim Elliot[9] and tens of thousands of others.

David and Jerusha's lives were brief, but their joy in heaven is great!

Reflection

David Brainerd hoped to marry Jerusha Edwards, but it was not part of God's plan for them. Imagine Jerusha Edwards's grief at his death. Yet God brought great glory to himself out of their short lives. When we experience intense disappointments in our lives, let us think of David and Jerusha and how God used their lives in a different way than they anticipated. They got to be together but not on this earth.

He will remove all of their sorrows, and there will be no more death or sorrow or crying or pain. REVELATION 21:4

October 5

What would you say in a last letter to your children?

IN APRIL 1573 Maeyken Wens was arrested along with four others as they met to study the Bible in Antwerp. Maeyken was the wife of an Anabaptist minister, Mattheus Wens, who by trade was a mason. The Anabaptists believed in believer's baptism and later called themselves Mennonites after their leader Menno Simons.

After their arrest, they were bound and placed in prison under the most severe conditions. Maeyken was repeatedly interrogated by priests, who tried to get her to deny her beliefs. When intimidation didn't work, they used torture. Still she would not deny her Lord.

Finally on **October 5, 1573,** Maeyken Wens and the four others arrested with her were sentenced to be burned at the stake. That day Maeyken wrote a final letter to her son Adriaen, a boy of about fifteen:

> O my dear son, though I am taken from you here, strive from your youth to fear God, and you shall have your mother again up yonder in the New Jerusalem, where parting will be no more. My dear son, I hope now to go before you; follow me thus as much as you value your soul, for besides this there shall be found no other way to salvation. Thus, I will now commend you to the Lord; may he keep you. I trust the Lord will do it if you seek him. Love one another all the days of your life; take little Hans on your arm now and then for me. And if your father should be taken from you, care for one another. The Lord keep you one and all. My dear children kiss one another once for me, for remembrance. Adieu, my dear children all of you. My dear son, do not be afraid of this suffering; it is nothing compared to that which shall endure forever. The Lord takes away all fear; I did not know what to do for joy when I was sentenced. Hence cease not to fear God because of this temporal death; I cannot fully thank my God for the great grace which he has shown me. Adieu once more, my dear son Adriaen; ever be kind to your afflicted father all the days of your life, and do not grieve him; this I pray all of you, for what I write to the oldest, I also mean to say to the youngest. Herewith I will commend you to the Lord once more. I have written this, after I was sentenced to die for the testimony of Jesus Christ, on the fifth day of October, in the year of our Lord Jesus Christ, 1573.
>
> Maeyken Wens

A MOTHER'S LEGACY

The following day Maeyken Wens and the other believers were prepared for execution. The executioner came to their cells and had them each stick out their tongues. He placed an iron clamp over the tongue, tightened it with a vice screw and then burned the tip of the tongue so it would swell and not be able to be pulled out of the clamp. These tongue screws prevented the victims from speaking out at their execution. Then the martyrs were marched to Antwerp's marketplace.

Young Adriaen could not stay away from his mother's execution and came, carrying three-year-old Hans, his youngest brother. However, when his mother was brought forward and tied to her stake, he fainted and didn't regain consciousness until his mother and the others had been burned.

Adriaen lingered behind after everyone had left the marketplace and went to search the ashes where his mother had been burned. There he found her tongue screw.

Reflection

What is the legacy that you wish to pass on to your children and grandchildren? It might be worthwhile to write letters to your children and grandchildren explaining what you hold dear and what you wish them to take from you. Such a letter is sometimes referred to as an "ethical will" and can be of much more value to our descendants than the possessions they might receive from our last will and testament.

I know that you sincerely trust the Lord, for you have the faith of your mother, Eunice, and your grandmother, Lois. 2 TIMOTHY 1:5

October 6

You have to be careful what you pray for.

In 1871 D. L. Moody was a well-known evangelical leader in Chicago.[10] Seven years before, at the age of just twenty-seven, he had founded the Illinois Street Church, which today is Moody Memorial Church. In the late 1860s he served as president of the Chicago YMCA and had a central role in building the first YMCA building in America, Farwell Hall, which had a seating capacity of three thousand. He preached on Sunday nights in Farwell Hall since the attendance had outgrown the Illinois Street Church.

At the time Moody was struggling with what God was calling him to do. He knew that he had to decide between being a social-religious organizer through the YMCA and being an evangelist. Deep down, Moody felt that God was calling him to a national evangelistic ministry, but rejected the idea because his ego was tied up in his Chicago projects.

His inner conflict began to diminish the power of his preaching. This became especially clear to two women in his church, Sarah Anne Cook and a Mrs. Hawxhurst. Cook, a recent immigrant from England and a Free Methodist, became convinced that Moody needed the baptism of the Holy Ghost and of fire. The women began making this a matter of earnest prayer. They sat in the front row and prayed whenever he preached.

The women shared their concern with Moody and eventually set up a regular Friday afternoon prayer time with him. Finally Moody's spiritual frustration was so great that on **October 6, 1871**, as they met for prayer, he rolled on the floor and tearfully asked God to baptize him with the Holy Spirit and fire.

The next Sunday night, October 8, Farwell Hall was full as Moody preached on "What then shall I do with Jesus which is called Christ?" He closed his message by saying, "I wish you would take this text home with you and turn it over in your minds during the week, and next Sabbath we will come to Calvary and the cross, and we will decide what to do with Jesus of Nazareth." Following the sermon his song leader, Ira Sankey, sang:

> *Today the Saviour calls,*
> *For refuge fly*
> *The storm of justice falls,*
> *And death is nigh.*

BAPTISM OF FIRE

Suddenly his voice was drowned out by the sound of fire engines rushing past the hall. Shouting could be heard in the streets, and Moody hurriedly closed the service.

Moody and Sankey left through the back door and saw flames reaching the sky to the southwest, upwind from the city's downtown. Moody rushed home to his family as the southwest wind reached almost hurricane force. It was the Great Chicago Fire, and it lasted until the following Wednesday. The fire destroyed Moody's house, the Illinois Street Church, and Farwell Hall.

Everything that held Moody to Chicago was in ashes. The only chain still binding him to Chicago was his own will. Weeks later as he quietly walked down a busy street in New York City, that last chain snapped, and he surrendered his will to God. Moody went on to become the leading evangelist in the English-speaking world at the end of the nineteenth century. He traveled over one million miles and presented the gospel by voice and written word to more than one hundred million people.

On the twenty-second anniversary of the Chicago Fire, Moody spoke reflectively: "I have never seen that congregation since, and I never will meet those people again until I meet them in another world. But I want to tell you of one lesson I learned that night, which I have never forgotten, and that is, when I preach, to press Christ upon the people then and there, and try to bring them to a decision on the spot. . . . I have asked God many times to forgive me for telling people that night to take a week to think it over."

Reflection

When we pray it is of utmost importance that we pray that God's will, not ours, be done. God desires that we conform our will to his. Moody learned this lesson the hard way. Remember to be careful what you ask of God because you just might get it!

May your will be done here on earth, just as it is in heaven.

MATTHEW 6:10

October 7

"Not by might, nor by power, but by my spirit, saith the Lord of hosts"
(Zechariah 4:6, KJV).

THESE WORDS of Zechariah were the motto of Jonathan Goforth,[11] and his life illustrated their truth. One of eleven children, Goforth was born on a farm near London, Ontario, in 1859. His spiritual pilgrimage began at the age of eighteen as he was struggling to finish high school. A Presbyterian pastor named Lachlan Cameron visited the school frequently to hold Bible studies. Goforth took a liking to the pastor and decided to visit his church. On his third visit Goforth felt as if the pastor were preaching directly to him. At the end of the sermon Goforth privately bowed his head and yielded himself to Christ.

Some time later when visiting his brother Will's farm fifteen miles away, Will's father-in-law gave Goforth a copy of *The Memoirs of Robert Murray M'Cheyne*. On the ride home in his horse and buggy, he started reading the story of the Church of Scotland pastor and soul winner. He became so engrossed in it that he tethered his horse to a tree and read until the sun was about to set. Captivated by M'Cheyne's burden for evangelism, Goforth resolved to devote his life to leading the unsaved to the Savior.

While still in high school, Goforth heard a missionary to the Far East express his heartbreak that he had not been able to find any young men to carry on the work that he had begun. Goforth heard the Lord asking, "Who will go for us and whom shall we send?" and he answered, "Here am I; send me." That hour marked the beginning of Jonathan Goforth's missionary career.

While attending Knox College in Toronto, he spent much time visiting the city's slums. It was in connection with his mission work in Toronto that he met Rosalind Bell-Smith, whom everyone knew as Rose, a member of a wealthy Episcopalian family and more important, a born-again Christian. Upon meeting him Rose noticed the shabbiness of his clothes but couldn't help being taken by the shining purpose in his eyes. A few days later she was able to sneak a peek at his well-worn Bible and found it filled with notes from cover to cover. She decided that this was the man she wanted to marry. Jonathan felt the same way, and they were married in October 1884. Four months later they sailed for China.

In China Jonathan and Rose and their growing family traveled from place to place doing evangelistic work. His ministry was truly blessed by God, and many hundreds came to know Christ through his preaching. But the hardships of missionary life cost them dearly—five of their eleven children died in China.

Goforth went to Korea to see firsthand the results of the revival of 1907 that occurred there. He returned to China with some Koreans who had participated, and together they brought the revival to China.

When nearly seventy years old, Goforth pioneered a new work in Manchuria and in a short period of time won thousands to Christ and trained over seventy evangelists to carry on the work. Even after going blind, he stayed on ministering for another year.

Returning to Canada in 1934, Goforth was much in demand as a speaker. Although in his mid-seventies and now blind, he spoke at 481 meetings in eighteen months.

His last Sunday in Toronto he spoke four times. Then on **October 7, 1936,** he traveled forty miles to give what would be his final address. The next morning Rose woke early, thinking Jonathan was still sleeping, but then she realized that he had passed into the land that is fairer than day.

A few weeks earlier he had said that he rejoiced to know that the first face he would see upon dying would be his Savior's, and now he saw him face-to-face.

Reflection

God took a Canadian farm boy and by his Spirit made him one of the most productive missionaries of all time. His secret was that he was wholly committed to God and trusted that he would work through him by his Spirit. What can you learn from Jonathan Goforth's life?

When the Holy Spirit has come upon you, you will receive power and will tell people about me everywhere—in Jerusalem, throughout Judea, in Samaria, and to the ends of the earth.　　ACTS 1:8

October 8

Hearing directly from God gets your attention!

GOD HAD greatly blessed his people, Israel, through Nehemiah, a Jew, who was the cupbearer to King Artaxerxes I of Persia (c. 465–424 B.C.). King Artaxerxes had made Nehemiah governor of Judah and as governor he had directed the rebuilding of the wall of Jerusalem in just fifty-two days (Nehemiah 1:1–6:16).[12]

However, restoration of the walls and gates was not the most important challenge facing the Jews returning to Jerusalem. Of far greater importance was their need for spiritual restoration. Therefore on **October 8, 445 B.C.**, Ezra the priest brought the scroll of the Law before an assembly of all the Jews in Jerusalem. He stood on a high wooden platform that had been built for the occasion. On the platform with Ezra were thirteen assistants, probably priests or Levites. The assembly included not only men and women but also all children old enough to understand the reading of the Law (8:1-4).

The date itself was significant, for in the Hebrew civil calendar this was the first day of the year. Today it is celebrated as New Year's Day, or Rosh Hashanah, meaning "the beginning of the year." Of this day God had instructed in the law, "You are to celebrate a day of complete rest. All your work must stop on that day. You will call the people to a sacred assembly—the Festival of Trumpets—with loud blasts from a trumpet" (Leviticus 23:24). The purpose was to assemble Israel to rejoice before the Lord.

Ezra unrolled the scroll at daybreak, and as he did so, everyone stood up. Before Ezra began to read, he praised the Lord, the great God whose word he was about to read, and all the people lifted their hands toward heaven and shouted, "Amen! Amen!" Then they bowed down and worshiped the Lord with their faces to the ground (Nehemiah 8:6).

When the people rose to their feet, Ezra began to read and continued until noon. Although the people stood for five to six hours, they listened attentively and began to weep as they realized that what they were hearing were the very words of God (vv. 2-9).

As the Law was being read, thirteen additional Levites circulated through the crowd, explaining what was being read so that everyone could understand it (vv. 7-8).

The people's response to the reading was to weep before the Lord, but Nehemiah, Ezra, and the Levites said to them, "Don't weep on such a day as this! For today is a sacred day before the Lord your God. . . . Go and celebrate with a feast of choice foods and sweet drinks, and share gifts of food with people who have nothing prepared. . . . Don't be dejected and sad, for the joy of the Lord is your strength!" They wanted the people to realize that in spite of their sins, their strength against their enemies in the coming years would be their joy in their Savior God (vv. 9-10).

The people then left the assembly in the early afternoon so they could prepare a holiday meal and celebrate with great joy, for they had heard God's words and understood them (v. 12).

The reading of the Law on **October 8, 445** B.C., was a turning point in the history of Israel. Up to then Israel had been a people whose religious life centered around the temple. On this day they became a people whose religious life centered on a book—God's book.[13]

Reflection

What part does the Bible play in your spiritual life? Do you prefer to read it yourself or to listen to what others have to say about its teachings? Are you a person of the Book? God works in the lives of his people using two agents, his Spirit and his Word. He controls his Spirit, but we are responsible to appropriate his Word in our lives.

I have hidden your word in my heart, that I might not sin against you.
PSALM 119:11

October 9

When all else fails, read the directions.

THE PREVIOUS day all of Israel had heard God's Law read to them.[14] Realizing how ignorant they were of it, the family leaders, priests, and Levites met with Ezra on **October 9, 445 B.C.**, to go over the Law in greater detail.

As they gathered around Ezra in the first group Bible study recorded in Scripture, they came to Leviticus 23:39-43. They read there that they were to build shelters or booths in which to live during the seven days of the Feast of Tabernacles, which was less than two weeks away. They apparently had been offering the prescribed sacrifices at the Feast of Tabernacles (Ezra 3:4) but had forgotten the commandment to live outside in handmade shelters to remind them of God's provision for them during their wilderness wanderings.

Realizing that his people were being disobedient to God's Law out of ignorance, Ezra commanded that a proclamation be made in Jerusalem and throughout all the Jewish towns telling the people to go to the hills to gather branches for making shelters. They would live in them during the Feast of Tabernacles, which would begin on October 22.

The people had almost two weeks to make their preparations, but it would be a busy time because October 17, just five days before the Feast of Tabernacles, was the Day of Atonement, or Yom Kippur. This was the one fast day stipulated in the Old Testament. No work was to be done on this day, and although men from other cities were not required to appear in Jerusalem, there was to be a sacred assembly of the Jewish men who were already there (Leviticus 23:27-28).

The Day of Atonement was the "Good Friday" of the Old Testament. On this day the high priest entered the Holy of Holies in the temple and made atonement for the sins of God's people. A sinner himself, the high priest first shed his usual garments, bathed himself, and then dressed in a white garment without ornamentation, symbolizing his role as a supplicant seeking forgiveness and also picturing the purity required of one entering God's presence. He then entered the Holy of Holies and sprinkled the blood of a sacrificial animal on the ark of the covenant, where the presence of God dwelt, thereby making atonement for the sins of God's people (16:1-34). This was a symbol of what the Lord Jesus would one day do. "Christ has now become the High Priest over all the good things that have come. He has entered that great, perfect sanctuary in heaven, not made by human hands and not part of this created world. Once for all time he took blood into that Most Holy Place, but not the blood of goats and calves. He took his own blood, and with it he secured our salvation forever" (Hebrews 9:11-12).

From the reading of the Law the previous day, Ezra, Nehemiah, and the Jewish leaders realized that they had forgotten to follow all of God's Law in the observance in the Feast of Tabernacles, so they sought to rectify it immediately.

Reflection

Ezra and the Jewish leaders of his day realized the necessity of under-standing all that God had revealed in order to serve him faithfully. Their knowledge of God's plan for the world was limited compared to what God subsequently revealed to us in the New Testament, but they sought to be faithful to him by understanding and obeying what they did have. Do you share that desire to be faithful to God's Word?

The law of the Lord is perfect, reviving the soul. The decrees of the Lord are trustworthy, making wise the simple. The commandments of the Lord are right, bringing joy to the heart. The commands of the Lord are clear, giving insight to life. Reverence for the Lord is pure, lasting forever. The laws of the Lord are true; each one is fair. They are more desirable than gold, even the finest gold. They are sweeter than honey, even honey dripping from the comb. They are a warning to those who hear them; there is great reward for those who obey them.   PSALM 19:7-11

October 10

He switched from the practice of law to pleading the cause of Christ.

In 1818 a twenty-six-year-old man named Charles Finney began a law apprenticeship in an attorney's office in Adams, New York. Although he had a limited formal education, within just three years he became a junior partner in the law firm.

As Finney studied law, the authors he read often quoted the Bible. Realizing his own ignorance of the Scriptures, he began to study them for himself.

When a new minister came to the local Presbyterian church, Finney began to attend. He got very little from the sermons and was rather skeptical of the whole concept of God answering prayer, but he loved music and volunteered to be the choir director.

Then in the summer of 1821 the pastor took a trip to visit his sick sister and told his replacement just to read sermons from a book. Surprisingly, the Holy Spirit began to move among the church members and Finney sensed that something was about to happen.

One day as Finney was returning from a legal appointment, he walked by a schoolhouse and heard a man praying inside. The words of that prayer stuck in his mind and affected him more than all the sermons he had heard previously. He started to spend a lot of time wondering about his own salvation.

Finney later recounted what happened on a particularly significant day, **October 10, 1821:**

> At an early hour I started for the office. But just before I arrived at the office, something seemed to confront me with questions like these: . . . "Did you not promise to give your heart to God? And what are you trying to do? Are you endeavoring to work out a righteousness of your own?"
>
> Just at that point the whole question of God's salvation opened to my mind in a manner most marvelous to me. . . . I saw then as clearly as I ever had in my life, the reality and the fullness of the atonement of Christ. I saw that his work was a finished work; that instead of having, or needing, any righteousness of my own to recommend me to God, I had to submit myself to the righteousness of God through Christ. It was full and complete, and all that was necessary on my part was to . . . give up my sins and accept Christ. Salvation, it seemed to me, instead

of being a thing to be wrought out by one's own works, was a thing to be found entirely in the Lord Jesus Christ, who presented Himself before me as my God and Savior.

Instead of going to his office, Finney went into a nearby woods and spent the morning wrestling with God in prayer until he reported, "I found that my mind had become most wonderfully quiet and peaceful."

The next day a client who was a deacon from his church came into his office and reminded him, "Mr. Finney, do you recollect that my case is to be tried at ten this morning?"

Finney replied, "Deacon, I have a retainer from the Lord Jesus Christ to plead His cause, and I cannot plead yours."

Stunned by his answer, the deacon only later came to understand what Finney meant when he himself shortly thereafter experienced the same changed life that Finney had.

Charles Finney went on to become the leading revivalist of the nineteenth century with approximately half a million people coming to Christ through the influence of his ministry. Beginning in upstate New York, his revivals swept through New York City, Philadelphia, Boston, and Rochester. In 1835 he became professor of theology at the newly formed Oberlin Collegiate Institute, now Oberlin College. He served as the college's president from 1851 to 1866, and it all started on that fateful day in 1821 when Charles Finney switched from the practice of law to pleading the cause of Christ.

Reflection

Like Charles Finney, we all face the choice of whether to trust our own righteousness to make us acceptable to God or to accept the forgiveness and righteousness offered by Jesus Christ. In which righteousness are you trusting?

∽◈∽

Now I will expose your so-called good deeds that you consider so righteous. None of them will benefit or save you.   ISAIAH 57:12

October 11

Why would anyone sail west to get to the east?

In 1451 a boy named Cristoforo Colombo was born in Genoa. We know him as Christopher Columbus. "Christopher" means "Christ Bearer," and he was undoubtedly named after St. Christopher, the patron saint of travelers. In those days people took the meaning of their name seriously, and Columbus took his name as a sign that he was to bear the name of Christ across the seas to those who didn't know him.

By the age of twenty, Columbus had already experienced shipwreck off the coast of Portugal. After making it to shore, he joined his brother in Lisbon. By 1484 the two brothers were employed as mapmakers. Columbus became convinced that the shortcut to the Orient was west. He calculated that the distance from the Canary Islands to Japan was 2,760 miles. He had obviously figured wrong, but God knew there was something important to discover just 150 miles farther than where Columbus thought Japan would be.

Columbus made a proposal to King John II of Portugal that he finance a westward expedition to the Orient but was turned down. He then became convinced that God wanted King Ferdinand and Queen Isabella of Spain to be his sponsors.[15] They finally agreed.

Before dawn on August 3, 1492, Columbus knelt on the dock to receive Holy Communion before rowing out to board the *Santa Maria* where his crew waited. Two accompanying ships, the *Pinta* and the *Nina,* were captained by Martin and Vicente Pinzon, two brothers who shared his vision.[16]

As his ship sailed westward toward the unknown, Columbus wrote in his journal Bible verses such as "Listen to me, all of you in far-off lands! The Lord called me before my birth; from within the womb he called me by name. . . . I will make you a light to the Gentiles, and you will bring my salvation to the ends of the earth" (Isaiah 49:1, 6).

On October 9 there was an emergency conference between Columbus and Martin and Vincente Pinzan. The brothers warned Columbus that they feared a mutiny unless they immediately turned back to Spain. Columbus was able to bargain with them for three more days, agreeing that if they had not sighted land by October 12, he would turn back.

The next day the convoy sailed hard, covering the second most miles of any day on the trip thus far. That day, for the first time, Columbus was openly challenged by his crew.

THE VOYAGE OF THE "CHRIST BEARER"

By **October 11, 1492,** the men were tense and the officers testy, but Columbus was confident that God would soon reveal the promised land. Then a shout went up from the *Pinta* that a reed and a small piece of wood that obviously had been shaped by a man were seen in the water. Next, the *Nina* sighted a small twig with roses on it. The mood of the crew was transformed. With their eyes glued to the horizon, Columbus and a seaman briefly saw a light at 10 P.M. that disappeared within a few minutes.

At 2 A.M. the next morning, just four hours before dawn on the third and final day before turning back, the lookout aboard the *Pinta* shouted, "Land! Land!" There in the moonlight they saw a low white cliff.

Columbus was the first person to set foot on land. He named the island San Salvador meaning, "Holy Savior." They all knelt in the sand with tears in their eyes as Columbus prayed, "O Lord, Almighty and everlasting God, by thy holy Word thou hast created the heaven, and the earth, and the sea; blessed and glorified be thy name and praised be thy majesty, which hath deigned to use us, thy humble servants, that thy holy Name may be proclaimed in this second part of the earth."

Reflection

To what extent do you believe that God was involved in Columbus's discovery of America, this "second part of the earth"? Do you believe Columbus was sincere in desiring the spread the gospel? Do you see any relationship between Columbus's goal and the later success of the gospel in the Americas?

∽≪⧫

Only ask, and I will give you the nations as your inheritance, the ends of the earth as your possession.   PSALM 2:8

October 12

Arrogance can spell ruin.

THE YEAR was 539 B.C., and the Babylonian Empire had dominated the Near East since 626 B.C. As king of Babylon, Nebuchadnezzar had taken the Jews captive to Babylon, where they still remained,[17] and Nabonidus, his son-in-law, now ruled the empire together with his son Belshazzar.

Cyrus II[18] king of Persia, now commanded the combined Medo-Persian forces against the Babylonians. Nabonidus was in charge of the Babylonian army in the field while Belshazzar was in charge of the city of Babylon. Herodotus, the Greek historian, reports, "A battle was fought at a short distance from the city, in which the Babylonians were defeated by the Persian king, whereupon they withdrew within their defenses. Here they shut themselves up and made light of this siege, having laid in a store of provisions for many years in preparation against this attack."

We see how lightly the Babylonians took this siege by what happened the next day. On **October 12, 539 B.C.**, in spite of the siege, King Belshazzar held a state banquet in his palace in the city of Babylon for a thousand of his nobles. As the wine was flowing freely, Belshazzar remembered the beautiful gold and silver cups that Nebuchadnezzar had taken from the temple in Jerusalem when he had defeated the Jews. Belshazzar gave orders to bring in the temple cups so that the king and his guests might drink from them (Daniel 5:1-4).

As they were drinking toasts to their idols, suddenly everyone saw the fingers of a human hand writing on the wall. The king turned pale with such fear that his legs gave way as terror gripped him (vv. 5-6).

Belshazzar immediately demanded that his enchanters, astrologers, and fortune-tellers be brought before him to interpret the writing. But none could. Now Belshazzar was even more alarmed (vv. 7-9).

When the queen mother heard what was happening, she hurried to the banquet hall and said to Belshazzar, "Don't be so pale and afraid about this. There is a man in your kingdom who has within him the spirit of the holy gods. . . . This man Daniel . . . is filled with divine knowledge and understanding. He can interpret dreams, explain riddles, and solve difficult problems. Call for Daniel, and he will tell you what the writing means" (vv. 10-12).

Daniel was summoned, and the king said, "I have heard that you have the spirit of the gods within you. . . . If you can read these words and tell me their meaning, you will be clothed in purple robes of royal honor, and you will wear a gold chain around your neck. You will become the third highest ruler in the kingdom" (vv. 13-16).

Daniel answered, "Keep your gifts or give them to someone else, but I will tell you what the writing means. . . . [Y]ou have defied the Lord of heaven and have had these cups from his Temple brought before you. You and your [guests] have been drinking wine from them while praising gods of silver, gold, bronze, iron, wood, and stone. . . . So God has sent this hand to write a message.

"This is the message that was written: MENE, MENE, TEKEL, PARSIN. This is what these words mean: *Mene* means 'numbered'—God has numbered the days of your reign and has brought it to an end. *Tekel* means 'weighed'—you have been weighed on the balances and have failed the test. *Parsin* means 'divided'—your kingdom has been divided and given to the Medes and Persians" (vv. 17-28).

That very night the Medo-Persian army diverted the waters of the Euphrates River that flowed through the city of Babylon. With the water in the riverbed reduced, the army was able to enter the city under cover of darkness. They captured Babylon and killed Belshazzar before his defenders knew what had happened (Daniel 5:30).

Reflection

Sometimes it seems as though the government is filled with corrupt officials. But God doesn't let them get away with it. Can you think of any examples of corrupt officials who have experienced the consequences of their behavior as Belshazzar did? What does that teach you about God?

All [God's] acts are just and true, and he is able to humble those who are proud.   DANIEL 4:37

October 13

Can God be trusted with our children?

THE EARLY years on the mission field were very difficult for Jonathan and Rose Goforth.[19] Four of their eight children died in their first twelve years in China. During the Boxer Rebellion of 1900, the family barely escaped with their lives.[20] They traveled home to Canada for a brief furlough and then returned to China with a new addition to their family, little Constance, who was born during the furlough.

Back in China, Jonathan's new responsibility was to evangelize one-third of the Changte region. On their way to the mission station, Jonathan told Rose about the plan he felt God had given him to reach this goal. He would send one of his assistants ahead to rent a place for the family to live for a month. Once there, Jonathan would preach in the streets or villages during the day while Rose would preach to women in their courtyard. Each evening they would hold a service in their home with Jonathan preaching and Rose playing the organ. At the end of the month they would move to another town, leaving behind an evangelist to teach the new believers.

Rose thought it sounded like a wonderful plan, but as they had five little ones, she was adamantly against it. She would remain at their home at the Changte mission station, and that was that. Having already buried four children in China, she couldn't bear the thought of losing another, and she was convinced Jonathan's plan would put the children's lives at risk.

As they made the long river journey to Changte, Jonathan continued to plead with Rose. He also loved their children dearly and couldn't bear the thought of losing another, yet God had given him an inexplicable peace that they would be safe if they followed this plan.

Finally Jonathan said to her, "Rose, I am so sure this plan is of God that I fear for the children if you disobey his call. The safest place for the children is the path of duty. You think you can keep your children safe in your comfortable home in Changte, but God may show you you cannot. But he can and will keep the children if you trust him and step out in faith!"

The Goforths reached their home at Changte on a Saturday evening. On Sunday morning Rose left the children with their faithful servant. Two hours later Rose returned to find their son Wallace ill. The doctor was called, and he diagnosed it as one of the worst cases of dysentery he had ever seen.

For two weeks Jonathan and Rose struggled for the child's life. Finally

A MOTHER'S AGONY

Wallace began to recover. When Jonathan felt confident that his son would survive, he left to begin his first evangelistic tour alone.

The day after Jonathan left, baby Constance became suddenly ill, just as Wallace had, only much worse. By the time Jonathan arrived, Constance was dying. As the two parents knelt beside her, Rose suddenly experienced a revelation of God's love in a way she hadn't considered before—as a Father. All of a sudden she was filled with the realization that her heavenly Father could be trusted to keep her children. It so overwhelmed her that she could only bow her head and pray, "O God, it is too late for Constance, but I will trust. I will go where you want me to go. But keep my children!"

Such peace and joy came over Rose that when Jonathan turned to her and sorrowfully said, "Constance is gone," she was comforted knowing that her baby's life had not been in vain.

Little Constance was buried next to two of her sisters on **October 13, 1902,** her first birthday. Armed with her renewed trust in God's faithfulness, Rose had two more children while they served as missionaries, but no more died in China.

Reflection

What lessons can you learn from the experiences of Rose Goforth? Are there things for which you find it difficult to trust God? Rose discovered that the path of faith is the path of obedience.

What is faith? It is the confident assurance that what we hope for is going to happen. It is the evidence of things we cannot yet see.

HEBREWS 11:1

October 14

Can persecution succeed?

BY THE 1530s Antwerp was on its way to becoming the richest and busiest city in Europe. Because of its port on the Scheldt River, Antwerp was Europe's center for international trade and finance. The whole region, known as Flanders, was under Spanish control. It became so prosperous that Charles V, emperor of the Holy Roman Empire, received half of all his tax revenue from there. Charles V, himself a native of Flanders, reciprocated by giving his native land many benefits—except for religious freedom. To Charles, national strength required religious unity.

When the Reformation began in 1517, it soon reached Antwerp, Europe's most cosmopolitan city. From Germany came Lutherans and Anabaptists, the forerunners of the Mennonites. From Switzerland and France came followers of Calvin[21] and Zwingli.[22] William Tyndale fled England and came to Antwerp to translate the Bible into English.[23]

Many Augustinian monks began preaching the principles of their fellow Augustinian Martin Luther.[24] One of them, James Porbst, a friend of Luther from Wittenberg, became prior of the convent in Antwerp and was an outspoken preacher of justification by faith. Fellow Augustinians in Dordrecht, the Hague, Utrecht, and Ghent all became vocal supporters of the Reformation. As early as 1520 some of Luther's books were being translated into Dutch.

Immediately the emperor and the Church mounted a vigorous counteroffensive. One Dominican friar said that he would like to fasten his teeth around Luther's throat and that he would proudly go to the Lord's Supper with Luther's blood dripping from his lips. A representative of the pope arrived in 1520 and with the emperor's blessing began burning books and preaching against heresy. Erasmus, the great intellectual living in Antwerp at the time, observed that the burning of books removed them only from the bookstores, not from people's hearts.

In 1521 Charles V, at the pope's request, specifically forbade the publishing or reading of the writings of Luther. He also ordered the secular courts to enforce that year's edict of the Diet of Worms of that year, which condemned Luther and his followers. Arrests began in 1522, and the first persons to be arrested were James Probst, the prior, and two close friends of Erasmus. Probst recanted but then after escaping from prison recanted his recantation.

The following year two Augustinian friars, Henry Voes and Johann Eck, were burned at the stake in Brussels—the first Protestant martyrs of Flanders. Erasmus observed that the martyrs made many Lutherans by their deaths.

In spite of the opposition and the mounting number of martyrs, interest in the gospel swelled in Antwerp. Every allusion to church corruption in speeches or plays was wildly cheered. A visitor from Italy to Antwerp was told by a leading citizen that if the revolt of the Anabaptists in Germany spread to Antwerp, twenty thousand men would rise up to join them. In 1527 the English ambassador reported that two-thirds of Antwerp's population "kept Luther's opinions."

Alarmed by this spread of heresy in Antwerp, the government issued an edict on **October 14, 1529,** that began a reign of terror. Death was decreed not only for all heretics but also for anyone who was not a theologian who discussed any article of faith or who failed to denounce the heretics he or she knew. The Spanish Inquisition[25] had arrived in Flanders, and the persecution continued for many years. During the sixteenth century in present-day Belgium, six hundred Protestant churches were destroyed and untold thousands were martyred.

This holocaust of Protestants was successful. Today less than one-third of a percent of Belgians are evangelical Christians.

Reflection

Christians of every age have been persecuted and martyred. Although by its very definition persecution is not pleasant, we should not be surprised when it happens to us. Our sufferings are nothing in comparison to the One who suffered for us.

∽◦∾

Dear friends, don't be surprised at the fiery trials you are going through, as if something strange were happening to you. Instead, be very glad—because these trials will make you partners with Christ in his suffering, and afterward you will have the wonderful joy of sharing his glory when it is displayed to all the world. 1 PETER 4:12-13

October 15

What happens when God captures the heart of an uneducated British parlor maid?

GLADYS AYLWARD was a mailman's daughter born near London in 1902. While working as a housemaid, she was converted to Christ at the age of eighteen. Immediately she set her heart on being a missionary to China. After being rejected by the China Inland Mission because she did not meet their educational standards, Gladys determined that she would go to China on her own and started saving almost all of her modest wages. Then in 1930 she heard of a seventy-three-year-old missionary in China, Jeannie Lawson, who was looking for an assistant. Immediately Gladys wrote, offering Miss Lawson her services. Finally the reply came that if Gladys could reach Tientsin (present-day Tianjin) on the coast of China, the missionary would take care of her from that point on.

On **October 15, 1932,** a small group of friends gathered in the Liverpool Street Station to see Gladys Aylward off to China. She traveled by train and boat to the Hague. From there she took the trans-Siberian train in spite of the danger as Russia and China were at war. At one point she was nearly detained in Russia, but she was eventually able to get to Tientsin. From there she finally joined Jeannie Lawson in the city of Yangcheng in the remote Shansi Province of northwest China. There the two women opened an inn. After Jeannie Lawson died, Gladys continued to operate it herself, entertaining her guests in the evenings by telling them Bible stories.

Gladys gained the trust of the mandarin of her city, who appointed her as the foot inspector to enforce Chiang Kai-shek's edict against binding the feet of young girls. She asked for permission to share her faith as she traveled doing her inspections, and it was granted. As a result, she had an open door to share the gospel with Chinese women. In 1936 Gladys became a citizen of China in order to identify herself even more with the people.

The late 1930s in China were chaotic as the Nationalist government fought the Communists and the Japanese. In the midst of the chaos Gladys was touched by the plight of the orphans and unwanted children and took in five of them.

In 1938 Japanese bombing raids began, the first one damaging Gladys's inn. With the Japanese army approaching, she set out for a remote mountain village with her five children, accompanied by forty of her converts. She had been to that village previously as the foot inspector and so was well received. There they took up residence in a large cave.

By 1940 Gladys had taken responsibility for nearly one hundred children—the majority of them war orphans. Realizing that she must lead them to safety, Gladys embarked on a 240-mile journey to Xi'an, the capital of the neighboring province, with her children. The trip was a harrowing experience as the Japanese soldiers were never far behind. Moving undetected with nearly one hundred children in tow placed an incredible strain on Gladys. When at last they reached their destination, Gladys collapsed both mentally and physically, suffering hallucinations and mental confusion. Fortunately, with time she fully recovered.

After being away nearly twenty years, Gladys was finally persuaded to visit England in 1949. There she won the hearts of the English people with her story of heroism and sacrifice, even dining with Queen Elizabeth. From her incredible adventures, Hollywood made the movie *The Inn of the Sixth Happiness,* starring Ingrid Bergman.

And it all began with a young English housemaid's putting her trust in Jesus.

Reflection

The story of Gladys Aylward should encourage all of us. Her main character qualities were that she desperately wanted God to use her and that she was determined not to let any obstacle stand in her way. How do you think God wants to use you? How can you overcome the obstacles in your life?

Jesus prayed this prayer: "O Father, Lord of heaven and earth, thank you for hiding the truth from those who think themselves so wise and clever, and for revealing it to the childlike. Yes, Father, it pleased you to do it this way!" MATTHEW 11:25-26

October 16

Be thou faithful unto death.

In 1534 King Henry VIII made himself head of the Church of England, separating it from the Roman Catholic Church.[26] This did not indicate a change in doctrine but merely meant that Henry VIII, not the pope, now controlled the English Church. However, Thomas Cranmer, the archbishop of Canterbury, the ecclesiastical head of the Church of England, was a committed Protestant believer. Cranmer appointed Hugh Latimer as royal chaplain. Latimer had experienced a dramatic conversion ten years earlier when another minister shared the gospel with him. Archbishop Cranmer appointed Nicholas Ridley as his own personal chaplain. Ridley, unlike Latimer, still espoused the Roman Catholic faith. However, in the following decade his thinking changed radically.

In the late 1530s the influence of Cranmer and Latimer, then a bishop, was growing. Henry VIII had unknowingly authorized the publishing of Tyndale's English translation of the Bible,[27] and Cranmer was pushing for a more Protestant liturgy.

Henry VIII became more dictatorial as he grew older. In 1539 he published his Six Articles, making belief in certain Roman Catholic doctrines obligatory and putting the growing number of Protestants in jeopardy. Latimer had to resign his bishopric because of the Six Articles. Ridley, whose views were gradually changing, became royal chaplain. Fortunately, after a year the king suspended enforcement of the Six Articles.

In 1547 Henry VIII died and was succeeded by his nine-year-old son, a sincere Christian, who became King Edward VI.[28] During Edward's reign, Archbishhop Cranmer had great influence, and the liturgy of English churches was changed from Latin to English. Ridley, by then a convinced evangelical, became a bishop, and Latimer, no longer a bishop, was actively preaching at least two sermons every Sunday. Unfortunately, Edward died in 1553 and was succeeded by his half sister, Mary Tudor, a Roman Catholic. She was crowned Queen Mary I and soon earned her nickname of "Bloody Mary."[29] Under Mary, all bishops were replaced by Roman Catholics, and Cranmer, Latimer, and Ridley were imprisoned, tried for heresy, and condemned to death.

On **October 16, 1555**, Latimer and Ridley were led out of prison to be burned at the stake. As the fire was lit, Latimer said, "Be of good comfort, Master Ridley, and play the man. We shall this day light such a candle by God's grace in England as I trust shall never be put out."[30]

THE SURPRISE ENDING

Cranmer was then "degraded," a formal ceremony in which all symbols of his office of archbishop were physically removed from him. Back in prison Cranmer was told that if he would recant he might be spared and given the opportunity to heal the divided church of England. After much pressure Cranmer finally signed a recantation denouncing Luther as a heretic and affirming the teachings of the Roman Catholic Church.

But Queen Mary I and the Catholic bishops had no intention of sparing Cranmer. They knew that the Reformation seemed to grow stronger with each martyrdom, so their plan was to show the folly of the movement through the collapse of a major leader. They planned to have Cranmer make a public statement of his conversion to Catholicism to show his weakness and *then* execute him.

But Cranmer had the last word. On the appointed day Cranmer was brought to the platform to speak to the assembled crowd. He confirmed his faith in God and in the Bible. Then to the horror of the church dignitaries, he said, "As for the pope, I refuse him, as Christ's enemy and Antichrist, with all his false doctrine." Amid an uproar, Cranmer was pulled off the platform, but he broke away and ran straight to the stake and stood resolutely to be burned.

The flames soon consumed him, but his brave denunciation destroyed forever the power of Roman Catholicism in England, making it a Protestant nation. The deaths of Latimer, Ridley, and Cranmer indeed lit a candle that has never been put out.

Reflection

Latimer and Ridley remained faithful throughout their imprisonment, whereas Cranmer temporarily weakened. Yet Cranmer's final repentance and faithful testimony had a greater impact on England than even the deaths of Latimer and Ridley. When you find yourself failing in your faithfulness to God, it's not too late to ask him to restore you and keep you faithful to the end.

Those who endure to the end will be saved.   MATTHEW 24:13

October 17

God sometimes used his prophets as motivational speakers.

For three and a half weeks Zerubbabel, the governor of Judah, and Jeshua, the high priest, had been directing the Jews who had returned with them from Babylonia as they rebuilt the temple in Jerusalem. The work was discouraging because the temple had lain in ruins for sixty-six years.

Previously the enemies of the Jews had been so successful in frightening and discouraging them that work had stopped for seventeen years. On **October 17, 520** B.C., as the rebuilding project was underway again, God sent a message to encourage and motivate the workers through the prophet Haggai (Haggai 2:1).[31]

Haggai said to Zerubbabel, Jeshua, and all the people, "Is there anyone who can remember this house—the Temple—as it was before? In comparison, how does it look to you now? It must seem like nothing at all! . . . Take courage and work, for I am with you, says the Lord Almighty. My Spirit remains among you, just as I promised when you came out of Egypt. So do not be afraid" (Haggai 2:3-5).

The original temple built by Solomon was ornate and luxurious. There was no way the workers could replicate its grandeur, and Haggai realized that this discouraged many of the workers. But God desired his people to be encouraged in spite of how insignificant the temple they were rebuilding might look.

So God gave them a glimpse of what the future temple would look like—in connection with the second coming of Christ. Of that time God said through Haggai to the discouraged temple builders, "In just a little while I will again shake the heavens and the earth. I will shake the oceans and the dry land, too. I will shake all the nations, and the treasures of all the nations will come to this Temple. I will fill this place with glory, says the Lord Almighty. The silver is mine, and the gold is mine, says the Lord Almighty. The future glory of this Temple will be greater than its past glory, says the Lord Almighty. And in this place I will bring peace. I, the Lord Almighty, have spoken!" (vv. 6-9).

Previously God had shaken the earth when he had made his covenant with them at Mount Sinai. "Moses led them out from the camp to meet with God, and they stood at the foot of the mountain. . . . And the whole mountain shook with a violent earthquake" (Exodus 19:17-18). God shook the earth again when Christ was crucified. "The earth shook, rocks split apart, and tombs opened" (Matthew 27:51-52). But the great shaking is yet to come. In a vision of the second coming of Christ, John saw "a great earthquake. . . . Then the stars of the sky fell to the earth. . . . And the sky was rolled up like a scroll and taken away. And all of the mountains and all of the islands disappeared" (Revelation 6:12-14; cf. Luke 21:25-27).

Through Haggai God helped the disheartened workers see that their building was part of a much bigger scenario—one in which the temple would eventually be rebuilt a final time to a grandeur greater than ever before (cf. Ezekiel 40:1–47:12).[32]

Reflection

God encouraged the discouraged temple builders by telling them of the glorious end of the project they were beginning. We, likewise, can become discouraged at the seeming insignificance of what God calls us to do. Yet it is all part of God's glorious perfect plan. No matter what our task, "the future glory . . . will be greater than its past" (Haggai 2:9).

The glory of the Lord filled the Temple.   EZEKIEL 43:5

October 18

Why is France today considered a mission field?

THE WARS of Religion began in France in 1562 between the Roman Catholics and the French Protestants called Huguenots. The Huguenots were led by the family of Henry of Navarre, a minor kingdom including a small portion of southern France and the present Spanish province of Navarre. Henry inherited the throne of Navarre from his staunchly Calvinist mother.[33] When his cousin King Henry III of France died in 1589, he became heir to the throne of France. His Calvinism made him an unacceptable candidate in Catholic France until he embraced Catholicism in 1593. He was then crowned King Henry IV.

Once he became king, however, he did not forget his Huguenot roots, and in 1598 he issued the Edict of Nantes. This agreement gave the Huguenots freedom of religion in certain areas of the country, civil equality, and fair administration of justice. It provided the Huguenots with a state subsidy for their troops and pastors and allowed them to retain control of approximately two hundred towns. The Edict of Nantes was historically unique in that it was the first time freedom was granted to two religions to coexist in a nation.

By the late 1600s Henry IV's grandson, Louis XIV, was king of France. But Louis XIV shared none of his grandfather's empathy for the Huguenots, and on **October 18, 1685,** he revoked the Edict of Nantes. All Huguenot worship and education were forbidden, and all Huguenot churches were either destroyed or turned into Catholic churches. Huguenot clergy were given fourteen days to leave France, but the remaining Huguenots were forbidden to emigrate. All children within France were to be baptized by a Catholic priest and raised as Catholics.

Mounted soldiers were housed in the homes of Huguenots. The troops were given license to do anything they pleased, short of murder. They forced their hosts to dance until they collapsed. They poured boiling water down their throats. They beat the soles of their feet and pulled out the hairs from their beards. The soldiers burned the arms and legs of their Huguenot hosts with candles and made them hold red-hot coals in their hands. They forced women to stand naked in the streets.

Some four hundred thousand "converts" were forced to attend Mass and receive the Eucharist. Those who spat out the wafers as they left the church were sentenced to be burned alive. Obstinate Huguenot men were imprisoned

THE EXTINGUISHING OF
PROTESTANTISM IN FRANCE

in dungeons and unheated cells. The women sometimes fared better as they were sent to convents, where they often received unexpectedly sympathetic treatment from the nuns.

Of the 1.5 million Huguenots living in France in 1660, over the next decades 400,000 risked their lives by escaping across the guarded borders. Geneva, a city of 16,000, welcomed four thousand Huguenots. Although they were Catholic, English kings Charles II and James II aided the Huguenot immigrants in their country. An entire quarter of London was soon populated with French workers. The elector of Brandenburg gave such a friendly reception to Huguenots that over a fifth of Berlin was French by 1697. Holland welcomed thousands and gave them citizenship. Dutch Catholics joined Protestants and Jews in raising money for Huguenot relief. Many Huguenots fled to South Carolina and to the other colonies as well.

At the height of the Reformation nearly half of the population of France was Huguenot. But as a result of the revocation of the Edict of Nantes and the intense persecution that followed, today less than one percent of the French shares the faith of the Huguenots, making France a mission field for the gospel.

Reflection

Why do you think God allowed the revocation of the Edict of Nantes? Were there any positive outcomes? Have you wondered why God allowed certain negative things to happen to you? Have you seen any positive outcomes to them? God often allows us to go through negative experiences without letting us know why. But someday when we get to heaven, he'll make it all plain.

I am the one who creates the light and makes the darkness. I am the one who sends good times and bad times. I, the Lord, am the one who does these things.   ISAIAH 45:7

October 19

Who determines who will die first?

IN THE 1550s the Anabaptists,[34] the early Baptists who developed into the Mennonites, experienced great persecution, particularly in Germany and the Netherlands. In January of 1558 Hans Smit, an Anabaptist pastor, and Hendrick Adams, a mature Christian layman, were meeting in a home in Aix-la-Chapelle, a town near the German-Dutch border, to study the Bible and pray with ten others. Suddenly the house was surrounded, and they were all arrested, both men and women. The next day a judge sentenced them, one by one, to prison.

Hans Smit, the pastor, was summoned before the judge a second time and asked how many people he had baptized and who they were. He replied firmly that he would rather die than tell. He was then tortured on the rack for half an hour, to which he willingly submitted. Then his interrogators asked him what he thought of the Eucharist. He answered, "I think much of it; but that which the priests use is not at all the true supper of Christ but a piece of idolatry." Upon hearing this, they tied Smit up and suspended him from the ceiling with a hundred-pound stone tied to his feet. But he kept the faith.

Finally his interrogators tried to reason with him, telling him that if he would renounce his baptism that they would deal with him favorably. When he answered that he would never renounce his faith as he believed it was taught in the Bible, they told him that Anabaptists were not allowed in Aix-la-Chapelle and that he must be killed. Smit's response was that if they killed him, they would have to answer for it before the Lord.

One of the councillors of Aix-la-Chapelle was violently opposed specifically to Hans Smit and Hendrick Adams. On one occasion when their interrogators were once again offering to pardon them if they would recant, Adams answered that he stood firm in his convictions. The vindictive councillor shouted, "Away with them, away with them, to death and the fire . . . no pardon should be offered them anymore!" Hendrick Adams looked him in the eye and said, "You will not live to see my death."

Hans Smit was sentenced to die first and Hendrick Adams three days later. On **October 19, 1558**, Smit was led through the city of Aix-la-Chapelle, singing joyfully as he went. He walked briskly to the stake, where he was strangled with a rope and his body burned.

But that is not all that happened on that day. The councillor who had so

"VENGEANCE IS MINE," SAITH THE LORD

eagerly sought the deaths of Smit and Adams was suddenly stricken violently ill. The nearer death came to him, the greater grew his despair. He began to cry out, plucking out his beard and confessing that he had sinned in judging many persons and that God would surely judge him for his bloodthirstiness. He also died on **October 19, 1558**.

Three days later Hendrick Adams was led to the place of execution. Like his pastor, he was strangled with a rope, then chained to the stake and burned. And like his pastor, he accepted it willingly.

God had spoken truth through Hendrick Adams. His accuser did not live to see his death.

Reflection

Jesus told us that if we as Christians are arrested and brought to trial for our faith, we should not worry ahead of time what we will say because God will give us the words to speak. Hendrick Adams is an illustration of how God will provide our words.

When you are arrested and stand trial, don't worry about what to say in your defense. Just say what God tells you to. Then it is not you who will be speaking, but the Holy Spirit.   MARK 13:11

October 20

God used some surprising people to save John Wesley's life.

IN 1742 and 1743 John Wesley[35] experienced great success preaching to the coal miners of Wednesbury, Darlaston, and Walsall, England. From his two trips to the area the Methodist Society grew to nearly four hundred, and Wesley established good relations with the Anglicans as well.

However, in early 1743 another itinerant Methodist preacher came through and thoroughly offended the Anglican vicar, turning his support for the growing Methodist work to opposition. The clergy of Wednesbury, Walsall, and Darlaston joined forces to attempt to destroy the local Methodist Society by spreading the rumor that cockfighting, bullbaiting, and prizefighting would cease if the Methodists were allowed to exist. As a result, windows were broken in Methodist homes, shops were looted, and several Methodist leaders were beaten.

When John Wesley returned to Wednesbury[36] on **October 20, 1743**, he preached at noon without disturbance, but that afternoon a mob from Darlaston accosted the five-foot-three Wesley and the Methodist leaders with him, threatening their safety. Wesley was able to talk to the ringleaders of the mob privately and actually win them over so that they promised to defend him. One woman even told the crowd, "This gentleman is an honest gentleman, and we will spill our blood in his defense." Soon after, the crowd dispersed.

Then several hours later the mob returned and forced Wesley and his Methodist supporters to go with them to the home of the justice of the peace in Walsall to bring charges against Wesley. However, by the time they got there, the justice of the peace was already in bed and the Darlaston mob had turned friendly. They dispatched fifty of their number to escort Wesley home, and the rest turned back to return to Darlaston.

Wesley and his escorts had hardly gone one hundred yards when they were met by a mob from Walsall. Wesley was suddenly in the middle of two traditional rivals, his Darlaston escorts and the mob from Walsall. The woman who had sworn to defend him charged the Walsall mob and knocked down several men. But she was soon overpowered and might have been killed if a champion prizefighter from Walsall, known as Honest Munchin, had not come to her aid.

The mob pulled Wesley and the Methodists down the steep streets to Walsall. Once there, as the crowd yelled threats, Wesley shouted, "Will you hear me?"

A CLOSE CALL

"No! No! Knock his brains out! Kill him!" the angry crowd shouted.

Wesley responded, "Which of you have I wronged?" Then he spoke of the love of God, and for a while they seemed to be listening. But after about fifteen minutes, Wesley's voice gave out, and as his words faded away, the crowd, led by Honest Munchin, yelled out, "Bring him away! Strip him!"

Wesley's voice miraculously returned, and he shouted, "You needn't do that: I will give you my clothes." Then he began to pray aloud, oblivious to all but the Lord Jesus.

His prayers were answered in a most unexpected way. Honest Munchin, the prizefighter, suddenly locked eyes with Wesley and stammered, "Sir, I will spend my life for you; follow me, and not one soul shall touch a hair of your head." Several others made their way to the front, said the same, and then formed themselves into a human shield around Wesley and the Methodists. The crowd was stunned by their leader's about-face and was momentarily quiet. But as they approached a bridge over a small stream, the shouts resumed, "Throw him in!" and a scuffle ensued. Honest Munchin broke the arm of one of the protesters and was able to muscle Wesley and his supporters through to safety.

John Wesley left Wednesbury the next day, but the results of his work continued. Honest Munchin and the young man whose arm was broken both joined the Methodist Society, with Munchin serving as a leader of the Wednesbury and Walsall Methodists until his death forty-six years later.

Reflection

Have you experienced God's protection in a frightening situation? Wesley entrusted himself to God's care, and God sent a surprising protector, the prizefighter leading the mob. We don't always know how God will protect us, but we know he has given us immortality until the day he has appointed for us to die.

∼✷∼

I will be with you, and I will protect you wherever you go.

GENESIS 28:15

October 21

Medical school didn't prepare him for this.

PAUL CARLSON was born in 1928, and from the time he was a boy he wanted to be a physician. He followed his dream, and after graduating from the Stanford University Medical School, he went into private practice.

Learning of the need for short-term missionaries, Dr. Paul and his wife, Lois, went to the Belgian Congo in 1961 to help with relief work. This experience led to a career commitment to medical missions in 1963. Dr. Carlson was assigned by the Evangelical Covenant Church to a hospital in the town of Wasolo in the Belgian Congo province of Ubangi.

In 1964 Communist rebel soldiers calling themselves Simbas infiltrated this area of the Congo, seizing Stanleyville (now Kisangani), the country's second largest city.

At the 1964 church conference in the Congo, Dr. Carlson led a Communion service in which he said, "We do not know what will happen in 1964—and in 1965—until we meet together again. We do not know if we will have to suffer and die during this year because we are Christians. But it does not matter. Our job is to follow Jesus. . . . My friends, if today you are not willing to suffer for Jesus, do not partake of the elements. . . . To follow Jesus means to be willing to suffer for him."

When Paul and Lois learned that the rebels were coming toward Wasolo, Paul took Lois and their two children to safety in the nearby Central African Republic and returned to Wasolo alone, staying in touch by radio. On September 9 he reported a disturbance in the town and said, "I must leave this evening."

The next report Lois heard was that Paul and three Catholic priests, friends of his, were captured and the hospital burned. Then in a short letter dated September 24, Paul wrote, "Where I go from here I know not, only that it will be with Him. If by God's grace, I live, which I doubt, it will be to His glory."

The last message was a scrap of paper dated **October 21, 1964.** He wrote, "I know I'm ready to meet my Lord, but my thoughts for you make this more difficult. I trust that I might be a witness for Christ. . . ."

Five days later the Simba radio announced that a mercenary named Major Carlson had been captured and would be brought to Stanleyville for trial. "Major" Carlson was held prisoner in a hotel and became the rebels' most publicized captive. Daily he was marched out for a mock execution but was beaten instead.

In late November Carlson was moved into another hotel with other American captives. As they talked together, Paul told them, "I can't think about the future. I can just live one day at a time and trust the Lord for that day."

After four days together, the roar of airplanes awakened the prisoners. "Outside! Outside!' a Simba screamed as he ran through the halls.

Once outside they looked up to see Belgian paratroopers descending from the sky. Carlson was among about 250 white hostages herded toward the city square and ordered to sit down. The sound of machine guns was everywhere. Suddenly the Simbas began firing into the crowd of hostages. Carlson and some others ran for a nearby house, where they had to climb over a masonry wall to reach the porch. Carlson motioned for another missionary to go over the wall first. The other missionary dove over and reached back his hand for Carlson. Five shots rang out and Paul Carlson fell dead in the street. Later that missionary said, "By letting me go first, Paul died that I might live."

His grave marker reads, "Greater love has no man than this, that one lay down his life for his friends."

Reflection

If you had been at the Communion service led by Paul Carlson when he asked only those willing to suffer for Christ to partake of the elements, would you have been a participant? It's not a question to be taken lightly. But when we consider Christ's sufferings, we see the pattern he set for those who follow him.

❧

But if we are to share his glory, we must also share his suffering.
ROMANS 8:17

October 22

Imagine a theological seminary with a faculty of one.

ARCHIBALD ALEXANDER was born to a Presbyterian family near Lexington, Virginia, in 1772.[37] At the age of seventeen he became the tutor for the family of a general in the army of the new nation. Mrs. Tyler, an elderly woman in the general's home, took young Archibald under her wing. She was a Baptist who viewed Presbyterians as sound in doctrine but often lacking the experience of spiritual rebirth.

The general hired a millwright for the mill on his plantation. One day the millwright, who also was a Baptist, asked Archibald whether he believed that to enter the kingdom of heaven one must be born again. Uncertain how to answer, Archibald answered yes. The millwright then asked him whether he had experienced the new birth. Archibald answered, "Not that I know of."

"Ah," said the millwright, "if you had ever experienced this change, you would know something about it!"

The conversation got Alexander thinking. Surely the new birth was in the Bible, but he had never heard the Presbyterians he knew talk about it.

Old Mrs. Tyler had poor eyesight and would frequently ask Alexander to read to her. Her favorite author was Puritan writer John Flavel. When Alexander learned that Flavel was a Presbyterian, he became very interested in learning what he had to say about the new birth.

On Sunday evenings Alexander was asked to read to the whole family. On one particular Sunday night he read the family a sermon of Flavel on Revelation 3:20, where Jesus says, "Behold I stand at the door and knock. . . ." As Alexander read the sermon, every word seemed to apply to him. By the time he finished, his voice was quivering with emotion. He laid down the book and ran to his room. Shutting the door, he fell to his knees and poured out his soul in prayer, inviting Jesus into his life. He had not prayed very long when he was overwhelmed by a joy that he had never experienced before. The joy was accompanied by a full assurance that, if he were to die, he would go to heaven.

Giving up tutoring, Alexander went to study theology at Liberty Hall (now Washington and Lee University) and entered the Presbyterian ministry. After serving as an itinerant minister on the Ohio-Virginia frontier, he became president of Hampden-Sydney College in 1796 at the age of twenty-four.

In 1807 Alexander became pastor of the Third Presbyterian Church of Philadelphia and moderator of the Presbyterian General Assembly. In his final address as moderator in 1808 he suggested the formation of a Presbyterian seminary in America. As a result of his leadership, Princeton Theological Seminary was founded in 1812 with Alexander as its sole faculty member for the first year. The first fall he had three students who were joined by six more in the spring and five more during the summer. Alexander's modest home served as library, chapel, and classroom. There the students studied and shared in his family worship. He continued teaching at Princeton Seminary until his death on **October 22, 1851.**

Archibald Alexander's heart can be seen in a prayer he penned shortly before his death:

O most merciful God! . . .Thou has a perfect right to dispose of me, in that manner which will most effectively promote thy glory: And I know that whatever Thou dost is right, and wise, and just, and good. . . . And when my spirit leaves this clay tenement, Lord Jesus receive it! Send some of the blessed angels to convey my inexperienced soul to the mansion which Thy love has prepared. And O! let me be so situated, though in the lowest rank, that I may behold Thy glory. May I have an abundant entrance administered unto me into the kingdom of our Lord and Savior, Jesus Christ; for whose sake and in whose name, I ask all these things. Amen.

Reflection

Archibald Alexander yearned to experience God's glorious heavenly kingdom. He became part of that kingdom when he was born again as a youth. Have you been born again? If not, invite the Lord Jesus to come into your life, and you can experience the joy of the new birth as Alexander did.

Jesus replied, "I assure you, unless you are born again, you can never see the Kingdom of God."   JOHN 3:3

October 23

What was it like to hear a legendary preacher from the past in person?

ON **OCTOBER 23, 1740,** twenty-five-year-old George Whitefield, the greatest evangelist of his day,[38] preached in Middletown, Connecticut. Nathan Cole, a farmer and carpenter, heard him and recorded his experience in his own words:

> [I]n the morning about 8 or 9 of the clock there came a messenger and said Mr. Whitefield preached at Hartford and Wethersfield yesterday and is to preach at Middletown this morning at ten of the clock. I was in my field at work. I dropped my tool that I had in my hand and ran home to my wife, telling her to make ready quickly to go and hear Mr. Whitefield preach at Middletown, then ran to my pasture for my horse with all my might, fearing that I should be too late. Having my horse, I with my wife soon mounted the horse and went forward as fast as I thought the horse could bear; and when my horse got much out of breath, I would get down and put my wife in the saddle and bid her ride . . . and so I would run until I was much out of breath and then mount my horse again, and so I did several times to favor my horse. We improved every moment to get along as if we were fleeing for our lives, all the while fearing we should be too late to hear the sermon, for we had twelve miles to ride double in little more than an hour. . . . And when we came within about half a mile or a mile of the road that comes from Hartford . . . to Middletown, on high land I saw before me a cloud of fog arising. I first thought it came from the great river, but as I came nearer the road I heard a noise of horses' feet coming down the road, and this cloud was a cloud of dust made by the horses' feet. It arose some rods into the air over the tops of hills and trees; and when I came within about 20 rods of the road, I could see men and horses clipping along in the cloud like shadows, and as I drew nearer it seemed like a steady stream of horses and their riders, scarcely a horse more than his length behind another, all of a lather and foam with sweat, their breath rolling out of their nostrils every jump. Every horse seemed to go with all his might to carry his rider to hear news from heaven for the saving of souls. . . . When we got to Middletown old meeting house, there was a great multitude, it was said to be 3 or

4,000 people, assembled together. We dismounted and shook off our dust. . . . When I saw Mr. Whitefield come upon the scaffold, he looked almost angelical; a young, slim, slender youth, before thousands of people with a bold undaunted countenance. . . . He looked as if he was clothed with authority from the Great God, and a sweet solemn solemnity sat upon his brow, and my hearing him preach gave me a heart wound. By God's blessing, my old foundation was broken up, and I saw that my righteousness would not save me.

Reflection

Mr. Cole had little education and probably was unaccustomed to writing, yet this event was so earth-shattering in its importance to him that he felt compelled to record it. How would you explain the great drawing power of young George Whitefield? Why do you feel Nathan Cole and the other thousands of people were so anxious to hear him?

People can't come to me unless the Father who sent me draws them to me. JOHN 6:44

October 24

"The truth is, a kernel of wheat must be planted in the soil. Unless it dies it will be alone—a single seed. But its death will produce many new kernels—a plentiful harvest of new lives" (John 12:24).

OCTOBER 24, 1851, was the funeral of Archibald Alexander, the first professor of Princeton Theological Seminary.[39] Under his leadership the school had become the leading seminary in the nation. The funeral was held in Princeton's First Presbyterian Church. The funeral procession then passed in front of Nassau Hall, where the college was located, before following Witherspoon Street to the cemetery. Leading the procession were the 250 students and the professors of the college.

One of the college students there that day was Robert Hamill Nassau, a young man with dreams of becoming a great orator or a famous soldier. To his surprise, the funeral produced in him a great longing for spiritual peace and purpose in life. A few weeks later, alone in a field near Princeton, he committed his life to Jesus Christ.

Nassau had taken an odd route to Princeton. He took the freshman-year course at Lafayette College, where his father was a professor. Apparently he was not ready for college, because the next year he attended the high school at Lawrenceville, New Jersey, which was run by his mother's brothers just down the road from Princeton. The following year he entered the College of New Jersey, as Princeton University was known at the time.

After graduating in 1854 at the age of nineteen, he taught for a year at Lawrenceville and then entered Princeton Theological Seminary. On Sundays, Nassau taught Sunday school at the town's black Presbyterian church. His first summer he asked the Presbyterian Board of Publication for the most difficult field in America—being a colporteur, a person who travels around distributing Bibles and Christian literature—and was given Missouri and Kansas. He spent his second summer as a missionary to the boatmen working along the Pennsylvania Canal.

During the school year he joined the "Brotherhood," a secret organization composed of students planning to go to the mission field. During Nassau's seminary days the twelve active members kept the challenge of foreign missions before the rest of the student body.

Upon graduating from the seminary in 1859, Nassau asked the Presbyterian Board of Foreign Missions to send him to the most difficult field they had.

LIFE OUT OF DEATH

They appointed him to their Corisco Mission in present-day Equatorial Guinea on the coast of West Africa. Nassau wrote in his journal, "Many of my acquaintances protested to me. And one said, 'What a fool you are, Nassau, to go to Africa to die!' " Nassau added, "I quietly determined not to die."

To prepare himself further, Nassau received his M.D. degree from the University of Pennsylvania in 1861. He was ordained in July of that year and in September was on Corisco Island off the coast of West Africa.

Nassau spent the next forty-five years in missionary service, mastering several African languages and establishing several mission stations. Somewhat conventional in his personal religious faith, he was anything but conventional in his missionary methodology. His well-loved Winchester rifle is referred to frequently in his journals, and he was a pioneer in using industrial training for evangelistic purposes. Most important, he helped translate the Old Testament and part of the New Testament into Benga, a dialect of Bantu.

Robert Nassau was a fruit of the life of Archibald Alexander. The death of Alexander was used by God to bring new life to Nassau, who in turn passed it on to hundreds in West Africa.

Reflection

We never know how we will affect those around us. The words shared at the funeral of Archibald Alexander were used by God to transform the life of one young man, whom God in turn used to transform the lives of many others. Remember the old familiar children's song "This little light of mine. I'm going to let it shine"? Let's do it.

◦◦◦

Don't hide your light under a basket! Instead, put it on a stand and let it shine for all.   MATTHEW 5:15

October 25

You never know when someone's words will change your life.

NAMED AFTER his grandfather, Casper Wyrtzen was born in 1913 in Brooklyn. Teased about his name in high school, he changed it to "Jack." His family occasionally attended the Unitarian church, but Wyrtzen grew up ridiculing religion. He dropped out of high school, joining the National Guard when he was eighteen.

In the Guard, Jack became friends with George Schilling, a heavy drinker. To everyone's surprise at camp their second summer, Schilling was a different person, reading his Bible and kneeling beside his cot every night to pray. Jack and the others made fun of him, but secretly Jack admired his friend's courage. Schilling persisted in handing Jack copies of the Gospel of John, and Jack persisted in tearing them up. Finally one day he read one of them.

Schilling asked Wyrtzen to play a trombone solo at a gospel service one night, and Wyrtzen agreed. Jack was upset by the preacher that night—so different from the gentle Unitarian pastors of his youth. This preacher pounded out a message of hellfire and brimstone that infuriated Jack. He left angry, but he couldn't stop thinking, *What if there is a heaven and hell?*

That night alone in his bedroom he realized that his anger was because of his pride and fear. He considered the possibility that Jesus did love him. Had Christ died for him? Jack finally slipped to his knees and committed his life to Jesus Christ.

The next morning when Schilling called to apologize for the preacher's words the night before, Jack responded, "When I got home, I got saved." He immediately followed his friend's example of daily Bible study and prayer but for several months told no one but Schilling of his new commitment, afraid that it would affect his dance band, the Silver Moon Serenaders, which had some prestigious gigs coming up. He was also quite sure that his girlfriend, Marge, would not be thrilled.

Several months later he received an astounding letter, "Honey, I'm saved, and I want you to be saved. But don't get saved until I get home because I want to save you. Love, Marge."

Amazed and delighted, Jack immediately sent a telegram back, "Dear Marge, Praise the Lord! I've been saved for the last few months, but I've been afraid to tell you. I'm so thankful the Lord has saved you. Jack."

Later that year a friend told Jack that his brother had died in a car accident two weeks earlier. Jack shared the gospel with him, but it was received with hostility. The friend said, "If you knew all about this heaven thing and that hell is for real, how come you never told me or my brother about it? If my brother had known, he might have believed. He could have been in heaven right now. But you never said a thing!"

Deeply convicted, Jack prayed that night, "Lord, never again will someone that I know die without hearing the gospel."

With George Schilling and two others, Wyrtzen began holding Sunday night evangelistic services in Brooklyn. Their vision enlarging, they contracted for thirteen Saturday night youth broadcasts on a powerful New York radio station. The first broadcast was on **October 25, 1941,** from the New York Gospel Tabernacle. At 7:30 P.M. these words rang out: "From Times Square New York, Word of Life presents Jack Wyrtzen with words of life for the youth of America."

The rallies grew until twenty thousand filled Madison Square Garden in 1944 and forty thousand filled Yankee Stadium in 1948. Wyrtzen opened Word of Life Camp at Schroon Lake, New York, in 1947, and from there camps were established throughout the world.

God wonderfully changed Jack Wyrtzen's life in order to change the lives of thousands of others.

Reflection

Jack Wyrtzen was driven by the desire to have everyone with whom he came in contact understand the gospel. After one missed opportunity, he never wanted to miss another. With whom do you believe God would have you share your faith? The first step is to start praying for them and then be ready to share when the opportunity comes.

∞

I am not ashamed of this Good News about Christ. It is the power of God at work, saving everyone who believes. ROMANS 1:16

October 26

Constantine was the first Christian emperor of the Roman Empire, but was he really a Christian?

His full name was Flavius Valerius Constantinus, but we know him as Constantine. He was the son of Constantius Chlorus, the western emperor of the Roman Empire, and his concubine, a barmaid named Helena. When his father died in 306, Constantine was proclaimed emperor by his father's troops. Meanwhile, back in Rome the Praetorian Guard proclaimed Maxentius as western emperor.

On **October 26, 312,** Constantine and his troops reached a point about five miles north of Rome, prepared to do battle with Maxentius the following day. Eusebius, a church historian living at the time, tells us that Constantine swore to him that he saw a flaming cross in the sky that evening with the Greek words for "In This Sign Conquer." He also reported that he had a dream that night in which Christ commanded him to have his soldiers mark their shields with the letters *chi* and *rho*, the first and second letters of the Greek word for "Christ," superimposed one upon the other. The next morning when he ordered his troops to put the inscription on their shields, it was a great encouragement to the many Christians in his army.

Meanwhile in Rome Maxentius spent the night before the battle engaged in sacrifices and divinations. The impending battle was shaping up to be between the army of Christ and the army of the Roman gods.

Maxentius decided to do battle directly in front of the Tiber River with the Milvian Bridge behind him, approximately a mile from the gates of Rome. His decision showed exceedingly poor judgment for if he lost, escape would be impossible. And lose he did to the outnumbered forces of Constantine. According to Eusebius, Constantine advanced "invoking the God of heaven, and his son and word our Lord Jesus Christ, the saviour of all." Maxentius was thrown into the Tiber along with many of his troops. His body was found the next day, and Constantine entered Rome as the undisputed emperor of the western empire.

The following year Constantine met with Licinius, emperor of the eastern empire, and issued the Edict of Milan, granting Christians freedom of worship along with compensation and return of confiscated church property.

An uneasy peace existed between Constantine and Licinius until 323 when

THE AMBIGUOUS EMPEROR

Constantine defeated Licinius in battle, becoming the sole emperor. He then founded the city of Constantinople (today's Istanbul) as capital of his empire.

Constantine is most remembered for his church policies. In addition to the Edict of Milan, he allowed bishops to settle civil lawsuits, he closed courts of law and workshops on Sundays, and banned gladiatorial games. He also took an active role in church affairs, summoning the Council of Nicea in 325.

But there was a darker side to Constantine. In 326 he had his wife, the sister of Maxentius, and one son executed under suspicious circumstances. He also never relinquished his position as chief priest of the pagan state religion, and his coins proclaimed his allegiance to the sun god. He delayed Christian baptism until shortly before his death. Yet whatever his personal spiritual state, because of Constantine, Christianity became the religion of the Roman Empire.

Reflection

Prior to Constantine Christians had experienced wave after wave of persecution. Then suddenly under Constantine it became the unofficial state religion. Do you think this was a positive development or a negative one? What are some of the benefits and drawbacks to Christianity's being the state religion?

All governments have been placed in power by God.   ROMANS 13:1

October 27

This professional baseball player spoke to larger crowds than he played for.

HIS NAME was Billy Sunday, and he was born near Ames, Iowa, in 1862. His father, a Union soldier, died before he saw his son. His Christian mother then married a man who deserted her. Unable to provide for all her children, she was forced to send Billy and a brother to an orphanage.

After high school Billy moved to Marshalltown, Iowa, where he played on the local state champion baseball team. His amazing speed attracted the attention of the manager of the Chicago White Stockings, and he signed with Chicago in 1883.

One Sunday afternoon in Chicago in 1886, Billy and some of his teammates went to a saloon and, after drinking their fill, went outside and sat down on the curb. Across the street a Christian band was singing and playing gospel songs that Billy remembered his mother singing years before in their log cabin. Overcome with nostalgia, Billy began to sob. One of the young men in the band walked over to him and said, "We are going down to the Pacific Garden Mission. Won't you come down to the mission?"[40]

Billy hesitated for a moment before jumping to his feet. He told his teammates on the curb, "I'm through. I am going to Jesus Christ. We've come to a parting of the ways." Sunday walked to the mission and fell down on his knees and into the arms of the Savior. Dreading his return to the ballpark the next day, he was pleasantly surprised to find his teammates supportive of what he had done.

Billy joined the Jefferson Park Presbyterian Church and regularly went to Bible studies at the YMCA. In 1888 he married Helen Thompson, the sister of the White Stockings batboy.

In 1891 Sunday ended his baseball career to work full time for the YMCA for a fraction of what he had earned as a baseball player. After two years he went to work as an advance man for evangelist J. Wilbur Chapman. When Chapman suddenly stopped traveling as an evangelist in 1895, he invited Sunday to hold evangelistic services for him in Garner, Iowa. Billy did so, using Chapman's sermon materials, and was never without invitations to preach from that time on. The Presbyterian Church did not license Sunday until 1898, and he wasn't ordained until 1903, but he never let that stand in his way.

PLAY BALL!

Sunday started out holding evangelistic crusades in small midwestern towns and gradually went to the larger cities of the Midwest and the East. His unorthodox preaching style, acrobatic antics, and flamboyant gestures attracted the press, making him a household name.

The climax of Sunday's services followed the sermon, when he invited members of the audience to "walk the sawdust trail" to the front, indicating their decision to commit their lives to Christ. His most successful crusade was in New York City, where 98,264 people "hit the sawdust trail" in ten weeks.

Much of Sunday's success was due to the organizational skills of his wife, Helen. At the peak of his career as an evangelist he had a full-time staff of twenty-three, including his song leader, Homer Rodeheaver. He preached to more than one hundred million during his lifetime, and hundreds of thousands put their faith in the Lord Jesus through his ministry.

Billy Sunday preached his last sermon on **October 27, 1935**, and forty-four came forward in the service. Ten days later he went to be with the Lord. No one else had done more than he in the early days of the twentieth century in America to keep the Christian faith vital and growing.

Reflection

How would you have reacted to Billy Sunday? Theologian J. Gresham Machen shared this reaction: "Much of it, I confess, left me cold. . . . But in the last five or ten minutes of that sermon, I got a new realization of the power of the gospel." Have you ever had a negative reaction to preachers with a unique style? What should be our criteria for evaluating preaching?

Dear brothers and sisters, when I first came to you I didn't use lofty words and brilliant ideas to tell you God's message. For I decided to concentrate only on Jesus Christ and his death on the cross.

1 CORINTHIANS 2:1-2

October 28

Capital punishment was freely administered in eighteenth-century England.

Sᴀʀᴀʜ Pᴇᴛᴇʀs, a friend of John Wesley's who shared his commitment to evangelism, felt a burden for the prisoners in London's Newgate Prison—especially those on death row. On October 9, 1748, she and a Christian friend went to see a prisoner named John Lancaster, who had requested a visit from them. They met that day in Lancaster's cell along with six or seven others also sentenced to death. As they sang a hymn together, read some Scripture, and prayed, the prisoners were in tears, convicted of their need for God. Lancaster told her how at one time he had attended church daily but then had drifted away. He became friends with a young man who was a thief, and they had become partners in crime. Now he was in prison, sentenced to death for breaking into a home and stealing nineteen yards of velvet.

This experience made Sarah Peters determined to do whatever she could for these men in their final days. Sometimes alone and sometimes with one or two others, Sarah visited these men almost daily as their execution dates approached. Deciding that it would be helpful to meet with each condemned prisoner individually to inquire about his spiritual condition, Sarah and her companions met first with John Lancaster. He lifted his eyes and his hands and after a moment said, "I thank God I do feel that he has forgiven me my sins. I do know it." They asked him how and when he first knew. He answered, "I was in great fear and heaviness till the very first morning you came hither first. That morning I was in earnest prayer, and just as St. Paul's clock struck five, the Lord poured into my soul such peace as I had never felt, so that I was scarce able to bear it. From that hour I have never been afraid to die. For I know, and am sure, as soon as my soul departs from the body, the Lord Jesus will stand ready to carry it into glory."

Six others told similar stories of how in the last days they had put their faith in Christ through the ministry of Sarah Peters.

The night before their execution they wanted to pray with Sarah one more time. She went to the prison at 10:00 P.M. but was not allowed to enter. The jailer did, however, allow six of the condemned men to spend their last night together in prayer in one cell.

At 6:00 A.M. the next morning Sarah Peters was admitted to the prison. As the cell was opened, the six men were rejoicing about their happy night of fellowship. John Lancaster was the first to be called out to have his leg irons removed. As the guard pounded off the irons, Lancaster exclaimed, "Blessed be the day I came into this place! O what a glorious work hath the Lord carried on in my soul since I came hither!"

When the guards led the prisoners into the prison yard to go to the execution site, Lancaster saw faithful Sarah, kissed her, and said, "I am going to paradise today. And you will follow me soon."

As the men were getting into the cart that would carry them to their execution, Lancaster said to his fellow prisoners, "Come, my dear friends, let us go joyfully, for the Lord is making ready to receive us into everlasting habitations."

John Lancaster and his friends were executed on **October 28, 1748.** Two days later Sarah fell ill with a fever. Her work with the prisoners completed, she contentedly praised God from her sickbed. Less than three weeks later Sarah Peters followed the prisoners to the "everlasting habitations."

Reflection

God used Sarah's compassion in ways she might never have imagined. Do you think that God can use you in ways you have never imagined? Always be open to the opportunities God places before you, and allow him to use you in new ways—his ways.

∽◎◇◎∽

Come, you who are blessed by my Father, inherit the Kingdom prepared for you from the foundation of the world. For . . . I was in prison, and you visited me.   MATTHEW 25:34-36

October 29

How would you like to have a godly theologian lead your nation?

ON OCTOBER 29, 1837, a son was born to the pastor of the Reformed state church in Maassluis, the Netherlands. His name was Abraham Kuyper, but his family called him "Bram."

Growing up in a pastor's home, young Kuyper felt himself more repulsed by than attracted to the church. Yet when he enrolled at the University of Leiden, he took the pretheology curriculum. At this time the theological faculties of the Dutch universities were being taken over by Modernism, which exalted human reason over divine revelation. Kuyper did not escape this influence. He entered the university a person of orthodox faith but within a year and a half had become a religious liberal.

Right before he was to enter the Leiden University Divinity School in 1858, his favorite undergraduate professor encouraged him to enter a theological essay contest comparing Calvin's view of the church with that of a Polish Reformer named Jan Laski. Kuyper scoured the libraries of Holland for the writings of Laski but found almost nothing. When he was about to give up his search, he suddenly found that his professor's father had the most complete collection of Laski's writings in all of Europe. Kuyper attributed this discovery to a direct act of the living sovereign God, and it had a profound effect upon his life. For the first time he began to experience doubt about his liberal theology.

The next major event in Kuyper's religious pilgrimage was reading an English novel given to him by his fiancée. It was *The Heir of Redclyffe* by the Christian author Charlotte Mary Yonge. Kuyper so identified with the proud hero of the story that when the hero knelt and wept before God with a broken and contrite heart, Kuyper did the same. The transaction that occurred at that moment Kuyper would only understand later. But from that moment on he found himself despising what he once admired and seeking what he once despised.

The final step in his pilgrimage came in his first pastorate. In his church was a group of individuals of low social status who knew more about the Bible than he did. They had a Calvinistic worldview that he envied, even though he had a doctorate in theology. The debates Kuyper had with these folk proved to be short lived because before long they had convinced him that the Bible taught God's sovereign grace. He later wrote, "Their unremitting perseverance has become the blessing of my heart, the rise of the morning star for my life."

A THEOLOGIAN BECOMES
PRIME MINISTER

The wisdom and faith of these simple people taught him to find rest for his soul "in the worship of a God who works all things, both the willing and the working, according to his good pleasure."

Now fully embracing orthodox Calvinism, Kuyper held major pulpits in Utrecht and Amsterdam. Taking up the cause for private schools, he joined the Anti-Revolutionary Party, which opposed godless revolution and made orthodox Calvinism a political force. Eventually he became the head of the party and beginning in 1874 served repeatedly as a member of one or the other of the houses of the Netherlands legislature. He edited his party's daily newspaper and wrote 16,800 editorials for it. In 1880 Kuyper and others founded the Free University of Amsterdam, dedicated to a Reformed theology. Kuyper became the professor of systematic theology.

In 1886 Kuyper led a break from the state church, founding "The Reformed Churches in the Netherlands." In the subsequent years he did his theological writing, authoring the *Encyclopedia of Sacred Theology* in 1898, *Calvinism* in 1899, and *The Work of the Holy Spirit* in 1900.

In 1901 Abraham Kuyper became prime minister of the Netherlands, holding the position for four years. As prime minister he was used of God to shape a nation.

Reflection

God created the institutions of church, state, and family—all three.
So many Christians just seek to represent God in one or two of these.
Abraham Kuyper was the supreme example of the well-rounded Christian who represented God in all three. Have you neglected one or more of these institutions? Determine that you will seek to represent God in all three.

∽♡✑

Show respect for everyone. Love your Christian brothers and sisters.
Fear God. Show respect for the king.   1 PETER 2:17

October 30

Where did the Roman Catholic Church and the Eastern Orthodox Church come from?

THE CRUCIAL date was **October 30, 451,** but there is a story that leads up to it.

In the early days of the Roman Empire, Rome was the imperial capital. The church there was the largest and wealthiest in the empire. By the middle of the third century its membership approached thirty thousand. It had no rival in the west.

In addition, certain early Christian writers from the second century on referred to Peter and Paul as founders of the church at Rome and to Rome's bishops as successors to the apostles. Yet this respect for the history of the church of Rome did not prevent these same writers from openly disagreeing with the bishop of Rome when they believed him to be in error. In fact, up to the time of Emperor Constantine (312–337)[41] the bishop of Rome exercised no authority outside the city.

As the church developed under Constantine, it naturally tended to follow the pattern of the empire, with the bishop of a provincial capital having authority over the bishops of the other cities of the province. In 325 the Council of Nicea recognized the bishops of Alexandria, Egypt; Antioch, Syria; and Rome as preeminent in their areas.

In 330 Constantine moved his residence from Rome to Constantinople, meaning "City of Constantine," today's Istanbul. Authority in the church moved east along with Constantine. Soon the bishop of Constantinople was considered to have authority equal to the bishops of Alexandria, Antioch, and Rome.

In 440 Leo I was elected bishop of Rome. He immediately proclaimed himself the supreme head of all Christendom. He established the ecclesiastical dynasty of Peter, which continues in the Roman Catholic Church today. In 451 Emperor Valentinian III put this into law, "As the primacy of the Apostolic See is based on the title of the blessed Peter, prince of episcopal dignity, on the dignity of the city of Rome, and on the decision of the Holy Synod, no illicit steps may be taken against this See to usurp its authority."

In 451 another church council was called at Chalcedon, a suburb of Constantinople. Approximately 450 bishops were invited, but no more than 340 were present at any one time. Although Leo did not attend himself, his influence was very evident. Thus, it was to everyone's surprise that on **October 30, 451**, the council gave the bishop of Constantinople authority equal to that of the bishop of Rome, making Constantinople for the east what Rome was for the west. The action of this council confirmed the independent authority of the bishop or patriarch of Constantinople over the eastern church.

Leo's representative at the council protested vehemently, but the decision stood. The church now had two heads: the bishop of Rome over the western church and the bishop of Constantinople over the eastern church.

In the sixth century the bishop of Rome came to be called the pope. The word *pope* comes from the word *papa* and originally was a reference to the fatherly care exercised by all bishops.

In subsequent centuries the Roman Catholic Church, as the western church came to be known, has remained monolithic. The eastern church subdivided into many self-governing ethnic Orthodox churches, which together compose a federation known as the Eastern Orthodox Church.

Reflection

The whole controversy between the eastern church and the western church was based upon the assumption that there is an office of "bishop" that is different from and has greater authority than the office of "pastor" or "elder." Do you think that is true? What church offices were present in the New Testament church?

It is a true saying that if someone wants to be an elder [Greek: "overseer" or "bishop"], he desires an honorable responsibility. For an elder [Greek: "presbyter" or "elder"] must be a man whose life cannot be spoken against. 1 TIMOTHY 3:1-2

October 31

What kind of people does God use to fulfill his purposes?

IN 445 B.C. Nehemiah, the cupbearer to the king of Persia, received permission from the king to go back to Jerusalem to rebuild the city's wall, which had been destroyed by the Babylonians 142 years earlier. To give Nehemiah the proper authority, the king appointed him governor of Judah. Nehemiah then returned to Jerusalem with an armed escort from the king. Under Nehemiah's direction the wall was rebuilt (Nehemiah 1:1–6:15).[42]

But Nehemiah knew that more than a wall was needed to accomplish God's purposes. Jerusalem needed to be filled with a people who had God's Word (7:4–8:18). But just hearing the word of God was not enough. The Jews who had returned to Jerusalem needed to repent of their sins and commit themselves wholeheartedly to the God of the Word (10:29). Only then would Jerusalem be secure.

When there was a change of rulers in Israel, there often was a covenant renewal ceremony in which the people confessed their sins and renewed their covenant under their new ruler. **October 31, 445 B.C.**, was the day for the Jews of Judah to renew their covenant with their Lord, taking an oath of allegiance to God under their new governor, Nehemiah.

They first had to confess their sins to God. Therefore, the people came together dressed in sackcloth to fast and to confess their sins and the sins of their ancestors. The Book of the Law of the Lord was read aloud to them for about three hours. Then for three more hours they took turns confessing their sins and worshiping the Lord their God (9:1-4).

In their prayer they confessed their years of serving other gods and their breaking of God's commandments. They took ownership of the sins that had brought the curse of God's covenant upon them and resulted in them being taken captive to Babylon. Even though Nehemiah was their governor, those who had returned to Jerusalem were still virtual slaves of Persia. They realized that their only hope was in turning back to God. As their Covenant Lord, he alone could lift the curse (vv. 5-37).

The leaders and people then gave an oath of allegiance to the Lord. They vowed to accept the curse of God if they failed to obey his law as given by Moses. They solemnly promised to follow faithfully all the commands, laws, and regulations of the Lord. They put their oath in writing and sealed it with the personal seals of the leaders (v. 38–10:29).

610

SECURITY TAKES MORE THAN WALLS

The covenant was thus renewed, and Nehemiah and all the people were now a people consecrated to God for his service and fit to live within the walls of his city, the newly secured Jerusalem.

Reflection

The ceremony by which we are to renew our personal covenant with God is the Lord's Supper. We are to make this our regular time of self-examination and confession of sin. Then, following the example of Nehemiah and the people of Judah, we are to renew our personal oath of allegiance to our Lord Jesus Christ.

As they were eating, Jesus took a loaf of bread and asked God's blessing on it. Then he broke it in pieces and gave it to the disciples, saying, "Take it, for this is my body." And he took a cup of wine and gave thanks to God for it. He gave it to them, and they all drank from it. And he said to them, "This is my blood, poured out for many, sealing the covenant between God and his people."   MARK 14:22-24

November 1

He was proceeding toward ordination in the Church of Scotland when he experienced the first of several mental breakdowns.

ALEXANDER CRUDEN was known as being mentally unstable, clueless in affairs of the heart, and an expert in Bible scholarship—quite an improbable combination.

Born in Aberdeen, Scotland, in 1699, Cruden completed a master of arts degree at Marischal College in Aberdeen and was proceeding toward ordination in the Church of Scotland when he experienced the first of several mental breakdowns. The breakdown was triggered by a disappointment in love, and he was placed in confinement for a short time.

Once recovered, he moved to London, where he worked first as a tutor, then as a proofreader, and finally as the French translator for an earl. After his dismissal for not knowing French well enough, he opened a bookstore in London in 1732. The bookstore was a success and earned him the honorary title of Bookseller to the Queen.

In 1736 he began work on a concordance of the Bible. His habit of meticulously tracing words through Scripture and his extensive study of the Bible made him eminently qualified for this endeavor. He completed the first edition in just eighteen months and in 1737 published *Cruden's Concordance*.

Unfortunately the book was not initially a financial success, causing him to lose his business. Cruden also was once again unlucky in love, this time making unwelcome advances toward a widow, triggering another bout with insanity. Again he was placed in what in that day was called a "private madhouse." After a few weeks he escaped by cutting through the bedstead to which he was chained.

In 1739 he issued a pamphlet on his confinement entitled *The London Citizen Exceedingly Injured, or a British Inquisition Display'd*. He subsequently brought a lawsuit over his confinement that he pleaded himself and lost. He then published a pamphlet of his trial.

In 1753 he was once again placed in an insane asylum for a short time. In between confinements his behavior could be described as eccentric at best. Cruden believed that God had appointed him as the public censor, especially regarding profanity and Sabbath keeping. He took upon himself the title Alexander the Corrector and in 1755 unsuccessfully petitioned Parliament to confer this title upon him officially. In this self-appointed role he went about London with a sponge, erasing from walls obscene graffiti and whatever else did not meet his approval. He solicited students to serve as his deputy-correctors.

He also ran unsuccessfully for Parliament and made frequent unwelcome and embarrassing contacts with various single women, including an attempt to marry the daughter of the lord mayor of London. To finance his misadventures he published pamphlets about his causes, including three entitled *The Adventures of Alexander the Corrector.*

Cruden finally found success as a proofreader, first for a daily newspaper and then for several editions of the Greek and Latin classics. His acute attention to detail served him well. He continued to revise his concordance and published two later editions in 1761 and 1769. These later editions produced both profit and recognition for Cruden. To this day they remain in print as the standard concordance for the King James Version of the Bible.

Although unquestionably eccentric and troubled, Alexander Cruden was a devout Christian and a gifted scholar. On **November 1, 1770,** he died while in prayer and was found still upon his knees.

Reflection

How did you react to the knowledge that Alexander Cruden had bouts with mental illness? What lessons can we learn from his life story? God used Alexander Cruden in spite of his limitations, and he can use us in spite of ours.

[The Lord] said, "My gracious favor is all you need. My power works best in your weakness."
2 CORINTHIANS 12:9

November 2

What do a lapsed Baptist, a member of the English landed gentry, and the inventor of synthetic acetate have in common?

WOULD YOU believe they were used by God to return the Jews to their land?

It all began in 1874 in the hamlet of Motol in what is today Belarus. Chaim Weizmann was born the third of fifteen children to Ezer Weizmann, who made a living cutting lumber and floating it down to the Baltic Sea. In spite of the family's meager resources, the children were able to attend the Orthodox Jewish school in their village and then go on to advanced training. All but one of Chaim's surviving siblings became either a scientist, a physician, a dentist, an engineer, or a teacher.

In 1900 Chaim received a Ph.D. in chemistry from the University of Fribourg and four years later became a professor of chemistry at the University of Manchester in England.

From childhood Weizmann had a passion for Zionism, the movement to reestablish a Jewish national state in Palestine. As a leading academic in England, he was able to use his position to meet the influential politicians of his day and to share with them his passion for Zionism.

Two of Weizmann's converts to Zionism were leaders of Parliament, Arthur Balfour and David Lloyd George. Balfour was the last representative of England's traditional landed class to lead England. Weizmann had a decisive discussion with Balfour in 1914, explaining that although the Jews were the main contributors to German culture, they had to hide their Jewishness to do so. This disclosure brought Balfour to tears and made him a committed supporter of Zionism.

David Lloyd George, a Welshman, was the grandson of a Baptist pastor. His father died when he was just one year old, leaving the family in dire poverty. His mother and her children were taken in and provided for by her brother, also a Baptist minister. David, however, lost his faith as a boy. As an adult and a leader of Parliament, he was infamous for his marital infidelity, having the same mistress for more than thirty years.

During World War I, Lloyd George, already a Zionist thanks to his contact with Weizmann, was put in charge first of the cabinet munitions portfolio and then of the whole war office. By 1916 England was facing a huge military logistic problem. It was running out of natural acetate, a crucial ingredient in the manufacture of munitions. Chaim Weizmann saved the day by quickly inventing a new process for extracting acetate from corn. The British would not run out of bullets!

Their gratitude for Weizmann's discovery served the cause of Zionism well when, also in 1916, Lloyd George became prime minister and Balfour his foreign secretary. As the British army fought the Ottoman Empire for control of Palestine, the British government issued the Balfour Declaration on **November 2, 1917,** to rally Jewish support for its effort. The key paragraph read, "His Majesty's Government views with favour the establishment in Palestine of a national home for the Jewish people . . . and will use their best endeavors to facilitate the achievement of this object."

The Balfour Declaration became the single most important document in the establishment of the state of Israel.[1] In 1949 Chaim Weizmann became Israel's first president.

God used Lloyd George, Balfour, and Weizmann to return the Jews to their land.

Reflection

Have you personally seen God accomplish his purposes through unbelievers? If so, what does that tell you about God? If God uses both believers and unbelievers to accomplish his purposes, think of what that implies regarding the range of requests that we can ask of him. Just as there are no limits to what God can do, there should be no limits to the scope of our prayers.

"Would I ever bring this nation to the point of birth and then not deliver it?" asks the Lord. "No! I would never keep this nation from being born," says your God. ISAIAH 66:9

November 3

What a difference a year can make.

On **November 3, 1745,** David Brainerd,[2] a twenty-seven-year-old missionary to the Indians of Crossweeksung, New Jersey, baptized fourteen converts. This was part of what he called "a remarkable work of grace" with which God had blessed his labors among the Native Americans of New Jersey and Pennsylvania.

David Brainerd was born in 1718 in Haddam, Connecticut, and orphaned at the age of fourteen. He was planning to farm the land he had inherited until he experienced a profound conversion in 1739. That same year he entered Yale, aspiring to the Congregational ministry.

At Yale he became a leader in the Great Awakening, a revival then sweeping New England. In his third year he was expelled from the university when he was overheard questioning the salvation of a faculty member. After his expulsion, he continued his studies for the ministry, living with a local minister. Subsequently he was licensed to preach and ordained as a Presbyterian minister. He became a missionary to the American Indians of New Jersey and Pennsylvania.

On that Sunday, **November 3, 1745,** Brainerd joyously baptized six adults and eight children. One of them was an eighty-year-old woman. Two of them were fifty-year-old men who were notorious drunkards before putting their trust in the Lord Jesus. One of the men was a murderer as well. Because of the terrible lives these men had led, Brainerd delayed baptizing them until he saw a radical change in their lives. But changed they were, and Brainerd finally felt at peace about baptizing them.

The baptisms of this day brought the total of baptized believers to forty-seven. Brainerd wrote in his journal, "Through rich grace, none of them have been left to disgrace their profession of Christianity by any scandalous or unbecoming behavior."

A year later this remarkable work of God among the Indians continued, but the work of David Brainerd was coming to a close. Brainerd, at the age of just twenty-eight, was dying of tuberculosis. He sadly realized that he must return to New England, where friends and family could care for him during his last days.

Desperately weak in body on **November 3, 1746,** Brainerd spent the day bidding farewell to his beloved Indian flock. He visited each family in their home and exhorted each person from God's Word. Tears flowed freely as he left each house. His farewells took most of the day, and in the evening he rode off, his mission completed.

A year later David Brainerd was dead at the age of twenty-nine.

Reflection

Our lives often have seasons. There are times when we are active in what God is doing and even see people put their faith in Christ. But there are other seasons when we are laid aside while others do the laboring. Ultimately all of us will come to a final season when we will die. We do not know the order or the length of our seasons, but what a comfort to know that Jesus is Lord of every season!

There is a time for everything, a season for every activity under heaven. A time to be born and a time to die. A time to plant and a time to harvest. A time to kill and a time to heal. A time to tear down and a time to rebuild. A time to cry and a time to laugh. A time to grieve and a time to dance.   ECCLESIASTES 3:1-4

November 4

The drinking of wine signaled both the beginning and the end of the spiritual pilgrimage of one of England's greatest preachers.

In 1779 Charles Simeon entered King's College at Cambridge University as an eager student with no particular allegiance to God. After three days he was appalled to learn that at Cambridge participation in the Lord's Supper was mandatory. In just three weeks he would have to eat the bread and drink the wine at Communion. His initial reaction was that Satan was probably more prepared for the Lord's Supper than he. An earnest soul, he determined that he must prepare himself immediately. He went out and bought the only Christian book he knew, *The Whole Duty of Man* by William Law, the great English devotional writer. As he read and reread it, he cried out to God for mercy. By the time he took Communion, he had made himself ill with his intense reading, fasting, and prayer.

Then as soon as he had taken Communion, he realized that Easter was coming when he would have to take it again. He sought out books on the Lord's Supper and pored over them. He remembered the sins of his life and mourned over them. He sincerely tried to repent and to exercise self-denial.

When Holy Week came, he read that in their sacrificial system the Jews transferred their sin to their sacrifice. The question entered his mind, *May I transfer my guilt to another? Has God provided an offering for me to which I may transfer my sins?*

On Wednesday of Holy Week he began to hope that he would find mercy. From Thursday through Saturday this hope increased more and more. Finally on Easter Sunday he awoke with these words on his lips: "Jesus Christ is risen today! Hallelujah! Hallelujah!" As he ate the bread and drank the wine of Communion, he felt a load being taken off his soul and a peace that he had never before experienced. He now knew that Jesus in his death had paid the penalty for his guilt and his sins.

Charles Simeon grew in his faith and went on to become vicar of Holy Trinity Church, Cambridge, where he served for fifty-four years as one of England's greatest preachers.

On **November 4, 1836,** exactly a week before his death, Charles Simeon drank a glass of wine that his doctor had prescribed for him. Stretching out his feeble arms, he pronounced a blessing on those in his room, "May all the blessings which my adorable Savior purchased for me with his tears, yea with his own precious life blood, be now given to me to enjoy, and to my two dearest friends . . . and to my two dear nurses. . . . I shall drink no more of that wine until I drink it new with my Redeemer."

A week later he was with his Redeemer in his kingdom.

Reflection

What does the Lord's Supper mean to you? Do you prepare yourself for it by taking a spiritual inventory and truly repenting of your sins? Taking the cup at the Lord's Supper can be just another church ritual, or it can be a renewal of your allegiance to the Lord of the Supper. Which is it for you?

Then he took a cup of wine, and when he had given thanks for it, he said, "Take this and share it among yourselves. For I will not drink wine again until the Kingdom of God has come."   LUKE 22:17-18

November 5

The God who controls the winds controls the nations.

IN THE seventeenth century the decades of the 1660s through the 1680s were tough times for God's people in England and Scotland. After the ascendancy of the Puritans to political power during the English civil wars of the 1640s and the execution of King Charles I, Oliver Cromwell, a Puritan Independent or Congregationalist, set up a commonwealth with himself as its head.[3] He took the title of Lord Protector, which he held until his death in 1658. His son Richard succeeded him as protector for one year before he resigned. During the Cromwells' rule the Puritans experienced the peak of their political power and enjoyed religious freedom.

The Presbyterians who controlled the English Parliament were no fans of the Cromwells. Therefore, in 1660 Parliament invited Charles II, the second son and successor of Charles I, to the throne. They were no doubt influenced by the fact that ten years earlier Charles II had become a Presbyterian in order to encourage Scottish support for his recovery of the throne. But Charles II turned out to be no friend of God's people. Under the Act of Uniformity of 1662 all ministers were given a deadline by which they had to give their public support of the Anglican Prayer Book and were required to receive Episcopal ordination if they had not yet been so ordained. This resulted in the "Great Ejection" in which about two thousand Presbyterian, Independent, and Baptist pastors were forced from their churches. The Five Mile Act of 1665 forbade non-Anglican ministers from coming within five miles of any British city or town.

Finally, on his deathbed in 1685, Charles II publicly acknowledged his conversion to Roman Catholicism, which he had kept secret for years. This explained his animosity toward the Presbyterians, who had brought him to the throne.

Charles II was succeeded by James II, another Roman Catholic. James II intensified the persecution of the Scottish Covenanters, who resisted the Episcopal form of government being forced upon the Church of Scotland. Many devout Presbyterians lost their lives. Since James II had pushed for a Catholic succession, the birth of his son brought the issue to a crisis. His daughter Mary had married William of Orange, who himself had strong claims to the throne of England. William, born in the Hague and raised as a follower of John Calvin, had become head of state of the Netherlands. The thought of James's

EVEN THE WIND AND WAVES
OBEY HIM

Catholic son as heir to the throne was too much for the Protestant nobles of England, and they invited William and Mary to take the throne.

On November 1, 1688, William set out with his navy across the English Channel, intending to invade England. The wind that propelled William's fleet was so strong that it kept many of the English ships imprisoned in the Thames River, unable to sail into the Channel to attack William. As William's fleet sailed along the English coast, martial music blared from the decks, and the lights stretching from stem to stern on each ship blazed through the evening sky. It was a stirring spectacle to the beleaguered Protestants of England. On **November 5, 1688,** William's fleet landed on English soil, and William of Orange and his troops began what has become known as the Glorious Revolution.

James II fled to France. The next month as the Protestants of England celebrated Christmas worshiping as they wished, James attended Mass in France.

God used the wind to keep England a Protestant nation.

Reflection

Have you ever seen God use the forces of nature to accomplish his purposes in your life? Has a storm or other natural disaster prevented you from doing something or going somewhere? Perhaps afterward you could see God's hand in it. Sometimes it is difficult to understand why certain things happen, but we can find comfort in knowing that God is in control of all things. Our faith is in a God who not only created the winds but also controls them to achieve his purposes. Our God is an awesome God!

Who is this man, that even the wind and waves obey him? MARK 4:41

November 6

When God chooses people, he often chooses the most unlikely ones.

THE YEAR was 1882 and the American preacher D. L. Moody[4] planned a week of meetings to evangelize the students of England's historic Cambridge University.

On Sunday, November 5, the first day of the meetings, many Christians from town and a few staunch Christians from the university attended a mass prayer meeting just before the first service. Moody spoke, and while some rejoiced at his message, others were appalled by his American accent and unsophisticated speech.

At eight o'clock the rented hall began to fill with rowdy university students, eventually numbering about seventeen hundred. The brave choir began singing, mocked by students singing back their own songs. While some of the students constructed a pyramid of chairs, another threw a firecracker against a window. Pandemonium reigned.

Then a door opened, and in filed D. L. Moody; his song leader, Ira Sankey; and several Christian faculty members and other clergy. A professor of botany offered an opening prayer with some students yelling out, "Hear! Hear!" Next Ira Sankey sang the hymn "The Ninety and Nine."[5] The audience listened in silence at first but then began beating the floor with their canes and umbrellas as they shouted, "Hear! Hear!" At the end of each song there were cries of "Encore." When the boisterous interruptions ruined Sankey's singing of "Man of Sorrows," he was close to tears. Several of the most offensive students were asked to leave, and Moody reminded the audience that this was not a political meeting.

Then Moody began to preach on Daniel in the lions' den. Moody's monosyllabic pronunciation, "Dan'l," was too much for the rabble-rousers, and they shouted back "Dan'l, Dan'l" each time Moody said the name. Whenever Moody used any American colloquialism or non-British pronunciation, there was loud laughter. The hecklers were led by a handsome young student in the front row. Moody kept looking him in the eye, but it was to no avail. Probably the majority of the students were listening, but the vocal minority made it difficult for them to do so.

As the students returned to the university after the meeting, Gerald Lander, the handsome heckler from the front row, loudly announced, "If uneducated men will come to teach the Varsity, they deserve to be snubbed."

FACING A HOSTILE AUDIENCE

The next morning, Monday, **November 6, 1882,** a bellboy knocked on Moody's hotel room door and handed him a personal calling card bearing the name "Mr. Gerald Lander."

Moody invited Lander to his room and recognized him instantly. The student said humbly, "I want to apologize, sir. And I've brought a letter of apology from the men."

Some of the more gentlemanly students, appalled at their companions' behavior, had written the apology and prevailed on Gerald Lander to deliver it. Reluctantly he went to Moody as an English gentleman who realized that he had overstepped the bounds of propriety. Moody had a long talk with Lander and got him to agree to come again that night to the meeting to prove the sincerity of his apology.

Little did Moody know that one day Gerald Lander, the disruptive leader of the students, would spend his life evangelizing southern China as a missionary.

Reflection

When we hear stories like that of Gerald Lander, we realize how unlimited God is in whom he draws to himself. We must never exclude any names from our prayer list thinking that it is unlikely that God will save them. Are there people for whom you have stopped praying, thinking their salvation unlikely? Don't give up! Our God specializes in accomplishing the unlikely.

Is anything too hard for the Lord?   GENESIS 18:14

November 7

God works through families—regardless of how dysfunctional they may be.

DUTTON LANE was born near Baltimore, Maryland, on **November 7, 1732,** the very same year George Washington was born. Sometime thereafter his father moved the family to Virginia near the North Carolina border.

Nearby in Sandy Springs, North Carolina, Shubal Stearns, a convert of George Whitefield, the leader of the Great Awakening,[6] had founded a Separate Baptist church in 1755 with the help of his brother-in-law Daniel Marshall. (During the Great Awakening revivalistic Baptist churches were called "Separate Baptist," and antirevivalistic ones were called "Regular Baptist.") Stearns and Marshall soon began evangelistic trips into Virginia, where one of the many who put their faith in the Lord Jesus and was baptized was Dutton Lane.

Lane soon began preaching himself, and when the first Separate Baptist church in Virginia was founded at Dan River in 1760, Dutton Lane was installed as its pastor. By 1772 he had five additional preaching positions with five assistants helping him.

In spite of God's blessing on his ministry, Dutton Lane also faced opposition. A man named William Cocker loudly boasted that he would rather go to hell than heaven if going to the latter required his becoming a Baptist. However, one day by chance Cocker heard Dutton Lane preach. His response was to fall to the ground, crying, "Lord, have mercy upon me! I am a gone man! What shall I do to be saved?" He soon was saved and became a Baptist on his way to heaven!

On another occasion an opponent by the name of James Roberts was traveling with a companion to obtain a warrant for the arrest of one of Lane's assistants. As they traveled at night a supernatural bright light shone around them, startling their horses. The bright light was followed by a thick darkness in which they could not see where they were going. Roberts understood this to be God's warning to him, and he immediately stopped opposing Dutton Lane.

Regrettably, Lane's greatest opposition came from his own father who told his mother that he would horsewhip her if she ever went to hear her son preach. On the one occasion when she did sneak away to hear her son, her husband whipped her on her return home.

Lane's father next determined that he was going to shoot his son. Lane's mother courageously reminded her husband that, when he went bird hunting, the birds had the opportunity to fly away before they were shot. She challenged her husband to give his son a similar opportunity and go hear him preach at least one time before he murdered him.

Lane's father accepted the challenge and went to hear his son. During the service he became convicted of his sins and soon trusted Jesus as the One who had paid the penalty for them. Dutton Lane then had the privilege of baptizing his father, who had sought to kill him.

Reflection

Have you experienced opposition to your faith from members of your family? How do you react to it? We need to remember that we are responsible only for our own behavior. If God changes us, those around us will act differently toward us. We can trust God's promise to work in our families.

Each of you must turn from your sins and turn to God, and be baptized in the name of Jesus Christ for the forgiveness of your sins. Then you will receive the gift of the Holy Spirit. This promise is to you and to your children, and even to the Gentiles—all who have been called by the Lord our God.   ACTS 2:38-39

November 8

To have faith or not to have faith—that is the question.

EDWARD D. GRIFFIN was born in 1770, the son of a wealthy Connecticut farmer. He went to Yale with the plan of studying for the ministry, but as he entered his senior year, he realized that he was unconverted. Horrified at the idea of going into the ministry without a personal faith, he turned to the study of law.

In July 1791 Griffin fell ill. On his sickbed, feeling miserable, Griffin began to think, *If I cannot bear this for a short time, how can I bear the pains of hell forever?* These thoughts refused to leave him, and within three months he had trusted in Jesus as his Lord and Savior and was headed for heaven.

Not long after, Griffin began to question his decision to become a lawyer. One Sunday after church as he walked up the stairs to his room, the question played through his mind over and over *And why should not you be a minister? And why should not you be a minister?* By the time he got to the top of the stairs, he resolved that he would seriously investigate the issue. He prayed earnestly that God would give him direction through the Bible. He opened his Bible repeatedly, and each time the passage he read pointed him toward, in his own words, "preaching the everlasting gospel and plucking souls as brands from the burnings." In less than forty-five minutes, he became certain that he was called to preach the gospel.

And preach he did. After training under Jonathan Edwards Jr., Griffin pastored a series of Congregational churches in New Salem and New Hartford, Connecticut, and in New Orange and Newark, New Jersey. In 1808 he became professor of preaching at Andover Seminary and from 1811 to 1814 was pastor of Park Street Church, Boston. Finally from 1821 to 1836 Griffin served as president of Williams College.[7]

The blessing of God on Griffin is almost unequaled in the history of American preachers. His ministry was one of almost unbroken revival. Wherever Edward Griffin went, the Holy Spirit drew people to Jesus. Griffin saw more people converted under his preaching than anyone since George Whitefield in the mid-1700s.[8] At one point during his years as president of Williams College there were only eighteen students out of the whole student body who had not committed themselves to Christ.

His passion for souls continued even as he was dying. To his grandchildren and to his servants he gave a parting challenge to meet him in heaven. To two grandsons he said, "You must give your heart to the Savior. Don't put it off another hour." To a granddaughter he pleaded, "Give your heart to the Savior while you are young."

Then on **November 8, 1837**, Edward Griffin was called home to be with his Savior forever.

Reflection

Do you know what God has called you to do? Edward Griffin had to wait until he had committed his life to the Lord Jesus before God showed him the plan for his life. Similarly for the rest of us, the first step to knowing God's plan for our lives is to wholeheartedly trust Jesus as our Lord and Savior. Then as we ask him for guidance, he will reveal his will to us just as he did to Edward Griffin.

Don't copy the behavior and customs of this world, but let God transform you into a new person by changing the way you think. Then you will know what God wants you to do, and you will know how good and pleasing and perfect his will really is. ROMANS 12:2

November 9

What would it have been like to spend a day with George Whitefield, the famous Anglican evangelist of the Great Awakening?

LET WHITEFIELD[9] tell you in the words of his journal for Sunday, **November 9, 1740.** He was just twenty-five years old at the time and was preaching in Philadelphia.

> Several came to see me with whom I prayed. Preached at eleven in the morning, to several thousands in a house built for that purpose since my departure from Philadelphia. It is a hundred feet long and seventy feet broad. Both in the morning and the evening, God's glory filled the house. . . . Great was the joy of most of the hearers when they saw me; but some still mocked. Between services . . . many friends being in the room, I kneeled down, prayed and exhorted them all. I was greatly rejoiced to look around them, because there were some who had been marvelous offenders against God. I shall mention two only. The first is a Mr. Brockden, recorder of deeds, etc., a man eminent in his profession, but for many days a notorious Deist. In his younger days, he told me, he had some religious impressions, but coming into business, the cares of the world so choked the good seed, that he not only forgot his God, but at length began to doubt of, and to dispute His very Being. . . . When I came to Philadelphia this time twelve-month, he had no curiosity to hear me. But a brother Deist, his choicest companion, pressing him to come to hear me, to satisfy his curiosity he at length complied with his request. It was night. I was preaching at the Court House stairs, upon the conference which our Lord had with Nicodemus. I had not spoken much before God struck his heart. . . . His family did not know he had come to hear me. After he came home, his wife, who had been at the sermon, came in also, and wished heartily that he had heard me. He said nothing. After this another of his family came in, repeating the same wish; and, if I mistake not, after that another, till at last being unable to refrain any longer, with tears in his eyes, he told them that he had been hearing me. . . . Though upwards of threescore years old, he is now, I believe, born again of God.
>
> The other is Captain H——l, formerly as great a reprobate as I have ever heard of, almost a scandal and reproach to human nature. . . . By

God's grace, he is now, I believe a Christian. Not only reformed but renewed. The effectual stroke, he told me, was given when I preached last spring at Pennytack. . . . Ever since, he has been zealous for the truth, stood firm when he was beaten, and in danger of being murdered sometime ago by many of my opposers; and in short shows forth his faith by his works. I mention these cases in particular, because I think they are remarkable proofs of the doctrine of God's eternal election and everlasting love. Whatever men's reasoning may suggest, if the children of God fairly examine their own experiences—if they do God justice, they must acknowledge that they did not choose God, but that God chose them.

Reflection

What do you think of Whitefield's statement that these converts did not choose God but God chose them? Our culture tells us that we have free will and that we are the captains of our own fate. If you are a Christian, have you considered the possibility that God chose you before you chose him?

∽৯৶

You didn't choose me. I chose you.   JOHN 15:16

November 10

On this day was born a man whom God used to change the course of history.

His name was Martin Luther, and he was born on **November 10, 1483,** in a peasant family in the town of Eisleben in Prussian Saxony.[10] The next day he was baptized and named after St. Martin, the saint for that day. Growing up, he was taught to pray to God and to the saints and to honor the church and its priests. Over time he became a devout worshiper of the Virgin Mary.

Luther enrolled at the University of Erfurt in 1501, receiving a bachelor of arts degree in 1502 and a master of arts in 1505.

That same year Luther was returning to Erfurt from a visit to his parents when he was overtaken by a violent thunderstorm. Terrified, Luther fell to the ground and cried out, "St. Anne, help me! I will become a monk." Fifteen days later Luther kept his vow and entered the monastery of the Hermits of St. Augustine in Erfurt. Two years later he was ordained a priest.

The following year Luther transferred to the University of Wittenberg, where he earned the doctor of theology degree in 1512. He received a permanent appointment as a professor of theology at the university, a position he held for life.

Luther probably would have lived out his life as a little-known university professor of theology had it not been for the following experience, told in his own words:

> I had been possessed by an unusually ardent desire to understand Paul in his epistle to the Romans. Nevertheless, in spite of the ardour of my heart, I was hindered by the unique word in the first chapter: "The righteousness of God. . . ." I hated that word "righteousness of God," because in accordance with the usage and custom of the doctors I had been taught to understand it philosophically as meaning, as they put it, the formal or active righteousness according to which God is righteous and punishes sinners and the unjust.
>
> As a monk I led an irreproachable life. Nevertheless I felt that I was a sinner before God. . . . Not only did I not love, but I actually hated the righteous God who punishes sinners. . . .
>
> Day and night I tried to meditate upon the significance of these words: "The righteousness of God is revealed in it, as it is written: The

righteous shall live by faith." Then, finally, God had mercy on me, and I began to understand that the righteousness of God is that gift of God by which a righteous man lives, namely, faith, and that this sentence— "The righteousness of God is revealed in the Gospel"—is passive, indicating that the merciful God justifies us by faith, as it is written: "The righteous shall live by faith." Now I felt as though I had been reborn altogether and had entered Paradise. . . .

Just as intensely as I had before hated the expression 'the righteousness of God', I now lovingly praised this most pleasant word. This passage from Paul became to me the very gate to Paradise.

After his rebirth, God went on to use Martin Luther to lead the Reformation and to found the Lutheran Church and Protestantism itself.

Reflection

Do you understand what it means to be justified by faith? It means that because Christ paid the penalty for our sins on the cross, God declares us righteous on the basis of our faith in Jesus Christ as Lord and Savior. We are justified when we first trust Christ, but then we are to continue trusting him day by day for the specifics of life. We are to live by faith.

This Good News tells us how God makes us right in his sight. This is accomplished from start to finish by faith. As the Scriptures say, "It is through faith that a righteous person has life." ROMANS 1:17

November 11

For the first time in recorded history, free men covenanted together to form a civil government with the authority to enact laws that the people promised to obey.

THE DATE was **November 11, 1620,** and the place was the *Mayflower,* anchored off the coast of Cape Cod. One hundred and two passengers including thirty-four children had spent seven weeks crossing the ocean from England. Of the passengers, sixteen men, eleven women, and fourteen children were Pilgrims, having been associated with the Separatist church in Scrooby, England. Refusing to conform to the Church of England, they had first sought religious asylum in Leyden, Holland. After twelve years there, they became concerned that their children would no longer identify themselves as English. Learning of the possibility of settling in America, they made arrangements with the Virginia Company to settle just south of the Hudson River within the northernmost boundary of the Virginia Charter. However, fierce winds blew them off course to the north—to the shores of Cape Cod.

They decided to settle on Cape Cod but then realized that since they would not be under the jurisdiction of the Virginia Company, they would be on their own because they had no agreement with the New England Company. On board the ship some of the non-Pilgrim bonded servants and those hired by contract greeted this newly revised plan as an opportunity for rebellion. The Pilgrim leadership saw that they must act quickly to prevent a mutiny.

The Pilgrim men then wrote up a compact, now known as the Mayflower Compact, and presented it to those on board. Forty-one of the sixty-five men signed it. Thirteen of those who didn't sign were sons of signers, covered by their fathers' commitments. The remaining men, nine servants and two hired sailors, were probably too sick to sign. The compact read:

> In the name of God, Amen. We whose names are underwritten, the
> loyal subjects of our dread Sovereign Lord King James by the grace of
> God, of Great Britain, France, Ireland, king, Defender of the Faith, etc.
> Having undertaken, for the glory of God and the advancement
> of the Christian Faith and honor of our King and country, a voyage
> to plant the first colony in the northern parts of Virginia, do by these
> presents solemnly and mutually in the presence of God and one

another, covenant and combine ourselves together into a civil body politic, for our better ordering and preservation and furtherance of the ends aforesaid, and by virtue hereof to enact, constitute and frame such just and equal laws, ordinances, acts, constitutions and offices from time to time, as shall be thought most meet and convenient for the general good of the colony. Unto which we promise all due submission and obedience. In witness whereof we have hereunder subscribed our names at Cape Cod, the 11th of November, in the year of the reign of our Sovereign King James of England . . . Anno Domini 1620.

Before leaving the Netherlands, the Pilgrims had knelt on the dock to ask God's blessing on their voyage, and now William Bradford recorded, "Being thus arrived in a good harbor and brought safe to land, they fell upon their knees and blessed the God of heaven."[11]

During their first winter, forty-seven people died including thirteen of the eighteen women. Only three families were left intact. These humble Christian men and women were to be the seeds of what would become the United States of America.

Reflection

In spite of all the hardships the Pilgrims experienced, their little government lasted and became a model for the entire nation. Acknowledging that their purpose was to glorify God, they covenanted together to enact laws "for the general good of the colony" and promised to abide by them. The Pilgrims had a clear vision and staked their very lives on following it. It is equally important for us to have a clear vision of God's purposes for ourselves and our families. What is your vision?

As for me and my family, we will serve the Lord.   JOSHUA 24:15

November 12

When God prompts you to pray for someone, you'd best take heed!

ON A COOL morning in a village near Bedford, England, in the 1870s, a widow named Mrs. Symons went to the door of her little cottage to watch the hounds run by, followed by the huntsmen. She always enjoyed waving to the children as they rode by on their ponies. On this particular morning she felt herself strangely drawn to the children of Captain Polhill-Turner, a family who often rode in the hunt. As the clatter of hooves faded away, Mrs. Symons was filled with the conviction that Jesus wanted her to pray for these children. And so she did, faithfully praying for them daily.

Captain Polhill-Turner, a wealthy member of Parliament, lived in a large country house with his six children. Nanny Readshaw cared for the children, and life proceeded in a well-planned and orderly fashion. Even the future careers of the three sons were already planned. The oldest would inherit the family estate, the second would join the English cavalry, and the youngest, Arthur, would enter the ministry. Growing up, Arthur's religious ideas were hazy. What little he knew came from Nanny Readshaw telling the children Bible stories and saying that Jesus was her friend.

Two critical events disturbed the well-ordered life of young Arthur Polhill-Turner. The first was when his oldest sister, Alice, suddenly announced that she was going to give up hunting and parties and serve Jesus. She had attended a mission service in Bedford, where she had trusted Christ as her Savior, unaware that Mrs. Symons and Nanny Readshaw had been praying for her all those years. Arthur found her subsequent efforts to evangelize him to be a nuisance.

The second event was a greater shock. In Arthur's last year of high school, his father died. As Arthur entered Cambridge University the following year, his father's death continued to weigh on him.

During his second year at Cambridge, Arthur was amused to read placards advertising the coming of an American evangelist, D. L. Moody,[12] and his song leader, Ira Sankey, to Cambridge. To him it was a joke that two uneducated Americans would come to Cambridge.

The first meeting was on a Sunday, and Arthur Polhill-Turner went out of curiosity. Although many of the students attending the meeting were rowdy, Arthur tried to listen to Moody's message in spite of the mayhem.

Arthur continued to go back every night. By Thursday the mood had changed, and at the end of the service many prominent students made their way to the inquiry room. That night Moody preached on the Prodigal Son, and Arthur realized the emptiness of his life. But back in his room Arthur was afraid of what it might mean to give himself wholeheartedly to Jesus. He returned to the meetings on Friday and Saturday, knowing he must trust Christ but afraid to do so.

On Sunday, **November 12, 1882,** a week after the first service, Arthur was back once again. In his sermon Moody quoted Isaiah 12:2: "Behold, God is my salvation; I will trust, and not be afraid: for the Lord Jehovah is my strength and my song; he also is become my salvation" (KJV). Suddenly Arthur understood. The words continued to ring in Arthur's ears as he joined in singing from the heart, "Just as I am, without one plea, but that Thy blood was shed for me . . . O Lamb of God, I come!"

At the close of the service Moody asked everyone who had received blessing during the week to stand as a token of their faith. Over two hundred stood, and one of them was Arthur Polhill-Turner. God led him to China, where he served as a missionary for the rest of his life.

Reflection

Do you ever find that you just can't get someone out of your mind? Perhaps God is prompting you to pray for that person. The two women in this story who prayed were an important part of God's plan. When you are praying and God brings someone's name to mind, rejoice that you, too, have been given a divine prayer assignment.

The earnest prayer of a righteous person has great power and wonderful results.   JAMES 5:16

November 13

God is in the business of changing lives.

No ONE is a better illustration of this than Augustine. He was born on **November 13, 354,** in the town of Tagaste in Numidia, North Africa, now Algeria. His parents named him Aurelius Augustinus. His father, Patricius, was a minor noble who desired above all else that Augustine become cultured. His devout but domineering mother, Monica, wanted above all else that her son become a Christian.

As a boy Augustine was the exact opposite of what his mother desired him to be. To her dismay he became an accomplished thief and liar.

At the age of twelve, Augustine was sent to school, first in the old Numidian city of Madiera and then in Carthage. During these years he added sexual promiscuity to his catalog of sins, taking a mistress by whom he fathered a son.

In spite of his immoral lifestyle, Augustine excelled academically. He became an accomplished Latin scholar and went on to study rhetoric and philosophy, eventually becoming a teacher of rhetoric.

Religiously, Augustine was attracted to the sect of the Manicheans, which believed in the eternal coexistence of two kingdoms—light and darkness—which were in an eternal struggle. When his mother, Monica, learned he had become a Manichean, she threw him out of the house.

Ambition brought Augustine to Rome in 383 and to Milan, the imperial capital, in 384 as a professor of rhetoric. There he met Ambrose, the bishop of Milan, who challenged him to consider Christianity.

Then came a warm day in July 386 that changed Augustine's life forever. Augustine was at his villa in Milan with his mother and his best friend, Alypius. That day Pontitian, an African Christian who was an officer of the imperial household, stopped for a visit. As they talked, Pontitian casually picked up a book lying on the table and was surprised to find it to be the epistles of Paul. That prompted Pontitian to relate how he had come to put his faith in Christ. He also told how two friends of his had decided to join a monastery and how their fiancées had also become Christians, dedicating themselves to virginity. Hearing the story of the two young women committing themselves to chastity pierced Augustine to the core. He suddenly realized that he was depraved and addicted to sex. How would he ever be able to extricate himself?

After Pontitian left, Augustine ran out of the house, overcome by his sin.

In despair he flung himself on the ground underneath a fig tree. There he babbled, "How long, how long? Tomorrow and tomorrow? Why not now? Why should there not be an end to my uncleanness now?"

Suddenly Augustine heard the plaintive voice of an unknown little girl singing a song with the simple words "Take up and read." To Augustine these words came as the voice of God himself. Jumping up, Augustine ran and got the book containing Paul's epistles. Opening its pages, his eyes fell on Romans 13:13-14: "We should be decent and true in everything we do, so that everyone can approve of our behavior. Don't participate in wild parties and getting drunk, or in adultery and immoral living, or in fighting and jealousy. But let the Lord Jesus Christ take control of you, and don't think of ways to indulge your evil desires."

Augustine later wrote, "Instantly as I reached the end of this sentence, it was as if the light of peace was poured into my heart, and all the shades of doubt faded away." He immediately went into the house and told his mother that her prayers had been answered.

Now a changed man, Augustine went on to become the bishop of Hippo in North Africa and the greatest theologian between the apostle Paul and John Calvin.[13]

Reflection

Augustine's life was transformed from gross immorality to total commitment to Jesus Christ. If you are a Christian, has God brought changes in your life? What have they been? If you are still on the way to becoming a Christian, what changes would you like God to make in you?

∽❧∾

Let the Lord Jesus Christ take control of you.   ROMANS 13:14

November 14

What's it like to starve?

GEORGE WHITEFIELD experienced starvation firsthand. Born in 1714, White-field entered Oxford University in 1734 and joined John Wesley's Holy Club.[14] At Oxford, Whitefield put his faith in the Lord Jesus. In 1737 Whitefield was ordained a preaching deacon in the Church of England and accepted the invitation of John and Charles Wesley to cross the Atlantic and join them in Georgia.[15]

Whitefield arrived in May 1738 at the age of twenty-three. After spending the summer preaching in Georgia, Whitefield felt that God would have him return home, and so on September 9 he boarded a ship returning to England.

On October 6 the ship experienced the worst storm the sailors had ever witnessed. Most of the fresh food washed overboard during the storm, making the future ominous indeed. Whitefield wrote in his journal, "All was terror and confusion, men's hearts failing them for fear, and the wind and the sea waging horribly. But God (forever be adored for his unmerited goodness) was exceedingly gracious unto me. I felt a sweet complacency in my will in submission to His. Many particular promises God has made me from His Word, that I should return in peace, flowed in upon my heart; and He enabled me greatly to rejoice."

By the end of October the daily ration was just a quart of water per day plus some salt beef and water dumplings. Several days later the passengers were informed that there was only a three-day supply of water left, if consumed at the current rate. As a result, the water ration was reduced to a pint a day.

Another violent wind arose on November 6 and drove the ship back many miles. Two little cakes made of flour and water and a tiny piece of salt beef were all that Whitefield had to eat as he lay sick on his cot. By now most on board were very weak and emaciated.

On November 10 Whitefield wrote in his journal, "Was much strengthened in our present distress by . . . our Saviour's turning the water into wine at the marriage at Cana. We have applied to Him as the holy Virgin did, and told Him in prayer that 'we have but very little water.' At present He seems to turn away His face, and to say, 'What have I to do with you?' But this is only because the hour of extremity is not yet come. When it is, I doubt not but He will now as richly supply our wants as He did theirs then."

By November 11 the daily rations were down to an ounce or two of salt beef, a pint of muddy water, and a small cake of flour and water. Whitefield wrote, "I have besought the Lord many times to send us a fair wind; but now He does not think it fit to answer me. I am wholly resigned, knowing that His grace will be sufficient for me and that His time is best."

The next day land was sighted, and on **November 14, 1738**, the ship arrived in Ireland. There was but half a pint of water left on the ship. A small boat was sent out to bring back food and water. Whitefield wrote, "As soon as the provisions came, we kneeled down and returned hearty thanks to our good God, who has heard our prayers, and sent His angel before us, to prepare our way."

Reflection

What is the worst trial that you have ever faced? Why do you think God allowed you to experience it? What lessons did you learn from it? Were you frustrated by God's timing? George Whitefield's acceptance of God's timing as best was amazing evidence of the depth of his faith. Are you willing to accept God's timing? God is never late, but he can be very last minute from our point of view.

∽◌◠

Dear brothers and sisters, whenever trouble comes your way, let it be an opportunity for joy. For when your faith is tested, your endurance has a chance to grow. So let it grow, for when your endurance is fully developed, you will be strong in character and ready for anything.

JAMES 1:2-4

November 15

One of the most famous Christian authors actually wrote only one book—a book that most of his readers have never heard of.

OSWALD CHAMBERS was born in Aberdeen, Scotland, in 1874, the son of a Baptist minister. As a teenager he accompanied his father to hear the famous Baptist preacher Charles Spurgeon.[16] Afterward, young Oswald told his father that if there had been an opportunity at the service, he would have given himself to the Lord. His father quickly answered, "You can do it now, my boy." And there on a London street with his father, Oswald Chambers quietly surrendered his life to Jesus Christ as his Savior and Lord.

After studying at Edinburgh University, Chambers entered Dunoon Gospel Training College in 1897 to prepare for the ministry. He then served as a tutor at the school for eight years. While he was there, his faith grew, and he developed a great zeal for evangelism. He next served as a traveling Bible teacher for the Pentecostal League of Prayer. In 1911 he became the first principal of the Bible Training College at Clapham Common, London. However, World War I soon exploded upon Europe, and the college was closed in 1915.

Chambers then joined the staff of the YMCA and with his wife, Gertrude, known to all as Biddy, was sent to Egypt to minister to the English and Australian troops stationed in Zeitoun and Ismailia. The YMCA constructed seventy-two-by-forty-foot "huts" constructed with "walls" of matting made of local reeds so that the army soldiers would have a place to come and relax. Chambers was to supervise them.

When he arrived in Zeitoun, he immediately put up a sign that read: "YMCA Study Hut Open 9 A.M. to 9 P.M. for Reading, Writing & Study. A Blackboard Lecture Each Evening at 7:30 P.M." Within a week he had four hundred soldiers packed in each night to hear him teach the Bible. Hundreds came to Christ. He wrote in his diary, "There are so many 'saved' souls waiting instruction, and they take it with zest. There is no difficulty at all in getting men to 'decide' for Christ, they do it readily."

In 1916 the YMCA planned evangelistic crusades throughout all the Egyptian military camps with Chambers as the evangelist. Chambers wrote in his diary of the meeting at the Ismailia camp: "We had some magnificent decisions, and I would not allow any singing or even bowing of heads but just told them to come out before all their comrades if they meant business, and out they came."

MY UTMOST FOR HIS HIGHEST

On October 17, 1917, Chambers returned from a Wednesday night prayer meeting feeling ill. Intense abdominal pain continued until finally on October 29 he allowed himself to be taken to the Gizeh Red Cross hospital. The surgeon operated immediately to remove Chambers's appendix. Chambers began to recover, but on November 4 he developed a blood clot, and on **November 15, 1917,** he died. His wife, Biddy, cabled back to England the simple message "Oswald in His Presence."

Chambers had written just one book before he died, *Baffled to Fight Better*, but he had kept a journal. Biddy was a trained court stenographer and had taken down word for word many of his hundreds of messages delivered at colleges and military camps.

Several years after Oswald's death, Biddy began editing his material into 365 daily readings and named it *My Utmost for His Highest*. She completed it in 1927, ten years after Oswald's death. Today the book remains among the top-ten Christian titles sold annually.

Biddy edited twelve more books from Oswald's material and published them under his name, never once mentioning her own.

Reflection

Oswald Chambers left a legacy both in the lives he influenced and in the words he spoke. What do you think will be your legacy? Not many of us will ever find our words in print, but all of us can make a difference in the lives of those around us.

Your lives are a letter written in our hearts, and everyone can read it and recognize our good work among you. Clearly, you are a letter from Christ prepared by us. It is written not with pen and ink, but with the Spirit of the living God. It is carved not on stone, but on human hearts. 2 CORINTHIANS 3:2-3

November 16

God used hymns in an unexpected way to save Protestantism in Germany.

THE THIRTY Years' War, lasting from 1618 to 1648, was a complex conflict that compressed various struggles into one ongoing conflagration. One of the primary contests was between the Catholics and Protestants of Germany.

By 1630 the Imperial Catholic armies were achieving great success, and the Protestant cause seemed hopeless. All of the Protestant princes had been defeated by the Catholic army, and the victors were preparing to extinguish every remnant of Lutheranism in Germany.

At this point King Gustavus Adolphus of Sweden decided to try to save Protestantism in continental Europe and landed in Germany with his small but well-trained army. The marquis of Brandenburg and the duke of Saxony supplied Gustavus with a few more troops. In a succession of swift victories, Gustavus defeated the Catholic army and marched victoriously across Germany.

Finally the Imperial Catholic army prepared to make a last stand against Gustavus at Lützen in southern Germany. There on the morning of **November 16, 1632,** Gustavus Adolphus commanded his army chaplain to lead his troops in worship. The king himself led the army in singing,

> *Fear not, thou faithful Christian flock;*
> *God is thy shelter and thy rock:*
> *Fear not for thy salvation.*
> *Though fierce the foe and dark the night,*
> *The Lord of hosts shall be thy might,*
> *Christ, thine illumination.*
>
> *Arise; arise, the foe defy!*
> *Call on the Name of God most high,*
> *That He with might endue you.*
> *And Christ your everlasting Priest,*
> *In all your conflicts shall assist,*
> *From strength to strength renew you.*

Gustavus then knelt in earnest prayer. A heavy morning fog prevented the Protestant forces from starting their attack. While they waited, Gustavus ordered the musicians to play Martin Luther's great hymn:

THE POWER OF HYMNS

A mighty fortress is our God, a bulwark never failing;
Our helper, He amid the flood of mortal ills prevailing.
For still our ancient foe doth seek to work us woe—
His craft and pow'r are great, and armed with cruel hate,
On earth is not his equal.

Did we in our own strength confide, our striving would be losing,
Were not the right Man on our side, the Man of God's own choosing.
Dost ask who that may be? Christ Jesus, it is He—
Lord Sabaoth His name, from age to age the same,
And He must win the battle.

As the fog began to lift, Gustavus himself prayed, "Jesus, Jesus, Jesus, help me today to do battle for thy holy name." He then shouted to his troops, "Now forward to the attack in the name of our God!" The troops answered back, "God with us," and they followed their king into battle.

The battle raged back and forth. At 11:00 A.M. Gustavus Adolphus fell from his horse mortally wounded. The cry went out, "The king is wounded," marking the turning point of the battle. In response, the Swedish army fiercely charged the enemy lines. By the end of the day the victory had been won, and German Protestantism was preserved. As they had sung earlier that day, "Though fierce the foe and dark the night, the Lord of hosts *was* their might." Gustavus Adolphus was victorious, albeit in death.

Reflection

When hymns or worship songs are sung in church, do you pay attention to the words? Do you allow God to minister to you through them? King Gustavus used the words of hymns to inspire and uplift his troops. Let them do the same for you.

❧

Let the Holy Spirit fill and control you. Then you will sing psalms and hymns and spiritual songs among yourselves, making music to the Lord in your hearts. And you will always give thanks for everything to God the Father in the name of our Lord Jesus Christ. EPHESIANS 5:18-20

November 17

How did a Gypsy boy grow up to be a great evangelist?

RODNEY SMITH was born in a tent in England in 1860 to illiterate Gypsy parents, Cornelius and Polly Smith.

When Rodney was a young boy, his oldest sister became very sick. The local doctor diagnosed it as smallpox and told the father to take his family and leave town at once. Cornelius set up camp outside of town. He stayed with his sick daughter in the wagon, and the rest of the family stayed in a tent a short distance away to keep from being infected. Unfortunately Rodney's brother and mother both came down with smallpox as well. As his wife lay dying, Cornelius asked, "Do you try to pray, my dear?"

"Yes," she answered, "I am trying, and while I am trying to pray it seems as though a black hand comes before me and shows me all that I have done, and something whispers, 'There is no mercy for you.' "

As a boy, Cornelius had heard the gospel while in prison, and so he told her what he had learned—that Christ died for sinners and that he was her Savior if she would look to him. After he finished, she threw her arms around him and kissed him. Cornelius went outside the wagon to weep, and as he did so, he heard her singing:

> *I have a Father in the Promised Land*
> *My God calls me, I must go*
> *To meet Him in the Promised Land.*

He hurried back into the wagon and asked, "Polly, my dear, where did you learn that song?"

She said, "I heard it when I was a little girl. One Sunday my father's tents were pitched on a village green, and seeing the young people and others go into a little . . . chapel, I followed them in, and they sang those words." She kept singing the words over and over. That children's song became a lifeline that pulled Polly from her darkness into God's light. She died the next day.

Several years later Cornelius himself determined he must turn to God. He went to a meeting at a mission hall where he was wonderfully converted. He came home a new man.

Observing the change in his father, young Rodney had a deep longing to experience the same change in his own life. One evening as he was sitting near

THE GYPSY EVANGELIST

his father's tent, Rodney asked himself the question, "Are you going to wander about as a gypsy boy and a gypsy man without hope, or will you be a Christian and have some definite object to live for?" He surprised himself when he answered his own question, "By the grace of God I will be a Christian, and I will meet my mother in heaven!"

A few days later, on **November 17, 1876,** Rodney went to the Primitive Methodist chapel in Cambridge determined that, if there was an opportunity, he would publicly give himself to Christ. At the end of the service the pastor invited those who wanted to give themselves to the Lord to come to the Communion rail. Rodney was the first to go forward. There in simple faith young Rodney Smith committed himself to Jesus Christ. He went home, and his father wept as Rodney told him that his prayers had been answered.

Rodney Smith became a great evangelist, known as "Gipsy Smith." He traveled widely, making over fifty trips to the United States to hold evangelistic meetings. Although uneducated, he was a winsome preacher. His straightforward messages and simple gospel songs brought thousands to Jesus Christ.

Reflection

Why do you think God often draws people to himself who we feel are unlikely candidates for becoming Christians? God specializes in the unexpected—he even had his Son be born in a stable and then die on a criminal's cross. This reminds us that since God is the God of the unexpected, no one is eliminated as a candidate for his kingdom.

Remember, dear brothers and sisters, that few of you were wise in the world's eyes, or powerful, or wealthy when God called you. Instead, God deliberately chose things the world considers foolish in order to shame those who think they are wise.   1 CORINTHIANS 1:26-27

November 18

"I, Benjamin, take thee Annie, to be my wedded wife, to have and to hold from this day forward, for better or for worse, for richer or for poorer, in sickness and in health."

IN 1876 when Benjamin Breckinridge Warfield made this vow to his bride, Annie Kinkead, he meant it with all of his being. Warfield was born in 1851 near Lexington, Kentucky. His father was a farmer and a published expert on raising cattle. His mother was the daughter of Rev. Robert Jefferson Breckinridge, a theologian at the Presbyterian seminary in Danville, Kentucky.

As a boy, Warfield made a public profession of his faith in the Lord Jesus and joined the Second Presbyterian Church of Lexington at the age of sixteen. His mother wanted him to be a minister, but while he was a student at Princeton University, his main academic interests were mathematics and science. He graduated with highest honors at the age of just nineteen and went off to Europe for graduate study in science. To everyone's surprise and his mother's delight, he wrote home in 1872 to announce that he had decided to enter the ministry instead.

He returned to the United States and entered Princeton Theological Seminary, graduating with the class of 1876. That summer he married Annie Kinkead, the daughter of a prominent Lexington attorney who had once represented Abraham Lincoln in a trial.

For their honeymoon the happy couple went to Europe, where Warfield was to study at the University of Leipzig. One day while they were hiking in the Harz Mountains of Germany, they were caught in a violent thunderstorm. Annie suffered a nervous breakdown from which she never recovered. She remained to some degree an invalid for the rest of her life.

Back in America, Warfield served nine years as professor of New Testament at Western Theological Seminary in Allegheny, Pennsylvania. In 1887 he was called to Princeton Theological Seminary as professor of Theology.

At Princeton, Warfield became his generation's leading exponent of Calvinistic theology in general and the authority of Scripture in particular. He was an outspoken critic of the liberal scholarship of his day and a prolific author. His collected works fill ten volumes.

In the midst of all his teaching and writing, Warfield was simultaneously caring for his beloved Annie. At first she was able to go on walks through the town of Princeton with her husband. When this became too difficult for her, they would walk together back and forth across the front porch of their home. Eventually she became bedridden and was seen by few others than her husband. By his own choice, Warfield spent nearly all of his nonteaching hours at home. Even with a busy academic schedule, he reserved time every day for reading to Annie. He was almost never away from his wife for more than two hours at a time.

During the last ten years of Annie's life, the Warfields only left Princeton once, to go on a vacation that he hoped would improve her health. In spite of the limitations placed on his life by her condition, no one ever heard one word of complaint from Warfield. In describing him a friend once said, "He has had only two interests in life—his work and Mrs. Warfield."

When Annie Warfield died on **November 18, 1915,** her husband had lovingly cared for her for thirty-nine years. Warfield himself died five years later.[17]

In spite of all the hours spent as caregiver to his wife, no other theologian of his time is as widely read today or has had his books in print as long as those of Benjamin Breckenridge Warfield. God blessed his faithfulness to his marriage vow.

Reflection

Are there things in your life that have not turned out as you had hoped? Are you able, like Benjamin Warfield, to be faithful and content in whatever situation God places you, or are you still struggling? God is most glorified when we are most satisfied with him.

I have learned the secret of living in every situation, whether it is with a full stomach or empty, with plenty or little. For I can do everything with the help of Christ who gives me the strength I need.

PHILIPPIANS 4:12-13

November 19

Do you know why most English towns have a Havelock Street, Road, or Square?

In 1815 a young Englishman named Henry Havelock joined the army as a second lieutenant. At that time promotions in the British army were purchased. When his father lost his fortune in 1820, Havelock realized that his only hope for advancement was in India, where they could be earned without purchase. Consequently in 1823 he embarked for India.

On the boat Havelock became friends with James Gardner, a young lieutenant. Gardner lent Havelock *Memoir of the Rev. Henry Martyn*, the story of the chaplain of the East India Company, who had made the same voyage in 1805 that Havelock was now making. Martyn had also been a bright, outwardly moral young man, similar to Havelock in many ways. After college Martyn had experienced a definite "conversion," a word that Havelock disliked intensely. Yet Havelock was struck by the last entry in Martyn's journal, made a few days before his death at age thirty-one, when he wrote of the sweet comfort of peace that he had received from God.

The next book Gardner lent to Havelock was by Thomas Scott. The author traced his spiritual journey from a position very similar to that of Havelock, telling of his pride in his own self-sufficiency and his denial of the deity of Christ. Scott had been slowly influenced by John Newton, the hymn writer and former slave trader,[18] and came to realize that Christ was the Son of God and placed his faith in him.

Despite his reservations, Havelock began to have a sense that Gardner, Martyn, and Scott were right and that faith in Jesus Christ might meet his own deepest needs. As Gardner guided him through the relevant Bible passages, Havelock came to know "a dear and merciful Saviour who will never cease to be kind to those who come to him in faith."

Havelock had a long and distinguished career in India. He served in the war against Burma (1824–1826), in the first Afghan war (1838–1842), in the first Sikh war (1845–1846), and in the invasion of Persia (1856).

Havelock particularly distinguished himself during the Indian mutiny of 1857, when the native regiments of the British army took control of large areas of India. From July through November Havelock won twelve battles against the mutineers in spite of being outnumbered every time. His son, Harry, served as his aide-de-camp.

"A DEAR AND MERCIFUL SAVIOR"

Of even greater satisfaction to Havelock than sharing military victories with his son was the personal victory Harry experienced. Young Harry had come to India with the belief that his father's faith was an unnecessary luxury. But as Harry spent day after day at his father's side, he came to share the widely held conviction that his father was the most brilliant soldier of his day. Harry realized that his father's success could not be separated from his absolute trust in Christ as his counselor and friend. Finally in November of 1857 Harry accepted his father's Savior as his own.

When news of Havelock's first three victories trickled back to London, he was promoted to major general and knighted. Unknown to him, on **November 19, 1857,** the queen made Havelock a baron, and Parliament voted lifetime pensions for both Henry and his son, Harry, a few days later.

When newspapers from London finally arrived in India reporting these adulations, what meant the most to Havelock was not that his name was now a household word throughout England but that the nation recognized him as a Christian general.

The day after reading those newspapers, Henry Havelock came down with dysentery and died four days later in the arms of his son. Harry wrote his mother, "His end was that of a just man made perfect."

Reflection

Henry Havelock let the world know that the secret to his success was his faith in Jesus Christ. Because he was empowered by God, he was able to bring glory to God in a way that all could see. Does being a Christian make a difference in your work? Do you consciously seek to glorify God as you fulfill your responsibilities?

❧

Let your good deeds shine out for all to see, so that everyone will praise your heavenly Father. MATTHEW 5:16

November 20

Did you know that the author of many of your favorite hymns was blind?

FANNY CROSBY was born in 1820 in Putnam County, New York. When she was just six weeks old, she caught a cold that caused inflammation in her eyes. When her parents called their family doctor, he was not at home and someone else came in his place. This stranger recommended that hot poultices be placed on her eyes, which tragically resulted in the loss of her eyesight. As news spread about her blindness, the man quickly left town and was never heard of again. Misfortune continued to follow the family as death claimed Fanny's father when she was but one year old.

When her grandmother first heard of Fanny's blindness, she said, "Then I will be her eyes." She became an important part of Fanny's life, spending hours describing flowers, birds, and beautiful sunsets to the little girl. Another important person entered Fanny's life when she was nine years old—a Mrs. Hawley, who schooled her in poetry and the Bible. Fanny spent much time memorizing both. By the age of ten she had memorized whole books of the Bible.

When Fanny was fifteen, she entered the Institution for the Blind in New York City. She studied there for seven years and then returned to teach at the school for eleven years. While a student there she developed her talent for writing verse. She was never proficient in Braille but rather depended upon her phenomenal memory. She composed and edited poems in her head.

In the fall of 1850 revival meetings were being held at the Thirtieth Street Methodist Church in New York City. Fanny and some of her friends went every night. Twice she went forward at the altar call but could not find the peace and joy she craved. On **November 20, 1850,** Fanny went forward for a third time, all by herself. The congregation was singing the old Isaac Watts hymn "Alas and Did My Savior Bleed." When they reached the last line of the last verse, "Here, Lord, I give myself away," Fanny was filled with joy and shouted, "Hallelujah!" She had given herself to her Savior.

She fell in love with Alexander Van Alstyne, a blind musician she met at the school for the blind. They married when she was thirty-eight and had one child, who died in infancy. Fanny kept her maiden name, which was unusual for the times, and was referred to as "Mrs. Crosby" for the rest of her life.

Fanny did not start writing hymns until eleven years after her conversion but then became one of the most prolific hymn writers in history. She wrote

BLIND BUT NOT HANDICAPPED

nearly nine thousand hymns before her death in 1915. Her well-known hymns include "Blessed Assurance," "Rescue the Perishing," "Jesus, Keep Me Near the Cross," "Pass Me Not," "Praise Him, Praise Him," "Saved by Grace," and "To God Be the Glory." Approximately sixty of her hymns are still in common use.

In addition to her hymn writing, Fanny Crosby was a popular speaker and traveled throughout the world. She went to the White House as guest of Presidents John Quincy Adams, John Tyler, Andrew Johnson, and Grover Cleveland. Her friends included many famous people, such as Horace Greeley, Henry Clay, and Jenny Lind. In spite of her fame, Fanny never missed an opportunity to present the gospel message to anyone who would listen.

Fanny Crosby never wanted sympathy because of her blindness. When a minister once expressed regret that God had not given her the gift of sight, her startling reply was, "If I had been given a choice at birth, I would have asked to be blind . . . for when I get to heaven, the first face I will see will be the One who died for me."

Reflection

Is there something about your appearance or your abilities that you would like to change? Fanny Crosby accepted herself just as she was, and God was able to use her mightily. What we see as limitations in our lives aren't limitations to God.

As Jesus was walking along, he saw a man who had been blind from birth. "Teacher," his disciples asked him, "why was this man born blind?" . . . Jesus answered, "He was born blind so the power of God could be seen in him." JOHN 9:1-3

November 21

What would it be like to live by faith, telling your needs only to God and to no one else?

GOD LEADS different people in different ways, but he led George Müller to trust him for everything in life and to let his needs be known to God alone.

Müller was born in Prussia in 1805, and though he trained for the Lutheran ministry, he led a degenerate life of petty thievery, once spending three weeks in jail. When he was a young man of twenty, a friend invited him to a private home, where on Saturday evenings there was prayer, hymn singing, Bible reading, and the reading of a printed sermon since it was illegal in Prussia for laymen to explain the Scriptures. Just hearing about such a gathering intrigued him. The meeting both puzzled and thrilled Müller. He realized that even though he was much better educated than the others present, he could not pray as eloquently as these simple tradesmen. That night Müller went home feeling that he had found what he was seeking. God had begun a work of grace in his heart, and he went to sleep peaceful and happy in Jesus.

God continued to work in his life, and in 1829 Müller went to London for training to be a missionary to the Jews. Upon meeting some of the first Plymouth Brethren, a group of Christians who functioned without a paid clergy, Müller became convinced of their teachings. Over the next few years he ministered at several Plymouth Brethren chapels in England.

Earlier in his life, while a student in Halle, Germany, Müller had observed the orphanages that August Francke, the German Pietist, had begun in 1696. Through the years he thought about founding an orphanage, but it was on **November 21, 1835,** after reading a book about Francke's life, that he felt God's definitely leading beyond the mere idea to a firm resolve to start an orphanage in Bristol, England. He immediately asked God for a building, funds to support it, and godly people to operate it. His orphanage was operational within five months and remained the major project of his life.

George Müller continually trusted God for the daily operations of the orphanage. **November 21, 1838,** three years after his decision to start the orphanage, is a case in point. On this particular day there was not a single halfpenny in the orphanage's coffers to buy bread for the evening meal. At one o'clock Müller prayed with his staff for their daily bread and told them that they must wait and see how the Lord would see fit to meet their need.

Feeling that he needed some exercise, Müller went out for a walk. On his way back, about twenty yards from his house he met a Christian brother, who gave him five pounds for the orphans. God put Müller in the right place at the right time to meet the man who made the donation.

Exactly one year later, on **November 21, 1839,** his journal provides another illustration of living by faith. On that day some small contributions were received at the orphanage, enough for the next day's breakfast but not enough for the next dinner. Müller described that day's staff meeting in his journal, "Our comfort . . . is 'The morrow shall take thought for the things of itself. Sufficient unto the day is the evil thereof.' Matt. 6:34. We separated very happy in God, though very poor, and our faith much tried."

Two and a half hours before dinner the next day a large box arrived at the orphanage with a generous contribution and some valuable articles that could be sold. The joy of George Müller and his fellow workers was indescribable, as God had once more provided for his orphans.[19]

Reflection

To what extent do you live by faith? Just as we were saved by faith, so we are to live by faith. George Müller's life exemplifies what it means to trust God for one's daily needs. Just as we are to trust God for our salvation, we are also to trust him for the specifics of life. Examine your life to determine the areas in which you need to put living by faith into practice.

We live by believing and not by seeing.   2 CORINTHIANS 5:7

November 22

Who died on November 22, 1963?

MANY WILL correctly answer, "President John F. Kennedy."

But also on that day another person died who was mightier in God's kingdom than President Kennedy. His name was C. S. Lewis.

His initials, "C. S.," stood for Clive Staples, but to his friends he was "Jack." Born near Belfast, Ireland, in 1898, he was raised as an Anglican. But at the age of ten his world was shaken when his mother died of cancer. Jack wanted nothing to do with a God so cruel as to take his mother. By his early teenage years he had become an atheist.

Jack graduated from Oxford University, where he studied philosophy and English literature. Oxford became his home for the rest of his life. He served the first thirty years of his academic career as a fellow of Magdalen College, Oxford. From there he went to the newly created chair of Medieval and Renaissance English at Cambridge University. While at Cambridge, he commuted back to Oxford on the weekends.

Jack's spiritual pilgrimage back to God began in 1926 with a conversation with another fellow of Magdalen College. Lewis was surprised to learn that his tough-minded, cynical friend believed in the Trinity. This revelation challenged Lewis's atheistic presuppositions.

His next step was a memorable bus trip he took on a spring day in 1929. Riding along, Jack pondered the various philosophers he had read. Taking Hegel's idea of the absolute and combining it with Berkeley's concept of Spirit, he conceived of a being he could call "God." He didn't know anything about this God, but when he got off the bus, he knew he believed something he hadn't before—that an absolute Spirit or God existed.

Some months later he began to formulate a mental vision of Absolute Spirit, conceiving of it as someone who said, "I am the Lord." Jack finally had to admit that God was God, and for the first time in years he prayed.

The next step in his spiritual pilgrimage came on a September evening spent with two friends, J. R. R. Tolkien, a Roman Catholic, and H. V. Dyson, an Anglican. As the three intellectuals discussed the authenticity and significance of Christian doctrines, Jack became more and more convinced that the events of the Bible had really happened.

But it was two years later, in 1931, that the real turning point came. On this particular afternoon Jack and his brother rode a motorcycle forty miles to visit the Whipsnade Zoo. Following them by car were three friends and a dog named Mr. Papworth. The Lewis brothers got there first, with time to relax with bottles of beer before their friends arrived. When the car pulled in, they all shared a picnic together before going into the zoo. Since dogs weren't allowed in the zoo, Jack stayed behind to babysit Mr. Papworth.

As Jack was relaxing in the park, feeling a pleasant tiredness from the long motorcycle ride, he realized that sometime during the previous few hours he had come to an important conclusion. He knew that when he had left for Whipsnade he did not believe that Jesus Christ was the Son of God, but somehow when he arrived, he believed! Without consciously thinking about it, he had passed from merely believing in God to trusting in him as his Savior.

In 1941 Lewis burst on the literary scene with *The Screwtape Letters*. Books then began to flow from his pen at an amazing rate, one or more a year. Titles such as *Mere Christianity, Surprised by Joy, A Grief Observed,* and The Chronicles of Narnia have been used by God to change the lives of people of all ages around the world.

C. S. Lewis is considered the most influential Christian author of the twentieth century—quite a leap from the atheism of his youth.

Reflection

The conversion of C. S. Lewis was certainly unusual. What is your explanation of what happened to him on the way to the zoo? His story is a graphic example of how God uses different means to bring different people to himself. Where are you in your spiritual pilgrimage?

Just as you can hear the wind but can't tell where it comes from or where it is going, so you can't explain how people are born of the Spirit.   JOHN 3:8

November 23

It is said that in life we pick our battles, but what if Satan picks us?

FOR JOHN KNOX, all of life was a battle. He was born in 1514 in Haddington, Scotland; educated at St. Andrews University; and ordained as a Catholic priest. However, by 1542 he, along with many of his contemporaries, had embraced the Protestant faith.

In 1547 Knox went to the Castle of St. Andrews, where he was appointed preacher to the garrison of Protestant soldiers there. In July of that year the Catholic French navy besieged the castle. The Scots held out valiantly for four weeks, but the castle fell, and Knox and the others were taken to France and made galley slaves for nineteen months.

Finally freed in 1549, Knox returned to England, where he was appointed preacher at Berwick and in 1551 chaplain to King Edward VI.[20] Knox's troubles renewed when Edward VI died in 1553 and was succeeded by Queen Mary I, who restored Roman Catholicism as the religion of her realm.[21] Knox along with many Reformers fled to the Continent, where he spent time with John Calvin[22] in Geneva.

Returning to Scotland in 1559, Knox became the leader of the Scottish Reformation. There he had repeated conflicts with Mary Queen of Scots. After she was deposed, her son became King James VI of Scotland,[23] and John Knox preached at his coronation.

The untiring labors of John Knox resulted in making Scotland the most Calvinistic nation in the world, yet his battle with Satan continued to the end. On Sunday, **November 23, 1572,** the day before he died, he shared with a friend: "I have been in meditation these two last nights upon the troubled kirk [church] of God, despised in the world, but precious in his sight. I have called to God for her, and commended her to Christ, her head; I have been fighting against Satan, who is ever ready for the assault; I have fought against spiritual wickedness and have prevailed; I have been as it were in heaven, and have tasted of its joys."

During the night his physician noticed how fitfully he was sleeping and asked him when he awoke how he was doing. Knox answered:

In my lifetime I have been often assaulted by Satan, and many times he hath cast my sins in my teeth, to bring me to despair; yet God gave me strength to overcome his temptations; and now that subtle serpent, who never ceased to tempt, hath taken another course, and seeks to persuade me that all my labors in the ministry, and the fidelity I have shown in that service, have merited heaven and immortality. But blessed be God that He hath brought to my mind that Scripture, "What hast thou that thou hast not received?" and "Not I, but the grace of God, which is in me," with which he hath gone away ashamed, and shall no more return. And now, I am sure my battle is at an end, and that I shall shortly, without pain of body or trouble of spirit, change this mortal and miserable life for that happy and immortal life that shall never have an end.

The very next day he entered the joy of his Lord that has no end. His battle with Satan was finally over.

Reflection

Do you at times feel as if you are battling Satan? In the description of the Christian's armor in Ephesians 6:13-18, there are two offensive weapons listed: the word of God (v. 17) and prayer (v. 18). We need to use them both.

~~~

Use every piece of God's armor to resist the enemy in the time of evil, so that after the battle you will still be standing firm. Stand your ground, putting on the sturdy belt of truth and the body armor of God's righteousness. For shoes, put on the peace that comes from the Good News, so that you will be fully prepared. In every battle you will need faith as your shield to stop the fiery arrows aimed at you by Satan. Put on salvation as your helmet, and take the sword of the Spirit, which is the word of God. Pray at all times and on every occasion in the power of the Holy Spirit. EPHESIANS 6:13-18

November 24

Playing "second fiddle" is a time-honored profession.

AMONG THE well-known leaders of the Reformation, Martin Luther[24] had Philip Melancthon; John Calvin[25] had Theodore Beza; and Ulrich Zwingli[26] had Johann Oecolampadius. Johann's real last name was Hausschein, which means "the light of the house" in German. He took the Greek equivalent, Oecolampadius, as his surname instead.

Johann Oecolampadius and Ulrich Zwingli, the better known of the two, were the reformers in German-speaking Switzerland. Zwingli led the Reformation in Zurich and Oecolampadius in Basel, the Athens of Switzerland—the wealthiest and most literary city. It was a commercial center as well, situated on the banks of the Rhine, bordering both Germany and France.

Oecolampadius was born in Germany in 1482. A precocious child, he began writing Latin poetry at the age of twelve and soon thereafter mastered Greek. According to Erasmus, the foremost intellect of his day, Oecolampadius was the second leading Hebrew scholar in the German-speaking world. Studying at the University of Tubingen, he became friends with Philip Melancthon, who was to become Luther's theologian.

In 1515 Oecolampadius was called to pastor the cathedral in Basel. The following year he received the degree of doctor of divinity. Ever the scholar, Oecolampadius assisted Erasmus in publishing his Greek New Testament. Job pressures caused him to leave Basel in 1520 to enter a monastery temporarily, but he returned in 1522 as preacher at the cathedral and professor of theology at the University of Basel, positions he held until his death.

It was also in 1522 that Oecolampadius became friends with Ulrich Zwingli, pastor of the Zurich Great Church. By this time he was deeply affected by the teachings of both Luther and Zwingli. He publicly attacked the doctrine of transubstantiation (the belief that in the Lord's Supper the bread and wine actually become Christ's body and blood), the abuses of the confessional, and worship of the Virgin Mary. Because of his vigorous campaign, the Mass was abolished in Basel.

The ministry of Oecolampadius, however, was not just a negative one. He preached and taught the Word of God. He instituted congregational singing in the services, and communicants participated in receiving both bread and wine.

In 1531 Zwingli was killed in a battle between the Reformed and Catholic cantons of Switzerland. The Zurich Reformers asked Oecolampadius to come to Zurich to replace Zwingli, but he declined their invitation. His ambition was not to take Zwingli's place as leader of the Reformation in Switzerland but to continue to minister in Basel.

Just five weeks later he fell gravely ill. Realizing he was dying, he shared the Lord's Supper with his family and servants. While they shed their tears, Oecolampadius told them, "This supper is a sign of my real faith in Jesus Christ, my Redeemer."

On the last night of his life as ten pastors of Basel stood around his bed, he inquired of one of them, "What is the news?"

The answer was, "Nothing," to which Oecolampadius replied, "Well, I will tell you something new. In a short time I will be with the Lord Jesus."

As dawn was beginning to break on **November 24, 1531,** he kept repeating the words of Psalm 51:1: "Have mercy upon me, O God, according to thy lovingkindness." As the sun rose, Oecolampadius, "the light of the house," was gone to shine like the sun in his Father's kingdom.

Reflection

Oecolampadius knew the role to which God had called him and faithfully fulfilled it. Do you know the role God has for you in his kingdom? If you are a child of God, God has given you at least one spiritual gift to exercise. If you aren't sure of your gift or your role, ask God to show you. You can also ask your Christian friends to help you identify your spiritual gift. God desires to use you for his glory!

∽◈◇

Christ . . . is the head of his body, the church. Under his direction, the whole body is fitted together perfectly. As each part does its own special work, it helps the other parts grow, so that the whole body is healthy and growing and full of love. EPHESIANS 4:15-16

November 25

People judge by outward appearance, but the Lord looks at a person's thoughts and intentions (1 Samuel 16:7).

H E WAS only five feet tall, and his huge head looked too large for his body. It looked even bigger with the large wig he wore. His nose was crooked, his eyes small and piercing, and his body frail. Physically there was nothing appealing about him.

He fell in love with a young woman and proposed to her, but her insensitive answer was, "I like the jewel but not the setting." He never married.

Who was this unfortunate person? His name was Isaac Watts, and he is considered to be the father of English hymnody.

Watts was born in Southhampton, England, in 1674. His father, a schoolmaster, was a devout Christian who was twice imprisoned for his faith. From his youth, Watts began to show his poetic genius. When he was eighteen, he complained to his father that the Psalms, which were the only songs used in his church, were poorly paraphrased for singing. Being a schoolmaster, his father challenged him to write something better. Young Watts did just that, and the next Sunday his first hymn was sung in the worship service. It contained a verse that proved to be prophetic of the contribution that Watts would make to English worship:

> *Behold the glories of the lamb*
> *Amidst His Father's throne;*
> *Prepare new honors for His Name,*
> *And songs before unknown.*

Within the next two years the youthful Watts wrote most of the 210 hymns contained in his *Hymns and Spiritual Songs* published in 1707, the first real hymnal in English.

In 1719 he published his *Psalms of David* in which he gave a New Testament perspective to the words of the Psalms. A familiar example is his version of Psalm 72:

> *Jesus shall reign where'er the sun*
> *Does his successive journeys run;*
> *His kingdom spread from shore to shore,*
> *Till moons shall wax and wane no more.*

THE UGLY POET

When Watts was thirty-eight and experiencing one of his frequent bouts of poor health, his good friend Sir Thomas Abney invited him to his estate for a week of recuperation. When no improvement was seen, the Abneys invited him to stay on. Watts became such a well-loved part of the family that he stayed there for the rest of his life—another thirty-six years!

Humanly speaking Watts had many strikes against him. He suffered ridicule for his appearance, rejection by the woman he loved, and continual poor health. Even his living situation was dependent upon the goodwill of a friend. Yet in spite of all that, Watts led a richly productive life. The night before he died he said, "I am a sinner; Christ is my Savior. I can let all else go; the finished work of Christ is all my hope. To depart and be with Christ will be far better."

Isaac Watts died on **November 25, 1748,** having written over six hundred hymns. His vision was to enable God's people to be able to sing the words of Scripture in meaningful poetic form. Many of his hymns, such as "O God, Our Help in Ages Past," "When I Survey the Wondrous Cross," and "Joy to the World," are still frequently sung today. The church continues to worship God through the words of Isaac Watts.

Reflection

How do you think you would have reacted to Isaac Watts? Do you, like most of us, look on the outward appearance or, like God, look upon the heart? Unfortunately we live in a culture that focuses on outward appearance. We venerate the beautiful and disdain the ugly. If that is our attitude, we will miss the Isaac Wattses of the world—and be the poorer for it.

People judge by outward appearance, but the Lord looks at a person's thoughts and intentions.   1 SAMUEL 16:7

November 26

William Grimshaw's funeral turned out very different from the one he had planned.

GRIMSHAW was born in 1708 in Lancashire, England. He went to Christ's College, Cambridge, intending to enter the ministry. During his third year he fell in with the wrong crowd, becoming, in his own words, "as vile as the worst." Still, he chose to enter the ministry, finding no incongruity between his behavior and his chosen profession.

Ordained in the Church of England in 1732, Grimshaw was assigned a church in West Yorkshire. He married a young widow, but within four years she tragically died, leaving him with two small children.

Already a troubled soul, Grimshaw was plunged into a deep depression. He sent his children away to be cared for by relatives. All he could think about was his own mortality and the necessity of making arrangements for his own funeral. On **November 26, 1739,** three weeks after his wife's funeral, he wrote, "The Form of My Burial." At that time funerals were followed by a feast at an alehouse, where alcohol flowed freely. In his written instructions he specified: "To attend my funeral I desire that 20 persons be invited (of my next relations and intimatest acquaintances) and be entertained in the following manner: Let 5 quarts of claret . . . be put in a punch bowl and be drunk in wine glasses round until done."

At this time an itinerant preacher began rebuking Grimshaw for his legalistic view of salvation. He said, "You are no believer in the Lord Jesus Christ. You are building on sand." Grimshaw tried to avoid the man, but the words "you are building on sand" kept haunting him.

In 1741 while visiting a friend, Grimshaw saw a book on a table and picked it up. As he opened it and discovered that the author was John Owen, the Puritan divine, a flash of heat flushed his face. Puzzled, he looked at the fireplace, wondering if the fire caused his sudden flush of heat. Opening the book again, he read the title, *The Doctrine of Justification by Faith*. Suddenly a second flash of heat swept over him. Astonished that it happened again, Grimshaw took it as a divine imperative that he was to read the book.

Taking the book back home, Grimshaw noted in the preface that Owen had written the book for people suffering from the same anguish and distress that he was experiencing. The book confronted the reader with the question

A JOURNEY FROM DEPRESSION
TO FAITH

of "whether he will trust unto his own personal inherent righteousness or, in full renunciation of it, betake himself unto the grace of God and the righteousness of Christ alone." To Grimshaw the choice was clear.

He later confided to a friend, "I was willing to renounce myself, every degree of fancied merit and ability, and to embrace Christ only for my all in all. O what light and comfort did I now enjoy in my own soul, and what a taste of the pardoning love of God!"

His ministry immediately changed, and he found peace and joy in his heart as well as his soul. He fell in love with a local girl, married her, and brought his children back home. Now his joy was complete.

He applied for a new parish and moved his family to nearby Haworth, where he ministered powerfully and effectively until his death in 1763.[27] Under his spiritual leadership the little-known village in Yorkshire became one of the leading centers of the Christian faith in all of England.

His funeral was quite different from the one he had planned years before. Vast crowds of loving parishioners followed his coffin to its final resting place. The pastor summarized the faith of William Grimshaw by saying, "Upon [Christ's] atoning blood and justifying righteousness alone, did every hope of his soul's acceptance with God depend."

Reflection

On what are you depending for your salvation? William Grimshaw's life went from utter despair to joyous faith when he put his trust in the finished work of the Lord Jesus Christ. Where will you put your trust?

~⌒~

When people work, their wages are not a gift. Workers earn what they receive. But people are declared righteous because of their faith, not because of their work.   ROMANS 4:4-5

November 27

If you had just listened to the best sermon you had ever heard, telling you what the will of God was, what would you do?

THE PLACE was Clermont, France, where Pope Urban II had called a church council. On the final day of the Council of Clermont, **November 27, 1095,** Urban II addressed the thousands assembled. Historians have deemed his sermon as possibly the most effective sermon of all time.

The burning issue for Urban II was that in 1076 the Seljuk Turks had captured Jerusalem from the Arabs and made life intolerable for any Christians living in Jerusalem or going there on a pilgrimage. Many Christians had been robbed and murdered.

The eloquent Urban II spoke in his native French to the crowds assembled in an open field:

> Ye men of the Franks . . . To you our words are spoken, and by you our message will be passed on . . . God orders it.
>
> From the borders of Jerusalem and the city of Constantinople evil tidings have come to my ears. . . . An accursed race, estranged from God has invaded the lands of the Christians in the East and have depopulated them by fire, steel and revenge. . . . These Turks have led away many Christians, captives, to their own country; they have torn down the churches of Christ or used them for their own rites. In some they stable their horses. . . .
>
> Who will avenge these wrongs, unless it be you who have won glory in arms? . . . If you would save your souls, then come forward to the defense of Christ. . . . Labor for everlasting reward. . . . You will earn the right to absolution from all your sins, and heaven is assured to any who may fall in this worthy undertaking. . . . The wealth of your enemies will be yours; ye shall plunder their treasures and return home victorious. . . . Take up your arms, valiant sons, and go—God guarding you. . . .

The crowd rose as one, chanting, "God wills it! God wills it!"

To this the pope answered, "It is the will of God! . . . You are soldiers of the cross. Wear on your breasts or shoulders the blood-red sign of the cross.

THE BEST SERMON EVER?

Wear it as a token that his help will never fail you, as the pledge of a vow never to be recalled."

Thousands immediately took the vow and sewed a cross on their garments. The message raced throughout Europe as it was spread by word of mouth. The next year the First Crusade left for Jerusalem accompanied by the rallying cry, "God wills it!"

The next two hundred years, the period of the Crusades, are the most embarrassing period of all church history.[28] Although the crusaders were able to capture Jerusalem and hold it for a period of time, the Near East in general and the Muslims in particular have never forgotten the murder, rape, and pillage that characterized the Crusades. Never in history have so many calling themselves Christians been so misdirected in their cause. Their actions demonstrated that most of them knew nothing of the faith they claimed to represent.

And it all began with an eloquent sermon proclaiming the will of God.

Reflection

Have you ever heard an eloquent sermon that, though moving, didn't contain the truth? After hearing Paul and Silas preach, the citizens of Berea studied their Bibles to make sure that they were hearing the truth. If it was necessary to check up on Paul and Silas, it is certainly necessary for us to check out the messages we hear before espousing them.

The people of Berea were more open-minded than those in Thessalonica, and they listened eagerly to Paul's message. They searched the Scriptures day after day to check up on Paul and Silas, to see if they were really teaching the truth. ACTS 17:11

November 28

Trusting the wrong person can be a fatal mistake.

JUST ASK Jan Hus. Jan Hus took his last name from Husinec, the town in southern Bohemia where he was born in 1373. He followed his mother's desire that he be a priest, primarily because it would bring him money and prestige. However, as he studied at the University of Prague, he felt his spiritual ardor growing.

After his ordination in 1402, Hus was appointed preacher at Bethlehem Chapel in Prague.[29] He also taught at the University of Prague. Shortly before Hus's appointment to his church, the writings of the English Reformer John Wycliffe had reached Prague by way of returning Czech students who had studied at Oxford. As Hus read the works of Wycliffe, he was drawn to the Reformer's views.

Hus preached godliness and vigorously attacked the sins and indiscretions of the clergy, claiming, "These priests . . . are drunks whose bellies growl with great drinking and are gluttons whose stomachs are overfilled until their double chins hang down." Needless to say this did not sit well with his fellow priests. But the people loved it and thronged to hear his controversial preaching.

Finally the pope published a papal bull, a decree calling for an investigation of the heresies of Wycliffe and Hus and condemning Bethlehem Chapel. Hus spoke out publicly against the bull with two thousand of his congregation expressing their willingness to stand behind him in his conflict with the pope.

Although excommunicated by the archbishop, Hus continued to preach since he had much more support in Prague than the archbishop did. As the pressure on him increased, Hus finally went into voluntary exile in 1412.

In 1414 Emperor Sigismund called a church council to be held in Constance in southern Germany. He invited Jan Hus, promising him safe conduct. Although warned by his friends not to go, Hus trusted the emperor's promise of protection and accepted his invitation.

Hus arrived safely in Constance, but three weeks later, on **November 28, 1414,** there was a knock on his door, and two bishops appeared to arrest him. Beyond the bishops, Hus could see that the house was surrounded by soldiers.

He was taken away and locked in a dark damp cell next to the latrines in the dungeon of a convent. Beset with fever and vomiting, Hus was soon near death. He was saved by a visit from the pope's physician and a move to a better cell.

Hus's supporters implored the emperor to honor his promise of safe conduct, but instead the emperor declared Hus to be the greatest heretic in the history of Christendom and therefore deserving of no protection.

Hus was brought to trial, and thirty charges were leveled against him. Many were completely frivolous, such as the charge that Hus claimed to be the fourth person of the Godhead. He rejected all the charges, but his denials were shouted down. The council found him guilty and sentenced him to be burned at the stake the same day. As the bishops ripped his vestments from his body, they cried, "We commit your soul to the devil."

When he was tied to the stake, he was given one last opportunity to recant. Hus replied, "God is my witness that . . . the principal intention of my preaching and of all my other acts or writings was solely that I might turn men from sin. And in that truth of the gospel . . . I am willing gladly to die today." As the flames shot up around him, he could be heard singing, "Jesus, Son of God, have mercy upon me."

The followers of John Hus down through the centuries developed into the Moravians[30] through whom John Wesley[31] and tens of thousands of others were converted. He may have lost the battle but not the war.

Reflection

Have you ever trusted someone, as Jan Hus trusted the emperor, who then let you down? What did you learn from that experience? The only One who is totally trustworthy is God, and it is only through his guidance that we can discern who around us is trustworthy.

❧

Trust in the Lord with all your heart; do not depend on your own understanding. Seek his will in all you do, and he will direct your paths. PROVERBS 3:5-6

November 29

Some important stories don't make the news.

ON NOVEMBER 29, 1947, headlines around the world proclaimed that the United Nations had voted to establish two separate states in Palestine, one Jewish and one Arab. The news brought joy to those longing for a national homeland for the Jews, and it brought bitter resentment to the Arabs.

However, another event happened that same day in Palestine that was to influence biblical studies forever. The story begins about a year earlier when three Bedouin teenagers, Muhammed Ahmed el-Hamed, Jum'a Muhammed Khalib, and Khalil Musa, made a momentous discovery while exploring a cave near the Dead Sea. They found three scrolls in an ancient jar.

In April 1947 an uncle of one of the boys took the scrolls to Bethlehem, the market town for the Bedouins, and showed them to a Muslim sheikh. The sheikh, seeing that they were not written in Arabic, assumed the language to be Syriac. He sent them to a Bethlehem shoemaker and part-time antiquities dealer known as "Kando."

Meanwhile, one of the boys, Khalil Musa, and some other Bedouins brought George Isaiah, a Syrian Orthodox merchant from Jerusalem, to see the cave. They found four more scrolls. Isaiah told the Syrian Orthodox Metropolitan in Jerusalem about the scrolls, and he offered to buy them.

In July, Jum'a, Musa, and Isaiah brought the four scrolls they had found to the monastery of the Syrian Orthodox Metropolitan but were mistakenly turned away. They then sold the four scrolls to the Bethlehem merchant Kando, who in turn sold them for $97.20 to the Metropolitan. Three additional scrolls were sold to another antiquities dealer for $28.35.

The Metropolitan sought out scholarly opinion to identify the scrolls that he had purchased. One of the experts he consulted was Eleazar Sukenik, a noted professor at the Hebrew University in Jerusalem.

At that time the British mandate was coming to an end, and the United Nations could not decide how to deal with the Jews and Arabs, making the situation in Palestine volatile. Though it was dangerous for a Jew to travel in an Arab area, when Sukenik learned that an antiquities dealer was selling ancient scrolls in the Arab city of Bethlehem, he was determined to go. On **November 29, 1947,** the very day that the United Nations voted to create a Jewish state, Sukenik made a secret trip to Bethlehem and purchased two of the scrolls. A month later he purchased a third.

SCROLLS FOR SALE

In 1954 the Syrian Orthodox Metropolitan tried to sell his four scrolls in the United States. He placed an ad in the *Wall Street Journal* reading, "The Four Dead Sea Scrolls—Biblical Manuscripts Dating Back at Least to 200 B.C. Are for Sale."

Sukenik's son, Yigael Yadin, an Israeli general and a leading archaeologist, was in the United States when the ad appeared. Through intermediaries Yadin was able to purchase the four scrolls for $250,000. Those four together with the three purchased by his father now reside in an exhibit in the Israel Museum called The Shrine of the Book.

The Dead Sea Scrolls, dating from the period 250 B.C. to A.D. 68, are the single most important archaeological discovery of all time. They apparently were part of the library of a Jewish sect, the Essenes, that lived at nearby Qumran. When the invading Roman armies reached southern Judea in A.D. 68, the Essenes hid their library in caves.

The scrolls range in length from the complete book of Isaiah to thousands of small fragments. At least one fragment from every Old Testament book except Esther has been found. Evidence shows that originally about three hundred books were hidden, a third of them portions of the Old Testament.

The greatest value of the Dead Sea Scrolls is that they demonstrate the accuracy of our current text of the Hebrew Old Testament, showing it to be virtually the same as that in 250 B.C.

Reflection

Isn't it reassuring to have evidence of how carefully God has superintended the transmission of the text of the Bible down through the centuries? What does it mean to you that our text of the Old Testament is nearly identical to what it was 2,250 years ago?

Do not add to or subtract from these commands I am giving you from the Lord your God. DEUTERONOMY 4:2

November 30

Almost everything in life pales in comparison to our love for our children and grandchildren.

Dwight Lyman Moody, born in 1837, was the greatest evangelist of his day.[32] He preached to more people than any of his contemporaries and was the catalyst of great revivals not only in the United States and Canada but also in England, Scotland, and Ireland.

Yet what meant more to Moody than even his evangelistic ministry was his family. He had three children, Emma, Will, and Paul Dwight. The arrival of his grandchildren brought Moody special joy. The first two, Will's daughter, Irene, and Emma's daughter, Emma, were born in 1895. Moody loved them dearly.

The arrival of his namesake, Dwight Lyman Moody, in November, 1897, added to his delight. But no one could foresee that his beloved grandchildren would soon precipitate his final crisis.

On **November 30, 1898,** while in Colorado, Moody received a telegram that stunned him. Little one-year-old Dwight, his pride and joy, had died. Heavy with grief, Moody wrote to the sorrowing parents:

I know Dwight is having a good time, and we should rejoice with him. What would the mansions be without children? He was the last to come into our circle, and he is the first to go up there! So safe, so free from all the sorrow we are passing through! I thank God for such a life. It was nearly all smiles and sunshine, and what a glorified body he will have, and with what joy he will await your coming! God does not give us such strong love for each other for a few days or years, but it is going to last forever, and you will have the dear little man with you for ages and ages, and love will keep increasing. The Master had need of him, or He would not have called him; and you should feel highly honored that you had anything in your home that He wanted.

I cannot think of him as belonging to earth. The more I think of him the more I think he was only sent to draw us all closer to each other and up to the world of light and joy. I could not wish him back, if he could have all earth could give him. . . . Dear, dear little fellow! . . . I have no doubt that when he saw the Saviour he smiled as he did when he saw you, and the word that keeps coming to my mind is this: 'It is well with the child. . . .' Thank God, Dwight is safe at home, and we will all of us see him soon.

Your loving father,
D. L. Moody

The following March little Irene fell ill with tuberculosis, and by August she was wasting away. Moody brought Will, his wife, May, and little Irene into his home to offer any help he could, but nothing could be done to save her. To their great sorrow, Irene died just eight months after her baby brother.

At the funeral Moody unexpectedly rose and spoke of Elijah "waiting in the Valley of Jordan so many years ago, for the chariot of God to take him home. Again the chariot of God came down to the Connecticut Valley yesterday morning about half-past six and took our little Irene home."

Grief weighed heavily on this grandfather's heart, and just four months later D. L. Moody himself was the one who was dying. He revived momentarily and said, "What does this all mean? I must have had a trance. I went to the gate of heaven. Why it was so wonderful, and I saw the children!"

His son, Will, asked, "Oh, Father, did you see them?"

Moody answered, "Yes, I saw Irene and Dwight." Moments later he was with them.

Reflection

Have you experienced the loss of someone close to you? Grief can be such an overpowering obstacle in our lives that it can seem impossible to overcome. The enormity of Moody's grief at the deaths of his grandchildren was matched only by the depth of God's comfort. Bring your loss to him and accept his comfort.

The Lord still waits for you to come to him so he can show you his love and compassion. For the Lord is a faithful God. ISAIAH 30:18

December 1

When peace like a river attendeth my way, When sorrows like sea billows roll . . .

WHEN 1871 dawned, Horatio Spafford was a happy man. His wife and four young daughters were a source of great joy and comfort. His real estate holdings in downtown Chicago were paying off handsomely with the city's rapid growth. Then in April of that year, the Great Chicago Fire consumed his real estate. But Spafford took comfort in the fact that his family had escaped the fire.

> *Whatever my lot, Thou hast taught me to say,*
> *"It is well, it is well with my soul."*

The Spaffords' loss was cushioned by a deep belief in the sovereign hand of God. They were friends of Dwight L. Moody[1] and had supported several of his crusades.

> *Though Satan should buffet, tho' trials should come . .*

In 1873 the Spaffords were overjoyed with the birth of their first son. But the boy lived only a short time. When the Spaffords buried his body, charred ruins still loomed over the cityscape. Chicago—and Spafford's business prospects—had barely begun to recover from the fire.

> *Let this blessed assurance control,*
> *That Christ has regarded my helpless estate,*
> *And has shed His own blood for my soul.*

God seemed to offer the Spaffords a much needed rest from the accumulated sorrow of their recent years. They had the opportunity to go to Europe to assist Moody with his next evangelistic campaign. While overseas they would not only be able to share the love of Christ but be able to visit the Holy Land. Their destination was Jerusalem, the very city where Christ's blood had made atonement for the sins of all those who would believe in him.

Just before Thanksgiving that year Horatio Spafford put his wife and daughters on the *Ville du Havre,* a ship bound for Europe. Business delayed his own departure, but he planned to follow in a few days.

Spafford awoke a week later to a horrible headline in the papers: The *Ville du Havre* had been struck by another ship in the mid-Atlantic and had sunk.

PEACE LIKE A RIVER

There was no initial word of any survivors. Then on **December 1, 1873,** Spafford received a telegram from his wife: "Saved. Alone."

> *And, Lord, haste the day when the faith shall be sight,*
> *The clouds be rolled back as a scroll,*
> *The trump shall resound and the Lord shall descend,*
> *Even so, it is well with my soul.*

Spafford boarded the next ship for Europe. The words of a poem that was forming in his head were on his heart as he passed over the watery grave of his four daughters, citizens now of the heavenly Jerusalem:

> *"Even so"—it is well with my soul.*

In the years to come Spafford and his wife made their permanent home in Jerusalem, where God blessed them with a second family of children. There they developed a ministry to the people who did not know the reality of Christ's peace like a river.

Reflection

When "sorrows like sea billows roll" in your life, as they have a way of doing, do you have "peace like a river"? Horatio Spafford's words were born out of a profound trust that God's purpose in his life was perfect. And God has a purpose just as real for each believer's life. No matter how bad things get, the believer can have peace, knowing that God is in control and that his will for us is best.

The Lord rules over the floodwaters. The Lord reigns as king forever.
The Lord gives his people strength. The Lord blesses them with peace.
PSALM 29:10-11

December 2

He was no stranger to the Bible or to church, but at the age of seventeen, he was still a stranger to a personal walk with God.

THE SUMMER of 1849 broke warm with promise in Hudson Taylor's heart, when at last God granted him the joyful realization of Christ's sufficiency for his sins.[2] Many years later Taylor recalled:

> Well do I remember that occasion, how in the gladness of my heart I poured out my soul before God, and again and again confessing my grateful love to Him who had done everything for me—who had saved me when I had given up all hope and even desire of salvation—I besought Him to give me some work for Him . . . that I might do for Him who had done so much for me. . . . I poured myself, my life, my friends, my all upon the altar, the deep solemnity that came over my soul with the assurance that my offering was accepted. The presence of God became unutterably real and blessed. . . . For what service I was accepted, I knew not. But a deep consciousness that I was not my own took possession of me, which has never since been effaced.

Taylor's inner change was outwardly visible that summer. He loved spending time in the Bible and in prayer. He was so filled with the joy and wonder of salvation that he used his free time to share his faith with others.

But as fall and then winter set in, a coldness crept over Taylor's spirit. He doggedly continued to do the things he felt a Christian should do. But Bible study and prayer lost their sweetness; he went to church only out of duty. His soul grew weary in its struggles with sin.

On Sunday, **December 2, 1849,** Hudson Taylor awakened feeling as sick in his physical body as he had been feeling in his spirit. When the rest of his family went to church and he was alone in the quiet house, he began a letter to his sister: "Pray for me, dear Amelia. Thank God I feel very happy in His love, but I am so unworthy of all His blessings. I so often give way to temptation. . . . Oh that the Lord would take away my heart of stone and give me a heart of flesh!"

Tormented by his thoughts, Taylor laid down his pen, and then, like Jacob of long ago, he decided that he would "lay hold of God and not let go except Thou bless me." What God did over the next few hours was so precious that Taylor never spoke of it in detail, but he did add this postscript to the letter: "Bless the Lord, O my soul, and all that is within me shout His praise! Glory to God, my dear Amelia. Christ has said 'Seek and ye shall find,' and praise His name, He has revealed himself to me in a an overflowing manner. He has cleansed me from all sin. . . . He has given me a new heart. Glory, glory, glory to His ever blessed Name! I cannot write for joy."

What filled Hudson Taylor with such praise? Six words from God that day, "Then go for me to China."

Hudson Taylor did go to China and founded the China Inland Mission, which became the largest missionary organization in the world.[3]

Reflection

Have you ever had an experience like that of Hudson Taylor when you laid hold of God and did not let him go until he blessed you? This was a major turning point in Hudson Taylor's life.

&

Jacob panted, "I will not let you go unless you bless me."

GENESIS 32:26

December 3

He was born in obscurity for a day that would live in infamy.

DECEMBER 3, 1902, marked the birth in Nagao, Japan, of Mitsuo Fuchida. His story, told in his own words, reveals the mark he left on history—and the mark God left on him.

> I must admit I was more excited than usual as I awoke that morning at 3:00 A.M. Hawaii time. . . . As General Commander of the Air Squadron, I made last minute checks on the intelligence information reports in the Operations Room before going to warm up my single-engine three-seater plane. . . .
>
> The sunrise in the east was magnificent above the white clouds as I led 360 planes towards Hawaii. I knew my objective: to surprise and cripple the American naval force in the Pacific. . . .
>
> Like a hurricane out of nowhere, my torpedo planes, dive-bombers, and fighters struck suddenly with indescribable fury. . . . It was the most thrilling exploit of my career. . . .
>
> With the end of the war my military career was over. . . . I became more and more unhappy, especially when the war crime trials opened in Tokyo. Though I was never accused, General Douglas MacArthur summoned me to testify on several occasions.
>
> As I got off the train one day in Tokyo's Shibuya Station, I saw an American distributing literature. He handed me a pamphlet entitled "I Was a Prisoner of Japan."
>
> What I read . . . eventually changed my life. On that Sunday while I was in the air over Pearl Harbor, an American soldier named Jacob DeShazer had been on K.P. duty in an army camp in California. When the radio announced the sneak demolishing of Pearl Harbor, he shouted, "Jap, just wait and see what we'll do to you!"
>
> One month later he volunteered for a secret mission with the Jimmy Doolittle Squadron—a surprise raid on Tokyo. . . . After the bombing raid, they flew on towards China but ran out of fuel and were forced to parachute into Japanese-held territory. . . . During the next 40 long months in confinement, DeShazer was cruelly treated . . . but after 25 months the U.S. prisoners were given a Bible to read. . . . There in a Japanese P.O.W. camp, he read and read—and eventually came to understand that the book was more than a historical classic.

"FROM PEARL HARBOR TO CALVARY"

After DeShazer was released, he returned to Japan as a missionary and in God's providence gave Fuchida the tract he had written. Fuchida continues:

> The peaceful motivation I had read about was exactly what I was seeking. Since the American had found it in the Bible, I decided to purchase one myself, despite my traditional Buddhist heritage.
>
> In the ensuing weeks I read this book eagerly. I came to the climactic drama—the Crucifixion. I read in Luke 23:34 the prayer of Jesus Christ at His death: "Father, forgive them for they know not what they do." I was impressed that I was certainly one of those for whom He had prayed. The many men I had killed had been slaughtered in the name of patriotism, for I did not understand the love that Christ wishes to implant within every heart.
>
> Right at that moment I seemed to meet Jesus for the first time. I understood the meaning of His death as a substitute for my wickedness and so in prayer, I requested Him to forgive my sins and change me from a bitter, disillusioned ex-pilot into a well-balanced Christian with purpose in living. . . .
>
> I believe with all my heart that those who will direct Japan—and all other nations—in the decades to come must not ignore the message of Christ. . . . He is the only hope for this troubled world.

Reflection

Mitsuo Fuchida came to know God personally through reading and studying the Bible, God's message to humanity. Do you regularly read and study the Bible? It has the power to change your life just as dramatically as it did Mitsuo Fuchida's.

Turn my eyes from worthless things, and give me life through your word. PSALM 119:37

December 4

"O for Friday! O for Friday! O Lord, give me patience to await thy appointed time!"

HIS JAILERS must have shaken their heads in disbelief, for Friday was the day appointed for John Nesbit's execution.

Like many other Scottish Covenanter martyrs,[4] John Nesbit spent the last days of his life in a jail cell. What set the Covenanters apart from other condemned prisoners was how they chose to spend their final days. They worshiped the Christ whom they would soon meet face-to-face and several wrote a Last and Dying Testimony. These are the words Nesbit left for posterity:

> Be not afraid at His sweet and lovely and desirable cross. For although I have not been able because of my wounds to lift up or lay down my head, but as I was helped, yet I was never in better case all my life. . . . God has so wonderfully shined on me with the sense of His redeeming, strengthening, assisting, supporting, through-bearing, pardoning and reconciling love, grace and mercy, that my soul doth long to be freed of bodily infirmities and earthly organs, that so I may flee to His Royal palace even the Heavenly habitation of my God, where I am sure of a crown put on my head, and a palm put in my hand, and a new song in my mouth, even the song of Moses and the Lamb, that so I may bless, praise, magnify and extol Him for what He hath done to me and for me. Wherefore I bid farewell to all my fellow-sufferers for the testimony of Jesus. . . .
>
> Farewell, my children, study holiness in all your ways, and praise the Lord for what He hath done for me, and tell all my Christian friends to praise Him on my account. Farewell, sweet Bible, and wanderings and contendings for truth. Welcome, death. Welcome, the city of my God where I shall see Him and be enabled to serve Him eternally with full freedom. . . . But above all, welcome, welcome, welcome, our glorious and alone God, Father, Son and Holy Ghost; into Thy hands I commit my spirit for Thou art worthy. Amen.

John Nesbit's Friday was **December 4, 1685.** He approached the gallows with eyes lifted up to heaven, his face shining. Then he jumped up on the scaffold and cried aloud:

My soul doth magnify the Lord! My soul doth magnify the Lord! I have longed sixteen years to seal the precious cause and interest of precious Christ with my blood. And now, now He hath answered and granted my request, and has left me no more ado but to come here and pour forth my last prayers, sing forth my last praise to Him in time on this sweet and desirable scaffold, mount that ladder, and then I shall quickly get home to my Father's House, see, enjoy, serve and sing forth the praises of my glorious Redeemer, for evermore world without end.

Reflection

Most of us spend our lives in denial regarding death. We think of it as something that happens to other people. We grieve when we hear of friends or relatives who have been told they are going to die. Yet we are all going to die; the only question is how soon. We may not face a martyr's death, as did John Nesbit, but unless the Lord Jesus returns first, we will all die. In light of this now is the time to prepare ourselves for our death and for standing before our Maker.

You were made from dust, and to the dust you will return.

GENESIS 3:19

December 5

About the year 1800 the mother of Allen Gardiner entered her little boy's bedroom and found him sleeping on the cold hard floor.

WHEN SHE asked him why, he replied that he intended someday to become a world traveler, and such an ambition required that one be accustomed to hardship.

Drawn by the romance of the sea, Gardiner joined the navy as a teenager. Navy life led him away from his mother's godly influence, yet he knew that she loved him and prayed continually for his salvation. When a letter informing him of his mother's death reached him at a port of call in China, a hunger for things Christian reawakened in him. In Lima he visited the site of the Inquisition and was sickened at the cruel instruments of torture.

Then his ship stopped in Tahiti. There Gardiner found an atmosphere of peace and rest. Missionaries had been there only a short time, but many people had been transformed. Gardiner attended church and was particularly impressed observing a native teaching small children.

His journal records the change that took place in his life as they approached South Africa: "The last time I visited this colony I was walking in the broad way and hastening by rapid strides to the brink of eternal ruin. Blessed be His name, who loved us and gave Himself for us, a great change has been wrought in my heart, and I am now enabled to derive pleasure and satisfaction in hearing and reading the Word of Life."

After his wife died in 1834, Gardiner's thoughts turned to the many people he had met on his naval adventures who had never heard about Jesus Christ. Gardiner longed for them to meet Jesus as he had and didn't care how many cold hard floors he'd have to sleep on to accomplish it.

That year he established the first mission station among the Zulus of South Africa. He won the Zulu king to the Lord, but a treacherous Dutch trader forced Gardiner to flee for his life back to England. In 1836 Gardiner, not one to be discouraged, turned his energies to the Indians of South America whom the Lord had laid on his heart during his navy days.

Gardiner remarried, and he and his family spent more than fifteen years in Chili and Argentina laboring to make the Patagonian Missionary Society a reality. He established a supply system from the Falkland Islands to support his endeavors. On **December 5, 1850,** he and six others landed on the island of Tierra del Fuego, or "The Land of the Fire." As they moved inland hoping for evangelistic success, hostile Indians drove them back to their small boat. They possessed only six months of rations and stretched them out as meagerly as they could, awaiting the scheduled supplies from the Falklands.

In January of 1852 the supply ship arrived—three months too late. Gardiner and his companions had slowly starved to death. His journal told the tale: "Poor and weak as we are, our boat is a very Bethel to our souls, for we feel and know that God is here. Asleep or awake, I am, beyond the power of expression, happy. . . . Great and marvelous are the loving-kindnesses of my gracious God unto me. I neither hunger nor thirst, though five days without food."

The story of Gardiner's death had a powerful impact on the Christians of England. Gardiner's Patagonian Missionary Society became the South American Missionary Society, and six years later eight more missionaries sailed below the equator. As they held a worship service on the shore, seven of them were slaughtered by Indians.

The Land of the Fire became a holy crucible, refining the South American Missionary Society for evangelizing South America. Today throughout southern Chile and Argentina tens of thousands of Christians are the result of its faithful efforts and a realization of Gardiner's dream.

Reflection

God is able to bring victory out of seeming tragedy. The death of Allen Gardiner raised up more missionaries than he could have recruited had he lived. His death brought the message of life to tens of thousands.

Jesus replied, "I am the bread of life. No one who comes to me will ever be hungry again. Those who believe in me will never thirst."

JOHN 6:35

December 6

"We don't know where they're going, but we're going to heaven."

JOHN AND BETTY STAM met at Moody Bible Institute, while both were studying to become missionaries to China. After going there separately under the China Inland Mission (CIM),[5] they were unexpectedly reunited and a year later were married. On September 11, 1934, their daughter, Helen Priscilla, was born, and by the end of November the Stams were installed in their new post in Tsingteh. Only twenty-seven and twenty-eight years old, with a newborn baby, they seemed at the beginning of their ministry, but on **December 6, 1934,** communist soldiers swept into Tsingteh and arrested the Stams.

John wrote to the CIM: "My wife, baby and myself are today in the hands of the Communists, in the city of Tsingteh. Their demand is twenty thousand dollars for our release. . . . God grant you wisdom in what you do, and us fortitude, courage and peace of heart. . . . The Lord bless and guide you, and as for us, may God be glorified whether by life or by death."

The Stams were forced to make a difficult march to the town of Miao-shou. Physically exhausted, they were horrified to hear the soldiers discuss plans to murder their baby to make the trip easier. Witnesses said that an old farmer stepped forward to object. When challenged by the soldiers to take baby Helen's place, the man agreed and was shot on the spot. Little Helen's life was miraculously spared.

Arriving in Miao-shou, the Stams were imprisoned until morning. Then soldiers bound them both and forced them to leave their baby behind. As they were marched through the streets, the soldiers called people to witness their execution. On a hill outside the village a local Christian doctor stepped forward to beg for their lives. The soldiers condemned him to die as well, and when John asked for mercy for the doctor, he was immediately beheaded. Betty fell on her knees beside John and was beheaded as well.

A Chinese evangelist named Lo was hiding with his family outside the village. Hearing of the executions, they came secretly into town, where villagers furtively pointed toward a silent house. Entering it, Lo found baby Helen, not three months old, miraculously safe after thirty hours alone.

Taking her with him, he went to the hill and found her parents' bodies. Hastily organizing his friends' burial, he spoke to the people who had gathered: "You have seen these wounded bodies, and you pity our friends for their suffering and death. But you should know that they are children of God. Their spirits are unharmed and are at the moment in the presence of their Heavenly Father. They came [here] not for themselves but for you, to tell you about the great love of God, that you might believe in the Lord Jesus and be eternally saved. You have heard their message. Remember, it is true. Their death proves it so. Do not forget what they told you—repent, and believe the Gospel."

Still in danger and penniless, the Lo family made their escape from Miaoshou with the baby. Pinned inside Helen's sleeping bag they found two five-dollar bills, along with clean diapers and clothes. It was all the Stams had been able to leave to Helen, but it was just enough to provide for their hundred-mile journey to safety.

Brought to her grandparents in Tsinan, Helen was found to be perfectly healthy. The news of the "Miracle Baby" and her parents' martyrdom spread around the world. In response, many hundreds pledged their lives to missionary service, and there was a great outpouring of prayer and support for the China Inland Mission. A fellow missionary in China wrote Betty's parents, "A life which had the longest span of years might not have been able to do one-hundreth of the work for Christ which they have done in a day."

Reflection

Are you surprised that God spared the baby and not the parents? Our times are in God's hands. He has numbered our days and given us immortality until the day he has chosen for our death.

You have decided the length of our lives. You know how many months we will live and we are not given a minute longer.   JOB 14:5

December 7

God promised good things to come.

ZECHARIAH, a priest and prophet, was born in Babylonia and returned to Jerusalem in 538 B.C. He began prophesying in the late fall of 520 B.C. and received eight visions from God on February 15, 519 B.C.[6]

A year and a half later the exiles who returned from Babylon and settled in the city of Bethel sent a delegation to Jerusalem, wanting to know whether they should continue to fast each summer as they had in Babylonia on the anniversary of the destruction of the temple in Jerusalem by Nebuchadnezzar.

On **December 7, 518 B.C.**, God gave the answer to their question to Zechariah:

"Say to all your people and your priests, 'During those seventy years of exile, when you fasted and mourned in the summer and at the festival in early autumn, was it really for me that you were fasting? And even now in your holy festivals, you don't think about me but only of pleasing yourselves. Isn't this the same message the Lord proclaimed through the prophets years ago when Jerusalem and the towns of Judah were bustling with people, and the Negev and the foothills of Judah were populated areas?' . . .

"This is what the Lord Almighty says: Judge fairly and honestly, and show mercy and kindness to one another. Do not oppress widows, orphans, foreigners, and poor people. And do not make evil plans to harm each other.

"Your ancestors would not listen to this message. They turned stubbornly away and put their fingers in their ears to keep from hearing. They made their hearts as hard as stone, so they could not hear the law or the messages that the Lord Almighty had sent them by his Spirit through the earlier prophets. That is why the Lord Almighty was so angry with them.

"Since they refused to listen when I called to them, I would not listen when they called to me, says the Lord Almighty. I scattered them as with a whirlwind among the distant nations, where they lived as strangers. . . ."

Then another message came to me from the Lord. . . . "Now the Lord says: I am returning to Mount Zion, and I will live in Jerusalem.

THE FUTURE OF JERUSALEM

Then Jerusalem will be called the Faithful City; the mountain of the Lord Almighty will be called the Holy Mountain. . . .

"All this may seem impossible to you now, a small and discouraged remnant of God's people. But do you think this is impossible for me, the Lord Almighty? . . . You can be sure that I will rescue my people from the east and from the west. I will bring them home again to live safely in Jerusalem. They will be my people, and I will be faithful and just toward them as their God." (Zechariah 7:5–8:8)

Then finally came the specific answer to the question of the delegation from Bethel:

"This is what the Lord Almighty says: The traditional fasts and times of mourning you have kept in early summer, midsummer, autumn, and winter are now ended. They will become festivals of joy and celebration for the people of Judah. . . .

"People from nations and cities around the world will travel to Jerusalem. . . . People from many nations, even powerful nations, will come to Jerusalem to seek the Lord Almighty and to ask the Lord to bless them." (8:19-22)

Reflection

In your opinion are these final promises of powerful nations coming to Jerusalem to seek the Lord something that has already happened or events that will occur following the second coming of Christ during the Millennium? What can you apply to your life from these words of God through the prophet Zechariah?

In the last days, the Temple of the Lord in Jerusalem will become the most important place on earth. People from all over the world will go there to worship.   MICAH 4:1

December 8

Being the author of best-selling books didn't prevent him from experiencing persecution.

RICHARD BAXTER was born at Rowton, Shropshire, England, in 1615. His father was converted to Christ about the time of his son's birth, and young Richard followed the faith of his father. A brilliant student, Baxter mastered books of theology while still in his teens. He was ordained into the Anglican ministry in 1638.

Baxter, a gifted intellectual, also had a pastor's heart for souls, which led to an almost complete conversion of his six-hundred-member congregation and a veritable social transformation of the town itself. On Sundays he reported, "You might hear a hundred families singing psalms and repeating sermons as you passed through."

His impassioned and eloquent preaching was so popular that galleries had to be added to his church to accommodate all those who came to worship. The congregation, in turn, reached out to the community at large. "Day and night they thirsted after the salvation of their neighbors," according to Baxter.

It was following his years in the army that Baxter began to write. He authored over 160 books including a paraphrase of the New Testament, a metrical version of the Psalms, and two volumes of poetry. His book *The Saints' Everlasting Rest* was among the most widely read English books of the seventeenth century.

He had a heart like Christ's for Christian unity, and his efforts to unite Protestant Christians on essential gospel truths met with success. Baxter founded the ecumenical "Worcester Association" for Protestant ministers, and Christians from varied denominations worshiped together regularly at his Kidderminster church.

He proposed a theological truce between the Calvinists and the Arminians, the two main doctrinal combatants of the day. It was Baxter who popularized the saying "In essentials unity; in nonessentials liberty; and in both charity."

But a man who seeks to draw people in is often misunderstood and even hated by those who seek to shut them out. As a Puritan within the Church of England, Baxter ran into trouble with the Anglican hierarchy when Charles II came to the throne and made him one of his chaplains. The Act of Uniformity of 1662 required all ministers to give unfeigned consent to the Anglican prayer book. This led to the Great Ejection of two thousand Puritan pastors from their churches—including Richard Baxter. In 1685 under King James II he was falsely accused of libel against the church, fined a large sum, and imprisoned for six months. When released, though seventy years old and ill, he plunged back into the harvest.

Baxter had always preached "as never sure to preach again, and as a dying man to dying men," and he delivered his final sermon with as much compassionate fire as his very first. Upon completion of his sermon, the aged pastor made his way wearily home to bed. There, in the company of beloved friends, he spent his final hours. "I bless God I have a well-grounded assurance of my eternal happiness," he whispered to his bedside companions, "and great peace and comfort within."

When his friends reminded him of the encouragement and comfort his books had been to others, he replied with humility, "I was but a pen in the hand of God. What praise is due a pen?"

He once wrote, "Our lives are. . . like a candle in a broken lantern, which a blast of wind may soon blow out." Richard Baxter's candle burned brightly until **December 8, 1691,** when the gentle breath of God blew out his temporal light and he entered into his everlasting rest.

Reflection

How do you evaluate the maxim "In essentials unity; in nonessentials liberty; and in both charity"? Have you had experiences in which this was not applied? How does one decide what are essentials and what are nonessentials?

~❧~

He is the one who gave these gifts to the church: the apostles, the prophets, the evangelists, and the pastors and teachers. Their responsibility is to equip God's people to do his work and build up the church, the body of Christ, until we come to such unity in our faith and knowledge of God's Son that we will be mature and full grown in the Lord, measuring up to the full stature of Christ. EPHESIANS 4:11-13

December 9

The Bible meant everything to Ulrich Zwingli, and the sword meant more than it probably should have.

In Zurich, Switzerland, stands the statue of a man holding a Bible in one hand and a sword in the other.

Courageous and resourceful, the Zurich pastor was ruthless in his pursuit of reform, persecuting defectors from the Swiss Reformation and taking up arms against the resistant Catholic cantons. The Lord Jesus said, "Those who use the sword will be killed by the sword" (Matthew 26:52).

Zwingli[7] perished on the battlefield of Kappel on October 11, 1531.

On **December 9, 1531,** Heinrich Bullinger succeeded Zwingli as pastor of the Zurich Great Church and leader of the Reformed movement in German-speaking Switzerland. Although a theological disciple of Zwingli, Bullinger was in many ways "greater than his master."

Born in 1504 in Bremgarten, Switzerland, Heinrich Bullinger was one of five sons of the village priest. His father paid the regional bishop a yearly tribute for the privilege of marriage (forbidden to the Roman Catholic clergy).

Heinrich was groomed for the priesthood himself from an early age. Studying in Cologne, Germany, in 1519, he was introduced to the writings of the church fathers. Their insistence on the priority of Scripture moved Bullinger into his own study of the Bible, which led to his further reading of the popular works of Martin Luther.[8] Seeds of reform were being sown in Bullinger's heart and mind.

Returning to Switzerland with his master's degree in 1522, Bullinger became abbot of a monastery in Kappel, where he taught the monks directly from the New Testament. A five-month assignment in Zurich introduced him to Zwingli and the foundations of the Swiss Reformation. Upon his return to Kappel, he convinced the abbot and all the monks of the truth of the Reformation.

In 1529 Bullinger's father declared himself a Protestant and was removed from his priesthood at Bremgarten. The townspeople, however, invited Heinrich to take his father's place as the church's first evangelical minister.

In Bremgarten, Bullinger's pastoral and teaching gifts became apparent. While there, he married Anna Adlischweiler, a former nun. Their marriage was loving and long, producing eleven children. All of their sons became Protestant ministers.

In 1531 when Ulrich Zwingli was killed, Zurich called on Heinrich Bullinger to take up the mantle of its fallen captain. He proved himself up to the task. Starting on the path that Zwingli had blazed, Bullinger soon forged his own way.

He was a devoted pastor whose home was constantly open to the hungry, the lost, the persecuted, and the spiritual seeker. Although his salary was meager, he refused any gifts, giving of his own small income to hospitals and institutions of mercy. The harried exiles of Bloody Mary's Catholic reign in England[9] found refuge in Bullinger's Zurich. When they returned home to England, they became leading Puritans.

Bullinger's preaching was powerful, and his pen never rested. For forty years he preached as often as seven times a week. He wrote commentaries on almost every book in the Bible, maintaining a remarkable correspondence with Christians and theologians all over the Protestant world. He corresponded with royalty as well.[10] His wise and persuasive words brought about many a needed compromise between doctrinal opponents within the Reformation, and his pastoral heart produced one of the first Protestant books for comforting the sick and dying. His writings outnumber those of Luther and Calvin[11] combined.

Meek, wise, and patient, Bullinger gave the Reformation what Zwingli probably would not have, even had he lived: order—both ecclesiastical and theological. When Heinrich Bullinger died in 1575, he left behind a church truly reformed. His legacy lives on in the Reformed and Presbyterian traditions.

Reflection

The Bible took priority in Bullinger's study and as a result, shaped his life. Is the Bible a priority in your life? In your devotions do you primarily read the Bible or books about the Bible? It's amazing how much light the Bible can shed on some of the books about it.

◦৽◦

Your word is a lamp for my feet and a light for my path.

PSALM 119:105

December 10

It was the first academic presentation of Protestantism in France, and it wasn't well received.

NICHOLAS COP, a professor of medicine and a good friend of twenty-five-year old John Calvin, a rising theologian,[12] had just been elected rector of the University of Paris. On All Saints Day, November 1, 1533, Cop delivered his inaugural speech to the faculty and students assembled at the Chapel of the Franciscan Observantines for the opening of the academic year. Under the guise of the topic "Christian Philosophy," what Cop actually delivered was an evangelical sermon. Using the first beatitude as his text, he passionately and convincingly stated that forgiveness of sin and eternal life are free gifts of God's grace that cannot be earned by good works. This was a shocking and bold statement by the rector, for this was a Roman Catholic university, and the convocation took place in a Catholic monastery! Never before in French academia had anyone publicly advocated the views of the Reformation. Despite the fact that Cop gave the traditional Catholic salutation to the Virgin Mary in his speech, the audience was not fooled. The theology of Luther[13] and Zwingli[14] clearly shone through. The university crowd was in an uproar, the faculty was furious, and the Franciscan monks went immediately to the Parliament of Paris crying heresy.

Cop was summoned to court to answer the charges brought against him. On his way to the court, a friend warned him that his life was in danger, and he quickly fled from Paris.

On **December 10, 1533,** Francis I, the king of France,[15] issued orders for the capture of Cop and for the punishment of the person who had warned him to flee. A reward of three hundred crowns was offered for the return of Nicholas Cop—dead or alive! He successfully fled to Basel, Switzerland.

This incident and similar ones convinced the king of France that Lutheran doctrines were spreading too quickly throughout France. He therefore adopted new, stricter measures to halt the Reformation and persecute its adherents. However, the march of Protestantism was growing and could not be stopped. The Reformers were not afraid to speak their beliefs and fight the system, even in the face of persecution and death.

Meanwhile John Calvin also fled Paris in the aftermath of the Cop affair. Calvin found a safe haven in Angoulême at the home of Louis de Tillet, where he was able to resume his theological studies and writing.

GHOSTWRITER?

In 1575 Theodore Beza, John Calvin's successor in Geneva, published a biography of Calvin in which he suggested that Calvin had actually written Nicholas Cop's infamous speech. A copy of the speech, although missing several pages, was found written in Calvin's handwriting among his papers. Whether Calvin wrote part or all of the speech remains an open question, but at the least he had strongly influenced Cop.

Reflection

Why do you think it was so scandalous for Nicholas Cop to preach that forgiveness of sin and eternal life are free gifts of God's grace? To what extent do you think his audience considered his propositions to be possibly true? What was your initial reaction when you first heard the gospel message?

༄

The Lord says, "These people say they are mine. They honor me with their lips, but their hearts are far away. And their worship of me amounts to nothing more than human laws learned by rote. Because of this, I will do wonders among these hypocrites. I will show that human wisdom is foolish and even the most brilliant people lack understanding."   ISAIAH 29:13-14

December 11

Forging a new life in a new land was fraught with danger.

THE PILGRIMS were Separatists from Scrooby, England, who refused to conform to the Church of England. They fled first to Holland and then to America, arriving at Cape Cod on the *Mayflower* in November 1620.[16] In early December a group of men set out from the *Mayflower* in a small boat to search for a place to establish their colony. The cold winds and spray from the sea quickly iced their cloaks. They reached the shore that evening exhausted and cold, and spent the next few days setting up temporary shelters and exploring the area to find the best land to settle. Early one morning they were attacked by Indians and narrowly escaped injury by huddling behind a makeshift barricade that shielded them from the arrows.

Eager to leave that unwelcome spot, they sailed in their little boat down through the bay, but a terrible storm forced them to land on an island off the coast. They spent two days there, observing the Sabbath with a day of rest.

The next day, Monday, **December 11, 1620,** the explorers arose at dawn and set sail from the island across the harbor and made their first landing at Plymouth. Armed and on the watch for any possible Indian encounters, the men searched the land. They were pleased with what they found. There were many streams to provide water as well as several cornfields that had been cleared by earlier inhabitants. Since this was the best land the Pilgrims had found since their arrival a month earlier, they decided this would be the place to settle.

They were so anxious to bring the good news to those waiting for them on the *Mayflower* that they decided to sail the twenty-five miles to the tip of Cape Cod across the open water instead of hugging the coast as they had originally done. They made it safely back in the late afternoon.

The return of the exploration party came as a great relief to those who awaited them; the men had been gone for a full week, and many had given them up for lost.

William Bradford returned to the *Mayflower* anticipating the embrace of his young wife, Dorothy. As William climbed aboard the ship amidst the joyful reunions, his eyes met the sorrowful stares of the other Pilgrims. As he searched for the warm smile of his wife, he realized that something was dreadfully wrong. Out of the crowd of sullen faces stepped William Brewster, an old friend and father figure to Bradford. He grasped Bradford's arm and gently pulled him aside. His words confirmed what Bradford now suspected: His wife was gone. She had fallen overboard and drowned before anyone could rescue her. She had been very depressed, and it is not unlikely that she took her own life.

Bradford was visibly shaken, and his loss might have sapped his will to see the new colony succeed. The man so many had leaned upon, was now the one needing support. Bradford's friends gathered around him in his time of need, mourned with him, and helped him deal with the doubts and questions that enshrouded his wife's death.

Within a year Bradford was elected governor of Plymouth Colony[17] and served in that capacity for most of the years between 1621 and his death in 1657.

Reflection

Imagine what December 11, 1620, must have been like for William Bradford. What feelings would you have had if you had been in his position? How does one recover from a shock like that?

"Lord, help!" they cried in their trouble, and he saved them from their distress.   PSALM 107:13

December 12

She stood just four feet three inches tall.

Two weeks before Christmas, on **December 12, 1840,** a baby girl was born into an aristocratic plantation family in Albermarle County, Virginia. Her name was Charlotte Diggs Moon, but everyone called her "Lottie." She grew to just four feet three inches, yet her intellect and force of personality were enormous. In a day when embroidery and dancing distinguished most young ladies, Lottie spoke six languages fluently and earned a master's degree in education from the Albermarle Female Institution in 1861, making her the most educated woman in the South. Lottie's older sister became the first female physician in the state.

Lottie came from a family of dedicated Southern Baptists and attended church most of her life. But at seventeen, Lottie was a staunch skeptic. Faith seemed antithetical to intellect, and Lottie had no need of it.

In December 1858 Dr. John Broadus, later to be one of the first four professors at Southern Baptist Theological Seminary, was holding evangelistic meetings for students at his Charlottesville Baptist Church. Lottie went to one of the services, intending to scoff.

That night after she went to bed, a barking dog kept Lottie awake. She was in the habit of using otherwise wasted hours to consider various intellectual propositions. That night she decided to ponder the merits of Christianity. As she lay in the dark, Lottie mentally reviewed Dr. Broadus's sermon, adding to it the Bible texts and arguments she'd heard throughout her life. By the time she got to the evangelist's altar call, the Spirit of God prompted her to respond, and Lottie Moon, the brilliant skeptic, believed. When she finished her prayer of commitment to Jesus, she realized that the dog had stopped barking.

At age thirty-three, Lottie was working as a teacher when she heard a call to missions "as clear as a bell." In July 1873 the foreign mission board of the Southern Baptist Convention appointed her its first unmarried woman missionary to China.

Lottie arrived in Shantung (now Shandong) Province that year and settled in the city of Tengchow (now Qingdao), where she opened a school for girls. Over time the focus of her ministry became personal evangelism among the poor. She wrote to her supporters: "I have never gotten so near the people in my life. . . . I have never had so many opportunities to press home upon their consciences their duty to God and the claims of the Savior to their love and devotion. I feel more and more that this is the work of God."

Through such letters, Lottie tirelessly advocated for the needs of the people in China. In 1888 she persuaded the women of the Southern Baptist Convention to take an annual missions offering on Christmas Eve. But by 1912, despite such gifts, thousands of people were dying of starvation every day in famine-ravaged Shantung Province. Lottie's cupboard was always open to the poor, even when she herself had to go without food.

On Christmas Eve that year, as Southern Baptist women collected their special missions offering, many were looking forward to meeting the woman who inspired their gifts. At seventy-two, Lottie Moon was coming home. But that same night, aboard a ship off Japan, she died—of complications from starvation. A few months before she had written, "If I had a thousand lives, I would give them all for the women of China."

Lottie Moon walked with God for fifty-four years and with the people of China for thirty-nine. She helped pioneer the role of unmarried women missionaries in evangelism and planted more than thirty Chinese churches. The Lottie Moon Christmas Offering continued after her death, and by 1995 it had raised over $1.5 billion dollars for missions.

Reflection

So often we judge people by their appearance. In the four-foot-three-inch Lottie Moon there was one of the great intellects of her time and, even more important, a heart completely dedicated to her Lord and to the people she served. Can you think of people that you have unfairly prejudged because of their appearance?

∽໑

The trouble with you is that you make your decisions on the basis of appearance. You must recognize that we belong to Christ.

2 CORINTHIANS 10:7

December 13

Not many believe they have heard the voice of God.

In 1292 Pope Nicholas IV died. For almost two and a half years the papal throne remained vacant while the cardinals bickered among themselves trying to elect the next pope. They were divided along family lines: the cardinals of the Colonna family against the cardinals of the Orsini family. Finally, one of the cardinals who himself wanted to be pope, Benedict Gaetani, reported that he had received a letter from a monk well known for his holiness who prophesied divine retribution on the cardinals if they did not soon choose a pope. When questioned, Gaetani identified the monk as the renowned hermit Peter of Morone. In a surprise compromise move, the cardinals decided to select the hermit monk, Peter of Morone, as the next pope.

In the stifling summer heat of 1294, the delegates sent by the cardinals made a 150-mile journey and a thousand-foot ascent up a mountain to inform the dumbstruck hermit that he had been elected pope. Scraggy and unwashed, eighty-five-year-old Peter of Morone declined at first but was finally persuaded to accept and took the name Celestine V.

With the new pope came quite a few changes. Celestine, who was a relatively uneducated man, could not understand Latin, so Italian became the language of official communication. Disapproving of the licentiousness of Rome, he made Naples the seat of the church. To make himself comfortable in the five-story castle that was to be his home, Celestine had a wooden cell constructed in one of the rooms. He avoided ceremonial banquets, preferring to live instead on bread and water in his cell. He commenced a program of giving away the church's money to the poor. The cardinals soon realized that they had made a terrible mistake in their selection of Celestine and were afraid that he would bankrupt the church.

In December 1294 Gaetani decided to take things into his own hands. He pierced a hole in the wall of Celestine's cell and put a small tube in it. In the middle of the night, Gaetani hissed into Celestine's cell: "Celestine, Celestine, lay down your office. It is too great a burden for you to bear." The cardinal continued this for many nights until Celestine, believing he had heard the voice of God himself, decided that he had better obey and resign from his papal office.

A mere fifteen weeks after he was brought down from his mountain sanctuary to celebrate his coronation, Pope Celestine V called his cardinals together to announce his plan to resign. While he had them assembled, he also took the opportunity to exhort them to send their mistresses to nunneries and to live in poverty as Jesus had lived. On **December 13, 1294,** after reading the formula of abdication written for him by Cardinal Gaetani, Pope Celestine V officially became Peter of Morone once again.

After Celestine's resignation, the cardinals quickly elected Cardinal Benedict Gaetani as his replacement. Gaetani took the name of Pope Boniface VIII. Peter of Morone wanted to return to his mountaintop in Morone, but Boniface, fearing that Peter might return one day to expose the new pope's foul play, had him imprisoned in the Castle of Fumone. Peter died two years later, still a captive.

Reflection

The story of the rise and fall of Pope Celestine V sounds very bizarre to us today. What do you believe God's purposes were in allowing this to happen? What lessons are to be learned from these events?

God let them go ahead and do whatever shameful things their hearts desired. ROMANS 1:24

December 14

Songwriter Philipp Bliss didn't like the unusual spelling of his first name, so as an adult he began using the extra "P" as a middle initial.

PHILIP P. BLISS grew up as a poor country boy in Rome, Pennsylvania. His love of music led him to fashion homemade musical instruments out of whatever materials he could find. At the age of ten he heard piano music for the first time. Entranced, he followed the sound into a woman's home. Startled at seeing a ragged, barefoot boy watching her, she immediately quit playing. Instead of fleeing, he cried, "O lady, play some more!"

Just as his love for music started at an early age so did his love for God. He once said that he could not remember a time when he "was not sorry for sin and did not love Christ." When he was fourteen years old, he went forward at a revival and made a public confession of his faith. Shortly after this he became a Sunday school teacher, a commitment he continued for the rest of his life. He found bringing his music to children particularly rewarding: "Think how readily children catch the meaning of a hymn, and how lasting may be its influence. . . . Cannot you, yourself, now remember the songs that you heard in childhood? More than this, can you not recall the very voice and manner in which they were sung? While the sermons—ably written, well delivered, with their flights of oratory and tender appeal—where are they? Their very texts forgotten!"

Although he received no formal musical training, he began writing songs and giving concerts full time at the age of twenty-six. He wrote both the words and music for most of his hymns. He was known for quickly writing entire songs after hearing one inspiring phrase or casual remark, creating the text and melody simultaneously. For example, after hearing D. L. Moody tell the story of a shipwreck caused by a problem in a lighthouse, he wrote, "Let the Lower Lights Be Burning." And while waiting for a train in Ohio he briefly slipped into a church and overheard the preacher saying, "To be almost saved is to be entirely lost." From this he wrote his well-known hymn "Almost Persuaded."

For a time Bliss worked for D. L. Moody in Chicago as a songwriter and singer for his evangelistic meetings.[18] On **December 14, 1876,** Philip Bliss and his wife unknowingly participated in what would be their last evangelistic service together. For the conclusion of the service, Bliss and his wife sang together "I Know Not the Hour When My Lord Shall Come."

"I KNOW NOT THE HOUR"

Later that month after visiting his boyhood home in Pennsylvania for Christmas, Bliss and his wife boarded a train to return to Chicago to minister with Moody. While crossing a railroad bridge near Ashtabula, Ohio, the bridge collapsed, plunging the train sixty feet down into a ravine. Observers saw Bliss escape the burning wreckage, but then crawl back through a window into the flames to search for his wife. Thirty-eight-year-old Bliss and his wife were among the more than one hundred passengers who perished in the tragedy.

At their funeral the last hymn they sang together publicly was sung, then with new meaning:

> *I know not the hour when my Lord shall come,*
> *To take me away to His own dear home,*
> *But I know that His presence will lighten the gloom,*
> *And that will be glory for me.*

> *I know not the form of my mansion fair,*
> *I know not the name that I then shall bear;*
> *But I know that my Saviour will welcome me there,*
> *And that will be heaven for me.*

Reflection

If you were to die suddenly in an accident, would the Savior welcome you to heaven? How do you know? In many ways, life is like a probation period to determine whether or not we will give our wholehearted allegiance to the Savior, whom God sent to redeem his people.

❧

Simon Peter replied, "Lord . . . You alone have the words that give eternal life. We believe them, and we know you are the Holy One of God." JOHN 6:68-69

December 15

The grace of God was truly a sweet sound in the ears of John Newton.

The life of John Newton consisted of many different seasons. His journey took him from the decks of slave ships in the 1740s to the pulpit in 1764.[19]

By his own admission, Newton's admiration of his wife approached levels of idolatry. He was passionately in love with her, an emotion that did not dim with the passing of the years. Consequently, as it became apparent that his wife's days were coming to a close, Newton's friends were concerned over what effect her death would have on him.

As his wife's health continued to deteriorate, John found his mind preoccupied with her well-being. "I have been watching with much feeling and too much anxiety my failing gourd, upon which a worm by the Divine appointment has been long preying."

Newton related his last communication with his wife on Sunday, December 12, 1790: "When I was preparing for church in the morning, she sent for me, and we took a final farewell as to this world. She faintly uttered an endearing compellation, which was familiar to her, and gave me her hand, which I held, while I prayed by her bedside. We exchanged a few tears; but I was almost as unable to speak as she was." That same evening Mrs. Newton lost her faculties of speech, sight, and hearing.

One of Newton's chief concerns as his wife's health failed was his own ability to model the truths he had spent so many years preaching from the pulpit. He had long emphasized the gospel's message of comfort to those who are afflicted. He had preached a God who was the foundation of truth, the comforter of all who suffer, and the source of strength and help to all who desire to be assisted. Now the author of "Amazing Grace, How Sweet the Sound" came to realize that he had to admit his need for God's grace in a time of his own great need.

In his memoirs he relates the result of this understanding: "From the time that I so remarkably felt myself *willing to be helped* I might truly say, to the praise of the Lord, 'My heart trusted in Him, and I was helped indeed.'"

It was only three days from the time his wife lost her ability to communicate that she drew her last breath. John sat faithfully by her side holding a candle by which he watched his beloved's life expire on **December 15, 1790.** He immediately knelt and thanked the Lord for her peaceful deliverance.

With the help of the Lord, Newton did not spend the days after his wife's departure mourning alone in his home. He preached three times before his wife was buried and preached at her funeral as well—with tears streaming down his cheeks.

Five years later, on the anniversary of her death, Newton reflected on his marriage and the passing of his wife in a poem:

> *Then let me change my sighs to praise,*
> *For all that He has done,*
> *And yield my few remaining days*
> *To Him, and Him alone.*
>
> *I hope to join her soon again*
> *On yonder happy shore,*
> *Where neither sorrow, sin, nor pain,*
> *Shall ever reach us more.*

God's grace was truly a sweet sound in the ears of John Newton.

Reflection

Whom do you love most in this world? Do you think you can trust God for his comfort if that person dies before you do? Will you meet again in heaven?

❧

God blesses those who mourn, for they will be comforted.

MATTHEW 5:4

December 16

It all happened just as the Bible said it would.

AFTER THE death of Alexander the Great in 323 B.C.,[20] four of his generals divided up his kingdom among themselves, with Seleucus gaining control of Babylonia and Ptolemy controlling Egypt. Palestine was under the rule of the Ptolemies until 198 B.C. when the Seleucid dynasty won control.

In the initial years of the Seleucid reign, the Jews enjoyed a period of brief tranquility. The Seleucid ruler Antiochus III permitted the Jewish people to worship according to their law.

In 187 B.C. Antiochus III was succeeded by his eldest son, Seleucus IV Philopater, and then by his youngest son, Antiochus IV Epiphanes, in 175 B.C.

The kingdom inherited by Antiochus IV Epiphanes was unstable. Antiochus's remedy for this was a vigorous program of Hellenization, introducing Greek culture and institutions throughout his kingdom. In his mind one of the unifying factors was religion. Therefore in about 169 B.C. he began to encourage his subjects to worship himself as the manifestation of Zeus. On coins he was called Theos Epiphanes, meaning "the manifest god." However, his enemies changed just one Greek letter in his name, making it Epimanes, meaning "madman."

One of the first disputes that Antiochus IV had to settle was between the Jewish high priest Onias III, who supported Egypt, and his brother Jason, who was a supporter of the Seleucids. By outbribing Onias, Jason secured the high priesthood and made Jerusalem a Greek city (1 Maccabees 1:10-15; 2 Maccabees 4:7-17). Then in 171 B.C. Menelaus, a friend of Jason, bid even more than Jason for the high priesthood. Because Antiochus needed money, he gave the position to Menelaus even though he was not a descendant of Aaron and thus was not qualified for the office. Jason fled to the territory of the Ammonites (2 Maccabees 4:23-29).

Menelaus then plundered the temple, causing the inhabitants of Jerusalem to riot. Jason returned to help the Jerusalemites avenge Menelaus's ravaging of the temple. Hearing that his high priest was being attacked, Antiochus interpreted this as a revolt against him and so determined to subdue Jerusalem (2 Maccabees 5:11-17). Returning there with Menelaus, he robbed the temple of its remaining treasures and then left the city under the control of one of his commanders (1 Maccabees 1:20-29; 2 Maccabees 5:18-22).

Antiochus then decided to make Palestine a buffer zone between himself and Egypt. He returned to Jerusalem, broke down the city walls, and made the old City of David into a military fortress. In his self-appointed role as Zeus Manifest, he ordered vigorous Hellenization and the elimination of the Jewish religion. He forbade Jews to keep the Sabbath, to offer sacrifices, or to circumcise and ordered the destruction of all copies of the Torah. Jews were ordered to offer unclean sacrifices and to eat the flesh of pigs—all forbidden by Jewish law (2 Maccabees 6:18).

The ultimate desecration of the Jewish temple occurred on **December 16, 167** B.C., when Antiochus ordered that an altar of Zeus be built on top of the altar of burnt offering, and swine's flesh was offered there to Zeus (1 Maccabees 1:41-64; 2 Maccabees 6:1-11).[21]

Nearly four hundred years earlier, the prophet Daniel had prophesied this exact event in Daniel 11:11-32. Antiochus fulfilled the prophecy precisely when his army took over "the Temple fortress, polluting the sanctuary, putting a stop to the daily sacrifices, and setting up the sacrilegious object that causes desecration" (Daniel 11:31).

Reflection

Antiochus's act of desecration is a precursor of the final act of desecration, which according to Jesus will occur shortly before his second coming. A few days before his crucifixion, Jesus said, " 'The time will come when you will see what Daniel the prophet spoke about [in Daniel 9:27]: the sacrilegious object that causes desecration standing in the Holy Place'—reader, pay attention!" (Matthew 24:15). In other words, Jesus is telling us to be watching for these signs as we await his second coming.

∼⌖∼

That day will not come until there is a great rebellion against God and the man of lawlessness is revealed—the one who brings destruction. He will exalt himself and defy every god there is and tear down every object of adoration and worship. He will position himself in the temple of God, claiming that he himself is God.　　2 THESSALONIANS 2:3-4

December 17

Queen Mary perceived him as a serious threat to her reign.

In 1553 England's newly enthroned Queen Mary I,[22] a committed Roman Catholic, wanted to impress her new subjects with her fair-mindedness. She called a convocation of the highest religious leaders in the Church of England to discuss its merits versus those of the Catholic Church. One of the Protestant leaders in attendance was John Philpot.

John Philpot was only a boy when King Henry VIII, eager to break his marriage vows, broke with the Catholic Church and made himself head of the Church of England.[23] Many continued to practice Catholicism, but the Reformation also took hold, and Philpot grew up a Protestant. At Oxford he studied law and languages. Later he was appointed archdeacon of Winchester and became a leading apologist for the Protestants.

At Queen Mary's convocation in 1553, Philpot and a few others boldly spoke in defense of the gospel. They were tolerated but ignored. Several months later Philpot published a book that reported vast portions of the closed-door discussions, making it clear that the convocation had simply been a political stratagem of the crown.

Shortly thereafter Philpot was arrested as Queen Mary perceived him as a serious threat to her reign. He was examined by bishops who Mary hoped would trap him into heresy or even convince him to turn his heart and pen to the Catholic faith. Philpot admitted that he wrote the book. But that admission was not enough to condemn him; even the Catholics had to agree that he had faithfully reported the proceedings. At his thirteenth and final examination the lord mayor brought a knife and a pig's bladder full of powder to try to seal their case. He said, "My lord, this man had a roasted pig brought unto him, and this knife was put secretly between the skin and the flesh thereof, and so it was sent to him in prison. Also this powder was sent to him . . . which when I did see, I thought it had been gunpowder and put fire to it, but it would not burn. Then I took it for poison and gave it to a dog. But it was not so. Then I took a little water, and it made as fair ink as I would ever write withal. Therefore, my lord, you see what a naughty fellow this is."

The incident had been fabricated by Queen Mary's supporters to condemn Philpot. It succeeded, and he was convicted of heresy and sentenced to burn at the stake. "Well, I must be content," he said, "for it is God's appointment. . . . I will never recant that which I have spoken, for it is most certain truth. And I will seal it with my blood."

At suppertime on **December 17, 1555,** the message was sent informing Philpot that he would be burned the following day. He said simply, "I am ready; God grant me strength and a joyful resurrection."

The next morning Philpot kissed the stake marked for his burning. "Shall I disdain to suffer at this stake," he asked the crowd, "seeing my Redeemer did not refuse to suffer vile death upon the cross for me?" Philpot recited Psalms 106, 107, and 108, the fire was lit, and he was with his Redeemer.

Reflection

Queen Mary's convocation was an effort to convert the Protestant leaders to Catholicism. When that was unsuccessful, she had them burned at the stake. It was similar to the experience of Jesus: When his opponents realized they could never win an argument with him, they determined to kill him. Why do you think people react in this way?

∽◈∼

Some of you are trying to kill me because my message does not find a place in your hearts.   JOHN 8:37

December 18

Who are the Good Shepherd's sheep?

HANUKKAH, sometimes called the Feast of Dedication or the Feast of Lights, is an eight-day celebration to commemorate the rededication of the temple in 164 B.C.[24] after it had been profaned by Antiochus IV Epiphanes three years earlier.[25]

In A.D. 32 Hanukkah began on **December 18**, and Jesus[26] was in Jerusalem for the celebration. He was in the temple walking through the section known as Solomon's Colonnade, where following his resurrection believers met to proclaim him as the Messiah (Acts 3:11–4:4; 5:12). There the Jewish leaders surrounded him and asked, "How long are you going to keep us in suspense? If you are the Messiah, tell us plainly" (John 10:24). It wasn't that they wanted to know whether he was the Messiah so that they could follow him; rather, they were trying to get him to make statements that they could use against him.

The reason that Jesus did not publicly claim to be the Messiah was that in first-century Palestine there were many popular political and military misconceptions about the Messiah with which Jesus did not want to identify. The popular conception of the Messiah was that he would be a conquering ruler, not a suffering servant whose kingdom would be neither political not military.

Jesus replied that his words and deeds pointed to him as the Messiah. He said, "The proof is what I do in the name of my Father. But you don't believe because you are not part of my flock. My sheep recognize my voice; I know them, and they follow me" (vv. 25-27). The implication is that the reverse is also true: those who are not part of his flock don't recognize his voice; Jesus doesn't know them, and they do not follow him.

Jesus went on to tell more of what he does for his sheep, saying, "I give them eternal life, and they will never perish" (v. 28). There is therefore a group of individuals, here called "his sheep," of whom it can be said, "They will never perish."

However, the focus is not on the power of eternal life but on the power of Jesus. He continues, "No one will snatch them away from me, for my Father has given them to me, and he is more powerful than anyone else. So no one can take them from me" (vv. 28-29). The security of Jesus' sheep lies with the Good Shepherd. As his sheep, we are not hanging on to him—he is hanging on to us. God the Father is more powerful than anyone in the universe, and so no one can steal his sheep.

Jesus' next words were blockbusters: "The Father and I are one" (v. 30). The Greek word for "one" used here doesn't mean that the Father and Son are one person but that they are one in action. Jesus does what the Father does and vice versa.

Hearing this, once again the Jewish leaders picked up stones to kill him. But Jesus asked them a simple question:

"At my Father's direction I have done many things to help the people. For which one of these good deeds are you killing me?"

They replied, "Not for any good work, but for blasphemy, because you, a mere man, have made yourself God."

Jesus replied, ". . . Why do you call it blasphemy when the Holy One who was sent into the world by the Father says, 'I am the Son of God'? Don't believe me unless I carry out my Father's work. But if I do his work, believe in what I have done, even if you don't believe me. Then you will realize that the Father is in me, and I am in the Father."

Once again they tried to arrest him, but he got away and left them. (vv. 32-39)

Why was he able to get away? Because his hour had not yet come.

Reflection

Are you one of the Good Shepherd's sheep? You can tell by whether or not you recognize his voice and you follow him. If you are one of his sheep, he has given you eternal life, and you will never perish.

The good shepherd lays down his life for the sheep.   JOHN 10:11

December 19

Everything that could possibly go wrong did.

MANY IN England, including King James I,[27] publicly claimed that the primary purpose in establishing the American colonies was to spread the gospel among the Indians. In truth, the primary motivation was greed. In 1606 the London Company was formed for the purpose of colonial expansion and trade. They obtained a royal charter to found a colony in Virginia. Without taking much time to prepare plans for the new colony, three ships carrying 105 colonists set out for the New World on **December 19, 1606.**

The company had a rough voyage. It took much longer than expected, forcing them to consume much of the rations en route that were to have sustained them through their first year. They constantly fought with each other, and because they had no form of government or authority structure, conflicts were difficult to resolve. In May the ships finally entered the Chesapeake Bay. The colonists named the river that flowed into the bay the James River and their colony Jamestown after their king.

These men were not fit to build a colony. With few laborers, carpenters, farmers, or blacksmiths among them, the group consisted primarily of "Gentlemen" who joined the enterprise without realizing the years of hard labor that would be necessary for the colony to achieve financial success. The quarreling that had started during their voyage continued on land. The Gentlemen refused to participate in any labor, desiring instead to set off in search of gold and pearls. Only one minister had been sent with them—an indication of how interested England really was in evangelizing the Indians. Rev. Robert Hunt was a man of God whose passion was spreading the gospel in the New World. However, his fellow colonists did not share his passion. He nailed a board between two trees for an altar and made an awning out of an old sail to serve as their church.

They arrived too late to plant spring crops and were quickly running out of food. They lived in continual fear of Indian attacks and suffered from illnesses caused from exposure, mosquitoes, and poor nutrition. Instead of drawing together or looking to God in their calamities, the rift between the Gentlemen and the others continued to widen, and no one showed any interest in Robert Hunt's continued pleas for repentance and reliance on God. By September 1607 half of the little colony had died.

Hunt's life was a vivid contrast. In addition to being a godly man of

THEY WENT WITHOUT GOD

prayer, he labored energetically, taking charge of building the first mill for the grinding of corn and becoming the primary caregiver for the sick. He pleaded with the Gentlemen to give up their arrogance, turn to God, and support the common cause of the colony, but his efforts were largely in vain.

In the winter of 1608 a fire destroyed their fort, storehouse, church, and some dwellings. Hunt lost all but the clothes he was wearing yet was not heard to complain.

The colony at Jamestown had become entirely dependent on the generosity of the Indians. Yet only Hunt thanked God for their assistance.

The sweltering heat in the summer of 1608 scorched the crops they planted. Starvation and disease claimed even more lives the second year than the first. Nine out of every ten people who embarked for Jamestown died. In 1609 there was no food left. Hunt himself succumbed to the conditions and died, leaving behind no one to take his place. This pattern continued for years. In March 1621 there were only 843 settlers in Virginia. During the next year 1,580 more people arrived but 1,183 died!

Even with this staggering death rate, the colonists refused to trust in God. Ship after ship arrived, with the investors always "forgetting" to send more ministers. In 1622 there were more than 1,200 settlers in ten plantations scattered throughout Virginia, but just three ministers. So much for spreading the gospel among the Indians!

Reflection

The story of Jamestown is a depressing litany. How do you think things might have been different had they trusted in God?

Do not forget the things I have done throughout history. For I am God—I alone! I am God, and there is no one else like me.   ISAIAH 46:9

December 20

In spite of his limitations, he answered God's call.

A. J. FREEMAN was blind in his right eye from birth. He immigrated to America from Sweden at the age of nineteen. In the summer of 1895 when he was twenty-seven, a coworker accidentally jabbed his thumb into Freeman's left eye while they were roughhousing. Freeman's remaining optic nerve was severed, leaving him totally blind.

Freeman visited many doctors and spent an entire year at the Illinois Eye and Ear Infirmary in Chicago under the care and supervision of the foremost eye specialist in the world. When even he was not able to help, Freeman sank into a deep depression. An unknown young man visited the hospital ward on an irregular basis and explained how Jesus Christ offered salvation. A Christian nurse also shared the same message with Freeman. Their words made him remember how his mother had shared the gospel with him in his youth. But lost in his depression, he spent his days plotting revenge on the man who had unwittingly blinded him.

Becoming suicidal one day, Freeman climbed up on the windowsill of his fifth-floor hospital ward, preparing to jump. As he trembled on the brink, a burning question flashed into his mind, *What shall become of me?* Just then an unseen nurse gripped his arm, preventing him from jumping. Immediately he fell to his knees and prayed for God to save him. From that time on he considered the window in the room his gateway to heaven since it marked the place where he had found life instead of death.

Freeman now had renewed hope that perhaps he had a purpose in life. Ambitious and hardworking by nature, he entered the School for the Blind in Jacksonville, Illinois, in the second year after his accident. There he learned the craft of broom making.

Freeman returned to his wife in Moline, Illinois, and started a broom factory. In a relatively short time, Freeman had fifteen men making brooms for him, producing more than six hundred brooms a day. In addition to his business venture he was being called upon by temperance and women's societies to sing and testify about Christ and the gift of salvation he had received. He began to spend so much time in this work that eventually his business began to suffer.

Freeman longed to serve the Lord full-time, but at the turn of the twentieth century such service was rarely remunerated, and he believed that his first

THE BLIND EVANGELIST

duty remained to support his family. In addition, he was unable to travel anywhere without a guide.

In 1902 at a revival at Freeman's home church, many people placed their faith in Jesus Christ. Freeman's own ten-year-old daughter, Esther, was among those who responded to the call to follow Christ. One night while walking to church with her father, Esther exclaimed, "Oh, Pa, I feel just like a new person." But Freeman, believing the gospel was too difficult for a child of ten to understand, continued to doubt her salvation. Then one day he and his wife came home to find Esther telling a group of children about Jesus and praying for their salvation. "This," said Freeman, "made me realize that the gospel is a power unto salvation also for little children who believe in their Saviour."

Esther could sing and soon began playing the mandolin with her father, and before long "Freeman and Esther" were well known locally as a singing group. Freeman's opportunities of service with Esther made the call to serve God more clear to him.

Finally, on **December 20, 1903,** at the age of thirty-five, Freeman was ordained to the ministry by the Swedish Free Church of Moline, Illinois, and became a full-time evangelist. Eventually more than twelve thousand persons came to put their faith in Jesus Christ through the preaching of the blind Swedish evangelist.

Reflection

Do you feel that you have physical or other handicaps that limit how God can use you? Maybe you just feel too shy or are too easily embarrassed. Just remember A. J. Freeman—for if God can use a blind Swedish immigrant, he can use you.

❧

Since I know it is all for Christ's good, I am quite content with my weaknesses and with insults, hardships, persecutions, and calamities. For when I am weak, then I am strong. 2 CORINTHIANS 12:10

December 21

My memory is nearly gone; but I remember two things: that I am a great sinner, and that Christ is a great Saviour.

J OHN NEWTON spent most of his early life at sea. The son of a merchant ship commander, midshipman of the British navy, and master of a slave ship, Newton knew the waters better than the shore at the age of twenty-three.

It was a great storm at sea that the Lord used as a beacon to cut through the darkness that had characterized Newton's early life.[28] From that point on, John Newton spent his life in the service of God, eventually becoming an Anglican clergyman and the author of many hymns including "Amazing Grace."

John Newton's final year was analogous to the setting of the sun.[29] He had gradually lost his hearing and sight and he could no longer recognize some of his closest friends. He declined to the point where he could not walk unaided.

In his closing months Newton clung to the truths he had spent years preaching from the pulpit and conveying through his writings. In his final month, Newton summarized the sufficiency of his failing mental faculties with these words, "My memory is nearly gone; but I remember two things: that I am a great sinner, and that Christ is a great Saviour."

In spite of his decline, Newton was able to describe the approaching end of his earthly life with great insight and anticipation: "I am like a person going on a journey in a stage-coach, who expects its arrival every hour, and is frequently looking out at the window for it." In another conversation, Newton said, "It is a great thing to die, and when flesh and heart fail, to have God for the strength of our heart, and our portion for ever. I know whom I have believed, and he is able to keep that which I have committed to him against that great day. Henceforth there is laid up for me a crown of righteousness, which the Lord, the righteous Judge, shall give me at that day."

On the Wednesday before his death, when someone asked him how he was doing, he replied, "I am satisfied with the Lord's will."

John Newton's final sunset came on Monday, **December 21, 1807,** when he died at the age of eighty-three. He was buried in his church of St. Mary Woolnoth, next to his wife, Mary, and niece, Miss Eliza Cunningham.

Newton wrote his own epitaph, which is engraved on a plain marble tablet in the church:

JOHN NEWTON,

CLERK

A SINNER SAVED BY GRACE

ONCE AN INFIDEL AND LIBERTINE,
A SERVANT OF SLAVES IN AFRICA,
WAS,
BY THE RICH MERCY OF OUR LORD AND SAVIOUR,
JESUS CHRIST,
PRESERVED, RESTORED, PARDONED,
AND APPOINTED TO PREACH THE FAITH
HE HAD LONG LABOURED TO DESTROY.
HE MINISTERED
NEAR XVI. YEARS AS A CURATE AND VICAR
OF OLNEY IN BUCKS,
AND XXVIII. AS RECTOR
OF THESE UNITED PARISHES.
ON FEBRY. THE FIRST MDCCL. HE MARRIED
MARY,
DAUGHTER OF THE LATE GEORGE CATLETT,
OF CHATHAM, KENT,
WHOM HE RESIGNED
TO THE LORD WHO GAVE HER,
ON DECR. THE XVTH. MDCCXC.

Reflection

As John Newton's memory began to fail him in old age, two thoughts remained as the foundation of his faith: that he was a great sinner and that Jesus was a great Savior. What thoughts would you want to characterize the end of your life?

King David spoke of this, describing the happiness of an undeserving sinner who is declared to be righteous: "Oh, what joy for those whose disobedience is forgiven, whose sins are put out of sight. Yes, what joy for those whose sin is no longer counted against them by the Lord."

December 22

He was licensed to preach by the Church of Scotland in 1661 at the age of twenty and preached in his last public sermon at the age of twenty-one.

THE SCRIPTURE doth abundantly evidence that the people of God have been persecuted sometimes by a Pharaoh on the throne, sometimes by a Haman in the state, and sometimes by a Judas in the church." The Pharaohs, Hamans, and Judases of Scotland hounded Hugh McKail to his death at the age of twenty-six.

McKail, who studied at the University of Edinburgh, was a scholarly young minister. He was a Covenanter—a group committed to preserving Presbyterianism and opposing any governmental control over the church. Pitted against the Covenanters was King Charles II, who came to the throne of England in 1660 and was intent on destroying the Presbyterian Church in Scotland by requiring adherence to the Church of England, of which he was the head.

After four years of hiding from the intense persecution, Hugh McKail was already dying of tuberculosis by the time he was captured in 1666. Taken before the tribunal in Edinburgh, McKail revealed nothing regarding the Covenanters. He was then subjected to a form of torture called the boot in which one of his legs was literally crushed. Miraculously stoic, he breathed no word of betrayal against his fellow Covenanters.

As soon as McKail's inquisitors considered him well enough recovered, they held another hearing. Refusing to plead guilty to rebellion against the Crown, McKail was sentenced to death by hanging. Hearing his sentence, McKail replied, "The Lord giveth and the Lord taketh away, blessed be the name of the Lord." Back in his cell he said to a friend, "O how good news: to be within four days' journey to enjoy the sight of Jesus Christ."

Hugh McKail was led out to the scaffold at two o'clock in the afternoon on **December 22, 1666.** Climbing the ladder to the scaffold dragging his mangled leg, he called down to those to be hanged after him, "Friends and fellow sufferers, do not be afraid; every step of this ladder is a degree nearer heaven." Then with the rope around his neck, he turned and addressed the crowd: "This is my comfort, I know that my Redeemer liveth. And now I do willingly lay down my life for the truth and cause of God, the Covenants and work of Reformation, which were once counted the glory of this nation; and it is for

THE SPIRIT AND THE BRIDE SAY, "COME"

endeavoring to defend this . . . that I embrace this rope . . . and that you may know what the ground of my encouragement in this work is, I shall read to you in the last chapter of the Bible."

After reading from Revelation 22 his closing words were:

> Here you see the glory that is to be revealed on me: a "'pure river of water of life"; and here you see my access to the glory and reward: "Let him who is athirst, come"; and here you see my welcome: "The Spirit and the bride say, 'Come.' "

I ascend to my Father and your Father, to my God and your God; to my King and your King, to the blessed apostles and martyrs, and to the city of the living God, the heavenly Jerusalem, to an innumerable company of angels, to the great assembly of the firstborn, to God the judge of all, to the spirits of just men made perfect, and to Jesus the Mediator of the New Covenant; and I bid you all farewell, for God will be more comfortable to you than I could be, and He will be now more refreshing to me than you can be. Farewell, farewell in the Lord!

Reflection

Can you imagine what it would be like to be tortured by inquisitors trying to obtain the names of your fellow Christians so that they in turn could be tortured? Hugh McKail had his leg crushed but refused to betray his Christian friends. How do you think he was able to endure the torture?

❧

I am willing to endure anything if it will bring salvation and eternal glory in Christ Jesus to those God has chosen. This is a true saying: If we die with him, we will also live with him. If we endure hardship, we will reign with him.   2 TIMOTHY 2:10-12

December 23

Why were they risking their lives for the chance of making contact with the Aucas?

Iɴ 1955 five missionary couples in the jungles of Ecuador were planning for a chance to share the gospel of Jesus Christ with the remote and fierce Auca tribe. They had been conducting "gift flights" over Auca territory, attempting to create awareness of their presence by dropping packages of clothing, food, and gadgets to the natives from a small plane.

On **December 23, 1955,** Nate Saint and Jim Elliot flew over Auca territory and dropped a gift package of clothing, a flashlight, and other trinkets. This time the missionaries received a package back from the Aucas, who tied it to a long cord the missionaries dropped from the plane. It was full of fish, peanuts, bananas, a parrot, and other meats. The gift from the Aucas greatly encouraged the missionaries, and four of the five couples met that same day to plan the trip that would bring them face-to-face with members of the Auca tribe.

The group began assigning the specific duties each member would be responsible for on the mission. Providing shelter in the jungle, packing food and supplies, maintaining a communication link with the home base, transporting those who were to go to and from the remote location, as well as other vital tasks, were all necessary for the success of the mission.

It was decided that the men would set up a camp on the beach near the location of the Aucas' main settlement. They chose January 3, 1956, for the mission as they knew they would need to arrive and depart before the onset of the rainy season, which would make takeoffs and landings impossible.[30]

As soon as the plans were finalized, the missionaries turned their attention to making Christmas in their camp in Arajuno as much like home as possible. A meal was prepared, and a Christmas tree was made from bamboo and decorated with tinsel to celebrate Jesus' birth.

Missionary Pete Fleming was still undecided as to whether he would accompany the other men on this trip. He waited on God in prayer continuously. For the wives it was a time of reflection and preparation for the dangers that were sure to confront their husbands on this mission. They knew it was possible they all could become widows as a result of this expedition. They also knew that the God they served held first place in the lives of each of their husbands. This fact seemed to hit home now more than ever.

A CONTEMPLATIVE CHRISTMAS

December 23 was also a day of self-reflection for the men. Why were they risking their lives for the chance of making contact with the Aucas?

Nate Saint summed up their sentiments: "If God would grant us the vision, the word *sacrifice* would disappear from our lips and thoughts; we would hate the things that seem now so dear to us; our lives would suddenly be too short, we would despise time-robbing distractions and charge the enemy with all our energies in the name of Christ. May God help us to judge ourselves by the eternities that separate the Aucas from a comprehension of Christmas and Him, who, though He was rich, yet for our sakes became poor so that we might, through His poverty, be made rich."

Reflection

During his college years Jim Elliot wrote in his journal, "He is no fool who gives what he cannot keep to gain what he cannot lose." Do these words ring true to you? What is their application in your life?

∽≫

Your attitude should be the same that Christ Jesus had. Though he was God, he did not demand and cling to his rights as God. He made himself nothing; he took the humble position of a slave and appeared in human form. And in human form he obediently humbled himself even further by dying a criminal's death on a cross. Because of this, God raised him up to the heights of heaven and gave him a name that is above every other name. PHILIPPIANS 2:5-9

December 24

The downpour of rain and snow turned into a downpour of bombs.

DURING the summer of 1944 the Allied forces had been experiencing great success in Europe against Adolph Hitler's German armies of the Third Reich. However, Hitler was biding his time, knowing that the upcoming winter weather would serve him well. The winter storms would prevent the Allied forces from using their air force, keeping the battles on the ground. The Germans had plenty of tanks and men but could not match the air power of the Allies. Hitler directed his forces "to benefit from the effect of surprise and to attack during a period when weather conditions are unfavourable for the enemy's aviation."

German meteorologists studied the historical weather patterns and settled on the beginning of December as the prime time to launch a major offensive. Sustained cloud cover was predicted for the second week of December, and Hitler planned surprise offensive attacks at Saint-Vith and Bostagne, Allied strongholds in Belgium. His objective was to make a swift breakthrough and capture Antwerp, thereby splitting the Allied armies. At 5:30 A.M. on December 16, 1944, German forces attacked, beginning the famous Battle of the Bulge. The stakes were high, for the German officers knew that if they were unsuccessful, this would be their last major battle.

The element of surprise was successful, and the Allied forces took heavy losses. The dense cloud cover and accompanying rain, wind, and snow made ground movements difficult and air strikes impossible. On December 22, in response to a directive from General George Patton, U.S. Army chaplain James O'Neill prayed over the Armed Forces Radio, "Almighty and most merciful Father, we humbly beseech Thee, of Thy great goodness, to restrain these immoderate rains with which we have to contend. Grant us fair weather for battle."

By that afternoon the winds began to shift. There was still dense cloud cover, but the cover was rising. For an hour that day the German troops at Bostagne got their first taste of Allied airpower while the Allies kept praying.

General Patton launched a ground attack the next day amidst a blinding snowstorm. The swirling snow on the ground made it difficult for the troops to distinguish friend from foe. The situation was desperate, and all they could do was to keep praying.

Although the skies did not clear enough for an air attack, planes were able to drop much-needed rations, fuel, and ammunition to the Allied ground troops. The pressure was on the Germans to win a quick victory. If the Allied planes could resupply their troops with such accuracy amidst a blinding snowstorm, what would they be able to do with bombs once the skies cleared?

On the evening of December 23 the Allied meteorologists on the air bases relayed the forecast for the next morning: "Clear, with visibility 5 to 8 kilometers. . . ." The rest of the weather report could not be heard due to the joyous cheering of the bomber crews. Tomorrow they would fly. Their prayers had been answered!

On **December 24, 1944,** Allied fliers in their Lightnings, Mustangs, Thunderbolts, B-17s, and Liberators buried the German ground troops with an endless barrage of bombs. The rain, wind, and snow had at last given way to a rain of bombs!

The siege of Bostagne was quickly over as the Germans were rendered defenseless. The Allies mounted a vast counteroffensive on January 3, and the Battle of the Bulge officially ended on January 16.

God had answered the Allies' prayers.

Reflection

God controls all things, including the weather. And the God who controls all things is a prayer-answering God. There need be no limitations on what we request from him.

Jesus rebuked the wind and the raging waves. The storm stopped and all was calm! Then he asked them, "Where is your faith?" And they were filled with awe and amazement. They said to one another, "Who is this man, that even the winds and waves obey him?" LUKE 8:24-25

December 25

There had been silence for forty-five years.

NICOLAE CEAUSESCU was dictator of Romania for twenty-five years. Referred to as "the Antichrist" by Romanians, he was unusually brutal and corrupt, even for a Marxist ruler. His reign was enforced by secret police called the Securitate, whose members were recruited largely from the state orphanages. Having as his goal a nation of 100 million people, Ceausescu outlawed contraceptives and abortions and penalized the unmarried and the childless. The most able male orphans were placed in cadet battalions in their early teens and indoctrinated into fierce loyalty to Ceausescu. As members of the Securitate, they were among the few Romanians who regularly had enough to eat.

In 1989 the Communist regimes of Europe were toppling, but Ceausescu felt that he was secure. The one problem of which he was aware was Romania's large Hungarian minority. There had been an active revolution in the Hungarian town of Timisoara, and Ceausescu had sent in the Securitate to put down the revolt. They did so with frightening force. Later a mass grave was discovered that was reported to contain the bodies of 4,630 Hungarians.

Feeling that he had dealt with the Hungarian problem, Ceausescu went on a scheduled visit to Iran. Once there, however, he received news that the Hungarian unrest was spreading, even to the capital city of Bucharest. He returned immediately and on December 21 addressed a crowd in front of the presidential palace. In the past, loudspeakers had supplied cheers and applause while the crowd listened in silence. This time the angry crowd shouted and hurled abuse at the dictator. Never having been treated like this before, Ceausescu stalked back into the palace followed by his furious wife, Elena.

As the situation escalated the next day, Ceausescu and his wife were forced to flee the presidential palace by helicopter. By this time the armed forces had turned against him, and the Ceausescus were captured as they fled.

On Christmas Day, **December 25, 1989,** a military court tried Ceausescu and his wife on charges of genocide and the murder of sixty thousand Romanians. They were quickly convicted and executed by a firing squad.

The residents of Bucharest wept openly as for the first time in forty-five years their church bells rang, proclaiming the death of the "Antichrist" and the birth of the Christ, as if the carol were written for that day:

> *I heard the bells on Christmas day*
> *Their old familiar carols play,*

THE BELLS OF CHRISTMAS

And wild and sweet the words repeat
Of peace on earth, goodwill to men.

I thought how, as the day had come,
The belfries of all Christendom
Had rolled along th' unbroken song
Of peace on earth, goodwill to men.

Till, ringing, singing on its way,
The world revolved from night to day,
A voice, a chime, a chant sublime,
Of peace on earth, goodwill to men.

And in despair I bowed my head,
"There is no peace on earth," I said,
"For hate is strong and mocks the song
Of peace on earth, goodwill to men."

Then pealed the bells more loud and deep:
"God is not dead, nor doth He sleep;
The wrong shall fail, the right prevail,
With peace on earth, goodwill to men."

Reflection

If you had been a Romanian living in Bucharest on that Christmas Day, how would you have felt when the church bells started to ring? Those under forty-five years of age had never even heard them before. What can we learn from the story of Nicolae Ceausescu?

∽◎◇

Suddenly, the angel was joined by a vast host of others—the armies of heaven—praising God: "Glory to God in the highest heaven, and peace on earth to all whom God favors." LUKE 2:13-14

December 26

Moody's transformation from businessman to Sunday school teacher, world evangelist, and spiritual giant could not be denied.

> *The sands of time are sinking, the dawn of heaven breaks,*
> *The summer morn I've sighed for, the fair sweet morn awakes;*
> *Dark, dark hath been the midnight, but dayspring is at hand,*
> *And glory, glory dwelleth in Immanuel's land.*

THUS SANG the congregation through their tears on **December 26, 1899,** as they celebrated the homegoing of one of Christendom's greatest evangelists, Dwight L. Moody.[31] The glorious birth they had celebrated just a day before stood complemented, not eclipsed, by the death they mourned that day. As Moody's favorite hymn rang throughout the church, "dayspring" truly was at hand, for at that moment Moody was beholding King Jesus.

> *The King there in his beauty without a veil is seen;*
> *It were a well-spent journey though sev'n deaths lay between:*
> *The Lamb with his fair army doth on Mount Zion stand,*
> *And glory, glory dwelleth in Immanuel's land.*

Moody's casket lay upon the shoulders of thirty-two young men, all of them from the Mount Hermon School for Boys, which Moody had founded. As they slowly moved to the front of the church, it was as if they helped their great teacher on the final steps of his "well-spent journey." That pilgrimage began in 1856, when Moody's enthusiastic initial profession of faith met some skepticism, and church leaders granted him probationary status for church membership. Moody would prove his Christian conviction many times over, however, and any skepticism quickly disappeared in the wake of his enormous spiritual influence. Moody's transformation from businessman to Sunday school teacher, world evangelist, and spiritual giant could not be denied. At his funeral, Rev. Dr. A. T. Pierson estimated that Moody, by voice and pen, touched over one hundred million souls throughout his ministry.

> *O Christ, He is the fountain, the deep sweet well of love!*
> *The streams on earth I've tasted, more deep I'll drink above:*

There to an ocean fullness His mercy doth expand,
And glory, glory dwelleth in Immanuel's land.

Second Corinthians 5:8 says that to be away from these bodies is to "be at home with the Lord," and God granted that grieving congregation an assuring grace that hour, as if to seal that very truth in their hearts. Moody's body lay in view of the congregation as they sang, wept, and listened to the testimonies of his life and impact. His son remarked that his face looked peaceful, reflecting that deep satisfaction the Christian experiences after leaving the streams of earth for the oceans of paradise. Then, as if they all stood in heaven with Moody, the gray clouds outside the church broke for a moment, and a shaft of sunlight shot through the back of the church. The beam narrowed upon the casket, then slowly moved up to Moody's face, illuminating it with pure, joyful radiance. Moody's son wrote: "The sunshine touched no other object; the face only was illumined, and then, as though its mission had been accomplished, its token from the upper world assured, the sun set behind the distant hill."

The bride eyes not her garment, but her dear bridegroom's face;
I will not gaze at glory, but on my King of grace;
Not at the crown He giveth, but on his pierced hand:
The Lamb is all the glory of Immanuel's land.

Reflection

What do you think your funeral will be like? How would you like it to be? Are you confidently looking forward to going to heaven? If you are not sure, make it your business to be sure before it's your funeral!

❦

Your eyes will see the king in all his splendor.   ISAIAH 33:17

December 27

Theological ideas alone cannot save, but they can be the seeds of spiritual transformation.

So IT WAS in the life of Ulrich Zwingli, who arrived on **December 27, 1518,** at Zurich, where he would play a crucial role in the Protestant Reformation.

Zwingli was not born an idealistic revolutionary. He was well educated and demonstrated a keen intellect. His training, not spiritual passion, led him into the ministry. In short, the ideas of the early church fathers made sense to Zwingli, but he lacked true spiritual devotion.

This rift between head and heart manifested itself earlier when, amid his persuasive sermons and popular ministry in the Swiss town of Glarus, someone exposed Zwingli's wanton relationship with a mistress. His conscience was pricked but not yet transformed. At this time Zwingli reluctantly accepted a post at Einsiedeln, a monastery and place of pilgrimage. There where indulgences promised a hollow forgiveness through material means, Zwingli turned his thoughts to the Scriptures, to the writings of the early church, and to his own heart.

As he preached there on God's grace, Zwingli began to find the rituals and trappings of the Roman Catholic Church lacking, and he publicly denounced the local seller of papal indulgences. Grace could not be bought and sold, he surmised, and while decrying the false hopes permeating this small town, Zwingli sought the Scriptures for an understanding of free grace. After all, his own soul was at stake.

God only knows when Zwingli discovered this saving grace, unmerited by pilgrimage or indulgence, but at Einsiedeln Zwingli confessed his own sins publicly and declared Christ's saving grace to be sufficient for the salvation of souls. Soon officials from Zurich noticed his powerful oratory. They had reservations about him, based on his past reputation, but he appeared changed. They soon invited him to become a priest at the Zurich Great Church. Europe would never be the same, and neither would Zwingli.

Zwingli entered a city primed for the Reformation. His employers had little idea they were hiring a Reformer, and Zwingli himself might not have known how much he would change. Zurich's citizens, known for their fine army and penchant for political independence, found themselves drawn to their new preacher. The message that a person could come to Christ individually, sin in hand, apart from the mediation of Rome, resonated with the people. In a revolutionary step Zwingli declared he would preach his own sermons on the Gospel of Matthew rather than follow the official Roman lectionary. The crowds responded enthusiastically, flocking to hear the Word of God fresh and newly proclaimed. Zwingli found himself preaching in the marketplace on Fridays so the crowds from surrounding villages might hear him. He proclaimed the sufficiency of faith in Christ, the deficiency of superstition and indulgences, the necessity of true repentance and godly living, and the importance of caring for the poor and needy, the widow and orphan.

And widows and orphans there would be. In the summer of 1519, while vacationing, Zwingli received a desperate call to return home. The plague had arrived. Three out of ten people died. Throughout this ravaged, desperate city, Zwingli diligently ministered. While attending to the sick and dying, he also became ill and lay for many days at death's door.

Zwingli eventually recovered and went on to become the leading figure in the Reformation in German-speaking Switzerland. But it was just a matter of time before war broke out between Protestants and the armies of the pope. A lifelong military chaplain, Zwingli died on the battlefield of Kappel in 1531, defending a threatened freedom: the preaching of the gospel he had come to know and love.

Reflection

What factors do you think contributed to the success of Zwingli's ministry? Are you surprised to learn that God mightily used a person who had a mistress in his early days as a pastor? What lessons can you learn from the life of Ulrich Zwingli?

Have mercy on me, O God, because of your unfailing love. Because of your great compassion, blot out the stain of my sins. Wash me clean from my guilt. Purify me from my sin. . . . Against you, and you alone, have I sinned; I have done what is evil in your sight. PSALM 51:1-4

December 28

His religion was real.

THE JAPANESE invaded Borneo in 1942. To escape capture, three Christian and Missionary Alliance (C&MA) missionaries, John Willfinger and Mr. and Mrs. Richard Lenham, fled into the jungle to live with Christians of the Murut tribe. Willfinger, a bachelor linguist, was anticipating his upcoming furlough and seeing his fiancée again. The Lenhams were working on a Murut translation of the Bible.

In July the three missionaries learned that a group of Europeans had been captured by the Japanese. In response, they moved to another Murut village in the northern part of Borneo. There they learned that three C&MA missionaries serving in eastern Borneo had been imprisoned by the Japanese.

Willfinger and the Lenhams assumed that the Japanese would find them. On September 19 a messenger brought a list of persons for whom the Japanese were searching. The names of all three were on the list. The messenger warned that anyone harboring fugitives would be severely punished.

"Stay," the Murut Christians pleaded. "We will take you where you cannot be found."

The three missionaries discussed what they should do and finally came to a decision. They told their Murut hosts, "You would have to lie to the Japanese. We would rather surrender than cause you to be disobedient to God's Word."

Willfinger explained in a "Whosoever Receives This" letter: "We feel that we could have successfully hidden, but at the risk of involving those Muruts who have been kind to us, and are desirous of hiding us. . . .Therefore we have decided to go to the enemy, trusting God as to the ultimate results."

He attached a list of the names and addresses of his loved ones to the letter, asking its receiver to "kindly send my love to my family and sweetheart."

The missionaries decided to separate. Willfinger desired to visit several tribal churches in eastern Borneo before turning himself in. The Lenhams, taking their precious Bible translations with them, set out for a Japanese post to the north. Several days later they walked into a Japanese prison camp and were immediately imprisoned. Mrs. Lenham miraculously was able to conceal the Gospel of Mark manuscript under wet clothing on the clothesline when the guards searched the women's quarters. A guard discovered the Gospel of Matthew in Mr. Lenham's possession, but after the war Mr. Lenham found it intact in a rubbish heap. Both Gospels were published for the Muruts by the British and Foreign Bible Society.

Willfinger completed his missionary tour and surrendered to the Japanese. On **December 28, 1942,** he was executed.

After the war, John Willfinger's Bible was discovered and inside the cover he had inscribed a poem:

> No mere man is the Christ I know,
> But greater far than all below.
> Day by day His love enfolds me,
> Day by day His power upholds me;
> All that God could ever be,
> That man of Nazareth is to me.
>
> No mere man can my strength sustain
> And drive away all my pain,
> Holding me close in His embrace.
> When death and I stand face-to-face;
> Then all that God could ever be
> The unseen Christ will be to me.

Below the poem he had written, "Hallelujah! This is real!"

Reflection

Is your faith real? As John Willfinger faced death, he found God's promises to be sure. You can too.

❧

As for God, his way is perfect. All the Lord's promises prove true. He is a shield for all who look to him for protection. For who is God except the Lord? Who but our God is a solid rock? 2 SAMUEL 22:31-32

December 29

As Judson faced the chains again, his heart quaked.

THE BRITISH forces advanced upon Burma, where Adoniram Judson, an American Baptist missionary, had already endured unspeakable horrors in prison for seventeen months. Falsely accused of espionage, he'd been out of prison less than two precious months. Now the Burmese government wished to negotiate with the British and ordered Judson to be their emissary. Because of Judson's extreme physical weakness his dear friend Dr. Jonathan Price volunteered to go in his stead, but the Burmese insisted that Judson be held in prison as surety for his return.

On **December 29, 1825,** the officials arrived, bearing the familiar, eerily clinking, blood-stained chains. At the chilling sight of them, the previous seventeen months of prison flooded back into Judson's battered mind once again.

He remembered the stench of dead, decaying rats, human excrement, disease, blood, sweat, vomit. He remembered the acrid taste of his cracking, dry mouth and the rotten food he'd forced down. He remembered the sight of other prisoners, sickened, tortured, dying, and the horrified expression of his wife as she beheld his miseries. He could feel the torment of his mangled feet, worn raw from the long barefoot marches in the blistering sun, mercilessly shackled to a bamboo pole hoisted above him, painfully stretched upward cutting off circulation, and bitten by mosquitoes for endless hours. But above all, Adoniram Judson recalled the evil sounds: the creak of the bamboo instruments of torture; the frenzied screams of the victims; the sneering laughter of the guards; the scrape of their knives being sharpened; and, worst of all, the haunting voice of the gong, suspended outside the prison, daily announcing the three o'clock execution hour for yet more prisoners (*Will it be me today? tomorrow? the next day?*). He'd done absolutely nothing to warrant those months of horror; the tyrannical king of Burma, hating foreigners and denying his people religious freedom, accused all white-skinned persons of collusion with the British. Nearly all were imprisoned, and many perished. Judson's prayer had been like his Savior's—he was willing to accept death, should the Lord will it, but also begged that the bitter cup be passed from him.

As Judson faced the chains again, his heart quaked. Could he survive it? Could his dear wife, Ann, bear it? During his last imprisonment, Ann had borne their daughter, Maria, now just eleven months old and frail. Would the little girl remember him? Would she even survive? Throughout the last two years Ann had endured a painful, lonely pregnancy, lobbied the queen for her husband's release, hidden their precious Burmese Bible translations and English-Burmese dictionary project, suffered with smallpox and spotted fever, and attended to her ailing newborn. Yet she had proven strong, but those sufferings and others had weakened her considerably. Just a few weeks before, when they had first heard Judson might be returned to the place of his worst tortures, it was almost too much for poor Ann. As they led him away, Judson prayed one more hopeful prayer for deliverance.

That prayer was answered miraculously soon. After just one night in a bearable local prison, the British insisted upon his freedom, and he was released. He and Ann returned to Rangoon, where they had spent their first ten years of ministry in Burma. Adoniram Judson's missionary endeavors would continue with enormous success for another twenty-four years.[32]

Reflection

While we are experiencing trials, it may seem as if they will last forever, but they do end. Even fatal illnesses end, albeit in death. When you suffer trials, be comforted with the realization that one day they will end.

After you have suffered a little while, he will restore, support, and strengthen you, and he will place you on a firm foundation. All power is his forever and ever. Amen.   1 PETER 5:10-11

December 30

When Titus Flavius Vespasianus was born on December 30, A.D. 39, no one suspected that he would one day fulfill prophecies of Jesus.

Tɪᴛᴜs's ꜰᴀᴛʜᴇʀ, Vespasian, achieved fame as a leader of the Roman legions in Britain in A.D. 43. Because of his father's achievements Titus was educated first in the palace of Emperor Claudius[33] and then of Nero,[34] becoming best friends with Claudius's son Britannicus. When Nero later poisoned Britannicus, Titus was present and drank some of the poisoned drink, becoming critically ill himself.

Having narrowly survived the Roman court, Titus served with distinction in the Roman army in Germany and Britain.

Back in Rome in A.D. 66 and part of Nero's entourage, Vespasian committed the outrage of falling asleep in front of the emperor. He was dismissed from Nero's court for being boorish and retreated to a small town to wait for the inevitable death sentence for offending the emperor.

However, to Vespasian's great surprise and relief, a revolt broke out in Judea and he was made commander of the Roman legions in Palestine sent to crush the revolt. In a very unusual move, Titus was put in command of one of his father's three legions. Not only was Titus too young for such a responsibility, but it was unprecedented for a son to command a legion in his father's army.

Titus played a prominent role in the Roman conquest of Galilee. Then in A.D. 68 Nero was assassinated in Rome. Because Titus had proven to be an able diplomat, his father sent him to Rome to pay his respects to Galba, the new emperor, but more important, to ascertain his family's standing with the new regime. However, by the time Titus had reached Corinth, he received news of Galba's assassination. He then openly advocated that his father take the throne himself. Titus returned to Judea and began to drum up support in Judea, Egypt, and Syria for his father's bid for the throne. Galba was succeeded by Otho and then Vitellius in quick succession, but on July 1, A.D. 69, Vespasian was proclaimed emperor by the Roman legions in Egypt and soon after that by the legions in Syria and Judea.

Titus replaced his father as supreme commander of the Roman legions in Judea. With virtually the whole country subdued except for Jerusalem, Titus advanced there with his troops, arriving just prior to the Feast of Passover in A.D. 70 with the latest siege equipment. In spite of the advancing Roman armies, historian Josephus reported that 1.1 million Jews crowded into the city for the feast. However, all the Christians in Jerusalem, heeding the words of Jesus recorded in Luke 21:20-21, fled the city and went to the city of Pella on the other side of the Jordan River.

Titus had sixty thousand soldiers. The Jews had twenty-five thousand fighters within the city, but they were divided into factions that fought with one another. The great masses of people caught in the siege were helpless pawns. Within the city starvation reigned. One mother even ate her own child.

Once the Romans had breached the city walls, fighting progressed from house to house. Titus intended to spare the temple, but a soldier threw a firebrand into it, and the whole edifice was soon in flames. Titus hurried to the temple, shouting to his troops to extinguish the fire, but no one listened. The temple burned to the ground, leaving only smoldering ruins. The Roman soldiers then sacrificed to their gods in the Holy Place. When the conquest was complete, the walls of the city were leveled.

All this happened just as Jesus had predicted thirty-seven years earlier. A foreign army came and surrounded Jerusalem (Luke 21:20), then burned it (Matthew 22:7) and completely destroyed the temple (Matthew 24:2).[35]

Titus succeeded his father as emperor in A.D. 79, but died two years later. He was immediately deified.

Reflection

Jesus taught that the reason God would destroy Jerusalem was that the Jews killed their Messiah (Matthew 21:33–22:7). Do you believe that? Why or why not?

∽⟐⌒

The king became furious. He sent out his army to destroy the
murderers and burn their city.　　　　　　MATTHEW 22:7

December 31

Boyle's keen mind was continually drawn to science.

SCIENCE has advanced so rapidly in the past few centuries that is hard to imagine that as recently as the Pilgrims' founding of Plymouth, "scientists" across Europe were still working to be the first to turn sand into gold and physicians used leeches to suck the "ill humors" out of their patients' blood.

Such was the world when Robert Boyle was born in Ireland in 1627. Boyle's father was the earl of Cork, and his mother died when Boyle was only three. When he was eight, he was enrolled at Eton, one of Great Britain's finest schools. There he displayed a precocious and fierce intelligence. But Boyle's ability to read Latin and Greek and do algebra without paper and pencil was not sufficient for an aristocratic young man's education. When Boyle was twelve, his father sent him to Switzerland to learn dancing, fencing, tennis, and French.

Years later Boyle wrote his biography, in which he named himself "Philatetus," Greek for "lover of virtue." In it he described an experience he had back in his school days in Geneva that changed the course of his life:

[He] suddenly awoke in a fright by loud claps of thunder and every clap was both preceded and attended with flashes of lightning so frequent and so dazzling, that Philatetus began to imagine them the sallies of that fire that must consume the world. The long continuance of that dismal tempest, when the winds were so loud, as almost drowned the noise of the very thunder, and the showers so hideous, as almost quenched the lightning, ere it could reach his eyes confirmed Philatetus in his apprehensions of the day of judgment's being at hand. Whereupon the consideration of his unpreparedness to welcome it, and the hideousness of being surprised by it in an unfit condition, made him resolve and vow that if his fears were that night disappointed, all his future additions to his life should be more religiously and watchfully employed. The morning came, and a serene cloudless sky returned, when he ratified his determination so solemnly, that from that day he dated his conversion.

That morning was **December 31, 1640.**

Boyle's keen mind was continually drawn to science. At Oxford College and on his father's estate, Boyle set up laboratories where he made painstaking inquiries into the properties of gases and other natural substances. At the root of all his discoveries was *order*. It was the basis of the empirical method of scientific inquiry he helped pioneer. He was among the first to demonstrate that substances are made up of atoms and the first to create a vacuum in which the effects of temperature and pressure on gases could be studied. He discovered Boyle's Law: When temperature is held constant, the volume of a gas varies inversely with the pressure applied to it.

But as devoted as he was to science, he was equally devoted to God. Boyle loved the Bible and believed nature was in concordance with theology. Although God would always know infinitely more than people do, he allowed them a glimpse into his perfection through the window of science. The ultimate goal of science, then, was to know and to worship God. But God also revealed himself to people in his Word. Boyle devoted his later life and much of his wealth to distributing the Bible, portions of which he arranged to have printed for the first time in Irish, Welsh, Indian, Turkish, and Malaysian.

Robert Boyle, the father of modern chemistry, died on December 30, 1691, exactly fifty years after the thunderstorm that awakened him to faith in God.

Reflection

Robert Boyle saw no contradiction between true science and the Bible. He believed that the ultimate goal of science was to know and worship God. Does it surprise you to learn that a famous scientist was a committed Christian who revered the Bible?

❧

The heavens tell of the glory of God. The skies display his marvelous craftsmanship.　　　　PSALM 19:1

CHRONOLOGICAL ORDER OF EVENTS

763 B.C.	June 15	Solar eclipse that dates the Old Testament
753 B.C.	April 21	The founding of Rome
597 B.C.	March 16	Nebuchadnezzar besieges Jerusalem the first time (JEREMIAH 22:24-30)
593 B.C.	July 31	Ezekiel called to be a prophet (EZEKIEL 1)
593 B.C.	August 8	Ezekiel is appointed a watchman for Israel (EZEKIEL 3)
592 B.C.	September 17	Ezekiel sees God's glory leave the temple (EZEKIEL 8)
591 B.C.	August 14	God pronounces judgment on Israel (EZEKIEL 20)
586 B.C.	July 18	Jerusalem falls to Nebuchadnezzar (JEREMIAH 39)
585 B.C.	January 8	Ezekiel learns Jerusalem has fallen (EZEKIEL 33)
585 B.C.	March 3	Message from God to Egypt (EZEKIEL 32)
573 B.C.	April 28	Ezekiel's vision of a future glorious temple (EZEKIEL 40–43)
539 B.C.	October 12	Medes and Persians defeat Babylon (Daniel 5)
536 B.C.	April 23	Daniel's vision of the future (DANIEL 10-12)
520 B.C.	February 15	Zechariah receives eight visions (ZECHARIAH 1:7-6:8)
520 B.C.	September 21	Jews resume building the temple (HAGGAI 1)
520 B.C.	October 17	God gives Israel a prophecy of the future temple (HAGGAI 2)
518 B.C.	December 7	God promises future blessing to Israel (ZECHARIAH 7-8)
516 B.C.	March 12	Jews finish rebuilding the temple (EZRA 6)

474 B.C.	June 25	Xerxes gives authority to the Jews to defend themselves against enemies (ESTHER 8)
458 B.C.	August 4	Ezra arrives in Jerusalem (EZRA 7)
457 B.C.	March 27	Jews divorce pagan wives (EZRA 9-10)
445 B.C.	October 2	Nehemiah and the Jews complete rebuilding of Jerusalem's walls (NEHEMIAH 6)
445 B.C.	October 8	Ezra reads the Law to the Jews (NEHEMIAH 8:1-12)
445 B.C.	October 9	Ezra studies the Law with the Jews (NEHEMIAH 8:13-15)
445 B.C.	October 31	Israel renews the covenant (NEHEMIAH 9-10)
331 B.C.	October 1	Alexander the Great defeats the Persian Empire
323 B.C.	June 10	Death of Alexander the Great
167 B.C.	December 16	Antiochus IV Epiphanes commits an abomination of desolation
161 B.C.	March 9	Maccabees defeat the Syrian general Nicanor
44 B.C.	March 15	Death of Julius Caesar
7 B.C.	May 29	Conjunction of planets preceding the birth of Christ
9	April 29	Jesus in the temple at age twelve (LUKE 2:41-52)
30	April 7	Jesus' first Passover during his ministry (JOHN 2:23-25)
32	September 10	Jesus at the Feast of Tabernacles (JOHN 7)
32	December 18	Jesus at the Feast of Dedication (JOHN 10:22-39)
33	March 28	Jesus enters Bethany (JOHN 12:1-8)
33	March 29	Jesus and the crowds at Bethany (JOHN 11:1–12:11)

33	March 30	Jesus' triumphal entry (LUKE 19:28-44 AND PARALLELS)
33	March 31	Jesus curses the fig tree and cleanses the temple (MARK 11:12-21)
33	April 1	Jesus' Olivet discourse (LUKE 21:5-36)
33	April 2	Jesus' Last Supper and trial before the Sanhedrin (LUKE 22:7–23:24 AND PARALLELS)
33	April 3	Jesus' crucifixion (JOHN 18:28–19:42 AND PARALLELS)
33	April 4	Jesus in the tomb (MATTHEW 27:62–28:15)
33	April 5	Jesus' resurrection (LUKE 24:1-49)
33	May 14	Jesus' ascension (ACTS 1:6-11)
33	May 24	Pentecost (ACTS 2:1-42)
39	December 30	Birth of Emperor Titus
41	February 8	King Herod Agrippa leaves Rome to return to his kingdom
42	January 25	Claudius becomes emperor
57	May 28	Paul meets with James the brother of Jesus in Jerusalem (ACTS 21:18-26)
57	June 2	Paul's arrest and public defense (ACTS 21:27–22:29)
57	June 3	Paul's defense before the Sanhedrin (ACTS 22:30–23:11)
57	June 4	Paul saved by his nephew (ACTS 23:12-31)
68	June 9	Nero commits suicide
70	September 2	Jerusalem destroyed by the Roman army
96	September 18	Assassination of Emperor Domitian
203	March 7	Martyrdom of Perpetua
250	January 3	Emperor Decius commands all citizens to sacrifice to Roman gods

303	February 23	Emperor Diocletian commands all churches be destroyed
312	October 26	Emperor Constantine sees a vision the night before defeating his rival
354	November 13	Birth of Augustine
363	June 27	Emperor Julian the Apostate replaced by Jovian, a Christian
394	September 5	Roman Christians under Theodosius I win the final battle against the followers of the Roman gods
395	January 17	Death of Emperor Theodosius I
417	January 27	Pelagians are excommunicated
420	September 30	Death of Jerome
451	October 30	Bishop of Constantinople given equal authority with the bishop of Rome
484	February 25	Huneric the Vandal orders all North African churches turned over to the Arians
632	June 8	Death of Mohammed
962	February 2	Otto I crowned emperor of the Holy Roman Empire
1095	November 27	Pope Urban II's sermon launches the Crusades
1098	June 14	Crusaders find "the holy lance"
1294	December 13	Pope Celestine V resigns
1413	September 25	John Oldcastle brought to trial for being a follower of Wycliffe
1414	November 28	Arrest of Jan Hus
1416	May 30	Jerome of Prague burned at the stake
1483	November 10	Birth of Martin Luther
1491	June 28	Birth of King Henry VIII of England

1492	August 2	Columbus's departure from Spain
1492	October 11	Columbus discovers America
1497	May 13	Excommunication of Savonarola
1498	September 16	Death of Tomás de Torquemada
1518	December 27	Arrival of Ulrich Zwingli in Zurich
1521	April 17	Arrival of Martin Luther at the Diet of Worms
1527	February 24	Michael Sattler forms the "Brotherly Union" of Anabaptists in Germany
1528	February 29	Patrick Hamilton, first Scottish Protestant martyr, burned at the stake
1528	June 18	Order given to arrest William Tyndale
1529	September 6	Georg Blaurock, Swiss Anabaptist, burned at the stake
1529	October 14	Death decreed for all Protestants in Antwerp
1531	November 24	Death of Johann Oecolampadius, leader of the Reformation in Basel
1531	December 9	Heinrich Bullinger succeeds Ulrich Zwingli as pastor of the Zurich Great Church
1533	December 10	King Francis I orders the arrest of Nicholas Cop, the rector of the University of Paris
1535	January 13	King Francis I outlaws printing in France
1536	May 19	Beheading of Anne Boleyn, second wife of King Henry VIII
1538	April 22	Geneva Council meets and expels John Calvin from Geneva
1542	September 20	Death of Martin Luther's daughter Magdalena
1546	February 22	Funeral of Martin Luther
1553	July 6	Death of King Edward VI of England

1554	February 12	Beheading of Lady Jane Grey, the nine-day queen of England
1554	March 4	Queen Mary I outlaws Protestantism in England
1555	January 22	Trial of John Bradford, English Protestant
1555	February 5	Rowland Taylor, English martyr, gives book of legacy to his son
1555	March 26	William Hunter, English Protestant, burned at the stake
1555	August 31	Robert Samuel, English Protestant, burned at the stake
1555	October 16	Hugh Latimer and Nicholas Ridley, former English bishops, burned at the stake
1555	December 17	John Philpot, English Protestant, receives word he will be burned at the stake the next day
1556	July 15	Julins Palmer, converted English Roman Catholic, sentenced to burn at the stake
1558	October 19	Martyrdom of Hans Smit, Anabaptist pastor
1561	January 31	Death of Menno Simons, founder of the Mennonites
1564	April 25	John Calvin writes his last will and testament
1569	January 20	Death of Miles Coverdale, English Bible translator
1570	June 26	Joost Verkindert, Antwerp Anabaptist, writes his brother before being burned at the stake
1572	August 24	The St. Bartholomew's Day Massacre
1572	November 23	John Knox testifies the day before his death

1573	October 5	Maeyken Wens, an Anabaptist, writes to her son the day before being burned at the stake
1586	July 7	Birth of Thomas Hooker, the founder of American democracy
1588	July 29	English defeat Spanish Armada
1603	March 24	James VI of Scotland becomes King James I of England
1606	December 19	Jamestown settlers set sail from England
1613	January 21	Birth of George Gillespie, Scottish theologian
1620	November 11	The Mayflower Compact presented and signed
1620	December 11	Pilgrims decide to settle at Plymouth
1621	March 22	Squanto meets the Pilgrims
1623	June 19	Birth of Blaise Pascal, French scholar
1626	April 14	Andrew Duncan, Scottish Presbyterian, writes his last will and testimony
1630	June 12	John Winthrop arrives at Salem
1632	June 21	Galileo is forced to recant his view that the earth circles the sun
1632	November 16	Death of Gustavus Adolphus, king of Sweden
1640	August 27	Henry Dunster is elected the first president of Harvard
1640	December 31	Conversion of Robert Boyle, the father of modern chemistry
1641	August 9	Death of Jonathan Burr, Puritan pastor in Massachusetts
1644	July 2	Oliver Cromwell wins the Battle of Marston Moor in the English civil war

1651	September 7	John Hazel, a Massachusetts Baptist, is sentenced by Governor Endecott
1661	March 20	Death of Samuel Rutherford, Scottish theologian
1661	May 27	Beheading of Archibald Campbell, earl of Argyll, in Scotland
1661	June 1	Hanging of James Guthrie, Scottish Covenanter
1666	December 22	Hanging of Hugh McKail, Scottish Covenanter
1678	February 18	John Bunyan's *Pilgrim's Progress* licensed to be printed
1680	July 22	Scottish Covenanter Richard Cameron killed in battle
1681	January 26	Martyrdom of Scottish Covenanters Isabel Alison and Marion Harvie
1681	July 27	Hanging of Donald Cargill, Scottish Covenanter
1684	March 5	Hanging of John Dick, Scottish Covenanter
1684	May 9	Hanging of John Paton, Scottish Covenanter
1685	May 1	Scottish Covenanter John Brown murdered by the king's troops
1685	May 11	Drowning of Margaret MacLachlan and Margaret Wilson, Scottish Covenanters
1685	October 18	King Louis XIV revokes the Edict of Nantes in France
1685	December 4	Hanging of John Nesbit, Scottish Covenanter
1688	February 17	Hanging of James Renwick, Scottish Covenanter
1688	November 5	Arrival of William of Orange in England

1690	May 2	Escape of the Waldensians from the French army
1691	December 8	Death of Richard Baxter, Puritan author
1692	September 22	Last execution of witches in Salem
1709	February 9	Five-year-old John Wesley saved from his burning home
1721	May 3	Norwegian missionary Hans Egede sails for Greenland
1727	July 19	Count Nicolaus von Zinzendorf divides the first Moravians into small groups
1732	November 7	Birth of Dutton Lane, Baptist pastor in Virginia
1735	May 5	George Whitefield writes to John Wesley of his conversion
1738	March 6	George Whitefield's last day in Gibraltar
1738	May 20	John and Charles Wesley pray all night for salvation
1738	May 26	John Wesley is concerned about not having joy after his conversion
1738	November 14	Boat with starving passengers including George Whitefield arrives in Ireland
1739	April 18	George Whitefield records his meeting with a recently converted Cambridge graduate
1739	July 12	Conversion of David Brainerd, missionary to the American Indians
1739	September 3	John Wesley learns of his mother's conversion
1739	November 26	William Grimshaw, an unconverted Anglican pastor, plans his funeral
1740	October 23	Nathan Cole, a Connecticut farmer, rides to hear George Whitefield preach

1740	November 9	George Whitefield preaches in Philadelphia
1741	July 8	Jonathan Edwards preaches on "Sinners in the Hands of an Angry God"
1741	September 14	George Frideric Handel completes his oratorio *Messiah*
1743	September 15	David Brainerd writes letter of apology to Yale appealing for readmission
1743	October 20	John Wesley almost killed by a mob
1745–46	November 3	David Brainerd's final year as a missionary to the Indians
1746	March 23	Indians of New Jersey experience revival under the ministry of David Brainerd
1746	May 6	Death of William Tennent, founder of the Log College
1746	June 20	France sends navy to attack the colonies
1747	October 4	Dying David Brainerd bids farewell to his fiancée, Jerusha Edwards
1748	March 21	Conversion of John Newton working on a slave ship
1748	October 28	John Lancaster, a recent convert, is executed in England for theft
1748	November 25	Death of Isaac Watts, English hymn writer
1751	February 10	John Wesley sprains his foot, leading to his marriage
1757	September 24	Death of Aaron Burr Sr. president of College of New Jersey (later Princeton)
1758	February 13	Jonathan Edwards inoculated unsuccessfully for smallpox
1763	July 3	Devereux Jarratt arrives back in America as an ordained priest of the Church of England

1766	May 17	Death of John Grimshaw, son of William Grimshaw
1767	September 8	Conversion of John Ryland Jr. under the preaching of George Whitefield
1770	March 10	Conversion of John Cowper, brother of the hymn writer William Cowper
1770	September 29	George Whitefield's last sermon
1770	November 1	Death of Alexander Cruden, compiler of concordance
1771	August 7	Francis Asbury answers the call for Methodist preachers to go to America
1775	April 19	Battles of Lexington and Concord
1775	June 16	Prayer meeting before the Battle of Bunker Hill
1776	February 1	Conversion of James Taylor, great-grandfather of Hudson Taylor
1778	August 11	Death of Augustus Toplady, English hymn writer
1779	August 1	Birth of Francis Scott Key
1789	March 17	Birth of Charlotte Elliott, English hymn writer
1790	December 15	Death of Mrs. John Newton, wife of pastor and hymn writer
1791	March 2	Death of John Wesley
1792	May 31	William Carey and others found a Baptist missionary society
1799	July 17	Death of Samuel Medley, English pastor and hymn writer
1801	August 6	The Cane Ridge Revival in Kentucky begins
1807	December 21	Death of John Newton, English pastor and hymn writer

1808	April 27	Birth of Milo Jewett, first president of Vassar College
1810	January 2	Edward Griffin, professor at Andover Theological Seminary, writes to family of a dying student
1810	June 29	Formation of the American Board of Commissioners for Foreign Missions
1812	March 11	The print shop of William Carey destroyed by fire in India
1812	June 24	The Baptist Missionary Society prays for the conversion of William Carey's son, Jabez
1817	January 11	Death of Timothy Dwight, president of Yale College
1819	June 6	Adoniram Judson, pioneer missionary to Burma, receives letter from first convert
1820	February 27	Asahel Nettleton leads revival in New York State
1820	August 25	Asahel Nettleton brings gospel to a group of women
1821	January 23	Lott Carey sails as first black missionary to Africa
1821	October 10	Conversion of Charles Finney
1823	May 25	Letter of Archibald Alexander, first professor at Princeton Seminary, to his aged mother
1824	August 26	Baptism of Karl Marx
1825	December 29	The last day in a Burmese prison for missionary Adoniram Judson
1827	April 26	Adoniram Judson writes to his mother-in-law about her granddaughter's death in Burma
1827	July 9	Wedding of Alexander Duff, missionary to India

1827	September 19	Last letter of Edward Payson, Congregational pastor, to his sister
1830	April 6	Founding of the Mormon Church
1832	October 3	Birth of Lina Sandell, Swedish hymn writer
1833	June 23	Ten-year-old Archibald Hodge writes letter to the heathen, later becomes professor of theology
1833	July 26	William Wilberforce learns that legislation freeing slaves in the British Empire will pass
1835	November 21	George Müller resolves to found an orphanage in Bristol, England
1836	November 4	Charles Simeon, Anglican preacher, addresses friends before he dies
1837	May 4	Jessie Hetherington, missionary to Australia, begins letter to her mother
1837	October 29	Birth of Abraham Kuyper, theologian and prime minister of the Netherlands
1837	November 8	Death of Edward Griffin, pastor, professor, and president of Williams College
1838	July 1	Titus Coan baptizes 1,705 converts in Hawaii
1838	July 16	Birth of John Clough, missionary to India
1839	March 8	Birth of Phoebe Palmer Knapp, American hymn writer
1839	July 25	Conversion of John Jasper, Virginia slave
1840	December 12	Birth of Lottie Moon, missionary to China
1843	January 29	Birth of William McKinley, twenty-fifth president of the United States
1844	September 13	Birth of Ann-Eliza Webb Young, nineteenth wife of Brigham Young

1845	September 1	Death of Sarah Boardman Judson, wife of Adoniram Judson, missionary to Burma
1846	June 13	James Caughey, American Methodist preacher, leaves Nottingham, England, after a revival
1846	July 10	Adoniram Judson, missionary to Burma, bids farewell to his children in America
1849	August 19	The last sermon of Samuel Miller, professor at Princeton Seminary
1849	December 2	Hudson Taylor is called to the mission field
1850	January 6	Conversion of Charles Spurgeon
1850	April 12	Death of Adoniram Judson, missionary to Burma
1850	November 20	Conversion of Fanny Crosby, blind hymn writer
1850	December 5	Missionary Allen Gardiner lands on Tierra del Fuego, an island off South America
1851	October 22	Death of Archibald Alexander, Princeton Seminary's first professor
1851	October 24	Funeral of Archibald Alexander, Princeton Seminary's first professor
1852	January 16	Death of Eddy Prentiss, three-year-old son of Elizabeth Prentiss, American hymn writer
1857	July 13	Hudson Taylor visits the missionary whose assistant he wishes to marry
1857	September 23	Beginning of the Fulton Street prayer meeting in New York City
1857	November 19	Queen of England makes Major General Henry Havelock a baron
1858	April 16	John Paton leaves Scotland as a missionary to the New Hebrides

1859	March 14	James McQuilkin begins a prayer meeting for revival in Ahogill, Ireland
1859	August 16	Charles Spurgeon lays the cornerstone for his London church, Metropolitan Tabernacle
1860	July 5	Missionary Francois Coillard's proposal of marriage is accepted
1860	September 28	Missionary Theodor Sonderman's church service turns into a revival in Jamaica
1862	April 11	Evangelist D. L. Moody arrives to minister to the wounded from the Battle of Shiloh
1862	August 17	The Sioux Uprising begins in Minnesota
1863	May 10	Death of Stonewall Jackson, Confederate general
1863	August 21	A day of prayer and fasting called by Jefferson Davis, president of the Confederacy
1864	May 18	Confederate General Joseph Johnston baptized by Lieutenant General Leonides Polk
1864	June 30	Confederate General Robert E. Lee's thirty-third wedding anniversary
1866	January 10	The boat carrying missionary Daniel Draper begins to sink
1867	July 24	Robert Annan, Scottish Christian, experiences God's presence
1868	January 15	Terminally ill missionary William Burns writes farewell letter to his mother
1869	September 4	Missionary Hudson Taylor learns his spiritual secret
1870	February 6	Death of wife of George Müller, founder of orphanages
1870	May 16	English general Charles Gordon visits a dying girl

1870	July 23	Death of Maria Taylor, wife of missionary Hudson Taylor
1871	January 12	Death of Henry Alford, English pastor, author, and hymn writer
1871	October 6	Evangelist D. L. Moody prays for a baptism of fire
1872	April 24	Celebration of Charles Hodge's fifty years of teaching at Princeton Seminary
1873	June 17	Evangelist D. L. Moody arrives in England to learn that no one was expecting him
1873	December 1	Horatio Spafford learns his children have drowned at sea
1874	February 4	Frances Ridley Havergal writes hymn "Take My Life and Let It Be"
1874	May 21	At a Moody service Ira Sankey sings "The Ninety and Nine," composing the melody as he goes
1876	November 17	Conversion of evangelist Gipsy Smith
1876	December 14	Philip P. Bliss and his wife sing together at their last evangelistic service
1878	June 22	Funeral of Charles Hodge, professor at Princeton Seminary
1878	August 13	Death of Elizabeth Prentiss, American hymn writer
1882	November 6	Cambridge student Gerald Lander apologizes to D. L. Moody for disrupting his service
1882	November 12	Conversion of Cambridge student Arthur Polhill-Turner
1884	August 5	Prime Minister Gladstone belatedly authorizes funds to rescue General Charles Gordon in Khartoum
1885	March 18	The Cambridge Seven arrive in China as missionaries

1892	February 11	Funeral of Charles Spurgeon, pastor of Metropolitan Tabernacle, London
1895	May 23	Malla Moe, Norwegian-American missionary to Africa, arrives at mission station
1897	January 19	Conversion of Mel Trotter at Chicago's Pacific Garden Mission
1898	November 30	Evangelist D. L. Moody learns of the death of his grandchild and namesake
1899	December 26	Funeral of evangelist D. L. Moody
1900	August 3	Missionary to China Lizzie Atwater writes a last letter to her family
1900	August 30	Martyrdom of Willie Peat and family, missionaries to China
1902	October 13	Burial of missionary Jonathan Goforth's infant daughter Constance in China
1902	December 3	Birth of Mitsuo Fuchida, lead Japanese pilot at the bombing of Pearl Harbor
1903	December 20	Ordination of A. J. Freeman, blind Swedish-American evangelist
1904	July 30	Death of missionary Hudson Taylor's wife, Jennie
1905	September 12	American socialists meet to organize
1906	January 28	Conversion of Oswald Smith, Canadian pastor
1906	March 25	Birth of Dawson Trotman, founder of the Navigators
1912	April 8	Will Moody, son of D. L. Moody, forces his brother, Paul, out of leadership of their father's schools
1912	April 15	English pastor John Harper evangelizes as the *Titanic* sinks

1913	April 9	Death of William Borden, missionary candidate
1914	January 14	Dr. Walter Wilson, Kansas City physician, dedicates himself to God
1915	November 18	Death of Annie Warfield, wife of B. B. Warfield, professor at Princeton Seminary
1917	November 2	Britain issues the Balfour Declaration
1917	November 15	Death of Oswald Chambers, YMCA chaplain in Egypt
1918	September 26	Corporal Alvin York earns the Congressional Medal of Honor in France
1921	February 16	Princeton Seminary professor B. B. Warfield teaches his last class
1923	March 19	Norwegian Sirianna Aas writes to her half brother in America
1924	February 3	Death of President Woodrow Wilson
1924	July 11	Eric Liddell is the first Scot to win a gold medal in track in the Olympics
1925	July 21	Tennessee jury finds John Scopes guilty of teaching evolution in a public school
1928	August 29	Ordination of W. A. Criswell, Southern Baptist pastor
1932	October 15	Gladys Aylward leaves England as a missionary to China
1933	August 10	Day of prayer and fasting leads to the founding of Wycliffe Bible Translators
1934	December 6	Chinese communist soldiers arrest missionaries John and Betty Stam
1935	October 27	Last sermon of evangelist Billy Sunday
1936	October 7	Last missionary address of Jonathan Goforth

1937	January 1	Death of J. Gresham Machen, Reformed seminary professor
1940	August 23	Missionaries are killed by Italian military in Ethiopia
1941	February 7	Billy Graham's second date with Ruth Bell
1941	August 22	Missionary Bill Bentley speaks at America's Keswick a week before his wedding
1941	October 25	First broadcast of Jack Wyrtzen's radio program *Word of Life*
1942	December 28	Execution of missionary John Willfinger in a Japanese prisoner-of-war camp in Borneo
1943	June 5	Wedding of Grady Wilson, later an associate evangelist to Billy Graham
1943	July 4	Missionaries return to the Wallamo tribe of Ethiopia after the Italian occupation
1943	September 9	Welshman Rees Howells leads prayer meeting at his Bible college for the Battle of Salerno
1944	February 28	Corrie ten Boom is arrested in Holland on suspicion of hiding Jews from the Nazis
1944	August 18	Death of John Sung, Chinese evangelist
1944	December 24	God answers prayer in the Battle of the Bulge
1945	February 21	Death of Eric Liddell, Olympic gold medal winner and missionary to China
1945	May 8	Missionary Judy Hyland arrives back in America from a Japanese prisoner-of-war camp
1945	August 15	Catholic priest Guido Scalzi meets a Baptist pastor in Italy
1947	November 29	Israeli scholar Eleazar Sukenik purchases Israel's first two Dead Sea scrolls

1948	May 15	British troops leave Palestine after Israel becomes a nation
1948	August 20	Bulgarian pastor Haralan Popov is threatened with death in prison
1951	January 18	Death of Amy Carmichael, missionary to India
1952	April 10	Arrest of Watchman Nee, Chinese Christian leader
1953	July 20	The last missionaries of the China Inland Mission are forced to leave China
1953	August 28	Bill Bright incorporates Campus Crusade for Christ
1954	May 22	The last day of Billy Graham's first London Crusade
1955	December 23	Missionaries to Ecuadorian Aucas make gift drop; receive first response from tribe
1956	January 9	Five missionaries to the Auca tribe are reported missing
1960	January 4	Death of Albert Camus, French existentialist
1963	May 12	Death of A. W. Tozer, American pastor and author
1963	November 22	Death of C. S. Lewis, English author
1964	January 24	Murder of Yona Kanamuzeyi, Rwandan pastor
1964	October 21	Last message from Dr. Paul Carlson, missionary to Belgian Congo
1967	February 20	D. James Kennedy holds first Evangelism Explosion Clinic
1967	June 7	Israel captures the Old City of Jerusalem
1973	January 7	Conversion of Johnny Hunt, pool shark
1973	March 1	Prime Minister Golda Meir of Israel sits next to Billy Graham at a White House dinner

1973	August 12	Conversion of Chuck Colson, President Nixon's hatchet man
1974	April 30	Mission officials learn of the kidnapping of Minka Hanskamp and Margaret Morgan in Thailand
1974	September 27	Conversion of Susan Atkins, member of the Manson family
1975	April 13	Assassination of N'Garta Tombalbaye, president of Chad
1976	July 14	Jimmy Carter receives the Democratic nomination for president of the United States
1978	March 13	Velma Barfield confesses to poisoning her fiancé
1981	February 26	Dr. David Martyn Lloyd-Jones, British pastor and author, asks his family not to pray for his healing
1981	July 28	Keith Green, singer and songwriter, dies in a plane crash
1985	February 19	Evon Herman contracts AIDS through a transfusion during the birth of her first child
1988	September 11	Edgar Whisenant's date for the Second Coming
1989	December 25	Execution of Nicolae Ceausescu, communist dictator of Romania
1992	June 11	The Auca Indians of Ecuador receive New Testaments in their own language
1995	January 5	Death of the father of John Ashcroft, who was serving as U.S. senator
1995	February 14	On anniversary of their engagement, Robertson McQuilkin communicates with his wife, who has Alzheimer's

1999	April 20	Rachel Scott is murdered at Columbine High School
2000	January 30	Kurt Warner is named the Most Valuable Player in the Super Bowl
2000	May 7	James Montgomery Boice announces to his congregation that he is rapidly dying of cancer

KEY TO SOURCE ABBREVIATIONS

ABD . . . . *Anchor Bible Dictionary*
ANB . . . . *American National Biography*
BDCM . . . . *Biographical Dictionary of Christian Missions*
BECNT . . . . *Baker Exegetical Commentary on the New Testament*
BKC . . . . *Bible Knowledge Commentary*
BST . . . . *The Bible Speaks Today*
CE . . . . *The Catholic Encyclopedia*
CH . . . . *Christian History* magazine
CT . . . . *Christianity Today* magazine
DAB . . . . *Dictionary of American Biography*
DCA . . . . *Dictionary of Christianity in America*
DCB . . . . *Dictionary of Christian Biography*
DNB . . . . *Dictionary of National Biography*
DPRTA . . . . *Dictionary of the Presbyterian and Reformed Tradition in America*
DRE . . . . *Dictionary of the Roman Empire*
DSCHT . . . . *Dictionary of Scottish Church History and Theology*
EAAR . . . . *Encyclopedia of African American Religions*
EARH . . . . *Encyclopedia of American Religious History*
EB . . . . *Encyclopedia Britannica*
EBC . . . . *Expositor's Bible Commentary*
EC . . . . *Encyclopedia of Christianity*
EDWM . . . . *Evangelical Dictionary of World Missions*
ISBE . . . . *International Standard Bible Encyclopedia*
NBC . . . . *New Bible Commentary*
NBD . . . . *New Bible Dictionary*
NICNT . . . . *New International Commentary on the New Testament*
NICOT . . . . *New International Commentary on the Old Testament*
NIDCC . . . . *New International Dictionary of the Christian Church*
NSHERK . . . . *New Schaff-Herzog Encyclopedia of Religious Knowledge*
OCBH . . . . *Oxford Companion to British History*
ODCC . . . . *Oxford Dictionary of the Christian Church*
ODP . . . . *Oxford Dictionary of Popes*
PE . . . . *Pope Encyclopedia*
TOTC . . . . *Tyndale Old Testament Commentaries*
WBC . . . . *Word Biblical Commentary*
WWCH . . . . *Who's Who in Christian History*
ZPEB . . . . *Zondervan Pictorial Encyclopedia of the Bible*

SOURCES

The authors consulted the following sources in researching material for this book. (The Key to Abbreviations is on page 757.)

January 1

Calhoun, David. *Princeton Seminary*. Edinburgh: Banner of Truth, 1996.

Hart, D. G. "Christianity v. Liberalism." In *More Than Conquerors*. Edited by John Woodbridge. Chicago: Moody, 1992. 313–6.

———. "Machen, (J)ohn Gresham (1881–1937)." DCA. 689–90.

Stonehouse, Ned B. *J. Gresham Machen*. Grand Rapids: Eerdmans, 1955.

January 2

Sprague, William B., ed. *The Life and Sermons of Edward D. Griffin*. Vol. 1. Edinburgh: Banner of Truth, 1987. 110–5.

January 3

Boer, Harry R. *A Short History of the Christian Church*. Grand Rapids: Eerdmans, 1995. 87–9, 100–4.

Dowley, Tim, ed. *Eerdmans Handbook to the History of Christianity*. Grand Rapids: Eerdmans, 1977. 77–80.

Healey, P. J. "Decius." CE. 4:666.

Smith, Michael A. "Cyprian of Carthage." In *Great Leaders of the Christian Church*. Edited by John Woodbridge. Chicago: Moody.

January 4

Sire, James W. "Camus the Christian." CT. 44 no. 12. October 23, 2000. 121–3.

January 5

Ashcroft, John. *Lessons from a Father to His Son*. Nashville: Thomas Nelson, 1998.

January 6

Dallimore, Arnold. *Spurgeon*. Edinburgh: Banner of Truth, 1988.

Spurgeon, C. H. *Autobiography*. Vol. 1.

Edinburgh: Banner of Truth, 1962. 78–96.

January 7

Hunt, Johnny M. and Gloria Cassity Stargel. "An Ugly Car, A Pretty Girl, and Mr. Pridgen." *Decision*. 42 (April 2001): 4–5.

January 8

Ezekiel 33:21–33.

January 9

Elliot, Elisabeth. *Through Gates of Splendor*. New York: Harper and Row, 1957.

Hitt, Russell. *Jungle Pilot*. Grand Rapids: Discovery, 1997.

Howard, David. "Heaven Soon: Jim Elliot Ecuador Martyr." In *More Than Conquerors*. Edited by John Woodbridge. Chicago: Moody, 1992. 73–8.

Liefeld, Olive. "The Impact of the Auca Five" in *Ambassadors for Christ*. Edited by John Woodbridge. Chicago: Moody, 1994. 127–33.

January 10

Murray, Ian H. *Australian Christian Life from 1788*. Edinburgh: Banner of Truth, 1988.

January 11

Curtis, Ken, et al. "The Second Great Awakening." On-line: http://www.gospelcom.net/chi/GLIMPSEF/Glimpses/glmps040.shtml.

Fox, Stephen. "Timothy Dwight." On-line: http://grove.ship.edu/ubf/leaders/dwight.htm.

Noll, Mark A. *A History of Christianity in the United States and Canada*. Grand Rapids: Eerdmans, 1998. 158–68.

January 12

Alford, Francis Oka. *Life, Journals and*

Letters of Henry Alford D. D. London: Rivingtons, 1874.

Bass, P. H. "Alford, Henry." NIDCC. 27.

Robinson, Charles Seymour. *Annotations upon Popular Hymns.* Cleveland: Barton, 1893. 481–2.

Ryden, E. E. *The Story of Christian Hymnody.* Rock Island: Augustana, 1959. 383–4.

January 13

Baird, Henry M. *History of the Rise of the Huguenots of France.* Vol. 1. New York: Scribner, 1879. 122–70.

Schaff, Philip. *History of the Christian Church.* Vol. 7. New York: Scribner, 1894. 296–321.

January 14

Edman, V. Raymond. *They Found the Secret.* Grand Rapids: Zondervan, 1984. 152–8.

January 15

Beaver, B. "Burns, William Chalmers." WWCH. 120.

Greenway, Roger S. "Burns, William Chalmers." EDWM. 152.

Hamilton, I. "Burns, William Chalmers." DSCHT. 114–5.

Hood, George A. "Burns, William Chalmers." BDCM. 102.

Miller, R. Strang. "William C. Burns." In *Five Pioneer Missionaries.* Edited by S. M. Houghton. Edinburgh: Banner of Truth, 1965. 93–169.

January 16

Prentiss, George Lewis. *More Love to Thee: The Life and Letters of Elizabeth Prentiss.* Amityville: Calvary, 1994.

January 17

Boer. *Short History of the Christian Church.* 140–50.

Dowley. *Eerdmans Handbook to the History of Christianity.* 139–42.

Fortescue, Adrian. "Theodosius I." CE. 14:577–8.

January 18

Arhyl, Saphir. "India." EDWM. 116.

Douglas, J. D. "Carmichael, Amy Wilson." EDWM. 168.

Murray, Jocelyn. "Carmichael, Amy Beatrice." BDCM. 16.

Norman, J. G. G. "Carmichael, Amy Wilson (1867–1951)." NIDCC. 194.

Tucker, Ruth A. and Walter L. Liefeld. *Daughters of the Church.* Grand Rapids: Zondervan, 1967. 291–306.

January 19

Bedroth, Margaret. "Rescued from Alcoholism: Mel Trotter 1870–1940." In *Ambassadors for Christ.* Edited by Woodbridge. 64–6.

January 20

Hoglund, K. "Coverdale, Miles." WWCH. 177.

Mozley. *Coverdale and His Bibles.* London: Lutterworth, 1953.

Rowden, Harold H. "Coverdale, Miles (1488–1569)." NIDCC. 267–8.

January 21

Barker, William. *Puritan Profiles.* Ross-Shire: Mentor, 1996.

Hodges, L. H. "Gillespie, George." DSCHT. 359–60.

Loughridge, Adam. "Westminster Assembly (1643)." NIDCC. 1039.

January 22

Ryle, J. C. *Five English Reformers.* Rev. ed. Edinburgh: Banner of Truth, 1981. 120–38.

Williamson, David. *History of the Kings and Queens of England.* New York: Konecky, 1988.

Williamson, G. A., ed. *Foxe's Book of Martyrs.* Boston: Little, Brown, 1965. 263–9.

January 23

Calenberg, Richard D. "Carey, Lott." EDWM. 162.

Fitts, Leroy. *Lott Carey: First Black Missionary to Africa.* Valley Forge: Judson, 1978.

Neely, Alan. "Carey, Lott." BDCM. 115.

January 24

Hefley, James and Marti Hefley. *By Their Blood: Christian Martyrs of the Twentieth Century.* 2nd ed. Grand Rapids: Baker, 1996. 500–1.

January 25

Armstrong, H. P. and J. Finegan. "Chronology of the NT." ISBE. Rev. ed. 1:686–93.

Brand, David C. "Agrippa." ABD. 1:98–100.

Hutchinson, J. "Claudius." ISBE. Rev. ed. 1:716–7.

Jones, Brian W. "Claudius." ABD. 1:1054–5.

Walls, A. F. "Aquila and Prisca, Priscilla." NBD. 3rd ed. 61.

Wood, A. S. "Apollos." NBD. 3rd ed. 57.

January 26

Smellie, Alexander. *Men of the Covenant.* Edinburgh: Banner of Truth, 1960. 435–8.

Thomson, John H. *A Cloud of Witnesses.* Harrisonburg, Va.: Sprinkle, 1989. 116–47.

January 27

Boer. *Short History of the Christian Church.* 161–2.

Douglas, J. D. "Pelagius." WWCH. 546–7.

I. W. "Pelagianism and Pelagius." DCB. 820–7.

Nash, Ronald H. "Augustine of Hippo, Philosopher and Theologian." In *Leaders of the Christian Church.* Edited by Woodbridge. 90.

January 28

Smith, Oswald J. *The Story of My Life.* London: Marshall, Morgan and Scott, 1962.

January 29

Morgan, H. Wayne. *William McKinley and His America.* Syracuse: Syracuse University Press, 1963.

Pierard, Richard V. and Robert D. Linder. *Civil Religion and the Presidency.* Grand Rapids: Zondervan, 1988.

January 30

Warner, Kurt and Michael Silver. *All Things Possible: My Story of Faith, Football, and the Miracle Season.* San Francisco: Harper, 2000.

January 31

Curtis, Ken, et al. "Menno Simons, Fugitive Leader." Online: http://www.gospelcom.net/chi/GLIMPSEF/Glimpses/glmps07.shtml.

Wenger, J. C., ed. *The Complete Works of Menno Simons, c. 1496–1561.* Scottdale: Herald, 1956.

February 1

Taylor, Dr. and Mrs. Howard. *Hudson Taylor in Early Years: The Growth of a Soul.* London: China Inland Mission, 1911. 3–27.

February 2

Schaff, Philip. *History of the Christian Church.* 4:283–4.

Walker, Williston. *A History of the Christian Church.* Rev. ed. New York: Scribner, 1959. 188.

February 3

Linder, R. D. "Wilson, Thomas Woodrow (1856–1924)." DCA. 1261–2.

Noll, Mark. "Woodrow Wilson: Fighting for a Just Peace." In *More Than Conquerors.* Edited by Woodbridge. 32–7.

February 4

Robinson. *Annotations upon Popular Hymns.* 301–2.

Smith, Jane Stuart and Betty Carlson. *Great Christian Hymn Writers.* Wheaton: Crossway, 1997. 79–84.

February 5

Williamson. *Foxe's Book of Martyrs.* 228–41.

Ryle, John Charles. *Light from Old Times.* Moscow, Idaho: Nolan, 2000. 121–34.

February 6

Garton, Nancy. *George Müller and His Orphans.* Westwood, N.J.: Revell, 1963.

Piper, John. *The Pleasures of God.* Portland: Multnomah, 1997.

February 7
Cornwall, Patricia. *Ruth: A Portrait*. New York: Doubleday, 1997.

February 8
Brand, David C. "Agrippa." ABD. 1:98–100.
Finegan, Jack. *Handbook of Biblical Chronology*. Rev. ed. Peabody: Hendrickson, 1998. 389.
Hoehner, Harold W. *Herod Antipas*. Cambridge: Cambridge University Press, 1972.
———. "Herod." ZPEB. 3:126–46.

February 9
Pollock, John. *John Wesley*. Wheaton: Harold Shaw, 1995.
Wood, A. Skevington. *The Inextinguishable Flame*. Grand Rapids: Eerdmans, 1960. 97–8.

February 10
"John Wesley and Women." CH. 1:25–7.
Pollock. *John Wesley*.

February 11
Bacon, Ernest W. *Spurgeon: Heir of the Puritans*. London: Allan and Unwin, 1967. 164–70.
Fullerton, W. Y. *Charles Haddon Spurgeon: A Biography*. Chicago: Moody, 1966.
Page, Jesse. *C. H. Spurgeon: His Life and Ministry*. London: Partridge, 1963. 137–60.
Pike, G. Holden. *Charles Haddon Spurgeon*. New York: Funk and Wagnalls, 1892. 342–78.
Skinner, Craig. *Spurgeon and Son: The Forgotten Story of Thomas Spurgeon and His Famous Father*. Grand Rapids: Kregel, 1999.
Smith, J. Manton. *The Essex Lad Who Became England's Greatest Preacher*. New York: American Tract Society, 1892. 161–9.

February 12
Luke, Mary. *The Nine Days Queen*. New York: Morrow, 1986.
Williamson. *Foxe's Book of Martyrs*. 192–8; 342–3.

February 13
Calhoun. *Princeton Seminary*. 1:8–9.
Hickman, Edward, ed. *The Works of Jonathan Edwards*. Edinburgh: Banner of Truth, 1974.
Levin, David, ed. *Jonathan Edwards: A Profile*. New York: Hill and Wang, 1969.
Piper, John. *God's Passion for His Glory: Living the Vision of Jonathan Edwards*. Wheaton: Crossway, 1998.

February 14
McQuilkin, Robertson. "Living by Vows." CT. 34. no. 14. (October 8, 1990): 38–40.
———. "Loving Muriel" in *Chicken Soup for the Golden Soul*. Edited by Jack Canfield et al. Deerfield Beach: Health Communications, 2000. 141–4.

February 15
Baldwin, Joyce C. *Haggai, Zechariah, Malachi*. TOTC. London: Inter-Varsity Press, 1972. 59–140
Lindsey, F. Duane. "Zechariah." BKC. 1:1545–59.

February 16
Calhoun. *Princeton Seminary*.
Lindsell, Harold. "Warfield, B(enjamin) B(reckenridge), (1851–1921)." NIDCC. 1030.
Stonehouse. *J. Gresham Machen*.

February 17
Blackie, John Stuart. *The Ideal of Humanity*. New York: Revell, n.d. 159–201.
Grant, M. "Renwick, James." DSCHT. 709–10.
Purves, Jock. *Fair Sunshine*. Edinburgh: Banner of Truth, 1968. 99–121, 195–203.
Smellie. *Men of the Covenant*.

February 18
Batson, E. Beatrice. "John Bunyan: The Man, Preacher and Author. CH. 5 no. 3. 1986. 6–7.
Harrison, Frank Mott. *John Bunyan: A Story*

of His Life. Edinburgh: Banner of Truth, 1995.

Piper, John. *The Hidden Soul of God*. Wheaton: Crossway, 2001. 41–78.

February 19

Herman, Doug. *Faith Quake: Surviving the Aftershocks of Tragedy*. Corsicana, Tex. Kauffman Burgess, n.d.

February 20

Kennedy, D. James. *Evangelism Explosion*. Wheaton: Tyndale, 1977.

Williams, Herbert Lee. *D. James Kennedy: The Man and His Ministry*. Fort Lauderdale: Coral Ridge, 1990.

February 21

Caughey, Ellen. *Eric Liddell: Olympian and Missionary*. Uhrichsville: Barbour, 2000.

Magnusson, Sally. *The Flying Scotsman: A Biography*. New York: Quartet, 1981.

February 22

Banton, Roland H. *Here I Stand*. New York: Abingdon, 1950.

MacCuish, Dolina. *Luther and His Katie*. Ross-Shire: Christian Focus, 1999.

Nuelsen, John Louis. *Luther: The Leader*. Cincinnati: Jennings and Graham, 1906.

February 23

Frend, W. H. C. *The Early Church*. 3rd ed. London: SCM, 1991. 115–25.

———. *The Rise of Christianity*. Philadelphia: Fortress, 1984. 456–64.

Newman, Albert Henry. *A Manual of Church History*. Vol. 1. Philadelphia: American Baptist. 166–71.

Potter, D. S. "Persecution in the Early Church." ABD. 5:231–5.

Schaff. *History of the Christian Church*. 2:633–74.

Tom, Pieter. "Diocletian (245–313)." NIDCC. 299.

February 24

Gross, Leonard. "Showing Them How to Die, How to Live." CH. 4 no. 1. 23.

February 25

"Arianism." EB Online: http://www.britannica.com/eb/article?eu=119959&tocid=46479&query=arianism.

Frend, W. H. C. *The Rise of Christianity*.

"North Africa, History of." EB. Online: http://www.britannica.com/eb/article?eu=119959&tocid=46479&query=huneric.

Victor of Vita. *History of the Vandal Persecution*. Translated by John Moorhead. Liverpool: Liverpool University Press, 1992.

February 26

Douglas, J. D. "Lloyd-Jones, David Martyn." WWCH. 427–8.

Lanning, R. B. "Dr. Martyn Lloyd-Jones: The Doctor." In *More Than Conquerors*. Edited by Woodbridge. 205–10.

February 27

Tyler Bennet and Andrew A. Bonar. *Asahel Nettleton and His Labours*. Edinburgh: Banner of Truth, 1854.

February 28

Temple, Todd and Kim Twitchell. *People Who Shaped the Church*. Wheaton: Tyndale, 2000. 315–22.

Wellman, Sam. "Corrie ten Boom" in *Faith's Great Heroes*. Edited by David Lindstedt. Uhrichsville: Barbour, 1989. 79–152.

February 29

Douglas, J. D. "Hamilton, Patrick." NIDCC. 449.

Hillyer, N. "Hamilton, Patrick." WWCH. 301.

Torrence, I. R. "Hamilton, Patrick." DSCHT. 390–1.

March 1

Cornwall. *Ruth: A Portrait*. New York: Doubleday, 1997. 218.

Graham, Billy. *Just As I Am: The Autobiography of Billy Graham*. San Francisco: Harper, 1997.

Pollock, John. *Billy Graham: Evangelist to the World*. Minneapolis: World Wide, 1979.

March 2

Pollock. *John Wesley.*

March 3

Alexander, Ralph. "Ezekiel." EBC. Vol. 6. Grand Rapids: Zondervan, 1986. 888–902.

March 4

Ashley, Mike. *The Mammoth Book of British Kings and Queens.* New York: Carroll and Graf, 1998. 638–40.

Durant, Will. *The Reformation.* Vol. 6 of *The Story of Civilization.* New York: Simon and Schuster, 1957.

Reid, W. S. "Henry VIII." WWCH. 312–4.

Toon, P. "Mary Tudor (1516–1558)." NIDCC. 640–1.

March 5

Douglas, J. D. "National Covenant," NIDCC. 694–5.

Purves. *Fair Sunshine.* 157–66.

March 6

Hamilton, I. "Whitefield, George." DSCHT. 897.

Lawson, J. Gilchrist. *Deeper Experience of Famous Christians.* Chicago: Glad Tidings, 1911. 173–86.

Whitefield, George. *George Whitefield's Journals.* London: Banner of Truth, 1965. 128–38.

March 7

Frend, W. H. C. *The Rise of Christianity.* 391–3.

Salisbury, Joyce E. *Perpetua's Passion: The Death and Memory of a Young Roman Woman.* New York: Routledge, 1997.

"Two Heroic Martyrs: Perpetua and Polycarp." CH. 27:12–4.

March 8

Brown, R. K. and M. R. Norton. *The One Year Book of Hymns.* Wheaton: Tyndale, 1995.

Gariepy, H. *Songs in the Night.* Grand Rapids: Eerdmans, 1996.

Kerr, P. *Music in Evangelism.* Glendale: Gospel Music, 1939.

March 9

Hoehner, H. W. "Maccabees." ISBE. Rev. ed. 3:196–200.

"Maccabees." EB. 15th ed. 11:224–6.

March 10

Ella, George Melvyn. *William Cowper: Poet of Paradise.* Dunham: Evangelical, 1993. 158–63.

March 11

Morgan, R. J. *On This Day.* Nashville: Nelson, 1997.

March 12

Ezra 5:1–6:16.

Haggai 1:5-6.

March 13

Barfield, Velma. *Woman on Death Row.* Minneapolis, World Wide, 1985.

March 14

Coad, F. Roy. *A History of the Brethren Movement.* Grand Rapids: Eerdmans, 1968.

Towns, Elmer and Douglas Porter. *The Ten Greatest Revivals.* Ann Arbor: Servant, 2000. 124–6.

March 15

Durant, Will. *Caesar and Christ.* Vol. 3 of *The Story of Civilization.* New York: Simon and Schuster, 1994. 194–208.

Green, Joel B. *The Gospel of Luke.* NICNT. Grand Rapids: Eerdmans, 1997. 121–9.

Potter, D. S. "Augustus." ABD. 1:524–8.

March 16

Merrill, Eugene H. *Kingdom of Priests: A History of Old Testament Israel.* Grand Rapids: Baker, 1996. 449–52.

Wiseman, D. J. "Carchemish." NBD. 3rd ed. 177.

Youngblood, R. F. "Carchemish." ISBE. Rev. ed. 1:616–7.

March 17

Robinson. *Annotations upon Popular Hymns.* 264.

Smith and Carlson. *Great Christian Hymn Writers.* 69–72.

March 18
Pollock, John. *The Cambridge Seven.* Chicago: InterVarsity, 1955.

March 19
Letters from Knut Stavig to Lars Stavig.
Vi Elske Knut: Letters of Lars Stavig.
Johnson, Norma and Oliver Swenumson, eds. *Across the Years: History of Sisseton South Dakota 1892–1992.* Watertown, South Dakota: Interstate, 1992.

March 20
Isbell, S. "Rutherford (or Rotherfurd), Samuel." DSCHT. 735–6.
Robinson. *Annotations upon Popular Hymns* 472–3.

March 21
Bull, Josiah. *John Newton.* Edinburgh: Banner of Truth, 1868.
Cecil, Richard. *The Life of John Newton.* Ross-Shire: Christian Focus, 2000.
Marten, Bernard. *John Newton: A Biography.* London: Heinemann, 1950.
Steer, Roger. *Guarding the Holy Fire.* Grand Rapids: Baker, 1999. 124–9.

March 22
Davis, William T., ed. *Bradford's History of Plymouth Plantation 1606–1646.* New Jersey: Barnes and Noble, 1908. 110–41.
Fleming, Thomas J. *One Small Candle: The Pilgrims' First Year in America.* New York: Norton, 1964. 160–74.
Marshall, Pieter and David Manuel. *The Light and the Glory.* Old Tappan, N.J.: Revell, 1977. 128–35.
Willeson, George F. *Saints and Strangers.* New York: Time, 1945. 184–228.

March 23
Edwards, Jonathan, ed. *The Life and Diary of David Brainerd.* Grand Rapids: Baker, 1997.
Piper, John. *The Hidden Smile of God.* 123–59.

March 24
Ashley. *The Mammoth Book of British Kings and Queens.* 630–50.
Benson, Bobrick. *Wide as the Waters: The Story of the English Bible and the Revolution It Inspired.* New York: Simon and Schuster, 2001. 199–263.
Bruce, F. F. "Bible (English Versions)." NIDCC. 127–9.
Sefton, Henry R. "James VI (of Scotland) and I (of England) (1566–1625)." NIDCC. 523.
Steer. *Guarding the Holy Fire.*

March 25
Bundy, D. D. "Trotman, Dawson Earle (1906–1956)." DCA. 1186.
Reapsome, James. "Trotman, Dawson E." EDWM. 971.
Senter, Mark. "Dawson Trotman and the Navigators." In *More Than Conquerors.* Edited by Woodbridge. 165–8.
Skinner, Betty Lee. *Daws.* Grand Rapids: Zondervan, 1974.

March 26
Williamson. *Foxe's Book of Martyrs.* 243–9.

March 27
Fensham, F. Charles. *The Books of Ezra and Nehemiah.* NICOT. Grand Rapids: Eerdmans, 1982.

March 28
Carson, D. A. *The Gospel according to John.* Leicester: Inter-Varsity, 1991. 424–30.

March 29
Hoehner, Harold W. *Chronological Aspects of the Life of Christ.* Grand Rapids: Zondervan, 1977.

March 30
Hoehner. *Chronological Aspects of the Life of Christ.*

March 31
Hoehner. *Chronological Aspects of the Life of Christ.*

Lane, William L. *The Gospel of Mark.* NICNT. Grand Rapids: Eerdmans, 1974. 398–430.

April 1
Eusebius. *Ecclesiastical History.* 3:5.
Hoehner. *Chronological Aspects of the Life of Christ.*

April 2
Allison, Dale C. *The New Moses.* Minneapolis: Fortress, 1993. 257.
Daube, David. *The New Testament and Rabbinic Judaism.* London: Athlone, 1956. 330–1.
Hoehner. *Chronological Aspects of the Life of Christ.*

April 3
Hoehner. *Chronological Aspects of the Life of Christ.*

April 4
Carson, D. A. "Matthew." EBC. 8:585–91.
Hagner, Donald A. *Matthew 14–28.* WBC. 33B. 860–78.
Hoehner. *Chronological Aspects of the Life of Christ.*

April 5
Hoehner. *Chronological Aspects of the Life of Christ.*

April 6
Fackler, M. "Smith, Joseph." WWCH. 628–9.
———. "Young, Brigham." WWCH. 739.
Hoekma, Anthony A. "Mormonism." NIDCC. 678–9.
Gerstner, John H. *The Theology of the Major Sects.* Grand Rapids: Baker, 1960. 41–52.
Martin, Walter. *The Kingdom of the Cults.* Minneapolis: Bethany, 1985. 166–226.

April 7
Hoehner. *Chronological Aspects of the Life of Christ.*

April 8
Brereton, Virginia L. "The Popular Educator." CH. 25:26–9.

Findlay, James. "The Northfield Schools." CH. 25:30–2.
Getz, G. A. "Moody Bible Institute." DCA. 769.
Hampton, V. and C. J. Wheeler. "Key People in the Life of D. L. Moody." CH. 25:12–5.

April 9
Bohrer, Dick. *Bill Borden.* Chicago: Moody, 1984.
Michel, D. J. "Borden, William Whiting." DCA. 177.
Tucker, Ruth A. "Borden, William Whiting." BDCM. 79.

April 10
Laurent, Bob. "Watchman Nee." In *Faith's Great Heroes.* 261–319.

April 11
Moody, William Revell. *The Life of D. L. Moody by His Son.* New York: Revell, 1900. 85–9.
Pollock, John. *Moody without Sankey.* London: Hodder and Stoughton, 1963.

April 12
Judson, Edward. *The Life of Adoniram Judson.* New York: Randolph, 1883.

April 13
Hefley and Hefley. *By Their Blood.* 411–5.
Johnstone, Patrick and Jason Mandryk. *Operation World.* 6th ed.

April 14
Howie, John. *The Scots Worthies.* Edinburgh: Banner of Truth, 1870. 110–4.
Wright, D. F. "Duncan, Andrew." DSCHT. 261–2.

April 15
Adams, Moody. *The Titanic's Last Hero.* West Columbia, S. C: Olive, 1997.

April 16
Paton, James. *The Story of Dr. John G. Paton's Thirty Years with South Sea Cannibals.* Revised by A. K. Langrudge. London: Hodder and Stoughton, 1924.

April 17

Bainton. *Here I Stand.*

Meyer, Carl S. "Luther, Martin (1483–1546)." NIDCC. 609–11.

April 18

Whitefield. *George Whitefield's Journals.* 253–5.

April 19

Stout, Harry. "Preaching the Insurrection." CH. 15 no. 2. 11–7.

April 20

Scott, Darrell and Beth Nimmo. *Rachel's Tears: The Spiritual Journey of Columbine Martyr Rachel Scott.* Nashville: Nelson, 2000.

Zoba, Wendy Murray. *Day of Reckoning: Columbine and the Search for America's Soul.* Grand Rapids: Baker, 2000.

April 21

Bunson, Matthew. "Rome." DRE. 362–7.

Smith, Clyde Curry. "Rome." NIDCC. 858–9.

Vos, H. F. "Rome." ISBE. Rev. ed. 4:228–36.

April 22

Armstrong, B. G. "Calvin, John." WWCH. 128–33.

Reid, W. S. "Calvin, John (1509–1564)." NIDCC. 177–9.

Schaff, Philip. *History of the Christian Church.* 8:347–438.

April 23

Wilson, R. D. and R. K. Harrison. "Daniel." ISBE. Rev. ed. 1:858–9.

April 24

Calhoun. *Princeton Seminary.*

Stewart, J. W. "Hodge, Charles (1797–1878). DPRTA. 122–3.

April 25

Armstrong. "Calvin, John." WWCH. 128–33.

Reid, W. S. "Calvin, John (1509–1564)." NIDCC. 177–9.

Reyburn, Hugh Y. *John Calvin: His Life,*

Letters, and Work. London: Hodder and Stoughton, 1914. 310–9.

April 26

Askew, Thomas. "Judson, Adoniram." EDWM. 528–9.

Judson, Edward. *The Life of Adoniram Judson.*

April 27

Taylor, James Monrow. *Before Vassar Opened.* Boston: Houghton Mifflin, 1914.

April 28

Alexander, Ralph H. "Ezekiel." EBC. 6:942–96.

April 29

Bock, Darrel L. *Luke.* BECNT. Grand Rapids: Baker, 1994. 1:259–75.

April 30

Hefley and Hefley. *By Their Blood.* 110–2.

May 1

Purves. *Fair Sunshine.* 65–73.

Smellie. *Men of the Covenant.* 401–8.

Thomson. *Cloud of Witnesses.* 535–7.

May 2

CH. 25:6–32

May 3

Block, N. E. "Egede, Hans (Povelsen)." BDCM. 196.

Johnstone and Mandryk. *Operation World.* 6th ed. 282–3.

Schuster, R. "Egede, Hans Povelsen." EDWM. 305.

May 4

Murray. *Australian Christian Life from 1788.* 253–5.

May 5

Dallimore, Arnold A. *George Whitefield: God's Anointed Son in the Great Revival of the Eighteenth Century.* Wheaton: Crossway, 1990.

———. *George Whitefield: The Life and Times of the Great Evangelist of the Eighteenth*

Century. 2 vols. Edinburgh: Banner of Truth, 1970.
Pollock. *John Wesley.*

May 6
Alexander, Archibald. *Biographical Sketches of the Founder and Principal Alumni of the Log College.* Princeton: Robinson, 1845.
Hope, N. V. "Tennent, William." WWCH. 663–4.
Logan, S. T. "Tennent, William." DCH. 1165.

May 7
Horton, Michael. "James Montgomery Boice: Servant of the Word." *Modern Reformation.* 9 no. 5 (September/October 2000): 10–1.

May 8
Hyland, Judy. *In the Shadow of the Rising Sun.* Minneapolis: Augsburg, 1984.

May 9
Thomson. *Cloud of Witnesses.* 359–64.

May 10
Chesebrough, David B. "The General Who Looked to God: 'Stonewall' Jackson." In *More Than Conquerors.* Edited by Woodbridge. 22–4.
———. "Jackson, Thomas Jonathan (Stonewall)." DCA. 586–7.
Hendersen, G. F. R. *Stonewall Jackson and the American Civil War.* 2 vols. London: Longmans Green, 1898.

May 11
Purves. *Fair Sunshine* 77–84.
Smellie. *Men of the Covenant.* 409–21.

May 12
de Rosset, Rosalie. "Chicago Prophet: A. W. Tozer." In *More Than Conquerors.* Edited by Woodbridge. 201–4.
Magnuson, N. A. "Tozer, (A)ldon (W)ilson (1897–1963)." DCA. 1182.
Temple and Twitchell. *People Who Shaped the Church.* 340–5.

May 13
Latourette, Kenneth Scott. *A History of*

Christianity. 2 vols. Peabody: Prince, 1975. 1:672–4.
Schaff. *History of the Christian Church.* 6:684–716.
Vos, H. F. "Savonarola, Girolamo." WWCH. 607–8.

May 14
Hoehner. "Chronology of the New Testament." NBD. 3rd ed. 193–9.

May 15
Johnson, Paul. *A History of the Jews.* New York: Harper, 1987.
Owen, G. Frederick. *Abraham to the Middle-East Crisis.* 4th ed. Grand Rapids: Eerdmans, 1957.

May 16
Elton, Godfrey. *Gordon of Khartoum.* New York: Knopf, 1954.

May 17
Cook, Faith. *William Grimshaw of Haworth.* Edinburgh: Banner of Truth, 1997.

May 18
King, D. D. *E. M. Bounds.* Minneapolis: Bethany, 1998.

May 19
Durant. *The Reformation.* 535–87.
Ives, E. W. *Ann Boleyn.* Oxford: Blockwell, 1986.
Lofts, Norah. *Ann Boleyn.* New York: Coward, McCann & Geoghegan, Inc., 1979.
Warnicke, Retha. *The Rise and Fall of Ann Boleyn.* Cambridge: Cambridge University Press, 1989.
Williamson. *Foxe's Book of Martyrs.* 107–33.

May 20
Comfort, G. A. "Wesley, Charles." WWCH. 708–9.
Partner, D. "Wesley, John." WWCH. 709–12.
Pollock. *John Wesley.*
Wood, A. Skevington. "Wesley, Charles (1707–1788)." NIDCC. 1033–4.
———. "Wesley, John (1703–1791)." NIDCC. 1034–5.

May 21
Ryden. *The Story of Christian Hymnody.* 425.

May 22
Cornwell. *Ruth: A Portrait.* 111–22.

May 23
Lingenfelter, J. "Moe, Malla." EDWM. 652.

Nilsen, M. and P. Sheetz. *Malla Moe.* Chicago: Moody, 1956.

Tucker, Ruth A. "Moe, Malla." BDCM. 463–4.

May 24
Hoehner. "Chronology of the New Testament. NBD. 3rd ed. 193–9.

May 25
Alexander, James. *The Life of Archibald Alexander, D.D.* Harrisonburg, Va.: Sprinkle, 1991.

Hope, N. V. "Alexander, Archibald." WWCH. 18.

May 26
Pollock, John. *John Wesley.* 102–9.

Slaate, Homer Alexander. *Fire in the Brand.* New York: Exposition, 1963. 88–94.

Wood, A. Skevington. "Wesley, John (1703–1791)." NIDCC. 1034–5.

May 27
Brown, K. M. "Campbell, Archibald." DSCHT. 126.

———. "Covenanters." DSCHT. 218–9.

Purves. *Fair Sunshine.* 195–203.

Smellie. *Men of the Covenant.* 89–105.

May 28
Bruce, F. F. *The Book of the Acts.* NICNT. Grand Rapids: Eerdmans, 1954. 428–32.

May 29
Buehler, W. W. "Wise-Men (NT)." ISBE. Rev. ed. 4:1084–5.

Kaufmanis, Karlis. "The Star of Bethlehem." *The Lutheran BOND.* (December 1970).

Kidger, Mark. *The Star of Bethlehem.*

Princeton: Princeton University Press, 1999.

May 30
Looser, Frieda. "The Wanderer." CH. 68:28–9.

Parker, G. H. *The Morning Star: Wycliffe and the Dawn of the Reformation.* Vol. 3 of *The Advance of Christianity through the Centuries.* Edited by F. F. Bruce. Grand Rapids: Eerdmans, 1965. 76–101.

May 31
Derham, A. Morgan. "Carey, William (1761–1834)." NIDCC. 192.

Fackler, M. "Carey, William." WWCH. 137–8.

Haykin, Michael. *One Heart and One Soul: John Sutcliffe of Olney, His Friends and His Times.* Durham: Evangelical, 1994.

Hedland, R. E. "Did You Know? Little Known or Remarkable Facts about William Carey." CH. 36:1–2.

Torbet, Robert. *A History of the Baptists.* Valley Forge: Judson, 1963.

June 1
Douglas, J. D. "Guthrie, James." DSCHT. 381.

Howie. *The Scots Worthies.* 257–68.

Purves. *Fair Sunshine.* 13–21.

Smellie. *Men of the Covenant.* 88–99.

June 2
Hoehner. "Chronology of the New Testament." NBD. 3rd ed. 193–9.

June 3
Hoehner. "Chronology of the New Testament." NBD. 3rd ed. 193–9.

June 4
Hoehner. "Chronology of the New Testament." NBD. 3rd ed. 193–9.

Stott, John R. W. "The Message of the Book of Acts: The Spirit, the Church and the World." BST. Downers Grove: Inter-Varsity, 1990.

June 5
Wilson, Grady. *Count It All Joy*. Nashville: Broadman, 1984.

June 6
Judson, Edward. *The Life of Adoniram Judson*. 124–32.
Johnstone and Mandryk. *Operation World*. 6th ed. 462–5.

June 7
Johnson. *A History of the Jews*.

June 8
Garraty, John A. and Peter Gay, eds. *The Columbia History of the World*. New York: Harper and Row, 1972. 259–67.
Johnstone and Mandryk. *Operation World*. 6th ed.

June 9
Angus, S. and A. M. Renwick. "Nero." ISBE. Rev. ed. 3:521–3.
Blaiklock, E. M. "Nero." ZPEB. 4:410–2.
Gasque, W. Ward. "Nero Claudius Caesar (37–68)." NIDCC. 699.

June 10
Milns, R. D. "Alexander the Great." ABD. 1:146–50.
Thomson, J. E. H. "Alexander the Great." ISBE. Rev. ed. 1:87–9.

June 11
Elliot. *Through Gates of Splendor*.
Liefeld, Olive. "The Auca Five." In *Ambassadors for Christ*. Edited by Woodbridge. 127–33.

June 12
Cooper, J. F. "Winthrop, John (1588–1649)." DCA. 1265.
Marshall and Manuel. *The Light and the Glory*.

June 13
The Triumphs of Truth and Continental Letters and Sketches from the Journal of the Rev. James Caughey as Illustrated in Two Great Revivals in Nottingham and Lincoln, England. Philadelphia: Higgins and Perkinpine, 1887.

June 14
Clouse, Robert G. "Crusades, The." NIDCC. 273–4.
Hallam, Elizabeth, ed. *Chronicles of the Crusaders: Eyewitness Accounts of the Wars between Christianity and Islam*. N.p. CLB. 1997.
Shelley, Bruce. *Church History in Plain Language*. Dallas: Word, 1982.

June 15
Kaiser, Walter C., Jr. *A History of Israel from the Bronze Age through the Jewish Wars*. Nashville: Broadman and Holman, 1998. 293–4.
Kitchen, K. A. and T. C. Mitchell. "Chronology of the Old Testament." NBD. 3rd ed. 186–93.
Merrill, Eugene. *A Historical Survey of the Old Testament*. 2nd ed. Grand Rapids: Baker, 1991. 97–100.

June 16
Marshall and Manuel. *The Light and the Glory*. 277–86.
Strauss, William and Neil Howe. *Generations: The History of America's Future*. New York: Morrow, 1991. 151.

June 17
Moody. *The Life of Dwight L. Moody*.
Pollock. *Moody without Sankey*.

June 18
"Did You Know?" CH. 16:4.
Duffield, G. E. "Tyndale, William." NIDCC. 990.
Edwards, Brian H. *God's Outlaw*. Darlington: Evangelical, 1976.

June 19
Bechtel, Paul M. "Pascal, Blaise (1623–1662)." NIDCC. 749.
Cailliet, Emil. *Pascal: The Emergence of Genius*. New York: Harper, 1945.

June 20
Foster, Marshall and Mary-Elaine Swanson. *The American Covenant: The Untold Story*. Thousand Oaks: Mayflower Institute, 1983.

June 21

Acworth, R. J. P. "Galileo." EC. 4:294–5.

Clouse, Robert. "Galileo Galilei." NIDCC. 399–400.

Durant, Will and Ariel. *The Age of Reason Begins*. Vol. 7 of *The Story of Civilization*. New York: Simon and Schuster, 1961. 600–12.

June 22

Calhoun. *Princeton Seminary*. 2:47–62.

Shelley, Bruce L. "Hodge, Charles (1797–1878)." NIDCC. 473–4.

June 23

Calhoun. *Princeton Seminary*. 1:192–3.

June 24

Haykin. *One Heart and One Soul*. 320–1.

Tucker, Ruth A. "William Carey's Less-than-Perfect Family Life." CH. 36:27–9.

June 25

Barabas, S. "Haman." ZPEB. 3:21.

"Esther." *NIV Study Bible*.

June 26

Van Braght, Thieleman J. *The Bloody Theater or Martyr's Mirror*. Scottdale: Herald, 1938. 851–2.

June 27

Frend. *The Rise of Christianity*. 593–617.

Norman, J. G. G. "Julian the Apostate." NIDCC. 555.

Schaff. *History of the Christian Church*. 3:41–60.

June 28

Ashley. *The Mammoth Book of British Kings and Queens*. 630–6.

Schnucker, Robert. "Henry VIII (1491–1547)." NIDCC. 461–2.

June 29

Detzler, W. A. "Haystack Prayer Meeting (1806)." DCA. 515.

———. "Mills, Samuel John, Jr. (1738–1818)." DCA. 741–2.

Johnstone and Mandryk. *Operation World*. 6th ed. 658.

Judson. *The Life of Adoniram Judson*. 16–35, 562.

Strong, William E. *The Story of the American Board: The Centenary of American Foreign Missions*. Boston: Pilgrim, 1910.

Tinder, D. G. "American Board of Commissioners for Foreign Missions." DCA. 44.

Wilson, E. A. "Judson, Adoniram (1788–1850)." DCA. 603.

June 30

Chesebrough, D. B. "Lee, Robert (E)dward (1807–1870)" DCA. 640–1.

Lee, Captain Robert E. *Recollections and Letters of General Robert E. Lee*. New York: Konecky and Konecky, n.d.

Nagel, Paul C. *The Lees of Virginia: Seven Generations of an American Family*. New York: Oxford University Press, 1990. 231–305.

July 1

Stowe, David M. "Coan, Titus." BDCM. 139.

Towns and Porter. *The Ten Greatest Revivals*. 104–9.

July 2

Charley, J. W. "Charles I (1600–1649)." NIDCC. 212.

D'Aubigné, J. H. Merle. *The Protector: A Vindication*. Harrisonburg, Va: Sprinkle, 1997.

Hope, N. V. "Charles I (1600–1649). WWCH. 152–3.

Sanderson, Edgar. *History of England and the British Empire*. London: Warne, 1893.

July 3

Jarratt, Devereux. *The Life of the Reverend Devereux Jarrett*. Baltimore: Warner and Hanna, 1806.

Steer. *Guarding the Holy Fire*. 137–52.

Weaver, C. D. "Jarratt, Devereux (1733–1801)." DCA. 588–9.

July 4

Hefley and Hefley. *By Their Blood*. 388–93.

July 5

Easterling, John. "Coillard, Francois." EDWM. 207.

Johnstone and Mandryk. *Operation World.* 685–8.

Longrove, D. W. "Haldane, James Alexander." DSCHT. 385.

———. "Haldane, Robert." DSCHT. 386–7.

Mackintosh, C. W. *Coillard of the Zambesi: The Lives of Francois and Christina Coillard of the Paris Missionary Society in South and Central Africa (1885–1904).* New York: American Tract Society, 1907.

Morgan. *On This Day.*

Spindler, Marc R. "Paris Evangelical Missionary Society." EDWM. 724–5.

June 6

Ashley. *The Mammoth Book of British Kings and Queens.* 20, 636–7.

Duffield, G. E. "Edward VI." EC. 4:17.

Durant. *The Reformation.* 579–87.

Petty, P. W. "Edward VI (1537–1553)." NIDCC. 333–4.

Smith, Preseved. *The Age of the Reformation.* New York: Holt, 1920. 310–7.

Williamson. *Foxe's Book of Martyrs.* 170–91.

July 7

Adams, James Truslow. "Hooker, Thomas." DAB. 5:199–200.

Cooper, J. F. "Cotton, John (1584–1652). DCA. 320–1.

Douglas, J. D. "Hooker, Thomas." WWCH. 326–7.

Harper, G. W. "Hooker, Thomas (1586–1647)." DCA. 551–2.

Shuffleton, Frank. "Hooker, Thomas." ANB. 12:137–9.

Toon, P. "Land, William." WWCH. 414–5.

July 8

Edwards, J. H. "Edwards, Jonathan (1702–1758)." DCA. 380–1.

Edwards, Jonathan. "Sinners in the Hands of an Angry God." CH. 4 no. 4. 32–4.

Mitchell, C. "Edwards, Jonathan." WWCH. 224–6.

Robertson, Pat. *America's Date with Destiny.* Nashville: Nelson, 1986. 49–59.

Tracy, Joseph. *The Great Awakening: A History of the Revival of Religion in the Time of Edwards and Whitefield.* Edinburgh: Banner of Truth, 1976. 213–6.

July 9

Douglas, J. D. "Duff, Alexander." EDWM. 292–4.

———. "Duff, Alexander (1806–1878)." NIDCC. 315.

Paton, William *Alexander Duff: Pioneer of Missionary Education.* London: Student Christian Movement, 1923.

Piggin, Stuart and John Roxborough. *The St. Andrews Seven: The Finest Flowering of Missionary Zeal in Scottish History.* Edinburgh: Banner of Truth, 1985.

Tucker, Ruth A. *From Jerusalem to Irian Jaya.* Grand Rapids: Zondervan, 1983. 134–6.

Walls, Andrew F. "Duff, Alexander." BDCM. 187–8.

July 10

Askey, Thomas A. "Judson, Adoniram." EDWM. 528–9.

Brackney, William H. "Judson, Adoniram." BDCM. 345–6.

Clasper, Paul. "Judson, Emily (Chubbock)." BDCM. 346.

Judson. *The Life of Adoniram Judson.*

Neely, Alan. "Judson, Sarah (Hall) Boardman." BDCM. 346–7.

Rober, Dana L. "Judson, Ann ("Nancy") (Hasseltine)." BDCM. 346.

July 11

Caughy. *Eric Liddell.*

Mitchell, David J. "Liddell, Eric Henry." BDCM. 400.

July 12

Edwards. *The Life and Diary of David Brainerd.*

Hunsicker, Ranelda. *David Brainerd.* Minneapolis: Bethany, 1999.

Norman, J. G. G. "Brainerd, David (1718–1747)." NIDCC. 151–2.

Piper. *The Hidden Smile of God.* 123–59.

July 13

Murray, Jocelyn. "Taylor, Maria (Dyer)." BDCM. 659.

Pollock, John *Hudson and Maria.* Ross-Shire: Christian Focus, 1996.

———. "Taylor, J(ames) Hudson (1832–1905)." NIDCC. 953.

Taylor, Dr. and Mrs. Howard. *Hudson Taylor in Early Years.*

July 14

Ariail, Dan and Cheryl Heckler-Feltz. *The Carpenter's Apprentice: The Spiritual Biography of Jimmy Carter.* Grand Rapids: Zondervan, 1996.

Baker, James T. *A Southern Baptist in the White House.* Philadelphia: Westminster, 1977.

Carter, Jimmy. *An Hour before Daylight: Memories of a Rural Boyhood.* New York: Simon and Schuster, 2001.

Linder, R. D. "Carter, James Earl, Jr. (1924–)." DCA. 227–8.

Pippert, Wesley G. *The Spiritual Journey of Jimmy Carter.* New York: Macmillan, 1978.

July 15

Williamson. *Foxe's Book of Martyrs.* 370–7.

July 16

McGree, Gary B. "Clough, John Everett." EDWM. 206.

Thompson, E. Wayne and David L. Cummins. *This Day in Baptist History.* Greenville: Bob Jones University Press, 1993. 272–3.

Torbet, Robert G. *Venture of Faith: The Story of the American Baptist Foreign Mission Society and the Women's American Baptist Foreign Mission Society 1814–1954.* Philadelphia: Judson, 1955. 254–63.

July 17

Robinson. *Annotations upon Popular Hymns.* 192–3.

Thompson and Cummins. *This Day in Baptist History.* 257–8.

July 18

Jeremiah 1:25, 39.

July 19

Firak, T. "Zinzendorf, Nicholaus Ludwig, Count von." WWCH. 742–5.

Lewis, A. J. "Baptized into One Spirit." CH. 1:24–5.

Norman, J. G. G. "Moravian Brethren." NIDCC. 676.

Pierard, Richard V. "Zinzendorf, Nikolaus Ludwig, Count von (1700–60)." NIDCC. 1071.

"The Rich Young Ruler Who Said Yes." CH. 1:7–9, 31–5.

July 20

Covell, Ralph R. "China." EDWM. 178–9.

Johnstone. *Operation World.* 5th ed. Grand Rapids: Zondervan, 1993. 163–9.

"The Miracles after Missions: An Interview with Kim-Kwong Chan." CH. 52:42–4.

Pollock, John C. "Taylor, J(ames) Hudson (1832–1905)." NIDCC. 953.

Steer, Roger. "Pushing Inward." CH. 52:10–8.

Tucker. *From Jerusalem to Irian Jaya.* 173–88.

July 21

Cherney, Robert W. *A Righteous Cause: The Life of William Jennings Bryan.* Boston: Little, Brown. 1985.

Marsden, G. M. "Scopes Trial." DCA. 1058–9.

Shelley, B. L. "Bryan, William Jennings (1860–1925)." DCA. 198.

July 22

Brown, K. M. "Covenanters." DSCHT. 218–9.

Douglas, J. D. "Charles II." DSCHT. 166.

———. "National Covenant." DSCHT. 166.

———. "Sanquhar Declaration." DSCHT. 620.

Grant, M. "Cameron, Richard." DSCHT. 124–5.

Lachman, D. C. "Ayrsmoss." DSCHT. 48.
———. "Solemn League and Covenant."
786–7.
Purves. *Fair Sunshine*. 39–51.
Stevenson, D. "Restoration." DSCHT. 910–1.

July 23
Murray, Jocelyn. "Taylor, Maria (Dyer)."
BDCM. 659.
Pollock. *Hudson and Maria*.
Tucker. *From Jerusalem to Irian Jaya*. 173–
83.

July 24
Tallach, John. *God Made Them Great*. Edinburgh: Banner of Truth, 1975. 119–35.

July 25
Hatcher, William E. *John Jasper: An
Unmatched Negro Philosopher and
Preacher*. New York: Negro Universities
Press, 1969.
"Jasper, John." EAAR. 393.
Thompson and Cummins. *This Day in
Baptist History*. 126–7.

July 26
Douglas, J. D. "Wilberforce, William."
WWCH. 719.
Nixon, R. E. "Milner, Isaac (1750–1820)."
NIDCC. 660–1.
———. "Milner, Joseph (1744–1797)."
NIDCC. 661.
———. "Wilberforce, William (1759–
1833)." NIDCC. 1046.
Pollock, John. *Wilberforce*. Tring: Lion,
1977.
Shelley. *Church History in Plain Language*.
384–9.
Williams, C. Peter. "Claphem Sect." NIDCC.
229–30.

July 27
Brown, K. M. "Covenanters." DSCHT.
218–9.
Dickson, J. A. "Bothwell Bridge." DSCHT.
90.
Douglas, J. D. "Cargill, Donald (Daniel)
(c. 1619–1680)." NIDCC. 192.
———. "Charles II." DSCHT. 166.

Grant, M. "Cargill, Donald." DSCHT. 137.
Purves. *Fair Sunshine*. 169–92.
Thomson. *A Cloud of Witnesses*. 1–26, 501–
10.

July 28
Green, Melody and David Hazard. *No
Compromise: The Life Story of Keith
Green*. Chatworth, Calif.: Sparrow, 1989.

July 29
Durant. *The Age of Reason Begins*. 30–8.
Motley, John Lothrop. *History of the United
Netherlands*. 2 Vols. New York: Harper,
1861. 2:458–536.
Norman, J. G. G. "Philip II (1527–1598)."
NIDCC. 773–4.
Petty, P. W. "Elizabeth I (1533–1603)."
NIDCC. 338–9.
Toon, P. "Elizabeth I." WWCH. 229.

July 30
Pollock. *Hudson and Maria*.
———. "Taylor, J(ames) Hudson (1832–
1905)." NIDCC. 953.
Taylor, Dr. and Mrs. Howard. *Hudson
Taylor and the China Inland Mission*.
London: China Inland Mission, 1918.
Tucker. *From Jerusalem to Irian Jaya*. 173–
88.

July 31
Alexander, Ralph H. "Ezekiel." EBC. 6:737–
996.

August 1
Ryden. *The Story of Christian Hymnody*,
479–81.

August 2
Johnson. *A History of the Jews*. 215–30.
Miller, Kevin A. "Why Did Columbus Sail?"
CH. 35:9–16.
Morgan. *On This Day*.
Morison, Samuel Eliot. *Admiral of the Sea:
A Life of Christopher Columbus*. Boston:
Little, Brown, 1942. 85–109.
Satinover, Jeffrey. *Cracking the Bible Code*.
New York: Morrow, 1997. 79.
Sellers, Ian. "Spain." NIDCC. 923–4.

Stewart, Roy A. "Anusim (Maranos)."
NIDCC. 52.

Toon, Peter. "Ferdinand V (1452–1516)."
NIDCC. 372.

Underwood, T. L. "Inquisition, The."
NIDCC. 511.

———. "Isabella of Castile (1451–1504)."
NIDCC. 518.

August 3

Bergman, Susan. "In the Shadow of the
Martyrs." CT. 40 (August 12, 1996):
18–25.

Hefley. By Their Blood. 15–25.

August 4

Fensham. The Books of Ezra and Nehemiah.
97–120.

Harris, R. L. "Ezra." ZPEB. 2:470–1.

Kidner, Derek. Ezra and Nehemiah: An
Introduction and Commentary. Vol. 2
of TOTC. Edited by D. J. Wiseman.
Leicester: Inter-Varsity, 1979. 61–7.

Wright, J. S. "Ezra." NBC. 3rd ed. 355.

August 5

Elton. Gordon of Khartoum.

August 6

Towns and Porter.The Ten Greatest Revivals
Ever. 79–82.

August 7

Norwood, Frederick A. The Story of American Methodism. Nashville: Abingdon,
1974. 73–223.

August 8

Alexander. "Ezekiel." EBC. 6:756–66.

August 9

Brook, Benjamin. The Lives of the Puritans.
3 vols. Morgan: Soli Deo Gloria, 1994.
2:463–6.

August 10

Hefley, James. "Apostle to the Lost Tribes:
William Cameron Townsend 1896–
1982." In Ambassadors for Christ. Edited
by Woodbridge. 118–26.

Hefley, James and Marti Hefley. Uncle Cam:
The Story of William Cameron Townsend

Founder of the Wycliffe Bible Translators
and the Summer Institute of Linguistics.
Waco: Word, 1974.

Hesselgrave, D. J. "Townsend, William
Cameron (1896–19820." DCA. 1182–3.

Tucker. From Jerusalem to Irian Jaya. 351–7.

August 11

Andrew, John S. "Toplady, Augustus
Montague (1740–1768)." NIDCC. 980.

Ryle, J. C. Christian Leaders of the Eighteenth
Century. Edinburgh: Banner of Truth,
1885. 358–84.

Ryden. The Story of Christian Hymnody.
290–3.

Smith and Carlson. Great Christian Hymn
Writers. 161–2.

August 12

Colson, Charles. Born Again. Old Tappan,
N.J.: Spire, 1977.

Vaughn, Ellen Santilli. "Watergate and
After: Chuck Colson and Prison Fellowship." In More Than Conquerors. Edited
by Woodbridge. 365–9.

Zoba, Wendy Murray. "The Legacy of Prisoner 23226." CT. 45 (July 9, 2001): 28–
35.

August 13

Prentiss. More Love to Thee.

Ryden. The Story of Christian Hymnody.
530–3.

Smith and Carlson. Great Christian Hymn
Writers. 135–7.

August 14

Alexander. "Ezekiel." EBC. 6:832–9.

August 15

Scalzi, Guido. "My Encounter with God."
In Testimonies of Fifty Converted Roman
Catholic Priests. Edited by Richard
Bennett and Maren Buckingham.
Edinburgh: Banner of Truth, 1994.
228–35.

August 16

Cook, Richard Briscoe. The Wit and Wisdom
of Rev. Charles H. Spurgeon. Containing
Selections from His Writings and a Sketch

of His Life and Work. New York: Treat, 1892.

Norman, J. G. G. "Spurgeon, Charles Haddon (1834–1892)." NIDCC. 928.

Toon, P. "Spurgeon, Charles Haddon." WWCH. 636.

Wayland, H. L. *Charles H. Spurgeon: His Faith and Works.* Philadelphia: American Baptist, 1892.

August 17

Blegen, Theodore C. *Building Minnesota.* Boston: Heath, 1938. 209–19.

Osgood, Phillips Endecott. *Straight Tongue: A Story of Henry Benjamin Whipple First Episcopal Bishop of Minnesota.* Minneapolis: Denison, 1958.

Riggs, Stephen R. *Mary and I: Forty Years with the Sioux.* Chicago: Holmes, 1880. 179–202.

August 18

Firak, T. "Sung, John." WWCH. 648–50.

Ling, Samuel. "Sung, John." EDWM. 918.

Lyall, Leslie T. *John Sung.* Rev. ed. London: China Inland Mission, 1956.

August 19

Calhoun. *Princeton Seminary.*

Kennedy, E. W. "Miller, Samuel (1769–1850)." DPRTA. 160.

August 20

Popov, Haralan. *Tortured for His Faith.* Grand Rapids: Zondervan, 1975.

August 21

Jones, John Williams. *Christ in the Camp.* Richmond: Johnson, 1887.

August 22

Hosier, Helen Kooiman. *100 Women Who Changed the Twentieth Century.* Grand Rapids: Revell, 2000. 334–40.

Tucker. *From Jerusalem to Irian Jaya.* 360–3.

August 23

Corwin, Gary R. "Bingham, Roland Victor." BDCM. 64–5.

Hay, Ian M. "Society for International Ministries (SIM)." EDWM. 886–7.

Hefley and Hefley. *By Their Blood.* 380–3.

August 24

Baird. *History of the Rise of the Huguenots in France.* 2:426–639.

Clark, R. E. D. "Bartholomew's Day, Massacre of St. (1572)." NIDCC. 108.

Curtis, A. Kenneth, J. Stephen Lang and Randy Peterson. *The 100 Most Important Events in Christian History.* Grand Rapids: Revell, 1991. 111–2.

Durant and Durant. *The Age of Reason Begins.* 346–55.

Johnstone. *Operation World.* 5th ed. 224–7.

Linder, Robert D. "Henry IV of France (1553–1610)." NIDCC. 460–1.

Morgan. *On This Day.*

August 25

Tyler and Bonar. *Asahel Nettleton.* 133–7.

August 26

Johnson, Paul. *Intellectuals.* New York: Harper, 1988. 52–81.

August 27

Fackler, M. "Dunster, Henry." WWCH. 216.

Mather, Cotton. *Magnalia Christi Americana or The Ecclesiastical History of New England.* 2 vols. Hartford: Andrus, 1953. 2:8–25.

August 28

Richardson, Michael. *Amazing Faith: The Authorized Biography of Bill Bright.* Colorado Springs: Waterbrook, 2000.

August 29

Criswell, W. A. *Standing on the Promises.* Dallas: Word, 1990.

August 30

Hefley and Hefley. *By Their Blood.* 15–27.

Tucker. *From Jerusalem to Irian Jaya.* 165–85.

September 1

Judson. *The Life of Adoniram Judson.*

September 2

Bruce, F. F. *The Spreading Flame: The Rise and Progress of Christianity from its First Beginnings to the Conversion of the English.* Grand Rapids: Eerdmans, 1958. 154–8.

Eusebius. *Ecclesiastical History.* 3:5.

Hoehner, H. W. "Chronology of the New Testament." NBD. 3rd ed. 198.

Johnson. *A History of the Jews.* 136–40.

Josephus, Flavius. *Wars of the Jews.*

Nolland, John. *Luke.* 18:35–24:53 Vol. 35c of WBC. Dallas: Word, 1993. 981–1014.

Owen. *Abraham to the Middle-East Crisis.* 153–67.

September 3

Gillies, John. *Historical Collections of Accounts of Remarkable Periods of the Success of the Gospel.* Edinburgh: Banner of Truth, 1981. 308.

Pollock. *John Wesley.*

Wood, A. Skevington. "Wesley, Charles (1707–1788)." NIDCC. 1033–4.

———. "Wesley, John (1703–1791)." NIDCC. 1034–5.

Wallace, Charles, Jr. "Like Mother, Like Son." CH. 69:18–9.

September 4

Covell, Ralph R. "Taylor, James Hudson." BDCM. 657–8.

Douglas, J. D. "Taylor, (James) Hudson." EDWM. 931.

Pollock. *Hudson and Maria.*

———. "Taylor, J(ames) Hudson (1832–1905)." NIDCC. 953.

Taylor, Dr. and Mrs. Howard. *Hudson Taylor's Spiritual Secret.* London: China Inland Mission, 1950.

September 5

Dowley, Tim, ed. *The Baker Atlas of Christian History.* Grand Rapids: Baker, 1997. 75.

Shelley. *Church History in Plain Language.* 91–107.

Wright, D. F. "Constantine the Great (c. 274/280–337)." NIDCC. 255–6.

September 6

Lender, Robert D. "Blaurock, Georg (c. 1492–1529)." NIDCC. 136–7.

Shelley. *Church History in Plain Language.* 247–51.

Thompson and Cummins. *This Day in Baptist History.* 6–7, 22–3, 50–2.

September 7

Mimkena, K. P. "Endecott, John (c. 1589–1665)." DCA. 391.

Thompson and Cummins. *This Day in Baptist History.* 275–6, 313–4, 366–8, 378–80.

September 8

Haykin. *One Heart and One Soul.*

September 9

Grubb, Norman. *Rees Howells: Intercessor.* Fort Washington: Christian Literature Crusade, 1997.

September 10

Beasley-Murray, George R. *John.* Vol. 36 of WBC. Nashville: Nelson, 1999.

Carson, D. A. *The Gospel according to John.* Leicester: Inter-Varsity, 1991.

Freeman D. "Tabernacles, Feast of." NBD. 3rd ed. 1148.

Hoehner. *Chronological Aspects of the Life of Christ.* 62.

Morris, Leon. *The Gospel according to John.* NICNT. Grand Rapids: Eerdmans, 1971.

September 11

Abanes, Richard. *End Time Visions: The Doomsday Obsession.* Nashville: Broadman and Holman, 1998. 93–105.

Alnor, William M. *Soothsayers of the Second Advent.* Old Tappan, N.J.: Revell, 1989. 15–33.

Chandler, Russell. *Doomsday: The End of the World through Time.* Ann Arbor: Servant, 1993. 273–74.

Whisenant, Edgar C. *On Borrowed Time: The Bible Dates of the 70th Week of Daniel, Armageddon and the Millennium.* Little Rock: By the author, 1988.

———. *The Rapture Rosh Hash Ana 1988 and 88 Reasons Why.* Little Rock: By the author, 1988.

Whisenant, Edgar and Greg Brewer. *The Final Shout Rapture Report 1989 1990 1991 1992 1993.* Nashville: World Bible Society, 1989.

September 12

Foster and Swanson. *The American Covenant*. xii–xviii.

Shafer, Paul W. and John Howland Snow. *The Turning of the Tides*. New Canaan: Long House, 1962.

September 13

Hexham, I. "Smith, Joseph, Jr. (1805–1844)." DCA. 1097–8.

Young, Ann-Eliza. *Wife No. 19 or The Story of a Life in Bondage Being an Exposé of Mormonism and Revealing the Sorrows, Sacrifices and Sufferings of Women in Polygamy*. Salem: Ayer, 1896.

September 14

Dinwiddie, Richard D. "Messiah: Behind the Scenes of Handel's Masterpiece." CT. 26 (December 17, 1982): 12–20.

Fuller-Maitland, John Alexander and William Barclay Squire. "Handel, George Frederick." DNB. 8:1161–75.

Kavanaugh, Patrick. *Spiritual Lives of the Great Composer*. Rev. ed. Grand Rapids: Zondervan, 1996. 26–34.

MacMillan, J. B. "Handel, George Frederic (1685–1759)." NIDCC. 450.

September 15

Edwards. *The Life and Diary of David Brainerd*.

Freundt, A. H. "Dickinson, Jonathan (1688–1747)." DCA. 355–6.

Hunsicker. *David Brainerd*.

Piper. *The Hidden Smile of God*.

September 16

Clouse, Robert G. "Torquemada, Tomás de (1420–1498)." NIDCC. 980.

Johnson, Paul. *A History of Christianity*. New York: Simon and Schuster, 1976. 306–7.

Schaff. *History of the Christian Church*. 6:533–54.

Toon, Peter. "Ferdinand V (1452–1516)." NIDCC. 372.

Underwood, T. L. "Inquisition, The." NIDCC. 511.

September 17

Alexander. "Ezekiel." EBC. 6:737–996.

McGreger, L. John. "Ezekiel." 4th ed. Leicester: Inter-Varsity, 1994. 716–44.

September 18

Aune, David E. *Revelation 1–5*. Vol. 52a of WBC. Dallas: Word, 1997.

Beale, G. K. *The Book of Revelation: A Commentary of the Greek Text*. Grand Rapids: Eerdmans, 1999.

Carroll, Scott T. "Patmos." ABD. 5:178–9.

Jones, Brian W. "Domitian." ABD. 2:221–2.

———. "Titus." ABD. 4:580–1.

Milns, R. D. "Vespasian." ABD. 4:851–3.

Toon, Peter. "Domitian, Titus Flavius (A.D. 51–96)." NIDCC. 308.

September 19

Cook, Faith. *Singing in the Fire: Christians in Adversity*. Edinburgh: Banner of Truth, 1995. 105–20.

Prentiss. *More Love to Thee*. 1–8.

September 20

MacCuish. *Luther and His Katie*.

September 21

Verhoef, Pieter A. *The Books of Haggai and Malachi*. NICOT. Grand Rapids: Eerdmans, 1987.

Wiseman, D. J. "Zerubbabel." NBD. 3rd ed. 1269–70.

September 22

Douglas, William O. *An Almanac of Liberty*. Garden City: Doubleday, 1954. 85.

Queen, Edward L., II. "Salem Witchcraft Trials." EARH. 2:581–2.

Stout, H. S. "Salem Witch Trial." DCA. 1041.

Strauss and Howe. *Generations*. 116–20.

Weinstein, Allen and Frank Otto Gatell. *Freedom and Crisis: An American History*. 3rd ed. New York: Random, 1981. 80–104.

September 23

Bendroth, Margaret. "What Wilt Thou Have Me to Do: Jeremiah Lanphier."

In *More Than Conquerors*. Edited by
Woodbridge. 336–9.

Marshall, Peter and David Manuel. *Sounding
the Trumpet*. Grand Rapids: Revell, 1997.
416–21.

Piper, John. *Desiring God: Meditations of a
Christian Hedonist*. Portland: Multnomah
Press, 1986. 148–50.

September 24

Calhoun. *Princeton Seminary*.

Kessler, Ben. "Shaping the Campus." *Princeton Alumni Weekly*. 101 (May 16, 2001):
24–31.

Piper. *God's Passion for His Glory*. 70–3.

———. *The Hidden Smile of God*. 122–57.

Sereno, Dwight. "Memoirs of Jonathan
Edwards." In *The Works of Jonathan
Edwards*. 2 vols. Edinburgh: Banner
of Truth, 1974. 1:clxxii–clxxvi.

September 25

Clouse, Robert G. "Lollards." NIDCC.
601–2.

———. "Wycliffe, John (c. 1329–1384)."
NIDCC. 1064–5.

Douglas, J. D. "Oldcastle, Sir John (Lord
Cobham) (c. 1378–1417)." NIDCC. 724.

Schaff. *History of the Christian Church*.
6:354.

Williamson. *Foxe's Book of Martyrs*. 1–44.

September 26

Perry, John. *Sgt. York: His Life, Legend
and Legacy*. Nashville: Broadman and
Holman, 1997.

September 27

Atkins, Susan. *Child of Satan, Child of God*.
Plainfield: Logos, 1977.

September 28

Towns and Porter. *The Ten Greatest Revivals
Ever*. 126–30.

September 30

Archer, Gleason L., Jr. *A Survey of Old
Testament Introduction*. Chicago: Moody,
1964.

Budrele, J. N. "Vulgate, The." NIDCC. 1024.

González, Justo L. *The Story of Christianity*.
Peabody: Hendrickson, 1999.

Metzger, Bruce M. *The Early Versions of the
New Testament*. Oxford: Clarendon,
1977. 330–62.

Schaff. *History of the Christian Church*.
3:205–14, 967–88.

Schnucker, Robert. "Jerome (Eusebius
Hieronymus) (c. 345– c. 419)." NIDCC.
528.

Unger, Merrill F. *Introductory Guide to the
Old Testament*. 2nd ed. Grand Rapids:
Zondervan, 1956. 82–114.

October 1

Hayden, R. E. "Persia." ISBE. Rev. ed.
3:776–80.

Judge, E. A. "Alexander." ZPEB. 1:97–100.

Milns, R. D. "Alexander the Great." ABD.
1:46–50.

Yamauchi, Edwin M. *Persia and the Bible*.
Grand Rapids: Baker, 1996.

Thompson, J. E. H. "Alexander the Great."
ISBE. Rev. ed. 1:87–9.

October 2

Kidner. *Ezra and Nehemiah*. TOTC.

Kitchen. "Geshem." NBD. 3rd ed. 406.

Wright, J. S. "Nehemiah." NBD. 3rd ed.
812–3.

———. "Sanballat." NBD. 3rd ed. 1057.

October 3

Ryden. *The Story of Christian Hymnody*.
188–93.

Smith and Carlson. *Great Christian Hymn
Writers*. 145–50.

October 4

Edwards. *The Life and Diary of David
Brainerd*.

Hope, N. V. "Brainerd, David (1718–1747)."
WWCH. 101–2.

Piper, *The Hidden Smile of God*. 122–59.

Thornbury, John. "David Brainerd." In
Five Pioneer Missionaries. Edinburgh:
Banner of Truth, 1965. 13–91.

October 5

Van Braght. *The Bloody Theater*. 979–91.

October 6

"Did You Know?" CH. 25:1.

Maas, David. "The Life and Times of D. L. Moody." CH. 25:5–11.

Marsden, G. M. "Moody, D. L. (Dwight Lyman)." WWCH. 483–5.

Moody. *The Life of D. L. Moody.*

Pollock. *Moody without Sankey.*

October 7

Goforth, Rosalind. *Jonathan Goforth.* Minneapolis: Bethany, 1986.

Kane, H. "Goforth, Jonathan (1859–1936)." WWCH. 227.

Rennie, I. S. "Goforth, Jonathan (1859–1936)." DCA. 485.

October 8

Fensham. *The Books of Ezra and Nehemiah.* NICOT.

Kidner. *Ezra and Nehemiah.* TOTC.

Williamson, H. G. M. "Nehemiah." NBC. 4th ed.

October 9

Fensham. *The Books of Ezra and Nehemiah.* NICOT.

Kidner. *Ezra and Nehemiah.* TOTC.

Williamson. "Nehemiah." NBC. 4th ed.

Jewitt, P. "Atonement." ZPEB. 1:408–13.

October 10

"Did You Know?" CH. 20:4.

Harvey, Bonnie C. *Charles Finney: Apostle of Revival.* Uhrichsville: Barbour, 1999.

Johnson, James E. "Charles Grandison Finney: Father of American Revivalism." CH. 20:6–9.

Shelley, Bruce L. "Finney, Charles G(randison) (1792–1875)." NIDCC. 376.

Rosell, G. M. "Finney, Charles Grandison." 439–40.

October 11

Marshall and Manuel. *The Light and the Glory.* 29–48.

Morison, Samuel Eliot. *Christopher Columbus, Mariner.* New York: Meridian, 1955.

October 12

Archer, Gleason L., Jr. "Daniel." EBC. 7:68–77.

October 13

Goforth. *Jonathan Goforth.*

October 14

Durant. *The Reformation.* 136–42, 631–7.

Edwards. *God's Outlaw.*

Johnstone. *Operation World.* 5th ed. 114–5.

Smith. *The Age of the Reformation.* 234–46.

October 15

Aylward, Gladys. *The Small Woman of the Inn of the Sixth Happiness.* Chicago: Moody, 1970.

Covell, Ralph R. "Aylward, Gladys." BDCM. 35.

Douglas, J. D. "Aylward, Gladys." EDWM. 101.

Norman, J. G. G. "Aylward, Gladys (c. 1900–1970)." NIDCC. 93.

Tucker. *From Jerusalem to Irian Jaya.* 249–54.

Wellman, Sam. *Gladys Aylward: Missionary to China.* Uhrichsville: Barbour, 1998.

October 16

Atkinson, James. *The Great Light: Luther and the Reformation.* Vol. 4 of *The Advance of Christianity through the Centuries.* Edited by F. F. Bruce. Grand Rapids: Eerdmans, 1968. 193–221.

Breward, I. "Cranmer, Thomas." WWCH. 179–80.

Durant. *The Reformation.* 523–601.

Petty, P. W. "Edward VI (1537–1553)." NIDCC. 333–4.

Pollard, Noel S. "Cranmer, Thomas (1489–1556)." NIDCC. 269–70.

Steer. *Guarding the Holy Fire.* 22–40.

Toon, P. "Latimer, Hugh." WWCH. 413.

———. "Mary Tudor." WWCH. 460–1.

———. "Ridley, Nicholas." WWCH. 589–90.

Williamson. *Foxe's Book of Martyrs.* 290–315.

October 17

Baldwin. *Haggai, Zechariah, Malachi.* TOTC.

October 18

Durant, Will and Ariel. *The Age of Louis XIV: A History of European Civilization in the Period of Pascal, Molière, Cromwell, Milton, Peter the Great, Newton, and Spinoza.* Vol. 8 of *The Story of Civilization.* New York: Simon and Schuster, 1963. 69–75.

Hope, N. V. "Henry IV." WWCH. 311–2.

Johnstone. *Operation World.* 5th ed. 224–7.

Langer, William. *An Encyclopedia of World History: Ancient, Medieval and Modern, Chronologically Arranged.* Rev. ed. Edinburgh: Harrap, 1948. 443.

Linder, Robert D. "Henry IV of France (1553–1610)." NIDCC. 460–1.

Norman, J. G. G. "Nantes, Edict of (1598)." NIDCC. 693–4.

Schlessinger, Arthur M., Jr., ed. *The Almanac of American History.* Rev. ed. New York: Barnes and Noble, 1993. 65.

October 19

Van Braght. *The Bloody Theater.* 588–90.

October 20

Pollock. *John Wesley.* 178–85.

October 21

Bergman, Susan. "The Shadow of the Martyrs." CT. 40 (August 12, 1996): 24.

Hefley and Hefley. *By Their Blood.* 515–36.

Tucker, Ruth. "Carlson, Paul." BDCM. 116.

———. *From Jerusalem to Irian Jaya.* 425–9.

October 22

Alexander. *The Life of Archibald Alexander.*

Calhoun. *Princeton Seminary.*

Hope, N. V. "Alexander, Archibald." WWCH. 18.

October 23

Whitefield. *George Whitefield's Journals.* 560–1. Reprinted from Cole, Nathan. "Spiritual Travels." *The William and Mary Quarterly.* 3rd series 7 (1950): 590–1.

October 24

Calhoun. *Princeton Seminary.*

Hornerk, Norman A. "Nassau, Robert Hamill." BDCM. 486–7.

Nichols, Robert Hastings. "Nassau, Robert Hamill." DAB. 13:390–1.

October 25

Wyrtzen, David. "Words of Life: Jack Wyrtzen and Radio Ministry." In *More Than Conquerors.* Edited by Woodbridge. 169–73.

October 26

Durant. *Caesar and Christ.* 653–64.

"Constantine the Great." EC. 3:155–6.

Eusebius. *Ecclesiastical History.* 9:9.

Frend. *The Rise of Christianity.* 473–515.

Hicks, C. "Constantine the Great." WWCH. 172–3.

Wordsworth, J. "Constantius I." DCB. 203–12.

Wright, D. F. "Constantine the Great (c. 274–337)." NIDCC. 255–6.

October 27

Dorsett, L. W. "Sunday, William (Billy) Ashley (1862–1935)." DCA. 1145–6.

Ellis, William T. *Billy Sunday: The Man and His Message.* Philadelphia: Universal, 1914.

Hannah, John. "Acrobatic Evangelist: Billy Sunday." In *More Than Conquerors.* Edited by Woodbridge. 152–5.

Rowdon, Howard R. "Sunday, William Ashley ("Billy") (1862–1935)." NIDCC. 940.

Schuster, R. D. "Sunday, William ("Billy") Ashley." WWCH. 647–8.

October 28

Ward, W. Reginald and Richard P. Heitenrater, eds. *The Works of John Wesley.* Nashville: Abingdon, 1991. 20:252–60.

October 29

Kuyper, Abraham. "Confidentially." In *Abraham Kuyper: A Centennial Reader.* Edited by James D. Bratt. Grand Rapids: Eerdmans, 1998. 45–61.

Vandenberg, Frank. *Abraham Kuyper.* Grand Rapids: Eerdmans, 1966.

Veltman, R. "Kuyper, Abraham." WWCH. 406–7.

October 30

Angel, G. T. D. "Chalcedon, Council of (451)." NIDCC. 208–9.

Clouse, Robert G. "Leo II, The Great, St. (c. 400–461)." NIDCC. 590.

Faulkner, Barbara L. "Eastern Orthodox Church." NIDCC. 322–5.

Shelley. *Church History in Plain Language.* 132–51.

October 31

Baltzer, Klaus. *The Covenant Formulary: In Old Testament, Jewish, and Early Christian Writings.* Oxford: Blackwell, 1971. 43–7.

November 1

Bruce, F. F. "Cruden, Alexander." DSCHT. 225.

Clouse, Robert G. "Cruden, Alexander (1699–1770)." NIDCC. 273.

"Cruden, Alexander." NSHERK. 3:314–5.

"Cruden, Alexander." ODCC. 3rd ed. 435.

Macray, William Dunn. "Cruden, Alexander (1701–1770)." DNB. 5:249–51.

November 2

Johnson, Paul. *A History of the Jews.* 423–31.

Pugh, Martin. "Balfour, Arthur James." OCBH. 75.

———. "Lloyd George, David." OCBH. 585.

November 3

Conforti, J. "Brainerd, David (1718–1747)." DCA. 181–2.

Edwards. *The Life and Diary of David Brainerd.*

Norman, J. G. G. "Brainerd, David (1718–1747)." NIDCC. 151–2.

November 4

Moule, Handley. *Charles Simeon: Pastor of a Generation.* Ross-Shire: Christian Focus, 1997.

November 5

Armstrong, Brian G. "William III (1650–1702)." NIDCC. 1048.

Brown, K. M. "Covenanters." DSCHT. 218–9.

Cairns, Earle E. *Christianity through the Centuries: A History of the Christian Church.* 3rd ed. Grand Rapids: Zondervan, 1958.

Charley, J. W. "Charles II (1630–1685)." NIDCC. 212–3.

Petty, P. W. "Cromwell, Oliver (1599–1658)." NIDCC. 271.

Sanderson. *History of England and the British Empire.*

Sellers, Ian. "Uniformity, Acts of." NIDCC. 995.

November 6

Pollock. *Moody without Sankey.* 229–32.

November 7

Shelley, Bruce L. "Stearns, Shubal (1706–1771)." DCA. 1131.

Spivey, J. T. "Separate Baptists." DCA. 1073.

Thompson and Cummins. *This Day in Baptist History.* 40–1, 421–3, 483–4, 486–8, 515–7.

November 8

Buss, D. G. "Griffin, Edward Dorr (1770–1837)." DCA. 500.

Sprague. *The Life and Sermons of Edward D. Griffin.*

November 9

Whitefield, George. *George Whitefield's Journals.*

November 10

Hillerbrand, Hans, ed. *The Reformation: A Narrative History Related by Contemporary Observers and Participants.* Grand Rapids: Baker, 1978. 27–8.

Meyer, Carl S. "Luther, Martin (1483–1546)." NIDCC. 609–11.

Schaff. *History of the Christian Church.* 7:105–45.

November 11

Fleming. *One Small Candle.* 1–112.

Marshall and Manuel. *The Light and the Glory*. 106–21.

Williams, D. R. "Pilgrims." DCA. 908.

November 12

Pollock. *The Cambridge Seven*. 35–41.

———. *Moody without Sankey*. 229–37.

November 13

Payne, Robert. "The Dark Heart Filled with Light." CH. 67:10–7.

Shelley. *Church History in Plain Language*. 140–7.

Wright, D. F. "Augustine of Hippo (354–430)." NIDCC. 86–8.

November 14

Pollard, Arthur. "Whitefield, George (1714–1770)." NIDCC. 1043–4.

Stout, H. S. "Whitefield, George (1715–1770)." DCA. 1251–3.

Whitefield. *George Whitefield's Journals*. 155–80.

November 15

McCasland, David. *Oswald Chambers: Abandoned to God*. Grand Rapids: Discovery House, 1993.

Norman, J. G. G. "Chambers, Oswald (1874–1917)." NIDCC. 210.

Taylor, J. "Chambers, Oswald (1874–1917)." DSCHT. 161.

Temple and Twitchell. *People Who Shaped the Church*. 57–62.

November 16

Clouse, Robert C. "Thirty Years' War (1618–48)." NIDCC. 970.

Ryden. *The Story of Christian Hymnody*. 91–2.

November 17

Norman, J. G. G. "Smith, Rodney ("Gipsy") (1860–1947)." NIDCC. 910–1.

Peterson, R. L. "Smith, Rodney ("Gipsy") (1860–1947)." DCA. 1099.

Smith, Gipsy. *Gipsy Smith: His Life and Work*. New York: Revell, 1913. 17–83.

November 18

Calhoun. *Princeton Seminary*. 2:118, 315–6.

Craig, Samuel G., ed. "Benjamin B. Warfield." In *Biblical and Theological Studies* by Benjamin Breckinridge Warfield. Philadelphia: Presbyterian and Reformed, 1952. xi–xlviii.

Hoffecker, W. A. "Warfield, Benjamin Breckinridge (1851–1921)." DCA. 1234–5.

Lindsell, Harold. "Warfield B(enjamin) B(reckinridge) (1851–1921)." NIDCC. 1030.

Nicole, Roger. "B. B. Warfield and the Calvinistic Revival." In *Great Leaders of the Christian Church*. Edited by Woodbridge. 343–6.

Piper, John. *Future Grace*. Sisters, Ore. Multnomah, 1995. 176.

November 19

"Havelock, Sir Henry." NSHERK. 4:172.

Pollock, John. *Way to Glory: The Life of Havelock of Lucknow*. Ross-Shire: Christian Focus, 1996.

Vetch, Robert Hamilton. "Havelock, Sir Henry (1795–1857)." DNB. 9:174–9.

November 20

Crosby, Fanny. *An Autobiography*. Grand Rapids: Baker, 1986.

Harvey, Bonnie C. *Fanny Crosby*. Minneapolis: Bethany, 1999.

Norman, J. G. G. "Crosby, Fanny (Mrs. F. J. Van Alstyne) (1823–1915)." NIDCC. 272.

Ryden. *The Story of Christian Hymnody*. 552–5.

Smith and Carlson. *Great Christian Hymn Writers*. 59–64.

Stanislaw, R. J. "Crosby (Van Alstyne), Fanny Jane (1820–1915)." DCA. 329.

———. "To God Be the Glory: Fanny Crosby." In *More Than Conquerors*. Edited by Woodbridge. 108–11.

November 21

Coad. *A History of the Brethren Movement*. 37–57.

Müller, George. *A Narrative of Some of the Lord's Dealings with George Müller*. 7th ed. London: Nisbet, 1869. 143–307.

Norman, J. G. G. "Müller, George (1805–1896)." NIDCC. 683.

November 22
Griffin, William. "C. S. Lewis: Scholar Pilgrim." In *More Than Conquerors.* Edited by Woodbridge. 118–26.

Ostlling, Joan. "Lewis, C(live) S(taples) (1898–1963)." NIDCC. 593–4.

Temple and Twitchell. *People Who Shaped the Church.* 168–75.

November 23
Durant. *The Reformation.* 607–20.

Greaves, Richard N. "Knox, John (c. 1514–1572)." NIDCC. 570–1.

Howie. *The Scots Worthies.* 48–66.

Kyle, R. G. "Knox, John." DSCHT. 465–6.

M'Crie, Thomas. *The Life of John Knox.* Glasgow: Free Presbyterian, 1991.

Shelley. *Church History in Plain Language.* 280–1.

November 24
Blackburn, William M. *Ulrich Zwingli: The Patriotic Reformer, A History.* Philadelphia: Presbyterian, 1868.

Clouse, Robert G. "Oecolampadius (1482–1531)." NIDCC. 722–3.

Durant. *The Reformation.* 410–4.

Schaff. *History of the Christian Church.* 8:107–16.

November 25
Gariepy. *Songs in the Night.* 67–9.

Robinson. *Annotations upon Popular Hymns.* 487–8.

Ryden. *The Story of Christian Hymnody.* 268–73.

Smith and Carlson. *Great Christian Hymn Writers.* 167–9.

November 26
Cook, Faith. *William Grimshaw of Haworth.* Edinburgh: Banner of Truth, 1997.

Pollock, John C. "Grimshaw, William (1708–1763)." NIDCC. 438.

November 27
Owen. *Abraham to the Middle-East Crisis.* 184–246.

Schaff. *History of the Christian Church.* 5:211–95.

November 28
Fudge, Thomas A. "To Build a Fire." CH. 68:10–8.

Schaff. *History of the Christian Church.* 6:358–88.

Shelley, Bruce L. "A Pastor's Heart." CH. 68:30–2.

Spinka, Matthew. "Hus, Jan (1373–1415)." NIDCC. 492–3.

November 29
Burrows, Millar. *The Dead Sea Scrolls.* New York: Viking, 1955.

Harrison, R. K. "Dead Sea Scrolls." ZPEB. 2:53–68.

La Sor, W. S. *Dead Sea Scrolls.* ISBE. Rev. ed. 1:883–97.

———. *The Dead Sea Scrolls and the Christian Faith.* Chicago: Moody, 1956.

Milik, J. T. *Ten Years of Discovery in the Wilderness.* London: SCM, 1959.

Pate, C. Marvin. *Communities of the Last Days: The Dead Sea Scrolls, the New Testament and the Story of Israel.* Downers Grove: InterVarsity, 2000. 29–51.

November 30
Moody. *The Life of Dwight L. Moody.*

Pollock. *Moody without Sankey.*

Weber, T. P. "Moody, (D)wight (L)yman (1837–1899)." DCA. 768–9.

December 1
Brown and Norton. *The One Year Book of Hymns.*

Morgan. *On This Day.*

December 2
Taylor and Taylor. *Hudson Taylor in Early Years.*

December 3
Fuchida, Mitsuo. "From Pearl Harbor to Calvary." Online: http://www.bli.org/pearlharbor/printmitsuo.htm.

Prange, Gordon W. *God's Samurai.* New York: Brassey's, 1990.

December 4
Purves. *Fair Sunshine.* 87–95.

December 5
Hefley and Hefley. *By Their Blood.* 595–6.
Scott, Lindy. "Gardiner, Allen Francis."
EDWM. 384–5.
Walls, Andrew F. "Gardiner, Allen Francis."
BDCM. 235–6.

December 6
Hefley and Hefley. *By Their Blood.* 57–60,
109, 524.
Miller, Kevin. "John and Betty Stam." CH.
52:37.
Taylor, Mrs. Howard. *The Triumph of John
and Betty Stam.* Philadelphia: China
Inland Mission, 1952.
Tucker. *From Jerusalem to Irian Jaya.*
421–4.

December 7
Zechariah 7:5–8:22.

December 8
Andrews, John S. "Hymns and Church
Music." In *Eerdmans Handbook to the
History of Christianity.* Edited by Tim
Dowley. Grand Rapids: Eerdmans, 1977.
426.
Baxter, Richard. *Richard Baxter.* Ross-Shire:
Christian Focus, 1998.

December 9
Meyer, Wilhelm Joseph. "Zwingli, Ulrich."
CE. 15:772–5.
Schaff. *History of the Christian Church.*
8:205–14.

December 10
Baird. *History of the Rise of the Huguenots
of France.* 1:53–4.
Cottret, Bernard. *Calvin.* Grand Rapids:
Eerdmans, 1995. 73–7.
McGrath, Alister E. *A Life of John Calvin.*
Oxford: Blackwood, 1990. 64–7.

December 11
Fleming. *One Small Candle.*
Marshall and Manuel. *The Light and the
Glory.*

December 12
Allen, Catherine B. *The New Lottie Moon
Story.* 2nd ed. Birmingham: Women's
Missionary Union, 1997.
Estep, W. R. "A Thousand Lives for
China: Lottie Moon." In *More Than
Conquerors.* Edited by Woodbridge.
56–62.
Pfester, Lauren. "Moon, Charlotte
("Lottie"). EDWM. 658.
Thompson and Cummins. *This Day in Bap-
tist History.* 537–9.
Tucker, R. A. "Moon, Charlotte ("Lottie")
Diggs (1840–1912)." DCA. 769–70.

December 13
"Boniface VIII." ODP. 206–8.
Brusher, Joseph S. *Popes through the Ages.*
Rev. ed. Princeton: Van Nostrand, 1964.
380–2.
"Celestine V, St." PE. 76–7.
"Celestine V, St. Peter." ODP. 206–8.
De Rosa, Peter. *Vicars of Christ.* New York:
Crown, 1988. 75–7.

December 14
Guest, William. *P. P. Bliss, Songwriter.* Bel-
fast: Ambassador, 1877.
Ryden. *The Story of Christian Hymnody.*

December 15
Bull. *John Newton.*
Cecil. *The Life of John Newton.*

December 16
Hoehner, H. W. "Maccabees." ISBE. Rev.
ed. 3:196–200.
Waltke, B. W. "Antiochus IV Epiphanes."
ISBE. Rev. ed. 1:145–6.

December 17
Ryle. *Light from Old Times.* 48–51.
Williamson. *Foxe's Book of Martyrs.*
316–21.

December 18
Carson. *The Gospel according to John.*
390–400.
Hoehner. *Chronological Aspects of the Life
of Christ.*

December 19

Elson, Henry William. *History of the United States of America*. New York: Macmillan, 1945.

Marshall and Manuel. *The Light and the Glory*.

December 20

Lindberg, Alfred E. *The Blind Swedish Evangel: Rev. A. J. Freeman*. Chicago: Mortenson, n.d.

December 21

Bull. *John Newton*.

December 22

Purves. *Fair Sunshine*. 25–35.
Howie. *The Scots Worthies*. 356–63.

December 23

Elliot. *Through Gates of Splendor*.

December 24

Durschmied, Erik. *The Weather Factor: How Nature Has Changed History*. New York: Arcade, 2000. 237–71.

December 25

Johnson, Paul. *Modern Times*. Rev. ed. New York: Collins, 1991.

December 26

Moody. *The Life of Dwight L. Moody*.

December 27

Atkinson. *The Great Light*. 129–51.
"Did You Know?" CH. 3. no. 1. 6.

December 28

Hefley and Hefley. *By Their Blood*. 176–7.

December 29

Judson. *The Life of Adoniram Judson*.

December 30

Johnson. *A History of the Jews*. 136–40.
Jones, Brian W. "Titus." ABD. 6:580–1.
Milns, R. D. "Vespasian." ABD. 6:851–3.
Owen. *Abraham to the Middle-East Crisis*. 153–66.
Schürer, Emil. *A History of the Jewish People in the Time of Jesus*. New York: Schocken, 1961. 245–75.
"Titus." DRE. 421–2.
"Vespasian." DRE. 443–4.

December 31

Grant, George and Wilbur Gregory. *The Christian Almanac*. Nashville: Cumberland, 2000. 765.
Holmes, A. F. "Boyle, Robert." WWCH. 100.
Hunter, Michael. "The Life and Thought of Robert Boyle." Online: http://bbk.ac.uk/Boyle/biog.html.

NOTES

Introduction

1. D. R. Wood et al., eds. "Chronology of the New Testament," in *New Bible Dictionary,* 3rd ed. (Downers Grove, Ill.: InterVarsity Press, 1996), 193–9.

January

1. See November 8.
2. See August 16 and February 11.
3. See March 16.
4. See July 31, August 8, September 17, August 14, March 3, April 28.
5. See July 18.
6. See December 23.
7. See June 11.
8. See August 11.
9. See July 8 and February 13.
10. See also August 13.
11. See October 27.
12. See June 18.
13. See October 16.
14. See June 28.
15. See May 19.
16. See January 13.
17. See July 2.
18. See March 20.
19. See July 6.
20. See February 12.
21. See March 4.
22. See April 7.
23. See February 8.
24. See May 28 and June 2, 3, 4.
25. See July 27.
26. See July 22.
27. See November 13.
28. See November 10, April 17, September 20, February 22.

February

1. See July 20, December 2, July 13, September 4, July 23, 30.
2. See July 6.
3. See March 4.
4. See November 21.
5. See also May 22, March 1.
6. See March 9.
7. See January 25.
8. See February 10, May 5, 20, 26, September 3, October 20, March 2.
9. See also February 9, May 5, 20, 26, September 3, October 20, March 2.
10. See also January 6, August 16.
11. See May 21.
12. See June 28.
13. See December 9.
14. See July 6.
15. See March 4.
16. See July 29.
17. See September 24.
18. See also July 8.
19. See July 12, September 15, November 3, March 23, October 4.
20. See October 12, March 12.
21. See September 21, October 17.
22. See also November 18.
23. See January 1.
24. See July 27.
25. See also May 7.
26. See July 11.
27. See November 10, April 17, September 20.
28. See April 21.
29. See October 26.
30. See September 6.
31. See August 25.
32. See November 10, April 17, September 20, February 22.
33. See June 18.

March

1. See also February 7, May 22.
2. See July 26.
3. See November 25.
4. See February 9, May 5, 20, 26, September 3, October 20, February 10.
5. See March 16.
6. See July 18.
7. See also July 31, August 8, September 17, August 14, January 8, April 28.

8. See June 28.
9. See July 29, March 24.
10. See July 6.
11. See February 12.
12. See January 22.
13. See October 16.
14. Compare with July 27.
15. See May 5.
16. See February 9, May 5, 20, 26, September 3, October 20, February 10, March 2.
17. See also November 14, April 18, October 23, November 9, September 29.
18. See November 20.
19. See December 16.
20. See May 31, June 24.
21. See September 21, October 17.
22. See February 15, December 7.
23. See July 18.
24. See July 18.
25. See February 7, May 22, March 1.
26. See November 12.
27. See July 20.
28. See January 21.
29. See also December 26.
30. See also December 15, 21.
31. See also November 11, December 11.
32. See July 12, September 15, November 3, October 4.
33. See also February 7, May 22, March 1.
34. See August 10.
35. See August 28.
36. See July 6.
37. See March 4.
38. See August 4.
39. See October 8, 9.
40. See also April 29, 7.
41. See March 29.
42. See April 3. *The text of this devotion is taken directly from John II, the New Living Translation Wheaton, Ill.: Tyndale House, 1996.
43. See also May 29, April 29, 7, December 18, March 28, 30–31, September 11, April 1–5, May 14.
44. See also May 29, April 29, 7, December 18, March 28–29, 31, September 11, April 1–5, May 14.

45. See April 1, September 2, December 30.
46. See also May 29, April 29, 7, December 18, March 28–30, September 11, April 1–5, May 14.

April

1. See also May 29, April 29, 7, December 18, March 28–31, September 11, April 2–5, 29, May 14.
2. See also September 2 and December 30.
3. See also May 29, December 18, March 28–31, Sepember 11, April 1, 3–5, May 14.
4. See also April 29, 7.
5. See also April 3.
6. See also May 29, April 29, 7, December 18, March 28–31, September 11, April 1, 4–5, May 14.
7. See also April 2.
8. See also May 29, April 29, 7, December 18, March 28–31, September 11, April 1–3, 5, May 14.
9. See April 5.
10. See also May 29, April 29, 7, September 11, December 18, May 28-31, April 1-3, May 14.
11. See also April 4.
12. See also September 13.
13. See also May 29, December 18, March 28–31, September 11, April 1, 3–5, May 14.
14. See also April 29, 2.
15. See also April 11, October 6, June 17, May 21, November 6, 12, 30, December 26.
16. See also July 20.
17. See also October 6, June 17, May 21, November 6, 12, 30, December 26, April 8.
18. See also June 6, April 26, July 10, September 1, December 29.
19. See also March 24.
20. See also November 10, September 20, February 22.
21. See also May 5, March 6, November 14, October 23, November 9, September 29.
22. See also June 16.
23. See also March 15.

788

24. See also January 25.
25. See also January 3, February 23.
26. See also October 26.
27. See also December 10.
28. See also April 25.
29. See also March 16, July 18.
30. See also October 12.
31. See also October 1, June 10.
32. See also December 16.
33. See also March 9.
34. See also June 23, 22.
35. See also December 10, April 22.
36. See also June 6, July 10, September 1, December 29, April 12.
37. See also March 16.
38. See also July 31, August 8, September 17, August 14, January 8, March 3.
39. See also July 18.
40. See also May 29, September 11, December 18, March 28–31, April 1–5, May 14.
41. See also April 7, 2.

May
1. See July 19.
2. See May 20.
3. See February 9, May 20, 26, September 3, October 20, February 10, March 2.
4. See March 6, November 14, April 18, October 23, November 9, September 29.
5. See March 6, November 14, April 18, October 23, November 9, September 29.
6. See July 12, September 15, November 3, March 23, October 4.
7. See September 24.
8. See also February 20.
9. See December 3.
10. See November 16.
11. See July 2.
12. See July 27.
13. See June 30.
14. See February 17.
15. See May 29, April 29, 7, 13, September 11, December 19, March 28–31, April 1–5, May 14.
16. See April 1.
17. See September 2.
18. See November 2.
19. See August 5.

20. See November 26.
21. See May 5, March 6, November 14, April 18, October 23, November 9, September 29.
22. See February 9, May 5, 20, 26, September 3, October 20, February 10, March 2.
23. See August 21.
24. See February 22.
25. See June 28.
26. See October 16.
27. See October 16.
28. See February 9, May 26, September 3, October 20, February 10, March 2.
29. See May 5, March 6, November 14, April 18, October 23, November 9, September 29.
30. See May 5.
31. See July 19.
32. See April 11, October 6, June 17, November 6, 12, 30, December 26.
33. See also February 7 and March 1.
34. See May 14.
35. See October 22, 24.
36. See July 19.
37. See May 20.
38. See also February 9, May 5, 20, September 3, October 20, February 10, March 2.
39. See also June 2, 3, 4.
40. See November 28.
41. See March 11, June 24.

June
1. See March 20.
2. See July 2.
3. See also May 28, June 3, 4.
4. See also May 28, June 2, 4.
5. See also May 28, June 2, 3.
6. See February 7, May 22, March 1.
7. See also June 29, December 29, April 26, July 10, September 1, April 12.
8. See also April 1.
9. See September 2, December 30.
10. See October 1.
11. See December 23 and January 9.
12. See also February 9, May 20, 26, September 3, October 20, February 10, March 2.

13. See November 27.
14. See also April 19.
15. See also April 11, October 6, May 21, November 6, 12, 30, December 26.
16. See also May 21.
17. See October 14.
18. See June 28.
19. See November 5.
20. See also June 23, April 24.
21. See June 22, April 24.
22. See also May 31, March 11.
23. See September 8.
24. See October 26.
25. See March 4.
26. See October 16.
27. See May 19.
28. See June 6, December 29, April 26, July 10, September 1, April 12.

July

1. See May 5, March 6, November 14, April 18, October 23, November 9, September 29.
2. See December 8.
3. See November 25.
4. See February 9, May 5, 20, 26, September 3, October 20, February 10, March 2.
5. See April 22, April 25.
6. See June 28.
7. See October 16.
8. See November 10, April 17, September 20, February 22.
9. See April 22, 25.
10. See December 27.
11. See September 6.
12. See February 13.
13. See June 6, December 29, April 26, 12.
14. See September 1.
15. See February 21.
16. See also September 15, November 3, March 23, October 4.
17. See July 8, February 13.
18. See also February 1, July 20, December 2, September 4, July 23, 30.
19. See July 6.
20. See March 4.
21. See October 16.
22. See November 25.

23. See March 16 and October 12.
24. See November 28.
25. See February 1, December 2, July 13, September 4, July 23, 30.
26. See February 3.
27. See July 27.
28. See July 27.
29. See February 1, July 20, December 2, July 13, September 4, July 30.
30. See March 21, December 15, 21.
31. See July 22.
32. See March 4.
33. See February 1, July 20, December 2, July 13, September 4, July 23.
34. See also August 8, September 17, August 14, January 8, March 3, April 28.

August

1. See also October 11.
2. See also August 30.
3. See also March 12, March 27, October 2, 8–9, 31.
4. See also May 16.
5. See February 9, May 5, 20, 26, September 3, February 10, March 2.
6. See also October 20.
7. See also July 31, September 17, August 14, March 3, January 8, April 28.
8. See May 5, 20.
9. See March 10.
10. See March 1.
11. See November 22.
12. See September 19.
13. See January 16.
14. See also July 31, August 8, September 17, March 3, January 8, April 28.
15. See also January 6, February 11.
16. See October 18.
17. See October 22, May 25, October 24.
18. See also May 10, 18.
19. See also June 30.
20. See August 10.
21. See also October 18.
22. See August 6.
23. See February 27.
24. See March 25.
25. See also August 3.
26. See July 6.

27. See February 12.
28. See March 4.
29. See June 28.

September
1. See also June 6, December 29, April 26, July 10, April 12.
2. See also April 1.
3. See December 30.
4. See February 9, May 5, 20, 26, October 20, February 10, March 2.
5. See also February 1, July 20, December 2, July 13, 23, 30.
6. See October 26.
7. See June 27.
8. See December 27.
9. See May 5, March 6, November 14, April 18, October 23, November 9, September 29.
10. See August 11.
11. See March 21, December 15, 21.
12. See May 31, March 11, June 24.
13. See April 29, 7, December 18, March 28-31, April 1-5, May 14.
14. See August 26.
15. See July 21.
16. See April 6.
17. See February 9, May 5, 20, 26, September 3, October 20, February 10, March 2.
18. See November 3, March 23, October 4.
19. See July 12.
20. See May 5, March 6, November 14, April 18, October 23, November 9, September 29.
21. See September 24.
22. See October 11.
23. See August 2.
24. See also July 31, August 8, 14, March 3, January 8, April 28.
25. See March 16.
26. See July 18.
27. See December 30 and September 2.
28. See August 13 and January 16.
29. See November 10, April 17, February 22.
30. See October 17, December 18, March 12.
31. See June 12.
32. See July 12, November 3, March 23, October 4.

33. See September 15.
34. See May 6.
35. See July 8, February 13.
36. See November 5.
37. See November 28.
38. See July 19.
39. See May 5, March 6, November 14, April 18, October 23, November 9.

October
1. See October 12.
2. See June 10.
3. See October 8, 9, 31.
4. See July 12, September 15, November 3, March 23.
5. See July 8 and February 13.
6. See February 9, May 5, 20, 26, September 3, October 20, February 10, March 2.
7. See May 31, March 11, June 24.
8. See October 7.
9. See December 23, January 9.
10. See also April 11, June 17, May 21, November 6, 12, 30, December 26.
11. See October 13.
12. See October 2.
13. See also October 9.
14. See October 8.
15. See also September 16.
16. See August 2.
17. See July 18.
18. See October 2.
19. See October 7.
20. See August 3.
21. See April 22, 25.
22. See December 27.
23. See June 18.
24. See November 10, April 17, September 20, February 22.
25. See September 16.
26. See June 28.
27. See June 18.
28. See July 6.
29. See March 4.
30. See July 15.
31. See also September 21, February 15, March 12.
32. See April 28.
33. See August 24.

34. See September 6.
35. See also February 9, May 5, 20, 26, September 3, February 10, March 2.
36. See also August 7.
37. See also May 25, October 24.
38. See also May 5, March 6, November 14, April 18, November 9, September 29.
39. See October 22 and May 25.
40. See also January 19.
41. See October 26.
42. See also October 2, 8–9.

November
1. See May 15.
2. See July 12, September 15, March 23, October 4.
3. See July 2.
4. See April 11, October 6, June 17, November 12, 30, December 29.
5. See May 21.
6. See May 5, March 6, November 14, April 18, November 9, September 29.
7. See also January 2.
8. See May 5, March 6, November 14, April 18, October 23, November 9, September 29.
9. See May 5, March 6, November 14, April 18, October 23, September 29.
10. See April 17, September 20, February 22.
11. See December 11, March 22.
12. See April 11, October 6, June 17, May 21, November 6, 30, December 26.
13. See April 22, 25.
14. See May 5.
15. See also March 6, April 18, October 23, November 9, September 29.
16. See January 6, August 16, February 11.
17. See February 16.
18. See March 21, December 15, 21.
19. See also February 6.
20. See July 6.
21. See March 4.
22. See April 22, April 25.
23. See March 24.
24. See November 10, April 17, September 20, February 22.
25. See April 22, April 25.
26. See December 27.

27. See also May 17.
28. See also June 14.
29. See also May 30.
30. See July 19.
31. See September 3, February 9, May 5, 20, 26, September 3, October 20, February 10, March 2.
32. See April 11, October 6, June 17, May 21, November 6, 12, December 26.

December
1. See April 11, October 6, June 17, May 21, November 6, 12, 30, December 26, April 8.
2. See July 20.
3. See February 1, July 13, September 4, July 23, 30.
4. See May 27, June 1, July 22, January 26, July 27, March 5, May 9, 1, 11, December 22, February 17.
5. See July 20.
6. See February 15.
7. See December 27.
8. See November 10, April 17, September 20, February 22.
9. See March 4.
10. See February 12.
11. See December 10, April 22, 25.
12. See December 10, April 22, 25.
13. See November 10, April 17, September 20, February 22.
14. See December 27.
15. See also January 13.
16. See November 11.
17. See also March 22.
18. See April 11, October 6, June 17, May 21, November 6, 12, 30, December 26, April 8.
19. See March 21. See also December 21.
20. See October 1, June 10.
21. See also March 9.
22. See March 4.
23. See June 28.
24. See March 9.
25. See December 16.
26. See also May 29, April 29, April 7, March 28–31, September 11, April 1–5, May 14.

27. See March 24.
28. See March 21.
29. See also December 15.
30. See also January 9 and June 11.
31. See also April 11, October 6, June 17, May 21, November 6, 12, 30, April 8.

32. See June 6, April 26, July 10, September 1, April 12.
33. See January 25.
34. See June 9.
35. See September 2, April 1.

INDEX

ABOUT THE AUTHORS

MIKE AND SHARON RUSTEN have successfully partnered together in marriage, parenting, business and now, in their newest collaboration, as coauthors.

Mike spent years as a perpetual student, receiving a B.A. from Princeton University, an M.A. from the University of Minnesota, an M.Div. from Westminster Theological Seminary (Philadelphia. a Th.M. from Trinity Evangelical Divinity School, and a Ph.D. from New York University. He also attended Dallas Theological Seminary and, with Sharon, the American Institute of Holy Land Studies, now Jerusalem University College. Sharon attended Beaver College and Lake Forest College and received a B.A. from the University of Minnesota. The Rustens have two grown children, Marta, a clinical psychologist, and Mark, a physician. Sharon, the only one in the family without a doctorate, is the undisputed facilitator of all.

Life for the Rustens has taken surprising turns, from owning a resort, Cascade Lodge, located on the North Shore of Lake Superior, to founding a Christian greeting card company, during which time Mike served on the board of directors of the Christian Booksellers Association.

Mike has an interest in politics, having served on the staff of one of the presidential campaigns in each of the past four elections. Sharon has gone from writing copy for greeting cards to scripts for Christian radio and is currently working with *Faith Matters,* a nationally distributed radio program featuring Leith Anderson.

The Rustens are members of Bethlehem Baptist Church in Minneapolis, where they are greatly blessed by the teaching of their pastor, John Piper.